THE CAMBRIDGE COMPANION TO
THE HEBREW BIBLE/OLD TESTAMENT

This *Companion* offers a concise and engaging introduction to the Hebrew Bible or Old Testament. Providing an up-to-date snapshot of scholarship, it includes chapters by twenty-three leading scholars specially commissioned for this volume. The volume examines a range of topics, including the historical and religious contexts for the contents of the biblical canon and critical approaches and methods, as well as newer topics such as the Hebrew Bible in Islam, Western art and literature, and contemporary politics. This *Companion* is an excellent resource for students at the university and graduate levels, as well as for laypeople and scholars in other fields who would like to gain an understanding of the current state of the academic discussion. The book does not presume prior knowledge, nor does it engage in highly technical discussions, but it does go into greater detail than a typical introductory textbook.

Stephen B. Chapman is Associate Professor of Old Testament in the Divinity School and Director of Graduate Studies for the Graduate Program in Religion at Duke University. He is also an affiliate faculty member in Duke's Center for Jewish Studies. He has published numerous essays and is author of *The Law and the Prophets* (2000) and *1 Samuel as Christian Scripture* (2016). He also coedited *Biblischer Text und theologische Theoriebildung* (2001).

Marvin A. Sweeney is Professor of Hebrew Bible at Claremont School of Theology and Professor of Tanak at the Academy for Jewish Religion (California). He has written highly regarded works on the Hebrew Bible, such as *Isaiah 1–39* (1996), *The Twelve Prophets* (2000), *King Josiah of Judah* (2001), *Reading the Hebrew Bible after the Shoah* (2008), *Tanak: A Theological and Critical Introduction to the Jewish Bible* (2012), *Reading Ezekiel* (2013), *Reading Prophetic Books* (2014), and *Isaiah 40–66* (2016). He coedited *New Visions of Isaiah* (1996), *Reading and Hearing the Book of the Twelve Prophets* (2000), *The Changing Face of Form Criticism for the Twenty-First Century* (2003), and other works.

(continued after index)

THE CAMBRIDGE COMPANION TO

THE HEBREW BIBLE/OLD TESTAMENT

Stephen B. Chapman
Duke University

Marvin A. Sweeney
Claremont School of Theology

CAMBRIDGE
UNIVERSITY PRESS

CAMBRIDGE
UNIVERSITY PRESS

University Printing House, Cambridge CB2 8BS, United Kingdom

One Liberty Plaza, 20th Floor, New York, NY 10006, USA

477 Williamstown Road, Port Melbourne, VIC 3207, Australia

314-321, 3rd Floor, Plot 3, Splendor Forum, Jasola District Centre, New Delhi - 110025, India

103 Penang Road, #05-06/07, Visioncrest Commercial, Singapore 238467

Cambridge University Press is part of the University of Cambridge.

It furthers the University's mission by disseminating knowledge in the pursuit of education, learning and research at the highest international levels of excellence.

www.cambridge.org
Information on this title: www.cambridge.org/9780521709651

First published 2016
4th printing 2019

A catalogue record for this publication is available from the British Library

Library of Congress Cataloging in Publication data
Names: Chapman, Stephen B., 1962– editor. | Sweeney, Marvin A.
(Marvin Alan), 1953– editor.
Title: The Cambridge companion to the Hebrew Bible/Old Testament /
[edited by] Stephen B. Chapman, Marvin A. Sweeney.
Description: New York : Cambridge University Press, 2016. | Series: Cambridge companions to religion | Includes bibliographical references and index.
Identifiers: LCCN 2015041664| ISBN 9780521883207 (hardback) |
ISBN 9780521709651 (paperback)
Subjects: LCSH: Bible. Old Testament – Introductions.
Classification: LCC BS1140.3.C35 2016 | DDC 221.6–dc23
LC record available at h ttp://lccn.loc.gov/2015041664

ISBN 978-0-521-88320-7 Hardback
ISBN 978-0-521-70965-1 Paperback

Contents

Tables, Maps, and Figures

Contributors

Samuel E. Balentine is Professor of Old Testament and Director of Graduate Studies at Union Presbyterian Seminary in Richmond, Virginia. He is the author of *Have You Considered My Servant Job?* (University of South Carolina Press).

Ehud Ben Zvi is a professor in the Department of History and Classics at the University of Alberta. He coedited *The Economy of Ancient Judah in Its Historical Context* (Eisenbrauns) and *Poets, Prophets, and Texts in Play* (Bloomsbury T & T Clark).

Adele Berlin is Robert H. Smith Professor Emerita of Hebrew Bible at the University of Maryland. She has been a Fellow at the Institute for Advanced Studies at the Hebrew University of Jerusalem and is currently at work on commentaries on Psalms and Song of Songs.

Marc Zvi Brettler is Bernice and Morton Lerner Professor of Jewish Studies at Duke University. He coedited the second edition of *The Jewish Study Bible* (Oxford University Press) and is writing a commentary on part of Psalms for the New Jewish Publication Society Commentary series.

William P. Brown is William Marcellus McPheeters Professor of Old Testament at Columbia Theological Seminary. He edited the *Oxford Handbook of the Psalms* and authored *Sacred Sense* (Eerdmans).

Stephen B. Chapman is Associate Professor of Old Testament and Director of Graduate Studies in Religion at Duke University. He is the author of *1 Samuel as Christian Scripture* (Eerdmans) and is writing a volume on *The Theology of Joshua* for Cambridge University Press.

John J. Collins is Holmes Professor of Old Testament Criticism and Interpretation at Yale Divinity School. He is the author of *Introduction to the Hebrew Bible* (Fortress) and *Scriptures and Sectarianism* (Mohr Siebeck).

Stephen L. Cook is Catherine N. McBurney Professor of Old Testament Language and Literature at Virginia Theological Seminary. He is the author of *The Social Roots of Biblical Yahwism* (Society of Biblical Literature) and *Reading Deuteronomy* (Smyth & Helwys).

Thomas B. Dozeman is Professor of Hebrew Bible at United Theological Seminary. He has written commentaries on Exodus (Eerdmans) and Joshua 1–12 (in the *Anchor Yale Bible*).

Nancy J. Duff is Stephen Colwell Associate Professor of Christian Ethics at Princeton Theological Seminary. She coedited a special edition of *Theology Today* focusing on the work of Dietrich Bonhoeffer.

John Goldingay is David Allan Hubbard Professor of Old Testament at Fuller Theological Seminary. He has published the three-volume *Old Testament Theology* and *Do We Need the New Testament?* (InterVarsity).

Frederick E. Greenspahn is Gimelstob Eminent Scholar of Judaic Studies at Florida Atlantic University and editor of the NYU Press series Jewish Studies in the Twenty-First Century.

David Lyle Jeffrey is Distinguished Professor of Literature and the Humanities in the Honors College of Baylor University. He is the author of *Houses of the Interpreter* (Baylor University Press) and the historical-theological commentary *Luke* (Brazos).

Victor H. Matthews is Dean of the College of Humanities and Public Affairs and Professor of Religious Studies at Missouri State University. He has published *The Cultural World of the Bible* and a second edition of *The Hebrew Prophets and Their Social World* (Baker Academic).

R. W. L. (Walter) Moberly is Professor of Theology and Biblical Interpretation at Durham University. He is the author of *The Theology of the Book of Genesis* (Cambridge University Press) and *Old Testament Theology* (Baker Academic).

Richard D. Nelson is W. J. A. Power Professor Emeritus of Biblical Hebrew and Old Testament Interpretation at Perkins School of Theology, Southern Methodist University. He contributed the volumes on Deuteronomy and Joshua in the *Old Testament Library* (Westminster John Knox).

Sharon Pace is Professor of Hebrew Bible at Marquette University. She contributed the volume on Daniel in the *Smyth & Helwys Bible Commentary* series.

Walid A. Saleh is an associate professor at the University of Toronto. He has published *The Formation of the Classical Tafsir Tradition* and *In Defense of the Bible* (Brill).

Kenton L. Sparks is a vice president and professor of biblical studies at Eastern University, St. Davids, Pennsylvania. He is the author of *God's Word in Human Words* (Baker Academic) and *Sacred Word, Broken Word* (Eerdmans).

Brent A. Strawn is Professor of Old Testament in the Candler School of Theology and Graduate Division of Religion at Emory University, where he is also affiliated with the Department of Middle Eastern and South Asian Studies and a Senior Fellow in the Center for the Study of Law and Religion. He is editor-in-chief of the *Oxford Encyclopedia of the Bible and Law*.

Marvin A. Sweeney is Professor of Hebrew Bible at Claremont School of Theology and Professor of Tanak and Chair of the Faculty at the Academy for Jewish Religion (California). He is the author of numerous volumes and studies, such as *Reading Prophetic Books* (Mohr Siebeck) and *Tanak: A Theological and Critical Introduction to the Jewish Bible* (Fortress).

James C. VanderKam is John A. O'Brien Professor of Hebrew Scriptures at the University of Notre Dame. He is the author of *From Joshua to Caiaphas* (Fortress) and *The Dead Sea Scrolls and the Bible* (Eerdmans).

Lawrence M. Wills is Ethelbert Talbot Professor of Biblical Studies at Episcopal Divinity School, Cambridge, Massachusetts. He is the author of *The Jewish Novel in the Ancient World* (Cornell University Press) and *Not God's People* (Rowman & Littlefield).

Abbreviations

AB	Anchor Bible
ABD	*Anchor Bible Dictionary*
ABLMS	*Assyrian and Babylonian Letters Belonging to the Kouyunjik Collections of the British Museum*
ABRL	Anchor Bible Reference Library
ACEBTSup	*Amsterdamse Cahiers voor Exegese en bijbelse Theologie: Supplement Series*
ANEP	*The Ancient Near East in Pictures Relating to the Old Testament*
AOTC	Abingdon Old Testament Commentaries
ASOR	American Schools of Oriental Research
ATANT	Adhandlungen zur Theologie des Alten und Neuen Testaments
BASOR	*Bulletin of the American Schools of Oriental Research*
BBB	Bonner biblische Beiträge
BEATAJ	Beiträge zur Erforschung des Alten Testaments und des antiken Judentum
BETL	Bibliotheca ephemeridum theologicarum lovaniensium
BIBInt	*Biblical Interpretation*
BIOSCS	*Bulletin of the International Organization for Septuagint and Cognate Studies*
BJS	Brown Judaic Studies
BKAT	Biblischer Kommentar, Altes Testament
BZABR	Beihefte zur Zeitschrift für altorientalische und biblische Rechtsgeschichte
BZAW	Beihefte zur Zeitschrift für die alttestamentliche Wissenschaft
BZNW	Beihefte zur Zeitschrift für die neutestamentliche Wissenschaft
CBC	Cambridge Bible Commentary
CBET	Contributions to Biblical Exegesis and Theology
CBQ	*Catholic Biblical Quarterly*
CRB	Cahiers de la Revue biblique
DJD	Discoveries in the Judaean Desert
DSD	*Dead Sea Discoveries*
FAT	Forschungen zum Alten Testament
FB	Forschungen zur Bibel
FC	Fathers of the Church
FOTL	Forms of the Old Testament Literature

FRLANT	Forschungen zur Religion und Literatur des Alten und Neuen Testaments
HBS	Herders biblische Studien
HCOT	Historical Commentary on the Old Testament
HSM	Harvard Semitic Monographs
HSS	Harvard Semitic Studies
HTR	*Harvard Theological Review*
HTS	Harvard Theological Studies
HUCA	*Hebrew Union College Annual*
IBT	Interpreting Biblical Texts
IEJ	*Israel Exploration Journal*
JBL	*Journal of Biblical Literature*
JBR	*Journal of Bible and Religion*
JESHO	*Journal of the Economic and Social History of the Orient*
JNSL	*Journal of Northwest Semitic Languages*
JPS	Jewish Publication Society
JQR	*Jewish Quarterly Review*
JSJ	*Journal for the Study of Judaism in the Persian, Hellenistic, and Roman Periods*
JSOTSup	Journal for the Study of the Old Testament Supplements
JSS	*Journal of Semitic Studies*
LAI	Library of Ancient Israel
LHBOTS	Library of Hebrew Bible/Old Testament Studies
LSTS	Library of Second Temple Studies
MdB	*Le Monde de la Bible*
NCB	New Century Bible
NCBC	New Century Bible Commentary
NEchtB	Neue Echter Bibel
NIBCOT	New International Bible Commentary on the Old Testament
NICOT	New International Commentary on the Old Testament
OBO	Orbis biblicus et orientalis
OTL	Old Testament Library
OtSt	*Oudtestamentische Studiën*
PEQ	*Palestine Exploration Quarterly*
RBL	*Review of Biblical Literature*
RevExp	*Review and Expositor*
RQ	*Römische Quartalschrift für christliche Altertumskunde und Kirchengeschichte*
SAHL	Studies in the Archeology and History of the Levant
SBLDS	Society of Biblical Literature Dissertation Series
SBLSS	Society of Biblical Literature Symposium Series
SBLWAW	Society of Biblical Literature Writings from the Ancient World
SBT	Studies in Biblical Theology
SBTS	Sources for Biblical and Theological Study
SHANE	Studies in the History of the Ancient Near East
SHCANE	Studies in the History and Culture of the Ancient Near East
SDSSRL	Studies in the Dead Sea Scrolls and Related Literature
StudBib	Studia Biblica

TOTC	Tyndale Old Testament Commentaries
UCOP	University of Cambridge Oriental Publications
VT	*Vetus Testamentum*
VTSup	Vetus Testamentum Supplements
WMANT	Wissenschaftliche Monographien zum Alten und Neuen Testament
ZAW	*Zeitschrift für die alttestamentliche Wissenschaft*

Introduction

STEPHEN B. CHAPMAN AND MARVIN A. SWEENEY

A remarkable diversification of religious scholarship occurred in the course of the twentieth century, uniquely affecting research on the Hebrew Bible or Old Testament. Once a relatively staid field framed within largely Protestant assumptions and expectations,[1] Hebrew Bible/ Old Testament scholarship has become a lively academic terrain of robust activity by Protestants, Catholics, Jews, secularists, and others.[2] Although still underrepresented, women and racial or ethnic minorities are thankfully now increasingly part of the scholarly conversation.

Moreover, the institutional context of this activity has also broadened significantly, with most of the work in the field currently being done at research universities (which might have religious studies departments and/or denominationally affiliated schools of religion or theology) rather than in free-standing theological schools. University religion departments routinely now include Jewish and Catholic biblical scholars, as well as scholars without any religious affiliation, and their students range across an extremely broad spectrum of religious backgrounds and commitments:

> There has been a major shift of the locus of biblical scholarship from Christian and Jewish theological faculties to the "secular" universities. University scholars in the field of biblical studies have not ceased universally to be Christians or Jews in their personal profession. Religious identity as Christian or Jewish still informs in many ways the views of biblical interpretation by such scholars. Now, however, these views must be expressed in an arena of scholars who represent various shades of Christian and Jewish life.[3]

Indeed, the diversification of the field has gone hand in hand with the dizzying institutional complexification of the modern university.

As this diversification has continued, the object of study in Hebrew Bible/Old Testament research has become increasingly challenging to define. Because alternative conceptions of the biblical canon exist, which

books are to be included for investigation? Because different text traditions are variously valued, is the field's interpretive goal the elucidation
of the Hebrew Bible, Greek Bible, or some combination of the two? Or
is "Bible" itself a problematic category?[4] Even the name of the field has
become unstable. "Old Testament" suggests a network of Christian hermeneutical presuppositions, a possible bias that has led to the increasing use of "Hebrew Bible," especially (but not exclusively) on the part
of Jewish scholars. Numerous other titles also have been proposed.[5] In
all these ways, there presently exists more vigorous debate about fundamental questions in the field than ever before. This debate is to be welcomed rather than regretted. Any time a field as traditional as this one
can become truly interesting again, it must be doing something right.

The goal of this *Cambridge Companion to the Hebrew Bible/Old
Testament* is twofold. The first goal is to exhibit in detail how the increasing diversity in biblical scholarship is no accident but results in part
from the nature of the Hebrew Bible/Old Testament itself. A completely
"neutral" point of standing is not possible with respect to this textual
collection, because its very identification and character are intrinsically
connected to specific communities of interpretation.

> Rather than having eliminated the religious influence on biblical
> interpretation, modernity has driven it underground, providing a
> blanket of secularism which permits scholars from diverse back-
> grounds to use common methods and a common language to com-
> municate with each other in a world where Jewish and Christian
> exegetes often find their work evaluated by individuals with differ-
> ent beliefs.[6]

In other words, while the history-of-religions approach has successfully
facilitated an "ecumenical" form of biblical scholarship, it has also done
so to an extent by glossing over unresolved religious differences. Many
of the current textbooks and handbooks in biblical studies neglect or
dismiss the Bible's traditional religious contexts, giving the impression
that the link between text and community can be bracketed out.[7] So
the first purpose of this *Companion* is instead to illustrate how the designations "Hebrew Bible," "Old Testament," and so on imply different things to different people depending on their religious and social
locations.

But awareness and recognition of genuine differences do not by
any means eliminate the possibility for successful common work. The
second goal of this *Companion* is thus to showcase the way in which

respected scholars from a variety of religious and scholarly traditions can mutually participate in fruitful collaboration, even though some of their operational presuppositions about the field may not actually match. Precisely because of the striking diversity of perspectives, methods, and goals within the field at present, this *Companion* provides a notable service by modeling how scholars with differing religious affiliations and commitments can engage productively in biblical scholarship together – without pretending to relinquish those affiliations and commitments from the outset.

In fact, we regret that this volume is not even more diverse than it is, although we also recognize that a single volume can no longer do justice to the diversity existing within our field. We hope, therefore, that this volume will be read alongside other introductory textbooks and guides, and that its publication will further enhance a developing conversation not only about the history of Israel and the character of the Hebrew Bible/Old Testament, but also about the nature of our field itself: its scope and its aims. In particular, this volume needs to be read together with other handbooks and resources that describe even newer methodological vantage points, especially with regard to contextual or "advocacy" approaches (e.g., feminist, African American, Native American, Hispanic/Latino/a, Asian) and interdisciplinary perspectives (e.g., postcolonial hermeneutics, disability studies, cultural criticism).[8] Our volume does not represent an effort to "define the field" and certainly does not intend to marginalize or exclude perspectives and topics that are left untreated – but only to offer one substantial, coherent exploration of various subfields of study relating to the Hebrew Bible/Old Testament.

Even though we could not fit everything between two covers, we hope this volume will provide a useful introduction to students and a helpful overview for colleagues, who may find (as we do) that it is more and more challenging, in these days of hyperspecialization, to look up from one's own furrow to the rest of the field in which we all are jointly laboring. Two other closely related *Cambridge Companions* appeared not long ago, and they continue to be well worth consulting.[9] This volume, however, is the first *Companion* to be focused exclusively on the Hebrew Bible/Old Testament. It has been in preparation for several years. During this period, we have done all we could to keep it current with the rapidly evolving secondary literature, but inevitably there will be certain omissions and oversights. Yet we remain confident that the volume represents a timely snapshot of significant contemporary scholarship on the Hebrew Bible/Old Testament. We have tried not to presume prior knowledge in the volume's treatment of various topics, but at the same time to introduce this complex body of scholarship at an advanced level.

We wish to thank Judith Heyhoe for her editorial assistance. Our thanks also go to the staff of Cambridge University Press for their patience, support, and expertise.

NOTES

1   See Ernest W. Saunders, *Searching the Scriptures: A History of the Society of Biblical Literature, 1880–1980* (Biblical Scholarship in North America 8; Chico, CA: Scholars Press, 1982).

2   See M. H. Goshen-Gottstein, "Christianity, Judaism and Modern Bible Study," *VTSup* 28 (1975): 83; Jacques Berlinerblau, " 'Poor Bird, Not Knowing Which Way to Fly': Biblical Scholarship's Marginality, Secular Humanism, and the Laudable Occident," *Biblical Interpretation* 10 (2002): 289; S. David Sperling, ed., *Students of the Covenant: A History of Jewish Biblical Scholarship in North America* (Atlanta: Scholars Press, 1992).

3   Ernest Frerichs, "Point, Counterpoint: The Interdependence of Jewish and Christian Interpretation of the Hebrew Bible," *Eretz Israel* 26 (1999): 42. Cf. John J. Collins, *The Bible after Babel: Historical Criticism in a Postmodern Age* (Grand Rapids, MI: Eerdmans, 2005), 9.

4   See further James E. Bowley and John C. Reeves, "Rethinking the Concept of 'Bible': Some Theses and Proposals," *Henoch* 25 (2003): 3–18; Robert A. Kraft, "Para-mania: Beside, Before and Beyond Bible Studies," *JBL* 126 (2007): 5–27.

5   As a reflection of this discussion, the compound title "Hebrew Bible/Old Testament" is used for this volume rather than a single title such as "Hebrew Bible," "Old Testament," "Jewish Scripture," or "Tanak." E.g., Marvin A. Sweeney, *Tanak: A Theological and Critical Introduction to the Jewish Bible* (Minneapolis, MN: Fortress, 2012). Each of these single titles implies particular prior assumptions about the object under study and the reasons for that study to be pursued. The compound title is intended to indicate a readiness to leave such questions open so that they are themselves part of what will be investigated. Since "Hebrew Bible" and "Old Testament" are the most widely used titles at present, they are the ones adopted in the combination. A combined form with a slash (i.e., "Hebrew Bible/Old Testament") is currently employed as a name for the field in several university graduate programs and a few other publishing ventures. E.g., *The Hebrew Bible/Old Testament: The History of Its Interpretation*, ed. by Magne Sæbø (Göttingen, Germany: Vandenhoeck und Ruprecht, 1996–2015). The debate over an appropriate title has also achieved a measure of wider cultural awareness; see William Safire, "On Language: The New Old Testament," *New York Times Magazine* (May 25, 1997): 20.

6   Frederick Greenspahn, "How Modern are Biblical Studies?" in *Minḥah le-Nahum: Biblical and Other Studies Presented to Nahum M. Sarna in*

Honour of his 70th Birthday, ed. by M. Brettler and M. Fishbane (Sheffield, England: JSOT Press, 1993), 179.

7   For an elaboration of this critique, see Jon Levenson, "Theological Consensus or Historicist Evasion? Jews and Christians in Biblical Studies," in Roger Brooks and John J. Collins, eds., *Hebrew Bible or Old Testament? Studying the Bible in Judaism and Christianity* (Notre Dame, IN: University of Notre Dame Press, 1990), 133.

8   For this purpose, we recommend the following publications: Steven L. McKenzie and Steven R. Haynes, eds., *To Each Its Own Meaning: An Introduction to Biblical Criticisms and Their Application*, rev'd. and expanded ed. (Louisville, KY: Westminster John Knox, 1999); Steven L. McKenzie and John Kaltner, eds., *New Meanings for Ancient Texts: Recent Approaches to Biblical Criticism and Their Applications* (Louisville, KY: Westminster John Knox, 2013); Carol A. Newsom, Sharon H. Ringe and Jacqueline E. Lapsley, eds., *Women's Bible Commentary*, 3d ed. (Louisville, KY: Westminster John Knox, 2012); Hugh R. Page, Jr., ed., *The Africana Bible: Reading Israel's Scriptures from Africa and the African Diaspora* (Minneapolis, MN: Fortress, 2010).

9   John Barton, ed., *The Cambridge Companion to Biblical Interpretation* (Cambridge University Press, 1998); Bruce Chilton, ed., *The Cambridge Companion to the Bible*, 2d ed. (Cambridge University Press, 2008).

Part I

Text and canon

1 Texts, titles, and translations

JAMES C. VANDERKAM

The twenty-four books that now constitute the Hebrew (and Aramaic) Bible or Protestant Old Testament (in which they are counted as thirty-nine books) were written at various times during the last millennium BCE. Scholars debate when certain parts of the Hebrew Bible were written or compiled, but there is general agreement that the last book to be completed was Daniel in c. 165 BCE. No original manuscript of any scriptural book has survived to the present. The first section of this chapter will survey the extant textual evidence for the Hebrew Bible.

I. TEXTS

This first section will describe the witnesses that have been available and studied for centuries, while the second section will treat the evidence discovered during the twentieth century in the Judean wilderness.

A. *The traditional witnesses.* The texts of all the books in the Hebrew Bible have long been known through two witnesses: the Masoretic Text (MT) and the Septuagint (LXX); the Samaritan Pentateuch (SP) has offered another ancient witness to the first five books. In addition, some other early versions that were at least in part based on Hebrew models have also been considered of value for the preservation and study of the text.

1. *The Masoretic Text (MT).* The traditional text of the Hebrew Bible is named the Masoretic Text because of the *masora*, or body of notes regarding its copying and reading, that was compiled to assist in transmitting it accurately. The MT consists of two parts: the consonantal component, which was the only element at first and which rests on much earlier manuscripts, and the vowels, accents, cantillation marks, and other notes that were added to the consonants by medieval Jewish experts called the *Masoretes*. The earliest copies of the MT or parts of it date from

the ninth and tenth centuries CE or shortly after: the Cairo Codex of the Prophets was copied in 896 CE, the Aleppo Codex (about three-quarters of the Hebrew Bible is preserved in the damaged copy) in c. 925 CE, and the Leningrad Codex (the entire Bible) in 1009 CE. In other words, the very earliest manuscripts are a full 1000 years and more distant in time from when the last book of the Bible reached completion.

The MT, which has been the Bible of Jews the world over since the Middle Ages, is a truly admirable production, the fruit of the labors of remarkable experts who went to extraordinary lengths to ensure the accuracy of the transmission of the text and to record its many special features. There are differences in readings between the copies, but these discrepancies are minor, though the Masoretes themselves preserved some variant readings through various devices. While there is no question about the impressive nature of the MT and the precision that characterized the copying of it, a different question is whether the wording of text so carefully preserved in it is the best Hebrew text attainable for these books. Experts agree that the question of the quality of the text must be examined book by book; in some cases, the MT preserves a careful, ancient form of the text (e.g., in Exodus); in others, it does not (e.g., the books of Samuel). Since it is in the original language of the books and is complete, the MT has enjoyed pride of place in the modern study and translation of the Hebrew Bible.

2. *The Septuagint (LXX).* The books of the Hebrew Bible were translated into the Greek language by Jewish scholars in the last three centuries BCE. There is no reliable information regarding when translating work began. A work entitled, The Letter of Aristeas, offers a story about the project for translating the books of the Law (Genesis through Deuteronomy) in the time of King Ptolemy II Philadelphus (283–246 BCE); it claims that seventy-two bilingual Jews from Palestine traveled at royal invitation and expense to Alexandria, Egypt, for the purpose of translating the books of the Law into Greek – a task they completed in seventy-two days. The story explains the name traditionally given to the Greek translation – the Septuagint (= the [translation of] the seventy, rounding off the number seventy-two for convenience) – but the amount of history preserved in it may be slight. There are citations from a Greek translation of parts of the Bible beginning around 200 BCE; consequently, translating work of some sort began before that time. The earliest form of

the LXX is called the Old Greek, and that Old Greek translation was later to be subjected to various kinds of revisions, often to bring it into closer conformity with a Hebrew text. Greek texts of the books became widely used not only by Jews who resided in primarily Greek speaking areas but also by Christians, for whom the Greek version became the Old Testament. As a result, readings from the LXX are found in the New Testament and other early Christian texts.

The Greek versions of the Bible exist in many copies. The oldest preserved ones are fragmentary papyri, some of which date from the second and first centuries BCE (found in Egypt and Palestine). For example, John Rylands' Papyrus 458 was inscribed in the second century BCE (on it, some verses from Deuteronomy 23–26, 28 survive) and Papyrus Fouad in approximately 100 BCE (containing a couple of fragments of Genesis and bits of Deuteronomy). The great codices (written with uncials), which contain Greek renderings of all books in the Hebrew Bible and more (the so-called apocryphal books and others, with the New Testament), date from the fourth and fifth centuries CE. The finest examples are Codex Vaticanus (= B; fourth century, generally regarded as the best guide to the Old Greek in almost all books), Codex Sinaiticus (= S; fourth century), and Codex Alexandrinus (=A; fifth century). There are also many minuscules of varying textual value. As will be noted later, caves 4 and 7 from Qumran contain copies of scriptural texts in Greek (Exodus, Leviticus, Numbers, and Deuteronomy) dating from the second century BCE to about the turn of the eras.

Some extant witnesses of the Greek translation are therefore much older than the earliest manuscripts of the MT. Nevertheless, the Greek has typically played a lesser role in modern translations of the Old Testament, perhaps mostly because it does not offer the text in its original language.

The Old Greek was rendered from Hebrew sources, but it is not always possible to retrovert that Hebrew source with confidence. Nevertheless, the translators often produced quite literal renderings of their base text and thus regularly offer a clear reflection of it. If the LXX faithfully represents its Hebrew base, that base differed in many instances from the readings found in the MT. At times, that presumed Hebrew model preserves better readings; at other times, poorer ones. To give just one example, the LXX differs from the MT in Genesis 4:8.

MT: Cain said to his brother Abel. And when they were in the field ...

LXX: Cain said to his brother Abel, "Let us go out to the field." And when they were in the field ...

Here the LXX (with the Samaritan Pentateuch and some MT copies) has the words of Cain that are implied by but not present in the MT.

Greek copies served as the basis for other ancient translations of the Scriptures. Prominent examples are the Old Latin, the Armenian, and the Ethiopic versions.

3. *The Samaritan Pentateuch (SP).* This name is given to the text of the Hebrew Bible used and preserved through the centuries by the Samaritan community. It contains, as the name indicates, only the first five books of the Hebrew Bible/Old Testament and only the consonantal text, written in the special Samaritan form of paleo-Hebrew. The SP, though the text rests on a much older foundation, survives exclusively in copies made in the Middle Ages or later. The earliest surviving copy may be Add. 1846, University Library Cambridge, which comes from early in the twelfth century CE.

The SP agrees with the MT in the vast majority of its readings. There are reported to be, however, about 6000 differences between the two – differences that from a textual standpoint frequently involve very minor matters such as spelling practices. A series of differences arises in Genesis 5, where in the SP the ages of the patriarchs are systematically lower than in either the MT or LXX – both of which have their own chronologies. Of the c. 6000 differences with the readings of the MT, the SP shares more than 1600 with the LXX. The SP is based on but expanded from a text like the MT. Among the expansions are instances in which the SP brings together into one place parallel material appearing in other places in the Pentateuch. There are also a few cases in which specifically Samaritan interests have made their way into the text. For example, an order identifying Mt. Gerizim as the chosen site for the temple is listed as the tenth commandment; the extra commandment was made possible by combining the first two into one. In such instances, it is most likely that they have been added to an older text form by Samaritan tradents.

These three witnesses, direct or indirect, to the text of the Hebrew Bible (or parts of it) have been used not only by their respective worshiping communities but also by scholars of the text as the basis for their work of research and translation.

4. *Other translations.* Three other ancient translations that were based in their own ways on Hebrew texts also should receive mention.

    a. *The Peshitta.* The translation of the books of the Hebrew Bible into the Syriac language took place over a period of time and was apparently the work of a number of translators. It may have been completed by the third century CE, and it did become the standard Bible for Syriac-speaking Christians. Some relatively old copies of it exist. For example, British Library Add. 14512 was copied in 459–60 CE and British Library Add. 14425 in 463–464 CE. The highly regarded Codex Ambrosianus dates from the sixth–seventh century CE. The Peshitta, a translation of the Scriptures from one Semitic language into another, shows evidence of a Jewish contribution to the work, especially in the translations of the first five books. The readings in the translation betray a high percentage of agreement with those in the MT.

    b. *The Vulgate.* The great disparity between the manuscripts of the Old Latin versions (translated from Greek models) led Damasus, Bishop of Rome, to commission Jerome in 382–383 CE to prepare a standard Latin edition of the entire Bible on the basis of a sound Greek text. Jerome began by revising Old Latin texts of the New Testament, but in his labors with the Old Testament books, he made use of Greek models. As his work progressed, he became more concerned about the discrepancies between readings of Greek copies and those in the Hebrew texts used by his Jewish acquaintances and debate partners. Accordingly, he started to make greater use of Hebrew manuscripts in his translating work. It seems unlikely that he produced the entire Vulgate (the name given the translation at a later time), but he did make a sizable contribution to this work that eventually became the Bible of the church in the West and for a long time the basis of Roman Catholic translations into English.

    c. *The Targums.* The word *targum* means "translation." It is applied to a series of renderings of the books in the Hebrew Bible into the Aramaic language widely used by Jewish people in Second Temple times. Little is known about the early history of the Targums (e.g., whether they were at first only oral and later reduced to writing), but some have been found among the Dead Sea Scrolls – a fact demonstrating that written forms of the Targums existed in pre-Christian times. There are several different Targums for the books of the law (Targum Pseudo-Jonathan, Targum Neophyti, the Fragment Targum, and Targum Onqelos), one for the Prophets (Targum Jonathan), and later translations of most of the Writings (except the ones with Aramaic sections in them [Ezra, Daniel]). While written Targums are attested at an early time, the Targums listed here are later in date. The Targums are valuable textually in that they were made from Hebrew texts, but they are also important for the history of interpreting the text because at times they expand on or otherwise alter their models in exegetical ways.

B. *Modern discoveries.* The twentieth century was a time of great archaeological discoveries that have significantly augmented the quantity and quality of the material available for study of the scriptural text and the history of transmitting it.

1. *The Dead Sea (Qumran) Scrolls.* Among the approximately 900 manuscripts identified by editors of the scrolls, approximately 230 qualify as copies of one or more scriptural books. The historical period in which the scrolls were transcribed begins in the third century BCE and continues to the first century CE, with most of them having been copied in the first century BCE or the first century CE. That is, they come from a time many centuries before the earliest manuscript copy of the MT and even of the LXX. It is likely that the Qumran copies reflect the situation with respect to the text of scriptural books not only at the small site of Qumran but also throughout the land of Israel because some of the scrolls – certainly the earliest ones – were brought to Qumran from elsewhere.

a. *Numbers of copies.* Only one of the many scrolls can be called complete: 1QIsaᵃ contains the entire book of Isaiah. All the others are fragmentary to one degree or another. Apart from one, every book in the Hebrew Bible is represented by at least one fragment among the Dead Sea Scrolls; the missing one is the book of Esther. Almost all the copies are inscribed in various styles of the square (or Assyrian) script, but twelve manuscripts were copied in paleo-Hebrew and at least five in Greek. The following list gives the numbers of identified Hebrew copies for each book of the Bible. The numbers in the list may not be exact because there are at times problems in determining whether a fragment belongs to a particular manuscript, but they should be close to accurate. The totals represented as "19–20" or "8–9" copies for a book indicate uncertainty about whether some fragments come from one or two copies; the numbers in parentheses express the actual number of scrolls involved in cases where more than one book was copied on a single scroll (they are counted once for each book; thus the larger totals for some books).

Genesis	19–20	Minor Prophets	8–9
Exodus	17 (15)	Psalms	36
Leviticus	13 (12)	Job	4
Numbers	7 (5)	Proverbs	2
Deuteronomy	30	Ruth	4
Joshua	2	Song	4
Judges	3	Ecclesiastes	2
1–2 Samuel	4	Lamentations	4
1–2 Kings	3	Daniel	8
Isaiah	21	Ezra	1
Jeremiah	6	1–2 Chronicles	1
Ezekiel	6	Nehemiah	1

The total for these figures, using the larger numbers in the uncertain cases, is 207; using the smaller numbers in those instances, it is 200.

b. *Other manuscripts.* The numbers are impressive, yet the ones listed are not the only witnesses to the scriptural texts found in the Qumran caves. As mentioned earlier, there are at least five copies of Greek translations: one for Exodus, two for Leviticus, one for Numbers, and one for Deuteronomy. Other small fragments may come from still more copies, though not enough text has survived to identify them. In addition, there are three manuscripts that have been identified as Targums – Aramaic translations of Hebrew Scriptures: one of Leviticus and two of Job, one of them extensively preserved.

Besides these scriptural copies, there are other kinds of works that are also valuable for a study of the text and its history. The caves at Qumran have yielded a series of commentaries on prophetic works. The writers of these works, called *Pesharim*, cite a passage from a scriptural book (occasionally books) and then explain its meaning. Having completed the commentary on that passage, they then move on to the next or another one found farther along in the book. These citations, and the many biblical citations in other scrolls (e.g., the Damascus Document), considerably augment the fund of information about the scriptural text in the Dead Sea Scrolls. There are also *tefillin* (phylacteries) and *mezuzot*, that is, collections of scriptural texts placed in a small container and attached to one's arm (and head; see, for example, Exod 13:9) or doorway (Deut 6:9). Since it is not always possible to distinguish the two types if only fragments are extant, the numbers may not be exact. But twenty-eight *tefillin* were found at Qumran (twenty-one in cave 4) and three at other sites; there are nine *mezuzot* from Qumran and one from Murabba'at.

2. *Texts from other Judean desert sites.* Several additional sites in the Judean desert have yielded copies of scriptural books. Not nearly as many were found in them as at Qumran, but their contributions are noteworthy nevertheless.

Masada (7). The finds at this famous site are securely dated in that they cannot be later than 73 CE, the date when the fortress was taken by the Romans.

Genesis	1
Leviticus	2
Deuteronomy	1
Ezekiel	1
Psalms	2

Murabba'at (7 [6])

Genesis	2
Exodus	1 (on the same manuscript as one of the Genesis copies)
Numbers	1
Deuteronomy	1
Isaiah	1
Minor Prophets	1 (a relatively well-preserved scroll)

Nahal Hever (3)

Numbers	1
Minor Prophets	1 (Greek, extensively preserved)
Psalms	1

Nahal Hever/Se'elim (2)

Numbers	1
Deuteronomy	1

Se'elim   (1)
   Numbers   1

Sdeir (1)
   Genesis   1

There are also copies of Joshua (1) and Judges (1) from an unknown location.

3. *Nature of the texts*. The texts, despite the limits caused by their fragmentary state of preservation, have made significant contributions to knowledge about the scriptural texts and their history.

a. *General comments*. The sum total of the scriptural manuscript evidence from Qumran permits some broad generalizations. First, they furnish the oldest original-language evidence for the many passages they represent, centuries older than any other evidence apart from some Greek papyri. The scrolls and scroll fragments from Qumran were copied in the period between the third century BCE and the first century CE. They are therefore several hundreds of years older than the most ancient Greek codices (fourth century CE), and they are, in many cases, a full millennium older than the first copies of the MT. In an age when all texts had to be hand copied, the earlier the evidence, the less opportunity there was for scribal lapses and other common copying errors to occur. There is no guarantee that older is better, but the ancient copies offer unique comparative evidence, allowing one to test whether the more recent (e.g., the MT) and the older copies are the same, almost the same, or quite different in their readings.

Second, it is worth emphasizing that the copies from the Judean wilderness provide evidence that scriptural texts were transcribed with care and precision by Jewish copyists. The differences between the Judean desert texts and, say, the MT are frequently slight, often ones that do not affect the meaning of the text (e.g., spelling changes, omission or addition of a conjunction, etc.). Statements in the Rabbinic literature describe the meticulous procedures used in copying scriptural texts; great care also was taken at an earlier time, as the Judean desert texts reveal. This should not, however, be taken to mean that the scribes were copying only one form of text; it does mean that whatever scriptural manuscript they were copying, they did the work with care.

b. *The textual picture.* The Qumran texts permit one to see that at the time (third century BCE–first century CE), there was a degree of fluidity in the wording of scriptural texts; there was not one completely uniform, accepted wording of a scriptural book such as Genesis, Isaiah, and so on. This is not to say that there was free variation in the wording of texts. Rather, within certain limits (in most cases), there were noticeable differences from manuscript to manuscript. Some examples will illustrate differing measures of variation (not including spelling practices).

Minor variation. Many differences in readings between manuscripts are the result of scribal lapses and addition/omission of small items such as the word *and* (one small letter in Hebrew). Examples of such largely insignificant variant readings include

Isa 6:3	MT:	Holy, holy, holy
	1QIsaᵃ	Holy, holy

For whatever reason, the Qumran copy has only two instances of *holy*. The omission from the familiar formula (if it was in fact omitted) is supported by no other ancient copy of Isaiah.

Gen 1:9	MT/SP	Let the waters be gathered into one place (= *mqwm*)
4QGenʰˡ	LXX	Let the waters be gathered into one gathering (= *mqwh*)

In this instance, two Hebrew words looking almost alike were confused.

Though it involves a larger stretch of text, the following example actually shows evidence of a simple scribal error that led to the omission of an entire paragraph:

1 Sam 10:27–11:1	MT	They despised him [Saul] and brought him no present. But he held his peace. Nahash the Ammonite went up ...
4QSamᵃ (IX frg. a 5–9)		They despised him and brought him no present. <blank>
		Now Nahash, king of the Ammonites, had been grievously oppressing the Gadites and the Reubenites. He would gouge out the right eye of each of them and would not grant Israel a deliverer. No one was

left of the Israelites across the Jordan whose
right eye Nahash, king of the Ammonites,
had not gouged out. But there were seven
thousand men who had escaped from the
Ammonites and had entered Jabesh-gilead.
    About a month later, Nahash the
Ammonite went up ...

The Hebrew expressions for "But he held his peace" (10:27 MT
[*wyhy kmḥryš*]) and "About a month later" (11:1 in 4QSamᵃ LXX
[*wyhy kmw ḥdš*]) are nearly identical. Their resemblance caused
a scribe to omit the intervening material; the defective text is
found in MT and all versions other than the Qumran copy and the
first century CE historian Josephus's paraphrase of this section
(*Antiquities of the Jews* 6.68–71). The Samuel manuscript itself is
defective in omitting the first of the two look-alike phrases, but it
reveals part of the mechanism that caused the omission.

Psalm 145	MT	[One verse is missing from this acrostic psalm: although each verse begins with a word starting with the successive letters of the alphabet, there is none for the letter *nun*, which should have appeared between vv. 13 and 14 and obviously was dropped from the text by scribal error.]
11QPsᵃ	LXX	Faithful is the Lord in all his words, and gracious in all his deeds.

The Hebrew word for *faithful* begins with *nun* and thus supplies
the missing verse.

Larger variation. More important for historical purposes are
textual variations that belong to a pattern. It is possible that in the
Qumran period, scribes, while copying precisely, still felt some
freedom to take a more active role with regard to a scriptural text
than simply transcribing it. One well-documented pattern in a
series of scrolls is to blend or combine wording from parallel passages. For example, the Ten Commandments are preserved in two
places – Exodus 20 and Deuteronomy 5. In the latter, the reason
for the Sabbath commandment is different from in the former:

Deut 5:15	MT	Remember that you were a slave in the land of Egypt, and the Lord your God brought you

out from there with a mighty hand and an
outstretched arm; therefore the Lord your
God commanded you to keep the Sabbath day.

Near the end of the passage, one of the Qumran copies (4QDeut^n) has an addition: "... to keep the Sabbath day and to hallow it. For in six days the Lord made heaven and earth, the sea, and all that is in them and rested the seventh day; so the Lord blessed the Sabbath day and hallowed it" (IV 4–7).

The addition is taken from Exod 20:11, part of the parallel version, where the motivation for the Sabbath rest is to imitate the pattern that God established in the first week. Combining material from parallel passages is a characteristic not only of some scriptural copies from Qumran but also of the SP, although in Deut 5:15, the SP does not add the material from Exod 20:11.

Broader variations. There are a few cases where sizable and systematic variations separate the witnesses, including those from Qumran. Some examples include entire books.

Jeremiah: The versions of the book of Jeremiah found in the MT and the LXX are of much different lengths. The MT Jeremiah is estimated to be some 13 percent longer than the LXX text. Among the fragmentary Hebrew copies of Jeremiah found at Qumran, two are similar to the longer readings of the MT and two align closely with the shorter readings of the LXX. The shorter version is generally regarded as textually superior; evidence from Hebrew manuscripts shows that the LXX translator(s) did not arbitrarily subtract text from their Hebrew model but rather rendered a Hebrew text that was much shorter than the traditional one, resulting in MT Jeremiah.

In general, one may say that manuscripts belonging to the textual traditions of the MT, the LXX, and the SP are found at Qumran, but these copies do not exhaust the data. Some copies do not fall into any of these categories and chart a different course textually. All these textual options were available at the time, and indeed, all of them are found at the one site of Qumran. There is no evidence that anyone was concerned about a certain fluidity in the texts of scriptural books.

c. *An end to fluidity.* Each of the texts found at the other sites, all of them a little later than the Qumran evidence, may fall into the pre-Masoretic category (though the books preserved at Masada are ones for which there were no variant literary editions) and suggest that by the end of the first or beginning of the second century CE the textual plurality apparent in the Qumran scrolls had given way to a far greater uniformity. There may well have been social and political reasons for this development in that the people who happened to use and copy this type of text became the central or nearly the only element in society engaged in such activity after the destruction of the temple in 70 CE.

II. TITLES

To this point, the survey has dealt with the books of the Hebrew Bible in general and the surviving early evidence for the texts. The concern in this section is groupings of books or how ancient writers referred to groups of them or even to all of them at once. In Second Temple times, the books would have been written on individual scrolls; only in a few cases would more than one book be copied onto a single scroll. Nevertheless, groups of scroll texts were identified and are referred to in the sources.

Traditionally, the Jewish canon of Scripture is divided into three sections: the Law, the Prophets, and the Writings. The Law designates Genesis through Deuteronomy – five books; the Prophets contains Joshua, Judges, Samuel, Kings (= Former Prophets), Isaiah, Jeremiah, Ezekiel, and the Twelve (= Latter Prophets – eight); and the Writings include Psalms, Proverbs, Job, the Song of Songs, Ruth, Lamentations, Ecclesiastes, Esther, Daniel, Ezra-Nehemiah, and Chronicles (though not necessarily in that order – eleven). Terms similar to those for the three divisions are present in ancient sources, but their precise meaning in them – how many and which books they intend – is often not entirely transparent.

A. *The Law and the Prophets.* The Hebrew Bible at times uses the word *law* in cases where it may refer to large parts of the Law, that is, the first five books of the Bible, but it is difficult to determine the precise meaning. For example, "Ezra had set his heart to study the law of the Lord, and to do it, and to teach the statutes and ordinances in Israel" (Ezra 7:10). Clearly *law* in this passage encompasses various sorts of legal material, but whether it means, say, Leviticus, parts of Leviticus, Leviticus and more, or something else, one cannot tell. Or Psalm 1:2 says of the righteous that "their delight is in the law of the Lord, and on his law they meditate day and night." Here as well the reference is too general to determine the identity of the law envisioned.

There are also passages that refer in a comprehensive way to the prophets, commonly in the phrase "all his servants the prophets" (see 2 Kings 17:13, 23; Jer 7:25; and many others). In these cases, however, the meaning is clearly the prophets themselves and not anything they might have written.

Of more importance in this context is the fairly widespread use of the phrase "the law and the prophets" in summarizing contexts. Juxtaposition of the two terms entails that written material is under consideration for both and that *prophets* does not mean the people who uttered prophecies. In some cases, the name *Moses* replaces *law*, but the meaning appears to be the same. The Rule of the Community, a text that describes the duties of members of the group responsible for the Dead Sea Scrolls, stipulates that they are "to do what is good and right before him, as he commanded through Moses and all his servants the prophets" (1QS 1.2–3; see also 8.15–16 and CD 7.15–18). Judas the Maccabee encouraged his troops "from the law and the prophets" before a battle (2 Macc 15:9), and Jesus told his audience: "'Do not think that I have come to abolish the law or the prophets; I have come not to abolish but to fulfill'" (Matt 5:17; see Luke 16:16). Paul said that he worshiped "the God of our ancestors, believing everything laid down according to the law or written in the prophets" (Acts 24:14), and when appealing to Jews in Rome, he tried "to convince them about Jesus both from the law of Moses and from the prophets" (Acts 28:23). *Law and Prophets* was the common designation for the Scriptures until early Christian times.

B. *Three entities.* In a few passages, the twofold "law and prophets" is expanded to include additional literature. An especially instructive set of examples occurs in the Prologue to the Greek translation of the Wisdom of Ben Sira, a prologue written by the author's grandson, who also happened to be the translator. Three times the grandson makes reference to the ancestral literature of his people in which wisdom and instruction are to be found: "Many great teachings have been given to us through the Law and the Prophets and the others that followed them." In the very next sentence he mentions "those who read the scriptures," apparently alluding comprehensively to the same writings. Continuing the idea of reading the Scriptures, he reports: "So my grandfather Jesus, who had devoted himself especially to the reading of the Law and the Prophets and the other books of our ancestors." Later, dealing with the difficulties involved in translating Hebrew, he notes about his grandfather's book: "Not only this book, but even the Law itself, the Prophecies, and the rest of the books differ not a little when read in the original."

A passage in the New Testament that is similarly meant as a comprehensive expression appears in Luke 24:44, part of Jesus's words to his disciples when he appeared to them after the resurrection: "Then he said to them, 'These are my words that I spoke to you while I was still with you – that everything written about me in the law of Moses, the prophets, and the psalms must be fulfilled.'" Again, it is helpful to notice that in the next verse the evangelist writes: "Then he opened their minds to understand the scriptures." (24:45). *The Scriptures* thus consist of the law of Moses, the prophets, and the psalms. The third category is debated: it may mean just the Psalms, or it could mean the books of Scripture not included in the law of Moses and the prophets because Psalms is often listed as the first book of the Writings in copies of the MT.

C. *The Scriptures.* As the examples from the Prologue to Ben Sira and Luke demonstrate, the three categories of books listed could be termed comprehensively *the scriptures.* The term is met in Greek sources, but as nearly as one can tell, there is no corresponding word in Hebrew or Aramaic texts from the time of the Second Temple. 1 Maccabees, a work composed in Hebrew, but of which only a Greek translation is available, does mention "the holy books" in 12:9, but nothing in the context clarifies which ones are meant – only that they provide encouragement.

Both the plural *the scriptures* and the singular *the scripture* are attested; the problem often is that the writers who employ these terms do not list the books they encompass. Although both Philo and Josephus use "the scriptures" and "scripture," the New Testament is a richer repository of such references as its writers attempt to show that the Scriptures found fulfilment in Jesus of Nazareth. In Luke 24, cited earlier, the author describes what Jesus did for the travelers to Emmaus: "Then beginning with Moses and all the prophets, he interpreted to them the things about himself in all the scriptures" (24:27; cf. v. 32).

III. TRANSLATIONS

Translators of the Hebrew Bible into modern languages are faced with a truly daunting task. Theoretically, they should take the full range of the textual evidence cited earlier into account in establishing the text to be rendered, but in practice the ideal may rarely be achieved – for quite understandable reasons. There have been many translations of the Bible into English in the last decades, and they often include in a preface a short explanation of the textual principles that guided the translators. By reading them, one can see that the textual base tends to be quite narrow, usually with few exceptions allowed.

A. *The Jewish Publication Society (JPS) Translation.* The JPS issued an English translation of the Bible in 1917, but a largely new one was later published in three stages: the Torah (1962), the Prophets (1978), and the Writings (1982). The three parts with revisions were brought together into one volume in 1985. It is certainly understandable that in a Jewish translation the basic principle would be "to follow faithfully the traditional Hebrew text" (*JPS Hebrew-English Tanakh,* xxiii) – that is, the MT, although the Preface to the 1985 edition notes five circumstances in which at least a footnote to the translation was felt to be necessary: (1) where the translators did not understand a word or expression; (2) where a different rendering of the MT was possible; (3) where an old rendering was so well known that it would probably be missed: the traditional translation was placed in a note introduced by the word *Others* (generally meaning it was in the 1917 translation); (4) where the understanding of a passage could be enhanced by another elsewhere in the Bible; and (5) where important variants are found in ancient manuscripts or versions of the Bible (xxiii–xxiv). The Introduction mentions special problems encountered in the many difficult passages in the Prophets. Where a reading in an ancient version or a proposed emendation clarifies the text, it is mentioned in a footnote (xxv). In the Writings, uncertain passages are indicated in the notes, but no emendations are offered (xxvi).

In the Preface to the 1999 Hebrew-English edition, the writers focus more on the Leningrad Codex because it is the Hebrew text printed in this edition. They use the Michigan-Claremont-Westminster electronic form of it – an extraordinarily accurate copy. Since the translation of 1985, with some revisions, is the text printed facing the Hebrew, the translation principles remain the same for this edition. The ancient versions play a decidedly modest role in the JPS translation.

B. *The New Revised Standard Version (NRSV).* The widely used NRSV (1989) is the latest embodiment of the translative tradition that goes back, via the Revised Standard Version (1952) and the American Standard Version (1901 [related to the British Revised Version of 1881–5]), to the King James Version and beyond. Bruce Metzger, chair of the NRSV Committee, sketched the principles at work in the translation in a preface called "To the reader."

For the Old Testament, the NRSV Committee has made use of the *Biblia Hebraica Stuttgartensia*. This is an edition of the Hebrew and Aramaic text as current early in the Christian era and fixed by Jewish scholars (the Masoretes) of the sixth to ninth centuries. The vowel signs, which were added by the Masoretes, are accepted in the main, but where a more probable and convincing reading can be obtained by assuming different vowels, a change has been made. No notes are given in such cases because the vowel points are less ancient and reliable than the consonants. When an alternative reading given by the Masoretes is translated in a footnote, this is identified by the words "Another reading is."

Departures from the consonantal text of the best manuscripts have been made only where it seems clear that errors in copying occurred before the text was standardized. Most of the corrections adopted are based on the ancient versions (translations into Greek, Aramaic, Syriac, and Latin), which were made prior to the time of the work of the Masoretes and which therefore may reflect earlier forms of the Hebrew text. In such instances, a footnote specifies the version or versions from which the correction has been derived and also gives a translation of the Masoretic Text (*The Harper Collins Study Bible*, xxvi).

Metzger explains later that in cases in which no version seemed to provide a satisfactory solution for a problematic text, conjectures were allowed, and these are indicated in footnotes with the letters "Cn" (= correction). To such notes, a translation of the MT is added (xxvii).

The NRSV, then, allows for more use of the versions in correcting the MT, but the MT remains the base text, and the version of the MT used is the Leningrad Codex (the basis for *BHS*), as in the JPS.

C. *The New American Bible.* As the title page announces, this Catholic translation, unlike earlier Catholic versions, was based on the original-language texts of the Bible, that is, not on the Vulgate. It appears from the Preface that the translators used the received text. A separate booklet containing textual notes was published for those who can control the original languages of the Bible. It explains cases in which the editors thought that a different reading than the traditional one was indicated by the early evidence. The Qumran manuscripts were consulted and used for correction.

D. *The New International Version (NIV).* Perhaps the most popular of the modern English translations, the NIV also bases its Old Testament section on the latest editions of the *Biblia Hebraica*, that is, the Leningrad Codex. The NIV identifies in footnotes any deviation from the consonantal text of the MT. Naturally, the translators consulted the ancient editions, including the Dead Sea Scrolls material. "Readings from these versions are occasionally followed where the Masoretic Text seemed doubtful and where accepted principles of textual criticism showed that one or more of these textual witnesses appeared to provide the correct reading. Such instances are footnoted" (Preface).

E. *The Revised English Bible (REB).* In the Preface to the predecessor to the REB, the New English Bible, the MT comes in for some heavy criticism and loses its place of priority: "The earliest surviving form of the Hebrew text is perhaps that found in the Samaritan Pentateuch." The MT, however, "is full of errors of every kind due to defective archetypes and successive copyists' errors, confusion of letters, omissions and insertions, displacements of words and even whole sentences or paragraphs; and copyists' unhappy attempts to rectify mistakes have only increased the confusion." As a result, the translators had plenty of opportunities to use the versions and conjectural emendation. But the Preface to the REB sounds far more pro-MT: it recognizes that the versions must be used ("in particular places their evidence may preserve the correct reading" [xvi]), but none of them is superior to the MT, which remained largely unaltered after the second century CE.

These examples show that translators, whether Jewish or Christian, follow generally the same rules – ones that are also at work in other translations such as *The New Jerusalem Bible*. The MT (as found in the Leningrad Codex) is the text, and departures from it occur only when there are problems in its readings. Judgments about what constitutes problems will vary, but the ancient versions serve as handmaidens to the MT, not as full witnesses to the text. It is a practical procedure if not always the best one, but what should one do when a case such as Jeremiah arises? There are two quite different forms of the book, and both are attested in Hebrew copies; many experts agree that the shorter form, found in the LXX and supported in part by two manuscripts from Qumran, is the more original form of the text. Obviously, the shorter form should appear in translations of Jeremiah, but it never does. Should both be presented to the reader? The weight of tradition exercises its force in decisions about the text to be translated, and at times, it clearly prevails over the evidence.

For practical purposes, it makes sense to select an existing text and to use that as the basis for translation, unless a reading is obviously wrong and a better one is available in another source or in a conjecture. Another procedure that is theoretically preferable would be to consult the full evidence, using recognized principles of textual criticism, and to establish an eclectic text – hypothetically, the "original" text – from that fund of readings. The workload would be enormous, but if divided among enough translators, it could be done. A disadvantage of this approach is that there would be disagreements about the best text in numerous instances and that any eclectic text is in a sense artificial, one that may never have existed.

FURTHER READING

Abegg, Martin, Peter Flint, and Eugene Ulrich. *The Dead Sea Scrolls Bible*. San Francisco: Harper, 1999.

Beckwith, Roger. *The Old Testament Canon of the New Testament Church and Its Background in Early Judaism*. Grand Rapids, MI: Eerdmans, 1985.

Flint, Peter, ed. *The Bible at Qumran: Text, Shape, and Interpretation* (SDSSRL). Grand Rapids, MI: Eerdmans, 2001.

Jellicoe, Sidney. *The Septuagint and Modern Study*. Oxford, UK: Clarendon Press, 1968.

Jobes, Karen H. and Moisés Silva. *Invitation to the Septuagint*. Grand Rapids, MI: Baker Academic, 2000.

Scanlin, Harold. *The Dead Sea Scrolls and Modern Translations of the Old Testament*. Wheaton, IL: Tyndale House, 1993.

Sundberg, Albert C. *The Old Testament of the Early Church* (HTS 20). Cambridge, MA: Harvard University Press, 1964.

Swete, Henry Barclay. *An Introduction to the Old Testament in Greek*. Cambridge University Press, 1914; reprint, Peabody, MA: Hendickson Publishers, 1989.

Tov, Emanuel. *Textual Criticism of the Hebrew Bible*, 3rd rev'd. ed. and exp. ed. Minneapolis, MN: Royal Van Gorcum, 2012.

Ulrich, Eugene. *The Dead Sea Scrolls and the Origins of the Bible* (SDSSRL). Grand Rapids, MI: Eerdmans, 1999.

2 Collections, canons, and communities
STEPHEN B. CHAPMAN

What is the best way to refer to the collection of books treated in this volume?

Answering that question is tricky, controversial, and revealing. Perhaps in no other discipline is there as much confusion and disagreement about what to call its own subject matter. Old Testament? Hebrew Bible? First Testament? Jewish Scripture? Tanakh? The profusion of proposed titles has resulted not only from a well-intentioned sensitivity to sociological diversity but also from an increased awareness of the fundamentally tradition-specific nature of this literature. Thus, the deeper question at stake in the current clash of titles is *whose* literature this collection is supposed to be. Because there is not simply one answer to this question, there is also not only one answer to the question of what to call it.

Sometimes it is claimed that only with the "New" Testament did Jewish Scripture become "old."[1] Indeed, as far as can be determined, the term "Old Testament" first appears toward the end of the second century CE as a literary title. After receiving an inquiry about the proper scope of Jewish Scripture (c. 170 CE), Melito, Bishop of Sardis, describes how he journeyed eastward to learn more accurately "the books of the old covenant" (*ta tēs palaias diathēkēs biblía*).[2] However, the terms "new covenant" and "old covenant" already appear in the Bible itself, although there they designate the divine-human relation more broadly, particularly with regard to legal obedience, and not exclusively a written document. The book of Jeremiah envisions a "new covenant with the house of Israel and the house of Judah" in which the law will become so internalized that instruction is no longer necessary (Jer 31:31–4). This "new covenant" is treated in the New Testament as having been fulfilled in Christ (Luke 22:20; 1 Cor 11:25; Heb 8:8, 13; 9:15; 12:24). Correspondingly, the term "old covenant" appears in the New Testament as a designation for Jewish biblical law (2 Cor 3:14; Heb 9:1).[3] Toward the end of the second century CE, Tertullian renders the Greek term "covenant" (*diathēkē*) by the Latin *testamentum* ("will"), a translation that reflects a growing association between "covenant" as a historical mode of divine-human interaction and "covenant" as a written record.[4] So there is no reason to view the late second-century usage of "Old Testament" as representing any major innovation. To the contrary, it reflects a gradual process of conceptual development rooted in Scripture itself.[5]

Yet Jewish Scripture did not seem "old" only to Christians. The book of 1 Maccabees (first century BCE?) depicts Mattathias exhorting his sons to exercise zeal, even at the cost of their lives, for "the covenant of our ancestors" (or "ancestral covenant"; 1 Macc 2:50). Just as in the New Testament, here too traditional Jewish Scripture is conceived as containing ancient written words of prophecy, now being fulfilled to the letter in the events of the Maccabean revolt (e.g., "in accordance with the word that was written" in 1 Macc 7:17, citing Ps 79:2–3). The Qumran community also remembered a "covenant of the ancestors" (CD 1:4; 3:10). Similarly, the Jewish historian Josephus, writing toward the end of the first century CE, describes Jewish Scripture as ancient and unchanging:

> It therefore naturally, or rather necessarily, follows (seeing that with us it is not open to everybody to write the records, and that there is no discrepancy in what is written; seeing that, on the contrary, the prophets alone had this privilege, obtaining their knowledge of the most remote and ancient history through the inspiration which they owed to God, and committing to writing a clear account of the events of their time just as they occurred) – it follows, I say, that we do not possess myriads of inconsistent books, conflicting with each other. Our books, those which are justly accredited, are but two and twenty, and contain the record of all time.
>
> Of these, five are the books of Moses, comprising the laws and the traditional history from the birth of man down to the death of the lawgiver. This period falls only a little short of three thousand years. From the death of Moses until Artaxerxes, who succeeded Xerxes as king of Persia, the prophets subsequent to Moses wrote the history of the events of their own times in thirteen books. The remaining four books contain hymns to God and precepts for the conduct of human life.
>
> From Artaxerxes to our own time the complete history has been written, but has not been deemed worthy of equal credit with the earlier records, because of the failure of the exact succession of the prophets.

> We have given practical proof of our reverence for our own Scriptures. For although such *long ages have now passed*, no one has ventured either to add, or to remove, or to alter a syllable; and it is an instinct with every Jew, from the day of his birth, to regard them as the decrees of God, to abide by them, and, if need be, cheerfully to die for them. Time and again ere now the sight has been witnessed of prisoners enduring tortures and death in every form in the theaters, rather than utter a single word against the laws and the allied documents.[6]

Here, roughly in the same period as the composition of the New Testament, the antiquity of Jewish Scripture is also affirmed within Jewish tradition.[7]

In other words, by the first century CE, *everyone* thought of Jewish Scripture as old. For devout Jews, Jewish Scripture was an unchanging, precisely written, supreme religious authority ("no one has ventured ... to alter a syllable"). Indeed, Scripture was worth dying for. More difficult to gauge is how much agreement existed about Scripture's scope (i.e., the number of books) and order (i.e., the arrangement of the books) or even the extent to which these considerations were viewed as important. Since Jewish Scripture does not provide much direct information about its own history, the work of historical reconstruction must operate on the basis of inference and meager extrabiblical evidence. Partly for this reason, the historical process of biblical canon formation remains much disputed within contemporary scholarship despite an already lengthy period of intensive investigation. Another reason for the intractability of the debate arises from the lack of any consensus about what key terms such as "scripture" and "canon" mean.

TERMINOLOGY

For some scholars, "scripture" refers to a writing or group of writings with a degree of sanctity within a particular community but at the same time a writing whose authority is not yet officially delimited and fixed. A "canon" is then formed when a scriptural collection is invested with even greater authority by being set apart from other writings and explicitly "closed." This distinction between scripture and canon was forcefully advocated by Albert Sundberg:

> [I]f we are to be able to write an accurate history of the canon ... we cannot continue to use the terms "scripture" and "canon" as synonyms, as has been the practice. This only leads to confusion.

Rather, in describing the history of the canon these terms should be differentiated. My proposal is that the term "scripture" should be used to designate writings that are regarded as in some sense authoritative, and the term "canon" used to designate a closed collection of scripture to which nothing can be added, nothing subtracted.[8]

The appeal of Sundberg's terminology lies in its apparent ability to describe the textual diversity now known to exist in antiquity, demonstrated above all by the manuscript finds at Qumran and other sites in the Judean desert.[9] Some of the "nonbiblical" books apparently held a degree of authority for at least certain streams of tradition in ancient Judaism, although they were not ultimately included in the Jewish biblical canon. Even some of the books that did later find a place in the canon existed at Qumran in multiple versions.[10]

Such textual pluriformity is frequently viewed as part of a general historical trajectory moving from cultural memory to sacred literature, a progressive pattern of development often presupposed by historical-critical scholars:

> Scripture, of course, began as tradition and only gradually *became* "Scripture"; and the collection of the Scriptures becomes canon retrospectively only through the historical developments of the community's ongoing trajectory of life, thought, and controversy.[11]

In this manner, the move to restrict the proper meaning of "canon" to a later stage of communal self-deliberation is also a move to postpone the religious authority of the biblical writings. To be sure, ancient Israel did not have a "Bible" that functioned the way the Bible does today in various religious communities. Yet the very preservation and editorial revision of the biblical writings, as successfully illuminated by historical-critical research, suggests that these writings were retained and transmitted *because* of their religious authority, not because they lacked it. Of particular interest is the manner in which editorial work now found in the biblical books themselves gives the appearance of being "canon conscious."

This "canon consciousness" can be perceived throughout the biblical traditions, although it functions in different ways. For example, the final three verses of Deuteronomy (Deut 34:10–12), most likely a late addition, offer a summary statement that reflects on the significance of the Mosaic legacy throughout the entire Pentateuch.[12] Similarly, the first chapter of the book of Joshua not only introduces the book but carefully negotiates both its literary continuity and discontinuity with respect to the Pentateuch. Joshua is Moses' clear successor, yet at the same time he inhabits an altered role as Israel's leader. His primary responsibility is now to follow "the book of the law" (Josh 1:7–8) that Moses left for Israel's instruction. Strikingly, the Hebrew phrase "meditate [√hgh] day and night" (Josh 1:8) is also found in Psalm 1:2, at the beginning of the Writings, the third section of the Hebrew canon – and these are the only two instances of this phrase used with reference to *torah* in the entire Bible.[13] Another kind of editorial interrelatedness is demonstrated by the shared material in the latter chapters of 2 Kings and the latter chapters of Isaiah (2 Kgs 18–20//Isa 36–39) and Jeremiah (2 Kgs 24–25//Jer 52). Finally, a dating scheme used within the Pentateuch and Former Prophets effectively sets the Maccabean rededication of the Jerusalem Temple (164 BCE) in the four-thousandth year after creation (1 Macc 4:36–59).[14]

In all these ways and many others, historical-critical research has actually demonstrated how the canonical impulse cannot be restricted to a late, secondary development but was already operative during the composition and editorial revision of the biblical books.[15] According to this alternate understanding, "canon" is not a late, extrinsic decision but a gradually forming religious grammar, a self-reinforcing pattern of communal thinking and acting that is given increasing expression within a body of texts. This line of thought, associated most closely with Brevard Childs, views the significance of "canon" not so much in terms of its fixity or even its authority but its intratextual influence over time as a developing sense of Scripture as a whole was brought to bear on the understanding of its various parts.[16]

RECONSTRUCTIONS

Ever since the nineteenth century, the process of canon formation has been reconstructed on the basis of the number and order of the canon's literary divisions.[17] The traditional canon of the Hebrew Bible contains three divisions: the Torah or Law (Pentateuch),[18] the Prophets, and the Writings. Most modern scholars have envisioned a three-stage linear process in which each of these divisions developed and closed in turn, one after the other.

As critical scholarship established a postexilic date for the Pentateuch, it also postponed even further the date of the prophetic division's canonization. The "closure" and promulgation of the Pentateuch was customarily dated to the time of Ezra, c. 444 BCE. Many of the prophetic writings were thought to have been already in existence in some form by that time. Indeed, several prophetic books were viewed as having their roots in the eighth century (e.g., Hosea, Amos, Isaiah, Micah). But even in the early postexilic period, it was believed, they were not yet final or "official." Their later canonization was demonstrated by the apparent presence of Persian and even Hellenistic material within their received form, as well as by the absence of all the prophetic books from the Samaritan Bible. The Samaritans, it was maintained, had separated from Judean Judaism toward the end of the fifth century (c. 432 BCE). Interestingly, Samaritan tradition did not appear to ascribe scriptural authority to the prophetic writings at all. In this fashion, the stabilization of the Pentateuch was increasingly treated not only as the first stage of a linear three-stage process of canonization but also as the creation of Israel's original "Bible." References to "the law of Moses" within the other two canonical divisions and the corresponding absence of comparable allusions to the Prophets and the Writings within the Pentateuch seemed to confirm the theory.[19]

The Prophets were usually thought to have been "closed" by the end of the third century (c. 200 BCE). One significant factor for this dating had to do with the absence of Maccabean-oriented editing within the Prophets. Another related factor was the absence of Daniel from the prophetic corpus. In Jewish tradition, Daniel is classed within the Writings. However, evidence from Qumran (4Q174 [4QFlor] 4.3), the New Testament (Matt 24:15) and Josephus (*Antiquities*, 10.264–68) suggests that Daniel was widely recognized as a prophet.[20] It stands to reason that there must have been some reason why Daniel did not appear in the Prophets, as would have been expected, and the reason given was that the prophetic corpus had already been "closed."

Finally, the Writings were thought to have stabilized by the turn of the millennium, only becoming officially "closed" toward the end of the first century CE as part of the deliberations of a Jewish council meeting at Jamnia (or Yavneh). A major factor in setting this late date was the hint of rabbinic debates about the status of certain biblical books at this time (m. Yad. 3.5). Also significant were references in the Writings and the apocryphal/deuterocanonical books to the prophetic corpus as Scripture. Thus, Daniel 9:2 alludes to "the books" containing "the word of the Lord to the prophet Jeremiah." The prophetic collection (with the Latter Prophets preceding the Minor Prophets) is rehearsed in canonical order within Sirach 48–49, with Malachi 4:5–6 [Heb. 3:23–24] cited in

Sirach 48:10 and the Minor Prophets cited as "the twelve prophets" in Sirach 49:10.

This linear three-stage reconstruction of canon formation still has some claim to being a majority view within scholarship, but the past three decades have not treated it kindly.[21] The Samaritan "schism" is now thought to have been a more gradual development and finally later than the fifth century BCE.[22] The idea of a canonical "council" meeting at Yavneh toward the end of the first century CE has been thoroughly discredited.[23] But even beyond questions of dating, the idea of canon formation as having proceeded *en bloc* (by division) increasingly seems artificial and out of step with critically reconstructed histories of how individual biblical books grew and developed literarily over time.

Some of the pressure against the three-stage theory has also come from scholars who are skeptical that even partial closure of the canon occurred in the Persian period, and who worry about the tendency of the three-stage theory to encourage an anachronistic view of Persian-period Israel. Several of these scholars want to postpone the existence of a canon until as late as the fourth century CE (e.g., McDonald). Other scholars have urged earlier dates, especially for the Writings, wanting to see the canon as largely established by the time of the Maccabean revolt (164 BCE), if not earlier (e.g., Beckwith, Freedman, and Leiman).[24] The description of Judas Maccabeus as having gathered up the scriptures that Antiochus Epiphanes sought to destroy (2 Macc 2:14–15; cf. 1 Macc 1:56–7) provides a degree of support for this latter view. However, the continued existence of other "noncanonical" books (as well as the absence of uniformity in this early canon's scope and order) casts significant doubt on the Maccabean revolt as setting the final date for the canon's formation.

A more basic issue has to do with the very idea of canonization in stages. Was it really the case that the Pentateuch was originally the sole "Bible" in Israel? And that the three divisions of Jewish Scripture were completed and "closed" in turn? How then were the more ancient portions of the Prophets and the Writings preserved and remembered while they existed as noncanonical texts? If, for example, some of the Psalms do reach back to the time of Solomon's Temple, as is frequently supposed, is it at all likely that they completely lacked canonical authority until the end of the first century CE? And if they existed in some quasi-scriptural or quasi-canonical state, how were they conceived and transmitted? How was their difference from the fully canonical writings maintained? Sundberg barely acknowledges these questions, let alone answers them.

As such questions indicate, an even more fundamental issue is what "canonization" is taken to mean. Does "canonization" in fact refer to a nationally imposed, legally binding decision to accept certain writings and only certain writings as an official standard of belief and practice? Or might "canonization" also be meaningfully employed to describe a collection of authoritative writings whose boundaries were still somewhat fluid and open? Insistence on the first viewpoint, which characteristically draws on Sundberg's distinction between "scripture" and "canon," inevitably leads to later dates for the canon of Jewish Scripture.[25] Reliance on the second viewpoint favors earlier dates, precisely by calling into question Sundberg's proposal. In dispute between the two sides is not so much the evidence itself, whether biblical or extrabiblical, but the significance of that evidence and how it fits into larger reconstructions relating to the history of Israel, early Judaism, and early Christianity. A crucial need for future research, therefore, is further exploration into the phenomenological aspects of canons and canon formation "on the ground." What *are* scriptural "canons" within religious communities? How do they actually form? How do they really function? Canon-oriented scholarship into comparative religious traditions has the potential to shed considerable light on the canonical dynamics within early Judaism and Christianity.[26]

As scholars have pushed the dates of many biblical books later into the Persian period, the distance between historical-critical theories concerning their formation and textual-critical investigation regarding their transmission has narrowed to the point of disappearance. In other words, the process of canon formation may in fact be glimpsed in later redactional work on the biblical books and the early textual variants of those books now known. This may mean, in turn, that the process of canonization was more intentional and more literary than has sometimes been thought, with some editorial work on the biblical books being done in order to fit them into a developing canon and present them as "scripture." The truism that none of the biblical books was *composed as* scripture may well turn out to be false or at least in need of considerable qualification. Related clichés that the Bible is more of a "library" or "anthology" similarly neglect the literary evidence of intratextual allusion and cross-referencing found within the canon. This evidence lends weight to an understanding of "canon" as a self-allusive unity and continues to destabilize the old linear three-stage paradigm. The canonical impulse does not first appear late in Israel's tradition, imposing ideological constraints on a literature that had previously been entirely non-systematic and nonreligious. Instead, the canonical impulse is deeply rooted in the production and transmission of this literature from the beginning and has given the canon its present shape.[27]

From this vantage point, "canonization" looks more like a matter of custom and usage than official decision making. In fact, there is no evidence that a representative body within Judaism has ever made an official decision regarding the contents of its biblical canon.[28] Even in Christianity, it can be argued that no ecumenical council has ever fully specified the complete contents of the biblical canon for the entire Christian church because the first such council to do so occurred at Trent (1546). By that time, the Orthodox and Protestant churches had already separated themselves from Roman Catholicism.[29]

TITLES

The uncertainties regarding the historical formation of this collection of authoritative writings generate further uncertainties about what to call it. Its traditional title in Christianity is "Old Testament." In recent years, however, this term has received criticism, both from inside and outside the Christian tradition. For some Christians, "Old Testament" conveys the impression of being outdated or passé.[30] Use of such terms as "Hebrew Bible" and "Jewish Scripture," not only in the academy but also within Christian worship, is advocated as a means of sending an important signal that this portion of the Christian Bible properly belongs to Jews and precedes the church, which therefore should read it as if "reading someone else's mail."[31] Moreover, for some scholars (both Christian and non-Christian), "Old Testament" is inappropriately confessional and should be replaced in academic usage with a more objective "neutral" term.

In response, others have noted that the "old" in "Old Testament" can instead be understood as "venerable" or "vintage" rather than "outmoded." Within Christian theology and in the logic of the two-part Christian Bible, "Old Testament" has an established place because it draws on Pauline discourse (2 Cor 3:14)[32] and ultimately the language of a "new covenant" within the Old Testament itself (e.g., Jer 31–4). This link can be seen most clearly in the Eucharistic "words of institution" found in Luke 22:30 and 1 Corinthians 11:25. From this perspective, referring to the "Hebrew Bible" in Christian worship runs the risk of an opposite danger: namely, conveying the impression that this portion of the Bible is not really "Christian" at all.[33] Even in an academic context, avoidance of the term "Old Testament" may lead to courses and curricula in which traditional Christian interpretation of the "Hebrew Bible" is never acknowledged or discussed, except perhaps as a foil.[34] Christological readings, for example, can be banished to history departments as quaint instances of illegitimate "precritical" interpretation.[35] So, too, courses titled "Christian Scripture" may deal exclusively with the New Testament and other writings from the early church.[36] Conversely, the danger of anachronism is actually just as great when it comes to interpretations of the Hebrew Bible articulated through the lens of rabbinic Judaism or, for that matter, through the prism of a modern materialism that from the outset rejects the Bible's theological perspectives as mere window dressing for what was *really* going on in ancient Israel.

Another part of the difficulty arises from the lack of acceptable alternatives. "Hebrew Bible" is a modern title, and it originally referred to the Hebrew-language Bible (in the Masoretic Text tradition) in contrast to the "Greek Bible" (or Septuagint). Using this title can usefully provide an effective pedagogical tool for calling attention to a number of crucial hermeneutical issues and subverting simplistic and misguided assumptions about the Bible. The main difficulty with the term "Hebrew Bible" is therefore not the fact that a couple of its sections are in Aramaic (Dan 2–7; Ezra 4–7) rather than Hebrew. The real problem is how "Hebrew Bible" implies the exclusion of the Greek septuagintal tradition. Sometimes this exclusion can be done on principle, as in the biblical translations of the Jewish Publication Society.[37] In this case, the exclusion is ultimately justified on religious rather than historical grounds. But sometimes exclusion is only implied, and in a manner that is conceptually muddled. On what basis, for instance, does one refer to septuagintal evidence at all when translating and interpreting the "Hebrew Bible"? It is at any rate confusing when some scholars use the term "Hebrew Bible" but then treat its contents in the book-order deriving from septuagintal tradition, with a four-part (rather than tripartite) format. Moreover, when "Hebrew Bible" is used in reference to Jews and Christian in antiquity, the term may disguise the fact that those Jews and Christians were actually using a Greek-language Bible.[38]

The Greek Bible still constitutes one of the most important textual witnesses to the history of the Bible's growth and transmission. To imply its negligible historical worth is highly problematic. Furthermore, some Christian churches, most prominently those in the Orthodox tradition, assign canonical standing to the Greek text.[39] The Greek Bible also contains a wider selection of books, called "apocryphal" by Protestants and "deuterocanonical" by Roman Catholics. When "Hebrew Bible" becomes the operative designation, these books may not receive due consideration despite their religious importance to the Orthodox, Catholics, and Anglicans.[40]

An additional problem with "Hebrew Bible" has to do with the very neutrality it supposedly honors. Does such "neutrality" exist? The notion that there are "objective" historical interpretations independent of interpretive communities is open to significant question.[41] In fact, "objective" efforts at biblical interpretation have invariably smuggled in their commitments through the back door and avoided the harder work of genuine dialogue across interpretive traditions only by maintaining a polite superficiality.[42] Whose "Bible" *is* the "Hebrew Bible" anyway? Is it more than a "Bible" of working scholars in the field? It is difficult to justify the "Hebrew Bible" as ancient Israel's "Bible" because it is not at all clear that ancient Israel *had* a "Bible" of the type that is familiar today.[43] Even for classical Judaism, the writings that function as an authoritative core are the Torah (= Pentateuch), the Mishnah, and the Talmud.[44] Officially, texts from the Prophets and Writings do not constitute direct sources of *halakah*, although they can still provide additional support and commentary. Whether Judaism is a "biblical" religion is indeed another current topic of debate.[45]

The perceived deficiencies of both "Old Testament" and "Hebrew Bible" have led to other proposals. Some advocate the Hebrew acronym "Tanakh" (= *T*orah + *N*evi'im + *K*etuvim for Torah + Prophets + Writings). One strength of this proposal is that it observes the genre distinctions used in antiquity without introducing another, possibly anachronistic term such as "Bible" or "canon." The acronym also already possesses a good degree of recognition within Jewish religious tradition, although historically it is of fairly late origin.[46] Yet the term is relatively unknown within Christian circles and once again threatens to foreclose the study of the Christian Old Testament, at least by implication. Additionally, it mirrors the threefold structure of the traditional Jewish canon and therefore will likely be either unacceptable or confusing to Christians, whose current Bibles are normally divided according to the fourfold structure derived from the Greek biblical tradition (i.e., Law + Former Prophets or Historical Books + Poetical Books + Latter Prophets [Major and Minor]). Similar strengths and weaknesses are presented by "Hebrew Scripture," "Jewish Scripture," or "Jewish Bible."[47] The Hebrew term "Miqra'" ("reading") was traditionally employed in Judaism, but it might be heard as excluding those parts of the canon not generally read in synagogue services.[48] The Hebrew term "Torah" ("law" or "teaching") has perhaps the strongest traditional claim as a title within Judaism – and good name recognition outside of Judaism – but the word is finally so elastic that its precise contents often remain unspecified and obscure.[49]

Another proposed title is "First Testament." Advocated by influential scholars such as John Goldingay, James Sanders, and Eric Zenger,[50] this term was intended to offer an end run around the problem of religious tradition by being entirely new but also something about which scholars from different religious traditions could agree.[51] Rather than being "neutral," however, the term is actually deeply problematic for many traditional Jews and Christians. For Jews, "first" implies the inevitability of a "second" testament no less than "old" implies "new."[52] Furthermore, a "first" testament implies not only a "second" testament but also possibly a third or fourth. Within Christian theology, "Old Testament" conveys the eventual emergence of the "New Testament" as well as the *finality* of that further revelation.[53] "First" is likewise ambiguous for estimations of comparative value. "First" might be understood as "primary" in a normative sense, but it might just as easily be heard as what is "initial."[54] What is "second" can sometimes be viewed as correcting and surpassing what is "first." Even more fundamentally, the implication of an open-ended numerical sequence subverts the significance of the canon as marking a critical boundary within the history of tradition. As much as the biblical canon can be described as continuing to undergo minor changes and developing into variant forms right down to the present day, there is also a major shift that needs to be explained within both Judaism and Christianity corresponding to the birth of biblical commentary.[55] At some point in the biblical tradition, the biblical text was no longer subject to broad-scale change and instead became the object of extratextual interpretation.

Yet the "Old Testament" is never called by that name in the New Testament either (with the possible exception of 2 Cor 3:14). Israel's Scriptures are instead known by genre categories such as "law" and "prophets" or sometimes by more authorial designations such as "Moses" and "prophets." Most often the New Testament simply cites "(the) scripture(s)." Only once does a threefold reference to "the law of Moses, the prophets, and the psalms" appear (Luke 24:44). Sometimes the New Testament can refer to the whole of the Old Testament as "law" (John 10:34; 15:25; 1 Cor 14:21; Rom 3:10–19) or "prophets" (Rom 1:2; cf. 3:2, "oracles of God"; Eph 2:20) or even the "wisdom of God" (Luke 11:49). The basic title is thus the compound form "Moses and the prophets" (Luke 16:29, 31; 24:27; John 1:45; Acts 26:22) or "the law and the prophets" (e.g., Matt 5:17–18; 22:40; Luke 16:16; Acts 28:23). By their very nature, these compound forms helpfully acknowledge the multivocality of the biblical canon and honor its diversity as well as its unity.

This kind of flexible naming is evident at Qumran, too. 1QS refers to "the hand of Moses and all his servants the prophets" (1:3; cf. 8:15–16; CD 5:21–6:1). The expression "law of Moses" appears a number of times as well (e.g., 1 QS 5:8; 8:22; CD 9:12; 15:2). There is also a reference to the "books of the prophets" (CD 7:17). Although the subject of ongoing discussion and debate, 4QMMT C 10–11 clearly acknowledges some kind of scriptural collection, citing at least "the book of Moses and the books of the prophets." Several scholars have further reconstructed "and the writings of David and the events of ages past," but this continuation is disputed.[56]

A term of art such as "Hebrew Bible/Old Testament" may well be the best solution for the immediate future because it grants the diversity of religious traditions using this scriptural literature and implies that there is significance to the relationship between text and community. Yet even this move has received criticism, both for being unclear and for sharing some of the same weaknesses as other alternatives.[57] What should be evident from the present discussion, however, is that no "objective" or "neutral" term exists for this body of literature, if by "objective" or "neutral" an identity apart from a concrete community of reading is meant. Such titles as "Old Testament," "Torah," and "Tanakh" are finally to be preferred because they signal this connection.[58]

In all likelihood, the future will see an increasing number of tradition-oriented approaches, in which Christians read the Old Testament as Christians and Jews read the Torah as Jews. The danger of this development lies in its potential to introduce a renewed sectarianism into biblical scholarship. But there is also potential for a more positive outcome. Partly a reaction to the superficial "ecumenism" of the past, the trend toward tradition-specific interpretation may, in turn, lead to a deeper form of interfaith dialogue in which differences are not simply pushed to the side at the outset in the name of some alleged lowest common denominator but candidly acknowledged and kept in view during the discussion.[59] In university contexts as well, there is a strong argument in favor of teaching the Bible with a sympathetic eye toward the multiple traditions that continue to use it rather than isolating the Bible from the history of its reception.[60] A reception-historical approach would include consideration of the Bible's use in the Western tradition of arts and letters as well as in contemporary religious communities.

The differences at issue relate not only to titles and reading practices but also to the scope and order of the biblical books, which vary among religious communities to this day. In the end, the title "Hebrew Bible," when advanced as a "neutral" academic term, is in fact the most difficult one to justify because apart from the interpretive tradition governing a concrete community there is no adequate basis from which to argue for a particular combination of the canon's scope and order. In other words, if the operative category is "the literature of Second Temple Judaism," then on purely historical grounds other books would need to be included and multiple formats opened to consideration. The "Hebrew Bible," as a construct of the modern academy, only exists in the same broad sense that a "Greek Bible" or an "English Bible" exists.

SCOPE AND ORDER

When and how the scope of the Jewish canon was determined are unknown. The evidence from Qumran suggests both that the canon was still somewhat open in practice, if not in theory, and that all the biblical books in the narrower canon (with the possible exception of Esther, which was not found at the site) already held a high position of authority.

Two different traditions of counting the books are known from antiquity. According to Josephus, the books of the Hebrew Bible are "but two and twenty" in number.[61] Because Josephus does not give an exact list, however, it is difficult to say with certainty what those twenty-two books were. He groups the books into three units of 5 + 13 + 4, most likely corresponding generally to something like Law + Prophets + Writings. If Ruth is counted with Judges, Lamentations with Jeremiah, and the Minor Prophets as a single book, then Josephus' canon closely approximates what is known from other sources.[62] Origen also later counts the books of the canon as twenty-two.[63]

According to another tradition, the books of the Hebrew Bible number twenty-four (4 Ezra 14:44–6; b. Baba Batra 14b-15a). Scholars disagree about which of these two traditions came first. Roger Beckwith argues strongly that the twenty-four-book count is older,[64] tracing it back to the time of Judas Maccabeus, whereas Lee McDonald is highly critical of any reconstruction claiming too much definition for the canon too soon.[65] No one misses the significance of the fact that the letters of the Hebrew alphabet also numbered twenty-two, which made for nice symbolism and a useful mnemonic device. But this connection does not lend decisive support to either side in the debate.

The order of the books of the Hebrew Bible is not uniform either. The Pentateuch is highly stable as a canonical division, almost always appearing in its familiar narrative sequence of Genesis, Exodus, Leviticus, Numbers, and Deuteronomy. The Prophets exhibit a degree of variation in the internal sequences of the Major Prophets and the Minor Prophets.[66] The Major and Minor Prophets also vary in terms of which precedes and which follows the other within the prophetic division as a whole. The Writings exist in quite a number of differing arrangements.[67]

For the most part, English-language Bibles observe an order derived from the Greek Bible, as inherited through the Latin Bible (or Vulgate). The primary characteristic of this order is its fourfold structure of Pentateuch, Historical Books (or Former Prophets), Poetical Books, and Latter Prophets (Major + Minor).[68] The Greek Bible, or Septuagint, is itself a Jewish Bible and began to be translated from the Hebrew c. 280–250 BCE, starting with the Pentateuch.[69] Until the discovery of the Dead Sea Scrolls, the oldest extant Hebrew Bibles dated from the tenth century CE, which meant that the Septuagint provided the primary witness to the state of the text 1,000 years earlier. Even after the Dead Sea Scrolls were found, beginning in 1946, the Greek biblical tradition has continued to be used to clarify important textual questions. It also plays a crucial role in exegetical work on the New Testament because the New Testament's authors appear to have read and relied on Old Testament Scripture largely in Greek translation.[70]

At the same time, references to "the" Septuagint obscure the nature of this translation, which was never uniform in character.[71] Nor does the Greek Bible ever appear to have had a standardized scope and order of its books. Three great codices of the Greek Bible, known as Alexandrinus, Sinaiticus, and Vaticanus, exist from the fourth–fifth centuries CE. All three differ in their scope and order, especially with regard to the books later designated "apocryphal" or "deuterocanonical."[72] Thus, Alexandrinus contains Tobit, Judith, 1–2 Esdras, and 1–4 Maccabees before the Psalms, with Wisdom and Sirach following the Writings; Sinaiticus includes Tobit, Judith, and 4 Maccabees before the Prophets, as well as Wisdom and Sirach after the Writings (but prior to Job). Only Vaticanus displays something like the fourfold order found in modern English-language Bibles, with the Poetical Books in the middle and the Latter Prophets at the end.[73] For this reason, characterizations such as "Christian order" and "Jewish order," as much as they usefully highlight contemporary differences, become misleading as descriptions of the situation in antiquity.[74] Indeed, some evidence indicates that *both* the threefold and fourfold arrangements have ancient Jewish roots.[75] The book of Sirach (c. 180 BCE) suggestively refers to law, wisdom, and prophecies (38:34b–39:1) rather than following the order of law, prophecies, and wisdom.[76] At one time it was thought that the fourfold order reflected a canon belonging to Jewish communities outside the land of Israel, particularly in Egypt. But the notion of an "Alexandrian canon" was largely demolished by Sundberg, who emphasized the canon's early lack of standardization.[77] Thanks to the pioneering efforts of Martin Hengel, among others, the old distinction between "Hellenistic" and "Palestinian" Judaism has completely broken down.[78] There was in fact much more cultural overlap and interaction between the two cultures than scholars had previously thought. With regard to the biblical text, there is now good evidence demonstrating that Greek manuscripts did exist in ancient Israel and that some early Greek biblical manuscripts were in fact revised in the direction of the developing Hebrew Bible (e.g., the prototheodotionic recension evident in texts such as 8HevXIIgr).[79] In this way, the Hebrew Bible continued to be known, exerting an influence on Greek biblical translations, even as the Greek Bible became more widely used (see Table 2.1).

The fundamental historical question regarding the relation between the smaller and larger Christian Old Testament canons is whether the smaller canon represents an earlier core or a secondary narrowing. In this regard, it remains highly significant that Philo of Alexandria (20 BCE–50 CE) almost never cites an apocryphal book, although he writes in Greek. Pentateuchal Scripture does predominate in Philo's work, but Philo cites from the Prophets and the Writings as well – just not nearly as often.[80] Philo also at one point refers explicitly to the biblical canon with a tripartite formula: "the laws, and the oracles given by inspiration through the prophets, and the psalms" (De Vita Cont. 25).

The Western church ultimately followed Augustine (354–430 CE) in recognizing the wider Old Testament canon. The Eastern Church tended only at first to favor the narrower canon. Nevertheless, a learned tradition throughout Christianity maintained awareness of Judaism's narrower canon into the medieval period. Doubts about the apocryphal books were expressed by Jerome, Athanasius, Cyril of Jerusalem, Gregory Nazianzus, Epiphanius, Rufinus, Gregory the Great, John of Damascus, Hugh of St. Victor, Nicholas of Lyra, Ximenes, and Cajetan.[81] In the Protestant Reformation, Martin Luther (1483–1546) rejected the apocryphal books because of their apparent support for prayers on behalf of the dead and purgatory (2 Macc 12:39-45; 15:12-16). However, some of the resistance to the apocryphal books also had humanistic roots. Until the modern period, these books existed only in Greek (i.e., without Hebrew exemplars), casting doubt on their authenticity.

Table 2.1. *Major canonical orders*

Jewish	Protestant	Roman Catholic	Greek Orthodox
Torah	*Pentateuch*	*Pentateuch*	*Pentateuch*
Genesis	Genesis	Genesis	Genesis
Exodus	Exodus	Exodus	Exodus
Leviticus	Leviticus	Leviticus	Leviticus
Numbers	Numbers	Numbers	Numbers
Deuteronomy	Deuteronomy	Deuteronomy	Deuteronomy
Prophets	*Historical Books*	*Historical Books*	*Historical Books*
Joshua	Joshua	Joshua	Joshua
Judges	Judges	Judges	Judges
1 Samuel	Ruth	Ruth	Ruth
2 Samuel	1 Samuel	1 Samuel	1 Kingdoms
1 Kings	2 Samuel	2 Samuel	2 Kingdoms
2 Kings	1 Kings	1 Kings	3 Kingdoms
Isaiah	2 Kings	2 Kings	4 Kingdoms
Jeremiah	1 Chronicles	1 Chronicles	1 Paralipomenon
Ezekiel	2 Chronicles	2 Chronicles	2 Paralipomenon
Hosea	Ezra	Ezra	1 Esdras
Joel	Nehemiah	Nehemiah	2 Esdras
Amos	Esther	Tobit	Tobit
Obadiah	*Poetical Books*	Judith	Judith
Jonah	Job	Esther	Esther
Micah	Psalms	1 Maccabees	1 Maccabees
Nahum	Proverbs	2 Maccabees	2 Maccabees
Habakkuk	Ecclesiastes	*Poetical Books*	3 Maccabees
Zephaniah	Song of Songs	Job	*Poetical Books*
Haggai	*Prophets*	Psalms	Psalms
Zechariah	Isaiah	Proverbs	Job
Malachi	Jeremiah	Ecclesiastes	Proverbs
Writings	Lamentations	Song of Songs	Ecclesiastes
Psalms	Ezekiel	Wisdom of Solomon	Song of Songs
Proverbs	Daniel	Sirach	Wisdom of Solomon

Jewish	Protestant	Roman Catholic	Greek Orthodox
Job	Hosea	*Prophets*	Sirach
Song of Songs	Joel	Isaiah	*Prophets*
Ruth	Amos	Jeremiah	Hosea
Lamentations	Obadiah	Lamentations	Amos
Ecclesiastes	Jonah	Baruch	Micah
Esther	Micah	Ezekiel	Joel
Daniel	Nahum	Daniel	Obadiah
Ezra	Habakkuk	Hosea	Jonah
Nehemiah	Zephaniah	Joel	Nahum
1 Chronicles	Haggai	Amos	Habakkuk
2 Chronicles	Zechariah	Obadiah	Zephaniah
	Malachi	Jonah	Haggai
		Micah	Zechariah
		Nahum	Malachi
		Habakkuk	Isaiah
		Zephaniah	Jeremiah
		Haggai	Baruch
		Zechariah	Lamentations
		Malachi	Letter of Jeremiah
			Ezekiel
			Daniel

Today, Jews and Protestants share a biblical canon with the same scope but a different order. Roman Catholics and the Orthodox both maintain the larger canon, although with minor differences in scope and order. The Ethiopian church possesses the largest canon of all, which includes all the apocryphal books as well as Jubilees and Enoch. However, there are still good reasons to speak of a single canon shared in different formats rather than multiple "canons." The difference in the arrangement of the Protestant and Jewish canons has yet to be shown to be materially significant.[82] Similarly, it is debated whether the presence or absence of the apocryphal books makes any difference today. A number of Protestant traditions are open to learning from the apocryphal books, although they may still restrict the source of their doctrine to the books of the narrower canon. Moreover, one of the reasons Protestants give for retaining the narrower canon is theological rather than historical in nature: by holding to its smaller scope, they continue to share their canon with Jews.

If the biblical canon is to preserve its usefulness and significance in the future, it will need to serve as a shared touchstone for as many discussion partners as possible. Hope for the future is still available from the past: the basic contents of the canon have been stable for 2,000 years and continue to provide a common inheritance for the Abrahamic faiths and Western civilization.

NOTES

1. E.g., Rolf Rendtorff, *The Canonical Hebrew Bible*, trans. by David E. Orton (Tools for Biblical Study 7; Leiden, Netherlands: Deo, 2005), 4; Heinz-Josef Fabry, "Das 'Alte Testament,'" in *What Is Bible?*, ed. by Karin Finsterbusch and Armin Lange (CBET 67; Leuven, Belgium: Peeters, 2012), 294: "Das Christusbekenntnis macht von jetzt an die heiligen Schriften Israels zum *'Alten* Testament'" (his emphasis).

2. Melito's account is related by the church historian Eusebius about 150 years later (see his *Ecclesiastical History*, 4.26.13–14). See further R. Mosis, "Die Bücher des 'Alten Bundes' bei Melito von Sardes," in *Schätze der Schrift*, ed. by A. Moenikes (Paderborner Theologische Studien 47; Paderborn, Germany: Schöningh, 2007), 131–76. Both Irenaeus (*Adv. Haer.* 4.28.1–2) and Tertullian (*Against Praxeas* 15) use similar language at about the same time as Melito. Clement of Alexandria, *Strom.* 5.85.1, also refers around this time to "the Old and New Testaments"; see Ulrike Mittman and Rouven Genz, "The Term and Concept of New Testament," in Finsterbusch and Lange, *Bible*, 323.

3. For the preceding information and further discussion, see Lee Martin McDonald, *The Origin of the Bible: A Guide for the Perplexed* (London: T & T Clark, 2011), 16–18. As McDonald notes, the term "covenant" already appears by itself in the legal material of the Old Testament, where it can be used as an umbrella term for the various provisions and teachings found there (e.g., Exod 19:5; 24:7–8).

4. Mittmann and Genz, "New Testament," 324.

5. So, too, the language of "new covenant," which is attested not only in the New Testament but already also at Qumran (e.g., CD 6:19; 8:21; 19:33–4; 20:12).

6. Josephus, *Against Apion*, trans. by H. St. J. Thackeray. (Loeb Classical Library; Cambridge, MA: Harvard University Press, 1966), 1:37–43 (emphasis added).

7. The frequently heard objection that Josephus' appeal to antiquity was strategic rather than accurate is considerably weakened by the presence of this same appeal in other early Jewish sources.

8. Albert C. Sundberg, Jr., "The Bible Canon and the Christian Doctrine of Inspiration," *Interpretation* 29 (1975): 356. Sundberg understood that the

term "open canon" could thus in theory be used as a synonym for what he called "scripture," but he argued against such nomenclature, maintaining that it would still imply too much fixity in the period prior to the canon's actual establishment.

9 See further James C. VanderKam, *The Dead Sea Scrolls and the Bible* (Grand Rapids, MI: Eerdmans, 2012).

10 Lee Martin McDonald, *The Biblical Canon* (Peabody, MA: Hendrickson, 2007); Eugene Ulrich, *The Dead Sea Scrolls and the Origins of the Bible* (SDSSRL; Grand Rapids, MI: Eerdmans, 1999).

11 Eugene Ulrich, "The Community of Israel and the Composition of the Scripture," in *The Quest for Context and Meaning: Studies in Biblical Intertextuality in Honor of James A. Sanders*, ed. by Craig A. Evans and Shemaryahu Talmon (Biblical Interpretation Series 28; Leiden, Netherlands: Brill, 1997), 341–2 (emphasis in original).

12 Joseph Blenkinsopp, *Prophecy and Canon* (Studies in Judaism and Christianity in Antiquity 3; Notre Dame, IN: University of Notre Dame Press, 1977).

13 Note, however, that the Psalms do not always begin the Writings. Sometimes the canon's third division begins instead with Ruth (as in b. Baba Batra 14b-15a) or Job (as in both the Leningrad and Aleppo codices) or Chronicles. See Rendtorff, *Hebrew Bible*, 5.

14 John H. Hayes, *An Introduction to Old Testament Study* (Nashville, TN: Abingdon, 1979), 24–5. Hayes notes that this dating scheme only works in the Hebrew (Masoretic) Text tradition and not with either the Samaritan Pentateuch or the Greek Bible. This variance in itself further supports its intentional construction in the MT.

15 Awareness of this kind of impulse is also growing in New Testament scholarship; see D. Moody Smith, "When Did the Gospels Become Scripture?" *JBL* 119(1) (2000): 3–20.

16 Brevard S. Childs, *Introduction to the Old Testament as Scripture* (Philadelphia: Fortress, 1979).

17 For the classic statement of this theory, see Herbert Edward Ryle, *The Canon of the Old Testament*, 2nd ed. (London: Macmillan, 1914). For a comprehensive account of the rise of this view, see Stephen B. Chapman, "Modernity's Canonical Crisis: Historiography and Theology in Collision," in *Hebrew Bible/Old Testament: The History of Its Interpretation*, Vol. III: *From Modernism to Post-Modernism, Part I: The Nineteenth Century – A Century of Modernism and Historicism*, ed. by Magne Sæbø (Göttingen, Germany: Vandenhoeck und Ruprecht, 2013), 651–87.

18 The term "Torah" also can be used to refer to the entire Hebrew Bible. Thus, Ezek 39:15 is cited as *torah* in b. Mo'ed Qatan 5a, and Ps 82:6 is similarly cited in b. Sanhedrin 91b. In the New Testament, John 10:34 quotes Ps 82:6 as "law," and 1 Cor 14:21 cites as "law" Isa 28:11–12.

19 Rendtorff, *Hebrew Bible*, 6.

20 See further Peter W. Flint, "The Daniel Tradition at Qumran," in *Eschatology, Messianism, and the Dead Sea Scrolls*, ed. by Craig A. Evans and Peter W. Flint (SDSSRL1; Grand Rapids, MI: Eerdmans, 1997), 41–60; Robert A. Kraft, "Daniel Outside the Traditional Jewish Canon: In the Footsteps of

M. R. James," in *Studies in the Hebrew Bible, Qumran, and the Septuagint Presented to Eugene Ulrich*, ed. by Peter W. Flint, Emanuel Tov, and James C. VanderKam (VTSup 101; Leiden, Netherlands: Brill, 2006), 121–33.

21   Cf. Karel van der Toorn, *Scribal Culture and the Making of the Hebrew Bible* (Cambridge, MA: Harvard University Press, 2007), 235: "Today this theory of canonization is no longer in favor with the scholarly community.... The history of the canonization of the Hebrew Bible has to be written anew."

22   James D. Purvis, *The Samaritan Pentateuch and the Origin of the Samaritan Sect* (HSM 2; Cambridge, MA: Harvard University Press, 1968). Although the Samaritans appear to have had their own temple on Mount Gerizim from the fifth century BCE on, the received form of the Samaritan Pentateuch must be dated to the Maccabean period on epigraphic grounds. On the possibility that the Samaritans may have later rejected portions of Jewish Scripture instead of never accepting them at all, see R. J. Coggins, *Samaritans and Jews: The Origins of Samaritanism Reconsidered* (Growing Points in Theology; Atlanta: John Knox, 1975). The earliest historical witness for a Samaritan canon consisting solely of the Pentateuch, so far as I know, is Origen (185–253 CE), *Commentary on John* 13.26 and *Against Celsus*, 1.49.

23   Jack P. Lewis, "Jamnia Revisited," in *The Canon Debate*, ed. by Lee Martin McDonald and James A. Sanders (Peabody, MA: Hendrickson, 2002), 146–62. The rabbinic gathering at Yavneh was a school, not a "council," and its discussion of biblical books addressed whether certain *already* canonical books should remain canonical rather than whether previously noncanonical books should be made canonical.

24   Roger T. Beckwith, *The Old Testament Canon of the New Testament Church and Its Background in Early Judaism* (Grand Rapids, MI: Eerdmans, 1985); David Noel Freedman, "The Symmetry of the Hebrew Bible," *Studia theologica* 46 (1992): 83–108; Shnayer Z. Leiman, *The Canonization of Hebrew Scripture: The Talmudic and Midrashic Evidence* (Transactions of the Connecticut Academy of Arts and Sciences 47; Hamden, CT: Archon Books, 1976).

25   This same methodological observation has been made in relation to investigations into the New Testament canon by John Barton, *Holy Writings, Sacred Text: The Canon in Earliest Christianity* (Louisville, KY: Westminster John Knox, 1997).

26   See, e.g., Margalit Finkelberg and Guy G. Stroumsa, eds., *Homer, the Bible, and Beyond: Literary and Religious Canons in the Ancient World* (Jerusalem Studies in Religion and Culture 2; Leiden, Netherlands: Brill, 2003).

27   Childs, *Introduction*, 77–9; Julio Trebolle Barrera, *The Jewish Bible and the Christian Bible*, trans. by Wilfred G. E. Watson (Grand Rapids, MI: Eerdmans, 1998), 157: "To some extent it can be said that the concept of canonicity accompanies the formation process of the OT from the beginning."

28   B. J. Schwartz, "Bible," in *The Oxford Dictionary of the Jewish Religion*, ed. by R. J. Z. Werblowsky and G. Wigoder (New York: Oxford University Press, 1997), 121–2.

29   Harry Y. Gamble, "Christianity, Scripture and Canon," in *The Holy Book in Comparative Perspective*, ed. by Frederick M. Denny and Rodney L. Taylor (Columbia: University of South Carolina Press, 1985), 44–5.

30   See further John F. A. Sawyer, "Combating Prejudices about the Bible and Judaism," *Theology* 94 (1991): 269–78; in response, R. W. L. Moberly, "'Old Testament' and 'New Testament': The Propriety of the Terms for Christian Theology," *Theology* 95 (1992): 26–32.

31   Paul van Buren, "On Reading Someone Else's Mail: The Church and Israel's Scriptures," in *Die Hebräische Bibel und ihre zweifache Nachgeschichte*, ed. by Erhard Blum, Christian Macholz, and Ekkehard W. Stegemann (Neukirchen-Vluyn, Germany: Neukirchener, 1990), 595–606. However, see as well van Buren's *According to the Scriptures: The Origins of the Gospel and the Church's Old Testament* (Grand Rapids, MI: Eerdmans, 1998), 92–3, where he qualifies his earlier formulation as "too simple."

32   See further Robert Davidson, "The Old Testament in the Church?" and William M. McKane, "Old and New Covenant (Testament): A Terminological Inquiry," in *Understanding Poets and Prophets; Essays in Honour of George Wishard Anderson*, ed. by A. Graeme Auld (JSOTSup 152; Sheffield, UK: JSOT Press, 1993), 114–26 and 227–35 (respectively).

33   This worry is articulated by John Barton, "Old Testament or Hebrew Bible?," in *The Old Testament: Canon, Literature and Theology* (Society for Old Testament Study Monographs; Burlington, VT: Ashgate, 2007), 83–9. Barton advocates the retention of "Old Testament" as a "neutral" term on the basis that it is "just what these books have been called in English for as long as they have had a name" (87–8), which rather badly misses the point. However, his concern that emphasis on the Jewishness of the Old Testament may serve to engender, rather than diminish, anti-Semitism needs to be taken seriously. The other difficulty with "Old Testament" as a neutral convention is that the practice will then evacuate the term's proper Christian meaning and turn it into something merely secular, as in Bruce Zuckerman, "Choosing Among the Strands: Teaching Hebrew Bible Survey to Undergraduates at a Secular University," in *Double Takes: Thinking and Rethinking Issues of Modern Judaism in Ancient Context*, ed. by Zev Garber and Bruce Zuckerman (Studies in the Shoah 26; Lanham, MD: University Press of America, 2004), 107–35.

34   Cf. Barton, "Old Testament," 89: "The Old Testament is indeed part of the heritage of Judaism, but that does not mean it is the exclusive heritage of what became mainstream rabbinic Judaism."

35   "Premodern" is a preferable term; traditional interpreters exercised significant critical discernment and not in such a different fashion as some contemporary scholars frequently assume. See F. E. Greenspahn, "How Modern are Modern Biblical Studies?," in *Minḥah le-Naḥum Biblical and Other Studies Presented to Nahum M. Sarna in Honour of his 70th Birthday*, ed. by M. Brettler and M. Fishbane (JSOTSup 154; Sheffield Academic Press, 1993), 164–82.

36   Christopher R. Seitz, *Word Without End: The Old Testament as Abiding Theological Witness* (Grand Rapids, MI: Eerdmans, 1998), 62, points out that even the lack of complementarity in a pairing such as "Hebrew Bible" and "New Testament" threatens to subvert the formal symmetry of the Christian Bible and thus diminish a sense of continuity between the two testaments. Also, on purely historical grounds, there may be more reason

to consider the New Testament a collection of *Jewish* literature than "Christian" literature!

37 JPS translations do not completely exclude consideration of Greek manuscripts, but they evidence a clear preference for the Hebrew text tradition whenever possible. See "Preface to the 1985 JPS Edition," in *The Jewish Study Bible*, ed. by Adele Berlin and Marc Zvi Brettler (Oxford University Press, 2004), xiii–xvi.

38 McDonald, *Biblical Canon*, 14.

39 See the comments of Amy-Jill Levine, *The Misunderstood Jew: The Church and the Scandal of the Jewish Jesus* (San Francisco: HarperCollins, 2006), 194: "Greek Orthodox students in the classroom were told that their language of 'Old Testament' was insensitive; their occasional protest that shifting the terminology to 'Hebrew Bible' erased their tradition went unheeded."

40 Levine, *Misunderstood Jew*, 194–5: "The shift in vocabulary to 'Hebrew Bible' thus creates a Protestant default. In attempting to avoid anti-Semitism, the shift in terminology promoted a generally unacknowledged anti-Catholicism."

41 See further Stanley Fish, *Is There a Text in This Class? The Authority of Interpretive Communities* (Cambridge, MA: Harvard University Press, 1980).

42 Jon D. Levinson, *The Hebrew Bible, the Old Testament, and Historical Criticism* (Louisville, KY: Westminster John Knox, 1993).

43 James Barr, *Holy Scripture: Canon, Authority, Criticism* (Philadelphia: Westminster, 1983), 5.

44 L. B. Wolfenson, "Implications of the Place of the Book of Ruth in Editions, Manuscripts, and Canon of the Old Testament," *HUCA* 1 (1924): 151–78.

45 See Ernest Frerichs, "The Torah Canon of Judaism and the Interpretation of Hebrew Scripture," *Horizons in Biblical Theology* 9 (1987): 13–25; Frederick Greenspahn, "Jewish Ambivalence Towards the Bible," *Journal of Hebrew Studies* 49 (2007): 7–21; Ziony Zevit, "From Judaism to Biblical Religion and Back Again," in *The Hebrew Bible: New Insights and Scholarship*, ed. by Frederick E. Greenspahn (New York University Press, 2008), 164–90.

46 See further Marvin A. Sweeney, "Tanak versus Old Testament: Concerning the Foundation for a Jewish Theology of the Bible," in *Problems in Biblical Theology: Essays in Honor of Rolf Knierim*, ed. by H. T. C. Sun et al. (Grand Rapids, MI: Eerdmans, 1997), 353–72; Tal Ilan, "The Term and Concept of TaNaKh," in Finsterbusch and Lange, *Bible*, 219: "This acronym is very late. It is found neither in the early Tannaitic nor in the late Amoraic strata of rabbinic literature."

47 Bernard M. Levinson, "The Development of the Jewish Bible: Critical Reflections upon the Concept of a 'Jewish Bible' and on the Idea of Its 'Development,'" in Finsterbusch and Lange, *Bible*, 386: "It seems the very term *Jewish Bible* represents a problematic form of modern political correctness that is neither historically nor hermeneutically accurate for the subject it seeks to describe" (italics in original).

48 Only a few prophetic texts are read as *haftarah* in the synagogue lectionary; for the texts and commentary, see Michael A. Fishbane, *Haftarot: The Traditional Hebrew Text with the New JPS Translation* (JPS Bible Commentary; Philadelphia: Jewish Publication Society, 2002). The Writings

are not included in the modern lectionary at all, although the five Megilloth (Song of Songs, Ruth, Lamentations, Ecclesiastes, and Esther) are read on religious festivals. There is some intriguing evidence that the Writings may have once been read in synagogue services despite frequent assumptions to the contrary; see Ben Zion Wacholder, "Prolegomenon," in Jacob Mann, *The Bible as Read and Preached in the Old Synagogue*, 2 vols. (New York: Ktav, 1971), 1:xxxv; cf. Beckwith, *Old Testament Canon*, 144, citing b. T. Shabbat 116b. The term Miqra' does possess an ancient pedigree; however, contemporary use of the term exhibits significant differences from its use within rabbinic literature. See Alexander Samely, "The Bible as Talked About: Reflections on the Usage and Conceptual Implications of the Term Miqra' in Early Rabbinic Literature," in Finsterbusch and Lange, *Bible*, 193–217.

49 See further Lawrence H. Schiffman, "The Term and Concept of Torah," in Finsterbusch and Lange, *Bible*, 173–91, esp. 191: "Ultimately, in medieval and modern times, the concept of Torah became synonymous with the whole of Judaism, even including sometimes local customs."

50 John Goldingay, *Old Testament Theology*, Vol. 1: *Israel's Gospel* (Downers Grove, IL: InterVarsity, 2003), 15; James A. Sanders, "First Testament and Second," *Biblical Theology Bulletin* 17 (1987): 47–9; Erich Zenger, *Das erste Testament: die jüdische Bible und die Christen* (Dusseldorf, Germany: Patmos, 1991).

51 In fact, the term does appear in the New Testament (Heb 8:7, 13; 9:1, 15, 18; cf. 10:9) in reference to the Old Testament's sacrificial instructions. Such usage could be understood as providing a biblical warrant for Christians to adopt the term, but it also should be taken into account that (1) the entirety of the Old Testament is apparently not in view and (2) the term is colored by its appearance in the New Testament only in Hebrews, that is, arguably its sharpest point of discontinuity with the Old Testament. See Erich Zenger, "Thesen zu einer Hermeneutik des Ersten Testaments nach Auschwitz," in *Eine Bibel – zwei Testamente: Positionen Biblischer Theologie*, ed. by Christoph Dohmen and Thomas Söding (Uni-Taschenbücher 1893; Paderborn, Germany: Schöningh, 1995), 143–58. Zenger attempts to ameliorate the supersessionistic connotation of the term by pointing out that it also appears, used more positively, in LXX Lev 26:45.

52 Goldingay, *Old Testament Theology*, 34: "Calling Israel's Scriptures 'the Old Testament' or 'the First Testament' identifies them as a Part One that has a Part Two. The terms 'Old Testament' or 'First Testament' indeed presuppose a Christian theological judgment on the significance of Israel's Scriptures."

53 Horst Seebass, "Erstes oder Altes Testament?" in *The Unity of Scripture and the Diversity of the Canon*, ed. by John Barton and Michael Wolter (BZNW 118; Berlin: de Gruyter, 2003), 27–43.

54 The expression "Prime Testament" represents an effort to articulate the notion of "primary" without the possible connotation of "initial." For this proposal, see André Lacocque, "The 'Old Testament' in the Protestant Tradition," in *Biblical Studies: Meeting Ground of Jews and Christians*, ed. by Lawrence Boadt, Helga Croner, and Leon Klenicki (Mahwah, NJ: Paulist Press, 1980), 120–43.

55 Esther Menn, "Inner-Biblical Exegesis in the Tanak," in *A History of Biblical Interpretation*, Vol. 1: *The Ancient Period*, ed. by Alan J. Hauser and Duane F. Watson (Grand Rapids, MI: Eerdmans, 1990), 75.

56 Eugene Ulrich, "The Non-Attestation of a Tripartite Canon in 4QMMT," *CBQ* 65(2) (2003): 202–14.

57 Seitz, *Word*, 72: "It is not clear if 'Hebrew Bible' is a parallel or a displacing term. The new convention might be parsed this way: 'Old Testament' is a term that arose within Christian (religious) circles and therefore points to that context of reading, while 'Hebrew Bible' is a more neutral term and could be used by readers without specific religious convictions of any sort. Not by accident, therefore, was the convention 'Old Testament/Torah' not to find its way into recent parlance, since it would cover different territory than 'Old Testament/Hebrew Bible.'"

58 Note the cautionary tale provided by Steven D. Fraade, "Response to 'Biblical Debates': Yes *and* No," in Finsterbusch and Lange, *Bible*, 154–5: "At my university, a long-standing introductory undergraduate course was once known as 'Introduction to the Old Testament.' However, when it was incorporated into the Program in Judaic Studies it was renamed 'Introduction to the Old Testament/Hebrew Bible.' In recent years, however, enrollments in that course had been dropping, in part because Jewish students found 'Old Testament' to sound too Christian, while Christian (and Jewish) students were put off by 'Hebrew Bible' as suggesting study of a text in Hebrew. This semester the instructor changed the title to simply "The Bible" (with the course description beginning, 'The writings common to both Jewish and Christian scripture'). Suddenly enrollments tripled."

59 See further Gavin Flood, "The Study of Religion as Corrective Reading," in *Fields of Faith: Theology and Religious Studies for the Twenty-First Century*, ed. by David F. Ford, Ben Quash, and Janet Martin Soskice (Cambridge University Press, 2005), 56–72; David F. Ford and C. C. Pecknold, *The Promise of Scriptural Reasoning* (Oxford, UK: Wiley-Blackwell, 2007).

60 James L. Kugel, "The Bible in the University," in *The Hebrew Bible and Its Interpreters*, ed. by William H. Propp, Baruch Halpern, and David Noel Freedman (Winona Lake, IN: Eisenbrauns, 1990), 143–65.

61 *Against Apion* 1:37–43; see the block quotation earlier.

62 See further D. L. Christensen, "Josephus and the Twenty-Two Book Canon of Sacred Scripture," *Journal of the Evangelical Theological Society* 29 (1986): 37–46; Steve Mason, "Josephus and His Twenty-Two Book Canon," in McDonald and Sanders, *Canon Debate*, 110–27.

63 See further Beckwith, *Old Testament Canon*, 185. There is a slender possibility that Jubilees 2:23–4 may provide a veiled reference to a twenty-two book canon. For discussion, see McDonald, *Biblical Canon*, 158–60.

64 Beckwith, *Old Testament Canon*, 235–73.

65 McDonald, *Biblical Canon*, 150–60.

66 For example, in b. Baba Batra 14b–15a, the order of the Latter Prophets is Jeremiah, Ezekiel, and Isaiah; in the Greek Bible, the first six of the Minor Prophets regularly appear as Hosea, Amos, Micah, Joel, Obadiah, and Jonah.

67 See Peter Brandt, *Endgestalten des Kanons: das Arrangement der Schriften Israels in der jüdischen und christlichen Bibel* (BBB 131; Berlin: Philo, 2001).

On the Writings, now see Timothy J. Stone, *The Compilational History of the Megilloth: Canon, Contoured Intertextuality and Meaning in the Writings* (FAT 2.59; Tübingen, Germany: Mohr Siebeck, 2013).

68 There are some English translations that differ in this regard; e.g., the New Jewish Publication Society (NJPS) translation reproduces the scope and order of the Masoretic canon.

69 See further Tessa Rajak, *Translation and Survival: The Greek Bible of the Ancient Jewish Diaspora* (Oxford University Press, 2009).

70 See Dietrich-Alex Koch, *Die Schrift als Zeuge des Evangeliums: Untersuchungen zur Verwendung und zum Verständnis der Schrift bei Paulus* (Beiträge zur historischen Theologie 69; Tübingen, Germany: Mohr Siebeck, 1986).

71 Leonard J. Greenspoon, "The Use and Abuse of the Term 'LXX' and Related Terminology in Recent Scholarship," *BIOSCS* 20 (1987): 21–9.

72 See further, James Keith Elliott, "Manuscripts, the Codex and the Canon," *Journal for the Study of the New Testament* 63 (1996): 105–23.

73 Even in Vaticanus, the Minor Prophets appear before the Major Prophets, and the Latter Prophets are followed by Daniel, which actually concludes the collection.

74 Note as well that some later Jewish Bibles separate the Megilloth from the rest of the Writings and place them as a unit between the Pentateuch and the Prophets, also yielding a fourfold pattern.

75 Cf. the argument of Wolfenson, "Implications of the Place of the Book of Ruth," that the tripartite structure of the Hebrew Bible emerged quite late (c. 100–150 CE), and that prior to that time the Prophets and the Writings were not fully distinguished from each other.

76 Melito's list (c. 150–200 CE) also reports what is apparently the Hebrew order as having the Poetical Books in the middle and the Latter Prophets at the end. See further Beckwith, *Old Testament Canon*, 183–4. Melito lists Esdras as the final book of the canon.

77 Albert C. Sundberg, *The Old Testament of the Early Church* (HTS 20; Cambridge, MA: Harvard University Press, 1964). Cf. Barrera, *Bible*, 229–33.

78 Martin Hengel, *Judaism and Hellenism: Studies in the Encounter in Palestine during the Early Hellenistic Period*, trans. by John Bowden (Philadelphia: Fortress, 1974); idem, *The "Hellenization" of Judaea in the First Century after Christ* (Philadelphia: Trinity, 1989).

79 See further, Dominique Barthélemy, *Les devanciers d'Aquila* (VTSup 10; Leiden, Netherlands: Brill, 1963); Emanuel Tov, *The Greek Minor Prophets Scrolls from Naḥal Ḥever: 8ḤevXIIgr* (DJD 8; Oxford, UK: Clarendon, 1990).

80 See J. Allenbach et al., eds., *Biblia Patristica: Supplément* (Paris: Éditions du centre national de la recherche scientifique, 1982). Of all the extracanonical books, Philo apparently refers only to Ben Sira and the Wisdom of Solomon, and only very rarely.

81 Raymond E. Brown, "Canonicity," in *The New Jerome Biblical Commentary*, ed. by Raymond E. Brown, Joseph A. Fitzmyer and Roland E. Murphy (Englewood Cliffs, NJ: Prentice-Hall, 1990), 1042A (66.41).

82 However, Levine, *Misunderstood Jew*, 199, engagingly employs a sports metaphor to express a fundamental difference between how she views the Jewish

Bible and the Christian Old Testament, particularly with regard to their respective conclusions (2 Chr 36:23 vs. Mal 4:4–6 [H 3:22–24]): "Christianity is football.... There is a linear sense to the Christian canon; one moves from the promise of the line of scrimmage to the goal of the (eschatological) end zone. Judaism, at least as understood by the canonical order, is baseball. The concern is to return to Zion, to go home."

FURTHER READING

Bartholomew, Craig, Scott Hahn, Robin Parry, Christopher Seitz and Al Wolters, eds. *Canon and Biblical Interpretation* (Scripture and Hermeneutics Seminar 7). Grand Rapids, MI: Zondervan, 2006.

Beckwith, Roger. *The Old Testament Canon of the New Testament Church and Its Background in Early Judaism.* Grand Rapids, MI: Eerdmans, 1985.

Brooks, Roger, and John J. Collins. *Hebrew Bible or Old Testament? Studying the Bible in Judaism and Christianity* (Christianity and Judaism in Antiquity 5). Notre Dame, IN: University of Notre Dame Press, 1990.

Chapman, Stephen B. *The Law and the Prophets: A Study in Old Testament Canon Formation* (FAT 27). Tübingen, Germany: Mohr Siebeck, 2000.

Cross, Frank Moore. *From Epic to Canon: History and Literature in Ancient Israel.* Baltimore, MD: Johns Hopkins University Press, 1998.

Finkelberg, Margalit, and Guy G. Stroumsa, eds. *Homer, the Bible, and Beyond: Literary and Religious Canons in the Ancient World* (Jerusalem Studies in Religion and Culture 2). Leiden, Netherlands: Brill, 2003.

Finsterbusch, Karin, and Armin Lange, eds. *What is Bible?* (CBET 67). Leuven, Belgium: Peeters, 2012.

Hengel, Martin. *The Septuagint as Christian Scripture.* Translated by Mark E. Biddle. Grand Rapids, MI: Baker Academic, 2002.

Lim, Timothy H. *The Formation of the Jewish Canon.* New Haven: Yale University Press, 2013.

McDonald, Lee Martin. *The Biblical Canon: Its Origin, Transmission, and Authority.* Peabody, MA: Hendrickson, 2007.

Seitz, Christopher R. *The Character of Christian Scripture: The Significance of a Two-Testament Bible* (Studies in Theological Interpretation). Grand Rapids, MI: Baker Academic, 2011.

Trebolle Barrera, Julio. *The Jewish Bible and the Christian Bible.* Translated by Wilfred G. E. Watson. Grand Rapids, MI: Eerdmans, 1998.

Part II

Historical background

3 The ancient Near Eastern context

KENTON L. SPARKS

During the nineteenth and early twentieth centuries, archaeologists began to recover the lost societies of the ancient Near East from Egypt, Mesopotamia, Syria, Anatolia, Persia and the Levant.[1] Many texts were unearthed in these digs, but at first the languages were unknown and the texts could not be read. Scholars managed to decipher the ancient scripts in a relatively short time, thanks to linguistic brilliance and the discovery of two multi-language texts, the Behistun Inscription of Darius (which permitted scholars to decipher the Akkadian script of Mesopotamia) and the Rosetta Stone (which permitted the same for Egyptian hieroglyphs). The feat of decipherment was so great that some of the world's best scholars doubted its accomplishment; these sceptics turned out to be wrong.

The texts from Mesopotamia had the most sensational effects in Europe and America. During the 1870s, scholars published Akkadian literature that was closely connected to the Bible. Some of these texts, which referred to Israel, Judah and their kings, were heralded as proof of the Bible's historicity and accuracy, but other texts created certain problems. Notable in this regard were *Enuma Elish*, the Gilgamesh Epic and the Sargon Birth Legend, which were, respectively, similar (for many, uncomfortably similar) to the creation story in Genesis, the biblical flood story and the story of Moses' birth. These texts appeared to undermine the supposed uniqueness of the Bible as the divine word. Some influential scholars began to think of Israel and its Bible as merely one small part of ancient Babylonian culture. Strong tensions soon emerged between the new field of Assyriology, which was discovering and publishing these new texts, and the field of Biblical studies, which was largely influenced by conservative Judaism and Christianity. The tensions persist to this day in some quarters of scholarship.

The 'pan-Babylonian' and 'parallelomania' approaches tended to assume that every similarity between Israelite and Mesopotamian literature was a result of borrowing from Mesopotamia.[2] For some, this meant that the writers of the Bible were reading and copying Mesopotamian texts, whereas others thought that the Bible reflected a degenerate memory of the more ancient and impressive Mesopotamian tradition. Scholars soon realized, however, that these theories offered deficient accounts of the matter.[3] They doubted that Israelite scribes living in Palestine, hundreds of miles from Mesopotamia, were reading and imitating cuneiform texts, and there were also clear differences between Israelite and Mesopotamian cultures. As a result, during the course of the twentieth century, scholars increasingly attributed these similarities to the general diffusion of religious and cultural ideas throughout the Near East. The Israelite scribes were not copying Mesopotamian texts – they were merely reflecting common religious and cultural patterns that permeated the ancient world.

In the last few decades, however, the pendulum respecting Mesopotamian influence has been modestly swinging the other way. Biblical texts once believed to come from early in Israel's history are now being dated to the exilic and post-exilic periods, at a point when the biblical writers actually lived in Mesopotamia or under its cultural influence. One result has been a renewed interest in the Near East and its literature among scholars and students of the Hebrew Bible. This chapter introduces that Near Eastern context.

Our discussion of the Near East is organised as a matrix that combines the contours of Near Eastern history with the history of Israel. Proceeding in this fashion allows readers to appreciate more readily the influence of Near Eastern culture on ancient Israel and its literature. The Appendix provides a chart of the history covered and a map of the region. Readers may wonder about the accuracy of the dates provided in the table and discussion. Because of their belief in the ominous nature of astronomical events, the Mesopotamians kept careful records of solar, lunar and planetary movements. By correlating these records with the dates given in Mesopotamian documents, scholars have been able to achieve quite precise dates for many events during the first millennium BCE. Dates for earlier periods are still relatively good but less precise; for instance, scholars often speak of the 'High', 'Middle' and 'Low' chronologies to describe three possible chronologies that suit the astronomical records from the early period.[4]

Modern resources for the study of the Near East are legion, but readers should be aware of the most important introductory books and sources.[5] Foremost among them is the multi-volume work edited by J. M. Sasson, *Civilizations of the Ancient Near East*, which includes a

wide variety of introductory articles on the history, culture and literature of the ancient world. The major introductory sources for the study
of Near Eastern literature are K. L. Sparks, *Ancient Texts for the Study
of the Hebrew Bible*, and a new volume edited by C. S. Erlich, *From
an Antique Land*. Standard English translations of Near Eastern literature include the *Context of Scripture* (ed. by W. W. Hallo) and the now
dated but still useful *Ancient Near Eastern Texts Relating to the Old
Testament* (ed. by J. B. Pritchard).[6]

ISRAEL'S ANCIENT NEAR EASTERN CONTEXT

A. Before Israel was, 3000–1200 BCE

The earliest Near Eastern civilizations arose in Egypt and Mesopotamia.
Writing was invented in both cultures prior to 3000, taking the form
of pictographic hieroglyphs in Egypt and a cuneiform ('wedge-shaped')
script in Sumer (lower or southern Mesopotamia).[7] As a rule the
Egyptians wrote on paper-like papyrus, which was much less durable
than the sun-dried or kiln-fired clay tablets used in Mesopotamia. This is
why archaeologists have recovered many more texts from Mesopotamia
than Egypt. Development of the Egyptian language and its written
scripts continued unabated down through history (progressively producing hieroglyphic, hieratic and demotic Egyptian), but as we will soon
see, the Sumerians and their language eventually disappeared.

The Sumerians developed a city-state culture in which each city
controlled its own suburbs, satellite towns and agricultural areas.[8]
Political power was shared in various ways by the king and the temple
of the city's chief deity. The most important cities were (from north to
south) Sippar, Kish, Nippur, Adab, Shuruppak, Umma, Lagash, Uruk,
Larsa, Ur and Eridu. Sumerian city-states were not large by modern or
even ancient standards; one of the largest, Lagash, comprised an area
of about 1,600 square kilometres and had a population of only 35,000
or so. Competition and war pockmarked this era of history, as one
city-state took control of another or even, on occasion, of Sumer as a
whole. Despite these political instabilities, the Sumerians produced
a significant literary tradition that included our oldest wisdom texts
(proverbs, riddles, dialogues and contest literature), epic tales of kings
and heroes (Enmerkar, Lugalbanda and Gilgamesh), hymns, prayers,
laments, love songs, magical incantations and numerous texts comparable to the biblical book of Genesis (a flood story, myths and a
king list similar to the genealogy in Gen 5).[9] We owe our copies of
these texts not to the Sumerian scribes alone but to the later Old

Babylonian scribes who inherited and preserved the Sumerian literary corpus.

During the second half of the third millennium, Sumerian culture was absorbed or displaced by a new culture whose language was Akkadian, a Semitic tongue related to the later biblical languages of Aramaic and Hebrew. These developments ushered in the Old Akkadian period.[10] Although scribes working in this period knew Sumerian and copied Sumerian texts, they adapted the Sumerian cuneiform script for writing their native Akkadian language. Sargon the Great (c. 2350–2300), King of Akkad, was among the most powerful of these early Semites. In contrast to Sumerian city-state culture, Sargon founded the first empire in Near Eastern antiquity, which lasted until about 2100. Notable from a literary standpoint is Sargon's daughter, Enḫeduanna, who wrote hymns and compiled a complete edition of the temple hymns of Sumer and Akkad. She was apparently the first female theologian and poet in the ancient world. Even so, the Sargonic dynasty eventually met its end. Scribes in the subsequent Ur III period provided a theological explanation for its fall in a famous text, the 'Curse of Akkad', which is comparable to Hebrew histories and prophecies that explain the respective falls of Israel and Judah.[11]

In connection with the Old Akkadian period, we should note the large administrative archive of twenty-fourth-century clay tablets recovered from ancient Ebla in Syria.[12] The Eblaite language was an East Semitic tongue closely related to Akkadian, but when the texts were first discovered, they were thought to be West Semitic (akin to Hebrew) and to reflect many historical connections with the events of early biblical history. These claims have now been thoroughly discredited, but the archive remains an important source of information about third-millennium Syria and the development of early urban cultures. Ebla was destroyed c. 2350 BCE (perhaps by Sargon the Great) but modestly recovered during the following Ur III period; its urban culture was finally brought to an end by the Hittites c. 1600 BCE.

The Ur III period (c. 2100–2000) was a last-gasp Sumerian 'renaissance' of sorts, after which the Sumerians seem to have disappeared for good.[13] As they faded into the cultural landscape, a new group of Semites – the Amorites – appeared on the scene, ushering in the Old Babylonian period (c. 2000–1600).[14] These Amorites were originally pastoralists, either nomadic or semi-nomadic, who came from steppes and desert fringes of Syria and the western desert and began to infiltrate the settled areas of Syria and Mesopotamia. It is unclear whether they were always in the area or migrated from somewhere else (or both). Their Semitic language differed from Akkadian (Amorite names are linguistically distinctive), but all the texts they have left are in Akkadian or Sumerian. Hammurabi (c. 1792–1750), the famous king of Babylon and founder of the Old Babylonian empire, was an Amorite. Numerous literary texts (hymns, prayers, omen texts and myths) and archival texts (legal and economic documents) come from this period, especially from the city of Sippar. Particularly significant for comparisons with the Hebrew Bible are the laws of Hammurabi and Eshnunna (cf. the biblical laws), the prophecies from Eshnunna (cf. biblical prophecy), the Gilgamesh Epic (cf. the heroic exploits of Jacob and Flood story) and the Atrahasis creation-flood myth (cf. Genesis 1–11).[15]

One archive contemporary with the Old Babylonian period is especially noteworthy. Archaeologists recovered over 20,000 texts from the city-state of Mari, in what is now modern Syria.[16] Its most famous ruler, Zimri-Lim, was an Amorite. Though he lived in a palace, he was kin to a major tent-dwelling tribal group of pastoralists. Because Mari society was composed of both tent-dwelling pastoralists and sedentary dwellers, many scholars believe that this archive – which contains numerous letters about life in Mari and its environs – provides a window into what life was like for the earliest Israelites and their immediate ancestors. In years past, a few scholars even suggested that Israel's earliest ancestors *were* Amorites (e.g., Abraham), but this is no longer widely believed. Nevertheless, it is generally recognised that the Mari texts shed considerable light on certain aspects of Israelite culture, such as Israel's pastoral lifestyle, prophecies (cf. the Mari prophetic letters and Israelite prophecy) and religious rituals.

Around 1600, forces from the east and west brought the Old Babylonian era to a close. From the west, a Hittite foray into Mesopotamia resulted in the sack of Babylon and an end of Hammurabi's dynasty (for discussion of the Hittites, see below). From the east, a new ethnic group appeared, called the Kassites, who seized power in Mesopotamia and ushered in the Middle Babylonian period (c. 1600–1200).[17] Little is known about the Kassites or their origins, but scholars credit them with copying and preserving the Mesopotamian literary tradition during the period. Among the creative literary works of the Kassite era were three wisdom texts, including *Ludlul Bel Nemeqi*, the Babylonian Theodicy and the standard version of the Gilgamesh Epic, which reframed the Old Babylonian version to accentuate the wisdom that Gilgamesh learned from his experiences.[18] All three texts questioned the validity of standard wisdom, which asserted that life has significance (contra Gilgamesh) and that human experience follows a predictable pattern of blessing for the righteous and punishment for evil (contra *Ludlul* and the Theodicy).

These pessimistic works are comparable with the biblical books of Job and especially Ecclesiastes, whose author was familiar with the Gilgamesh Epic and perhaps with the other texts as well.[19]

Before the Kassites ruled Babylon, a new civilization was brewing in Anatolia (modern Turkey). These people, known as the Hittites, came to the fore around 1700 and eventually created an empire that lasted for about two centuries (c. 1400–1200).[20] The Hittites spoke an Indo-European language distantly related to English. They are best known for their sack of Babylon and for the large archive (30,000 texts) left behind at the Hittite capital of Ḫattusha. Among these texts are historical texts, treaties, administrative texts, instructions, laws, myths, prayers, festivals, omens and rituals. The treaties and rituals, in particular, are quite comparable to some texts in the Hebrew Bible (cf. the Hittite scapegoat rites and Lev 16), as are the laws (cf. biblical law) and the priestly instructions (cf. Leviticus).[21] During a significant stretch of the Late Bronze Age, the Hittites fought with Egypt for control of the Levantine coast. The conflict ended in a truce that lasted over fifty years (c. 1260–1200), at which point the Hittite Empire collapsed under pressure from the Sea Peoples (see below) and from other factors that are not wholly understood (a likely factor was climate change). Biblical references to the Hittites do not refer to the Hittite Empire but were inspired by the smaller Neo-Hittite states created by Hittite refugees in southwest Anatolia and northern Syria after the empire's fall.[22] These states date between the twelfth and seventh centuries and included the likes of Carchemish, Karatepe, Kummah, Gurgum, Melid, Tabal, Mukish and Hamath. King Toi of Hamath, who sent an emissary to David in 2 Samuel 8:9–10, was a Neo-Hittite king.

Four ancient cities contemporary with the Kassites and Hittites should be mentioned, mainly because of the textual evidence each provides. The first is the city-state of Ugarit.[23] Located on a strategic trade route on the northern Levantine coast, this trade centre reached its cultural height from about 1450 to 1200. Two factors make it especially important for students of the ancient world and Hebrew Bible. First, scholars at Ugarit adapted the Mesopotamian cuneiform medium for writing their own language. The key innovation in this adaptation was to replace the Akkadian syllabic system (which involved several hundred signs) with an alphabetic system using only thirty letters. Second, there exists a large corpus of texts from Ugarit. The stash includes archival texts as well as numerous ritual and mythical texts that reflect religious themes and concepts similar to those found in the Hebrew Bible. For instance, the gods El and Baal and the goddess Asherah are prominent at Ugarit and in the Bible's descriptions of the Canaanite religion. Also comparable to the Hebrew Bible are the Ugaritic legends of Aqhat and Kirta, whose motifs are at some points reminiscent of the patriarchal stories in Genesis. For these reasons, the Ugaritic texts are regarded as the best source of information about the religious beliefs of ancient Canaan, which lay about 300 kilometres to the south of Ugarit.

The second important archive involves over 500 texts recovered from ancient Alalakh.[24] The texts, which date to the eighteenth, seventeenth and fifteenth centuries, are mainly administrative records which cast comparative light on ancient Israel's cultural and religious institutions; the best-known text, a biographical inscription of King Idrimi (fifteenth century) on his own statue, has been compared to the story of David's rise in 1 Samuel and to the heroic tales in Judges.

A third archive was unearthed at the ancient Hurrian city of Nuzi (in northern Mesopotamia).[25] Hurrian culture dominated upper Mesopotamia and Syria for significant stretches of the second millennium (c. 1600–1350), during which it established an empire (Mitanni) that rivalled Egypt and the Hittites. Scholars once believed that customs reflected in Nuzi's fifteenth- and fourteenth-century Akkadian texts were similar to, and thus confirmed, the antiquity of the patriarchal stories in Genesis, but today this is widely doubted; the Nuzi texts provide only general cultural background for our understanding of ancient Israel.[26]

A fourth important archive from this period was unearthed at Emar, in modern Syria.[27] Over eight hundred texts dating between the late fourteenth and early twelfth centuries were discovered. About half of these are archival records, but the balance is made up of lexical, literary and ritual texts. The ritual texts include anointing rituals and festivals which are similar to those described in the Hebrew Bible.[28]

Let us now consider ancient Egypt. Egyptian power ebbed and flowed throughout this period. The cultural high points were the Old Kingdom, Middle Kingdom, New Kingdom and Late Period, with phases of political and economic weakness between them. Scholars refer to these three low points as the first, second and third intermediate periods.[29]

The Old Kingdom (c. 2700–2150) is best known for the great pyramids that it produced in the vicinity of Memphis, Egypt's capital.[30] It is likely that the heavy burden of resources needed for these building projects ushered in the social and economic decline of the first intermediate period. From a literary standpoint, the most significant texts produced were the Instructions of Hardjedef and Ptahhotep (both from the Old Kingdom) and of Merkare (from the first intermediate period).[31] These texts are comparable to the biblical book of Proverbs. Also important were the rituals and incantations that gave one life after death.[32] Scholars call these 'Pyramid Texts', for the obvious reason that they were collected and inscribed on the passages and chambers of pyramids. The genre developed during the course of Egyptian history, yielding the Middle Kingdom 'Coffin Texts' and then the New Kingdom 'Book of the Dead'. During the Old Kingdom, the opportunity for an afterlife was limited to the pharaohs, who were viewed as deities, but by the New Kingdom, the genre was democratised and offered eternal bliss to other Egyptians. The myths used in this funerary literature are often reminiscent of the biblical creation stories.[33]

Egypt recovered from the first intermediate period during the Middle Kingdom (c. 2050–1650), with the city of Thebes emerging as Egypt's capital. Modern scholars often regard this era as the cultural high point of Egyptian literature.[34] Our most significant corpus of Near Eastern short stories and novella literature comes from this period.[35] The best known of these texts is the Story of Sinuhe, in which an Egyptian exiled to Syria/Palestine rises to power in a foreign setting; biblical scholars have compared this to the Joseph Story (Gen 37–50), in which an Israelite exiled to Egypt rises to power. Middle Kingdom scribes also composed instructional wisdom texts, akin to those produced in the Old Kingdom and later in the New Kingdom.

The second intermediate period, which brought the Middle Kingdom to a close, was ushered in by the rise of a foreign Asiatic regime. These Asiatics slowly infiltrated Egypt from the east and eventually became numerous enough to seize power. The Egyptians called them the Hyksos, meaning 'ruler(s) of foreign countries'.[36] The Hyksos ruled Egypt for about a century, from 1650 to 1550, until the Egyptians pushed them back into Syria/Palestine. Some scholars believe that the biblical Exodus story may reflect faint memories of the Hyksos expulsion from Egypt (as did the Jewish historian Josephus already in antiquity). But true or not, this much is clear: the Hyksos experience had a profound effect on the Egyptian psyche during the New Kingdom period (c. 1550–1100).[37]

In order to protect Egypt from future Asiatic incursions from the east, New Kingdom pharaohs – especially Thutmose III, Seti I and Rameses II – aggressively fought for control of Palestine and Syria, eventually turning Canaan into an Egyptian province (or close to it). The objective was not merely to control Canaan but also to establish a buffer territory between Egypt and the large nations to the north, including Mittanni (at the beginning of the New Kingdom) and the Hittites (at the end of the New Kingdom). Egypt eventually established peace with both nations. Another motivation for Egyptian control of Palestine was economic; the

New Kingdom coincided with the Late Bronze Age (1550–1200 BCE), a period of extensive international trade and cultural exchange. Control of the trade routes in Palestine and Syria allowed Egypt to exploit the benefits of this economic activity.

From the New Kingdom, the Amarna Letters provide an historical window into fourteenth-century Palestine.[38] The letters are reports from Egypt's vassals in Palestine and thus describe events as they were unfolding in the provinces. There are no signs of Israel or of any Israelite tribes in the letters, but the Canaanites report that bands of outlaws, called *Ḥapiru*, were roaming the area, making mischief, and sometimes seizing control of cities and regions. Some scholars believe that there may be some link between these *Ḥapiru* and the Hebrews, but this is a matter of considerable debate. Speculation about a connection between the Hebrews and the Amarna era was originally fuelled by the religious reforms of Pharaoh Akhenaten (Amenhotep IV, 1367–1350), a 'monotheist' of sorts who abolished Egypt's standard cults and built a new capital city called Akhetaten (modern el-Amarna), where he established a cult centre devoted to the worship of Aten, the sun disk. At one time it was believed that Israel's Mosaic monotheism was inspired by Akhenaten's reforms, but it is now recognized that Amarna religion was not really monotheistic. Both the god and pharaoh were worshipped, and the existence of other gods was admitted (hence, Amarna religion is better described as monolatry). Many readers will know the name of Akhenaten's son, King Tut (Tutankhamon, 1347–1339), whose tomb treasures have been displayed at museums throughout the modern world. The Egyptians gave him a lavish burial because he eliminated the Amarna religion and restored the traditional worship of the god Amon.

For students of the Hebrew Bible, the most significant comparative texts from the New Kingdom period are the instructions and love songs.[39] The Instructions of Amenemope were known to Israelite scribes, who actually adapted and included parts of them in the book of Proverbs (Prov 22:17–23:14). As for the love songs, these are comparable in expression, tone and content to Song of Songs.

Egyptian control in Palestine began to wane around 1200–1150 BCE into what would become the Third Intermediate Period (c. 1100–650). A chief cause for the decline seems to have been the arrival of the Sea Peoples, who were migrating into the region from the Aegean Sea area.[40] It is not known what prompted these migrations, but the effect is evident: the Hittite Empire and Ugarit were destroyed, and Egypt lost its territories in Asia and narrowly escaped destruction. It was during this period of unparalleled social upheaval that Israel's ancestors first began to settle in Palestine.

B. The Near East during the Israelite settlement and Early Period, 1200–1000 BCE

The settlement of the Israelites (or proto-Israelites) in the central highlands of Palestine and in Transjordan is visible in the archaeological record; similar settlements appeared in areas of Transjordan which would later become Ammon, Moab and also, perhaps, Edom (depending on when one dates the settlement there).[41] Chronologically, these settlements first appeared around 1200. This was near the end of Egypt's long-standing control of Palestine during the Late Bronze Age (1550–1200). Textual sources from this period are relatively scant, but this much is sure: the fourteenth-century Amarna Letters do not mention either Israel or any of the Israelite tribes, nor do any of the Late Bronze Egyptian texts which list cities and locations in Palestine. The first reference to Israel appears in a stele of Pharaoh Merneptah, which dates c. 1200.[42] Otherwise, the stele conveys little, except that Israel was a 'people' rather than a political nation and that it was considered an enemy of Egypt at the time.

The Philistines (one of the Sea Peoples) arrived on the coast of Palestine around 1150.[43] The arrival is confirmed by intersecting pieces of evidence from the Bible, Egyptian texts and archaeology (which reveals a distinctive Philistine pottery type). As the Hebrew Bible recalls it, Israel faced a potent and technologically superior foe in the Philistines. Given the military victories scored by the Sea Peoples all along the Levantine coast, and even well inland, this cannot be a surprise. Nor can it be a surprise that the earliest Israelite heroes – its 'judges' and first kings, Saul and David – secured their fame by fighting off the Philistines. Inscriptions and archaeological evidence from later periods show that the Philistines eventually adopted the language of Canaan and assimilated to the local culture, but they retained a distinctive Philistine identity well into the Iron Age.

The Arameans were another group appearing on the scene in this period.[44] Like the Sumerians, Semites, Amorites and Kassites before them, their origins are uncertain, though they seem to have been nomadic or semi-nomadic pastoralists living in the steppe-lands of the Euphrates, especially in Syrian regions. According to the Assyrian annals, the Arameans first began to encroach on settled areas around 1100, eventually forming a series of relatively small states in Syria, including Bit-Adini, Bit-Agusi, Guzana, Sam'al, Hamath and Damascus; to these one could add the minor Aramean states just to the north and east of Israel, Geshur, Maacah and Zobah. Some of these states (particularly those in northern Syria) also have been described as 'Neo-Hittite' because a significant contingent of the population was Hittite in background. The Arameans spoke a Semitic tongue called Aramaic, which is similar to Hebrew and eventually became the *lingua franca* of the entire Near East. Because Aramaic was commonly written on perishable papyrus, little from the literary traditions of Aramean culture has survived. The major textual sources are the inscriptions, which are numerous and important for reconstructing the history of this region during the first half of the first millennium.[45] Biblical and Near Eastern sources reveal that Israel had an on-again, off-again relationship with the Arameans (especially with Damascus), sometimes fighting alongside the Arameans and at other times fighting against them. The biblical story of Jacob and Laban reflects this relational ambiguity, insofar as the two men (one Israelite, the other Aramean) are ethnically associated but nevertheless enact a treaty to prevent further hostilities between them.

Also blossoming during this period were the Phoenician cities on the Mediterranean coast of Syria, just north of Israel.[46] These cities – Aradus, Byblos, Sidon and Tyre – were already important trade centres in the Late Bronze Age, when cedar wood and purple-red dyes (extracted from native molluscs) were the key staples of their trade activity. During the Iron Age, this trade continued, but it was accompanied by their ever-expanding colonisation of sites in the Mediterranean basin (citizens of these colonies are called the Punic peoples). The Israelites apparently coveted Phoenician wood products, which they purchased for use in the construction of royal palaces and temples. From a literary standpoint, artefacts from Phoenicia are meagre, amounting to a few royal inscriptions. Current understanding of Phoenician religion, literature and culture is cobbled together by correlating information from these inscriptions with texts from ancient Ugarit, the Bible, Egypt (especially the 'Story of Wenamon'), Mesopotamia (the Assyrian annals) and the much later history of Phoenicia by Philo Biblius.[47]

To summarise: one reason that the Israelite settlement was possible in this period was the power vacuum created in Syria/Palestine around 1200 by the withdrawal of Egypt from Asia, the collapse of the Hittite Empire and the relative weakness of Mesopotamia. Small regional states began to emerge in the area, including the Neo-Hittite states in northern Syria, the Aramean states in southern Syria and the nations of Israel, Ammon and Moab (and perhaps Edom) in Cis- and Transjordan.

C. The Near East during the early and divided monarchy, c. 1000–722 BCE

The 'regional states' era of Syro-Palestinian history continued until the Assyrians began to threaten the area in the mid-ninth century. The Israelite monarchy, which took shape beforehand during the reigns of Saul, David (c. 1000–960) and Solomon (c. 960–930), was one of many states comprising this political and economic fabric.[48] Though few scholars would question the historicity of David and Solomon, or of their predecessor, Saul, many scholars doubt that their kingdoms were as large as the Bible suggests. The early Israelite kings are not mentioned in any contemporary ancient documents, and there is a vigorous debate about whether the archaeological evidence in Israel supports the historicity of an economically and politically significant 'United Monarchy'. Today many scholars believe that the kingdoms of Saul, David and Solomon were relatively small, covering an area limited mainly to the highlands of Cisjordan and portions of Transjordan. Two pieces of Near Eastern evidence nevertheless suggest that the biblical sources describing this period reflect on-the-ground circumstances in the early monarchy.

The first is that the stories of David and Solomon are similar to other works of ancient propaganda, written to defend kings against charges that threatened their power and to critique their political opponents.[49] In the case of David, the books of 1–2 Samuel drew upon sources that criticised Saul and defended David against the charge that he was a Philistine mercenary who ruthlessly murdered his political opponents. The comparative exemplars include several Hittite apologies (Telepinu Edict and Apology of Ḫattušili III), an Assyrian text (Apology of Esarhaddon), Babylonian texts (The Sins of Nabû-šuma-iškun and Verse Account of Nabonidus), Persian texts (Cyrus Cylinder and Bisitun Inscription of Darius) and a late papyrus which contains the remnants of Neo-Assyrian propaganda (Tale of Sarbanapal and Sarmuge).[50] The second piece of evidence suggesting the antiquity of the biblical account is an inscription by Pharaoh Sheshonq in which he claims to have invaded Syria/Palestine during the late tenth century.[51] According to the Bible, this took place during the reign of Rehoboam of Judah, not long after the reigns of David and Solomon (see 1 Kgs 14:25). So, on this point at least, the Bible accurately reflects events from early in the monarchy.

Competition between Israel and the other regional states for land, resources and trade routes was inevitable. One of the first casualties of this competition was Israel itself, which divided into two smaller states, Israel and Judah. The Bible preserves memories of the conflict between the northern and southern Hebrew states, as well as between Israel and nearby states such as Aram, Ammon and Moab. Several ninth-century inscriptions cast further light on this contextual situation. An Aramaic stele discovered in northern Israel, at Tel Dan, celebrates an Aramean victory of Israel (the Tel Dan Stele), as does the Mesha Stele erected by a Moabite king.[52] In both cases, it seems that the situations described in these foreign texts can be tolerably correlated with events recounted in the Hebrew Bible (see 1 Kgs 19:16–17; 2 Kgs 3:4–5; 2 Kgs 9–10).[53]

Although archaeological evidence confirms that the material cultures of Israel, Judah, Ammon, Moab and Edom were similar, numerous inscriptions suggest at least one significant but unsurprising religious difference between them.[54] The inscriptions show that Yahweh was the national deity in Israel and Judah, Chemosh in Moab, Qaus in Edom and Milkom in Ammon (where Milkom was probably identified with the name El); these further suggest that each of the male deities had a female consort, the two examples being Asherah as Yahweh's consort and Ashtar-Chemosh as Chemosh's consort. All this evidence squares fairly well with biblical descriptions of religion in the region.

As noted earlier, Assyria began to exert its influence in Syria/Palestine during the mid-ninth century, ushering in the Neo-Assyrian period.[55] This era is historically well documented because of the Assyrian annals, a genre that memorialized the king's name in year-by-year accounts of his military, civic and religious deeds. The texts specifically mention Assyrian contact with Ahab of Israel (853), Jehu of Israel (841), Joash of Israel (796), Menahem of Israel (740; 738) Ahaz of Judah (734), Pekah and Hoshea of Israel (732), Hezekiah of Judah (701) and Manasseh of Judah (c. 674). Also mentioned in the annals is the re-conquest of the north and its capital in 720 by Sargon II, this being a follow-up operation after Samaria was taken by Shalmaneser V in 722 (as confirmed by Babylonian Chronicle 1).[56]

Assyria's first major foray into the region, by Shalmaneser III (858–824), was halted at Qarqar in 853 by a coalition of states that included Ahab of Israel and numerous Aramean and Neo-Hittite states (cf. the Bible and Assyrian annals). The Assyrians also faced difficulties elsewhere in the empire, including a threat from Urartu in the north (in the vicinity of Lake Van) and from Babylonian insurrections close to home.[57] As a result, Syria/Palestine was relatively free of Assyrian interference for about thirty years (840–810). During this period. Aram/Damascus emerged as *the* influential power in Syria/Palestine.[58] Israel and Judah were constantly threatened by it and lost territory to its kings, Hazael and Ben-hadad. These circumstances are reflected in Hebrew stories about the prophet Elisha (see 2 Kgs 6–7).

Assyria eventually returned to the region, reasserting control during the reigns of Adad-nirari III (810–783) and Tiglath-pileser III (744–727). Expansion of the empire was militaristic, of course, but as a rule it was fuelled by voluntary submission to Assyria. Nations which submitted voluntarily became client states of Assyria, but those which resisted faced stricter terms and became vassal states. The political relationships established between Assyria and its vassals were expressed in vassal treaties, which stipulated the behaviour of the vassal and promised an Assyrian attack, and divine destruction, for any signs of rebellion. If the vassal relationship failed, the Assyrians often converted the rebellious territory into a province with an Assyrian governor. As the empire expanded, Tiglath-pileser implemented a new imperial policy known as 'double deportation', in which population groups were exchanged between conquered territories. In northern Israel, this policy eventually created an ethnically diverse population, which would later be called 'Samaritans'. For parts of this period, Israel was a pro-Assyrian vassal, but an anti-Assyrian turn prompted an Assyrian assault and the conquest of the north in 722; from that time forward, Israel became an Assyrian province called 'Samarina'.

The Bible's history of this period is found in 1–2 Kings. Though this history was written in Judah or perhaps even during the Exile, scholars have deduced that its author (or authors) had access to historical records from the northern kingdom, which northern refugees apparently brought to the south after Israel's fall.[59] The sources were similar to (and perhaps inspired by) a Mesopotamian genre known as the 'chronicle', which provided year-by-year lists of significant events that took place during the reign of each king.[60] Most of the surviving chronicles are Babylonian and date after the northern kingdom, but there were earlier chronicles – including Assyrian chronicles – compiled by Mesopotamian scribes. A major difference between the chronicles and the aforementioned Assyrian annals is that the annals were politically propagandistic, whereas the chronicles were not.

D. The Near East from Judah to the Exile, c. 722–586 BCE

Judah was generally ignored by Assyria but became a tribute-paying vassal, in exchange for Assyria's help, when Israel and Aram attempted to force Judah into a coalition against Assyria (c. 734). The first Judean rebellion against Assyria was mounted by King Hezekiah in 701, with disastrous results.[61] Sennacherib destroyed Judah's cities, ravaged its countryside, deported thousands and exacted heavy tribute; Judah became a rump state composed of Jerusalem and its immediate environs.

During the subsequent reign of Manasseh, the nation of Judah recovered significantly, however, benefitting from its participation in the robust economy of the Assyrian Empire.

Back in Assyria, Sennacherib found it necessary to crush a rebellion in the ancient and holy city of Babylon. This was an act of impiety in the eyes of many, which Sennacherib's son, Esarhaddon, attempted to set right. Esarhaddon invested heavily in Babylon and in rebuilding and renewing its religious centres. Texts from the reigns of Sennacherib (704–681), Esarhaddon (680–669) and Assurbanipal (888–627) reflect an ideological battle between the pro-Babylonian and anti-Babylonian elements in Assyria (see Ordeal of Marduk, Sin of Sargon and Kummaya's Dream Vision).[62] These were works of religious and political propaganda, comparable to the priestly literature now ensconced in parts of the Pentateuch.

Under Assurbanipal, the Assyrian Empire reached its greatest limits, stretching from the far reaches of Persia in the east to Egypt in the west. Assyrian interests in the west were advanced by a close and mutually supportive political relationship between the empire and Egypt's twenty-sixth dynasty in Sais.[63] Scholars refer to this era of Egyptian resurgence as the 'Late Period' (c. 650–332). Assurbanipal helped the Saites push the Nubian-controlled twenty-fifth dynasty out of Egypt by providing military support and mercenary troops. Among these mercenaries were Judeans, whose ancestors later show up in Elephantine (the far south of Egypt) as a mercenary force for the Persians. The end result of these developments was a kind of *Pax Assyriaca* in the region, from which Judah greatly benefitted. In the end, however, this vast empire proved unstable. Within fifteen years of Assurbanipal's death (627), the Assyrian capital of Nineveh fell to the emerging Babylonian Empire (612). The last remnants of Assyria were defeated in 609.

Before considering Babylon, two further details about Assyrian literature should be noted. First, one of its kings, Assurbanipal, must be thanked for the many Mesopotamian texts now known. He assembled a massive library in Nineveh containing copies of almost all the important texts from Mesopotamia's literary tradition. Second, in the case of the Assyrian texts themselves, many are comparable to biblical literature. Foremost among these are the Neo-Assyrian annals (comparable to Hebrew historiography), prophetic oracles (comparable to the biblical prophetic books) and treaties (comparable to Deuteronomy).[64] This last example is particularly interesting because of its connection with King Josiah's religious reform in Judah (c. 620), during which a copy of Deuteronomy was 'found' in the temple. Given that Deuteronomy is similar to Assyrian treaties and that Josiah was essentially rebelling against Assyria, this suggests that the biblical book was written as a resistance document, which expressed that Yahweh, not the Assyrian king, was Judah's overlord.

Babylon's defeat of Assyria at the end of the seventh century ushered in the Neo-Babylonian era, but Babylonian strength was brewing earlier.[65] Already in the ninth century, texts refer to Chaldean tribes who lived in the marshy areas of the lower Tigris and Euphrates rivers. At the time, there were three population groups in the region, including native Babylonians, the Chaldeans and the semi-nomadic Arameans. The last group lived on the social periphery and was indifferent to Babylonian politics, but the first two groups were politically active. In the years leading up to the defeat of Assyria, Babylonian nationalism resurfaced again and again, prompting Assyrian efforts to quell the rebellion. During the eighth and seventh centuries, the throne of Babylon alternated between Babylonians, Assyrians and Chaldeans. One of these kings was the Chaldean, Merodach-Baladan (721–710), who is mentioned in Isaiah 39. But it was another Chaldean, Nabopolassar (625–605), who finally defeated Assyria and thus secured Babylon's independence and laid the foundations for the Neo-Babylonian Empire. Upon his death, his son Nebuchadnezzar II (604–562) reigned in his stead, fresh on the heels of a victory over Egypt at Carchemish in 605.

Because Judah had allied itself with Egypt, one of Nebuchadnezzar's first actions with regard to Judah was military. In 597, he moved to depose Jehoiakim, the Egyptian-appointed king of Judah (who had briefly turned to Babylon but then switched his allegiance), but by the time Nebuchadnezzar reached Jerusalem, Jehoiakim had died and his son, Jehoiachin, was on the throne. After a successful siege of Jerusalem, Nebuchadnezzar exacted tribute, deported families of social and political influence (including King Jehoiachin and the prophet Ezekiel) and placed Jehoiachin's uncle, Zedekiah, on the throne. It is of critical importance to notice the difference between Assyrian and Babylonian deportation policies. Whereas Assyria's double-deportation policy had the effect of diluting the identities of conquered peoples (because it intermixed various groups), Babylon's single-deportation policy had the opposite effect. By settling Jews as discrete communities within a foreign Mesopotamian context, the policy actually reinforced a Jewish sense of identity and solidarity. Were it not for this policy difference, it is possible that the Hebrew Bible as we know it would not exist.

When an insurrection arose in Babylon some ten years later, King Zedekiah of Judah again turned to Egypt and rejected Babylonian rule. But Nebuchadnezzar quickly dispelled the rebellion and then moved swiftly against Judah. The siege of Jerusalem began in 588 and ended with the city's fall in 586. Nebuchadnezzar destroyed the city and temple and deported more people to Babylon. The government was moved by Babylon to the city of Mizpah, where a Judean named Gedaliah took the helm as governor.

The twin deportations in 597 and 586 began the 'Babylonian' Exile. This name does not indicate that a majority of Jews were deported to Mesopotamia; rather, it indicates that many were deported, including influential Jews who carried with them the ideological banner of Judean identity. Biblical religion was radically shaped by these exiled scribes, politicians, prophets and people of means. Insofar as the Exile took these Jews to Mesopotamia and caused many others to flee to Egypt, it can rightly be said that one effect of Babylonian imperialism was the emergence of Diaspora Judaism. And because the language of the Chaldeans was Aramaic (as it was for many others in Syria and Mesopotamia), another effect was that Jews in Babylon became speakers of that language. Palestinian Jews would eventually follow suit when Aramaic – already a long-standing diplomatic language – emerged as the *lingua franca* of the Persian era.

E. The Near East during the exilic and post-exilic period, c. 586–331

Nebuchadnezzar's empire was never as large as Assyria's. He was unable to add Egypt to his holdings, nor was he able to annex Media and Persia in the east. Yet the period was a Babylonian renaissance nonetheless, during which he undertook many building projects that transformed Babylon into the greatest city of antiquity. Babylon's famous "Hanging Gardens," one of the seven wonders of the ancient world, are often credited to him. While undertaking these grand projects in Babylon and elsewhere, Nebuchadnezzar often contended with insurrections within the empire and foreign threats to it. So far as is known, his last military action in the case of Judah was in 580, when he responded to rebels who killed his Judean governor, Gedaliah. More deportations from Judah then followed. After Nebuchadnezzar's death in 562, Evil-Merodach came to the throne for two years. He is familiar to Bible readers as the king who released Jehoiachin from prison and established a permanent ration for his support (as is confirmed by a cuneiform ration docket that mentions 'King Yaukin of Judah'). Several short-lived kings succeeded Evil-Merodach before a usurper king, Nabonidus (555–539), seized the throne. Nabonidus was notorious in antiquity for his decision to reject Babylon's gods and withdraw to the Arabian oasis of Tema, some 500 miles from Babylon. Memories of this move (which Babylonian priests described as bizarre) are preserved in an Akkadian text called the 'Verse Account of Nabonidus', in a Jewish text called the 'Prayer of Nabonidus' and in the biblical book of Daniel, where the tale of Nebuchadnezzar's madness should be traced back to Nabonidus.[66] Babylonian elites thus welcomed the arrival of the Persian king, Cyrus (559–530), when he took control of Babylon in 538.

Whence came the Persians? They shared Indo-European roots with the neighboring Medes.[67] According to Neo-Assyrian annals, the eighth-century Assyrian kings fought with and made vassals of Median peoples to the east. The Medes were at the time an amalgam of decentralized chiefdoms, but at the end of the seventh century, these groups unified and established a capital at Ecbatana. The Medes then joined forces with Babylon and were instrumental in the final defeat of their old enemy, Assyria. Cyrus of Persia (who was actually Cyrus II, son of Cambyses I and grandson of Cyrus I) appeared on the scene some fifty years later. Approaching Media from his homeland to the south, he conquered the Medes and unified the entire Iranian plateau under Persian rule. His dynasty was the Achaemenid Dynasty, a name that honoured his great great grandfather, Achaemenes.

No previous empire compared in size with the Achaemenid (Persian) Empire, which eventually stretched from the border of India in the east to Egypt in the west. What accounted for its success? There is no question that the Achaemenids used military might to create and maintain this empire, but it is equally clear that their policies were not as severe as those followed by Assyria and Babylon. The Achaemenids often attempted to win the support of the conquered territories through acts of political and economic generosity. For example, Cyrus decreed that Jewish exiles could return home in 538, Darius (522–485) commissioned the rebuilding of the Jerusalem Temple in 520 and Artaxerxes I (464–525) sponsored the legal reforms of Ezra (458) and the restoration of Jerusalem by Nehemiah (444).[68] Nearly identical policies were followed elsewhere in Persia. The Achaemenids decreed the return of all exiled peoples to their native lands, rebuilt and restored many temples (especially in Babylon), sought out natives to implement political policies (e.g., Udjahorresnet of Egypt was selected by Cambyses) and commissioned the codification of native law (e.g., of Egyptian law by Darius). These were indeed magnanimous acts of kindness for the native populations, but the Persians greatly benefitted as well. For example, the rebuilding of the temple and the promulgation of Ezra's law brought more order and stability to Judah, and Nehemiah's wall and economic reforms made Jerusalem a suitable capital for the new Persian province of Yehud. Equally beneficial for Persia was the co-opting of the native religion for its political purposes. Cyrus claimed that the Babylonian god Marduk selected him to become the deliverer of Babylon, a message that apparently resonated with the Babylonians, who welcomed him into their city.[69] Similar claims were made by some Jews, for whom Cyrus became Yahweh's anointed deliverer of Israel (see Isa 45:1).

During the Achaemenid period, Jews were scattered across the empire from east to west. Ancient texts provide tantalising glimpses into their lives.[70] One Akkadian text refers to a settlement called *al Yaḫuda* ('city of Judah'), the Babylonian name for Jerusalem that apparently attests to exiled Jews who named their Mesopotamian settlement after the homeland capital. Also from Mesopotamia is the fifth-century Murašû archive, which belonged to a family of merchant bankers in Nippur. Among its clients and creditors are numerous Jews who owned houses and land, suggesting that a large community of Jews must have lived in Nippur, being both prosperous and tolerably assimilated to Mesopotamian society.

Turning to Persian-era Egypt, several collections of Aramaic texts attest to Jewish life there. Foremost among them is the Elephantine archive recovered on the Nile in the deep south of Egypt, which contains texts that belonged to members of a Jewish military colony. The colony was established by the Persians but, as mentioned earlier, had roots probably going back to Judeans stationed in Egypt by the Assyrians. Mundane but telling legal and business documents appear in the archive, as well as a collection of communal texts associated with Jedaniah – a priest, probably the high priest – of the Jewish temple at Elephantine. Here one finds correspondence with the Persians in which the Jews requested permission to rebuild their temple, previously destroyed by local Egyptians. Persia granted the request but further stipulated that Egyptian Jews could offer only meal and incense at the new temple, in keeping with the Jewish law that reserved flesh offerings for the Jerusalem Temple. From this at least two things can be inferred: first, that Jews in Egypt were not wholly committed to the theological standards of Jerusalem Jewry and, second, that the Persians were in the business of promoting religious harmony in the empire. It is unclear how these developments square with the famous schism in Palestinian Jewry between the party of Ezra/Nehemiah, centred in the Temple community of Jerusalem, and Jews in the north, where the Samaritan sect built a competing temple on Mt. Gerazim in the sixth/fifth century (eventually destroyed by the Jewish Hasmoneans in the second century).[71]

Given the size, prosperity and sophistication of the Persians, one might expect that they left behind many literary texts for modern scholars to read and study. But alas, as in the case of ancient Israel, it seems that their literature was written on perishable papyrus. What we do have are thousands of administrative tablets recovered from Persepolis, which was one of three Persian capitals (along with Susa and Ecbatana).[72] These texts were written in cuneiform Elamite, the native language of Persia. Modern knowledge of Persian religion and literature has been pieced together from a fairly small corpus of royal inscriptions, Greek sources (especially the histories of Herodotus) and, later, Persian texts. The most distinctive feature of Persian theology was its Zoroastrian dualism, which pitted the goodness of the great god Ahura-Mazda against the evil of Ahriman. The Persians believed that Ahura-Mazda would eventually win this cosmic battle, ushering in a day of final judgement for humanity. Many scholars believe that this theology modestly inspired the rise of similar ideas in Jewish apocalyptic texts, but it contrasted sharply with Mesopotamian theology, which offered no after-life and admitted the morally capricious nature of its deities.

What brought the Persian Empire to its end? Persia exhausted much of its military energy in establishing and preserving its territories in Asia Minor and Macedonia, where the Greeks were its chief enemy. The Persians hoped to take the Greek mainland itself, but Greek victories against Darius I at the Battle of Marathon (490) and against the Persian navy and land forces of Xerxes I (480–479) put an end to this dream. In the end, these battles only fomented Greek anger towards Persia, eventually spelling trouble for the empire. And Persia faced significant difficulties in Babylon and Egypt as well. The Babylonians and Egyptians were always fiercely independent societies and were heavily taxed by the Persians, so they were ever anxious to throw off the Persian chains. The violent suppression of revolts in Egypt and Babylon by Xerxes I (485–465) cannot have helped matters. The main point is that the Persian Empire eventually fell because of inherent instabilities within the empire, as well as because it faced a determined and potent external enemy: the Greeks.

Mention of the Greeks leads to Alexander of Macedon, better known as Alexander the Great. He inherited his small Macedonian (Greek) Empire from his father (Philip II) in 336 and hoped to extend it into Asia Minor, where other Greeks – especially the Ionians – remained under Persian rule.[73] He campaigned under the banner of Greek liberation, but it seems that his true agenda was always the defeat of Persia and an empire in the east. By 332, he had successfully defeated the Persians and taken control of Anatolia, the Levant, Egypt, Mesopotamia and Iran. Alexander's imperial policy was culturally sensitive and similar in this respect to that of Persia, but he added a new element to the mix: one of his first orders of business was to colonize the new provinces with Greeks. This he did not by settling Greeks in native towns but by establishing new Greek cities. Among the most famous of these was Alexandria in Egypt. From this point forward, the Hellenisation of the Near East rapidly accelerated and continued all the way down to the Romans and Byzantium, ending only with the Islamic conquest c. 635 CE. Intellectuals across the new empire, which was even larger than that of the Persians, found themselves reading and writing Greek. Native histories written in the new language included a history of Phoenicia (by Philo Biblius), of Egypt (by Manetho), of Babylon (by Berossus) and of the Jews (Josephus).

Following his conquest of Persia, Alexander campaigned further east in India, returning to Babylon about a decade later. It was there that he suddenly died in 323, supposedly from malaria. Because his sons were minors (and one was mentally disabled), the empire was divvied up among his four generals, the *Diadochi* (Greek for 'successors'). Only two of the four resulting polities are directly relevant to Near Eastern history, the Ptolemies in Egypt and the Seleucids in Syria/ Mesopotamia. To simplify an incredibly complex era of history, the two Hellenistic nations contended for control of the Levantine coast and its trade routes for a century, with the Ptolemies enjoying the upper hand until 198 BCE. At that point, the Seleucids seized control of the Levant and, hence, of the Jewish homeland.[74]

Jews in Palestine prospered under the Ptolemies and, at first, under the Seleucids. But in the third decade of Seleucid rule, Antiochus IV Epiphanes began to persecute traditional Jews who were resisting Hellenism. The persecution began with the conquest of Jerusalem in 168, which was followed by a series of royal decrees that abolished the legitimacy of Jewish law and religious practice. Many Jews were killed, copies of the Torah were burned and the Temple in Jerusalem was turned into a temple of Zeus. Jewish tradition recalls this as a simple matter of religious persecution, but the motivations behind it were more complex. Antiochus was interested in Jerusalem's temple treasures and was promised these if he helped the pro-Hellenistic Jews wrest control of the high priesthood and Temple from conservative Jews. Conservative Jewry responded to these developments militantly and in their religious literature. The military response was a rebellion, led by the Maccabean family in 164 (the Maccabean Revolt), which eventually secured a native Jewish dynasty called the 'Hasmonean Dynasty'. Victory did not come quickly, however. The first military successes were in 164, but the last vestiges of Seleucid power were only expunged during the reign of John Hyrcanus (134–104), the true founder of the Hasmonean Dynasty. As for the Jewish literary response, this took the form of numerous apocalyptic texts that predicted God's intervention in history and his destruction of the Greek oppressors.[75] The Jews were not alone in composing these anti-Hellenistic texts. Similar texts were written in Egypt (The Demotic Chronicle) and in Babylon (The Dynastic Prophecy).[76] One of the Jewish apocalyptic works was the Book of Daniel, the latest significant piece of literature in the Hebrew Bible (c. 167–164).

APPENDIX

Table 3A.1. *Ancient Near Eastern history*

Archaeological period	Mesopotamia	Egypt	Syria/Palestine
Early Bronze (3100–2100)	Sumerian and Old Akkadian periods	Old Kingdom	Ebla
Middle Bronze (2100–1550)	Old Babylonian period; the Amorites	First Intermediate period, Middle Kingdom and Second Intermediate period	Mari, Amorites
Late Bronze (1550–1200)	Middle Babylonian/ Kassite period; Nuzi	New Kingdom	Ugarit
Iron I (1200–1000)	Neo-Assyrian period	Third Intermediate period	Sea Peoples, Early Israel, the Arameans
Iron II (1000–600)	Neo-Babylonian period	Late period	Israel and Judah Babylonian Exile
Iron III (600–330)	Persian period	Persian period	Persian period
Hellenistic period (330)	Hellenistic period	Hellenistic period	Hellenistic period

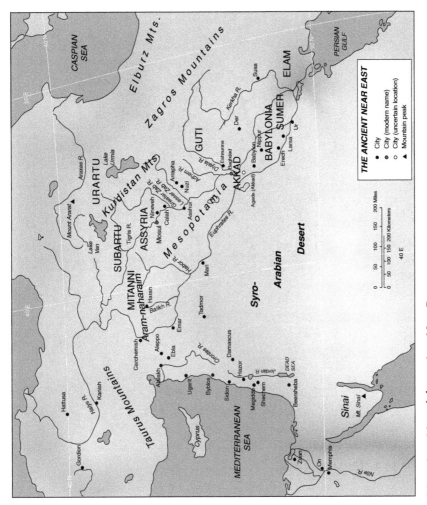

Map 3.A.1. Map of the ancient Near East.

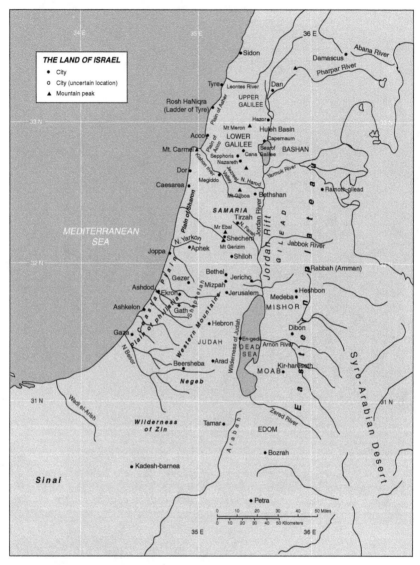

Map 3A.2. The Land of Israel.

NOTES

1   For background on the following discussion, see Kevin J. Cathcart, 'Age of Decipherment: The Old Testament and the Ancient Near East in the Nineteenth Century', in *Congress Volume: Cambridge 1995*, ed. by J. A. Emerton (VTSup 66; Leiden, Netherlands: Brill, 1997), 81–95; M. W. Chavalas, 'Assyriology and Biblical Studies: A Century and a Half of

Tension', in *Mesopotamia and the Bible: Comparative Explorations*, ed. by M. W. Chavalas and K. L. Younger (Grand Rapids, MI: Baker, 2002), 21–67 (hereafter *MB*).

2 See Mogens Trolle Larsen, 'The "Babel/Bible" Controversy and Its Aftermath', in *Civilizations of the Ancient Near East*, 4 vols., ed. by Jack M. Sasson (New York: Scribners, 1995), 1: 95–106 (hereafter *CANE*); Samuel Sandmel, 'Parallelomania', *JBL* 81 (1962): 1–13.

3 B. Landsberger, 'Die Eigenbegrifflichkeit der babylonischen Welt', *Islamica* 2 (1929): 355–72; W. W. Hallo, 'Compare and Contrast: The Contextual Approach to Biblical Literature', in *The Bible in the Light of Cuneiform Literature*, ed. by W. W. Hallo, B. W. Jones and G. L. Mattingly (Lewiston, NY: Mellen, 1990), 1–30.

4 Paul Åström, ed. *High, Middle or Low?* (Gothenburg, Sweden: Åströms Förlag, 1987); Frederick H. Cryer, 'Chronology: Issues and Problems', *CANE* 1: 651–64.

5 *CANE*; Kenton L. Sparks, *Ancient Texts for the Study of the Hebrew Bible* (Peabody, MA: Hendrickson, 2005) (hereafter *ATSHB*); Carl S. Erlich, *From an Antique Land: An Introduction to Ancient Near Eastern Literature* (Lanham, MD: Rowman & Littlefield, 2008) (hereafter *FAL*); W. W. Hallo, ed., *The Context of Scripture*, 3 vols. (Leiden, Netherlands: Brill, 1997–2002); J. B. Pritchard, *Ancient Texts Relating to the Old Testament*, 3rd ed. (Princeton, NJ: Princeton University Press, 1969).

6 For other important translation collections, see *ATSHB*.

7 For background on the languages discussed in this article, see Steven L. McKenzie and John Kaltner, eds., *Beyond Babel: A Handbook for Biblical Hebrew and Related Languages* (Atlanta: Society of Biblical Literature, 2002).

8 Harriet Crawford, *Sumer and the Sumerians* (Cambridge University Press, 1991); Gonzalo Rubio, 'Sumerian Literature', in *FAL*, 11–74; Georges Roux, *Ancient Iraq*, 3rd ed. (New York: Penguin, 1992), 1–145.

9 *ATSHB*, 58–9, 64–5 (wisdom), 273–8 (epics), 85–7, 90–9, 102 (hymns, prayers, laments), 307–13 (myths), 345–8 (king lists).

10 Sabrina Franke, 'Kings of Akkad: Sargon and Naram-Sin', in *CANE* 2: 831–41; Benjamin R. Foster, 'Akkadian Literature', in *FAL*, 137–214; Roux, *Ancient Iraq*, 146–60.

11 *ATSHB*, 284–5 (Curse of Akkad).

12 Lucio Milano, 'Ebla: A Third-Millennium City-State in Ancient Syria', in *CANE* 2: 1219–30.

13 Jacob Klein, 'Shulgi of Ur: King of a Neo-Sumerian Empire', in *CANE* 2: 843–58; Rubio, 'Sumerian Literature'; Roux, *Ancient Iraq*, 161–78.

14 Roux, *Ancient Iraq*, 169–20; Jack M. Sasson, 'King Hammurabi of Babylon', in *CANE* 2: 901–16; Keith N. Schoville, 'Canaanites and Amorites', in *Peoples of the Old Testament World*, ed. by Alfred J. Hoerth, Gerald L. Mattingly and Edwin M. Yamauchi (Grand Rapids, MI: Baker, 1994), 157–82 (hereafter *POTW*); Robert M. Whiting, 'Amorite Tribes and Nations of Second-Millennium Western Asia', in *CANE* 2: 1231–42.

15 On these texts, see *ATSHB*, 227 (prophecies), 275–8 (Gilgamesh), 313–14 (Atraḫasis), 421–3 (laws).

16 Daniel E. Fleming, *Democracy's Ancient Ancestors: Mari and Early Collective Governance* (Cambridge University Press, 2004); Jean-Claude Margueron, 'Mari: A Portrait in Art of a Mesopotamian City-State', in *CANE* 2: 885–99.

17 For more on the Kassites and the Middle Kingdom, see Walter Sommerfeld, 'The Kassites of Ancient Mesopotamia: Origins, Politics, and Culture', in *CANE* 2: 917–30.

18 *ATSHB*, 62–3 (*Ludlul*, Babylonian Theodicy), 275–8 (Gilgamesh).

19 John Day, 'Foreign Semitic Influence on the Wisdom of Israel and Its Appropriation in the Book of Proverbs', in *Wisdom in Ancient Israel*, ed. by J. Day, R. P. Gordon and H. G. M. Williamson (Cambridge: University Press, 1995), 55–70.

20 Billie Jean Collins, *The Hittites and Their World* (Atlanta: Society of Biblical Literature, 2007); J. G. Macqueen, 'The History of Anatolia and of the Hittite Empire: An Overview', in *CANE* 2:1085–1106.

21 *ATSHB*, 77–8 (instructions), 164–5 (rituals), 426–7 (laws).

22 J. David Hawkins, 'Karkamish and Karatepe: Neo-Hittite City-States in North Syria', in *CANE* 2: 1295–1308.

23 Wayne T. Pitard, 'Voices from the Dust: The Tablets from Ugarit and the Bible', in *MB*, 251–75; W. H. van Soldt, 'Ugarit: A Second-Millennium Kingdom on the Mediterranean Coast', in *CANE* 2: 1255–66.

24 Richard S. Hess, 'The Bible and Alalakh', in *MB*, 209–21.

25 For Nuzi, Mitanni and Hurrian culture, see Maynard P. Maidman, 'Nuzi: Portrait of an Ancient Mesopotamian Provincial Town', in *CANE* 2: 931–47; Gernot Wilhelm, 'The Kingdom of Mitanni in Second-Millennium Upper Mesopotamia', in *CANE* 2: 1243–54.

26 See John Van Seters, *Abraham in History and Tradition* (New Haven, CT: Yale University Press, 1975), 65–103.

27 Daniel E. Fleming, 'Emar: On the Road from Harran to Hebron', in *MB*, 222–50; John Huehnergard, 'Emar Texts', in *The Oxford Encyclopedia of Archaeology in the Near East*, 5 vols., ed. by Eric M. Meyers (Oxford University Press, 1997), 2: 239–40 (hereafter *OEANE*); J.-C. Margueron and Marcel Sigrest, 'Emar', in *OEANE* 2: 236–9.

28 See *ATSHB*, 165, 169, 172.

29 For a more detailed overview of Egyptian history, literature and culture, see William J. Murnane, 'The History of Ancient Egypt: an Overview', in *CANE* 2: 691–718; Jan Assmann, *The Mind of Egypt* (New York: Metropolitan Books, 2002); Susan Tower Hollis, 'Egyptian Literature', in *FAL*, 77–136.

30 A. J. Spencer, *Early Egypt: The Rise of Civilisation in the Nile Valley* (Norman: University of Oklahoma Press, 1995).

31 *ATSHB*, 66–8.

32 Regarding the Egyptian funerary literature, see *ATSHB*, 192–6.

33 *ATSHB*, 323–4.

34 Detlef Franke, 'The Middle Kingdom of Egypt', in *CANE* 2: 735–48.

35 For these texts, including the Story of Sinuhe, see *ATSHB*, 253–6.

36 James M. Weinstein, 'Hyksos', in *OEANE* 3: 133–6; Donald B. Redford, *Egypt, Canaan, and Israel in Ancient Times* (Princeton, NJ: Princeton University Press, 1992), 98–124.

37   Kenneth A. Kitchen, 'Pharaoh Rameses II and His Times', in *CANE* 763–74; Redford, *Egypt, Canaan, and Israel in Ancient Times*, 152–282.

38   Betsy M. Bryan, 'Amarna, Tell el-', in *OEANE* 1: 81–6; Shlomo Isre'el, 'Amarna Tablets', in *OEANE* 1: 86–7.

39   See *ATSHB*, 70–1, 135–9,

40   Trude Dothan, 'The "Sea Peoples" and the Philistines of Ancient Palestine', in *CANE* 2: 1267–80.

41   For a discussion and bibliography, see Kenton L. Sparks, 'Religion, Identity and the Origins of Ancient Israel', *Religion Compass* 1(6) (2007): 587–614.

42   *ATSHB*, 389–90.

43   Trude Dothan and Moshe Dothan, *People of the Sea: The Search for the Philistines* (New York: Macmillan, 1992).

44   William M. Schniedewind, 'The Rise of the Aramean States', in *MB*, 276–87.

45   See the Aramaic inscriptions treated in *ATSHB*, 463–76.

46   Edward Lipiński, 'The Phoenicians', in *CANE* 2: 1321–33; William A. Ward, 'Phoenicians', in *POTW*, 183–206.

47   See *ATSHB*, 266–7 (Wenamon), 364 (Assyrian Annals), 400 (Philo Biblius).

48   For the relevant historical background, see J. Maxwell Miller and John H. Hayes, *A History of Ancient Israel and Judah*, 2nd ed. (Louisville, KY: Westminster John Knox, 2006).

49   Steven L. McKenzie, *King David: A Biography* (New York: Oxford University Press, 2000).

50   For these texts, see *ATSHB*, 392–3 (Telepinu), 395–6 (Ḫattušili), 365 (Esarhaddon), 373 (Nabû-šuma-iškun), 379 (Nabonidus), 397–8 (Cyrus), 398–400 (Darius), 291–2 (Sarbanapal and Sarmuge).

51   *ATSHB*, 390.

52   See *ATSHB*, 466 (Mesha), 467–8 (Tel Dan).

53   William M. Schniedewind, 'Tel Dan Stela: New Light on Aramaic and Jehu's Revolt', *BASOR* 302 (1996): 75–90.

54   Sparks, 'Religion, Identity and the Origins of Ancient Israel'.

55   Roux, *Ancient Iraq*, chaps. 18–22.

56   For the texts and references, see Mordecai Cogan, 'Chronology (Hebrew Bible)', in *The Anchor Bible Dictionary*, 6 vols., ed. by David Noel Freedman (New York: Doubleday, 1992), 1: 1002–11 (hereafter *ABD*).

57   Paul E. Zimansky, 'The Kingdom of Urartu in Eastern Anatolia', in *CANE* 2: 1135–46.

58   Wayne T. Pitard, *Ancient Damascus* (Winona Lake, IN: Eisenbrauns, 1987).

59   S. R. Bin-Nun, 'Formulas from the Royal Records of Israel and Judah', *VT* 18 (1968): 414–32.

60   *ATSHB*, 363–76.

61   See Miller and Hayes, *A History of Ancient Israel*, 400–37.

62   *ATSHB*, 244–5 (Kummaya), 290 (Sin of Sargon), 321 (Ordeal).

63   William Y. Adams, 'The Kingdom and Civilization of Kush in Northeast Africa', in *CANE* 2: 775–90; Alan B. Lloyd, 'The Late Period, 664–323 B.C.', in *Ancient Egypt: A Social History*, ed. by B. G. Trigger (Cambridge University Press, 1983), 279–348.

64   *ATSHB*, 227–9 (oracles), 364–8 (annals), 441–3 (treaties).

65   For more on the Babylonians and Chaldeans, see Bill T. Arnold, *Who Were the Babylonians?* (Atlanta: Society of Biblical Literature, 2004).

66   *ATSHB*, 379 (Verse Account); F. G. Martínez and E. J. C. Tigchelaar, *The Dead Sea Scrolls: Study Edition*, 2 vols. (Grand Rapids, MI: Eerdmans, 1997–8), 1: 486–89 (Prayer of Nabonidus).

67   Burchard Brentjes, 'The History of Elam and Achaemenid Persia: An Overview', in *CANE* 2: 1001–22; Edwin M. Yamauchi, 'Persians', in *POTW*, 107–24.

68   It is possible that the reforms of Ezra took place after Nehemiah's mission, during the fourth century reign of Artaxerxes II.

69   For this text, see *ATSHB*, 397–8.

70   See *ATSHB*, 41–2 (Murašû)], 48–50 (Elephantine), 379 (al Yaḫuda).

71   Ephraim Stern and Yitzhak Magen, 'Archaeological Evidence for the First Stage of the Samaritan Temple on Mount Gerizim', *IEJ* 52 (2002): 49–57.

72   *ATSHB*, 52.

73   N. G. L. Hammond, *The Macedonian State: Origins, Institutions, and History* (Oxford, UK: Clarendon, 1989); Simon Price, 'The History of the Hellenistic Period', in *The Oxford History of Greece and the Hellenistic World*, ed. by John Boardman, Jasper Griffin and Oswyn Murray (Oxford University Press, 1988), 364–89.

74   For Jewish history in this period, see Victor Tcherikover, *Hellenistic Civilization and the Jews* (New York: Atheneum, 1975); Shaye J. D. Cohen, *From the Maccabees to the Mishnah*, 2nd ed. (Louisville, KY: Westminster John Knox, 2006).

75   For many examples, see James H. Charlesworth, ed., *The Old Testament Pseudepigrapha*, 2 vols. (Garden City, NY: Doubleday, 1983–5), 1.

76   *ATSHB*, 244 (Dynastic Prophecy), 246–7 (Demotic Chronicle).

FURTHER READING

Assmann, Jan. *The Mind of Egypt: History and Meaning in the Time of the Pharaohs*. Translated by A. Jenkins. New York: Metropolitan Books, 2002.

Collins, Billie Jean. *The Hittites and Their World*. Atlanta: Society of Biblical Literature, 2007.

Ehrlich, Carl S., ed. *From an Antique Land: An Introduction to Ancient Near Eastern Literature*. Lanham, MD: Rowman & Littlefield, 2008.

Foster, Benjamin R., ed. *Before the Muses: An Anthology of Akkadian Literature*, 3rd ed. Bethesda, MD: CDL Press, 2005.

Hallo, W. W., ed. *The Context of Scripture*, 3 vols. Leiden, Netherlands: Brill, 1997–2002.

Lichtheim, Miriam, ed. *Ancient Egyptian Literature*, 3 vols. Berkeley: University of California Press, 1971–1980.

Miller, J. Maxwell and John H. Hayes. *A History of Ancient Israel and Judah*, 2nd ed. Louisville, KY: Westminster John Knox, 2006.

Pitchard, James B., ed. *Ancient Near Eastern Texts Relating to the Old Testament*, 3rd ed. Princeton, NJ: Princeton University Press, 1969.

Redford, Donald B. *Egypt, Canaan, and Israel in Ancient Times*. Princeton, NJ: Princeton University Press, 1992.

Roux, Georges. *Ancient Iraq*, 3rd ed. New York: Penguin, 1992.

Sasson, Jack M., ed. *Civilizations of the Ancient Near East*, 4 vols. New York: Scribners, 1995.

Simpson, William Kelly, ed. *The Literature of Ancient Egypt: An Anthology of Stories, Instructions, Stelae, Autobiographies, and Poetry*. New Haven, CT: Yale University Press, 2003.

Snell, Daniel C. *Life in the Ancient Near East, 3100–332 B.C.E.* New Haven, CT: Yale University Press, 1997.

Sparks, Kenton L. *Ancient Texts for the Study of the Hebrew Bible: A Guide to the Background Literature*. Peabody, MA: Hendrickson, 2005.

4 The history of Israelite religion

BRENT A. STRAWN

The "history of Israelite religion" may be provisionally defined as the attempt, by various means and methods, to reconstruct the religious thinking and practices of the ancient Israelite people during the periods reflected in or most directly pertinent to the biblical texts themselves – namely, the Late Bronze Age through the Persian Period/Iron Age III (1500–332 BCE).[1] However, even this provisional definition faces immediate problems. First, the chronological range is extensive. Consequently, the amount of evidence available is massive, even for what is, comparatively speaking, a relatively small geographical region. Hence, the task of describing "Israelite religion" as a comprehensive phenomenon, not to mention its history – which would include matters of emergence, influence, development, and so forth – is herculean. Second, the provisional definition is complicated by additional challenges, including the nature of the sources available to us, the interpretation of nontextual material, and a host of specific questions pertaining to the biblical texts themselves, not the least of which is whether and how they ought to play a role in the study and definition of Israelite religion in the first place.

Given the complexity inherent in the subject, this chapter cannot hope to address all these issues and questions, as important as they are. Instead, it will provide a brief overview of the history of the study of Israelite religion before discussing three important issues that have been the subject of significant recent (re)investigation. These issues, which concern the sources, locus, and content of Israelite religion, are critical ones that pertain to any endeavor to write the history of ancient Israelite religion.

I wish to thank Patrick D. Miller, Christopher B. Hays, Joel M. LeMon, Bill T. Arnold, and Stephen B. Chapman for their help with this chapter.

A BRIEF HISTORY OF THE HISTORY OF
ISRAELITE RELIGION

Prior to the late eighteenth and early nineteenth centuries, when artifacts from Mesopotamia and Egypt began to come to the attention of Western Europeans, discussions of Israelite religion were entirely dependent on the Bible and the few classical sources that existed that could shed light on the subject (e.g., Berossus, Manetho, Herodotus, Philo of Byblos, and Lucian). The classical texts were typically scrutinized, if not chastened, by the biblical evidence, which was, at this point in time, deemed superior a priori. The "discovery" (from the Western perspective) and early exploration of Egypt and Mesopotamia inaugurated the quest to gather artifacts from these ancient locales.² Among the spoils were inscribed remains, and scholars quickly set out to decipher scripts and languages that had been forgotten for millennia. Breakthroughs came in 1822 when Champollion deciphered Egyptian and, only slightly later, when the work of Rawlinson, Hincks, and others converged sufficiently to crack the cuneiform script of Akkadian used in ancient Mesopotamia. These milestones enabled the direct study of sources unfiltered by classical lenses that were both later in time and foreign in origin or by biblical lenses that were admittedly ancient but still foreign. For the first time in quite literally thousands of years, scholars could read native texts from the regions and civilizations of the ancient Near East. This afforded them an until-then-unimagined ability to assess the cogency of both the biblical and classical texts about various locales, peoples, and practices, as well as to investigate the influence of those selfsame subjects on – or, at least, their relationship with – the biblical and classical materials.

Another crucial moment in this history came in 1928–9 with the discovery of Ugarit, a Late Bronze Age city-state on the Syrian coast, and the deciphering of its native language, Ugaritic. Although written in cuneiform, the Ugaritic script was alphabetic, and its orthography and grammar were more closely related to Hebrew than to Akkadian. Great insight was immediately gained on the history of the Hebrew language in light of this earlier northwest Semitic linguistic cousin. More important for the study of Israelite religion, however, was the fact that while the citizens of Ugarit worshipped many deities, two were of immediate relevance to the study of the Hebrew Bible. First was the head of the pantheon, El or *'Ilu*, whose name was equivalent to one of the main terms used of Israel's deity in the Old Testament (Ugaritic *il*; Hebrew *'ēl*). Second was the vibrant storm god known as Baal or *Baʿlu* (Ugaritic *bʿl*; cf. Akkadian *bēl*; Hebrew *baʿal*), literally "lord" or "owner," also known from the Old Testament as an important god of the Canaanites and a frequent threat to Israelite worship of Yahweh (see, e.g., 1 Kgs 18:20–40). A third deity, a goddess named Athiratu (Ugaritic *a̱trt*), also was of interest because her name is equivalent to the Hebrew word *'ăšērâ*, which apparently refers to either a deity or a cult object related to this goddess (see later). Of these three, Baal initially received the most attention because there were at least six tablets devoted to a Baal "cycle" that recounted this god's rise to prominence, his relationship to El, his battle with the god of death (Ugaritic *mt* = Môtu), his profile as a storm god, and his death and subsequent revivification.[3] The Ugaritic tablets offered, or so it seemed, a firsthand, "insider" perspective on the "Canaanite religion" discussed in the Hebrew Bible. So, just as slightly earlier scholars could assess the value of the Bible's information on major ancient Near Eastern powers such as Egypt, Babylonia, and Assyria with the help of Egyptian and Mesopotamian texts, they could now begin to assess the Bible's information on the land, religion, and culture of ancient Israel/Palestine, on "Canaan," and therefore on the "Canaanites" themselves.

Accompanying this progress in the study of ancient Near Eastern texts was the explosion and maturation of archaeological work done in ancient Israel/Palestine. In a brief period of time in the latter half of the twentieth century, archaeology of the southern Levant went from "biblical archaeology," in which a primary goal was to demonstrate the veracity of the biblical text or at least relate archaeological discoveries to the Bible, to "Syro-Palestinian archaeology," which conducts its business no differently than excavations in any other part of the world and is often quite content to leave references to the Bible aside altogether.[4] Regardless of this development and any correlative theorizing of the relationship of the Bible to archaeology (or lack thereof),[5] the study of Israelite religion received enormous impetus from archaeological discoveries in the twentieth century. Among countless examples, one should mention numerous epigraphic discoveries, including the important inscriptions from Khirbet el-Qom and Kuntillet 'Ajrud (see later). Alongside these inscribed remains, the study of iconography has proved to be an increasingly important and revelatory area for Israelite religion.

The upshot of all these discoveries and developments – including in many areas that were not mentioned earlier[6] – is nicely summarized by Frank Moore Cross:

> [T]here has been a cascade of new, extra-biblical resources that give us new aids and insights and controls, and indeed require that we go

back to the biblical sources and reexamine old work based on biblical literature alone.[7]

The language of control and requirement that Cross uses here is quite telling. In brief, the situation that obtained prior to these discoveries is now exactly and precisely *reversed*: no longer is the Old Testament the source and judge of ancient texts or cultures; instead, those ancient texts and cultures are now the source and judge of the Hebrew Bible. And the earlier historical reconstructions often do not withstand this shift.

That said, it should be observed that as scholars have done this new work, the results have been mixed. On one side stand those who assert that Israelite religion was radically different from that of its ancient Near Eastern congeners, including and especially the indigenous religion of ancient Canaan.[8] This is a position found within the Bible itself, most clearly, perhaps, in the book of Deuteronomy. On the other side are those scholars who have found more and more evidence of continuity – or, at best, very little discontinuity – between early Israelite religion and what has been found at Ugarit (and elsewhere),[9] which has shed light on the nature of "Canaanite" or "West Semitic"/"West Asian" religion.[10] This second perspective believes that, for all intents and purposes, Israelite religion *was* Canaanite religion. This position, too, finds support within the biblical texts. There are hints, for example, that the full vision of Deuteronomy stems from a later period and was never systematically achieved, if only because the prophets find it necessary to call the people (back?) to exclusive devotion to Yahweh. In this way, Deuteronomy – whatever its compositional and redactional history or putative date – is seen not as the standard from which Israel fell (as in the first perspective) but rather as a later evolution or achievement that emerged from what was, on the ground, a far more complex and messy religious context.

It is clear that these two opposed perspectives – and the many that lie on the continuum between them – depend a great deal on a number of prior questions. Debates over the continuity between Israelite and Canaanite religion, for example, are closely linked to debates over the Exodus and the rise of early Israel: whether or not there was an exodus group at all, how large and significant it was if it existed, the identity of the villagers that inhabited the highlands in the Late Bronze Age/Iron Age I periods, and so on. One suspects, then, that the marked difference of opinion on many points of Israelite religion may not be due to new data per se so much as assumptions and interpretations regarding the data at hand, whether new or old. If so, things seem to be at something of an impasse, and we might well wonder how these large and significant debates are to be (re)negotiated.

THREE IMPORTANT ISSUES: THE SOURCES, LOCUS, AND CONTENT OF ISRAELITE RELIGION

Given the thorough interpenetration of the study of Israelite religion with a number of other areas of study, as well as logically prior methodological assumptions, it seems unlikely that the largest questions will be resolved any time soon. The profound interconnection between the history of Israelite religion and other subjects is not simply a *problem* to be solved, however; it is also a *major result* of recent research, highlighting a central point about the study of Israelite religion – namely, that religion is to be found everywhere, lurking in some aspect or nook of virtually every discourse about ancient Israel, its land, its literature, and its cultural features.

Limitations of space preclude engaging the full range of issues at work in the scholarly history sketched earlier. It must suffice to discuss three important issues that (1) remain significant areas of inquiry and debate, (2) showcase recent developments in the field, and/or (3) must be addressed and answered (even if only temporarily) for further progress in the study of Israelite religion to be made. Given the interconnectedness of the study of ancient Israelite religion, it should come as no surprise that these three critical issues are not easily disentangled but, instead, profoundly interrelated.

The sources of Israelite religion: texts and/or archaeology and/or iconography and/or ... ?

The first issue, appropriately, concerns the sources. Simply put, what is the best data set for reconstructing ancient Israelite religion? Is it textual material or is it archaeological and artistic remains? From the start, it would seem obvious that all these sources are legitimate and that each should be used. However, perhaps owing to the prior hegemony of the biblical texts, not to mention the rush of new discoveries, the question is a live one, with the relationship between the biblical and nonbiblical materials often viewed antagonistically.[11] Not infrequently one encounters positions that eschew the biblical evidence, mostly because of its (supposed) lateness and ideological overlay, favoring instead the archaeological data, which are then touted as both objective and unmediated.[12] Such a judgment is not without some truth, but in some contexts it also seems related to a developmental process in which fields of study that began as "handmaidens" to the study of Scripture have eventually come of age, including, it would seem, the age of rebellion against "parental" authority.

Whatever the case, everyone agrees that the study of Israelite religion has been transformed by new archaeological discoveries and their interpretation. It is that latter element, however, that is the rub. How are these discoveries to be *interpreted*? And how are they to be integrated, if at all, with the biblical material? And which arena, the textual or archaeological, should lead and which should follow? These questions permit no easy answers. Even so, a few comments can be made on this important issue of sources.

First, the picture of Israelite religion that emerges from the archaeological data, especially when they are correlated with the biblical material, is one of *complexity*. It is clear that Israelite religion "on the ground" was far more diverse than the picture one gets from a simplistic reading of the Bible alone, though one must be quick to point out that the Bible itself is far from univocal on these matters – a point sometimes underestimated by scholars who downplay the biblical evidence. Moreover, one suspects that the relatively recent emphasis on complexity in Israelite religion is related to broader intellectual emphases on globalization, pluralism, and diversity. If so, then it is likely that future assessments of antiquity will continue to highlight additional features of Israelite religion. Be that as it may, it remains a fact that Israelite religion was a complicated and variegated phenomenon – better, *phenomena*.[13] It is also a fact that careful assessment of the biblical sources, not just the archaeology alone, reveals as much.

Second, the texts that must be studied for the history of Israelite religion include both the biblical texts and nonbiblical epigraphic remains (the latter often included with "archaeology" writ large). Both approaches present problems and possibilities.

1. With regard to the *biblical texts*, modern biblical scholarship has shown nothing if not that the Bible is a mosaic and that not all of its elements are of one piece. On the one hand, this greatly complicates its use as a historical source since the Old Testament is, in the words of William G. Dever, a "curated artifact" – clearly old, but lacking critical information about its original provenience.[14] On the other hand, biblical scholars have also proffered a vast number of hypotheses (often contradictory) regarding when exactly this or that text is to be dated, with various historical and religious significances to be drawn from the dating. These researches into the history of the

biblical text deserve as serious a consideration as the study of the archaeological record.

2.   As for the *epigraphic texts*, they both "confirm and challenge the picture of Israelite religion given in the Bible."[15] Among other things, *confirmation* is found in the facts that (a) with the (possible) exception of the Khirbet el-Qom and Kuntillet 'Ajrud inscriptions, Yahweh is the only Israelite deity mentioned in the major inscriptions, and (b) the personal names that have been recovered are similarly and predominantly Yahwistic, except for some Baalistic personal names found in the Samaria ostraca, a situation not unexpected if the biblical text is to be believed (cf., e.g., 1 Kgs 16:32; Jer 23:13).[16] *Challenge* is found in the Khirbet el-Qom and Kuntillet 'Ajrud texts, which, while perhaps representing a minority perspective, are nevertheless significant for that very reason. Though the full significance of these finds is debated, many scholars take it as self-evident that these inscriptions indicate some sort of veneration of the goddess Asherah, known also from Ugarit. Also challenging to the biblical perspective are the personal names that include Baal as the theophoric element.

Third, all data require interpretation. It is not correct to say that artifacts are mute or opaque; neither is it right to believe that texts are manifestly transparent. The point is simply that whatever the realia or media involved, interpretation by definition involves external considerations and models for understanding – in a word, hermeneutics. So it is the case that despite the evidence adduced about Yahwistic personal names and what it may say about the lack of polytheism in the monarchic period, the usefulness of these names nevertheless can be legitimately doubted,[17] with some scholars placing confidence instead in the Khirbet el-Qom and Kuntillet 'Ajrud inscriptions, which might seem to demonstrate the opposite conclusion. Still other scholars have challenged the significance of the latter texts in light of other considerations – the peripheral location of Kuntillet 'Ajrud, for instance, or its apparent nature as a caravanserai, not a religious center proper. Debate over these finds continues. The point is simply that the data must be weighed as much as counted, and adjudication is seldom, if ever, an obvious or simple process. That process is made even more difficult because it is a deeply hermeneutical one.

Fourth, whenever possible, texts and artifacts should accompany one another in archaeological interpretation. Ideally, one wishes for textual discoveries "explaining" the significance or meaning of a cultic assemblage or an anepigraphic seal. In reality, such situations rarely obtain. And yet, an abundance of textual data *is* found in the Bible (despite its curated nature) that is available for interpretive use. That the biblical data should play a role in archeological interpretation is less a prescriptive statement than a descriptive one.[18] Said differently, while one can produce an image of Israelite religion solely from "dirt archaeology," it will surely be a less complete or interesting one than a portrait produced by the integration of textual (biblical and otherwise) and archaeological sources.

Fifth, archaeology has recovered both written and nonwritten remains. Among the latter are not just architectural ruins, human tools, traces of foodstuffs, and/or environmental indicators of various sorts (e.g., seeds, animal bones, etc.) but also iconographic materials. While the application of iconography to the study of the biblical text and/or Israelite religion is a relatively recent phenomenon, it has already yielded a number of important studies, with more appearing all the time.[19] The most important of these for the study of Israelite religion is Othmar Keel and Christoph Uehlinger's *Gods, Goddesses, and Images of God in Ancient Israel*, which offers a diachronic reconstruction of Israelite religion via iconography with minimal recourse to the biblical text.[20]

The study of images is helpful on a number of fronts. Iconographic data stand somewhere between textual material of whatever sort and aniconic/anepigraphic remains. While few images from ancient Israel/Palestine contain accompanying text describing their significance or identifying their constituent parts, the history of image use, especially when compared with other images in related contexts, affords insight into an image's meaning. That is to say, there is a kind of iconographic "syntax" or "grammar" that aids in interpretation.[21] This very point emphasizes, of course, that images, no less than other data, also require interpretation. That granted, the information images convey is not solely illustrative. Instead, it is often quite generative, as, for example, in the study of imagistic language (especially metaphor) used in the biblical texts; at other times, it is cautionary, chastening overly hasty and inexpert assessments of certain key artifacts.

To sum up this first issue of sources: a symbiotic relationship exists – or *should* exist – between textual and archaeological data in their respective contributions to the study of Israelite religion. One cannot have one without the other, or, said differently, each needs the other, though this greatly complicates matters and stretches the skills of the individual scholar. In any case, Arnold is right to describe a current stalemate between the archaeological approach, on the one hand, and the tradition historical approach to the Bible, on the other hand. In this respect things have not progressed much beyond the mid-twentieth-century debate between the schools of Albright and Alt/Noth.[22] If the study of the history of Israelite religion is to proceed, it must somehow move beyond this impasse. The way forward will involve uniting the best of archaeological, textual, and iconographic approaches without neglecting any potentially useful source.

The locus of Israelite religion: "official" versus "popular" religion

The issue of locus in Israelite religion is closely related to that of sources. Since Rainer Albertz's breakthrough work in 1978, it has become fashionable to speak of personal/popular versus official/normative loci in Israelite religion.[23] This dyad can be parsed in several ways and is frequently compounded with additional elements. An often-encountered interpretation of the dichotomy correlates "personal/popular" religion with the "folk religion" of Kuntillet 'Ajrud or the later Jewish colony at Elephantine, which is marked by syncretism or outright polytheism; "official/normative" religion, however, is often associated with elites and characterized as "orthodox," however that term is defined and understood in ancient periods (as monotheistic, perhaps, or as "pure" Yahwism). "Popular religion" is thus regularly associated with average people and the domestic cult of the family;[24] "official religion" is associated with centers of power – namely, the monarchy, the priesthood, and the temple cultus. To correlate religious locus with religious source, one might say that popular religion is found (mostly) in the archaeological record; official religion (mostly) in the Bible or, at least, among the priests or scribal culture that is purportedly responsible for production of the biblical texts.[25]

While there is no doubt some truth to this dyadic presentation, it is equally true that an overly precise dichotomy between "popular/folk" and "official/normative" religion suffers from several disadvantages and problems. To begin with, it seems a somewhat Romantic (if not explicitly Marxist) depiction of the struggle between the haves and the have-nots. To be sure, earlier scholarship often privileged the viewpoint of the haves, but a simple reversal of the imbalance is unlikely to get us any nearer to reality. Indeed, the fact that in one scholarly generation one group has been favored, whereas, more recently, another group has been the focus of scholarly attention indicates that the schema is ultimately less helpful than would appear at first blush. Then, too, the applicability of postindustrial socioeconomic categories (on which presentations of the dichotomy often depend) to what was a relatively small, often colonized, and certainly preindustrial Iron Age society may be debated. To be sure, the disparity between an average farmer and the Israelite monarch would have been considerable; however, outside the king's immediate circle, it is likely that the majority of people had more in common than not, especially socioeconomically. Undoubtedly, socioeconomic differences did exist and would have been even more apparent to natives on the ground, but fantastic disparity, even in religious practices, seems unlikely, especially in later periods when the society increasingly became economically interrelated.[26]

Zevit has recently challenged the official/popular dichotomy, arguing that these categories do not correspond to known social referents in ancient Israel. While there were elites, officials, a state, a populace, and the "man on the street," the "data do not support the proposition that a particular type of pattern or credo or praxis may be associated" with just one (or each) of these; instead, underlying all "was some minimal Israelitish *koiné*, of credo and praxis, similar to the 'common Judaism' of Late Antiquity."[27] Rather than speak of "official" or "popular" religion, then, it is better to discuss religion among groups that are clearly attested in the data: the individual, the father's house, the clan, the tribe, the people/public. Moreover,

> there is no reason to assume that cultic observances at the level of the father's house were less formal, regulated, or tradition-bound than at the poly-tribal level, and because there is no reason to assume any significant difference in formality between the observances of consanguine groups and those of affiliations of unrelated individuals, the ... dichotomies [of official cult and popular religion] simply do not apply.... [They] lack a social or ideological referent in the culture of ancient Israel.[28]

An overly simplified dichotomy is also problematic because, as already noted, the biblical texts themselves – those selfsame texts that are often thought to be the product of elite, normative religion – are far from univocal on religious matters. The Hebrew Bible acknowledges struggles between different religious groups at various times in Israel's history; at some points the biblical texts even admit of the validity or vitality of other deities (or their symbols) at least among some of these groups.[29] It would seem, then, that those elite persons responsible for the Bible did a rather poor job "norming" their normative religious text. To respond to this objection by asserting that the texts bore authentic reminiscences that had to be preserved is certainly possible but also posits a concern on the part of the "orthodox" for antiquarianism and truth-telling that trumps their commitment to religious ideology – a position that strains credulity, at least according to the way these "orthodox" are often portrayed by scholars emphasizing (if not somehow also preferring) "folk religion." It may be both easier and simpler, then, to posit that the texts, in details concerning *both* "heterodox" *and* what became "normative" Yahwism, are less anachronistic than is often thought to be the case.[30] In short, the religion of the people on the ground may have been more like the religion of the people as described in the texts, especially insofar as the biblical picture is complex and variegated, and insofar as that picture is (if and when it can be) supported by extrabiblical data. Moreover, it should not be forgotten that the biblical texts portray how the syncretistic or polytheistic tendency at times belonged not to the general populace but to the upper echelons, especially the monarchy. Indeed, popular religion seems sometimes to have been marked by pietistic resistance to official religion (see, e.g., Elijah vs. Ahab and Jezebel in 1 Kgs 16:31–21:29). Here, too, overly reified understandings of the official/ popular dichotomy are shown to be unhelpful, if not erroneous.

So, while we definitely have to posit "internal religious pluralism" (Albertz) in ancient Israel, we also must consider the possibility that the range of options may have been more limited – or, said differently, more closely related – than is often imagined. This is Zevit's point about the religion of known social groups within ancient Israel. It receives further support from Routledge's work on Egyptian religion. Against the long-standing opinion that the Egyptian masses had no contact with official/state religion and that such religion was therefore of little or no significance to them, Routledge argues that a number of close parallels exist between the official religion of the state temples and the popular religion practiced by everyday people.[31] These parallels include similar offerings, performed in similar fashion, and said with similar prayers. Furthermore, people participated in the outer courts of official temples, where they often engaged in rites "directly parallel to the daily ritual performed on the god's statue in the sanctuary."[32] Still further, the architecture, iconography, and rituals practiced in small, local chapels indicate "that the religion of these chapels is parallel to, not independent of, official religion."[33] Routledge concludes that any bifurcation of Egyptian religion into a dichotomy of official and popular religion "misses much of its complexity and meaning."[34] This is not to say that no differences exist; rather, Routledge wants to argue that the two poles were

> integrated and defined through state temples and religious practice. This was not a bipartite religious system practiced by two

non-communicating groups. Treating religious practice as an integrated whole allows a wider role for the temple in ancient Egyptian society and explains the willingness of the people to participate in the economic, political, and religious life of those temples. Indeed, the construction of consent ... is a much stronger force in legitimizing a given social order than is direct coercion. As C. Bell has stated, religious practices and rituals are central elements in the ideological systems that create and negotiate tacit consent between social groups with potentially different interests. Such central social dynamics are neglected when a bifurcation of religious practice is assumed.[35]

To be sure, there are marked differences between ancient Egyptian religion and ancient Israelite religion, but the analogues are weighty, including Routledge's observation that the general populace in Egypt had access to the outer courts of the temple and that petitions of the people were heard there.[36] Certainly the same held true for Israel. In fact, it might be even more true of Israel, which lacked at least some of the apparatus that accrued to the Egyptian religious system.

Equally important is Routledge's attention to symbolic literacy rather than practical literacy in religious participation.[37] Practical literacy would likely be needed by a priest or official functionary, especially a scribe, but would not necessarily be required for an average, partially literate or even totally illiterate person who was nevertheless symbolically or ritually literate: able, that is, by various means such as memorization or by ritual, architectural, and iconographic clues, to participate in religious activities that otherwise would appear to depend on full, practical literacy or elite knowledge. Formal or elite religious education, in brief, may not have been the barrier it is often thought to be to full religious participation.[38]

These considerations bring official and popular religion closer than they have been construed by some scholars in recent years. A closer relationship might, in turn, help to explain more easily why the normative Yahwism that eventually became encapsulated in the biblical texts was able to survive in the first place. At least part of the reason would be because that type of Yahwism was not altogether discontinuous from the practiced religion of earlier periods by real, regular people. Let it be stressed again: more complexity and religious diversity than what is envisioned by the Bible is a given, and yet what is allowed, even mandated, in the traditions found within the Bible must represent an important, perhaps even dominant (at least at some points) element within that complexity, even as that element is itself complex. Otherwise, the coercive mechanisms that would explain the later religious triumph of normative Yahwism become increasingly difficult to imagine and hard to locate in time and space with any certainty.[39] "Normative, official Yahwism" may well have triumphed, then (at least in part), because it was not solely a late, elite, or predominantly small phenomenon vis-à-vis a putatively early, widely practiced, and massively polytheistic folk religion.[40]

Once again, the data, biblical and otherwise, complicate any simple presentation. So, just as there are multiple sources for the history of Israelite religion, the same situation obtains with regard to its locus: there are no doubt *multiple loci* for Israelite religion, even if they may be closer to one another than often surmised.

The content of Israelite religion: "theology" or "practice/ritual"?

The third important issue, concerning the *content* of Israelite religion, follows naturally from the second. What is the precise content of ancient Israelite religion? Is it formal ideational content, perhaps even of a "systematic" sort,[41] that would presumably be the product of higher echelons within the religious structure (i.e., "official" or "state" arenas)? Or is it the various religious practices performed by average, everyday people with little or no knowledge of the implicit or explicit ideational content pertaining thereto, assuming that such content even existed?[42] We can designate these two options with the terms "theology" for the former and "practice" or "ritual" for the latter.

In many ways, this question of "theology" versus "practice/ritual" is related to a much older one: namely, whether the study of Israelite religion should be a *historical* one, oriented toward Israel's *religious practices* and their *diachronic* development, or a *theological* one, oriented toward the *ideational content* of the textual remains (preeminently the Old Testament), mostly in a *synchronic* mode. This older question goes back at least as far as Gabler's famous inaugural address at the University of Altdorf in 1787, which, according to many scholars, drove a wedge between dogmatic theological inquiry and critical historical study.[43] It also gave birth to a disciplinary distinction between the study of Israelite religion (understood as a mostly historical, diachronic, and purportedly objective pursuit) and "Old Testament theology" (treated as a more literary, synchronic, and subjective or existentially engaged approach). Debates over which approach is superior have raged ever since. Cross, for instance, has recently (re)asserted that "[i]f we propose to study the history of the religion of Israel today we must be

governed by the same postulates which are the basis of modern historical method. Our task must be a historical not a theological enterprise."[44]
Somewhat ironically, however, Cross's own work has been criticized
for being overly beholden to presuppositions favoring the superiority
of Israelite religion over Canaanite religion, thus skewing his results.[45]
Evidently, one person's objective history is another person's subjective
theology.

The issue of religious content is also profoundly connected to the
issue of sources. Which sources are to be valued above the others, or how
are the different (often equivocal) sources to be adjudicated? If archaeological data are privileged and are largely understood to be at odds with
the content of the biblical text, what then? Is the latter "only" theology
that can be safely ignored in light of the superior extrabiblical data? At
times it appears that scholars who favor archaeological sources believe
that such sources reveal only rituals or religious practices, not theology
proper, which is then thought to be a later by-product or development
of some sort. But many artifacts, especially *religious* ones (e.g., altars,
votive objects, etc.), and epigraphic data with religious content (e.g.,
divine names or theophoric personal names) bear witness to or betray
ideational beliefs. This would suggest that "theology" (generously
defined for the moment) is not an inappropriate or anachronistic category in the study of ancient Israelite religion and is profoundly related to
issues and practices of religion and ritual.[46] A complete and total bifurcation of practice and belief is therefore suspect and can actually smack of
older antiritual interpretations of Catholicism by Protestants or Judaism
by Christians, as if ritual practices never or seldom involve belief content. Patrick D. Miller has written that

> it is difficult to comprehend how that [bifurcation] works, except
> that it makes it easier to deal with a lot of archaeological data where
> there is no interpretive clue as to what the data indicate about
> "belief," that is, what prompts this site, this figuring, this vessel,
> and so forth. Assuming that there is no thought behind the practice
> simply because there is no written text is dubious. Further, there is
> much written text that has much to say about belief and cannot be
> avoided in writing about this topic or interpreting the data.[47]

A safer course of action, then, seems to be to hold practice and belief
together, viewing practice as related to belief and having at least implicit
belief content. "Theology" is an appropriate word for such belief content, if that term is understood as things having to do with the divine
realm and with the way they impinge on the nondivine world.

In Smith's concise formulation: "Out of experience comes literature, and out of religious experience comes religious literature."[48] Such
religious literature is obviously found in the Hebrew Bible, but traces, at
least, of the same are also found in inscriptions that bless in the name of
Yahweh or in personal names that use Yahweh's name as the theophoric
element, or another god's name for that matter. Smith's formulation also
may be extended to *religious objects* (e.g., artifacts, statues, iconography,
and cult sites) that bear a relationship to religious ideas and practices.
These, too, are brought forth from religious experience. Yet at this point
we are thrown back to the issues of source and locus because many of
these objects, artifacts, and sites are not forthcoming about their religious content or their points of origin, at least not explicitly or obviously
so. This difficulty must not be understood as indicating that they have
no such content, only that extreme caution must be exercised in deduc-
ing or interpreting what is and is not there.

The history of Israelite religion therefore must deal with *both* "theology" and "practice/ritual." Recent definitions of Israelite religion recognize as much:

> [R]eligion ... is *the service and worship of the divine or supernatural
> through a system of attitudes, beliefs, and practices.*[49]

and

> *Israelite religions are the varied, symbolic expressions of, and appro-
> priate responses to the deities and powers that groups or commu-
> nities deliberately affirmed as being of unrestricted value to them
> within their worldview.*[50]

It is unfruitful, then, to parse "religion," "practice," or "ritual" as
completely nonideational and non-belief-related and to pursue such a
detheologized version as an end run around theological content. To be
sure, there are indubitably major differences between Israelite religion –
again, understood as *both* practice and belief – in the Neo-Assyrian
period and the religion evident in, say, a contemporary Jewish *Siddur*,
let alone the catechism of the Catholic Church. But recognizing those
differences ought to free one to investigate their nature.

Finally, it is obvious from the history of the discipline that theological concerns, contemporary and otherwise, bear on and relate to
questions in the study of Israelite religion.[51] This partially explains
the heat, if not light, that is produced at the intersection of these
separable-but-not-fully-discrete studies. This point is increasingly recognized even in archaeological circles, which may be evidence of a new

synthesis of what has been often viewed in polarized fashion.[52] A further benefit of (re)uniting ritual and belief, "religious practice" and "theology," is that such a (re)union transcends the tired distinction of practice and ideas so as to get at a better understanding of all aspects of Israelite religion, including, perhaps, its effects. If the Hebrew Bible is to be believed, there can be no ultimate separation of practice and belief – for example, of the importance of God's gracious acts, on the one hand, and Israel's concretized, obedience in response, on the other hand.[53] Such a conclusion is not without significant theological as well as historical merit.

NOTES

1 Some scholars would include the Greco-Roman period because this was formative for certain late biblical materials (e.g., Daniel) or because of important text finds (e.g., Qumran) dating from that era. Most material-cultural histories of Israelite religion have not gone past 332 BCE, however, because the Hellenistic period represents a marked shift in influences and archaeology.

2 For some of this history, see John A. Wilson, *Signs and Wonders upon Pharaoh: A History of American Egyptology* (University of Chicago Press, 1964); and Mogens Trolle Larsen, *The Conquest of Assyria: Excavations in an Antique Land 1840–1860* (London: Routledge, 1996 [Dutch orig: 1994]).

3 The Baal cycle and other important Ugaritic texts are conveniently collected in Simon B. Parker, ed., *Ugaritic Narrative Poetry* (SBLWAW 9; Atlanta: Scholars Press, 1997).

4 See, e.g., William G. Dever, "Syro-Palestinian and Biblical Archaeology," in *The Hebrew Bible and Its Modern Interpreters*, ed. by Douglas A. Knight and Gene M. Tucker (Minneapolis, MN: Fortress, 1985), 31–74; Dever, "Biblical and Syro-Palestinian Archaeology: A State-of-the-Art Assessment at the Turn of the Millennium," *Currents in Biblical Research* 8 (2000): 91–116; Dever, "Syro-Palestinian and Biblical Archaeology: Into the Next Millennium," in *Symbiosis, Symbolism, and the Power of the Past: Canaan, Ancient Israel, and Their Neighbors from the Late Bronze Age through Roman Palaestina*, ed. by William G. Dever and Seymour Gitin (Winona Lake, IN: Eisenbrauns, 2003), 513–27. More generally, see P. R. S. Moorey, *A Century of Biblical Archaeology* (Louisville, KY: Westminster/John Knox, 1991), esp. 114–78.

5 For a recent collection of essays on the topic, see Barry M. Gittlen, ed., *Sacred Time, Sacred Place: Archaeology and the Religion of Israel* (Winona Lake, IN: Eisenbrauns, 2002).

6 E.g., discoveries in Phoenicia, Philistia, Aram/Damascus, Transjordan, Hatti, Persia, various Syrian sites (esp. Emar), Mari, and, to a lesser degree, locations such as Urartu, Elam, pre-Islamic Arabia, and Bronze/Iron Age Greece.

7 Frank Moore Cross, "Introduction to the Study of the History of the Religion of Israel," in *Inspired Speech: Prophecy in the Ancient Near East: Essays*

in Honor of Herbert B. Huffmon, ed. by John Kaltner and Louis Stulman (JSOTSup 378; New York: T & T Clark, 2004), 8–11 (11).

8   For scholars emphasizing Israel's uniqueness, see, e.g., Yehezkel Kaufmann, *The Religion of Israel: From Its Beginnings to the Babylonian Exile,* trans. and abridged by Moshe Greenberg (New York: Schocken, 1972 [1960]); G. Ernest Wright, *The Old Testament Against Its Environment* (SBT 2; London: SCM, 1950); and, most recently, John H. Walton, *Ancient Near Eastern Thought and the Old Testament: Introducing the Conceptual World of the Hebrew Bible* (Grand Rapids, MI: Baker Academic, 2006).

9   Serious problems beset any easy identification of the Ugaritic data with the indigenous religion that was practiced in more southern parts of the Levant and that can be deduced from the biblical material. This point granted, there seems to be enough convergence between these data sets to justify their careful correlation.

10 Strong emphasis on continuity can be found in, e.g., Beth Alpert Nakhai, *Archaeology and the Religions of Canaan and Israel* (ASOR Book 7; Boston: American Schools of Oriental Research, 2001); William G. Dever, *Did God Have a Wife? Archaeology and Folk Religion in Ancient Israel* (Grand Rapids, MI: Eerdmans, 2005); and Mark S. Smith, *The Early History of God: Yahweh and the Other Deities in Ancient Israel,* 2d ed. (Grand Rapids, MI: Eerdmans, 2002), though with important differences and nuances.

11 As late as the 1960s and 1970s, most histories of Israelite religion were still largely confined to the biblical texts and the then-contemporary under-standings of their composition, integrity, and accuracy. See, e.g., Helmer Ringgren, *Israelite Religion,* trans. by David E. Green (Philadelphia: Fortress, 1966 [German orig. 1963]), 4–14; and Georg Fohrer, *History of Israelite Religion,* trans. by David E. Green (Nashville, TN: Abingdon, 1972 [German orig. 1968]), 24–5. Ringgren does not mention archaeology at all in his discussion of sources; Fohrer says only that archaeological data "are particularly helpful in illuminating the external circumstances of Israelite religion, and contribute to our understanding of the primary source, the OT," but immediately adds, "[t]hey seldom have anything to say about the content of religious belief" (25).

12 See, e.g., Nakhai, *Archaeology and the Religions of Canaan and Israel,* 2, 192; Dever, *Did God Have a Wife?,* esp. 74–6.

13 Use of the plural "religions" in the works of Richard S. Hess, *Israelite Religions: An Archaeological and Biblical Survey* (Grand Rapids, MI: Baker Academic, 2007) and Ziony Zevit, *The Religions of Ancient Israel: A Synthesis of Parallactic Approaches* (London: Continuum, 2001) is decisive and representative in this regard.

14 William G. Dever, *Recent Archaeological Discoveries and Biblical Research* (Seattle: University of Washington Press, 1990), 9.

15 Patrick D. Miller, "Israelite Religion," in Knight and Tucker, eds., *Hebrew Bible and Its Modern Interpreters,* 206, n. 3.

16 See Jeffrey H. Tigay, *You Shall Have No Other Gods: Israelite Religion in the Light of Hebrew Inscriptions* (HSS 31; Atlanta: Scholars Press, 1986); Tigay, "Israelite Religion: The Onomastic and Epigraphic Evidence," in *Ancient Israelite Religion: Essays in Honor of Frank Moore Cross,* ed. by Patrick D.

Miller, Jr., Paul D. Hanson, and S. Dean McBride (Philadelphia: Fortress, 1987), 157–94. Note also Johannes C. de Moor, *The Rise of Yahwism: The Roots of Israelite Monotheism*, rev. ed. (BETL 91; Leuven, Netherlands: University Press, 1997), 10–40, who likewise highlights El-based personal names.

17 The personal names might be unhelpful given social conventions, family traditions, or even uncertain etymologies; moreover, even at Ugarit, there is but one attestation of a personal name that includes the goddess Athirat's name; see Theodore J. Lewis, "Israel, Religion of," in *The Oxford Companion to the Bible*, ed. by Bruce M. Metzger and Michael D. Coogan (Oxford University Press, 1993), 333–4; John Day, *Yahweh and the Gods and Goddesses of Canaan* (JSOTSup 265; London: Sheffield Academic Press, 2000), 226–8.

18 See, e.g., J. Maxwell Miller, "The Ancient Near East and Archaeology," in *Old Testament Interpretation: Past, Present, and Future: Essays in Honor of Gene M. Tucker*, ed. by James Luther Mays, David L. Petersen, and Kent Harold Richards (Nashville, TN: Abingdon, 1995), 259: "[I]n instances where archaeological evidence and the Old Testament record are brought together, the Old Testament record invariably plays a major role in interpreting the archaeological evidence." On this score, one might note the title of the useful compendium of archaeological data on ancient Israel by Philip J. King and Lawrence E. Stager, *Life in Biblical Israel* (LAI; Louisville, KY: Westminster John Knox, 2001).

19 The pioneering work was Othmar Keel, *The Symbolism of the Biblical World: Ancient Near Eastern Iconography and the Book of Psalms*, reprint ed., trans. by Timothy J. Hallett (Winona Lake, IN: Eisenbrauns, 1997), which appeared in German in 1972. Since then, Keel and his students (often called the "Fribourg School") – especially Silvia Schroer, Christoph Uehlinger, Thomas Staubli, and Jürg Eggler, among others – have produced numerous important studies, many of which are found in the series *Orbis biblicus et orientalis*. See the thorough discussion in Izaak J. de Hulster, "Illuminating Images: An Iconographic Method of Old Testament Exegesis with Three Case Studies from Third Isaiah," Ph.D. dissertation, University of Utrecht, 2007; and, more briefly, de Hulster, *Iconographic Exegesis and Third Isaiah* (FAT II.36; Tübingen, Germany: Mohr Siebeck, 2009).

20 Othmar Keel and Christoph Uehlinger, *Gods, Goddesses, and Images of God in Ancient Israel*, trans. by Thomas H. Trapp (Minneapolis, MN: Fortress, 1998). Note also Silvia Schroer and Othmar Keel, *Die Ikonographie Palästinas/Israels und der Alte Orient: eine Religionsgeschichte in Bildern*, 3 vols. to date (Fribourg, Switzerland: Academic Press, 2005); as well as the in-process *Iconography of Demons and Deities in the Ancient Near East: An Iconographic Dictionary with Special Emphasis on First-Millennium BCE Palestine/Israel*, ed. by Jürg Eggler, Christoph Uehlinger, et al.; available online at: www.religionswissenschaft.uzh.ch/idd/.

21 See Keel and Uehlinger, *Gods, Goddesses, and Images of God*, 7–13, 393–6; also Brent A. Strawn, "Imagery," in *Dictionary of the Old Testament: Wisdom, Poetry and Writings*, ed. by Tremper Longman and Peter Enns (Downers Grove, IL: IVP Academic, 2008), 306–14; further, de Hulster, *Iconographic Exegesis and Third Isaiah*, esp. 23–104.

22   Bill T. Arnold, "Religion in Ancient Israel," in *The Face of Old Testament Studies: A Survey of Contemporary Approaches*, ed. by David W. Baker and Bill T. Arnold (Grand Rapids, MI: Baker, 1999), 392–3. For more on these schools, see Megan Bishop Moore, *Philosophy and Practice in Writing a History of Ancient Israel* (LHBOTS 435; New York: T & T Clark, 2006).

23   Rainer Albertz, *Persönliche Frömmigkeit und offizielle Religion: religionsinterner Pluralismus in Israel und Babylon* (Calwer Theologische Monographien 9; Stuttgart, Germany: Calwer, 1978). See also Rainer Albertz, *A History of Israelite Religion in the Old Testament Period*, 2 vols., trans. by John Bowden (OTL; Louisville, KY: Westminster John Knox, 1994 [Germ orig. 1992]), esp. the charts on 1:21, 106 and 2:443 and the discussions there.

24   For the importance of family religion, see esp. J. David Schloen, *The House of the Father as Fact and Symbol: Patrimonialism in Ugarit and the Ancient Near East* (SAHL 2; Winona Lake, IN: Eisenbrauns, 2001); and Karel van der Toorn, *Family Religion in Babylonia, Syria and Israel: Continuity and Change in the Forms of Religious Life* (SHCANE 7; Leiden, Netherlands: Brill, 1996).

25   For the Bible's emergence from elite scribal culture, see, e.g., Karel van der Toorn, *Scribal Culture and the Making of the Hebrew Bible* (Cambridge, MA: Harvard University Press, 2007); William M. Schniedewind, *How the Bible Became a Book: The Textualization of Ancient Israel* (New York: Cambridge University Press, 2004); and, more polemically, Dever, *Did God Have a Wife?*

26   See, e.g., Paula McNutt, *Reconstructing the Society of Ancient Israel* (LAI; Louisville: Westminster John Knox, 1999), 154–72, esp. 158–9, who states that social stratification and economic inequalities were pronounced in peasant societies largely because there was no middle class. That point granted, the upper class was likely to be exceedingly small, relegating the vast majority of people to the same (lower) class. While McNutt lists professional classes that may have been associated with royalty or elites (ibid., 167–8, 199–200), it may legitimately be doubted that all of these belonged to, or necessarily constitute, an upper class per se.

27   Ziony Zevit, "False Dichotomies in Descriptions of Israelite Religion: A Problem, Its Origin, and a Proposed Solution," in *Symbiosis, Symbolism, and the Power of the Past: Canaan, Ancient Israel, and Their Neighbors from the Late Bronze Age through Roman Palaestina*, ed. by William G. Dever and Seymour Gitin (Winona Lake, IN: Eisenbrauns, 2003), 232.

28   Ibid.

29   See the data collected in Karel van der Toorn, Bob Becking, and Pieter W. van der Horst, eds. *Dictionary of Deities and Demons in the Bible*, 2nd ed. (Grand Rapids, MI: Eerdmans, 1999).

30   Perhaps also that the religion itself (notwithstanding the complexity already acknowledged) was less heterodox or that the heterodoxy that existed was less heterodox than often suspected.

31   Carolyn Routledge, "Parallelism in Popular and Official Religion in Ancient Egypt," in *Text, Artifact, and Image: Revealing Ancient Israelite Religion*,

ed. by Gary Beckman and Theodore J. Lewis (BJS 346; Providence, RI: Brown Judaic Studies, 2006), 223–8.

32 Ibid., 232.

33 Ibid., 234.

34 Ibid., 237.

35 Ibid., 238. Routledge's reference to Catherine Bell is to Bell's *Ritual Theory, Ritual Practice* (Oxford University Press, 1992), 204–18.

36 Routledge, "Parallelism in Popular and Official Religion in Ancient Egypt," 230–1.

37 Ibid., 226–30.

38 It might be further noted that in Egypt of the Old and Middle Kingdoms, service in the sanctuaries fell to lay priests who also worked in other vocations. Only later was the lay priesthood replaced by a class of priestly officials; see Sigfried Morenz, *Egyptian Religion*, trans. by Ann E. Keep (Ithaca, NY: Cornell University Press, 1973 [German orig. 1960]), 101; Denise M. Doxey, "Priesthood," in *The Ancient Gods Speak: A Guide to Egyptian Religion*, ed. by Donald B. Redford (Oxford University Press, 2002), 315–22. It seems that a similar situation obtained in Israel for some religious officiants, if only because the Levites, e.g., are said to reside in towns throughout the land (Num 35:2, 8; Deut 12:12; 14:27, 29; Joshua 21; Neh 11:20). In short, both scenarios, Egyptian and Israelite, provide for a healthy intermixture of religious officials and the regular populace.

39 Van der Toorn argues that canonization means "a limited number of texts . . . [being] imposed upon a particular community for all members, for all times" (*Scribal Culture*, 7–8; further 205–32). Perhaps so, but one wonders if some sort of totalitarian mechanism must be posited if the general populace had no role or awareness whatsoever in the production and use of the texts in question. General ignorance of the texts and their production is precisely what van der Toorn implies: "Scribes wrote for scribes. To the public at large, the books of the Bible were icons of a body of knowledge accessible only through the oral instruction presented by religious experts. The text of the Hebrew Bible was not part of the popular culture. The Bible was born and studied in the scribal workshop at the temple. In its fundamental essence, it was a book of the clergy" (ibid., 2). Much depends here on "oral instruction" and the "text of the Hebrew Bible."

40 Cf. Robert P. Gordon, "Introducing the God of Israel," in *The God of Israel*, ed. by Robert P. Gordon (UCOP 64; Cambridge University Press, 2007), 6: "A form of Yahwism that was polytheistic and undifferentiated from other pluriform systems of worship would have been an improbable matrix for the world's monotheistic faiths."

41 For the inevitability of systematization, see Rolf P. Knierim, *The Task of Old Testament Theology: Substance, Method and Cases* (Grand Rapids, MI: Eerdmans, 1995), 475–86, esp. 548. Already in 1929, Walther Eichrodt argued that even historical investigations of the "religious thought world" of the Old Testament must be systematic ("Does Old Testament Theology Still Have Independent Significance within Old Testament Scholarship?" in *Old Testament Theology: Flowering and Future*, rev.

ed., ed. by Ben C. Ollenburger [SBTS 1; Winona Lake, IN: Eisenbrauns, 2004], 24).

42   There is debate in ritual studies on precisely this latter point. See, e.g., Bell, *Ritual Theory, Ritual Practice; and eadem, Ritual: Perspectives and Dimensions* (New York: Oxford University Press, 1997). For biblical studies proper, see Ithamar Gruenwald, *Rituals and Ritual Theory in Ancient Israel* (Leiden, Netherlands: Brill, 2003); and Gerald A. Klingbeil, *Bridging the Gap: Ritual and Ritual Texts in the Bible* (Winona Lake, IN: Eisenbrauns, 2007).

43   See Johann P. Gabler, "An Oration on the Proper Distinction Between Biblical and Dogmatic Theology and the Specific Objectives of Each," in Ollenburger, ed., *Old Testament Theology*, 497–506.

44   Cross, "Introduction to the Study of the History of the Religion of Israel," 8.

45   So Delbert R. Hillers, "Analyzing the Abominable: Our Understanding of Canaanite Religion," *JQR* 75 (1985): 253–69.

46   One might compare the frequent and non-problematic employment of the term "theology" in Egyptology. See, e.g., Jan Assmann, *The Search for God in Ancient Egypt*, trans. by David Lorton (Ithaca, NY: Cornell University Press, 2001 [German orig. 1984]).

47   Review of Dever, *Did God Have a Wife?* in RBL 07/2007; available online at: www.bookreviews.org/pdf/4910_6305.pdf. The converse also might be worried about: if no belief inheres with the practice, then one must not extrapolate beliefs behind the practice, and yet many archaeologists do precisely that. See, extensively, Dever, *Did God Have a Wife?*

48   Mark S. Smith, "Recent Study of Israelite Religion in Light of the Ugaritic Texts," in *Ugarit at Seventy-Five*, ed. by K. Lawson Younger, Jr. (Winona Lake, IN: Eisenbrauns, 2007), 1–25 (5).

49   Hess, *Israelite Religion*, 15 (his emphases; see also 22).

50   Zevit, *Religions of Ancient Israel*, 15 (his emphases).

51   See, e.g., Arnold, "Religion in Ancient Israel," 418–20; Erhard S. Gerstenberger, "The Religion and Institutions of Ancient Israel: Toward a Contextual Theology of the Scriptures," in Mays et al., eds., *Old Testament Interpretation: Past, Present, and Future*, 263, 266; W. Zimmerli, "The History of Israelite Religion," in *Tradition and Interpretation: Essays by Members of the Society for Old Testament Study*, ed. by G. W. Anderson (Oxford, UK: Clarendon, 1979), 374; and esp. Miller, "Israelite Religion," 218 and *passim*.

52   E.g., P. R. S. Moorey, *Idols of the People: Miniature Images of Clay in the Ancient Near East: The Schweich Lectures of the British Academy 2001* (Oxford University Press, 2003), 5; Zevit, *Religions of Ancient Israel*, 36–7 (but, for his own perspective, see 79); and Dever, *Did God Have a Wife?*, which makes a number of large theological claims on the basis of archaeological data.

53   See Gary A. Anderson, "Introduction to Israelite Religion," in *The New Interpreter's Bible*, ed. by Leander E. Keck et al. (Nashville, TN: Abingdon Press, 1994), 1:277.

FURTHER READING

Albertz, Rainer. *A History of Israelite Religion in the Old Testament Period*, 2 vols. (OTL). Translated by John Bowden. Louisville, KY: Westminster John Knox, 1994 (German orig. 1992).

Beckman, Gary M., and Theodore J. Lewis, eds. *Text, Artifact, and Image: Revealing Ancient Israelite Religion* (BJS 346). Providence, RI: Brown Judaic Studies, 2006.

Cross, Frank Moore. *Canaanite Myth and Hebrew Epic: Essays in the History of the Religion of Israel*. Cambridge, MA: Harvard University Press, 1973.

Day, John. *Yahweh and the Gods and Goddesses of Canaan* (JSOTSup 265). Sheffield Academic Press, 2000.

Dever, William G. *Did God Have a Wife? Archaeology and Folk Religion in Ancient Israel*. Grand Rapids, MI: Eerdmans, 2005.

Dever, William G. and Seymour Gitin, eds. *Symbiosis, Symbolism, and the Power of the Past: Canaan, Ancient Israel, and Their Neighbors from the Late Bronze Age through Roman Palaestina*. Winona Lake, IN: Eisenbrauns, 2003.

Hadley, Judith M. *The Cult of Asherah in Ancient Israel and Judah: Evidence for a Hebrew Goddess* (UCOP 57). Cambridge University Press, 2000.

Hess, Richard S. *Israelite Religions: An Archaeological and Biblical Survey*. Grand Rapids, MI: Baker Academic, 2007.

Keel, Othmar, and Christoph Uehlinger. *Gods, Goddesses, and Images of God in Ancient Israel*. Translated by Thomas H. Trapp. Minneapolis, MN: Fortress, 1998.

Miller, Patrick D. *The Religion of Ancient Israel* (LAI). Edited by Douglas A. Knight. Louisville, KY: Westminster John Knox, 2000.

Miller, Patrick D., Paul D. Hanson, and S. Dean McBride, eds. *Ancient Israelite Religion: Essays in Honor of Frank Moore Cross*. Philadelphia: Fortress, 1987.

Smith, Mark S. *The Early History of God: Yahweh and the Other Deities in Ancient Israel*, 2d ed. Grand Rapids, MI: Eerdmans/Dearborn, MI: Dove, 2002 [1990].

Zevit, Ziony. *The Religions of Ancient Israel: A Synthesis of Parallactic Approaches*. London: Continuum, 2001.

5 The Hebrew Bible and history

MARC ZVI BRETTLER

In modern parlance, the term "history" is used in two main senses: the past and (written) depictions of the past, often called "historiography." These two senses live in an uncomfortable tension because the past is a set of events that transpired once and can never be recaptured exactly. Instead, various efforts can be made to capture these events in some form – most often through a writing system that can tell *certain aspects* of what really happened. Societies desire to recapture the past at particular points in time for particular reasons.

The introductions to the two great Greek histories that are often thought of as the beginning of history in the fifth century BCE, *The Histories* by Herodotus and *The History of the Peloponnesian War* by Thucydides, offer explicit reasons for trying to recapture the past. Herodotus opens his work

> Herodotus of Halicarnasssus, his *Researches* [Greek: *historiai*] are here set down to preserve the memory of the past by putting on record the astonishing achievements both of our own and of other peoples; and more particularly, to show how they came into conflict.[1]

Thucydides opens

> Thucydides the Athenian wrote the history of the war fought between Athens and Sparta, beginning the account at the very outbreak of the war, in the belief that it was going to be a great war and more worth writing about than any of those which had taken place in the past.... This was the greatest disturbance in the history of the Hellenes.... For though I have found it impossible, because of its remoteness in time, to acquire a really precise knowledge of the distant past or even of the history preceding our own period, yet, after looking back into it as far as I can, all the evidence leads me to conclude that these periods were not great periods either in warfare or in anything else.[2]

No comparable introduction is found in any text from the ancient Near Eastern world. In contrast to these two works, ancient Near Eastern accounts are typically anonymous, do not have introductions, and do not offer explicit reasons why they have been written.

This may suggest that it is best to avoid the term "history" for the Bible and, perhaps, the pre-Hellenistic ancient world. Many surveys of history writing do in fact exclude the Bible, beginning with the classical world.[3] Yet it is not clear that we should be shackled to this understanding of history as "researches," namely, as critical historiography based on careful interrogation and combination of sources. Although etymology is one way of defining terms, it is not the only way, and there is no reason that we should give priority to an understanding of history that emphasizes its roots in research – namely, on critical examination of various sources to see which is correct. Furthermore, as a growing number of classical historians are recognizing, if critical examination of sources is the key to defining what should or should not be considered history, much of Greek historiography, including Herodotus, might not be considered history either. In fact, the idea of critical historiography really only developed in a serious and consistent fashion in German universities in the nineteenth century with Leopold von Ranke and others.[4] Thus, an understanding of history limited to an attempt to map[5] the past through an accurate narrative, presented chronologically, using sources in a critical, objective fashion, would exclude speaking of not only the Bible as history but also Herodotus, the other classical historians, and indeed much written about the past until the last two centuries.

For these reasons, if we want to speak of pre–modern history at all, it is best to define history in an open-ended fashion as "a depiction of a past." We know that in the ancient Near Eastern world such depictions took many forms. In ancient Mesopotamia, for example, scribes wrote chronicles, annals, and even letters to gods.[6] Kings set up steles to commemorate their victories, and palace walls often were decorated with historical scenes that could be "read" chronologically from left to right, just as the Akkadian writing system could be read in that direction – some even contain labels that explain the events depicted.[7] It is likely that ancient Israelites, too, had a wide variety of ways of depicting a past. They may have decorated palace walls and may have erected victory steles, but none of these has survived. They also told a wide variety of stories about a past, but many of these are in no way reflected in the current text of the Hebrew Bible and have been lost. Instead, we are left with highly reworked depictions of a past, as preserved in the Hebrew Bible.

The Hebrew Bible contains many narratives that depict a past, the definition of history preferred here. This definition is narrower than that used earlier – it only includes narratives, because the Bible is a narrative text. Yet for some this will still be an uncomfortably broad definition of history. It discusses "a past" rather than "the past." Also, narrative (often understood as *X* telling *Y* about *Z*) is a broader term than a "story," which needs to have a beginning, middle, and end. It is nevertheless crucial to be as broad as possible because considering only narratives that present *the* past would introduce insuperable problems: given the paucity of extrabiblical evidence bearing on the historicity of the Bible, how can it be known which narratives succeed in telling *the* past? And how would this be measured – would such a text be historical if it were more than 51 percent historically correct? What if it had some details correct but exhibited major gaps and some fanciful additions? (This is indeed the case for many biblical historical narratives.) It is thus best to use the definition of "a narrative that presents a past" when considering biblical texts as history and to examine the extent of these narratives in the Hebrew Bible, their different types, and the different reasons for their depictions.

It is possible to look at these issues because the Bible has a sense of a past that is distinct from the present and offers many texts that narrate, in one version or another, this past. The biblical references to memory, specifically to the Hebrew root *zkr*, "to remember," make it clear that the Israelites saw the past and present as distinct. The predominance of this motif may not be obvious to a person who reads the Bible in translation, where this same root can lie behind different English words, as seen here:

Exodus 13:3 And Moses said to the people, "*Remember* this day, on which you went free from Egypt, the house of bondage, how the Lord freed you from it with a mighty hand: no leavened bread shall be eaten."[8]

Deuteronomy 15:15 *Bear in mind* that you were slaves in the land of Egypt and the Lord your God redeemed you; therefore I enjoin this commandment upon you today.

Psalm 77:12 I *recall* the deeds of the Lord; yes, I *recall* Your wonders of old;

Psalm 78:42 They did not *remember* His strength, or the day He redeemed them from the foe;

Psalm 105:5 *Remember* the wonders He has done, His portents and the judgments He has pronounced,

Psalm 137:1 By the rivers of Babylon, there we sat, sat and wept, as we *thought of* Zion.

Biblical texts even reflect the notion that the past may be fundamentally different from the present. This is seen in many texts where God is called on to act as in the past, as in Isaiah 51:9–10:

> 9 Awake, awake, clothe yourself with splendor. O arm of the Lord! Awake as in days of old, as in former ages! It was you that hacked Rahab in pieces, that pierced the Dragon. 10 It was you that dried up the Sea, the waters of the great deep; that made the abysses of the Sea a road the redeemed might walk.

In these poetic verses, the prophet living during the turmoil of the Babylonian Exile in the sixth pre-Christian century asks God to be the God of old – he wants the present to be like the imagined past. In so doing, it is noteworthy that he recalls what we would consider mythological time, when, according to some creation traditions in ancient Israel, God became king after killing various mythological deities (Rahab, Dragon, and Sea).[9] He also recalls historical time, the redemption from Egypt (v. 10). Israel did not make a fundamental distinction between historical and mythological time – what is narrated in both verses is history because both verses describe a past.

Such consciousness of the past as different from the present is not limited to poetic texts, such as Isaiah 51, or the many psalms that ask God to act as of old. It is found, for example, in Judges 6:13, where Gideon, a judge, a type of military leader, says to an angelic messenger: "Where are all His wondrous deeds about which our fathers told us, saying, 'Truly the Lord brought us up from Egypt'? Now the Lord has abandoned us and delivered us into the hands of Midian!" Thus stories were told in ancient Israel about a past, and various biblical authors were conscious that the past differed in fundamental ways from the present. The Torah suggests that the story of liberation from Egypt was a key story; this is especially reinforced in the fivefold repetition of the phrase "Remember/Bear in mind that you were a slave in (the land of) Egypt" in Deuteronomy (5:15; 15:15; 16:12; 24:18, 22). This motif emphasizes the geographical (Israel vs. Egypt) and social status (free vs. slave) differences between past and present, and reinforces what is often called "historical consciousness," namely, that the past is different from the present.

Given the extent that historical consciousness pervades the Bible, it is not surprising that the Bible contains so many historical texts (or, again, narratives depicting a past). Much of the Torah is history in this sense. It is narrated in the past or perfect.[10] Even though approximately half of the Torah contains laws, these are embedded in narratives about a past – laws told to Israel, for example, at Sinai in Exodus, at the Tent of Meeting in the Priestly literature, or in the fortieth year of wandering in the wilderness in Deuteronomy. Although some ancient Near Eastern law collections are independent, containing only laws, others appear within narrative frameworks, such as Hammurabi's legal collection, which has both a prologue and an epilogue.[11] In Israel, all the legal corpora contained in the Torah are now in a larger narrative set in a past. Law is set or contextualized in history.

This is especially clear in Deuteronomy, which opens

> 1 These are the words that Moses addressed to all Israel on the other side of the Jordan. – Through the wilderness, in the Arabah near Suph, between Paran and Tophel, Laban, Hazeroth, and Di-zahab, 2 it is eleven days from Horeb to Kadesh-barnea by the Mount Seir route. – 3 It was in the fortieth year, on the first day of the eleventh month, that Moses addressed the Israelites in accordance with the instructions that the Lord had given him for them, 4 after he had defeated Sihon king of the Amorites, who dwelt in Heshbon, and King Og of Bashan, who dwelt at Ashtaroth [and] Edrei. 5 On the other side of the Jordan, in the land of Moab, Moses undertook to expound this Teaching.

Deuteronomy contains eleven chapters of material depicting a past, including some laws, before finally getting to what is often called the "Deuteronomic law collection," beginning in chapter 12. Although the other law collections do not contain as extensive a narrative frame, they are all framed in a past. Thus, even though the Torah is often understood as, and even translated as, "law," this is incorrect. Torah means "instruction," and the stories of the Torah, and the laws embedded in these stories function as instruction.

These narratives about a past continue through the four books of the Former Prophets: Joshua, Judges, Samuel, and Kings. (I am using the Hebrew understanding of book counting in the Bible, where Samuel and Kings are each a single book.) They are even found in the Major Prophets, though not in large number. The small prophet Jonah is set in a past, and several prophets, though they are most interested in the present and the future, recount a past for a variety of reasons. For example, Ezekiel 16 and 23 contain sordid allegories of Israel's past as justification for its current punishment. This aligns well with a common use, perhaps the most common use of history in many cultures: to explain the present.[12] Two of the large prophetic books contain prose material probably taken from (some form of) Kings: Isaiah 36–9 and Jeremiah 52. These chapters were most likely inserted by an editor to show that the main predictions of these prophecies came true. In other words, they were added to show that as predicted by Isaiah, King Sennacherib of Assyria did not capture Jerusalem, and just as predicted by Jeremiah, Jerusalem and the Temple were destroyed. Here too, the reason why history is written conforms to what we know of other cultures, where it often serves to legitimate.

Even the final section of the Hebrew Bible, *Ketuvim* or Writings, is suffused with history. Although "historical psalms" are not a formal genre – in other words, the psalms that mention a past do not have a common structure – more than a dozen psalms do mention a past. These include Psalm 78, the second longest in the Psalter; Psalm 89, about the eternal promise of dynasty to David; and the lengthy section Psalms 105–7. History is absent in Proverbs, but by the definition we are using, Job is set in a past (1:1 "There *was* a man in the land of Uz named Job. That man *was* blameless and upright; he feared God and shunned evil"), as are the following books of Ruth, Lamentations, (sections of) Ecclesiastes, Esther, Daniel, Ezra-Nehemiah, and Chronicles. In sum, using this broad definition of history, much more than half of the Bible should be considered history.

A cursory examination of these texts, however, suggests that they are of many different types – Jonah, for example, shares little resemblance to Samuel. This variety is not surprising – just as history could be told in Mesopotamia differently in palace reliefs, annals, letters, stele, and chronicles, a variety of types of history-telling developed in ancient Israel. In addition, even though the Bible is considered to be a "book," it is not a book in the Western sense, written by a single author in a period of months or years. It is an anthology, written over a period of a millennium, in different countries by different authors with different interests and different influences. It is thus not surprising that it should incorporate so many different ways of depicting a past.

The broadest distinction between various types of historical writings in Israel is between poetry and prose. Most biblical historical texts are in prose, although some texts are in poetry. For example, it seems that there was a tradition in ancient Israel for women to welcome warriors back from battle in poetry, as in 1 Samuel 18:7: "The women sang as they danced, and they chanted: Saul has slain his thousands; David, his tens of thousands!" A similar tradition may be true of the ancient Song of the Sea in Exodus 15, attributed in one place to Moses (v. 1) and later to Miriam (vv. 20–1). Following a Mesopotamian pattern, laments over the destructions of cities were typically in poetry.[13] As suggested by Psalms, much cultic speech was poetic because high-register speech was used for speaking to God in the Temple. Thus, when psalms have reason to recall a past, they do so in poetry. Some scholars even suggest that poetry was the predominant mode of recounting a past in ancient Israel and that sections of the prose narratives in the Torah are based on original poetic epic sources, but there is little evidence to support this theory.[14]

The prose texts that depict a past differ widely. Some, like the book of Jonah, depict a period of approximately one week in four chapters – one chapter per day or two. The book of Kings depicts approximately four centuries in forty-seven chapters – about one chapter per eighty years. It is difficult to believe that these two books served the same purpose or derived from the same circle of storytellers. The adjacent prose books of Samuel and Kings are also quite different: the fifty-five chapters of Samuel focus on two kings, Saul and David, while the forty-seven chapters of Kings focus on over forty kings. There is even a significant disparity concerning the nature of stories within a single book such as Judges. The life of the judge Shamgar is narrated in a single verse (3:31): "After him came Shamgar son of Anath, who slew six hundred Philistines with an oxgoad. He too was a champion of Israel." In contrast, the life of Samson is told in four chapters that form a cycle – they are composed of disparate stories loosely tied together[15] and are full of juicy details about Samson, his women, his temper tantrums, and his relation to God. Here, too, it is clear that the stories eventually incorporated into Judges are from different hands and reflect different interests, styles, and skills.

It is hard to determine the specific reasons why particular stories were told, the particular people or group that told them, and when they were told. Answering these questions is of utmost importance for understanding how particular stories may be used for reconstructing the history of Israel because these factors determine to a large extent the shaping and reshaping of stories. Certain issues concerning the dating and composition history of texts that were hardly contested a decade ago – such as the ability to use the biblical Hebrew language to date the composition of texts, or the compositional history of particular texts such as Kings, or the literary relation between various biblical texts such as Samuel/Kings and Chronicles – have been reopened, so historical terra firma can be elusive for any particular text.

These issues are of fundamental importance as we try to understand why any particular text was written, as may be seen from the following example. The story in Genesis 11:1–9 tells of the construction by humanity, and the destruction by God, of the Tower of Babel. Who wrote this story and why? Is it an early story, written perhaps by a Judean before the Babylonian exile, composed primarily to explain the origin of many languages and the dispersion of humanity, with the author standing in awe of the prestigious Babylon? Or is it a story written in the Babylonian Exile, mocking Babylon by describing a destroyed ziggurat and identifying the Israelite God as responsible for its destruction? Without hints about who wrote the story, why, and when, it is difficult to choose between these two interpretations.

Although most stories remain as ambiguous and problematic as Genesis 11:1–9, there are some texts that contain explicit information about why they are told and others that contain certain features providing strong indications of why they were told. Isaiah 51:9–10, examined earlier, belong to the first category: a past is narrated so that God will reenact it. Psalm 106 is similar – it tells of God's beneficent acts to a rebellious Israel, emphasizing that even though Israel sinned again and again (vv. 44–6),

> [w]hen He saw that they were in distress, when He heard their cry, He was mindful of His covenant and in His great faithfulness relented. He made all their captors kindly disposed toward them.

It then concludes with the request (v. 47) "Deliver us, O Lord our God, and gather us from among the nations, to acclaim Your holy name, to glory in Your praise" – in other words, requesting that God act as of old.[16] Psalm 78:6–8 suggest a different reason why history could be narrated:

> [T]hat a future generation might know – children yet to be born – and in turn tell their children that they might put their confidence in God, and not forget God's great deeds, but observe His commandments, and not be like their fathers, a wayward and defiant generation, a generation whose heart was inconstant, whose spirit was not true to God.

In other words, a past was sometimes recounted for didactic reasons so that people would follow the wishes of a beneficent God. Unfortunately, no prose historical text recounts so explicitly, as do these psalms, why a past is being recalled.

The result is only various hints about why particular texts preserve a past. Such clues suggest, not surprisingly, that history was written for many of the same reasons it is written now: to explain (for political reasons, for religious reasons, etc.), to legitimate, and to entertain, among other reasons.[17] Sometimes an author was influenced by more than one reason for writing history (e.g., he or she was interested in creating an entertaining story that illustrated a religious point). Many of these reasons are not mutually exclusive and are even mutually reinforcing. In the ancient Near East, religion and politics were closely allied. In other cases, a story was told and retold and/or written and rewritten by different people in different settings, reflecting different interests, so that the story was recast, but not completely, and its original and secondary purposes may still be seen.[18] These reasons for why narratives about a past were written in antiquity are little different from those currently in use, with one significant difference – there was no interest in the past for its own sake, what is sometimes called "antiquarian interest."

As noted earlier, a wide variety of texts in the Bible reflect a curiosity in explaining the present, especially as it relates to a past and to the physical and geographical world around Israel. In older biblical scholarship, such texts were called "etiologies," from Greek *aitiologia*, "giving a reason for." Unfortunately, the study of etiologies has fallen out of fashion in more recent biblical scholarship.

Biblical historical texts contain many etiologies. Often, but not always, they contain the Hebrew phrase ʿal-kēn, translated as "therefore" or something similar. Etiological texts can be short or long. For example, Genesis 10:9 contains a brief etiology of a popular saying: "He was a mighty hunter by the grace of the Lord; hence (ʿal-kēn) the saying, 'Like Nimrod a mighty hunter by the grace of the Lord.'" Genesis 11:1–9, the Tower of Babel story, is a longer etiology, concluding "that is why (ʿal-kēn) it was called Babel, because there the Lord confounded (bālal) the speech of the whole earth; and from there the Lord scattered them over the face of the whole earth." A similar long etiology is found at the end of the story of Jacob striving with an angel in 32:23–33: "That is why (ʿal-kēn) the children of Israel to this day do not eat the thigh muscle that is on the socket of the hip, since Jacob's hip socket was wrenched at the thigh muscle." Almost by definition, the phrase ʿal-kēn marks a narrative that has a strong interest in explaining something.

Stories can be etiological even when such a phrase is missing. A classical case of this implied etiology is seen when the wife of Lot, Abraham's nephew, is turned into a pillar of salt when fleeing from Sodom (Gen 19:26). It is *as if* the text is saying "ʿal-kēn there is a person-like salt formation near the Dead Sea – the remains of Lot's wife."

Sometimes the biblical text even preserves double etiologies, which offer two reasons for something. For example, Genesis 21:31 notes "Hence (ʿal-kēn) that place was called Beer-sheba, for there the two of them swore an oath" based on the connection between Sheba and the word nišběʿû, "swore an oath," suggesting that the well is so-called because it is "the well of oath-taking." Yet the previous verses (28–30) mention seven (*šebaʿ*) ewes three times – this word too is connected by context to "Sheba," suggesting that the well is where seven ewes sanctified a covenant. Thus the end of Genesis 21:31 contains two etiologies for the name Beer-Sheba, one explicitly marked with *ʿal-kēn*, the other not. It is likely that many of the biblical texts about a past are etiological, though often this is not marked as clearly as the cases noted here, with the result that this intention is missed. The desire to explain the present through the past is a fundamental human instinct.

Many societies also produce works about a past for political reasons. A past may be invented of whole cloth, or real past events may have been shaped, sometimes even radically, by "spin doctors" to make a particular point. This is easy to discern in modern times, where we have a large number of sources whose authors are known to us, and we can even sometimes see how events that we have witnessed are "spun" in such a fashion that they are hardly recognizable. In antiquity, it is difficult to see how narratives manipulate the past, but we can sometimes see cases where texts express an extremely implausible position that would have political advantages to one party or another. For example, many scholars have shown how the material in the middle of the book of Samuel is written to express a smooth transition from Saul to David and to quiet any suggestion that David had a hand in Saul's death. This is such a strong theme at the end of 1 Samuel and the beginning of 2 Samuel that some scholars have insisted on reading against the grain and have claimed that David was complicit in Saul's death![19] Most scholars are led to the position that this material is highly ideological and politically shaped by noting certain repeated themes. Most significantly, the text goes to great pains to show that David had several legitimate opportunities to kill Saul when Saul was persecuting David, but David instead spared him (1 Sam 24 and 26) and even rebuked one of his warriors who wanted to kill Saul (1 Sam 26:9): "Don't do him violence! No one can lay hands on the Lord's anointed with impunity." We may debate the extent to which such chapters, insisting on a smooth and legitimate transition, are entirely made up or merely reflect a significant touching up of earlier stories, but it is clear that they, and many other biblical stories, are written from a political slant. Many readers fail to notice this dimension because they read the Bible exclusively as a religious text.

Biblical texts about a past are certainly also written for religious reasons. This was illustrated earlier with certain historical psalms, some of which were composed, incorporating traditions about a past, to evoke God's compassion or to convince God to act. History written or rewritten for religious reasons is also found in prose accounts. For example, one of the most discussed accounts in the Bible concerns the Judean king Manasseh, who reigned in the mid-seventh century BCE. At the beginning of his accounts in both Kings and Chronicles, his many sins are listed. 2 Chronicles 33:11–13 then reads

> so the Lord brought against them the officers of the army of the king of Assyria, who took Manasseh captive in manacles, bound him in fetters, and led him off to Babylon. In his distress, he entreated the Lord his God and humbled himself greatly before the God of his fathers. He prayed to Him, and He granted his prayer, heard his plea, and returned him to Jerusalem to his kingdom. Then Manasseh knew that the Lord alone was God.

Biblical scholars continue to debate whether there is *any* truth to these verses – for example, they note that the king of Assyria would have brought Manasseh to Nineveh, the Assyrian capital, not to Babylon. But whether this account has any historical value is not of concern here; what is relevant is that it is currently fashioned to show how even the most horrendous person can be forgiven if he humbles himself before God.

In other words, Manasseh is shaped by the author of Chronicles as a paradigm of the efficacy of repentance, a sharp contrast to the message of such texts such as Jonah 3:9 (another biblical historical text), which states concerning divine forgiveness: "*Who knows* but that God *may* turn and relent? He *may* turn back from His wrath, so that we do not perish." 2 Chronicles 33 has shaped a past based on its author's religious concerns. The book of Job – a theological work set in a past but clearly interested in its author's present – is only slightly different from Chronicles. Both present a past. Chronicles uses sources and is in prose, whereas it is unclear whether Job uses sources and is mostly poetry, but both are narratives depicting a past in order to shape, clarify, and influence the religious beliefs of their readers.

Many biblical historical texts play a central role in legitimizing various institutions or ideas. For example, it is clear that one purpose of the scroll of Esther is to legitimize the festival of Purim; this is stated explicitly in Esther 9:26: "For that reason (*'al-kēn*) these days were named Purim, after *pur* [a lot]." Several verses in the story of the binding of Isaac suggest that one form of the story[20] is interested in presenting Abraham's willingness to sacrifice Isaac as legitimating the hold of his children on the land of Israel (Gen 22:16–18):

> By Myself I swear, the Lord declares: Because you have done this and have not withheld your son, your favored one, I will bestow My

blessing upon you and make your descendants as numerous as the stars of heaven and the sands on the seashore; and your descendants shall seize the gates of their foes. All the nations of the earth shall bless themselves by your descendants, because you have obeyed My command.

In some cases, this legitimization is accomplished through typology or prefiguration.[21] For example, in Genesis 12:10–20, Abram, the first patriarch, is depicted as going down to Egypt (because of a famine in Canaan), deceiving and despoiling the Egyptians who are inflicted with "mighty plagues," and being expelled from Egypt after being enriched. The details of this story, and even particular phrases, match the account of the Israelite enslavement and liberation from Egypt. Abraham is a "type" for Israel, prefiguring what will later happen to his descendents. Genesis 12:10–20 pretells the exodus, placing it already at the beginning of the story of Israel, and thus makes it (even) more entrenched in the national consciousness. In other words, the author is here telling a symbolic story, which is not meant *literally* to depict the past of the *literal* Abram. There are other cases where the Bible incorporates stories depicting *a* past that were likely not meant to be read as depicting *the real* past, but these are often difficult to discern. We cannot be positive about the hints that ancient Israelite authors would have provided to express the idea that "even though I am depicting a past, do not read me as meaning to map the real past, but read me as writing for some other reason."

It is likely that some stories incorporated in the Bible were written primarily to entertain audiences. It is difficult to know exactly when and where such stories were told, though Judges 14 suggests that riddles were told as part of wedding entertainment – maybe stories were told then too. We also know that stories were told in the context of family education, as suggested, for example, by Exodus 13:14a: "And when, in time to come, your son asks you, saying, 'What does this mean?'" In any case, it is likely that the book of Jonah, in which a man named Jonah (Hebrew for "dove") is swallowed by a "big fish" on his way to Nineveh (which means "the city of the fish"), was written in part to entertain. The same is true of many of the episodes in Judges, which seem to have their origin in hero stories, most likely originally told orally – they often mock Israel's enemies.[22] 1 Samuel 24, which depicts Saul as relieving himself while David and his gang are all watching, uses scatological humor at Saul's expense. It is difficult to know the social setting of this entertainment – how seriously should we take the idea of some earlier scholars that stories were told around the campfire? – but it is clear that ancient societies had the same need for entertainment that we have.[23] Unfortunately, humor and entertainment are culturally bound notions, so it is difficult to pinpoint all the cases of humor and entertainment in the Bible – but it is certain that such cases are present.

It is impossible to illustrate all the reasons why authors in ancient Israel wrote down traditions narrated in the past (or perfect) tense, but it is clear that a sense of curiosity explains many of these traditions in their current form. Conspicuously absent from this list is any "antiquarian interest." Although there are cases where authentic old sources are cited in biblical texts,[24] they are not quoted simply because they are known – they are quoted to fit in with various purposes of the types noted earlier. In general, biblical history was like most premodern history; it was interested in the present, not in the past, although it could cite or create texts about a past in the service of the present.

This understanding of why narratives about a past were written and eventually incorporated into the Bible has important implications for how these texts, comprising much of the Bible, should be used by the modern scholar who wishes to reconstruct the history of ancient Israel. Given that the Bible is a compilation, each biblical text narrating a past needs to be evaluated on its own. Our initial assumptions should not be either that the text is true unless it can be falsified or that the text is false unless it can be verified. The beginning position should be that the text narrates a past that may or may not map in an accurate way what really happened and that like any historian, we need to use various criteria to judge whether or not the particular text is representing the real past in some way. We need to determine the distance between the putative event and the text – and for most biblical historical texts, this distance is great, suggesting (if we use the norms of most modern historians) that we must use these texts with great caution, if at all. Like normal historians, we need to ask whether this narrative about a past is likely intending to tell the real past – or is it, like *Alice in Wonderland*, a didactic and/or entertaining work of fiction set in a past? This question, as noted earlier, is difficult to answer because it is hard to determine exactly what textual clues ancient Israelite authors used to say "I am trying to tell the real past" versus "I am creating a (symbolic) story set in the past." Finally, stories constantly change, especially as they move from one social setting to another. It is impossible to go far behind the written stories that we now have, even though we strongly suspect that many of them have oral antecedents[25] – but we cannot recreate these antecedents. We also do not have a good idea of the different authors and settings that contributed to the story in its final form and thus cannot judge how each changed the story, obscuring its possible original relation to real events.

Considering all these factors, it is not prudent to base the history of Israel predominantly on the biblical text, as so many modern historians have done – the biblical texts are centuries later than the events they purport to narrate, we are not even sure which texts are purporting to narrate the past and which are symbolic, and we do not know much about any of those figures who transmitted these stories in both their oral and written forms.

This means that if we want to reconstruct the history of Israel as part of the history of the ancient Near East, nonbiblical sources (often written close to the events they depict and in known social settings, often the royal court) are far superior sources to the Bible. If we want to understand sections of biblical books, for example, in their historical context, we may not simply take the account of Kings, remove references to God, and assume that we are left with an accurate historical background. Two simple cases show the dangers of such a procedure. First, the Omri of the Bible – about whom relatively little is narrated in 1 Kings 16 other than (v. 25) "Omri did what was displeasing to the Lord; he was worse than all who preceded him" – is quite different from the powerful Omri described in the Moabite Mesha inscription and alluded to in Assyrian inscriptions. Second, the biblical Ahab and the Ahab known from inscriptions are also very different.[26] It is the Omri or Ahab that we may reconstruct from the inscriptions rather than from the Bible that provides useful background either for constructing ninth-century history of Israel or serving as background for ninth-century biblical writings, if there are any.

This does not mean that these narratives depicting a past have no value to the modern historian of ancient Israel. In many cases, we can use them to understand the ideology of their authors rather than the period that they purport to tell. For example, it is generally acknowledged that the Judean King Manasseh was the focus of attention by many later authors, who reshaped his reign several times. If we can isolate these authors, date them, and place them, then we can use the different depictions of Manasseh as a case example illustrating the hopes and fears of various authors, most likely living before, during, and after the Babylonian exile. Thus, from these Manasseh texts, we can learn more about the authors than we can about Manasseh. These attitudes of the biblical authors are also part of history. Yet here as well we must be cautious about overgeneralizing, as the following example from Ezra-Nehemiah illustrates.

The late book of Ezra-Nehemiah is depicted, correctly I believe, as displaying an extreme position against intermarriage. Many scholars go further, however, and view the book as giving voice to widespread intolerance to intermarriage in the postexilic period. But how do we know how representative Ezra-Nehemiah is? Does it depict a common attitude or the attitude of some small subgroup that for some reason managed to get its voice into the canon? What of the attitude expressed in the book of Ruth, which many scholars see as dating from this period – perhaps written as a polemic against Ezra-Nehemiah, insisting instead that loving-kindness (Hebrew *ḥesed*) is more important than genealogy and that intermarriage in certain situations is not problematic? In this case, rather than taking Ezra-Nehemiah as the norm, we should say that in the postexilic period there was a debate concerning the importance of lineage and Jewishness, with Ruth representing one position and Ezra-Nehemiah the other. It is impossible, as far as I know, to date or place either of these works precisely, so we are left, as historians, simply knowing that these ideologies existed, but without a clear sense of who expounded them when, how they may have interacted, whether either one reflects a majority ideology, and so on. Thus even here the conclusions that may be derived from the biblical historical texts, especially relating to their authors' ideologies, may be too anemic for the typical historian.

I have written about the Bible as history and have left archaeology aside. Contrary to popular opinion, archaeology is as much an art as a science. One reputable scholar, for example, may date a set of city gates to the tenth century and thus use them to support the biblical account of the majestic Solomonic kingdom, whereas another reputable scholar may date the same finds a century later and claim that no extensive Solomonic kingdom ever existed.[27] In examining the impact of archaeology on understanding the Bible, we must learn from the history of scholarship. After the city of Megiddo was excavated, some scholars found "Solomonic stables" there, but these are now recognized as neither Solomonic nor stables.[28] These buildings, like any structure or piece of pottery, had to be interpreted – and their early excavators *mis*interpreted their date and their function. I worry that current archaeologists, despite having significantly better tools, are making some of the same interpretive errors as they reconstruct ancient history from artifacts.

Furthermore, there is one period for which we do have many unambiguous archaeological findings bearing on the Bible: the period of the so-called conquest. These findings illustrate the highly problematic nature of the predominant story found in Joshua, in which hundreds of thousands of Israelites conquer nearly the entire land of Canaan. Many cities that were supposedly destroyed by the Israelites, according to Joshua, were not destroyed at that time, according to the current archaeological record – and some were not even inhabited.[29] In sum, archaeology is not (yet?) fully a science, and artifacts must be interpreted and do not offer history in a straightforward manner. And when they do yield clear signs about what happened in the past, they suggest in some cases that the narratives about a past in the Bible have elements that may be historically accurate and, in some cases, elements that are historically inaccurate. Thus archaeology has little constructive bearing on the Bible as history, though it is useful for understanding certain aspects of ancient Israelite history. Instead, we are left with a large number of biblical texts depicting a past, texts that must be subjected to many different types of analyses so that we can understand why particular authors, living in particular periods and settings, decided to shape those texts in the particular form(s)[30] that they have come down to us.

For those who have studied the nature of premodern historical writing, there should be little that is surprising here. The interest in facts for their own sake is a relatively modern interest, and Israel's use of narratives that depict a past is similar to that of its neighbors. The first words of the Hebrew Bible are *bĕrē'šît bārā' 'ĕlōhîm* – "When God began to create" – they are not "read me as the actual history of what happened." Based on analogies and our understanding of various concepts connected to the rise of history writing, we need to make a decision about how best to read these accounts of a past – and there is nothing in the biblical text to suggest that they should be read as "*the* history of *the* past." The nature of biblical texts is captured most elegantly by the Jewish historian Yosef Hayim Yerushalmi, who in his survey of Jewish history writing notes: "Israel is told that it must be a kingdom of priests and a holy nation; nowhere is it suggested that it become a nation of historians."[31]

NOTES

1   Herodotus, *The Histories*, trans. by Aubrey de Sélincourt; rev. by A. R. Burn (Harmondsworth, UK: Penguin, 1979), 41.
2   Thucydides, *History of the Peloponnesian War*, trans. by Rex Warner (London: Penguin, 1972), 35.
3   See, e.g., John Burrow, *A History of Histories: Epics, Chronicles, Romances and Inquiries from Herodotus and Thucydides to the Twentieth Century* (New York: Knopf, 2008); and Donald R. Kelley, *Faces of History: Historical Inquiry from Herodotus to Herder* (New Haven, CT: Yale University Press, 1998).

4   For a survey of Europe, see Donald R. Kelley, *Fortunes of History: Historical Inquiry from Herder to Huizinga* (New Haven, CT: Yale University Press, 2003); for the American scene, see Peter Novick, *That Noble Dream: The "Objectivity Question" and the American Historical Profession* (New York: Cambridge University Press, 1998).

5   For this understanding, see John Lewis Gaddis, *The Landscape of History: How Historians Map the Past* (New York: Oxford University Press, 2002).

6   On the variety of genres in Mesopotamian historical writing, see Jean-Jacques Glassner, *Mesopotamian Chronicles* (Atlanta: Society of Biblical Literature, 2004), 3–99.

7   See, e.g., David Ussishkin, *The Conquest of Lachish by Sennacherib* (Tel Aviv: Tel Aviv University Press, 1982).

8   All translations follow the New Jewish Publication Society version of the Bible (NJPS).

9   For a discussion of these myths, see Bernard F. Batto, *Slaying the Dragon: Mythmaking in the Biblical Tradition* (Louisville, KY: Westminster/John Know, 1992).

10 The exact nature of the Hebrew verbal system continues to be debated.

11 See the collection by Martha T. Roth, *Law Collections from Mesopotamia and Asia Minor* (Atlanta: Scholars Press, 1995).

12 See, e.g., Paul Connerton, *How Societies Remember* (Cambridge University Press, 1989), 3: "Thus we may say that our experiences of the present largely depend upon our knowledge of the past, and that our images of the past commonly serve to legitimate a present social order."

13 Adele Berlin, *Lamentations: A Commentary* (OTL; Louisville, KY: Westminster John Knox, 2002), 26–30.

14 Shemaryahu Talmon, "Did There Exist a Biblical National Epic?" in his *Literary Studies in the Hebrew Bible: Form and Content* (Jerusalem: Magnes, 1993), 91–111.

15 Marc Zvi Brettler, *The Book of Judges* (London: Routledge, 2002).

16 It is widely recognized that v. 48 is editorial and not part of the psalm itself.

17 Gordon S. Wood, *The Purpose of the Past: Reflections on the Uses of History* (New York: Penguin, 2008).

18 This is especially evident in the book of Judges, where stories were edited together to create a message that has no relation to why the individual stories were written; see Brettler, *Judges*.

19 Baruch Halpern, *David's Secret Demons: Messiah, Murderer, Traitor, King* (Grand Rapids, MI: Eerdmans, 2001).

20 Many scholars view verses 15–18 as secondary.

21 On typology and prefiguration, see Marc Zvi Brettler, *The Creation of History in Ancient Israel* (London: Routledge, 1995), 48–61.

22 For one such example, see ibid., 79–90.

23 Yehuda T. Radday and Athalya Brenner, *On Humour and the Comic in the Hebrew Bible* (JSOTSup 92; Sheffield, UK: Almond Press, 1990).

24 Marc Zvi Brettler, "Method in the Application of Biblical Source Material to Historical Writing (with Particular Reference to the Ninth Century BCE)," in *Understanding the History of Ancient Israel*, ed. by H. G. M. Williamson (Oxford University Press, 2007), 305–36.

25 Susan Niditch, *Oral World and Written Word: Ancient Israelite Literature* (Louisville, KY: Westminster John Knox, 1996).
26 For an analysis of these inscriptions, see Mordechai Cogan, *The Raging Torrent: Historical Inscriptions from Assyria and Babylonia Relating to Ancient Israel* (Jerusalem: Carta, 2008).
27 Some of this debate is reflected in Israel Finkelstein and Amihai Mazar, *The Quest for the Historical Israel* (Atlanta: Society of Biblical Literature, 2007).
28 For the older view, see plates 741–2 in James B. Pritchard, *Ancient Near East in Pictures Relating to the Old Testament*, 2nd ed. with suppl. (Princeton, NJ: Princeton University Press, 1969), 232; many now consider these structures to be storehouses.
29 William G. Dever, *Who Were the Early Israelites and Where Did They Come From?* (Grand Rapids, MI: Eerdmans, 2003), 37–74.
30 The plural "forms" is appropriate because in some cases biblical books are extant in more than one edition.
31 Yosef Hayim Yerushalmi, *Zakhor: Jewish History and Jewish Memory* (Seattle: University of Washington Press, 1982), 10.

FURTHER READING

Brettler, Marc Zvi. *The Creation of History in Ancient Israel*. London: Routledge, 1995.
Davies, Philip R. *Memories of Ancient Israel: An Introduction to Biblical History Ancient and Modern*. Louisville, KY: Westminster John Knox, 2008.
Dever, William G. *What Did the Biblical Writers Know and When Did They Know it? What Archaeology Can Tell Us About the Reality of Ancient Israel*. Grand Rapids, MI: Eerdmans, 2001.
Grabbe, Lester L. *Ancient Israel: What Do We Know and How Do We Know It?* London: T & T. Clark, 2007.
    ed. *Can a "History of Israel" Be Written?* (JSOTSup 245). Sheffield Academic Press, 1997.
Liverani, Mario. *Israel's History and the History of Israel*. London: Equinox, 2005.
Miller, J. Maxwell, and John H. Hayes. *A History of Ancient Israel and Judah*, 2nd ed. Louisville, KY: Westminster John Knox, 2006.

Part III

Methods and approaches

6 Historical-critical methods

JOHN J. COLLINS

"Historical criticism" is the name usually given to what may be termed "mainline" biblical criticism over the last three centuries or so, although it is increasingly in dispute in recent years. James Barr has rightly insisted that it is misleading to speak of "the historical-critical method": "there are *methods* used by historical-criticism, but there is no such thing as *the* historical critical method."[1] Whether the adjective "historical" is always appropriate also may be questioned.[2] For purposes of this chapter, historical-critical methods are those which take account of the fact that the biblical texts were written long ago, in a cultural matrix very different from our own, and that attempt to understand the texts first of all in the context of that ancient setting. Historical considerations are a necessary part of that discussion because it requires at least an approximate idea of the time, place, and circumstances of composition. The goal of this inquiry, however, is not necessarily historical in a narrow sense. It might just as well be the theology or rhetoric of the text, seen in light of its historical context.

To say that texts are written in specific times and places and that historical context is germane to interpretation may seem to be stating the obvious. One need only look, however, at an ancient interpreter such as Philo of Alexandria to see that the point has not always been appreciated. The historian Peter Burke has argued that "medieval men lacked a sense of the past being different in quality from the present."[3] In the case of the Bible, there was no point in differentiating the time when the different books were written because they were all supposed to come from God. The rise of biblical criticism is sometimes traced back to the recovery of classical antiquity and ancient manuscripts in the Renaissance. German Protestants have tended to see its origin rather in the Reformation, which set the authority of the *sola scriptura* over against that of the Church.[4] There can be little doubt that the Reformation contributed to the importance attached to the biblical text in its original context, but it certainly did not lead immediately to a wholesale adoption of historical exegesis. Another impetus came from the Enlightenment and the writings of Spinoza and the English Deists.⁵ It is with the Enlightenment that the human origin of the Bible was first emphasized, and the miraculous events and revelations that it narrates were subjected to critique. The Enlightenment emphasis on epistemology, the critical reflection on the warrants for knowledge, was especially important in this regard. Historical criticism developed hand in hand with German historiography in the nineteenth century and adopted the same methods of source analysis. Yet another impulse, in the same century, came from the Romantic movement, which emphasized the expressive character of literature and was especially influential in the rise of form criticism. In fact, historical criticism, broadly conceived, has reacted to and been influenced by just about every major intellectual movement since the Reformation.

The nature and focus of historical-critical methodologies also have changed over the centuries. The nineteenth century was arguably the great age of historiography, especially in Germany, characterized especially by von Ranke's famous ideal: to describe the past as it really was. (This was not a matter of collecting dry facts; von Ranke was an idealist who wanted to penetrate to the essence of history.) Julius Wellhausen, a quintessential historical critic, stood in the tradition of German historiography and had no time for biblical theology, which he regarded as a dubious enterprise. His attempt to reconstruct the history of the religion of Israel was based on an analysis of the sources of the Pentateuch (known as JEDP).⁶ While Wellhausen was not concerned with the minutiae of source criticism to the same degree as some of his successors, historical criticism came to be closely identified with source criticism in some quarters and even remains so today.

In the twentieth century, historical criticism developed along two quite distinct lines. On the one hand, a series of methods (form criticism and redaction criticism) was developed, primarily in Germany, for the literary analysis of the text, and with a view to identifying its earliest stages and tracing its diachronic development. On the other hand, historical criticism became closely allied to archeology and the recovery of the ancient Near Eastern background of the text. This latter approach dominated North American scholarship in the early and middle twentieth century, through the influence of W. F. Albright and his students. It also was embraced with enthusiasm in Israeli scholarship.

THE GERMAN TRADITION

The form-critical approach of Hermann Gunkel was in many ways antithetical to Wellhausen's approach because it moved the focus away from
major authors and sources to the smallest units of text and the underlying oral tradition.[7] Gunkel's concerns were primarily literary, dealing
with the genre of texts, but he attached great importance to the typical
setting of a genre and thereby attempted to ground the method in the
historical specificity of an ancient culture. The method, then, was no
less historical critical than that of Wellhausen. In fact, later practitioners
of form criticism often tended to use the analysis of forms as a way to
establish the earliest stage of the text.

Both source criticism and form criticism were concerned primarily
with what Robert Alter has called "excavative" scholarship.[8] They were
used to recover the earliest forms of the text, which often were the sole
objects of scholarly concern. Redaction criticism was developed to coun-
terbalance this tendency and shift the emphasis to the way in which
the various components of the biblical text were put together. (Closely
related to this was tradition history, exemplified in the work of Martin
Noth, which sought to trace the transmission of the various biblical
traditions. This enterprise often focused on oral tradition, especially in
Scandinavian scholarship.[9]) Redaction criticism, too, could be done in a
historical-critical perspective. The redactors or editors could be treated
as authors, who worked in specific times and places. Gerhard von Rad's
reconstruction of the Yahwist is a classic illustration of the method.[10]
While each of these methods (source, form, and redaction criticism) was
distinct in its emphasis, they were generally viewed as complementary
ways of tracing the growth of the biblical corpus.

The common complaint against this entire scholarly tradition
(which is still flourishing, especially in Germany) is that it led to the
eclipse of biblical narrative by breaking up the text into its component parts. Redaction criticism tried to address that problem to some
degree, but it still focused much of its attention on distinguishing diachronic layers in the text. Accordingly, a reaction has arisen (especially
in English-speaking countries) that focuses rather on the final form of
the text. David Gunn and Danna Nolan Fewell list three widespread
criticisms of the source/form/redaction approach to biblical texts:

> First, the paucity of external controls (such as datable literary texts
> or historical records from ancient Israel) left the process prone to
> circular argument.... Second, the analysis of sources, fundamental

to the method, was basically dependent on aesthetic premises which were often arbitrary and rarely acknowledged. Sources were determined by criteria such as vocabulary use and "contradiction" according to what seemed to the critic to be consistent with the style and thought processes of a single author.... Third, historical criticism accorded a privilege to the notion of "original" which is both problematic in itself ... and also devastating to the value of the text most people actually read, namely the final canonical text.[11]

The shift to the "final form" of the text has been advocated both on purely literary and on theological grounds. Even the final form could, in principle, be addressed in a historical-critical way, if an attempt was made to see the final editing of the text in its historical context.

It also should be noted that the leading advocate of a canonical focus, Brevard Childs, retained a place for form and redaction criticism as guides to the way in which the canonical text was shaped. In most cases, however, concern for the final form of the text has been quite ahistorical and has attempted to view the text without regard to its historical context. This tendency in biblical criticism corresponded to a movement in literary criticism called the "new criticism," which tried to read texts as artifacts in their own right, apart from considerations of authorial intention or setting. That movement has now faded in literary criticism and been replaced to a great degree by a new historicism.

There is no doubt that the division of texts into multiple layers has often been (and, especially in German scholarship, continues to be) carried to excess. The increased attention to the final form of the text in recent years is a salutary, and overdue, corrective. Nonetheless, there is equally no doubt that many biblical texts are composite and took shape over extended periods of time, and this fact cannot be ignored in a modern reading. The Pentateuch was not composed like a modern novel and cannot be read like one either. Even Robert Alter, who has done more than anyone to advance the literary reading of the Bible, speaks of "composite artistry." Consequently, the attempt to distinguish layers in a text remains worthwhile and cannot be dispensed with. But critics of the method have made a valid point that the distinction of sources is not an end in itself and that our ability to distinguish layers is often more limited than practitioners of the method have been willing to recognize.

THE ALBRIGHTIAN APPROACH

A quite different kind of historical criticism, associated with the work of William Foxwell Albright and his students, was dominant in North

America for much of the twentieth century. This approach relied less on the minute analysis of texts and more on the correlation of the text with either archaeological data or ancient Near Eastern texts and inscriptions. While Albright's student John Bright produced a classic *History of Israel*,[12] many members of the school were concerned more with the history of religion or in some cases simply with language and philology. The Anchor Bible Commentary series was conceived by Albright, and while it has grown more diverse over the years, it has retained the emphasis on Near Eastern context that characterized the Albrightian school.

Like the German tradition, this mode of scholarship also has been criticized, with some justice, for switching interest away from the text itself to its "background." It also has been criticized for failure to give due attention to questions of literary form and genre and for a tendency to accept the biblical text too readily at face value. Bright's *History of Israel* is a case in point. At the same time, this line of scholarship has been very fruitful. Archeology and the study of the ancient Near East have shed enormous light on the biblical text and are indispensable for understanding the referential aspects of the text. Indeed, it is has been argued that from the perspective of contemporary literary criticism, "everything we can learn about ancient Israel, its history, religion, culture, economy, climate, geography, politics, is potentially relevant for the interpretation of Israel's literature."[13] Consequently,

> the formalist modes of literary theory ... are in need of supplementation ... with the type of knowledge traditionally generated by the recently much maligned Albrightian school of criticism. Literary critics who have embraced formalist theories as a means of avoiding having to deal with the diachronic elements of literary study have only been deceiving themselves.[14]

But equally it must be granted that the Albrightian approach needs to be supplemented by a concern for the text in its final form and by sensitivity to its literary character.

RECENT DEVELOPMENTS

Some of the more recent developments in biblical scholarship are also fundamentally historical critical in the sense that they take account of historical context, even when they are presented as liberating alternatives to the historical criticism of the previous generation. Norman Gottwald observed acutely that biblical scholarship since the Renaissance has been prejudiced to a degree by the social location of its practitioners: "without taking serious account of the sociopolitical tensions in industrialized capitalist Europe, they naively clung to the goal of the disinterested humanities without facing the reality that large segments of the European population were effectively omitted from their vision."[15] His early work, *The Tribes of Yahweh*, is informed by sociological theory and has clear ideological commitments. (The dedication page cites an anonymous tribute to the people of Vietnam.) Yet it is essentially a work of historical reconstruction that stands or falls on its marshaling of the historical evidence. The same might be said of much feminist scholarship. It is now a truism that biblical scholarship was practically a monopoly of (white) males before the last quarter of the twentieth century and that it paid very little attention to issues concerning women. That situation has changed considerably in recent decades, though not universally. Some feminist critics, such as Phyllis Trible, have relied on literary and rhetorical criticism, with little attention to historical context.[16] Others, however, have tried to appreciate both the lives of ancient women and the biblical text in the context of ancient Near Eastern society. So, for example, Tikvah Frymer-Kensky used the mythology of the ancient Near East as the backdrop and foil for her discussion of women in the Bible.[17] Carol Meyers, an archaeologist, focused rather on the society behind the text, in classic historical-critical fashion.[18] The fact that these scholars bring to the text questions that had been neglected by earlier scholars does not make their work any less historical critical.

The same might be said of the more recent phenomenon of postcolonial criticism. R. S. Sugirtharajah has complained that "though historical criticism was liberative particularly to the Western, white and middle class, it had a shackling and enslaving impact on women, blacks and people of other cultures."[19] Historical criticism (and also literary and other forms of criticism) has never been exempt from the prejudices of its practitioners. But to read, say, the book of Ezra with an eye to the dynamics of colonialism is still to read it historically. Equally, to read the story of the conquest with an eye to the way it has been used to legitimate colonial expansion is also a historical reading, arguably a better and more nuanced historical reading than that of some classic historical-critical treatments.[20]

Even within literary criticism, the so-called new historicism or cultural poetics now affirms "the historicity of texts and the textuality of history," in the phrase of Louis Montrose.[21] In contrast to the strictly ahistorical approach of the new criticism, more recent literary critics acknowledge "the cultural specificity, the social embedment, of all modes of writing – not only the texts that critics study but also the texts in which we study them."[22] Historical criticism, in some form, is alive and well not only in biblical studies but also in the humanities in general.

It may be objected, however, that many of these newer approaches to historical study violate one of the sacred canons of the older historical criticism: they disavow the pursuit of objectivity and not only acknowledge but also celebrate the engaged and interested character of scholarship. New historicists, who affirm not only the historicity of texts but also the textuality of history, mean that "we have no access to a full and authentic past, a lived material existence unmediated by the surviving textual traces of the society in question."[23] All texts, both primary and secondary, are "ideologically marked." We cannot ignore the processes by which the past is constructed or invented. Moreover, knowledge of the past is no longer conceived as an end in itself. According to Elisabeth Schüssler Fiorenza, the main task of a critical feminist hermeneutics is "to articulate the theological authority of women."[24] Readings that advance the cause of liberation must be given the benefit of the doubt and so forth. In short, much of the more recent scholarship that might be described as broadly postmodern still may take historicity very seriously, but it also raises fundamental questions about the nature of historical criticism.

THE PRINCIPLES OF HISTORICAL CRITICISM

The classic formulation of the principles of historical criticism is that of Ernst Troeltsch in 1898. These principles are summarized as follows by Van Harvey:

1. the principle of criticism, by which [Troeltsch] meant that our judgments about the past cannot simply be classified as true or false but must be seen as claiming only a greater or a lesser degree of probability, and as always open to revision;
2. the principle of analogy, by which he meant that we are able to make such judgments of probability only if we presuppose that our present experience is not radically dissimilar to the experience of past persons; and
3. the principle of correlation, by which he meant that the phenomena of man's historical life are so related and interdependent that no radical change can take place at any one point in the historical nexus without effecting a change in all that immediately surrounds it. Historical explanation, therefore, necessarily takes the form

of understanding an event in terms of its antecedents and consequences, and no event can be isolated from its historically conditioned time and place.[25]

To these, Harvey would add the principle of autonomy, which is associated especially with Immanuel Kant and the Enlightenment.[26]

On the one hand, the historian, or the biblical critic, must be free from constraint by authority, either clerical or secular. One cannot work with integrity if the conclusions one has to reach are prescribed in advance. On the other hand, this principle warns against undue influence from received opinion. In the words of historian R. G. Collingwood, "so far from relying on an authority other than himself, to whose statements his thought must conform, the historian is his own authority."[27] As Harvey observed, the principle of autonomy represented a radical change in the morality of knowledge. Where medieval culture had celebrated belief as a virtue and regarded doubt as sin, the modern critical mentality regards doubt as a necessary step in the testing of knowledge and sees belief as an obstacle to rational thought.

Perhaps the most basic of these principles is Troeltsch's principle of criticism. The results of scholarship are never final. This, in fact, is simply the human condition, but it is perhaps especially true in historical scholarship, where today's assured results may be overturned by tomorrow's excavation. Therefore, in theory at least, historical criticism is incompatible with dogmatic certainty. Critics of historical criticism sometimes accuse it of being a quest for "some kind of absolute truth."[28] At least insofar as Troeltsch's principles are representative of historical criticism, quite the opposite is the case.

Neither Troeltsch nor Harvey mentions objectivity as a principle of historical criticism. There is surely a general assumption in historical criticism that the meaning of a text can be established in an objective manner, but this assumption is more complicated than it may seem. The meaning intended by an ancient author can only be reconstructed tentatively, and texts clearly can take new meanings in new circumstances. Contrary to what is often alleged, historical criticism does not necessarily reduce a text to a single meaning. But historical critics usually assume a hierarchy of meanings and regard the original historical context as basic or primary.

The principles set out earlier are not necessarily representative of all who would describe themselves as historical critics. Few, if any, scholars are autonomous in the sense that Harvey requires, and the field has never been free of dogmatism. But the shortcomings of practitioners do not invalidate the principles. We may take it that the principles represent an ideal to which most historical critics would subscribe, even if they do not always attain it in practice.

CRITIQUES OF HISTORICAL CRITICISM

As a mode of biblical criticism, historical criticism has always had its detractors. It is often said that it imprisons the text in the past and does not allow it to speak to the present, but this criticism is superficial. To be sure, there are plenty of examples of historical-critical studies that are antiquarian and have little relevance to nonspecialists, but literary studies can be trivial, too. Historical criticism is not inherently antiquarian. There is no better way to bring a text to life than by reconstructing a historical context in which it might have been composed.

Some of the detractors of historical criticism are simply religious conservatives. Troeltsch himself concluded that the principles of historical criticism were basically incompatible with traditional Christian faith insofar as it is based on a supernaturalist metaphysics.[29] Wellhausen felt obliged to resign from a theological faculty; Robertson Smith and Charles A. Briggs were subjected to heresy trials. The Fundamentalist movement in the United States was in large part a reaction to historical criticism and the relativism it implied. In the Roman Catholic Church, the Modernist movement, which embraced historical criticism, was condemned by the papacy. The mainline churches, including the Catholic Church, eventually made their peace with historical criticism and have even come to view it as a bulwark against the more corrosive relativism of postmodernism.[30] But historical criticism, with its attempt to explain the Bible as a historical human product, remains anathema to fundamentalist Christians and at least some Orthodox Jews.

The issue that most frequently troubles theological conservatives is the principle of analogy. Troeltsch and Harvey are often accused of having a closed universe and of undue dogmatism in excluding the possibility of miracles or divine intervention. So Richard R. Niebuhr argued that historical thinking requires an openness to the uniqueness and novelty of past events and that a historian cannot rule out in advance the possibility of such events.[31] The recent *Biblical History of Israel* by Provan, Long, and Longman goes further. The authors find no reason to believe "that an account that describes the unique or unusual is for that reason to be suspected of unreliability."[32] "Common human experience" is a mirage of eighteenth-century rationalism.

In fact, regardless of how Troeltsch may have understood the principle of analogy, there is no reason why historical criticism should deny the possibility of anything. It is not concerned with establishing possibility, but probability. If someone wants to argue for the historicity of an exceptional or even unique event, which can only be explained by appeal to divine intervention (say, the Exodus or the Resurrection), he or she must assume the burden of proof by establishing as far as possible what happened and providing arguments as to why the supernatural explanation is probable. That burden is not easily assumed. It is not the business of the historical critic to disprove the supernaturalist interpretation, only to explain the events as far as possible in historical terms. The principle of analogy, then, should not be conceived as a doctrine (or denial) of metaphysics. It simply reflects the limits of human understanding. If something were to happen for which there is no analogy in human experience, it would be incomprehensible. Appeals to divine intervention take us outside the proper realm of historical-critical explanation.

Conservative scholars also object to the principle of autonomy. According to Provan, Long, and Longman, "what is commonly referred to as 'knowledge of the past' is more accurately described as 'faith in the testimony,' in the interpretations of the past offered by other people."[33] They acknowledge, briefly, that testimony may be unreliable, but they articulate no criteria for evaluating it. Rather, they insist that "autonomous thinking is entirely compatible with fundamental reliance on the word of others, as a path to knowledge."[34] In practice, they do not question the reliability of the biblical "testimony" at all. But such a "hermeneutic of belief" surrenders the hard-won gains of the Enlightenment with respect to critical thinking and cannot be accepted as critical at all.

There is, however, a serious issue to be raised with respect to the autonomy of the scholar. Jon Levenson acknowledges the importance of academic freedom but insists on the social character of knowledge:

> It is not at all the case, however, that the contemporary academy has found a way to dispense with all social processes for the validation of knowledge.... Instead of setting forth a sharp dichotomy between autonomy and submission to a collective body, therefore, we would be wiser to note the inevitable correlation between the character of a social body and the nature of the knowledge it validates.[35]

The scholar, in short, does not work in a vacuum but depends on the standards, criteria, and conventions of the academic community. The academy is a community of interpretation, with its own presuppositions and traditions, just as are the synagogue and the church.

It is by now a commonplace of hermeneutics that there is no exegesis without presuppositions.[36] There is no such thing as pure reason, detached from all tradition, so the critic can never be completely autonomous. Historical criticism, too, is a tradition. But then, asks Levenson, "why follow Troeltsch's three axioms, augmented by ... [the] principle of autonomy, if they are not intrinsic to human rationality but themselves partake of historical and cultural particularity?"[37] Here Levenson allies himself, somewhat improbably, with the theological agenda of Brevard Childs, which is based on the status of canonicity as a statement of Christian belief.[38] Levenson does not share Childs's Christian postulates, but he welcomes his approach because it subordinates historical criticism to religious faith. Levenson's position here (why one tradition rather than another?) is not especially new. It is broadly in line with "nonfoundationalism," an influential movement in twentieth-century philosophy that holds that there is no objective, universally valid way of grasping reality that is independent of specific historical-cultural traditions. Truth is not the correlation of mind and reality but a matter of coherence within a shared set of beliefs. Nonfoundationalism has often been adapted for apologetic ends in Christian theology with the significant modification that there is no secure foundation except belief in Christ.[39]

The validity and value of historical criticism do not require that its principles be intrinsic to human rationality or that they not arise from a particular cultural tradition. The question is whether it is able to give an adequate account of its subject matter, one that is satisfactory in our present time and circumstances. One test of the adequacy of a tradition is the degree to which it can accommodate new insights and adapt to changing circumstances. It makes a great difference here whether the tradition in which one stands is itself dogmatic or rather abides by Troeltsch's principle of criticism. Scholarship is, in effect, an ongoing conversation. Everyone enters the conversation with some presuppositions, and some positions are accepted as given around the table. What is essential to historical criticism, and indeed to critical thinking of any kind, is that everything in principle is open for discussion. Any position, no matter how venerable, can be challenged by new arguments and evidence. Of course, the challenger usually will have an uphill battle. Entrenched positions are not lightly abandoned, nor should they be. But the history of biblical scholarship over the last half century shows that challenges can indeed succeed. In the end, arguments are not settled by appeals to authority but by the quality of evidence and argument.

The challenge of postmodernism

Levenson's insistence on the social character of knowledge is related to the most fundamental problem confronting historical criticism in the postmodern era, the possibility of objective knowledge. While postmodernism is a name applied to a wide range of thinkers and trends, the following sketch of the phenomenon by Terry Eagleton is reasonable:

> By "postmodern" I mean, roughly speaking, the contemporary movement of thought which rejects totalities, universal values, grand historical narratives, solid foundations to human existence and the possibility of objective knowledge. Postmodernism is skeptical of truth, unity and progress, opposes what it sees as elitism in culture, tends towards cultural relativism, and celebrates pluralism, discontinuity and heterogeneity.[40]

Perhaps the most widely shared characteristic of postmodernists is a rejection of "objectivity," or of the distinction between the subjective and the objective. Objectivity is no more than a pretense that masks the vested interests of the interpreter. If everyone has a power-seeking agenda, then it is better to have these agendas out in the open. Typically, postmodernists also deny that they are claiming absolute truth for their own positions, although in some cases this modesty is belied by their rhetoric. They are also suspicious of consensus, on the grounds that it suppresses minority views.

Another common postmodernist assumption is that there is no univocal, unambiguous meaning. Any text is open to multiple interpretations. Some would deny that a text has any meaning apart from the reader who "constructs" it. But at least the idea of a single meaning is anathema. In the words of A. K. M. Adam, postmodernists "suspect that any univocity is the product of an interpretive violence that suppresses ambiguity by a will to unity."[41]

There is some range of attitudes among postmodern critics as to whether the text can be said to set limits to valid interpretation. The more extreme postmodernists regard all interpretations (both scholarly and popular) as equally valid as long as they are not absolutized.[42] Not all postmodernist critics would go so far, but the issue of validity in interpretation is problematic in postmodernist criticism.

At least some postmodernist critics deny that time is an essential consideration in meaning.[43] Yvonne Sherwood speaks of "hurling all kinds of contemporary idioms/preoccupations – all kinds of ropes of analogy – out to the shores of the ancient text in the hope that they will form some kind of attachment and in the process rearrange and reanimate the over-familiarized text."[44] In contrast, for historical criticism, anachronism is a cardinal sin.

All of this obviously presents a challenge to historical criticism as traditionally conceived. Some formulations of postmodernism are more congenial than others. The kinds of limitless possibilities envisioned by some postmodernist critics leave one to wonder why one should bother with criticism at all. A Bible that can mean anything means nothing. There is need of some basic consensus on the limits of valid interpretation. As Robert Alter has insisted, "The words of the text afford us at least a narrow strip of solid ground in the quagmire of indeterminacy, because the words a writer uses, despite the margin of ambiguity of some of them, have definite meanings, and no critic is free to invent meanings in order to sustain a reading."[45] Historical criticism does not require that texts have a single meaning, and there is no reason why a historical critic should not appreciate ambiguity. Redaction criticism was based on the assumption that texts could be reused and acquire new meanings in new contexts. But historical criticism definitely assumes that there are limits to what a text may mean. Not all postmodernists would disagree. In the words of Mieke Bal,

> The text is not an object upon which we can operate; it is another subject that speaks to us. We can listen, and just as in real life, we will hear our own voice reflected; yet we cannot attribute just anything to the other speaker. If we shout too loud, so that the other is reduced to silence, we will lack arguments to make our case. This is the point of rational argumentation, of the attempt to give evidence in the text while we do not believe interpretations can ever be truly based on it. It is not a matter of empirical proof; it is a matter of plausible interaction.[46]

Respect for the other is one of the basic principles of postmodernism. This principle demands respect also for the otherness of the text and, accordingly, some measure of objectivity in the range of possible meanings. The classic Albrightian model of historical criticism safeguarded the otherness of the text by attention to its ancient Near Eastern context and by requiring competence in ancient Near Eastern literature and civilization. The postmodernist emphasis on multivalence is salutary insofar as it cautions against a naive positivism and the premature assumption that one meaning is "the" meaning. But, as even a relatively ahistorical literary critic such as Alter realizes, historical philology sets limits to the possible meanings of a text.

That said, there is no reason for historical critics to object to anachronistic analogies. The question is how the analogies are used and what the issue is that is under consideration. Anachronism becomes a problem only in questions of historical meaning, and even then anachronistic analogies can still have heuristic value.

Perhaps the most troubling aspect of the critique of objectivity is the observation that declarations of objective fact are often implicated in claims to power. This is the basis for the common charge that historical criticism has had an enslaving effect on women, blacks, and people of minority cultures. The story of the conquest is a case in point. Until very recently, it was invariably read from an Israelite point of view, with no concern for the rights of the conquered people. (The moral issue here is independent of the historical accuracy of the biblical account.) The Canaanites are excluded from moral concern. This reading of the biblical text has had far-reaching implications when it is used to legitimate other conquests, such as the European conquest of North America or the modern Israeli conquest of Palestine. David Clines has noted that biblical interpreters tend to accept the value judgments of the biblical text without question. So, for example, they tend to accept the judgment of the prophets that the destruction of Israel was fit punishment for social inequities and reflected the will of Yahweh, rather than viewing it as a consequence of the balance of power in the ancient Near East.[47] A historical critic could quite accurately argue that the Bible does not forbid slavery and that it does not condone homosexuality. Even the basic statement of Genesis 1, "male and female he created them" has proved to be more complicated than it might have seemed because it marginalizes people of ambiguous sexuality.

None of this, however, seems to me to indict historical criticism as such. Historical critics are quite right to observe that the Bible condones slavery and condemns homosexuality. But the implications of these observations for modern society are a separate issue and depend on one's view of biblical authority. The failure to take account of the Canaanite perspective on the conquest is a failure to be adequately, or comprehensively, historical. The kind of critique offered by Clines can be conceived as pushing historical criticism to its logical conclusions, in a way that historical critics have traditionally failed to do. This is true more generally of the postmodern concern for "voices from the margins" that have often been ignored in the past. Historical criticism as such has no bias against the margins, but its practitioners are often prisoners of their own social location.

Some aspects of postmodernism, then, can be conceived as a kind of radicalization of historical criticism, an approach that appreciates historical contingency to a new degree. Not all aspects of postmodernism can be accommodated in this way. Historical criticism remains a modernist rather than postmodernist enterprise insofar as it is based on the assumption that some interpretations can be established with greater relative probability than others.

CONCLUSION

The critiques that have been directed against historical criticism are of different kinds. Some are reflections of theological conservatism, but not all. It is useful to distinguish between critiques of the practice of historical criticism and those that pertain to its basic principles. The practice of historical criticism has been transformed in recent years by new perspectives that have been brought to bear on it, especially by women and minorities of various kinds, whose voices were largely excluded in the past. Most important here has been the realization of the textuality of history and the degree to which both ancient texts and modern scholarship reflect the interests of their authors. Some fundamental questions also have been raised about the principles that have governed historical criticism hitherto. The principle of analogy should be understood as a pragmatic guide rather than as a metaphysical dogma, but it remains fundamental to critical study. The idea of autonomy must be seriously qualified to recognize the social character of knowledge, but the qualification should not be used as an excuse for the uncritical acceptance of all biblical "testimony." The principle of criticism remains most fundamental of all because it requires that historical criticism remains open to new questions and continues to adapt to a changing cultural environment.

Historical criticism has served biblical studies well. To a great degree it has freed the Bible from the shackles of fundamentalism. It has created an environment in which Jews, Catholics, Protestants, and even atheists can collaborate in the study of the ancient texts. It is not the only valid way to approach the text. Biblical criticism has been enriched in recent years by the development of new methods, especially literary ones, that are often ahistorical but nonetheless enlightening. Yet, as F. W. Dobbs-Allsopp has argued, "literary study of whatever kind, and especially of the Hebrew Bible, cannot escape history."[48] The fact remains that the Bible was written long ago, in a culture remote from our own. If biblical scholarship ignores the historical otherness of the text, it seriously diminishes our ability to understand it.

NOTES

1   James Barr, *History and Ideology in the Old Testament. Biblical Studies at the End of a Millennium* (Oxford University Press, 2000), 32.
2   John Barton, *The Nature of Biblical Criticism* (Louisville, KY: Westminster John Knox, 2007), 31–68.
3   Peter Burke, *The Renaissance Sense of the Past* (New York: St. Martin's Press, 1969), 1. Cf. Jon D. Levenson, *The Hebrew Bible, The Old Testament, and Historical Criticism* (Louisville, KY: Westminster John Knox, 1993), 88.
4   E.g., Hans-Joachim Kraus, *Geschichte der historisch-kritischen Erforschung des Alten Testaments*, 3rd ed. (Neukirchen-Vluyn, Germany: Neukirchener Verlag, 1982).
5   Edgar Krentz, *The Historical-Critical Method* (Philadelphia: Fortress, 1975), 16–22.
6   Julius Wellhausen, *Prolegomena to the History of Israel* (Atlanta: Scholars Press, 1994 [1885]).
7   Gene M. Tucker, *Form Criticism of the Old Testament* (Philadelphia: Fortress, 1971).
8   Robert Alter, *The Art of Biblical Narrative* (New York: Basic Books, 1981).
9   For an overview, see Douglas A. Knight, *Rediscovering the Traditions of Israel* (Missoula, MT: Scholars Press, 1973).
10 Gerhard von Rad, "The Form-Critical Problem of the Hexateuch," in *The Problem of the Hexateuch and Other Essays* (New York: McGraw-Hill, 1966), 1–78.
11 David M. Gunn and Danna Nolan Fewell, *Narrative in the Hebrew Bible* (Oxford University Press, 1993), 7–8.
12 John Bright, *A History of Israel* (Philadelphia: Westminster, 1959).
13 F. Dobbs-Allsopp, "Rethinking Historical Criticism," *Bib Int* 7 (1999): 235–71 (250).
14 Ibid., 251.
15 Norman K. Gottwald, *The Tribes of Yahweh: A Sociology of the Religion of Liberated Israel, 1250–1050 B.C.E.* (Maryknoll, NY: Orbis, 1979).
16 Phyllis Trible, *God and the Rhetoric of Sexuality* (Philadelphia: Fortress, 1978).
17 Tikva Frymer-Kensky, *Reading the Women of the Bible* (New York: Schocken Books, 2002).
18 Carol L. Meyers, *Discovering Eve: Ancient Israelite Women in Context* (New York: Oxford University Press, 1988).
19 R. S. Sugirtharajah, "Critics, Tools, and the Global Arena," in *Reading the Bible in the Global Village: Helsinki*, ed. by H. Räisänen et al. (Atlanta: Society of Biblical Literature, 2000), 49–60 (52).
20 Keith Whitelam, *The Invention of Ancient Israel: The Silencing of Palestinian History* (London: Routledge, 1996).

21 Louis A. Montrose, "Professing the Renaissance: The Poetics and Politics of Culture," in *The New Historicism*, ed. by H. Aram Veeser (London: Routledge, 1989), 15–36 (20).

22 Ibid.

23 Ibid. Compare Hayden White, *Tropics of Discourse* (Baltimore, MD: Johns Hopkins University Press, 1978).

24 Elisabeth Schüssler Fiorenza, "Feminist Hermeneutics," in *Anchor Bible Dictionary*, ed. by David N. Freedman et al. (New York: Doubleday, 1992), 2: 785.

25 Van A. Harvey, *The Historian and the Believer: The Morality of Historical Knowledge and Christian Belief* (New York: Macmillan, 1966), 14–15.

26 Ibid., 39.

27 R. G. Collingwood, *The Idea of History* (Oxford University Press, 1946), 236.

28 See Gunn and Fewell, *Narrative in the Hebrew Bible*, 7.

29 Harvey, *The Historian and the Believer*, 5.

30 E.g., Joseph A. Fitzmyer, S. J., *The Interpretation of Scripture: In Defense of the Historical-Critical Method* (New York: Paulist Press, 2008).

31 Richard R. Niebuhr, *Resurrection and Historical Reason* (New York: Scribners, 1957).

32 Iain Provan, V. Phillips Long, and Tremper Longman, III, *A Biblical History of Israel* (Louisville, KY: Westminster John Knox, 2003), 70–2.

33 Ibid., 36.

34 Ibid., 48.

35 Levenson, *Hebrew Bible*, 121.

36 Hans- Georg Gadamer, *Truth and Method* (New York: Crossroad, 1975).

37 Levenson, *Hebrew Bible*, 120.

38 Brevard S. Childs, *Biblical Theology in Crisis* (Philadelphia: Westminster, 1970), 99.

39 Harvey, *Historian and the Believer*, 205–30, characterizes this approach as "hard perspectivism."

40 Terry Eagleton, *After Theory* (New York: Basic Books, 2003), 13.

41 A. K. M. Adam, "Post-modern Biblical Interpretations," in *Dictionary of Biblical Interpretation*, ed. by John H. Hayes (Nashville, TN: Abingdon, 1999), 2: 305–9.

42 E.g., Daniel Patte, *The Ethics of Biblical Interpretation: A Reevaluation* (Louisville, KY: Westminster John Knox, 1995).

43 A. K. M. Adam, *What is Postmodern Biblical Criticism?* (Minneapolis, MN: Fortress, 1995), 305.

44 Yvonne Sherwood, *A Biblical Text and Its Afterlives: The Survival of Jonah in Western Culture* (Cambridge University Press, 2000), 291.

45 Robert Alter, *The Pleasures of Reading in an Ideological Age* (New York: Simon & Schuster, 1989), 224.

46 Mieke Bal, *Death and Dissymmetry: The Politics of Coherence in the Book of Judges* (University of Chicago Press, 1988), 240.

47 D. J. Clines, "Metacommenting Amos," in *Interested Parties: The Ideology of Writers and Readers of the Hebrew Bible* (Sheffield Academic Press, 1995), 76–93.

48 Dobbs-Allsopp, "Rethinking Historical Criticism," 235.

FURTHER READING

Adam, A. K. M. *What is Postmodern Biblical Criticism?* Minneapolis, MN: Fortress, 1995.

Barr, James. *History and Ideology in the Old Testament: Biblical Studies at the End of a Millennium.* Oxford University Press, 2000.

Barton, John. "Historical-Critical Approaches." In *The Cambridge Companion to Biblical Interpretation.* Edited by John Barton. Cambridge University Press, 1998. 9–20.

   The Nature of Biblical Criticism. Louisville, KY: Westminster John Knox, 2007.

Collins, John J. *The Bible after Babel: Historical Criticism in a Postmodern Age.* Grand Rapids, MI: Eerdmans, 2005.

Dobbs-Allsopp, F. W. "Rethinking Historical Criticism." *Biblical Interpretation* 7 (1999): 235–71.

Harvey, Van A. *The Historian and the Believer.* New York: Macmillan, 1966.

Hens-Piazza, Gina. *The New Historicism.* Minneapolis, MN: Fortress, 2002.

Kraus, Hans-Joachim. *Geschichte der historisch-kritischen Erforschung des Alten Testaments,* 3rd ed. Neukirchen-Vluyn, Germany: Neukirchener Verlag, 1982.

Krentz, Edgar. *The Historical-Critical Method.* Philadelphia: Fortress, 1975.

Levenson, Jon D. *The Hebrew Bible, the Old Testament, and Historical Criticism.* Louisville, KY: Westminster John Knox, 1993.

Morgan, Robert, with John Barton. *Biblical Interpretation.* Oxford University Press, 1988.

7 Social science models

VICTOR H. MATTHEWS

A social science reading of the biblical narrative is an exploration into the world that produced the text. With an emphasis on establishing both the "plain meaning" of the text and how it would have been "heard" by the ancient audience, social science methods delve into the human character of the storytelling process. These methods represent a multidisciplinary approach, taking advantage of the theoretical models created over the last century by psychology, sociology, geography, and anthropology. In employing these models, its primary aim is to explore the social dimensions that are evident in the biblical narrative. This method also can be used to recreate ancient social situations through the analysis of sociolinguistic, rhetorical, economic, political, and social forces. In the process, it takes into account and interprets human reactions to particular social and environmental conditions, as well as physical and psychological stresses.

Because social scientific criticism is not based on a single approach or methodology, its eclectic analysis of biblical materials is often criticized for being too speculative or too jargon laden for others to appreciate. To be sure, to apply social science models effectively, it is necessary to step out of the familiar paths of biblical interpretation, to embrace the writings of sociologists and anthropologists, and to engage in the dual form of interpretation known as "ethnoarchaeology," which combines an examination of material culture with textual references. Thus, for instance, when the topic under consideration is the social transition from village-tribal culture to centralized government and a bureaucratic state, disparate sets of data must be examined and a variety of models employed.

Over the past fifty years, social science models have ranged from a functionalist approach (which examines the various parts of a cultural system and how they interact to maintain a society) to conflict models (which examine how friction between worldviews and ideologies based on cultural self-interest transforms social structure and promotes change). Those who espouse the cultural-materialist approach place an emphasis on economic and technological factors as the catalyst for social change, whereas others point to the forces that lead to the rise of particular political institutions (e.g., chiefdoms and monarchies) as part of a larger set of factors, including environmental and resource management, kinship structures, religious hierarchies, and regional politics. Ultimately, it becomes clear that there is value in each of these approaches, but the reconstruction of the social world of ancient Israel does not rest on any one or any particular combination of models. Like the social sciences themselves, the interpretative process is a dynamic and ever-shifting imaginative arena, and what is essential is allowing one's perspective to be open to new ideas, methods, and possibilities as data are added to the mix.

Social scientific criticism's primary value is found in its recognition and examination of the social character of human existence. Evidence for how a society expresses and defines itself can be seen in its architectural design, its storytelling, its various forms of ritual performance (whether sacred or mundane), its legal statements, and the establishment of personal and group identity. In addition, underlying political, religious, and economic forces can provide further insight into why certain stories are found in the Bible, why these stories emphasize certain items while ignoring or omitting others, and in what way the framework of an emerging Israelite religion among the other ancient Near Eastern religions shaped these ancient people and their understanding of the world. In this chapter, a variety of social science models will be explained, and examples will be provided to demonstrate their effectiveness as interpretative methods in the study of the Bible.

USING SOCIAL SCIENTIFIC METHODS

A social science reading of the biblical narrative is not always an easy task. Cultural meaning is sometimes embedded in a story in a very offhanded manner and may not be immediately discerned. The basic understanding of the social sciences is that social interaction between individuals and groups is defined and regulated by a set of customs, traditions, and expectations. It is these rules of social conduct that can be identified in any culture and then be used to help explain, at least in part, why certain acts are deemed appropriate/beneficial and others are not. Of course, there is always the issue of just how much an *etic* (or "outsider") perspective can penetrate into the "insider" social meanings, institutions, and associations of another culture (the *emic* perspective).

Narrative and social gaps are in fact already a reflection of the emic perspective of the storyteller at work. In modern Western society, few any longer have an intimate knowledge or understanding of life in a small agricultural community of approximately 75 to 150 people, one that depends for its survival on the rains coming in their proper season and the harvest producing enough to sustain them throughout the coming year. Furthermore, since modern society tends to glorify the individual, it is difficult to think in terms of the group (outside of the military, a sports team, or a large extended family). This makes contemporary readers less sensitive to the cultural nuances contained in the biblical narrative, and it often requires setting aside modern preconceptions about what life was like in ancient times. Social science models can facilitate this interpretative process.

Of course, no one social science model can be touted as the most reliable or most useful for reconstruction of the ancient world. While some scholars may favor a particular method or theory, most choose to take a more eclectic approach, applying a variety of social theories to what is revealed by the ancient textual material and the exposed archaeological data. By taking a more objective stance on the relative value of these models, the researcher and reader can engage in continuous self-evaluation and restructuring of the interpretative approach as needed.

To simplify this process, it is best to establish a set of social categories or concepts that help to define the social relationships and actions that are graphically described in the biblical text. These include social identity and kinship, equations of honor and shame, principles of reciprocity, concepts associated with spatiality, and the basic rules of social interaction in speech, gesture, and action.

Identity and kinship

Among the most important of social science concepts is personal and group identity. It encompasses self-awareness as well as recognition of ethnic groups, kinship ties, social and economic status, gender, age, legal principles, and power relationships by others inside and outside one's own community. Each culture determines and reacts to identity through its manner of address and speech, its attitudes toward persons in various recognized social categories and relationships, and its methods of protecting established measures of identity through legal and customary means. Ancient Israel considered itself a collective society, with the most important social and legal categorizations firmly based on kin-ship. Individual identity was submerged into that of the household and extended kinship group. A person's identity, his or her status and level of worth to the group, therefore was based on an ascribed sense of place that was determined by physical location, blood relations, and acquired associations granted to that individual by others (patron-client relations).

Thus, in the biblical narrative, the storyteller makes it clear that in ancient Israel every person establishes his or her identity by a claim of kinship affiliation (*X*, son of *X*, of the tribe of *X*); by reference to a spe-cific town, village, or territory; by the clothing worn; by spoken dialect; and by patterns of social interaction. Of course, the storyteller and the ancient audience were fully aware of these identity factors, and they only required a sort of "shorthand" social reference. Modern readers are less socially aware of the elements of identity in ancient Israel, and one of the tasks of social scientific models is to provide analysis of these references. To illustrate how this social process operates, note the fol-lowing examples:

Clothing as an identity marker
Within a society that continually assessed and judged the character and virtuous behavior of its members, clothing functioned as an extremely important source of cultural symbolism and categorization. Garments served as social props, providing a way to cover the body to keep it warm or shaded, to distinguish gender differences, and to add either a sense of utility or "fashion" to personal appearance. Clothing signaled rank as well as social condition (e.g., mourning or celebration). It communi-cated personal identity and thereby provided both a verification of social identity and an opportunity for the confusion of identity that sometimes served as a narrative ploy by a storyteller.

In Genesis 38:14, Tamar is identified by Judah and his household as a widow by the garments that she habitually wears. When she removes them, she becomes another person with an entirely different social iden-tity. Combined with her spatial setting, outside the household and sitting beside the road all alone, she is perceived to be a prostitute by Judah and is addressed in an entirely different manner than if he had identified her as his widowed daughter-in-law (Gen 38:15–16). Such social confusion is also at the heart of the legal pronouncement in Deuteronomy 22:5 that forbids any form of cross-dressing. This portion of the Deuteronomic Code states that neither men nor women may wear the clothing of the other gender to prevent gender-identity confusion and presumably to avoid committing an even greater social infraction.

At times, it is convenient to flaunt one's identity with clothing to establish who is of high status or authority (see the kings' robes of office in 1 Kgs 22:10). It is also possible to hide one's identity, and this is the basis for King Ahab's actions in 1 Kings 22:30. Having been warned by the prophet Micaiah that his army will be routed in the coming battle, Ahab disguises himself before he goes to fight. However, his ally, King Jehoshaphat, wears his robes of office as he leads his men against the Syrians. In this way, Ahab's identity is masked, but the enemy focuses on Jehoshaphat, who is clearly identified as a king. The result is a major defeat for the Israelites, and Ahab's disguise, like Saul's when he goes to meet the witch of Endor (1 Sam 28:8–10), proves ineffective in saving him from his fate.

Social affiliation as an identity marker
Only the incurably diseased, bandits, or stateless persons lacked social affiliation in ancient Israel. As such, they were unable to conduct business, arrange marriages, engage in religious rituals, or establish patron-client arrangements. They were truly liminal persons because they could not respond to the question of their identity based on their kinship or household ties. Social interaction was based on this expectation, and when identity was uncertain, it became the first order of business to make it clear who a person "belonged to" in society. A clear example of this situation is found in Genesis 32:17. Realizing that he is traveling with a large enough household to intimidate everyone he meets, Jacob tells his servants how to respond when his brother Esau asks them, "To whom do you belong?" He instructs them to say, "They belong to your servant Jacob." In this case, the men are bound as servants to Jacob's household, and they derive their identity from that affiliation.

In a similar manner, Boaz asks his field boss, "To whom does this young woman belong?" (Ruth 2:5–7). The response provides several levels of identification: she is a "Moabite, who came back with Naomi from the country of Moab." Further information about her personal character is offered as well because the servant takes note of her diligence in working without rest while gleaning in the field. Boaz's question, the answer to which he probably already knew, formalizes for the community and the audience the basic elements of Ruth's social identity. Women in this traditional culture are classed by their place of origin as well as their affiliation with a household or as a member of a specific community. It is possible that the further statement about her hard work is intended to defuse any cultural hostilities by counterbalancing the fact that she is a Moabite and therefore an outsider.

Concern that some associations are potentially harmful or danger-ous also contributes to choices made by characters in the biblical narra-tive. In Judges 19:12, the Levite is given the chance to stop for the night at Jebus. However, the Levite refuses, saying, "We will not turn aside into a city of foreigners, who do not belong to the people of Israel." In this case, it is ethnic identity and a lack of affiliation with a particular group that form the basis for his decision. Of course, the irony at this point in the story is that he apparently makes the correct social deci-sion by stopping at the Benjaminite village of Gibeah. The storyteller then plays on the reversal of social expectation, leaving the Levite to be invited into the home of a resident alien, with the result that his life is threatened and his concubine raped and killed.

Social status as an identity marker

It is clear that social status can and does change as elements of identity vary and that sometimes identity must be defended when it is chal-lenged. A prime example is found in 1 Samuel 25:6–11, when David sends some of his men to request supplies from a large landowner named Nabal. They are instructed to explain that David's forces had protected Nabal's herders, that David is Nabal's "son," and that on a feast day it would be expected for them to receive "whatever you have at hand" as a gift. The weight of social expectation here is based on the principle of reciprocity, in which the receipt of a service or gift in turn requires a matching service or gift to maintain the honor of both par-ties. Nabal is identified by the storyteller as "a man of Maon," a very rich man with 3,000 sheep and 1,000 goats, and also a "surly and mean" fellow, who is a Calebite (1 Sam 25:2–3). All of this stands in contrast to David, who as an outlaw running from Saul's forces has demonstrated his ability to protect Nabal's resources and now finds it necessary to ask for assistance for his men. Rather than play the host, Nabal refuses to recognize any facet of David's identity by saying, "Who is David? Who is the son of Jesse?" (25:10), and accuses him of being a man who has broken away from his master, possibly a reference to David's out-law status after fleeing from Saul. David's immediate reaction is to defend his identity by eliminating this man's household, and he is only restrained from doing so by another narrative twist that sends Nabal's wife, Abigail, to David's camp. She takes up the social role that her husband had chosen to ignore, and her speech before David offers not only the supplies he had requested but full political fealty as a client of the future king (25:18–31). In this way, David's identity is restored and enhanced by Abigail's statement.

The rather fragile nature of political identity in the period of the early monarchy is also displayed in an episode in 2 Samuel 19:18–23. After David's victory over his rebellious son, Absalom, he is met by delegations of people hoping to reaffirm their affiliation with his administration or to repair broken political ties. Among them is Shimei, "a man of the family of the house of Saul," who had cursed David when the king was forced to flee his capital city (2 Sam 16:5–8), calling David a murderer and a scoundrel (labels that denied David's identity as the true king). Shimei now asks for mercy and forgiveness, and he repeatedly refers to David as his lord and king. David is magnanimous in accepting this restoration of his identity in the eyes of a client, and he even rebukes members of his royal party who are calling for Shimei's execution. In this way, David demonstrates that he has been restored to full power and once again can be identified as the king (19:22).

Honor and shame

Social science models often draw on studies of more recent Mediterranean and Middle Eastern cultures and then make comparisons to parallels in the comparable social descriptions found in the biblical text. Of course, the biblical storytellers only provide details concerning social interaction that they feel are necessary for the story, and they seldom take the time to explain everyday acts or behaviors. This requires caution in making comparisons but does not negate their value. For example, studies of villagers in modern traditional societies have shown that they classify behavior by employing labels of honor and shame. Such labels may be applied either with words or gestures, facial expressions, or the tone of voice. Interestingly, labels do not indicate as much about the actions of a household as how the village as a whole reacts to those actions.

The principles of hospitality rituals in modern Bedouin cultures are a case in point. An apparent hospitality protocol is found in Genesis 18 when Abraham entertains three visitors. Modern studies of hospitality, and a close reading of Genesis 18, demonstrate a tie between the social obligation attached to playing the host and the desire to transform the different (or the "other") into, at least temporarily, the familiar and the safe. Plus a built-in incentive is also found in the ability to acquire honor through the proper performance of social obligations for both the host and the guest(s). Although it appears that there is a limitless ability to add to one's store of honor and thereby contribute to elevated status, moderation is also demanded. Seeking honor for its own sake rather than contributing to the well-being of the community demonstrates a lack of self-control and is to be avoided (Prov 25:27–8). Conversely, failure to meet social expectations or to reject what a society deems to be honorable behavior results in being labeled as antisocial, criminal, and shameful to oneself and to the community in general.

Every regulated society draws a line between appropriate and inappropriate behavior. Although legal codes and judicial interpretations function as one fairly straightforward method of defining legal and illegal actions and providing incentives and disincentives, they are seldom the only methods employed. Often a culture chooses to explain the value of right action and the consequences of wrong action in storytelling or in wisdom sayings, and these popular means of social shaping in ancient Israel were based on the concepts of honor and shame. Following are some examples to illustrate how these concepts helped to regulate behavior.

Ascribed or acquired honor

Despite the fact that Jacob worked fourteen years to provide a bride price for his wives, his uncle Laban did not give his daughters Leah and Rachel a dowry at the time they married Jacob. As a result, the sisters were shamed and, according to custom and the laws of reciprocity, were relegated to the status of concubines, who had no dowry. To help overcome this social stigma, Leah expressed the hope that a measure of the honor due a wife from her husband would be the result of her having borne six sons to Jacob (Gen 30:20). In this way, she reconstructed her honor by fulfilling the socially expected role as a mother – in particular, the mother of sons. Even though it was her husband whom she hoped to please, the value of children to the community as a whole also would have enhanced her position and level of honor.

According to the laws of the Decalogue, the Israelites were to engage in proper worship and to refrain from antisocial acts such as theft, murder, and adultery. One of these laws (Exod 20:12) required each person to "honor your father and your mother," and this commandment functioned not only as an acknowledgment of the debt owed to parents but also as a recognition of the right to honor acquired by elders who had guided their households and the community. There was additionally a multigenerational aspect to this law because it helped to ensure that each successive generation cared for the needs of the previous one. The logic associated with the basic principles of reciprocity required that this same honor and respect were due to God, as the father and master of the people (Mal 1:6).

As part of the narrative designed to demonstrate Saul's qualifications to become Israel's first king (actually a tribal chief, given the level of political organization at that point), Saul was portrayed as an obedient son who spent several days hunting for his father's lost donkeys (1 Sam 9:3–10). Frustrated in his search, Saul's own honor was expanded when he was willing to listen to his servant's advice to seek out a "man of God," who was "held in honor," because "whatever he says always comes true." This description matches the qualifications for a true prophet, as described in Deuteronomy 18:15–22. Saul gained honor by association when he met Samuel, ate a meal with the prophet, and then was anointed as Israel's leader (1 Sam 9:22–10:1).

A recitation of honorable behavior is found in Psalm 15:2–5, providing a model that could easily be translated into the values of any well-ordered society. In this case, the proper pattern of social interaction, defined as right behavior, included to "walk blamelessly and do what is right and speak the truth." This meant that one should avoid slander, do no evil thing to friends, or make complaint against neighbors. In contrast, the wicked were to be despised, and honor was only to be given to those who "fear[ed] the Lord." Oaths had to be kept despite the cost, money could not be lent at interest, and no bribe could be accepted because it corrupted the courts and injured the weak. Each of these acts contributed to one's honor in the eyes of the community and helped protect weaker groups (widows, orphans, and strangers) from harm or exploitation (see also Prov 3:35).

Shameful behavior and acquired shame
Honor also could be lost and replaced by a range of conditions from simple embarrassment to shame. In 1 Samuel 15:17–19, Samuel condemned Saul for failing to carrying out the divine command to "utterly destroy ... the Amalekites." Caught with the evidence of his actions, Saul eventually acknowledged his sin and pleaded with Samuel to "honor me now before the elders of my people and before Israel" (1 Sam 15:30) so that he would not be shamed before the supporters he needed to remain the tribal chief. In this case, honor was denied because it had been forfeited. To the editor of these stories, the last thing that the prophet would be concerned with was Saul's public image.

The internal struggles for succession to the throne included an example of how women could be exploited for the political advancement of their male relatives. 2 Samuel 13 contains the story of Amnon's plot to weaken his brother Absalom's claim as David's heir. When Amnon demanded that his half-sister Tamar "lie" with him (2 Sam 13:12–13), her response was filled with social indicators as well as personal despair. She called Amnon "my brother," identifying their kinship relationship.

She pleaded, "do not force me, for such a thing is not done in Israel," indicating that other cultures might engage in such "vile" acts as incest and rape, but not Israel. She pointed out that her resulting shamed condition would make her an outcast in their society and that he would "be as one of the scoundrels in Israel." Then she suggested a solution, asking him to speak to the king and arrange their marriage – honorable rather than shameful behavior.

All her arguments could not deter Amnon because there were no witnesses, and his honor was not publicly damaged. Tamar displayed her stolen honor by tearing her garment, one specifically identifying her as one of the "virgin daughters of the king" (2 Sam 13:18–19). However, the storyteller, by including Tamar's argument, indicates to the audience that shame is attached to these actions and will have an effect in future events. Amnon was murdered two years later by Absalom's agents as a means of restoring Absalom's honor and, of course, removing a political rival (13:28–9).

Spatiality

Every culture constantly defines the places in which its members live, the neighboring areas with which they occasionally come into contact, and the imagined worlds that they will never see. As demonstrated in the models developed by critical geographers, space (the concept that functions as the mental placeholder for where we physically or mentally exist) can be divided into distinct categories. "Firstspace" is used to identify physical locations that can be mapped and that are considered to be physical realities, such as villages, rolling plains, and valleys. "Secondspace" provides a label for imagined space or ideas about space, including the attribution of sacred character to a place or the imagined qualities of utopias such as the Garden of Eden. "Thirdspace" is the portion of "firstspace" that is considered lived space, those places where people eat and sleep, work, conduct business, and spend time gossiping with neighbors.

This spatial framework provides the scholar with a means of describing how space was perceived in ancient Israel and how the biblical storyteller manipulated that ancient cultural understanding of space to provide a setting for a story or to signal certain actions or outcomes to the audience. When applying these concepts, it is possible to classify how space is associated with political events and the pronouncement or enactment of legal proceedings. Attention to space also enables the archaeologist, historian, and biblical scholar to better understand the use of domestic and monumental architectural designs and the basic character of economic activities at the city gate or on the threshing floor.

When the biblical storyteller describes a specific place or topographic feature, it often appears superficial because the intended audience would have already been intimately familiar with that place or feature. They knew what it was like to step out the dimensions of a field (1 Kgs 21:16–18), journey with their animals to new pastures (Gen 37:12–14; Ps 23:2–3), shelter during a storm (Isa 4:6), and smell the dreadful aromas emanating from a battlefield (Job 39:25). All these experiences were part of their collective memory of the spaces they had visited or had been told about. They were geographic "insiders," and it therefore took little description to conjure up a spatial image in their minds. For modern readers, narrative gaps and descriptive omissions instead can lead to baffled expressions and a loss of meaning.

Once it becomes clear that space is one of several factors in building a story, then place and placement become more than just window dressing. Instead, a critically important role is attached to the physical places where the Israelites engaged in tasks such as pottery making (Jeremiah 18), worship and sacrificial rituals (1 Sam 1:3), commercial activity (Prov 31:24), and assembling to hear the words of a king or prophet (2 Sam 19:8; Jer 7:2). Then, when space and time are joined within the story, the actions of the characters take on new purpose. Thus, when Boaz called together the elders of Bethlehem in the gate area to discuss Naomi's legal problem in Ruth 4:1–2, the question must be asked: why in the gate area rather than at his house? What "secondspace" connotations does the gate area have that allowed it to be transformed from an entrance to a good place for a legal forum? Having called to these men to sit with him, what factors gave these members of the community the authority and status to hear his plea and come to a consensus that would return the community to social balance? Clearly, much of what went on in this episode was based on the use of space as well as the social understanding of what could be accomplished in that place on that occasion.

By playing on the familiar landscape that made up their world, storytellers were able to use space by combining first-, second-, and third-spaces to provide basic physical descriptions of surrounding geography and topography while at the same time exploring idealized images or dimensions. For instance, the phrase "from Dan to Beersheba" (2 Sam 3:10) can denote a political boundary of the Promised Land, an expression of the covenant, and the national identity of the Israelites.

Of course, many narratives contain references to physical geography in order to facilitate movement of the characters and to provide mental signposts for the audience. For example, when Saul is directed by his father to search for some stray donkeys, the storyteller informs the audience that Saul and his servant "passed through the hill country of Ephraim and passed through the land of Shalishah" and eventually as far as "the land of Zuph" (1 Sam 9:4–5). In this instance, the ancient audience could imagine the journey and any physical obstacles Saul might have faced, perhaps applauding his diligence. If modern readers also choose to take the time to discover more about this physical space, they, too, can draw on some of what the original audience experienced.

It is important to realize as well that physical locations have elements of "imagined space." For example, Elisha's house in 2 Kings 5:9 consists of physical dimensions and occupies a defined space (= firstspace). Presumably, this dwelling served all the functions of lived space necessary to house and protect the prophet and his servant Gehazi (= thirdspace). However, it also represents a place of hope for the leprous Syrian general Naaman, who sought out the prophet to obtain a cure for his disease (a secondspace concept). Beyond its physical reality as a destination and a dwelling place, this house then becomes the focal point for a confrontation with the general, eventually leading him to give up a portion of his personal identity or status and submit to the instructions of the prophet transmitted to him by Gehazi. In the process, the storyteller takes the reader to the Jordan River and augments its physical characteristics by constructing a mental and miraculous image of healing power: the general is cured by following Elisha's instructions. The result is an expansive and geographically universal statement of faith by the Syrian, proclaiming that "there is no God in all the earth except in Israel" (2 Kgs 5:16).

The most familiar space in the biblical narrative is the city. So many narratives revolve around Jerusalem, Bethel, Shechem, and Samaria that a fairly clear understanding can be developed of their physical locations. These narratives also convey the defensive qualities of cities and their strategic importance to kings, merchants, generals, and priests. But cities are known for their secondspace qualities, too: Jerusalem/Zion becomes the "new Eden" for the exiles who hope to return to the Promised Land (Ezek 47:1–12; Zech 14:8), and Bethel's character is submerged into its association with King Jeroboam and his designation of this city as the "king's sanctuary" (Amos 7:13). Samaria, Israel's capital city, is caricatured as Jerusalem's corrupt "elder sister" (Ezek 16:46), who taught the younger "girl" and is eventually surpassed by Jerusalem's abominations (16:51).

Discourse analysis

Various social science models have been developed to analyze conversation and discourse. When dealing with the embedded dialogues in the biblical narrative, these techniques open up new possibilities for critical exploration of the text and the storytelling process. In particular, it becomes crucial to study how interacting speakers orient themselves to each other and to the context in which they operate. The "turn taking" of the speakers reflects not only their words but also their comparative social status, their respective gender(s), and their physical and social setting – all of which serve as elements of the frame or orientation of the speakers (see the shifting characteristics and manner of address by Judah and Tamar in Genesis 38). When dialogue is added to the mix of sensory and background information contained within the frame (i.e., sights and sounds of a marketplace or public building), the character of the discourse, the shifting tone, and the conversational strategies employed by each speaker all contribute to the overall picture.

Social interaction consists of a constantly shifting kaleidoscope of social and physical frames that vary as scenes and participants change. These frames are mental projections that are shaped by a person's understanding of the world and the things that inhabit or structure it. They also consist of idealized and real impressions, based on previously acquired data that help to define and explain the social situation. They form the context within which all social interaction takes place. Only when the frame is comprised of a set of socially understandable elements is it considered a true frame and not a creation of the fantastic (compare the commonplace frame of Solomon's dedication of the Jerusalem Temple in 1 Kings 8 with the visions of strange beasts in Daniel 7).

When using a narrative form, the storyteller tends to create a believable frame within which the characters play their part, and each element conforms to expected social understandings or expectations. But when the storyteller disrupts or breaks the frame, dramatic possibilities arise. This narrative tool is facilitated by an assumption on the part of the audience that certain personal qualities (e.g., status, rank, and power relationships) associated with the physical and social setting of a story are fully understood and that activity within the described setting follows a logical set of rules of behavior. Furthermore, the assumption also is made that standard speech patterns will conform to what would be expected within that frame. Of course, storytellers and their characters do not always play by the rules. The basic variability in human interaction allows the frame to be shifted and even endangered by a speaker's words, and it is at this point that the storyteller has the opportunity either to drive home a character's role or allow the character to succumb to the power and persuasiveness of another (see David's confrontation with Michal in 2 Sam 6:20–3).

An excellent example of attempted frame busting is found in the confrontation between the prophets Jeremiah and Hananiah (Jeremiah 27–8). Jeremiah is attempting to create public consensus regarding his message that the people of Jerusalem should accept the "yoke of Babylon" and not oppose Nebuchadnezzar's rule or military efforts against their leaders. Jeremiah graphically illustrates his position by wearing an ox yoke on his neck (27:2) and proclaims God's promise that "any nation that will bring its neck under the yoke of the king of Babylon and serve him, I will leave on its own land … to till it and live there" (27:11). Hananiah rejects this strategy first with a prophetic statement diametrically opposed to Jeremiah's words: "Thus says the Lord of hosts, the God of Israel: I have broken the yoke of the king of Babylon. Within two years I will bring back to this place all the vessels of the Lord's house.… I will bring back to this place King Jeconiah … and all of the exiles" (28:2–4). He then steps into the public arena, stripping Jeremiah of his ox yoke and breaking it as a way of showing how God will break the yoke of the king of Babylon (28:10–11). Both the dumbfounded Jeremiah and the witnesses to this event are faced with a case of cognitive dissonance, a situation in which there are two apparently true statements spoken, although only one, in reality, can be true.

Will Jeremiah's carefully developed frame be broken, and will Hananiah's defiant attitude then become the dominant frame for the people of Jerusalem? The answer comes when Jeremiah restores his control over the situation. He appears in public proclaiming that God will impose an unbreakable and even heavier iron yoke so that the nation will be forced to serve King Nebuchadnezzar (Jer 28:14). Then, using the socially understood definition of a true prophet as the basis for his curse and his denial of Hananiah's true vocation (see Deut 18:15–22), Jeremiah predicts his opponent's death within the space of only one year (Jer 28:15–17).

Another useful social scientific model is based on the idea of "positioning theory." Each participant in a dialogue establishes a favorable position but may be forced as the conversation progresses to shift or defend that position. According to this model, first-order positioning involves making an assertion. If that statement is accepted, then the position holds. However, if it is disputed (= second-order positioning), then some resolution of the disagreement is necessary. During the course of this debate, the narrator or one of the characters may turn to the audience and say something about the views being expressed in an attempt to clarify or win the day for one side or the other (= third-order positioning).

Absalom's solicitation of advice from Ahithophel and Hushai in 2 Samuel 17:1–14 provides a useful illustration of positioning theory. Ahithophel takes the position that Absalom's troops should immediately pursue David (while the deposed king is "weary and discouraged"). With a quick victory, Absalom will bring all the people to his side and peace to the nation (2 Sam 17:1–4). Wishing for a second opinion, Absalom calls on Hushai to speak to the court. This "double agent" (see 2 Sam 15:32–4) takes a position hostile to Ahithophel's advice. He counsels delay while the usurper gathers a vast army "from Dan to Beer-sheba, like the sand by the sea" that can overwhelm David even if he takes shelter in a fortified city (17:7–13). And, to remind the audience of the political background to this confrontation, the storyteller includes a narrative aside that "the Lord had ordained to defeat the good counsel of Ahithophel, so that the Lord might bring ruin on Absalom" (17:14).

Completing this brief survey of social science models employed in discourse analysis is "mental space theory." According to this analytical technique, mental spaces and cognitive connections are constructed as a discourse unfolds. Mental spaces can be thought of as temporary containers or locations for relevant information about a particular object or person. Because these pockets of understanding are constructed during the course of dialogue, they are unique and temporary in the sense that they only relate to a particular ongoing discourse. Mental space theory also allows a way to represent information about a place and/or person in contexts where its/their properties may have changed.

Thus, in the sentence "Joseph is governor over the land of Egypt," a certain mental space is created that supplies a portion of Joseph's identity. This mental space is established based on the information provided and the culture's understanding of a particular social role. Joseph would be costumed in the official garments of office, and his manner of speech would be authoritative, so his brothers do not recognize him as their kinsman (Gen 42:6–8). When Joseph finally decides to reveal his identity, it is difficult for his brothers to create a new and separate mental space for this Egyptian governor. Their image of this official has been blinded by a "counterfactual conceptualization" that, in turn, required Joseph to make a special effort and to reveal information that only his family would know (45:1–15). The changing situation required the creation of altered mental space to coincide with a new understanding of reality.

FURTHER READING

Carter, Charles E. and Carol L. Meyers, eds. *Community, Identity, and Ideology: Social Science Approaches to the Hebrew Bible*. Winona Lake, IN: Eisenbrauns, 1996.

Esler, Philip F., ed. *Ancient Israel: The Old Testament in Its Social Context*. Minneapolis, MN: Fortress, 2006.

Gunn, David M. and Paula M. McNutt, eds. *"Imagining" Biblical Worlds: Studies in Spatial, Social and Historical Constructs in Honor of James W. Flanagan* (JSOTSup 359). Sheffield Academic Press, 2002.

Lawrence, Louise J. and Mario I. Aguilar, eds. *Anthropology and Biblical Studies: Avenues of Approach*. Leiden, Netherlands: Deo, 2004.

McNutt, Paula. *Reconstructing the Society of Ancient Israel*. Louisville, KY: Westminster/John Knox, 1999.

Matthews, Victor H. *More than Meets the Ear: Discovering the Hidden Contexts of Old Testament Conversations*. Grand Rapids, MI: Eerdmans, 2008.

Matthews, Victor H. and Don C. Benjamin. *Social World of Ancient Israel, 1250–587 BCE*. Peabody, MA:Hendrickson, 1993.

Miller, Robert D. *Chieftains of the Highland Clans: A History of Israel in the 12th and 11th Centuries B.C.* Grand Rapids, MI: Eerdmans, 2005.

Simkins, Ronald A. and Stephen L. Cook, eds. *The Social World of the Hebrew Bible: Twenty-Five Years of the Social Sciences in the Academy* (Semeia 87). Atlanta: Society of Biblical Literature, 1999.

8   Literary approaches to the Hebrew Bible

ADELE BERLIN

Literary approaches to the Bible are actually quite ancient, but the modern academic approaches and methodologies that are subsumed under this rubric date from the middle of the twentieth century.[1] Early seeds were sown by biblical scholars who did comparative work with ancient Near Eastern texts. Newly discovered Ugaritic poetry bore a remarkable resemblance to biblical psalms in its use of parallelism and the combination of so-called word pairs in parallel lines, as well as in shared divine imagery. From another direction came James Muilenburg's "rhetorical criticism" (an outgrowth of form criticism), in which the focus was on the distinctiveness of each text. This distinctiveness was ascertained by examining its stylistic traits, especially on the patterning of words and themes, rather than concentrating on the features it shared with other texts in its genre.[2] A third precursor was the work of the formalist Vladimir Propp, whose *Morphology of the Folktale* described the underlying plot development and the functions of main character types in folktales. In a quite different move from Muilenburg's, Proppian analysis of biblical narratives put the spotlight on universal narrative structures that the Bible shared with other literatures and provided a new way to understand them.[3]

But the field of biblical scholarship at large really took notice when several literary scholars applied literary criticism to the narratives of the Hebrew Bible: first, Erich Auerbach, who compared the narrative styles in Homer and the Bible, and then, most famously, Robert Alter and Meir Sternberg, who developed more thorough-going modes of analyzing biblical narrative derived from the study of modern fiction.[4] (A similar phenomenon occurred in New Testament studies at about the same time; Northrop Frye and Frank Kermode are among the early notables.) In fact, when many people think of literary approaches to the Bible, they think of narrative poetics of the type first demonstrated by Alter and Sternberg, and then by a host of successors from among both literary and biblical scholars. Biblical scholars until that point had been oriented toward historical and philological disciplines, and literary analyses came as something of a revelation, opening as they did the doors to new kinds of interpretation. It was not long, however, before a range of applications of current literary theory and practice to the biblical text found a secure place in the field of biblical studies.

Because of the popularity of narratology during the last decades of the twentieth century, narrative dominated the literary-critical scene in biblical studies.[5] Poetry, which would seem to be the most obvious candidate for literary study, was a distant second, with studies of it focused largely on its formal structures and devices such as parallelism, meter, and poetic tropes. Major exceptions were Meir Weiss (*The Bible from Within*) and Robert Alter (*The Art of Biblical Poetry*), both of whom used "new critical" literary approaches (Weiss called his approach "total interpretation"). Legal discourse was almost entirely absent from literary consideration. Now, however, nonnarrative sections of the Bible are also receiving literary scrutiny.[6] Reflecting the history of the field, this chapter, too, will privilege narrative over the other genres. Regrettably, it will touch on feminist studies of narrative only briefly. Feminist studies have had a significant impact on the literary study of biblical narrative and deserve a separate essay.[7]

There is not one literary approach but many, and they change to reflect developments in the field of literary criticism. As one new literary theory or school followed another, each, in turn, was fruitfully applied to the Bible: e.g., new criticism, formalism, structuralism, reader-response criticism, feminism, and various types of postmodernism.[8] Observations were made about the fabric of biblical discourse, the patternings of words and structures, and narrative poetics – the way a story is told, its point of view, characterization, plot symmetries, and compositional techniques. Then new questions were raised – about the representation and role of women, the power structures reflected in the texts, and the ideology of texts and readers. The result was a greater awareness of the process of interpretation, of how meaning is made by texts and/or by readers. The notion that a text has a single eternally correct meaning was challenged and replaced by the notion that it possesses potentially a multitude of meanings, that its meaning is "indeterminate."

Because literary analyses of biblical narratives are so numerous and so diffuse, with a wide variety of underlying assumptions and reading strategies, no single piece of writing can do justice to the topic. More to the point, writings such as this chapter tend to reflect the interests and judgments of their authors. While scholarship is global, we all work within a subset of academic communities, defined variously by such things as our training and skills, geographical location, languages we can read, religious affiliation (or absence thereof), and implied audiences, as well as the big three of social location – race, class, and gender. So I will discuss the developments that I consider most central to the topic, and even here, I cannot aim for completeness. Rather than presenting only theories or descriptions of literary approaches, I have selected one pericope to track through a variety of interpretations, for a concrete example is the best way to grasp the nature of the diversity of literary approaches and their results.

First, though, let me suggest a broad definition of what literary approaches are and what they are trying to accomplish. The overarching purpose of a literary inquiry is a better understanding of the text – its construction, its forms of expression, its meaning and significance, and/or its relationship to nontextual events or to other texts.

Literature is a verbal construction of a world, analogous to the visual construction of the world in art. It may represent the real world (in which case it may appear historical even when it is not) or a nonreal world (e.g., heaven, Sheol, or apocalyptic visions). It may represent the real world realistically or not (earlier scholars sometimes mistook realism, or verisimilitude, for historicity). A literary interpretation of the Bible probes the Bible's construction of the world and analyzes the forms of expression through which that world is constructed. It examines modes of discourse, literary conventions and assumptions, and context. It seeks to show how the Bible imagines the world and what message that image conveys. I would say that whenever we ask what the text means or how it creates meaning, whenever we engage in an act of interpretation, we are, in some way, espousing a literary approach.

HISTORICAL CRITICISM VERSUS LITERARY CRITICISM

The opposition between historical and literary criticism is no longer altogether valid – and perhaps never was. Source criticism (once known as "literary criticism"), the epitome of what is most often regarded as historical criticism, along with form criticism and redaction criticism, has always had a literary dimension. After all, Hermann Gunkel, the father of form criticism, was essentially involved in studying narrative and poetic genres. However, early proponents of a literary approach, notably Alter and Sternberg, as well as David M. Gunn and Danna Nolan Fewell, set their work in opposition to historical criticism. They maintained that while historical critics sought to get behind the text to its pretextual and early textual origins (a "diachronic" approach), literary critics concentrated on the final product, the text as it now stands (a "synchronic" approach). Additionally, historical critics assumed the text to be a conglomeration of sources, but literary critics approached it as a coherent unity.[9]

These differences initially alienated biblical scholars who were committed to historical inquiry, but in recent years, both sides have drawn closer to each other, especially with the advent of postmodernism, which has changed not only the literary enterprise but also the historical enterprise. Few source critics today think of the biblical redactors as mechanical cutters and pasters but rather as sentient authors and editors who borrowed and often rewrote earlier traditional material for new purposes. They are therefore more attuned to a nuanced literary analysis of the texts.[10] For their part, postmodern literary critics no longer view the text as an independent entity isolated from its historical context (as new critics such as Alter did). So the study of historical and cultural context is as vital to literary scholars as it is to historical scholars. As modernism gave way to more developed modes of postmodernism, specifically new historicism, the path was smoothed for the reintegration of historical concerns into literary study.[11] It is no longer an oxymoron to approach a biblical passage with both literary and historical interests; in fact, good scholarship demands both.

LITERARY APPROACHES TO BIBLICAL NARRATIVE

We begin in the 1970s and early 1980s with the study of the poetics of biblical narrative, that is, the "grammar" or building blocks of narrative discourse and structure, and its conventional modes of expression. The identification of these features derives from modern literary criticism, in which close reading is combined with narrative theory. Included are characterization, point of view, plot structure, foreshadowing, type scenes, and various uses of repetition. More specific points may be the ways that characters are referred to (often by relational terms such as "son" or by ethnic terms or titles), whether speeches are repeated exactly or with changes in wording, whether the narrator and the characters share the same point of view, whether the plot unfolds in chronological order, and other similar questions. Other characteristics of biblical narrative have been noticed, such as the general absence of detailed description for its own sake and the reliability of the narrator. Narrative poetics aims mainly to ascertain the compositional techniques and building blocks of the narrative.

The interesting question is how these techniques have been used to interpret biblical narratives. There is also the question of the gaps in the narrative (all narratives have gaps) and the ways the reader may fill them in. In other words, how much of the interpretation is dictated by the text and how much by the reader. For my case study, I have chosen Genesis 34, the Dinah episode, because through it we can see how the same narrative techniques may lead to different interpretations, and also because the diverse readings of this story exemplify the development of literary approaches to the Bible, including feminist approaches and especially the modern and postmodern divide.

This story is sometimes called "The Rape of Dinah," but because not everyone agrees that Dinah was raped,[12] I prefer the more neutral title, "The Story of Dinah." But even this title is misleading because, as I read it, the story is really more about Jacob and his sons, Simeon and Levi, than about Dinah (just as the "Binding of Isaac" in Genesis 22 is about Abraham, not his son, and "The Story of Amnon and Tamar" in 2 Samuel 13 is really more about Absalom). But perhaps our story is not about individuals at all. Stephen A. Geller refers to it as "The Sack of Shechem," thereby highlighting the location, not the characters. Already we see disagreement about what the point of the story is, who its hero is, and how to explain the sexual encounter.

Meir Sternberg, a text-oriented interpreter, devoted a chapter to Genesis 34 in his 1985 book, *The Poetics of Biblical Narrative* (445–75). Sternberg's larger thesis is that the Bible is a "foolproof" composition whose message any competent reader (knowledgeable about biblical narrative poetics) can discern. Sternberg, the competent reader par excellence, is a brilliant expositor of narrative poetics, which becomes the basis for his interpretation of the story.[13] He insists that the narrator views the two brothers, Simeon and Levi, as the heroes.

Sternberg points to specific instances where the narrative garners sympathy for Simeon and Levi. He finds that these two brothers look good in contrast to Jacob, the other brothers, and the Hivites. In the first four verses, Dinah is repeatedly referred to as the daughter of Jacob, thereby positioning Jacob as the person responsible for her. Yet, when Jacob hears that his daughter has been defiled, he does nothing; he keeps silent until his sons come home. Simeon and Levi, by contrast, are enraged, and it is they, not the father, who seek to defend the honor of the family.

According to Sternberg, the reader may side with the Hivites on two counts – that Shechem fell in love with Dinah and that the entire community of Hivites was willing to undergo circumcision, as Simeon and Levi stipulated. But, suggests Sternberg, the Hivites lose the reader's sympathy when they cast the agreement as a financial deal, forgetting that the issue for the brothers is a matter of honor. Then, out of the blue, in verse 26 we learn that Dinah had all the while been in Shechem's house. Simeon and Levi, after killing all the male Hivites, bring Dinah out of Shechem's house. Sternberg accuses the Hivites of having taken Dinah as a hostage, perhaps to use her to blackmail her relatives into a marriage arrangement, an action that fully justifies the brothers' deceit in making the agreement with the Hivites. Simeon and Levi are, in Sternberg's view, on a rescue mission, not a wanton massacre.

At the end of the story, Jacob confronts Simeon and Levi for having angered the Canaanite neighbors, who may attack the weaker Israelites. But Simeon and Levi are given the last word: "Should our sister be treated like a whore?" This question indicates to Sternberg (and others) that family honor trumps friendly relations with neighbors. It also points Sternberg toward the meaning of the story as a whole. He says that the concern of Simeon and Levi has been "to redress the wrong done to their sister and the whole family, which includes *the prevention of an exogamous marriage*" (472, italics added). The idea of exogamous marriage will reappear later.

Sternberg was attacked vociferously by Dana Nolan Fewell and David M. Gunn in a 1991 article.[14] They reject his notion of foolproof composition in favor of the possibility of multiple interpretations or conflicting competent readings. Basing their analysis on the same narrative poetics – that is, the same techniques of storytelling – they arrive at a different interpretation. They do not evaluate Jacob's silence negatively, arguing instead that it reflects caution and concern for the well-being of the family. They question whether Dinah was held hostage, interpreting her presence in Shechem's house as an act of her own free will, now that Shechem loved her. Fewell and Gunn see Simeon and Levi not as the idealists that Sternberg sees but as self-centered and vengeful, defending their own honor, not the honor of their sister. For Fewell and Gunn, the offense committed is against Dinah, not against the male members of the family, and they fault Simeon and Levi for failing to understand this.

Unlike Sternberg's text-oriented approach, Fewell and Gunn's reader-oriented approach does not permit them to ask what the author's purpose was in telling this story but only to discuss how readers can read it. They dismiss the idea that the story is about exogamous marriage and read it instead as a story about "rights vs. responsibility." To Fewell and Gunn, Sternberg's reader holds normative values that hinge on an ethics of rights, whereas Fewell and Gunn's reader "responds with an ethics of responsibility, where relationships, care, and consequences shape moral choices" (209). They therefore admire Jacob, whose initial silence and final criticism of the brothers they see as a sign of sensitivity and concern for consequences – as opposed to the brothers, who insist on their rights no matter what the consequences.

I doubt that either Sternberg or Fewell and Gunn would entirely convince today's readers, but they are usefully set side by side to show how different assumptions lead to different results. The main issues that separate Sternberg from Fewell and Gunn are threefold. First, how much of the meaning is made by the text and how much by the reader? For the text-oriented Sternberg, all meaning resides in the text. For Fewell and Gunn, all meaning resides in the reader; theirs is a reader-oriented approach. Second, whose meaning are we searching for? Sternberg is looking for the meaning that the story had for an ancient Israelite, whereas Fewell and Gunn seek the meaning(s) it has for today's reader. Fewell and Gunn read the story in light of their own contemporary values, whereas Sternberg aims to uncover the values of the biblical narrator/author.[15] Third, can interpretation be objective? Sternberg claims that his is an objective reading, whereas Fewell and Gunn claim that no reading can be objective (yet they can and do claim that their reading is a right reading and Sternberg's is not).

These differences between Sternberg, on the one hand, and Fewell and Gunn, on the other, mark the divide between modernism and postmodernism. As David Gunn says elsewhere,

> I used to think that the dividing line in biblical scholarship was that between "historical criticism" and "literary criticism." But that is patently not the case. The divide is between modern and postmodern. Put very baldly, it is the difference between a project that reaches for the unity, stability, and truth of the text, and one that seeks the fractures, instabilities, and multivalences of a text which "itself" is protean. Meir Sternberg's poetics ... are modern.[16]

Needless to say, Fewell and Gunn are postmodern.

However, the great divide that Gunn sees between modernism and postmodernism is not as absolute as it may sound, although it was initially useful to distinguish the newer approach from the older one. As modernism is giving way to postmodernism, postmodernism itself is evolving. On the question of whether meaning resides in the text or in the reader, a compromise position seems to be the current consensus: interpretation is a joint effort between reader and text. The postmodernist Robert Carroll, generally sympathetic to reader-oriented strategies, concluded

> I would however not want to advocate too strongly a reader-response ideology for all reading strategies. Texts deserve greater distance, more respect and engagement than reader-response approaches would allow. Without some oppositional element provided by texts over against the reading self the text will be swamped by the over-whelming subjectivities of readers. There must be space for the text to contribute something to the hermeneutic process.[17]

Concomitantly, while few today would argue that the text has one original, permanently fixed, and recoverable meaning, today's postmodernism no longer limits itself to reading a text solely from the reader's current (i.e., social, political, etc.) perspective, as Fewell and Gunn did. It is now perfectly legitimate, indeed desirable, to investigate meaning in earlier times and places. In other words, the pendulum has swung back to attending to writers as well as to readers, to writers of the biblical text and writers of earlier interpretations, as well as to contemporary readers (see later, on the history of biblical interpretation). Moreover, although it may operate with different questions and rules and arrive at different conclusions, postmodernist scholarship (especially new historicism) often sounds "modernist" in that it is just as "distanced from the text" and just as sure that it has reached the proper understanding. That favorite term of early postmodernists, "indeterminacy of meaning," is rarely invoked these days. Rather, postmodernists insist that writers and readers are ideologically influenced and that the job of postmodernists is to uncover the ideologies of writers and readers. Nevertheless, the ideology of many a postmodern scholar goes unacknowledged no less than it did among modernists. Postmodernists criticize modernists for naively buying into the Bible's ideology, but postmodernists need to guard against buying in too strongly to their own ideologies.

So let me advocate what I will call a "postmodern modernism" that I see developing in certain areas of biblical studies (described later). Knowing that our interpretations are conditioned by our own times, learning, and values – that is to say, our interpretation can never be uncontaminated by our own perspective – we can still recognize the difference between ourselves and the object of our investigation, the ancient text. Our goal should not be to re-create the text in our own image but to gain access to it across the distance of time and culture as best we can. This will, of necessity, require posing questions that are meaningful today, for each generation of interpreters searches for something different. The result likely will be that we will understand the ancient authors and readers in a way that they might not have understood themselves, for they would not have used our categories of knowing, and we need to understand things in our own terms. At the same time, though, we should not collapse the difference between us and them. Their world is not our world, their ideologies are not our ideologies, and I see no reason to judge their values against ours, as some scholars insist on doing.[18]

NEW HISTORICISM AND CULTURAL STUDIES: READING FOR ETHNICITY AND GENDER

Issues of identity and ideology, particularly those relating to gender, social class, or ethnicity, have captured the spotlight in contemporary literary studies, especially in new historicism and/or cultural studies.[19] New historicists see the text as a reflection of the institutions and/or ideology from which it arose, and they want to reveal those cultural, social, political, or religious institutions and ideologies. New historicists read biblical texts for what they can tell us about the Bible's religious and political ideologies and institutions.[20]

This is a move back to a more text-centered approach and a more historical approach than early postmodernists such as Fewell and Gunn advocated. The ideology of the current reader is not the acknowledged focus (although it may lurk behind the interpretation); it has been replaced by the ideology of the text. At the same time, new historicism is a reaction against new criticism (from whence Alter came), for it views the text as a historical artifact. The text is not a detached, independent object but grew out of a particular historical moment and needs to be understood in the context of that historical moment (albeit by posing to it questions that could only be posed today). The important historical moment for the new historicist is the time when the text was created, not the time the text purports to be describing. New historicists would not use the Dinah story to reconstruct the early history of the patriarchs and their Canaanite neighbors; they would not see it, as earlier scholars did, as a record of an early conflict involving the tribes of Simeon and Levi in the region of Shechem. Rather, they ask how and why the Israelite past was being presented at the time the story was written. In other words, how is the story using the past to talk about the ancient present?

But when was the story written? Here a would-be new historicist encounters the perpetual problem of the dating of biblical texts. And suddenly, historical criticism and redaction criticism, those old efforts to date texts and to discover their textual history, formerly disdained by literary scholars from new criticism to early postmodernism, once again become relevant to literary interpretation.

Let us survey a few studies of Genesis 34 that I gather loosely under the rubric of new historicism or cultural studies. Stephen A. Geller, in a 1990 essay, declares our story to be a voice for two related themes that form part of the dominant religion of the Bible, especially in Deuteronomic theology: the prohibition of intermarriage with Canaanites and the demand for their total extermination, strongly worded in Deuteronomy 7:1–5 (see also Exod 34:11–16).[21] Geller reads the story on two levels: the narrative level and the typological level. Typological readings are usually associated with Christian exegesis of the Old Testament as foreshadowing the New Testament, but typology is an interpretive strategy used by the rabbis, too, and is even found within the Bible itself.[22] In typological interpretation, persons or events are viewed as figures that are historically real themselves but also prefigure later persons and events.

On the narrative level, this story is an episode in the family history of Jacob, a story of crime and punishment. On the typological level, the more significant level for Geller, it foreshadows events in the national life of later Israel, specifically the Josianic reforms in 621 BCE, famous for their eradication of idolatrous practices (note the eradication of the altars, pillars, and posts in Deuteronomy 7 and Exodus 34). By this time, the real Canaanites were long gone; "Canaanite" had become an abstraction, a code word for all that was religiously alien to Israel. The Canaanites (Hivites) in our story, says Geller, represent the Judean opponents of Josiah's reform – the heretical priests of the *bamot*, the outlawed places of sacrifice, and their followers. As "Canaanites," they are also associated with licentious sexual practices, another feature of the Bible's portrait of Canaanites, wherein sexual relations with Canaanites leads Israel to apostasy. Geller finds sexual licentiousness in Shechem's behavior. The invitation to intermarriage that follows is the very thing against which Deuteronomy warns.

Geller interprets the story as a polemic from the time of Josiah. Yairah Amit, who also reads typologically, dates the story to the time of Ezra and finds in it a hidden polemic against the Samaritans.[23] Like Geller, Amit does not take "Canaanites" literally. For her, they represent the Samaritans, the group whom the returning Judeans opposed and in contrast to whom they constituted their Judean/Jewish identity. For both Geller and Amit, a typological interpretation trumps a literal interpretation. The significance of the story is in the way the remembered or invented past serves the ideological agenda of an author writing either during the late Judean monarchy (Geller) or in postexilic times (Amit). In both explanations, "Canaanite" stands for "the other," those from whom Israel differentiates itself as it defines its identity.

Taking an altogether different tack, focusing on sex as a social marker of power and authority and using a feminist anthropological approach bolstered by examples from Greek and Roman literature, Helene Zlotnick finds that Genesis 34 is not about a crisis generated by a rape but a clash between two marital strategies or ideologies: arranged marriage and abduction marriage.[24] Jacob and his family had the tradition of arranged marriages, but Shechem's action is a case of abduction marriage. The strategy of abduction marriage is known from the classical world, often in foundational stories, and so Zlotnick concludes that "the episode of Dinah's 'rape' proved as critical as were the rapes of the Sabine women for the foundation of the Roman state, and of Lucretia for the demise of the Roman monarchy and the rise of the Republic."[25] As an Israelite foundation story, "[t]he affair of Dinah put an end to any ideology of coexistence in patriarchal Canaan."[26] Zlotnick does not date the story, but she, like Geller and Amit, sees it as speaking to the issue of Israelite identity.

Abduction marriage supplies the reason that Dinah remained in the house of Shechem, from which her brothers "rescue" her. According to Zlotnick's interpretation, they are not rescuing a rape victim but annulling an abduction marriage. The abduction marriage explanation also leads us to reconsider the meaning of the punch line that closes the story: "Should our sister be treated like a whore?" The issue is not sexual looseness, or even premarital sex per se, but the authority of the family to regulate marriages. The term *zônâ*, generally translated as "whore/ prostitute," refers to a woman who engages in a sexual relationship outside of a formal union, not only to a "woman for hire." The brothers do not consider abduction marriage to be a legal marriage. In their eyes, Shechem acted as though Dinah were independent and accessible, like a prostitute, a woman not under the authority of a father, brother, or husband. Abduction marriage denies Dinah's family any authority over her and is therefore an insult to the honor of the family. This is what angers Simeon and Levi.

But why, then, is not Jacob angry and insulted? Complicating the conflict between marriage strategies, in Zlotnick's view, is the guest-host relationship that obtains between Jacob and the Hivites. Jacob, a newcomer to the area, is the guest of the Hivites, the native residents. He and his hosts are bound by the accepted rules of the guest-host relationship, involving reciprocity and voluntary association. This guest-host relationship becomes strained as a result of the abduction marriage, clearly offensive to the Israelites and perhaps not the norm among the Hivites either. Zlotnick explains Jacob's silence not as callous indifference (as Sternberg does) or as concerned restraint (as Fewell and Gunn do) but as his inability to reconcile marriage by abduction with the Hivites' obligation as hosts. What is Jacob, as a guest, to do when his hosts have imposed a type of marriage arrangement that is anathema to his own family? Zlotnick interprets the offer of marital and economic exchanges later in the story as the Hivites' attempt to repair the damaged guest-host relationship, a relationship that Jacob apparently would have liked to preserve, but his sons rendered null and void.

Geller, Amit, and Zlotnick all demonstrate, in different ways, the current interest in gender, ethnicity, identity, and power. Zlotnick concentrates on gender, while Geller and Amit are more concerned with ethnic distinctions. These three studies differ substantially in their interpretations, but they all find the significance of our story in what it says about the establishment of Israel's identity, an identity shaped in contrast to a Canaanite identity (whether "Canaanite" is taken literally or symbolically). They illustrate how, increasingly in postmodern studies, ethnic identity is becoming the focus of much biblical interpretation. The Bible is seen as the primary locus of the expression of Israel's identity – its past, its values and worldview, and its place among the nations of the world.

Notice that, unlike Fewell and Gunn, the interpreters whom I have called "new historians" are not focused on the values of today's readers but on ancient values, as read with the benefit of today's interests in gender and ethnicity. Some might say that this is a distinction without a difference, that the new historians are reading today's issues or their own ideologies into the text no less than Fewell and Gunn did. That, alas, is often true and, some would say, unavoidable, but I think that the focus on the ancient context of the story is significant. At the least, it shows that we can and should attempt to read the story in an ancient context. There is nothing wrong with posing today's questions to an ancient text – we have always done so, and it is impossible not to. My own view of academic biblical scholarship is that it has a responsibility to inquire into the meaning(s) for an ancient audience (I avoid the term "original audience," for each redaction of a passage gives it a new original audience) and not simply to make the Bible meaningful for today's readers. I want to suggest that a primary distinction in biblical studies will soon no longer be between modernism and postmodernism, as it was when Gunn wrote, but between different postmodernisms: those that contextualize the text and its interpretation historically and those that do not. If we take seriously the idea that a text may have different interpretations (and the interpretations of Genesis 34 presented here surely confirm that assumption), we should be investigating those differences and trying to understand how and why they came about. This brings me to the history of biblical interpretation.

INNER BIBLICAL INTERPRETATION AND THE HISTORY OF INTERPRETATION

Inner biblical interpretation, the earliest stage in the history of biblical interpretation, is generally dealt with separately from literary approaches, but it is essentially a literary operation. It is concerned with how and why earlier traditions are alluded to, reformulated, updated, and interpreted in later writings that now form part of the biblical canon (e.g., the use of the Torah in Psalms or Chronicles' rewriting of Samuel-Kings).[27] Inner biblical interpretation reveals the presence of a dynamic process of reinterpretation. It also attests to a process that renders the notion of "original meaning" meaningless. The meaning of the earliest sources that lie behind the Torah text is buried in an overlay of layers of subsequent meaning. Later authors, editors, or redactors never intended for the earliest meaning to survive. They overwrote it because they wanted to promote their own take on ancient traditions. The final product, the Torah as a whole, took on yet another interpretative life as the raw material for subsequent rewritings and reinterpretations in later works, some of which later became canonical and some of which did not. When the Bible was canonized and its text could no longer be altered, commentary on the text substituted for rewriting the text, resulting in all manner of new meanings.[28]

The study of inner biblical interpretation and the continuation of its exegetical program in postbiblical literature (and beyond) has ignited much interest in recent decades, marking, in terms of the history of biblical studies, a move away from the early stages of the formation of the Bible (its origin and pretextual sources) to the later development of biblical writings, after a body of them had gained some authority in the community and were therefore studied, interpreted, and echoed in new compositions. I attribute this move at least in part to the rise of postmodern thought.[29] If, as postmodernism suggests, there is not one definitive meaning for a text but multiple possible meanings, the question shifts from "What does the passage mean?" to "What does the passage mean in a given time and place?" Meaning is always historically and socially contextualized. Related questions are "Who produced and controlled the meaning?" and "Who benefited from a particular interpretation?"

Like earlier reader-oriented approaches, on the one hand, the history of interpretation replaces interest in the text with interest in its interpreters and their interpretations. The scholarly gaze moves away from the biblical text itself and rests instead on the reader, the ancient interpreter, as the maker of meaning. On the other hand, like new historicism, the history of interpretation is essentially a recovery of the history of ideology.

What does the early history of biblical interpretation have to say about Genesis 34? How was this story understood within the Bible and in ancient times? Genesis 49:5–7 is often, although not universally, taken to be an allusion to the Dinah story, and it was clearly understood this way by certain ancient readers.[30] Without Genesis 34, the reference to the lawless weapons of Simeon and Levi in Genesis 49 would be obscure or unintelligible.

> Simeon and Levi are a pair;
> Their weapons are tools of lawlessness.
> Let not my person be included in their council,
> Let not my being be counted in their assembly.
> For when angry they slay men,
> And when pleased they maim oxen.
> Cursed be their anger so fierce,
> And their wrath so relentless.
> I will divide them in Jacob,
> Scatter them in Israel.

These verses are part of Jacob's deathbed speech to his sons, foretelling their destinies. In actuality, of course, this is poetic hindsight – a retrojection of later tribal allotments and fortunes into the mouth of the father of those tribes. Because Jacob is speaking, it is not surprising that his opposition to the brothers' action here coincides with that in Genesis 34. This does not prove that the author of Genesis 34 "intended" to condemn the brothers, but it indicates how a later writer (re)interpreted and recontextualized the story to explain why neither Simeon nor Levi ultimately had land allotments.[31] This is part of a larger agenda in Genesis that promotes the tribe of Judah over the tribes of the earlier-born sons. It is feasible that Genesis 34, too, is also part of this agenda, in which case the reader would condemn Simeon and Levi there also.[32]

However, many readers during the Greek and Roman periods (also known as the Second Temple period) were loath to condemn the actions of Simeon and Levi, and went out of their way to justify them and vilify the Hivites.[33] Among their explanations are that Simeon and Levi were acting on God's command for vengeance, or were guided by an angel, or had a heavenly sword and that the Hivites deserved to be destroyed because they were rapists, immoral pagans, and lacked proper hospitality to strangers. Simeon and Levi, seen as opponents of Jewish intermarriage, become the heroes, for, since Ezra, endogamous marriage had become an important issue in the definition of Jewish identity. In addition to promoting then-current ideas of Jewish identity, these interpretations eliminate the moral ambiguity of the story and turn it into a smooth, unproblematic tale of Jewish heroism against a foreign enemy. The Hellenistic Jewish writers retell the story, as they do other biblical stories, as part of a larger agenda to justify the Bible and biblical Jewish behavior that might otherwise sound primitive or unjust to a reader steeped in Greek cultural values (modern readers have an analogous problem).[34] This does not necessarily mean that these interpreters were making up their interpretations from whole cloth. They may have been drawing on more ancient traditions of interpretation. By the same token, though, there seems little doubt that they are shaping the meaning of the story to the needs and tastes of their times.[35] Interpretation always takes place in a historical context.

The contemporary acts of interpreting the Bible and studying its past interpretations form a complementary pair of literary approaches to the Bible. Both are nowadays occupied with the recovery of ideology. The first inquires into the ideology of the biblical text; the second examines the ideology of the interpreters. Another way to say this is that the first is concerned with how the Bible constructs its meaning of the world and the second with how interpreters construct their meaning of the Bible.

NOTES

1 This chapter contains some material that was first published in my article, "Literary Approaches to Biblical Literature: General Observations and a Case Study of Genesis 34," in *The Hebrew Bible. New Insights and Scholarship*, ed. by F. Greenspahn (New York and London: New York University Press, 2007), 45–75. See also now Adele Berlin, "From scripture to literature. Modern ways of reading the Bible." In *Interpreting Scriptures in Judaism, Christianity and Islam: Overlapping Inquiries*, ed. by Mordechai Z. Cohen and Adele Berlin, with the assistance of Meir M. Bar-Asher, Rita Copeland, and Jon Whitman (Cambridge: Cambridge University Press, forthcoming), 326–335. For a sense of literary approaches to the Hebrew Bible in earlier periods, see Alex Preminger and Edward L. Greenstein, eds., *The Hebrew Bible in Literary Criticism* (New York: Ungar, 1986).

2 James Muilenburg, "Form Criticism and Beyond," *JBL* 88 (1969): 1–18.

3 A good example is Jack M. Sasson, *Ruth: A New Translation with a Philological Commentary and a Formalist-Folklorist Interpretation* (Baltimore, MD: Johns Hopkins University Press, 1979).

4 Erich Auerbach, "Odysseus' Scar," in *Mimesis: The Representation of Reality in Western Literature* (Princeton, NJ: Princeton University Press, 1957 [1946]),1–20; Robert Alter, *The Art of Biblical Narrative* (New York: Basic Books, 1981), which was preceded by several articles in *Commentary*; Meir Sternberg, *The Poetics of Biblical Narrative* (Bloomington: Indiana University Press, 1985).

5 The listings in Mark Alan Powell, *The Bible and Modern Literary Criticism: A Critical Assessment and Annotated Bibliography* (New York: Greenwood Press, 1992), show that the great preponderance of entries is on narrative. For a survey of the work done on biblical narrative, see D. M. Gunn, "Hebrew Narrative," in *Text in Context*, ed. by A. D. H. Mayes (Oxford University Press, 2000), 223–52.

6 This is increasingly seen in many commentaries. For overviews of the description of biblical poetry and of the study of that poetry, see Adele Berlin, "Introduction to Hebrew Poetry," in *New Interpreters Bible*, Vol. IV, ed. by Robert Duran et al. (Nashville, TN: Abingdon, 1996), 301–15; Berlin, "Poetry, Hebrew Bible," in *Dictionary of Biblical Interpretation*, Vol. 2, ed. by John H. Hayes (Nashville, TN: Abingdon, 1999), 290–6; W. G. E. Watson, "Hebrew Poetry," in *Text in Context*, 253–85. As for individual studies of specific texts, one of the earliest examples is Francis Landy, *Paradoxes of Paradise: Identity and Difference in the Song of Songs* (Sheffield, UK: Almond Press, 1983). Among numerous recent works on poetic texts, I would mention Carol A. Newsom, *The Book of Job: A Contest of Moral Imaginations* (New York: Oxford University Press, 2003); Yvonne Sherwood, *The Prostitute and the Prophet: Hosea's Marriage in Literary-Theoretical Perspective* (Sheffield Academic Press, 1996), and Tod Linafeldt, *Surviving Lamentations: Catastrophe, Lament, and Protest in the Afterlife of a Biblical Book* (University of Chicago Press, 2000). On literary readings of legal texts, see Baruch J. Schwartz, תורת הקדושה: עיונים בחוקה הכוהנית שבתורה (Jerusalem: Magnes and Hebrew University, 1999); James W. Watts, *Reading Law: The Rhetorical Shaping of the Pentateuch* (Sheffield Academic Press, 1999); and Assnat Bartor, "The Representation of Speech in the Casuistic Laws of the Pentateuch," *JBL* 126 (2007): 231–49.

7 There is a large body of work on feminist studies of both a practical and a theoretical nature. See Elisabeth Schüssler Fiorenza, "Feminist Hermeneutics," in *Anchor Bible Dictionary*, Vol. 2, ed. by David N. Freedman et al. (New York: Doubleday, 1992), 783–91; A. Brenner and C. Fontaine, eds., *A Feminist Companion to Reading the Bible* (Sheffield Academic Press, 1997); J. Cheryl Exum, "Feminist Study of the Old Testament," in *Text in Context*, 86–115 (with extensive bibliography); Esther Fuchs, "Feminist Approaches to the Hebrew Bible," in *The Hebrew Bible: New Insights and Scholarship*, ed. by F. Greenspahn (New York University Press, 2008), 76–95.

8 For more on these terms, see the essay adapted by Adele Berlin and Marc Zvi Brettler, "The Modern Study of the Bible," in *The Jewish Study Bible*, ed. by

Adele Berlin, Marc Zvi Brettler, and Michael A. Fishbane (New York: Oxford University Press, 2004), esp. 2090–6; Carl R. Holladay, "Contemporary Methods of Reading the Bible," in *The New Interpreter's Bible*, Vol. 1 (Nashville, TN: Abingdon Press, 1994–2004), 125–49, esp.136–49; Mark Allan Powell, "Bible and Modern Literary Criticism," in *The Cambridge Companion to Biblical Interpretation*, ed. by John Barton (Cambridge University Press, 1998). Hayes, *Dictionary of Biblical Interpretation*, contains entries on "Cultural Studies"; "Ideological Criticism"; "Literary Theory, Literary Criticism, and the Bible"; "Post-Colonial Biblical Interpretation"; "Reader-Response Criticism"; and "Strucutralism and Deconstruction."

9 See David M. Gunn and Danna Nolan Fewell, *Narrative in the Hebrew Bible* (Oxford University Press, 1993), 7–10. They add that historical critics see the text as having one stable meaning that can be revealed objectively, whereas literary critics see the text as unstable, possessing many meanings, and containing within itself the seeds of its own deconstruction. Interpretation is therefore a subjective act. However, I would not assign these last distinctions to the contrast between historical and literary criticism. Sternberg, definitely not a historical critic, also operates with the assumption that the text has one stable meaning that can be retrieved objectively.

10 See F. W. Dobbs-Allsopp, "Rethinking Historical Criticism," *Bib Int* 7 (1999): 235–71. Dobbs-Allsopp stresses the ongoing importance of historical criticism to the literary study of the Bible and wants to rethink traditional historical criticism from a postmodern perspective.

11 David M. Carr, *Reading the Fractures of Genesis: Historical and Literary Approaches* (Louisville, KY: Westminster John Knox, 1996), 11, makes a similar observation: "Already this survey suggests a potential convergence between recent postmodern synchronic studies and recent diachronic studies. Just as diachronic studies are focusing more on illuminating the present form of the text, synchronic studies are displaying increasing interest in the very textual disunity that was often the mainstay of transmission history."

12 Those who question whether Shechem raped Dinah include Lyn M. Bechtel, "What if Dinah Is Not Raped? (Genesis 34)," *JSOT* 62 (1994): 19–36; and "Dinah," in *Women in Scripture*, ed. by C. Meyers et al. (Boston: Houghton Mifflin, 2000), 69–71; Joseph Fleishman, "Shechem and Dinah – In the Light of Non-biblical and Biblical Sources," *ZAW* 116 (2004): 12–32; Richard Elliott Friedman, *Commentary on the Torah* (HarperSanFrancisco, 2001), 116; Tikva Frymer-Kensky, *Reading the Women of the Bible* (New York: Schocken Books, 2002), 181–3; Mayer Gruber, "A Re-examination of the Charges Against Shechem Son of Hamor," *Beit Mikra* 157 (1999): 119–27; Hilary Lipka, *Sexual Transgression in the Hebrew Bible* (Sheffield, UK: Sheffield Phoenix, 2006), 184–99; John Van Seters, "The Silence of Dinah (Genesis 34)," in *Jacob – Commentaire à plusieurs voix de Gen 25–36; mélanges offerts à Albert de Pury*, ed. by Jean-Daniel Macchi and Thomas Römer (Geneva: Labor et Fides, 2001), 239–47; and Ellen J. van Wolde, "Love and Hatred in a Multiracial Society: The Dinah and Shechem Story in Genesis 34 in the Context of Genesis 28–35," in *Reading from Right to Left: Essays on the Hebrew Bible in Honour of David J. A. Clines*, ed. by J. C. Exum and

H. G. M. Williamson (Sheffield Academic Press, 2003), 435–49. For a different view, see Susanne Scholz, *Rape Plots: A Feminist Cultural Study of Genesis 34* (New York: Peter Lang. 2000); "Through Whose Eyes? A 'Right' Reading of Genesis 34," in *Genesis: The Feminist Companion to the Bible*, 2nd series, ed. by A. Brenner (Sheffield Academic Press, 1998), 150–71; and "Was It Really Rape in Genesis 34? Biblical Scholarship as a Reflection of Cultural Assumptions," in *Escaping Eden: New Feminist Perspectives on the Bible*, ed. by Harold C. Washington, Susan L. Graham, and Pamela L. Thimmes (New York University Press, 1998) 182–98. The idea that Dinah was raped was upheld recently by Yael Shemesh, "Rape Is Rape Is Rape: The Story of Dinah and Shechem (Genesis 34)," *ZAW* 119 (2007): 2–21, who, while not accepting the interpretation that abduction marriage is the issue in our story, insists that abduction marriage constitutes rape.

13   Sternberg's assumption that any competent reader will discern the text's meaning is obviously faulty when one realizes that a number of scholars, including Fewell and Gunn, as well as Yairah Amit (Sternberg's student), all use the same analysis of narrative poetics but reach quite different conclusions about the story's meaning.

14   "Tipping the Balance: Sternberg's Reader and the Rape of Dinah," *JBL* 110 (1991): 193–211. Meir Sternberg responded the following year in "Biblical Poetics and Sexual Politics: From Reading to Counterreading," *JBL* 111 (1992): 463–88.

15   As Gunn and Fewell state in *Narrative in the Hebrew Bible*, 9, "we read these narratives as we might read modern novels or short stories, constructing a story world in which questions of human values and belief ... find shape in relation to our own (and our readers') world(s)." In contrast, Sternberg's search for the ancient meaning is closer to historical-critical approaches.

16   Gunn, "Hebrew Narrative," in *Text in Context*, 226. For some of the tensions between modern and postmodern approaches, see John J. Collins, *The Bible after Babel* (Grand Rapids, MI: Eerdmans, 2005).

17   R. P. Carroll, "The Reader and the Text," in *Text and Context*, 24. See also Berlin, "The Role of the Text in the Reading Process," *Semeia* 62 (1993): 143–7.

18   This program resembles the part of David Clines' program that he calls "understanding," which is the "Enlightenment project to which most scholars ... still subscribe," whose goal is the "fair-minded, patient, and sympathetic re-creation of the meaning, significance and intentions of the ancient text in its own time." Clines maintains that this requires acknowledging that "the biblical text is an ideological production, that the interpreter is reading the text from within a particular ideological formation, and that the ideologies of ancient Israel are historically and culturally far removed from the ideologies of our own day" (*Interested Parties: The Ideology of Writers and Readers of the Hebrew Bible* [Journal of the Study of the Old Testament Supplement 205; Gender, Culture, Theory 1; Sheffield Academic Press, 1995], 19). The second aspect of Clines' program is "critique," which is the evaluation (both positive and negative) of the ancient ideologies by our own standards. Here Clines wants "to collapse the historical distance between the text and ourselves," which seems to me to undermine his program of "understanding." Clines finds this move ethically responsible.

I reject Clines' program of "critique" for biblical studies just as I reject it for Assyriology or any other area; "the ethics of reading" does not concern me.

19   I use these terms in a broad and benign sense without the radical political overtones that accompanied their birth. As with other avant garde movements, their popular acceptance tames them.

20   As Robert P. Carroll put it, new historicism "seeks to construct a cultural poetics of the Bible" ("Poststructuralist Approaches: New Historicism and Postmodernism," in *Cambridge Companion to Biblical Interpretation,* 57). Sternberg, too, moved from the poetics of narrative to the poetics of culture in his *Hebrews between Cultures: Group Portraits and National Literature* (Bloomington: Indiana University Press, 1998), xxii.

21   "The Sack of Shechem," *Prooftexts* 10 (1990): 1–15. Geller's work resembles van Wolde's in its general conclusion about monoethnicity and in its author's revulsion of ancient values, but it is much more nuanced and developed, and historically contextualized.

22   Michael A. Fishbane, *Biblical Interpretation in Ancient Israel* (Oxford, UK: Clarendon, 1985), 350–79.

23   Yairah Amit, *Hidden Polemics in Biblical Narrative,* trans. by Jonathan Chipman (Leiden, Netherlands: Brill. 2000), 189–217. For a related view, see Bernd Jørg Diebner, "Gen 34 und Dinas Rolle bei der Definition 'Israels,'" *Dielheimer Blätter zum Alten Testament* 19 (1984): 59–76), who does not date the story to the time of Ezra but asks how it would have been read at that time.

24   *Dinah's Daughters: Gender and Judaism from the Hebrew Bible to Late Antiquity* (Philadelphia: University of Pennsylvania Press, 2002), 33–48. That this was an abduction marriage receives support from an independent study by Joseph Fleishman ("Shechem and Dinah"; see also Fleishman, "Why Did Simeon and Levi Rebuke Their Father in Genesis 34:31?" *JNSL* 26 [2000]: 101–16). Fleishman does not employ a feminist or an anthropological approach, and he gets his proof from ancient Near Eastern legal texts and from biblical and rabbinic material, not from classical sources, as Zlotnick does.

25   *Dinah's Daughters,* 26.

26   Ibid., 41–2.

27   The major work in this area is Fishbane, *Biblical Interpretation in Ancient Israel.* Developing the idea from his teacher, Nahum Sarna, Fishbane demonstrated that later parts of the Bible often interpret earlier parts. His aim was to show that the types of interpretation known from rabbinic sources were already inherent in the Bible itself. For an overview, see Sommer, "Inner-Biblical Interpretation," in *The Jewish Study Bible,* 1829–35.

28   Jeremy Cohen, in tracing the career of a single verse from the Bible through medieval exegesis, makes a related observation: "the role of interpretation in the formation of the biblical text is for this book a methodological premise.... A historical study of biblical interpretation may not casually presume that at the moment of its composition a scriptural text possessed a clear, indisputable meaning from which all subsequent understanding of that text departed. It is difficult if not impossible to determine whether a text ever had an original, uninterpreted meaning; more often than not, the

qualitative distinction between this meaning and later, interpretative expositions is untenable. The extant text of the Bible itself derives from several lengthy processes of transmission, reflection, and revision; it never did have a single, absolute value that the historian can recover" (*"Be Fertile and Increase, Fill the Earth and Master It": The Ancient and Medieval Career of a Biblical Text* [Ithaca, NY: Cornell University Press, 1989], 11).

29   Other reasons include the publications and scholarship on the Dead Sea Scrolls, the availability of other works from the Second Temple period, and a general rise in interest in this period. Foremost in promoting interest in ancient biblical interpretation is James Kugel. See his *The Bible as It Was* (Cambridge, MA: Belknap, 1997) and now *How to Read the Bible: A Guide to Scripture, Then and Now* (New York: Free Press, 2007). For some overviews, see Devorah Dimant, "Use and Interpretation of Mikra in the Apocrypha and Pseudepigrapha," in *Mikra: Text, Translation, Reading, and Interpretation of the Hebrew Bible in Ancient Judaism and Early Christianity*, ed. by Martin Jan Mulder (Philadelphia, PA: Fortress Press, 1988), 379–420, esp. 396–9; Hindy Najman, "Early Nonrabbinic Interpretation," in *The Jewish Study Bible*, 1835–44; and Moshe Bernstein, "Interpretation of Scripture," in *Encyclopedia of the Dead Sea Scrolls*, Vol. 1, ed. by Lawrence H. Schiffman and James C. VanderKam (Oxford University Press, 2000), 376–83.

30   Kugel, *Bible as It Was*, 234, points out that 4 Macc 2:19–20 took Genesis 49 as an allusion to Genesis 34. He words his statement craftily and noncommitally, saying that Genesis 49 "seemed to interpreters to shed light on the true significance of this incident. For while the story of Dinah is not explicitly mentioned elsewhere in the Hebrew Bible, interpreters from earliest times found an allusion to it at the end of the book of Genesis." We do not know whether or not Kugel himself sees an allusion to the Dinah story in Genesis 49.

31   The Levites were assigned to divine service and therefore did not have private agricultural holdings; the tribe of Simeon was absorbed into the tribe of Judah. Compare the poem in Deuteronomy 33, which praises Levi as the priestly tribe (with no reference to Genesis 34) and omits Simeon altogether.

32   Source critics identify both passages as belonging to J, a Judean source. David M. Carr (*Reading the Fractures of Genesis*, 304), a source critic informed by literary approaches, concludes that both Genesis 34 and Gen 49:5–7 are part of the work of a pro-Judean author who reshaped earlier material in the Jacob and Joseph stories for the purpose of promoting the tribe of Judah by disqualifying earlier-born sons of Jacob, including Simeon and Levi.

33   The summary in Frymer-Kensky, *Reading the Women of the Bible*, 341, is useful and has served as the basis for some of my remarks here. Kugel, *Bible as It Was*, 233–44, offers excerpts of the texts and brief explanations. For in-depth studies of specific writings on Genesis 34, see Tjitze Baarda, "The Shechem Episode in the Testament of Levi: A Comparison with Other Traditions," in *Sacred History and Sacred Texts in Early Judaism: A Symposium in Honor of A. S. van der Woude*, ed. by J. N. Bremmer and F. García Martínez (Kampen, Netherlands: Pharos, 1992), 11–73; John J. Collins, "The Epic of Theodotus and the Hellenism of the Hasmoneans," *HTR* 73 (1980): 91–104); Louis H. Feldman, "Philo, Pseudo-Philo, Josephus, and Theodotus on the

Rape of Dinah," *JQR* 94 (2004): 253–77; James Kugel, "The Story of Dinah in the Testament of Levi," *HTR* 85(1) (1992): 1–34; Judith H. Newman, *Praying by the Book: The Scripturalization of Prayer in Second Temple Judaism* (Atlanta: Scholars Press, 1999), 123–38; S. R. Pummer, "Genesis 34 in the Jewish Writings of the Hellenistic and Roman Periods," *HTR* 75 (1982): 177–88; and Angela Standhartinger, "'Um zu sehen die Töchter des Landes.' Die Perspektiv Dinas in der jüdisch-hellenistichen Diskussion um Gen. 34," in *Religious Propaganda and Missionary Competition in the New Testament World: Essays Honoring Dieter Georgi*, ed. by Dieter Georgi et al. (Leiden, Netherlands: Brill, 1994), 89–116.

34 See Feldman, "Philo, Pseudo-Philo, Josephus."
35 How much of ancient interpretation reflects earlier exegetical tradition and how much reflects the author's own ideology remain questions. Kugel, "Story of Dinah," stresses the former, whereas Feldman, "Philo, Pseudo-Philo, Josephus," argues for the latter.

FURTHER READING

Barton, John, ed. *The Cambridge Companion to Biblical Interpretation.* Cambridge University Press, 1998.
Berlin, Adele, and Marc Zvi Brettler, eds. *The Jewish Study Bible.* New York: Oxford University Press, 2004.
Carr, David M. *Reading the Fractures of Genesis: Historical and Literary Approaches.* Louisville, KY: Westminster John Knox Press, 1996.
Fishbane, Michael A. *Biblical Interpretation in Ancient Israel.* Oxford, UK: Clarendon, 1985.
Kugel, James. *How to Read the Bible: A Guide to Scripture, Then and Now.* New York: Free Press, 2007.
Mayes, A. D. H., ed. *Text in Context.* Oxford University Press, 2000.
Weitzman, Steven. "Before and After the Art of Biblical Narrative." *Prooftexts* 27(2) (2007): 191–210.

Part IV

Subcollections and genres

9 The Pentateuch and Israelite law

THOMAS B. DOZEMAN

THE LITERATURE OF THE PENTATEUCH

THE LITERATURE OF THE PENTATEUCH

The Pentateuch includes the first five books of the Hebrew Bible: Genesis, Exodus, Leviticus, Numbers, and Deuteronomy. The books separate into two unequal parts: Genesis and Exodus-Deuteronomy.[1] Genesis traces the ancestral origins of Israel. It is composed in narrative, with no single character dominating the story. Exodus through Deuteronomy recounts the Israelite salvation from Egypt, the wilderness journey, and the revelation of law at the divine mountain. These books are a mixture of narrative and law, with Moses emerging as the central character. The literary structure and the central themes of the pentateuchal books can be summarized as follows.

Genesis: creation of the world and origin of the ancestors

Genesis narrates the creation of the world (Genesis 1–11) and the ancestral origins of Israel (12–50). It traces the evolution of the world through a series of genealogies that narrow from all humanity (2:4a, heaven and earth; 5:1, Adam; 6:9, Noah; 10:1, Noah's sons; 11:10, Shem) to the Israelite ancestors (11:27, Terah; 25:12, Ishmael; 25:19, Isaac, 36:1, Esau; 37:2, Jacob). Genesis 1–11 narrates a broad sweep of time, which includes nearly two millennia (1,876 years) between the creation of the first human (Gen 1:26–7) and the birth of Terah, the father of Abraham (Gen 11:24). Genesis 12–50 narrows in scope to chronicle the family history of Israel, which takes place over a period of an additional 360 years (i.e., year 1876 to year 2236). The main subject matter concerns the first three generations of Israelites, represented by Abraham (Gen 11:27–25:18), Isaac (Gen 25:19–35:29), and Jacob (36:1–50:26). Genesis ends with the fourth generation of Israelites (i.e., Joseph and his brothers) settling in Egypt (Gen 47:9). Two themes dominate the narrative of the ancestors: the divine promises of many descendants and a homeland (Gen 12:1–4).

A central feature of the literature in Genesis is the repetition of stories. Representative examples in Gen 1–11 include two accounts of creation (Genesis 1 and 2), two genealogies of humanity (Gen 4:17–26 and 5), and two versions of the flood (Genesis 6–9). The story of the ancestors in Gen 12–50 is also characterized by repetition. There are two accounts of God entering into covenant with Abraham (Genesis 15, 17), two versions of Hagar being driven away into the wilderness from the camp of Abraham and Sarah (Gen 16:1–14; 21:8–21), two episodes in which Jacob establishes a worship site at Bethel (Gen 28:11–28; 35:1–8), and no fewer than three occasions on which Abraham and Isaac falsely present their wives as sisters to foreign kings (Genesis 12, 20, 26).

Exodus, Leviticus, Numbers, Deuteronomy: the biography of Moses and the salvation of the Israelite people

Moses emerges as the central character in Exodus, Leviticus, Numbers, and Deuteronomy. He is idealized as the savior of the Israelites and the mediator of divine law. Exodus through Deuteronomy is framed by the birth (Exodus 2) and death (Deuteronomy 34) of Moses, so the majority of the pentateuchal literature is confined to the 120 years of his life (the years 2586–2706) as compared with the millennia that transpire in Genesis. During his career, Moses liberates Israel from Egypt (Exodus 5–14), leads them into the wilderness (Exodus 15–18; Numbers 11–21), and twice mediates divine law, initially at the mountain of God to the first generation of Israelites (Exodus 19–Numbers 10) and again to the second generation on the plains of Moab (Deuteronomy). The leadership of Moses over the period of two generations also indicates a further distinction between the books of Exodus, Leviticus, and Numbers from Deuteronomy.

Exodus, Leviticus, and Numbers: Moses and the first generation of Israelites

Exodus, Numbers, and Leviticus are nearly inseparable in the literary design of the Pentateuch and clearly distinct from Genesis and Deuteronomy. Exodus 1 sets the stage for the story of the Exodus. It indicates a significant break in time (Exod 1:6) from the events in Genesis, later described as a period of 430 years, making the date of the Exodus the year 2666 (Exod 12:40–1). During this period of time, the original family of seventy has grown into a large nation (Exod 1:5, 7), which threatens Pharaoh (Exod 1:8–10). He enslaves the Israelites (Exod 1:11–14) and slaughters the male infants to maintain population control (Exod 1:15–22). The central themes of the book of Exodus are the power of Yahweh to rescue the Israelite people from slavery (Exodus 2–15), the divine leading of the people through the wilderness (Exodus 16–18), and the revelation of law through the building of the tabernacle at Mount Sinai (Exodus 19–40).

Leviticus and Numbers continue the setting of the Israelite encampment at Mount Sinai (Lev 1:1; Num 1:1) in order to build on the themes of the construction of the tabernacle, the appearance of the glory of Yahweh, and the revelation of law from the book of Exodus. Leviticus describes the sacrificial rituals of the tabernacle (Leviticus 1–7), the ordination of the priesthood to mediate the rituals (Leviticus 8–10), the rules of purity (Leviticus 11–16), and the ethics of holiness (Leviticus 17–27). Numbers extends the ethics of holiness from the worship practices outlined in Leviticus to the social world of the Israelite people by describing a religious community organized around the sanctuary (Numbers 1–10). Once organized, the people leave the divine mountain and set out for the promised land of Canaan, where the first generation dies because of their lack of faith in the leadership of Moses and in the power of Yahweh to fulfill promises (Numbers 11–21). Numbers closes with a story of the continuing divine care of the Israelites in the wilderness (Numbers 22–4), a warning against intermarriage (Numbers 25), and descriptions of the promised land (Numbers 26–36).

Deuteronomy: Moses and the second generation of Israelites
According to the book of Deuteronomy, the first generation of Israelites has died in the wilderness, and Moses is teaching the second generation on the last day of his life. Moses' instruction progresses from the recounting of the Exodus, the wilderness journey, and revelation of the Decalogue (Deuteronomy 1–11) to the promulgation of further law (Deuteronomy 12–26), the list of blessings and curses that are tied to the observance of the law (Deuteronomy 27–28), and a concluding section on the establishment of the covenant between Yahweh and Israel as well as poetry and the account of Moses' death (Deuteronomy 29–34). Moses dies on Mount Nebo (Deut 34:1–8) at the conclusion of his teaching.

The story of Moses is also characterized by repetition. The narrative of the Exodus includes two accounts of Moses' commission and the revelation of the divine name, Yahweh (Exodus 3, 6), contrasting versions of the plagues (Exodus 7–10), and multiple accounts of the destruction of the Egyptian army (Exodus 14–15). The same technique of repetition continues in the story of the wilderness journey, where there are also multiple accounts of the Israelites' fear of conquest and loss of the Promised Land (Numbers 13–14). These instances of repetition are reminiscent of

Genesis, where multiple versions of the same story also occur. But the significance of repetition in the story of Moses exceeds the book of Genesis because of the recurrence of the revelation of law over two generations. The Decalogue (Exodus 20), the Book of the Covenant (Exodus 21–23), and the priestly legislation for the tabernacle (Exodus 25–40, Leviticus, and parts of Numbers) are promulgated to the first generation and the laws of Deuteronomy to the second. The law codes create an extensive series of repetitions beyond the narratives. Examples include two mountains of revelation (Sinai in Exodus and Horeb in Deuteronomy), two versions of the Decalogue (Exodus 20; Deuteronomy 5), conflicting cultic calendars (Exod 23:14–17; Leviticus 23; Numbers 27–8; Deuteronomy 16), competing views of sacrifice (Leviticus 1–7, Deuteronomy 15), and different laws concerning warfare (Numbers 31; Deuteronomy 20).

A central task in interpretation of the Pentateuch is thus to explain the repetition of the stories and the laws, and to identify the author(s) of the literature. The history of interpretation divides between the premodern and modern periods. Interpreters in the premodern period assumed the authorship of Moses and the unified meaning of the different stories and law codes. The modern period introduced a more critical study of the Pentateuch as a composition of many anonymous authors and one that contains a collection of narratives and laws with conflicting themes.

PRECRITICAL INTERPRETATION OF THE PENTATEUCH

Mosaic authorship

The author of the Pentateuch is not identified within the literature. Yet authorship became closely associated with Moses because of his central role in Exodus through Deuteronomy. The Mosaic authorship of the Pentateuch was reinforced by scattered references to writing in Exodus, Numbers, and Deuteronomy. Only God and Moses write in the Pentateuch. God writes laws (Exod 24:12), the architectural plans for the tabernacle (Exod 31:18), the names of the elect in a special book (Exod 32:32), and the tablets containing the Decalogue (Exod 34:1; Deut 4:13; 5:22; 9:10; 10:2–4). Moses writes four distinct genres of literature: prophecy about holy war (Exod 17:14), laws (Exod 24:4; 34:27–8; Deut 31:9, 34), the history of the wilderness journey (Num 33:2), and a song (Deut 31:9, 22).

Mosaic authorship is most likely extended in Deuteronomy 31:24–6 to include the entire book of Deuteronomy, described as the "book of the torah" (meaning "book of the law"). Joshua 8:31–4 identifies the "book of the torah" as the "torah of Moses" (see also Josh 23:6; 1 Kgs 2:3; 2

Kgs 14:6; 23:25). The "torah of Moses" may refer only to the book of Deuteronomy throughout these citations. But over time, the designation came to represent all pentateuchal literature. Thus, when Ezra the scribe returns from Persia after the exile (sometime in the fifth century BCE), the "torah of Moses" that he reads publicly was associated with the entire Pentateuch (see Ezr 3:2; 7:6; Neh 8:1; and also 2 Chr 23:18; 30:16; 34:14). In the process, Moses was also idealized as an inspired author. Thus, his authorship became important for attributing divine authority to Torah. It also laid the foundation for a belief that the Pentateuch contained one, unified message because it had one divinely inspired author.

Jewish and Christian interpretation

Mosaic authorship of the Pentateuch was assumed in Jewish Hellenistic, Rabbinic, and early Christian writings. Philo, a Hellenistic Jewish author writing in the first century CE, provides an early example in his commentary on creation, stating, "Moses says ... 'In the beginning God created the heaven and the earth' "(*Works of Philo*, op. 26). Josephus also asserts that Moses authored the first five books (*Against Apion* 1:37–40). The Rabbis, too, state, "Moses wrote his own book" (*B. Bat* 14b). At the same time, its origin was divine (*Sanh* 99a). Early Christian writers reinforced the Mosaic authorship of the Pentateuch. The Apostle Paul refers to the Pentateuch as the "law of Moses" (1 Cor 9:9). The author of the Gospel of Luke expresses the same thought when the Pentateuch is indicated by simple reference to its author "Moses" (Luke 24:27) and later described as the "law of Moses" (Luke 24:44). These examples indicate two important developments in premodern interpretation of the Pentateuch. First, Mosaic authorship of the Pentateuch emerged within tradition and not from historical-critical study of its literary composition. Second, Mosaic authorship became important for attributing divine authority to Scripture. The Rabbis provide an illustration when they conclude that "God spoke Torah to Moses, who wrote down the words" (*B. Bat.* 15a).

However, even in the absence of modern critical study, questions about Mosaic authorship arose. The Rabbis, for example, continued to debate whether Moses could have written the account of his own death in Deut 34:5–12 (*B. Bat* 15a; *Menah.* 30a). Jewish medieval commentators noticed other problems. Abraham Ibn Ezra, a twelfth-century CE Spanish interpreter, noted passages in Deuteronomy that Moses could not have written, such as the phrases "beyond Jordan" (Deut 1:1), because Moses never crossed the Jordan River.[2] Doubts about Mosaic authorship of the Pentateuch, however, remained at the periphery of interpretation, and the problem of repetition in the narratives and laws did not provide a hermeneutical starting point for interpreting pentateuchal literature. Thus, despite a variety of literary problems, the authoritative teaching of tradition concerning Mosaic authorship of the Pentateuch was accepted without serious or widespread opposition, and as a result, Jewish and Christian interpreters sought a unified message in Torah from its single author, Moses.

Critical interpretation of the Pentateuch

The Renaissance and the Protestant Reformation introduced a more critical stance toward religious tradition and authority, expressed in the slogan *sola scriptura*.[3] This claim meant that only Scripture and not traditional teaching could represent divine instruction on all questions of faith and practice. Study of Scripture, therefore, was used as a countervoice to the authority of church tradition.[4] The reformers' critical stance toward tradition eventually would call into question Mosaic authorship because it, too, rested on the authority of traditional teaching. John Calvin and Benedict de Spinoza illustrate the emergence of historical criticism of the Pentateuch and the eventual rejection of Mosaic authorship.

Emergence of historical criticism and the rejection of Mosaic authorship

John Calvin (1509–64) never himself questioned Mosaic authorship of the Pentateuch. In the "Preface" to *The Four Last Books of Moses in the Form of a Harmony*, Calvin states that "what was dictated to Moses was excellent."[5] And in the introductory "Argument" to *The First Book of Moses Called Genesis*, he makes clear his quest to discern the intention of Moses as a source of divine revelation.[6] Uncovering Mosaic intention often served polemical purposes, refuting the claims of papal authority.[7] It also brought literary repetitions and potential contradictions into clearer focus. For example, Calvin is aware of two creation stories in Genesis 1 and 2 and of the name changes for God from Elohim (in Genesis 1) to Yahweh (in Genesis 2). Such repetition, however, does not prompt questions about Mosaic authorship, nor does it challenge the assumption that the Pentateuch contains a unified message about creation. Instead, the two creation stories are for emphasis, according to Calvin. In the same way the multiple accounts of Abraham (Genesis 12, 20) and Isaac (Genesis 26) presenting their wives as sisters to foreign kings is not the result of different authors but a reflection of history because it happened three times.[8]

Benedict de Spinoza (1634–77) shared the reformers' rejection of traditional religious authority. He stated in the "Preface" of his *Theologico-Political Treatise* that blind adherence to religious authority without free rational and critical inquiry is nothing more than superstition rooted in fear, resulting in prejudice and violence.[9] Thus, Spinoza agreed with the reformers' claim of *sola scriptura* as a means of opposing the tyranny of tradition. But Spinoza went far beyond Calvin and the reformers. He rooted the superstition of religious tradition in the interpretation of Scripture itself. The clearest evidence of such superstition was the "ungrounded and even irrational" claim of Mosaic authorship.[10] Spinoza reviewed the problems of Mosaic authorship that were noted by Ibn Ezra and others, such as third-person references to Moses (i.e., "Moses talked with God") or anachronisms in the comparison of Moses to later prophets (i.e., "there was never a prophet in Israel like Moses"). The conclusion, writes Spinoza, is "clearer than the sun at noonday that the Pentateuch was not written by Moses, but by someone who lived long after Moses."[11] Spinoza introduced a whole new problem that has dominated the historical-critical study of the Pentateuch in the modern era. It is that "the history of the Bible is ... untrustworthy."[12] Calvin never entertained such a possibility. For Spinoza, the defense of the Mosaic authorship of the Pentateuch advances the unreliable character of Bible, and those who advocate for it provide one more instance of the superstition of traditional religious authority. In view of this situation, he writes that the new aim of biblical interpretation is to uncover "a trustworthy history of the sacred writings."[13] Three principles shape his new approach to the Pentateuch: (1) a reliable history must be built on a study of the Hebrew language, (2) knowledge of the Bible must arise only from a study of the text and not from traditional teachings about it, and (3) the interpreter must identify the genuine authors of the biblical books, who were channels of divine revelation.[14]

Identification of anonymous authors

Spinoza's principles of interpretation laid the groundwork for the modern study of pentateuchal narrative and law as a quest for anonymous authors whose identification would provide a window into the history and the religion of ancient Israel. The repetitive nature of the narratives and the laws led interpreters to presume that many anonymous authors contributed to the composition of the Pentateuch, and that the literature could not be harmonized into a single, unified message. Two goals comprise the core of the historical-critical study of the Pentateuch. First, repetitions and contradictions were separated, not harmonized,

into different bodies of literature ("sources" and "law codes") to identify authors with distinct religious worldviews. Second, interpreters
sought to arrange the order in which the authors wrote, thus fashioning
the history of Israelite religion. The identification of literary contradictions with distinct authors and the establishing of a relative chronology
became the basic building blocks for historical critics in establishing
the "trustworthy history of the sacred writings" advocated by Spinoza.
Some shared Spinoza's belief in divine inspiration; others did not. In
either case, though, the quest for anonymous authors created tension
with the traditional teaching that the Torah was written by Moses and
thus contained one unified message. Jean Astruc and W. M. L. de Wette
provide early examples of the identification of anonymous authors in
narrative and legal literature in the Pentateuch.

Jean Astruc and the identification of two narratives

Identification of the anonymous authors of the narratives of the
Pentateuch arose from an inductive study of the literature, especially
in the book of Genesis. Lack of chronology, repetition, and contradiction of content were considered indicators of different writers. The
divine names emerged as an important starting point for tracing the literary thread of the distinct bodies of literature and identification of the
authors. In some stories, the deity is named Elohim (translated "God"
in the New Revised Standard Version [NRSV]), and in others, Yahweh
(translated "LORD" in the NRSV). The opening chapters of Genesis provide an example. The deity is "Elohim" in Gen 1:1–2:3 but "Yahweh
Elohim" ("LORD God," NRSV) throughout Gen 2:4–25. Calvin saw this
already in his commentary on Genesis but interpreted it as a literary
technique by Moses for emphasis. Historical critics, by contrast, judged
the different divine names to be a contradiction, revealing authors with
distinct views of the deity.

Jean Astruc (1684–1766) separated the literature in Genesis 1–Exodus
2 into sources A and B based on the divine names.[15] The author of A used
the divine name, Elohim, whereas B preferred Yahweh. For Astruc, the
two creation stories (Gen 1:1–2:3 and 2:4–25) form a doublet that represents conflicting views of creation. The accounts of the patriarchs
(Abraham and Isaac) falsely presenting their wives as sisters to foreign
kings are also stories from different authors, who refer to the deity with
distinct names. When Abraham first lies to Pharaoh about Sarah (Gen
12:10–20), it is Yahweh who sends plagues on the Egyptians. Thus,
it is an episode in source B, according to Astruc. But when Abraham
repeats this action with Abimelech (Gen 20:1–18), Elohim, not Yahweh,

threatens the king with disease and death, indicating a story in source A. The divine name Yahweh returns in the account of Isaac, Rebekah, and Abimelech (Gen 26:1–16), making it an episode in source B, along with the first story of Abraham and Sarah in Egypt (Gen 12:10–20). Astruc employed historical-critical methodology to confirm the Mosaic authorship of the Pentateuch. He argued that the anonymous sources A and B were pre-Mosaic and used by Moses in composing the Pentateuch. Subsequent interpreters would identify the anonymous authors well beyond the time of Moses and thus support Spinoza's conclusion concerning the non-Mosaic authorship of the Pentateuch.

W. M. L. de Wette and the identification of two laws

The starting point of W. M. L. de Wette's (1780–1859) research was the repetition of Moses' mediation of divine law twice in the Pentateuch to subsequent generations of Israelites. First, he transmits law at Mount Sinai in the year of the Exodus (Exodus 19–Numbers 10) and then a second time, forty years later, on the plains of Moab (Deuteronomy). De Wette provided a new direction for interpreting this repetition by focusing on the second body of law contained in the book of Deuteronomy.[16] He noted that the story of Moses comes to an end at the close of Numbers. His impending death is confirmed (Num 27:12–14), the land of Canaan is divided (Num 26:52–6), and Joshua is appointed as his successor (Num 27:15–23). Somewhat unexpectedly, Deuteronomy begins the story anew by repeating much of the material that occurs in Leviticus and Numbers. New law is given (Deuteronomy 4–5, 12–25), the story of Israel's wilderness journey is retold (Deuteronomy 1–3), many specific laws repeat (Leviticus 26; Deuteronomy 28), Joshua is appointed a second time to succeed Moses (Deuteronomy 31), and God tells Moses again of his impending death (Deuteronomy 31, 34). The repetitions suggest that the history of Moses is essentially complete at the close of Numbers.

De Wette also noted that Deuteronomy's style of writing and religious outlook were unique.[17] He judged the language to be more reflective and theologically sophisticated than the literature in Genesis through Numbers, with distinctive phrases (e.g., "that you may live in the land which Yahweh our God gives you") and a unique view of the cult, which advocated worship at a single sanctuary (Deuteronomy 12). The theme of centralized worship was at odds with the biblical portrait of Israel as having many sanctuaries throughout the Mosaic (e.g., Exod 20:24–5) and monarchical (e.g., Saul in 1 Samuel 13; David in 1 Samuel 21; and Solomon in 1 Kings 3) periods. As a consequence, de Wette argued that Moses could not have written the book of Deuteronomy. No trace of the

wilderness community or its form of worship in Deuteronomy was evident in the stories of Israel's life in the land under either the judges or
the monarchy.[18] He concluded that the earliest portions of Deuteronomy
were written in the closing years of the monarchical period, during the
Josianic reform (621 BCE), which introduced the centralization of worship (2 Kings 22–23). De Wette's fixing of the date of Deuteronomy to
the end of the monarchical period became a fulcrum for establishing the
chronology of the literature in the Pentateuch. Deuteronomy was a separate account of the origin of Israel, written at a later point in time than
the laws in Exodus through Numbers. The influence of de Wette continues into the present, especially the conclusion that the Book of the
Covenant is an older law code than the laws in Deuteronomy 12–26.[19]

Julius Wellhausen and the documentary hypothesis

Astruc's identification of multiple narratives and de Wette's description
of two law codes became building blocks in the modern interpretation
of the Pentateuch. But identification of the authors, the nature of the
literature, and the process by which the Pentateuch was formed were
far from settled. Astruc's sources quickly took on the names of the deity
prominent in each. Thus, scholars such as Johann Gottfried Eichhorn
(1752–1827) referred to Elohistic (E) and Yahwistic (J for the German
term, Jahwist) sources.[20] Other interpreters began to identify more than
two authors from the divine names. Already in 1798, Carl David Ilgen
suggested a three-source theory of composition in Genesis, with two
Elohistic authors.[21] Herman Hupfeld (1796–1866) addressed the problem
anew with his distinction between Elohist one (E[1]) and two (E[2]), in which
E[1] was a foundational document beginning with creation in Genesis 1
and continuing through the book of Joshua, whereas E[2] had a more narrow focus on the patriarchal literature beginning in Genesis 12.[22] This
separation would eventually lead to the renaming of E[1] as the Priestly
(P) code, which would result in the identification of four distinct bodies
of literature in the composition of the Pentateuch: J (Yahwistic source),
E (Elohistic source), D (Deuteronomy), and P (Priestly source).

The research of Julius Wellhausen (1844–1918) typifies this kind of
work and illustrates its impact for interpreting the history of Israelite
religion.[23] The innovative aspect of Wellhausen's contribution concerns
the Priestly source, which is focused on cultic law associated with the
wilderness tabernacle (i.e., Exodus 25–31, 35–40; Leviticus; Numbers
1–10).[24] Prior to Wellhausen, interpreters identified the Priestly source
as the oldest body of literature in the Pentateuch. Its presumed antiquity was indicated by the various designations E[1], the "Older Elohist,"

the "foundation document," the "main stock," and the German word *Quelle* (Q), meaning source, spring, or origin. It was considered the foundational text on which other documents were added. As a result, interpreters assumed that the revelation of law, the tabernacle cult, and its priestly hierarchy were part of the earliest history of ancient Israel, preceding even the prophets and kings of the monarchical period. This was de Wette's position. He assumed that Deuteronomy was a reinterpretation of the tabernacle legislation (e.g., Exodus 25–40; Leviticus).

Wellhausen proposed just the reverse, that the Priestly source depended on Deuteronomy and that its author wrote after the Josianic reform in 621 BCE, probably as late as the postexilic period. De Wette himself had provided the clue. He had demonstrated that centralized worship was an innovation in Deuteronomy, which was evident in the polemical tone of the book. Multiple sanctuaries are repeatedly condemned, while the law of a single sanctuary is carefully outlined. However, the Priestly author is so dependent on Deuteronomy, Wellhausen contended, that there is no need for further argument about centralized worship at a single sanctuary. It is simply assumed. The absence of conflict indicated a much later date, when Israel was a theocracy in the postexilic period, organized around one sanctuary and ruled by clergy now separated between Aaronide priests and Levites, something that is also lacking in Deuteronomy. This late dating of P provides the basis for the classic theory of the "documentary hypothesis," in which the order of the sources in the Pentateuch is explained as J, E, D, and P.[25]

Accordingly, Wellhausen's research on the Priestly source had far-reaching implications for interpreting the history of ancient Israelite religion. Neither Mosaic authorship nor even the Mosaic period plays a role in his interpretation of the Pentateuch, nor is the literature unified in theme or composed by a single author. Instead, the Pentateuch was judged to be an anthology with competing views of theology, worship, and social life. J and E are narratives from the monarchical period, with J written in the southern kingdom of Judah, whereas E was a northern version of the same story (although Wellhausen did not work out the literary separation between the two sources in any detail and often simply employed the designation JE [= "Yehowist"] as a more general reference to the two bodies of literature). Yet, it was clear to Wellhausen that both J and E were written earlier than Deuteronomy and the Priestly source. They assume multiple cultic sites, a mode of worship closely tied to agrarian life, and a minimal role for law. Wellhausen placed the two histories in the early Assyrian period (ninth–eighth centuries BCE). The D source remained firmly fixed as the document of the Josianic reform in the late seventh century BCE. And now P was judged to be a late history from the postexilic period, not earlier than the fifth century BCE.

Once the sources were dated and interpreted in chronological order, the different laws provided a window into the development of Israelite religion. The various festival calendars in the source documents provide an illustration. Wellhausen argued that J and E were organized around harvest festivals (Exod 23:14–17; 34:21–3). In D (Deuteronomy 16) and especially P (Leviticus 23), worship became more abstracted from nature, until the festivals were no longer attached to harvest cycles. The central role of law envisioned in D and P, moreover, emerges late in the history of Israel, according to Wellhausen, and not at its origin as the pentateuchal story suggests. As a consequence, the prophets represent an older form of religion, prior to the legal traditions of D and P. Wellhausen concluded that Moses, the lawgiver at the wilderness tabernacle in P, is a literary fiction, meant to lend authority to the Priestly theocracy and cult of the postexilic period.

MODIFICATIONS TO THE DOCUMENTARY HYPOTHESIS

The documentary hypothesis continues to be a model for interpretation of the Pentateuch, even though it has undergone extensive criticism and revision. Five areas of research have modified the documentary hypothesis while maintaining its basic framework: (1) the emergence of form criticism and tradition history, (2) the broader study of law within the context of the ancient Near East, (3) the combining of the J and E sources, (4) the literary scope of the sources, and (5) the reevaluation of the Priestly source.

Form criticism and tradition history

The methodology of form criticism shifted the focus of interpretation of the Pentateuch from the authors of the written sources to the origin of the individual stories as oral tradition. This shift marginalized the creative role of the authors in the documentary hypothesis and emphasized, instead, the influence of oral tradition in the formation of the Pentateuch. Form critics wanted to know what social setting (or *Sitz im Leben*) would have produced the oral stories because these were judged to be the most creative stage in the development of the Pentateuch. Hermann Gunkel (1862–1932) probed the oral, preliterary stage of the pentateuchal literature rather than the composition of the sources.[26] He concluded that Wellhausen's sources of the Pentateuch were collections of more ancient etiological legends and not the creation of an author.

Jacob's dream at Bethel (Gen 28:10–17) provides an example. It is an independent story that is meant to explain the presence of a sanctuary at the location of Bethel ("house of El"). The focus on oral stories also developed into the study of larger units of oral tradition, such as cultic legends of the Exodus or the establishment of covenant.[27]

Although the focus on the formation of oral tradition challenged the creative role of the authors, it did not represent a rejection of the documentary hypothesis. Instead, the authors of the sources became collectors of traditional material. Thus, the story of Jacob's dream at Bethel was no longer viewed as a composition of the J author but rather as an example of traditional material preserved in the J source. The emphasis on oral tradition also shifted interpretation to the premonarchical period as the truly creative time in the formation of Israelite tradition, in comparison with the monarchical and exilic periods in the documentary hypothesis. The shift in emphasis encouraged earlier dating for formation of the J and E sources – as is evident in the work of Gerhard von Rad and Martin Noth, who merged the study of oral tradition and source criticism in their interpretation of the Pentateuch.[28] Both interpreters assume a creative oral stage in the formation of pentateuchal tradition, a clearer separation of the sources of J and E than is evident in the work of Wellhausen, and a much earlier date for the J source in the period of the united monarchy (tenth century BCE), even while they continued to research within the framework of the documentary hypothesis.

Comparative study of ancient Near Eastern law

The study of Israelite law within the context of the ancient Near Eastern legal tradition also created tension with the documentary hypothesis, although without requiring interpreters to abandon the theory. Central to Wellhausen's thesis was that law developed late in Israelite tradition and that the oldest form of Yahwism was more charismatic and nonlegal. This hypothesis influenced the dating of the literature in the Pentateuch. Thus, for example, the more limited role of the Book of the Covenant in the J source eventually gives way to the prominent role of law and covenant in the later composition of the book of Deuteronomy and in the P source.

The comparative study of law in the ancient Near East raised two areas of tension with the documentary hypothesis. First, it became apparent that legal traditions are ancient, going back to the third millennium (e.g., the Laws of Ur-Nammu).[29] The antiquity of law in the ancient Near East called into question the developmental view of Israelite religion that undergirded the documentary hypothesis. This change in perspective is evident in A. Alt, who sought the origin of law in the premonarchical period by exploring the ancient character of Israel's legal traditions.[30] Second, the comparative study of ancient Near Eastern law also prompted scholars to detach the laws of the Pentateuch from their narrative context in order to study them as distinct genres of literature with their own oral and literary development. Alt again provides an example, with his distinction between casuistic law (or "case law") and apodictic law (or "absolute law").[31] B. Bäntsch illustrates the isolation of an entire law code from its narrative context in concluding that the Book of the Covenant was independent and only later incorporated into the E source.[32] Research on law in the Pentateuch had the same effect as the form-critical study of narrative. It tended to identify the creative formation of the law codes independently from the pentateuchal sources, transforming the authors of the sources into collectors of legal tradition. Thus, M. Noth wrote of the Book of the Covenant, "It is probable that this collection once formed an independent book of law, which has been inserted into the pentateuchal narrative as an already self-contained entity."[33]

The incomplete character of the E source

The E source remained somewhat undefined already in the work of Wellhausen, and its presence in the Pentateuch continued to be questioned by advocates of the documentary hypothesis. The E source represents the non-P stories in the Pentateuch where the divine name "Elohim" occurs.[34] It is less formulaic than P, emphasizing a prophetic interpretation of Israel's origins. Central examples in Genesis include the second episode of Abraham falsely presenting Sarah as his sister to Abimelech of Gerar (Genesis 20) and the testing of Abraham in the divine command to sacrifice Isaac (Genesis 22). Examples in Exodus through Numbers include the use of the name "Elohim" in the story of the midwives (Exod 1:15–21), the call of Moses (Exodus 3), the meeting between Moses and Jethro (Exodus 18), and the theophany at Sinai (Exodus 19). This list is not exhaustive, but it already indicates a central problem, namely, the scarcity of material in the Pentateuch that can be attributed to the Elohistic author.[35]

The limited literary basis for E has raised questions about its independence from the Yahwistic source. This was evident in Wellhausen's use of the symbol JE, and scholars have continued to debate whether there ever was an independent E source. If it existed, most of the document is now lost because the literature of J, D, and P dominates the Pentateuch. Those who favor the existence of an E source locate that document in the northern kingdom, with a time of composition around the eighth century BCE.[36] Those who reject the hypothesis interpret the E stories as additions to the J source.[37] In either case, it is possible for interpreters to suspend a decision on the strength of the documentary hypothesis simply by referring to JE as one body of literature in the Pentateuch while continuing to work within the framework of the sources.[38]

The literary scope of the sources

Interpreters debated the extent of the sources, especially whether they continue into the book of Joshua, where the conquest of the land is narrated. The central theme of the promise of land to the ancestors throughout the Pentateuch suggests that the story would continue into the account of the conquest in Joshua. Yet the language of that book creates literary problems. Wellhausen already noted that even though Joshua presupposes the Pentateuch, the character of the literature is not the same, with the book often appearing to be a supplement to the entire Pentateuch rather than a specific source.[39] In the end, Wellhausen concluded that sources J and E did include an account of the conquest of the land and that P ended in Deuteronomy. Those who agreed with Wellhausen spoke of a six-book Hexateuch (Genesis through Joshua) rather than a five-book Pentateuch (Genesis though Deuteronomy),[40] whereas others even extended the P source into the book of Joshua.[41] Martin Noth disagreed, arguing instead that the motifs in Joshua reflected only the language of Deuteronomy and not the sources in Genesis through Numbers.[42] As a result, Noth restricted the scope of the sources to Genesis through Numbers, which introduced the new term, "Tetrateuch," as setting the boundaries of J, E, and P.[43] Noth also separated Deuteronomy (D) from the Tetrateuch and combined it with the Former Prophets (Joshua, Judges, Samuel, and Kings), which formed a single body of literature that he described as the "Deuteronomistic History."[44] Even with these significant alterations, Noth continued to research within the framework of the documentary hypothesis.

The date of the Priestly source

Wellhausen's identification of P as the latest source in the Pentateuch was a linchpin in the formation of the documentary hypothesis. It provided the basis for the judgment that priestly ritual was a late development in Israelite religion. Research by Y. Kaufmann, J. Milgrom, I. Knohl, and others has demonstrated the dynamic character of ritual, law, and priestly hierarchy throughout the religious development of ancient Israel, in contrast to the position of Wellhausen, who saw the rituals of the tabernacle as wooden innovations from the exilic or post-exilic period.[45] As a consequence, Wellhausen's evaluation of the Priestly source has undergone revision, prompting some interpreters to date the P source earlier than the exilic and postexilic periods or to identify more than one Priestly source. R. E. Friedman, for example, identifies two Priestly sources while maintaining the basic structure of the documentary hypothesis: the first is a response to the Josianic reform (P[1]), and the second is a response to the exile (P[2]), which corresponds more closely to the date of Wellhausen.[46]

ALTERNATIVES TO THE DOCUMENTARY HYPOTHESIS

The documentary hypothesis was formulated in relationship to other competing theories of the formation of the Pentateuch. Already in the eighteenth century interpreters questioned whether continuous themes could be identified in sources that run throughout the Pentateuch because of the complexity of the literature. Alexander Geddes (1737–1802)[47] and J. S. Vater (1771–1826)[48] advocated a fragmentary hypothesis in which independent literary units, especially laws, were woven together to form the larger story of the Pentateuch. Heinrich Ewald (1803–75) suggested yet another hypothesis, in which a base document was supplemented by additional material.[49] Alternative theories of the composition of the Pentateuch continue into the present time. The following summary will focus on four areas of ongoing research: (1) interpretation of the present form of the Pentateuch in conjunction with its history of composition, (2) the late dating of the Yahwistic literature, (3) methodological problems surrounding the relationship between tradition history and the literary composition of the Pentateuch, and (4) reinterpretation of sources as redactions.

Interpretation of the present form of the Pentateuch

Emergence of a new literary approach to the Bible in the late twentieth century heightened tensions with the theoretical assumptions of source criticism. The starting point of the documentary hypothesis was recognition of literary repetitions, revealing contradictions in content and, in turn, allowing for identification of different authors (J, E, D, and P) who lived at different times. The narrow focus on the individual sources, however, left the present form of the Pentateuch unexplained.

The literary turn in the late twentieth century focused interpretation more intensely on the present form of the Pentateuch. In so doing, interpreters raised new questions about the function of repetition and the conflicting content of the narratives and laws in the Pentateuch. The rhetorical criticism of James Muilenburg,[50] the literary readings of Robert Alter,[51] the inner-biblical exegesis of Michael Fishbane,[52] the thematic study of the Pentateuch by David Clines,[53] and the canonical criticism of Brevard Childs[54] all located, in different ways, strategies of coherence in the biblical text that did not conform to the notions of literary unity undergirding the documentary hypothesis. These interpreters did not advocate a return to the presuppositions of the premodern period, in which the Pentateuch was assumed to have one author and one unified meaning. The multiauthored nature of the Pentateuch was assumed. But a greater focus on the late formation of the Pentateuch and its present literary design underscored how the repetition and mixing of traditions need not constitute simple contradiction but could instead function as literary devices to correlate competing texts and thus encourage multiple interpretations of the same story or law.

Often the more synchronic literary readings of the Pentateuch were undertaken independently from the diachronic focus of the documentary hypothesis so that they did not directly challenge source criticism. But they did change the nature of the discussion with regard to the techniques of composition, repetition, inner-biblical links between literature, and what constitutes the literary coherence of the Pentateuch. And these insights then had the potential to alter the documentary hypothesis. For example, David Carr argued that the divine names, Yahweh and Elohim, or the repetition of stories such as the wife-sister episodes, required both synchronic and diachronic interpretation,[55] whereas Bernard Levinson illustrated that competing laws may actually be in conversation with each other.[56] In the case of Carr, attention to the present literary design of the Pentateuch resulted in identification of only two authors in the book of Genesis (non-P and P), whereas Levinson was able to describe an exegetical tradition that correlated pentateuchal law codes by means of hermeneutical transformations.

The late date of the Yahwist

There is growing debate concerning the authorship and date of J. Throughout the modern historical-critical period, a strong consensus dated the Yahwistic source to the early monarchy. Wellhausen placed J in the ninth to eighth centuries BCE. Subsequent scholars such as Gerhard von Rad pushed the date of J to the tenth century BCE. In either case, there was agreement that ancient Israel began to write historical narrative early in the monarchical period. Scholars did raise questions of genre. Could such writing be called history, or were other categories, such as epic, myth, legend, or folklore, more appropriate?[57] Within this debate, however, there was general agreement that some form of historiography emerged during the early monarchical period, and this consensus influenced the interpretation of ancient Israelite religion. An early date for J allowed interpreters to use it as an avenue for discerning the social and religious worldview of the monarchy. It also assumed that the J source was written to support the rise of kings and the formation of the Israelite state. According to Gerhard von Rad, it reflected the "Solomonic Enlightenment."[58]

Interpreters are increasingly arguing for a later date to the Yahwistic literature. The hypothesis of Martin Noth, in which he separated the Tetrateuch from the Deuteronomistic History, has tended to provide the framework for the debate. The central arguments surround the relationship of the Yahwist literature in the Tetrateuch to Deuteronomy (D) and the Deuteronomistic History (Joshua, Judges, Samuel, and Kings). In 1970s, H. H. Schmid undertook a literary study of Yahwistic stories, terminology, and themes.[59] He concluded that there was similarity between the J literature in Genesis, Exodus, and Numbers and the prophetic themes and genres in the Deuteronomistic History (e.g., the commissioning of Moses in Exodus 3–4 is a prophetic genre repeated in Judges and Samuel). Schmid argued that the J literature was the product of the Deuteronomistic writers, who wrote during the exilic period, which accounts for the thematic emphasis on blessing, nationhood, and the promise of land. Martin Rose extended the thesis of Schmid, concluding that the J version of the Tetrateuch was written to be a prologue to the Deuteronomistic History.[60] Christoph Levin developed a similar position concerning the late date of the J literature. He identified the corpus as a post-Deuteronomistic redaction. The exilic Yahwist, according to Levin, was critical of the centralization of the cult in the book of Deuteronomy, advocating, instead, the ability of Yahweh to be present with the Diaspora Jews of the exile.[61]

John Van Seters also reinterpreted the Yahwist within the framework of Noth's separation of the Tetrateuch and the Deuteronomistic History. He, too, argued that the Tetrateuch was written to be the prologue to the Deuteronomistic History and thus was composed later than Deuteronomy and the Deuteronomistic History. This conclusion, as is also the case with Rose and Levin, reverses the literary relationship between the Tetrateuch and Deuteronomy in the documentary hypothesis.[62] Like Schmid, Van Seters focused on terminology and the relationship between Genesis, Exodus, and Numbers, on the one hand, and Deuteronomy and the Deuteronomistic History, on the other. But he has also added the comparative study of historiography to sharpen the characterization of the J prologue in the Tetrateuch as ancient history writing, concluding that J is similar to Greek historiography in the Persian period.[63]

Even though these interpreters employ the word "Yahwist" to describe the author of the Tetrateuch, their theories of the composition of the Pentateuch have nothing to do with the documentary hypothesis. The anonymous author, whether writing as a redactor or a historian, is not identified by the use of the divine name "Yahweh." The composition is not part of the social development of the monarchy under David and Solomon but is actually critical of the monarchical period. These interpreters agree that the Yahwist shares many of the perspectives found in the Deuteronomy and the Deuteronomistic History, while also providing a later reinterpretation of its central themes.

Methodological problems between tradition history and the literary composition of the Pentateuch

The question of whether continuous themes could be identified in the sources of the Pentateuch/Hextateuch has lingered throughout the modern period of interpretation, but it intensified with the emergence of form criticism and tradition history. R. Rendtorff returned to this problem in the 1970s by reevaluating the synthesis of Martin Noth and Gerhard von Rad, which had come to dominate study of the Pentateuch in the mid-twentieth century.[64] Noth's identification of the five themes in the Pentateuch (patriarchal promise, Exodus, Sinai, wilderness wandering, and land) provided the framework for Rendtorff's study, whereas the thesis of von Rad concerning the creative role of the Yahwist author in combining the themes presented the problem. Rendtorff argued that neither Noth nor von Rad had sufficiently examined how the individual stories within the five themes developed into the larger literary complexes. The reason was their dependence on Gunkel, who did not develop a methodology for discerning the dynamics of literary formation; his focus remained, instead, too general and moved too quickly from oral tradition to written sources. Thus, von Rad's assumption concerning the creative role of the Yahwist in fashioning a comprehensive story of salvation was based on tradition history without demonstrating a literary cohesion between the passages ascribed to the Yahwist.

Rendtorff's study of the intermediate formation of the traditional material indicated that the themes underwent literary development independently and were only related to each other at a later stage by collectors, not source authors. Study of the theme of the promise to the ancestors indicated its central role in Genesis but near absence in the account of the Exodus, suggesting the late combination of these bodies of literature, perhaps by Deuteronomistic tradents. Rendtorff's thesis implied breakdown of the documentary hypothesis in general and loss of the Yahwist in particular. It also suggested that the story of salvation history in the Pentateuch/Hexateuch is a very late creation in the history of ancient Israel, not earlier than the Babylonian Exile.

The hypothesis of Rendtorff has given rise to a wide range of research that is presently incomplete. Erhard Blum extended the work of Rendtorff in two studies, first on the ancestral material and then on the story of Moses. The research on the ancestral material yielded a complex history of composition, whereas the Moses story investigation resulted in a more streamlined hypothesis focused on two exilic and/or postexilic compositions: a lay-oriented work that reflected themes from the book of Deuteronomy and the Deuteronomistic History ("D-Komposition" [KD]) and a priestly oriented work that included the traditional literature of the P source ("P-Komposition" [KP]).[65] These independent documents were combined in the Persian period to form the Pentateuch. Joseph Blenkinsopp's identification of a Deuteronomic corpus and a Priestly stratum of literature, which were combined in the Persian period, also corresponds to many aspects of Blum's hypothesis.[66]

Study of the individual complexes of the Pentateuch has also continued beyond the ancestral literature. Marcus Witte has researched the independent development of Genesis 1–11.[67] Thomas Dozeman investigated the formation of the Exodus and the Sinai material within Deuteronomistic and Priestly tradition.[68] Albert de Pury and Thomas Römer have argued that the combination of different complexes is first evident in the Priestly source and not in the KD of Blum, thus pushing formation of the Pentateuch to an even later date.[69] Konrad Schmid has advanced a similar argument by identifying the book of Genesis as an origin tradition distinct from the story of Moses and the Exodus, making the relationship of Genesis to Exodus through Kings a significant development in formation of the Pentateuch (now conceived as a nine-book collection, or "Enneateuch").[70] A common thread throughout the different interpretations is an abandonment of the documentary hypothesis and a later dating of the pentateuchal literature to the exilic and postexilic periods.

Reinterpretation of sources as redactions

The role of redactors to combine distinct sources was a central feature in the documentary hypothesis. Wellhausen, for example, attributed the combination of the J and E sources to a "Yehowist" redactor. Subsequent interpreters have begun to attribute a more prominent role to redactors, which over time has intensified conflict with the documentary hypothesis. Identification of extensive redactions left only minimal literature that could be assigned to the traditional sources, as in the work of Lothar Perlitt, who attributed large portions of the narrative and law in Exodus 19–34 to Deuteronomistic redactors rather than to the J and E sources.[71] The combination of sources and extensive redactions also resulted in complex theories of composition, such as Erich Zenger's identification of successive stages of narrative cycles from the monarchical period as reflecting multiple revisions, including the incorporation of law codes in the "Exilic Historical Work" and the further additions of the P source and Deuteronomy in the "Exilic History."[72]

Interpreters are increasingly limiting or abandoning the sources of the documentary hypothesis and attributing the entire composition of the Pentateuch to redactors. Christoph Levin identifies the Yahwist as an exilic editor or redactor who fashioned literary fragments into the foundational document of the Tetrateuch. Frank M. Cross argues that the Priestly tradition was not a source but a supplement to early non-Priestly tradition because of the incomplete character of the narrative.[73] Jean-Louis Ska agrees with Cross while adding that P is not simply a supplement to early literature but a more critical revision.[74]

Many interpreters are beginning to attribute a significant role to post-Priestly redactor(s) in the composition of the Pentateuch. This interpretation represents a reversal of the documentary hypothesis. In this view, the P source is not judged to be the last source but the first to provide the basic structure of the Pentateuch. The P source undergoes expansion and revision by post-Priestly authors, who merge the language of Deuteronomy and the Priestly source. Thomas Römer, Konrad Schmid, and Jan Christian Geertz attribute a significant role to the post-Priestly redactor in the composition of the Pentateuch and the Former Prophets.[75] Eckart Otto and Reinhard Achenbach provide an even more nuanced description of the post-Priestly composition of the Pentateuch and Joshua, which includes three redactions: a hextateuchal redaction that is inclusive, prophetic, and focused on the land; a pentateuchal redaction that emphasizes Torah; and a theocratic redaction that identifies Israel as a people organized around the temple.[76] Although the research on the post-Priestly composition of the Pentateuch/Hexateuch/ Enneateuch is ongoing and includes significant variation, the effect of the research is to push the composition of the literature even later, from the monarchical and exilic periods into the late Persian period.

SUMMARY

This review has sought to demonstrate the dynamic and incomplete character of the research on the Pentateuch. Debate over its formation, genre, and the best description of its anonymous author(s) is far from settled. Interpreters continue to argue both for sources and for a process of supplementation to account for the formation of the Pentateuch. Yet there is also a trend toward progressively later dating of the Pentateuch, which will undoubtedly have implications for interpreting Israelite religion and the formation of the canon. Early historical critics disputed the historical presentation of the Mosaic age. The loss of the Yahwist of the Solomonic Enlightenment has prompted contemporary interpreters to dispute the biblical portrait of the monarchical period, especially the united monarchy[77] but also the social circumstances of the Exile.[78] The later dating of the Pentateuch suggests further that the creative era for the emergence of the Yahwism represented in the Torah is a postexilic accomplishment, not a monarchical achievement, which is prompting scholars to explore more carefully the formation of the Pentateuch in the Persian and even the Hellenistic periods.[79]

NOTES

1   R. Knierim, *The Task of Old Testament Theology: Substance, Method, and Cases* (Grand Rapids, MI: Eerdmans, 1996), 351–79.

2   See C. Houtman, *Der Pentateuch: Die Geschichte seiner Erforschung neben einer Auswertung* (CBET 9; Kampen, Netherlands: Pharos, 1994), 22–7; and J. Blenkinsopp, *The Pentateuch: An Introduction to the First Five Books of the Bible* (ABRL; New York: Doubleday, 1992), 2–3.

3   For discussion of *sola scriptura* as it developed in Martin Luther's Leipzig Disputation of 1519 and subsequently through Calvin, see H.-J. Kraus, *Geschichte der historisch-kritischen Erforschung des Alten Testaments* (Neukirchen-Vluyn, Germany: Neukirchener Verlag, 1969), 6–9.

4   Ibid., 6.

5   J. Calvin, *The Last Four Books of Moses in the Form of a Harmony I*, trans. by C. W. Bingham (Grand Rapids, MI: Eerdmans, 1950), xiv.

6   J. Calvin, *The First Book of Moses Called Genesis I*, trans. by J. King (Grand Rapids, MI: Eerdmans, 1948), 58–9.

7   Calvin, *Last Four Books of Moses I*, 29.

8   Calvin, *Genesis I*, 109.

9   B. de Spinoza, *A Theologico-Political Treatise Containing Certain Discussions Wherein Is Set Forth that Freedom of Thought and Speech Not Only May, Without Prejudice to Piety and the Public Peace, Be Granted; But Also May Not, Without Danger to Piety and the Public Peace, be Withheld*, trans. by R. H. M. Elwes (New York: Dover, 1951), 7.

10 Ibid., 120, 126.
11 Ibid., 124.
12 Ibid., 120.
13 Ibid.,
14 Ibid., 101–3.
15 J. Astruc, *Conjectures sur les mémoires originaux dont il paroit que Moyse s'est servi pour composer le livre de la Génèse. Avec des remarques, qui appuient ou qui éclairissent ces conjectures* (Brussels, 1753). See E. O'Doharty, "The Conjectures of Jean Astruc, 1753," *CBQ* 76 (1953): 300–4.
16 W. M. L. de Wette, *Dissertatio critico-exegetica qua Deuteronomium a prioribus Pentateuchi Libris diversum, alius cuiusdam recentioris auctoris opus esse monstratur; quam ... auctoritate amplissimi philosophorum ordinis pro venia legendi AD XXVII* (Jena, 1805); and *Beiträge zur Einleitung in das Alte Testament* (Halle, 1806–7). See J. W. Rogerson, *W. M. L. de Wette Founder of Modern Biblical Criticism: An Intellectual Biography* (JSOTSup 126; Sheffield Academic Press, 1992).
17 For a summary of the language in the book of Deuteronomy, see M. Weinfeld, *Deuteronomy and the Deuteronomic School* (Oxford University Press, 1972).
18 J. Wellhausen describes de Wette as "the epoch-making pioneer of historical criticism" (*Prolegomena to the History of Israel*, trans. by J. S. Black and A. Menzie from the German 6th ed. [Atlanta: Scholars Press, 1994], 4–5).
19 See F. Crüsemann, *The Torah: Theology and Social History of Old Testament Law*, trans. by A. W. Mahnke (Minneapolis, MN: Fortress/Augsburg, 1996); E. Otto, *Wandel der Rechtsbegründungen in der Gesellschaftsgeschichte des Antiken Israel: eine Rechtsgeschichte des "Bundesbuches" Ex XX 22 – XXIII 13* (StudBib 3; Leiden, Netherlands: Brill, 1988); and B. W. Levinson, *Deuteronomy and the Hermeneutics of Legal Innovation* (New York: Oxford University Press, 1997). Compare J. Van Seters, *A Law Book for the Diaspora: Revision in the Study of the Covenant Code* (New York: Oxford: 2002).
20 J. G. Eichhorn, *Einleitung ins Alte Testament* (Leipzig, Germany: Weidmann, 1780–3).
21 C. D. Ilgen, *Die Urkunden des Jerusalemischen Tempelarchivs in ihrer Urgestalt also Beytrag zur Berichtigung der Geschichte der Religion und Politik aus dem Hebräischen mit kritischen und erklärenden Anmerkungen, auch mancherley dazu gehörigen Abhandlungen Theil I: Die Urkunden des ersten Buchs von Moses* (Halle, Germany: Hemmerde und Schwetschke, 1798).
22 H. Hupfeld, *Die Quellen der Genesis und die Art ihrer Zusammensetzung* (Berlin: Wiegandt und Grieben, 1853).
23 J. Wellhausen, *Die Composition des Hexateuchs und der Historischen Bücher des Alten Testament*, 3rd ed. (Berlin: Georg Reimer, 1899); and *Prolegomena to the History of Ancient Israel*. See D. A. Knight, *Julius Wellhausen and His Prolegomena to the History of Israel* (Semeia 25; Chico, CA: Scholars Press, 1983).
24 For discussion of the research on the Priestly source, see T. Pola, *Die ursprüngliche Priesterschrift: Beobachtungen zur Literarkritik*

und Traditionsgeschichte von Pg (WMANT 70; Neukirchen-Vluyn, Germany: Neukirchener, 1995). For a summary of the language and style of the Priestly source, see S. E. McEvenue, *The Narrative Style of the Priestly Writer* (Analecta Biblica 50; Rome: Biblical Institute, 1971).

25   For a summary of the sources of the Pentateuch, see O. Eissfeldt, *The Old Testament: An Introduction* (Oxford, UK: Basil Blackwell, 1965).

26   H. Gunkel, *Genesis*, 3rd ed. (Göttingen: Vandenhoeck & Ruprecht, 1910). See W. Klatt, *Hermann Gunkel: zu seiner Theologie der Religionsgeschichte und zur Entstehung der formgeschichtlichen Methode* (Göttingen, Germany: Vandenhoeck und Ruprecht, 1969); and M. A. Sweeney and E. Ben Zvi, eds., *The Changing Face of Form Criticism for the Twenty-First Century* (Grand Rapids, MI: Eerdmans, 2003).

27   See I. Engnell, *A Rigid Scrutiny: Critical Essays on the Old Testament*, trans. by John T. Willis (Nashville, TN: Vanderbilt University Press, 1969); and D. A. Knight, *Rediscovering the Traditions of Israel: The Development of the Traditio-Historical Research of the Old Testament, with Special Consideration of Scandinavian Contributions* (SBLDS 9; Missoula, MT: Society of Biblical Literature, 1973).

28   G. von Rad, "The Form-Critical Problem of the Hexateuch," in *The Problem of the Hexateuch and Other Essays* trans. by E. W. T. Dicken (New York: McGraw-Hill, 1966) 1–78; and M. Noth, *A History of Pentateuchal Traditions*, trans. by B. W. Anderson (Chico, CA: Scholars Press, 1981).

29   M. T. Roth, *Law Collections from Mesopotamia and Asia Minor*, 2nd ed. (SBLWAW 6; Atlanta: Scholars Press, 1997).

30   A. Alt, *Essays on Old Testament History and Religion*, trans. by R. A. Wilson (Oxford, UK: Basil Blackwell, 1966).

31   A. Alt, "The Origins of Israelite Law," in ibid., 79–132.

32   B. Bäntsch, *Das Bundesbuch: Exod. xx 22-xxiii 33. Seine ursprüngliche Gestalt, sein Verhältnis zu den es umgebenden Quellschriften und seine Stellung in der alttestamentlichen Gesetzgebung* (Halle, Germany: Max Niemeyer, 1892).

33   M. Noth, *Exodus*, trans. by J. S. Bowden (OTL; Philadelphia: Westminster Press, 1962) 173.

34   See A. W. Jenks, *The Elohist and North Israelite Traditions* (ABLMS 22; Missoula, MT: Scholars Press, 1977); and A. Graupner, *Der Elohist: Gegenwart und Wirksamkeit des transzendenten Gottes in der Geschichte* (WMANT 97; Neukirchen-Vluyn, Germany: Neukirchener, 2002).

35   See, however, the extensive identification of the E source in the book of Exodus by W. Propp, *Exodus 1–18* (AB 2A; New York: Doubleday, 1999).

36   H. W. Wolff, "The Elohistic Fragments in the Pentateuch," in *The Vitality of Old Testament Traditions*, 2nd., ed. by W. Brueggemann and H. W. Wolff (Atlanta: John Knox Press, 1982) 67–82.

37   W. Rudolph, *Der "Elohist" von Exodus bis Josua* (BZAW 68; Berlin: A. Töpelmann, 1938).

38   See B. A. Levine, *Numbers 1–20* (AB 4A; New York: Doubleday, 1993); and H. Seebass, *Numeri 10,11-22,1* (BKAT IV/2; Neukirchen-Vluyn, Germany: Neukirchener, 2003).

39 Wellhausen, *Composition*, 118–36.

40 See O. Eissfeldt, *Hexateuch-Synopse: die Erzählung der fünf Bücher Mose und des Buches Josua mit dem Anfange des Richterbuches in ihre vier Quellen zerlegt und in deutscher Übersetzung dargeboten samt einer in Einleitung und Anmerkungen gegebenen Begründung* (Leipzig, Germany: Hinrich, 1922).

41 See N. Lohfink, "Priesterschift und die Geschichte," in *Congress Volume: Göttingen, 1977*, ed. by W. Zimmerli VTSup 29; Leiden, Netherlands: Brill, 1978), 189–255; J. Blenkinsopp, "The Structure of P," *CBQ* 38 (1976): 275–92; and E. Cortese, *Josua 13–21: ein priesterschriftlicher Abschnitt im deuteronomistischen Geschichtswerk* (OBO 94. Göttingen, Germany: Vandenhoeck und Ruprecht, 1990).

42 M. Noth, *Das Buch Josua*, 2nd ed. (HAT 7; Tübingen, Germany: Mohr Siebeck, 1971).

43 M. Noth, *A History of Pentateuchal Traditions*, trans. by B. W. Anderson Chico, CA: Scholars Press, 1981).

44 M. Noth, *Überlieferungsgeschichtliche Studien I: die sammelnden und bearbeitenden Geschichtswerke im Alten Testament*, 2nd ed. (Tübingen, Germany: Mohr Siebeck, 1957). The English translation of Part 1, *The Deuteronomistic History* (JSOTSup 15; Sheffield Academic Press, 1981).

45 Y. Kaufmann, *The Religion of Israel: From its Beginnings to the Babylonian Exile*, trans. and abridged by M. Greenberg (University of Chicago Press, 1960); J. Milgrom, *Leviticus 1–16* (Anchor Bible 3A; New York: Doubleday, 1991); and I. Knohl, *The Sanctuary of Silence: The Priestly Torah and the Holiness School* (Minneapolis, MN: Fortress Press, 1995). See also M. Haran, *Temples and Temple-Service in Ancient Israel: An Inquiry into the Character of Cult Phenomena and the Historical Setting of the Priestly School* (Oxford, UK: Clarendon Press, 1978).

46 R. E. Friedman, *Who Wrote the Bible?* (San Francisco: Harper, 1987).

47 A. Geddes, *The Holy Bible or the Books Accounted Sacred by Jews and Christians: Otherwise Called the Books of the Old and New Covenants: Faithfully Translated from Corrected Texts of the Originals with Various Readings, Explanatory Notes and Notes and Critical Remarks, Vol. I (Pentateuch and Joshua)* (London: J. Davis, 1792); Geddes, *Critical Remarks on the Hebrew Scriptures: Corresponding with a New Translation of the Bible*, Vol. I: *Containing Remarks on the Pentateuch* (London: Davis, Wilks, and Taylor, 1800).

48 J. Severin Vater, *Commentar über den Pentateuch, mit Einleitungen zu den einzelnen Abschnitten der eingeschalteten Übersetzung von Dr. A. Geddes merkwürdigen critischen und exegetischen Anmerkungen und einer Abhandlung über Mose und die Verfasser des Pentateuchs*, Vols. I–III (Halle, Germany: Waisenhaus Buchhandlung, 1802–5).

49 H. G. A. Ewald, *Die Komposition der Genesis: Kritisch untersucht* (Braunschweig, Germany: Ludwig Lucius, 1823).

50 J. Muilenburg, "Form Criticism and Beyond," *JBL* 88 (1969): 1–18.

51 R. Alter, *The Art of Biblical Narrative* (New York: Basic Books, 1981).

52 M. A. Fishbane, *Biblical Interpretation in Ancient Israel* (Oxford University Press, 1985).

53 D. J. A. Clines, *The Theme of the Pentateuch* (JSOTSup 10; Sheffield Academic Press, 1999).

54 B. S. Childs, *Introduction to the Old Testament as Scripture* (Philadelphia: Fortress, 1979).

55 D. M. Carr, *Reading the Fractures of Genesis* (Louisville, KY: Westminster John Knox, 1996).

56 Levinson, *Deuteronomy and the Hermeneutics of Legal Innovation.*

57 J. W. Rogerson, *Myth in Old Testament Interpretation* (BZAW 134; Berlin: de Gruyter, 1974).

58 See von Rad, *The Problem of the Hextateuch and Other Essays;* and H. W. Wolff, "The Kerygma of the Yahwist," in *Vitality of Old Testament Traditions,* 41–66.

59 H. H. Schmid, *Der sogenannte Jahwist: Beobachtungen und Fragen zur Pentateuchforschung* (Zurich: Theologischer Verlag, 1976).

60 M. Rose, *Deuteronomist und Jahwist: Untersuchungen zu den Berührungspunkten beider Literaturwerke* (ATANT 67; Zurich: Theologischer Verlag, 1981).

61 C. Levin, *Der Jahwist* (FRLANT 157; Göttingen, Germany: Vandenhoeck & Ruprecht, 1993).

62 J. Van Seters, *Prologue to History: The Yahwist as Historian in Genesis* (Louisville, KY: Westminster John Knox, 1992), and *The Life of Moses: The Yahwist as Historian in Exodus-Numbers* (Louisville, KY: Westminster John Knox, 1994).

63 J. Van Seters, *In Search of History: Historiography in the Ancient World and the Origins of Biblical History* (New Haven, CT: Yale University Press, 1983).

64 R. Rendtorff, *Das überlieferungsgeschichtliche Problem des Pentateuch* (BZAW 147; Berlin: de Gruyter, 1977). English translation: *The Problem of the Process of the Transmission in the Pentateuch,* trans. by J. J. Scullion (JSOTSup 89; Sheffield, UK: JSOT Press, 1990).

65 E. Blum, *Die Komposition der Vätergeschichte* (WMANT 57; Neukirchen-Vluyn, Germany: Neukirchener, 1984), and *Studien zur Komposition des Pentateuch* (BZAW 189; Berlin: de Gruyter, 1990).

66 Blenkinsopp, *The Pentateuch.*

67 M. Witte, *Die biblische Urgeschichte: redaktions- und theologiegeschichtliche Beobachtungen zu Genesis 1, 1–11, 26* (BZAW 265; Berlin: de Gruyter, 1998).

68 T. B. Dozeman, *God on the Mountain: A Study of Redaction, Theology and Canon in Exodus 19–24* (SBLMS 37; Atlanta: Scholars Press, 1989), and *God at War: Power in the Exodus Tradition* (New York: Oxford University Press, 1996).

69 A. de Pury, "Situer le cycle de Jacob: Quelques réflexions, vingt-cinq ans plus tard," in *Studies in the Book of Genesis: Literature, Redaction and History,* ed. by A. Wénin (BETL 155; Leuven: Leuven University Press/Peeters, 2001), 213–41; and T. Römer, *Israels Väter: Untersuchungen zur Väterthematik im Deuteronomium und in der deuteronomistischen Tradition* (OBO 99; Fribourg, Germany: Universitäts Verlag, 1990).

70   K. Schmid, *Erzväter und Exodus: Untersuchungen zur doppelten Begründung der Ursprünge Israels innerhalb der Geschichtsbücher des Alten Testaments* (WMANT 81; Neukirchen-Vluyn, Germany: Neukirchener, 1999). See also T. B. Dozeman and K. Schmid, eds., *A Farewell to the Yahwist? The Composition of the Pentateuch in Recent European Interpretation* (Symposium Series 34; Atlanta: Scholars Press, 2006).

71   L. Perlitt, *Bundestheologie im Alten Testament* (WMANT 36; Neukirchen-Vluyn, Germany: Neukirchener, 1969).

72   E. Zenger, *Die Sinaitheophanie* (FB 3; Würzburg, Germany: Echter Verlage, 1971).

73   F. M. Cross, *Canaanite Myth and Hebrew Epic: Essays in the History of Religion* (Cambridge, MA: Harvard University Press, 1973).

74   J-. L. Ska, "Quelques remarques sur Pg et la derniére rédaction du pentateuque," in *Le pentateuque en question: Les origines et la composition des cinq premiers livres de la Bible à la lumiére des recherches récentes*, ed. by A. de Pury et al. (MdB; Genève: Labor et Fides, 1989), 95–125, and "De la relative indépendance de l'écrit sacerdotal," *Bib* 76 (1995): 396–415.

75   Römer, *Israels Väter*; Schmid, *Erzväter und Exodus*; J. C. Gertz, *Tradition und Redaktion in der Exoduserzählung: Untersuchungen zur Endredaktion des Pentateuch* (FRLANT 186; Göttingen: Vandenhoeck und Ruprecht, 2000). See also J. C. Gertz, K. Schmid, and M. Witte, eds., *Abschied vom Jahwisten: Die Kompostion des Hexateuch in der jüngsten Diskussion* (BZAW 315; Berlin: de Gruyter, 2000).

76   E. Otto, "Die nachpriesterschriftliche Pentateuchredaktion im Buch Exodus," in *Studies in the Book of Exodus*, ed. by M. Vervenne (BETL 126; Leuven, Netherlands: Leuven University Press, 1996), 61–111, and *Das Deuteronomium im Pentateuch und Hexateuch: Studien zur Literaturgeschichte von Pentateuch und Hexateuch im Lichte des Deuteronomiumrahmens* (FAT 30; Tübingen, Germany: Mohr Siebeck, 2000); and R. Achenbach, *Die Vollendung der Tora: Studien zur Redaktionsgeschichte des Numeribuches im Kontext von Hextateuch und Pentateuch* (BZABR 3; Wiesbaden, Germany: Harrassowitz, 2002).

77   See T. L. Thompson, *Early History of the Israelite People: From the Written and Archaeological Sources* (Studies in the History of the Ancient Near East 4; Leiden, Netherlands: Brill, 1992).

78   L. L. Grabbe, ed., *Leading Captivity Captive: 'The Exile' as History and Ideology* (Journal of the Study of the Old Testament Supplement 278; European Seminar in Historical Methodology 2; Sheffield Academic Press, 1998).

79   G. N. Knoppers and B. M. Levinson, eds., *The Pentateuch as Torah: New Models for Understanding Its Promulgation and Acceptance* (Winona Lake, IN: Eisenbrauns, 2008).

FURTHER READING

Blenkinsopp, J. *The Pentateuch: An Introduction to the First Five Books of the Bible* (ABRL). New York: Doubleday, 1992.

Campbell, A. F. and M. A. O'Brien. *Sources of the Pentateuch: Texts, Introductions, Annotations.* Minneapolis, MN: Fortress Press, 1993.

Crüsemann, F. *The Torah: Theology and History of Old Testament Law.* Translated by A. W. Mahnke. Minneapolis, MN: Fortress, 1996.

Eissfeldt, O. *The Old Testament: An Introduction.* Translated by P. R. Ackroyd. New York: Harper & Row, 1965.

Houtman, C. *Der Pentateuch: die Geschichte seiner Erforschung neben einer Auswertung* (CBET 9). Kampen, Netherlands: Pharos, 1994.

Levinson, B. M., ed. *Theory and Method in Biblical and Cuneiform Law: Revision, Interpolation and Development* (JSOTSup 181). Sheffield Academic Press, 1994.

Pury, A. de and T. Römer, eds. *Le pentateuque en question: Les origines et la composition des cinq premiers livres de la Bible à la lumiére des recherches récentes.* MdB. Geneva: Labor et Fides, 1989.

Ska, J.-L. *Introduction to Reading the Pentateuch.* Winona Lake, IN: Eisenbrauns, 2006.

10   The Former Prophets and historiography

RICHARD D. NELSON

The books of the Former Prophets tell a connected history-like story. Beginning with triumphal conquest (Joshua), the story moves through premonarchic disorder (Judges) and the emergence of kingship (1 and 2 Samuel), to a moralizing description of the deeds of the kings of Israel and Judah, and finally to the catastrophic collapse of each kingdom (1 and 2 Kings). For the most part, this story is told and evaluated from a perspective derived from Deuteronomy. Despite the unity provided by thematic and chronological linkages, however, the final form of each of the four books also has its own authenticity as an independent literary work.

CONNECTIONS AND DIVISIONS

The connected narrative of the Former Prophets is established by plot linkages between the four books (and back to narratives reported in Deuteronomy), by the intermittent appearance of linguistic features rooted in the book of Deuteronomy, by an evolution of common themes, and by the binding force of pervasive structural patterns. The most evident book-to-book linkages include

- Initiation in Deuteronomy of subjects that later unfold in Joshua: Joshua's task (Deut 1:38; 3:28; 31:3, 7; Josh 1:2–9), Canaanite fear (Deut 2:25; Josh 2:9–12), tribes east of the Jordan (Deut 3:18–20; Josh 1:12–15), and the death of the wilderness generation (Deut 1:35; 2:14–16; Josh 5:4–7).
- From Deuteronomy 31:7–8; 34:1–6 to Joshua 1:1–9 (transition from Moses to Joshua).
- From Joshua 24:29–31 to Judges 2:6–10 (death of Joshua and dismissal of the national assembly).
- From Judges 13:1, 5; 15:20; 16:31 (Samson begins to deliver the Israelites from the Philistines for twenty of their forty-year

oppression) to 1 Samuel 4:1–7:2 (further oppression by them) and then to 1 Samuel 7:7–14 (victorious exploits of Samuel).

- From 2 Samuel 15–20 to 1 Kings 1 (sequential insurgencies of Absalom, Sheba, and Adonijah).

Language and theology echoing Deuteronomy also provide connecting factors among these books. Deuteronomistic language is concentrated at points of theological commentary such as Joshua 1 and 23, 1 Samuel 12, 1 Kings 8, and 2 Kings 17. However, it is also extensively distributed in smaller interpretive units such as Joshua 2:10–11, Judges 2:7–23 and 10:6–8, 1 Kings 2:2–4, and the summary judgments on the kings of Israel and Judah. (Deuteronomistic language is markedly less visible in Samuel than elsewhere.) However, this does not mean that every element of Deuteronomy's theology is faithfully reproduced, especially with regard to kingship and the legitimacy of pre-Solomonic altars.[1]

Themes common to these four books include flawed (as opposed to faithful) leadership, religious apostasy, and the law of Moses. There is repeated emphasis on divine promise, punishment, and deliverance.

Structural unity is provided by a pattern of theologizing summaries that mark major shifts in Israel's situation: Joshua 1 (conquest), Joshua 23 (postconquest situation), 1 Samuel 12 (kingship), 1 Kings 8 (temple), 2 Samuel 7 (Davidic dynasty), and 2 Kings 17 (destruction of the Northern Kingdom). Chronology is a second factor holding the overall story together. The 480 years from the Exodus to the start of Temple construction (1 Kgs 6:1) is reflected in chronological notices in Deuteronomy, Joshua, Judges, and Samuel. Overlapping this pattern is a chronology of kings that begins with Saul and David (1 Sam 13:1; 2 Sam 5:4; 1 Kgs 2:11) and dominates the book of Kings. A third unifying element is the forecast of some event and its subsequent occurrence in a later book (Josh 6:26 and 1 Kgs 16:34 [textually uncertain]; 1 Sam 2:27–36 and 1 Kgs 2:27; 2 Sam 7:13 and 1 Kgs 8:20).

At the same time, each of these four books has an independent final form as a self-contained unit. Material inserted at the end or beginning of the books breaks the connections noted earlier and demonstrates their later independent transmission.

- Judges 1:1–2:5 (successful and unsuccessful conquest)
- Judges 17–21 ("no king in Israel")
- 2 Samuel 21–4 (chiastic unit concerning David)

Joshua and Judges are clearly delineated by topic and begin with introductory formulas ("after the death of"). Samuel begins by introducing a new major character. The start of Kings is less natural and obvious. Evidence from the Septuagint and Josephus indicates that some transmission traditions began the book at 1 Kings 2:12. Masoretic tradition considered Samuel and Kings as single books, recognizing that no change of topic or narrative interruption divides 1 Samuel from 2 Samuel or 1 Kings from 2 Kings. Septuagintal tradition instead acknowledged the larger narrative unity by treating Samuel-Kings as a single entity (Reigns) divided into four books. The associated subdivision of Samuel and Kings in Christian (and eventually Jewish) practice recognizes that the dividing formula "after the death of" (from Josh 1:1 and Judg 1:1) is echoed in 2 Samuel 1:1 and 2 Kings 1:1.

The relationship of the Former Prophets to the Pentateuch or Tetrateuch is a vexing issue. Because their connection to Deuteronomy is so strong (something especially true of Joshua), the question has to do with the original function of Deuteronomy as either the last book of a Pentateuch or an independent new start after a Tetrateuch. Deuteronomy does not really advance the Genesis-Numbers story but leaves Israel exactly where it had been at the end of Numbers – on the plains of Moab with the promise of the land unfulfilled. An important question is whether a D source occurs in the Tetrateuch, particularly in Exodus. In any case, the *present* forms of both Deuteronomy and Joshua have conclusions designed to integrate them into the preceding books (Deut 34:10–12; Josh 24:2–10).

DEUTERONOMISTIC HISTORY

Biblical scholarship speaks of the unity of Deuteronomy and the Former Prophets under the rubric "Deuteronomistic History" (DH). The thesis of a large-scale historiographic work influenced by the theology of Deuteronomy has been vigorously debated, especially in regard to composition, sources, social setting, and date. The phrase "Deuteronomistic History" communicates scholarly conviction about four points. First, some more or less unified compositional process, inspired by the ideology of Deuteronomy, produced an extended account of Israel's life in the land. Whether one should think of an author, one or more editors, or a scribal school behind this process is a matter of contention. Second, the absence of Deuteronomistic language from large expanses of text (along with literary connections and purposes on a scale smaller than that of the Former Prophets as a whole) indicates the use of prior sources. The extent and date of any such sources is controversial, however, as is the degree to which any such sources are historically trustworthy. Third, this far-reaching literary undertaking was impelled by some significant event or crisis. Sharp controversy swirls around whether this critical compositional moment was the reform of Josiah (or Hezekiah) or the defeat and exile by the Babylonians. Fourth, internal inconsistencies in perspective and theme (or at least emphasis) cause most scholars to propose various revisions or additions to an original core. No agreement exists as to whether this core was preexilic or exilic. Some point to revisions triggered by Babylonian exile; others, to Persian imperialism. Still others judge that later supplements and revisions were caused not so much by national crisis as by the successive layering of varying theological interests, specifically torah piety and prophetic principles.

Revisions to the original hypothesis of a single, exilic DH (Martin Noth, 1943) emerged in the 1970s and have flourished and diversified since the 1980s.[2] Two competing approaches have dominated discussion, the *block model* and the *layer model*. Layer-model advocates (sometimes called the "Göttingen School") postulate that two supplementary redactions took place after the foundational work of an exilic historian and that these can be traced throughout the base text as insertions and overlays. Initially, Rudolph Smend distinguished one or more DtrN (N = "nomistic") layers emphasizing obedience to law and added in order to prevent a loss of identity in the alien environment of exile. Walter Dietrich subsequently located an earlier layer with an interest in prophecy (DtrP). In the layer model, then, the decisive motivations leading to redaction are all situated in the Exile, and individual themes (law and prophets) are consigned to consecutive literary strata. Advocates of the block model (initially advanced by Frank Cross) explain irregularities in DH by postulating that the work of a preexilic historian (termed Dtr[1]) was later carried forward and revised by an exilic editor (Dtr[2]). Dtr[1] is usually dated in or shortly after Josiah's reign and is thought to provide support for his policies. Alternative forms of the theory point to Hezekiah's reform either as the date of initial composition or as a later but still preexilic author's point of focus. Block-model theorists propose updating and rewriting in the Exile to convert a basically optimistic history into a reflection on defeat and exile.

New approaches continue to be suggested. Recently, Thomas Römer has formulated a compromise between competing compositional models by advocating a three-stage process. In the first stage, royal scribes in the neo-Assyrian period produced a library of shorter scrolls. Among these was a propagandistic version of Samuel-Kings that underscored Josiah's Davidic legitimacy. Another was a version of Deuteronomy-Joshua emphasizing Judah's possession of its land, based in part on Assyrian models. In a second stage, these individual documents were linked together into a "Deuteronomistic History" intended to come to terms with the crisis of defeat and exile. Speeches or editorial discourses from a Deuteronomistic perspective organized this work. A third stage continued redaction into the Persian period, stressing segregation, monotheism, and integration of the exilic community.[3]

Marvin Sweeney proposes a different three-stage model. A Hezekiah-era DtrH culminated with 2 Kings 18–20, as evidenced by changes in the regnal formulas in Kings and correlation of the leadership theme in Judges with pro-Hezekiah ideology. During the reign of Josiah, the work was edited and expanded. This Josianic DH included 2 Samuel 10–12, which casts aspersions on David and thus celebrates Josiah by contrast. Finally, an exilic edition of DH took the form of a history of the Davidic monarchy's fate in order to explain the demise of the dynasty. This exilic DH used Athaliah's incorporation of the Omri/Ahab heritage into Judahite dynastic succession to contend that the doom predicted by Elijah on Omri's house eventually led to the downfall of the house of David.[4]

There is no generally accepted solution to the problem of the composition of DH. Some see this as a fatal embarrassment to the whole theory. However, a *somewhat* unified DH, perhaps produced over several generations, seems to be the only logical way to account for pervasive Deuteronomistic language and perspectives, the use of inherited source materials, and linkages connecting Deuteronomy through 2 Kings.

SOURCES

The question of what sources DH may have incorporated continues to be of interest. Previously, a generally accepted list would have included

- A pre-Deuteronomistic collection of conquest narratives within Joshua 2–11 using fearful enemy reaction and the figure of Joshua to systematize individual stories into a unified conquest of Canaan.
- Possibly a book of premonarchic deliverers ("judges" in DH's parlance).
- An Ark of the Covenant story (1 Samuel 4–6; 2 Samuel 6) describing the ark's itinerary up to its installation in Jerusalem.
- A Rise of David narrative (1 Sam 16:14–2 Sam 5:12) coordinating stories about David and Saul to affirm that David was God's choice.
- A Succession Narrative (2 Samuel 9–2 Kings 2) recounting family struggles and palace intrigues leading to Solomon's accession.

- An Elijah-Elisha cycle (1 Kings 17–19, 21; 2 Kings 1–8).
- Three (annalistic or historiographic) sources cited in Kings (1 Kgs 11:41; 14:29; 15:31).

A different way of understanding DH's source material is offered by Antony Campbell, who theorizes that a connected "Prophetic Record" lies behind much of 1 and 2 Samuel and 1 Kings up to 2 Kings 10:28. This document chronicled the prophetic guidance of Israel's destiny up to the reform of Jehu.[4] Yet another approach is Graeme Auld's proposal of a "Book of Two Houses," traceable in a supposed common-source text shared by Samuel-Kings and Chronicles. This ran from the death of Saul to the removal of Jehoiachin.[5]

The hypothesis of a "succession history" has fared poorly in recent scholarship. There is no longer agreement that such a source ever existed. On the one hand, one cannot deny a substantial cohesiveness of style and plot, especially in 2 Samuel 13–20. Although there is a wide narrative gap between the revolt of Sheba (2 Samuel 20) and the jump to David as an old man in 1 Kings 1–2, the similarities between Adonijah and Absalom (2 Sam 15:1; 1 Kgs 1:5–6) remain a telling sign of unity. The most serious problem is that the so-called succession history has no real beginning. Starting with Michal's childlessness (2 Sam 6:23) would seem to require the inclusion of the Ark of the Covenant story, which has its own independent plot and different ideological interests. Second Samuel 7:11b, 16 introduces the topic of succession, but the chapter as a whole has other interests, and these particular verses are most likely Deuteronomistic. Succession hovers in the background of 2 Samuel 9 (David's generosity to Mephibosheth), but the concern here is really David's inheritance of Saul's house and not David's eventual successor. Succession plays no role in chapter 10, which seems abrupt and off topic, yet the situation described is needed to set up the Bathsheba episode leading to Solomon. The Bathsheba affair itself is framed in a self-contained way by 11:1 and 12:26–31, yet is set into the military situation of chapter 10.

The problem of the beginning of a supposed succession narrative is compounded by the constant assumption that the reader is conversant with previous material. One can hardly start a narrative with 2 Samuel 11:1! What is "the year" referred to? Who is Joab? As the story unfolds, other figures such as Abishai, Abiathar, and Zadok suddenly appear. Can the reader really understand the incident with Mephibosheth in chapter 9 without reference to the friendship between David and Jonathan? The "Sons of Zeruiah" motif of 19:22 requires the background narrated in 1 Samuel 26:6–8 and 2 Samuel 2:18–23. 1 Kings 2:5 refers to events in

Joab's career detailed in 2 Samuel 3. The afflictions that Abiathar shared with David (1 Kgs 2:26) seem to refer to 1 Samuel 22–3.

Even if an earlier connected source running from 2 Samuel 11 (or 6 or 9?) through 2 Kings 2 can be assumed, is its topic really the succession to David's throne? The theme of succession emerges unambiguously only in 1 Kings 1. Other themes seem more dominant: political tensions, family dysfunction, the relationship of the sexes, and David's use and preservation of power. The narrative is not really pro-David. He is manipulated by others into confessing his crimes and into allowing Absalom to return, and when old and impotent, he is again manipulated. He unthinkingly sends Tamar to Amnon, fails to punish the resulting rape, forgives Absalom his fratricide, and is overly solicitous about Absalom's death. He orders a retributive blood bath on his death bed. Nor is the story actually very pro-Solomon either. Three passages about God and Solomon (2 Sam 11:27b; 12:24–5; 17:14b), usually assumed to give us the view of the author, are now often understood as insertions. The story of Solomon's birth is problematic. He comes to the throne only through the schemes (and lies?) of Nathan and Bathsheba. His first royal act is a series of brutal liquidations. Perhaps we should move beyond a simplistic and propagandistic game of "pro" and "anti" and allow for artistic ambiguity. After all, Ahitophel and Joab are simultaneously incriminated and admirable, and the characters of Bathsheba and Nathan are deeply ambiguous.[6]

There is more consensus about the "Rise of David" as a source, although this is more a series of incidents pasted together than a continuing narrative. The theme of opposition between Saul and David as God's choice is clear (1 Sam 16:14; 18:12). Both kings seek divine guidance, but with very different results (cf. 23:1–12 with 28). Songs (18:7; 21:11; 29:5) and paired narratives (24 and 26) are characteristic features. The genre of an apology of a usurper and defense against charges is known in Near Eastern literature.[7] Perhaps the legitimacy and divine election of the two competing kingdoms is the real topic, however, with David standing for Judah and Saul for Israel.

LITERARY STUDIES

Perhaps because the historical realities behind these books seem increasingly out of reach and dubious, there has been an upsurge in narratival, rhetorical, and other sorts of literary studies, often focusing on whole books in their final, canonical forms and foregrounding matters of plot, character, reader response, and the like. Such approaches have proven especially popular in Judges and Samuel. Perhaps a mild caveat is in order, however. Insofar as the ancient writers and readers of these books thought they were writing and reading something akin to *history*, it may be a methodological error (akin to genre misidentification) to bracket off that particular concern and deal with these books as examples of creative narrative artistry. Are we justified in treating texts – originally having some pragmatic or purposeful goal (one thinks also of parenesis, law, or prophetic admonition) and directed to a specific historical context – as *literature* in the more modern and artistic sense of the term?

HISTORY AND HISTORIOGRAPHY

To what degree, then, were the Former Prophets intended to be *history*? We should not be led astray by the great difference between them and modern notions of proper history writing. Of course, the divine causation model the biblical writers use as an explanatory tool is totally opposed to the philosophical basis of modern history writing. Of course, their interpretations are more blatantly partisan and their assessment of sources and inherited traditional materials more naive than anything a modern historian would tolerate. However, it does not appear that these ancient authors simply invented material to make their points or intentionally mischaracterized the documents before them or the traditional stories they had heard. The preservation of competing views and traditions, sometimes put into the background but still not eliminated, suggests exactly the opposite. The books of the Former Prophets are historiography, albeit of a premodern and theological sort. Their authors intended to recount and explain the past largely as they encountered it in their sources or at least felt the need to modify or "correct" sources instead of merely inventing something completely new. Historiography intends to be about reality because it keeps faith with its sources (whether oral or written, traditional or annalistic). These authors and scribes related the past as they thought it had taken place or should have taken place and intended to refer to real people and real events, no matter how far short of our standards they may have fallen.[8]

Historiography seeks not only to narrate the past but also to make judgments about it. History is an ideological and interpretive enterprise. Historians write because they have convictions about both past and present and want to communicate their beliefs. They tell a story about the past to contemporary readers for a purpose. This may be to explain something about the present on the basis of the past, to legitimate change or resist it, or to define national or religious identity. The books of the

Former Prophets claim Israel's ancestral lands in the face of opposition (Joshua), urge religious loyalty (Judges), legitimate the dynasty of David (Samuel), and explain defeat and exile (Kings).

Historiography makes value judgments in at least four ways. The first of these is in the *selection* of events and people. Thus, Kings totally fails to mention the battle of Qarqar (853 BCE), one of the most important events in the reign of Ahab. At the same time, it portrays the important ruler Omri in a mere eight verses, boiled down basically to "he did evil" (1 Kgs 16:21-8). A second tool of evaluation is *organization*. Historians impose structure on the past and supply links between events, offering a unified interpretive outlook. They can follow a chronological scheme, focus on certain themes, or trace repeated patterns. Judges presents a cyclical pattern of apostasy and deliverance. The "Rise of David" contrasts Saul's decline with David's rise to royal power. An example of an extended organizing pattern is the repeated "after the death of" formula (Josh 1:1; Judg 1:1; 2 Sam 1:1; 2 Kgs 1:1). Analogies provide another organizational tool. Examples in Kings include "mothers disputing about their children" (1 Kgs 3:16-28; 2 Kgs 6:26-31) and "wisdom and folly with visitors" (1 Kgs 10:1-13; 2 Kgs 20:12-19). Historical *causation* is a third approach to interpretation. In place of modern concerns with geography, climate, economics, technology, and sociology, biblical (and other ancient) historians regularly cite divine will and action as the cause of events. Psychological (1 Kgs 1:6), social (1 Kgs 12:4), or geopolitical (Judg 18:27-8; 2 Kgs 17:4) factors are not ignored, but critical events are caused primarily by the passions and purposes of God. A fourth tactic is *editorialization* on the meaning of events, as in the periodic discourses interpreting past events and preparing for what is to come (Joshua 1 and 23, 1 Samuel 12, 2 Samuel 7, 1 Kings 8, and 2 Kings 17) or in prophetic announcements such as 1 Kings 13:1-3 and 2 Kings 22:15-20.

The modern historian must use these books with the greatest care. Folktales and legends abound and certainly dominate Joshua, Judges, and Samuel. Examples of potentially trustworthy information are administrative lists such as 1 Kings 4:2-19 or geographical materials such as Joshua 15:20-62 and 18:21-8. Some poems are older than the prose accounts that surround them and may provide useful historical information (Josh 10:12-13; Judges 5). Possibly reliable sources may stand behind Joshua's tribal boundary descriptions, the rosters of David's officials and heroes (2 Sam 8:16-18; 20:23-6; 23:8-39) and information apparently derived from inscriptions and annals (1 Kgs 14:25-8; 2 Kgs 20:20).

224 Richard D. Nelson

JOSHUA

Joshua begins with the death of Moses, the "servant of the Lord," and the handover of leadership to Joshua (1:1–2). It ends in a parallel way with the death of Joshua, now himself "servant of the Lord," and a changeover to a new generation (24:29–31). Speeches enclose the plot action in chapters 1 and 23–4. Joshua is held together by numerous interconnections. Rahab (2) leads to Jericho (6), which, in turn, leads to Achan's sin (7), which provides the background for the battle over Ai (8). The command to go across the Jordan (1:2, 11) leads to a procession involving the powerful Ark (3–4), which, in turn, prepares for the encirclement of Jericho. Successes at Jericho and Ai motivate the Gibeonites' trick (9) and the coordinated opposition of southern Canaanite kings (9:1–2; 10), whose defeat, in turn, triggers a corresponding coalition of northern kings (11). Joshua gives orders to the east Jordan tribes (1:12–18) and, as the book draws to a close, releases them (22:1–6). God makes promises in chapter 1 and then keeps them (11:23; 21:43–5). Joshua's two final warning speeches celebrate conquest and land (23:3–4, 9–10; 24:11–13).

The book falls into three acts: conquest (1–12), land allotment (13–21), and warnings about the future (22–4). The stories that provide the backbone of the first act (conquest; 1–12) began as oral folktales linked to localities: city ruins (6:26; 8:28), commemorative markers (4:20; 7:26), and features of the landscape (4:9; 5:3; 10:27; 11:5). These were linked together into a connected narrative of conquest victories by the theme of enemy fear at the news of Israel's success (2:9; 5:1; 9:1–2; 10:1–2; 11:1). These stories recount the triumphs of Yahweh as "Divine Warrior," as demonstrated by victory oracles (6:2; 8:1, 7, 18), by application of the ban (6:21; 8:26; 10:28–40; 11:11–14, 20), and by miraculous events and panic at Jericho, Ai, and throughout chapters 10 and 11. The campaign is organized geographically: central (6–8), south (9–10), and north (11). A summary list of conquered kings in chapter 12 emphasizes the extent of Israel's triumph and also leads into the second act, land allotment.

Allotment (13–21) reshapes geographical data into a narrative of apportionment by divine guidance. References to the east Jordan tribes (13:7–32; 22:1–6) bracket this section. Tribal boundary descriptions and city lists are used to give substance to a narrative that first reviews what Moses distributed (13), next describes the border allotment for the three most important tribes (14–17), and then a somewhat different process of survey, partition, and apportionment by lot to the remaining tribes

(18–19). Chapters 20 and 21 cover the two interrelated topics of cities of refuge and Levitical cities. Interspersed into this overall narrative are stories about other aspects of land allocation: keeping promises (14:6–15; 15:13–19; 17:3–6) and solving problems (17:14–18; 19:49–50).

The third act involves *warning*. In chapter 22, conflict over an altar built by the east Jordan tribes urges national cohesiveness and loyalty to Deuteronomy's ideal of a single sanctuary. In 13:1, reference to his old age initiated Joshua's division of land. Now the same motive triggers his two final speeches (23:1). These speeches urge future loyalty and obedience and warn of danger. Chapter 23 interprets the meaning of the conquest. Earlier hints of partial failure (15:63; 16:10; 17:12–13) now take on greater meaning (23:12–13). Chapter 24 expounds on God's election of Israel from Genesis through Joshua. Both warn that the future holds great danger (23:15–16; 24:19–20).

JUDGES

Judges might be called dogmatic historiography. A theological pattern about disobedience and repentance dominates its presentation of traditional materials. Topically and structurally the book divides into 1:1–2:5 (incomplete conquest), 2:6–16:31 (deliverers), and 17–21 (liberty as license). It begins with the death of Joshua, narrated twice (1:1; 2:6). The first mention of Joshua's death leads to a renewed campaign of conquest led by Judah, which for that tribe is victorious. The other tribes are notably less successful. Although formerly Joshua 1 was taken to be a genuine source offering a more realistic view of the conquest than Joshua, today is it generally viewed as a pastiche made up from material from Joshua along with other traditions. This first section introduces the themes of retribution (with Adoni-bezek), wise and tricky speech (Achsah), deception (Bethel), and God's punishment for apostasy (Bochim). Dan's dilemma prepares for Samson and the tribe's move north.

Parallels between chapters 1 and 17–21 bracket the central part. The "sons of Israel" (New Revised Standard Version [NRSV], "the Israelites") begin their campaign in 1:1 and disperse in 21:24. The question of 1:1 is repeated in a darker mode in 20:18. The ban is enforced in 1:17 and 21:11 as sacral war degenerates into civil war, and the same expression for setting fire appears in both 1:8 and 20:48.

The second mention of Joshua's death leads into the main action (2:6–16:31). The incomplete conquest of chapter 1 has left foreigners in the land, and these enemies overshadow the rest of book. Alternative explanations for their continued existence are given: punishment for sin (2:20–1), a test of loyalty (2:22–3; 3:1), or to provide training in war (3:2).

The central section of Judges is structured by a drifting pattern. Events seem stuck in a repeated sequence of disobedience and temporary repentance. A broad sketch of the cycle is set forth in 2:11–19: apostasy, divine anger, oppression, a judge who delivers, and then a return to apostasy to start over. This pattern is not carried through mechanically, however. A bare-bones narrative about Othniel (3:7–11) serves as an illustration and adds further items that are carried through for other judges: the people's "cry" along with a period of "rest." Another variation is that the Othniel narrative picks up Yahweh's anger from the introduction (2:14; 3:8), but this item will only reappear in the introduction to Jephthah (10:7). The Ehud story adds that the enemy was "subdued" (3:30), which also then becomes part of the full pattern. Scholarship tends to explain these irregularities by different layers of composition, but this approach assumes that authorial consistency is the same thing as tedious inflexibility. The pattern in its fullest form introduces and concludes Ehud, Deborah/Barak, and Gideon, but items are missing for Jephthah. A review interlude (10:11–16) interrupts the introduction of Jephthah with comments that highlight Israel's inconstancy and God's graciousness. With Samson, the pattern stalls partway through. There is apostasy and oppression (13:1), but no cry to God. The enemy is not subdued, nor is there rest. Given Samson's failings in leadership and personal life, his career ends with the crisis of Philistine oppression still unresolved. Samson only "begins to deliver" (13:5, cf. 25).

The very different so-called minor judges who appear before and after Jephthah (10:1–5; 12:[7]8–15) derive from a (probably artificial) list of civil officials who succeeded each other with diverse terms of service. This earlier document was likely the source for the idea that the six deliverers, whose stories were originally transmitted independently, ought to be considered as "judges" (2:16–19) who ruled over all Israel (3:10; 15:20; 16:31) and who succeeded one after the other. This development would have been facilitated by Jephthah's place in both categories, as minor judge (12:7) and renowned deliverer. Scholarship tends to assign this act of authorial creativity to DH, along with the book's Deuteronomistic language and theology (cf. 2:1–3:6; 6:7–10; 10:6–16) and the chronology of the major judges (in round numbers of twenty, forty, and eighty years). Many suggest that DH used an earlier book of deliverers, an opinion based largely on the detection of supposedly non-Deuteronomistic framing elements and differences between the clearly DH preface of 2:7–19 and the pattern as it actually plays out in the subsequent narratives.

The concluding section (17–21) shifts from drifting ambiguity to outright catastrophe. The problem is no longer inconsistent loyalty or external enemies but self-centered ("right in their own eyes") chaos caused by the absence of a king's authority (17:6; 18:1; 19:1; 21:25). "No king" means theft, reprehensible religious practices, rape and murder, civil war against Benjamin, and irregular marriage arrangements. This downward trend, however, was already present in the middle section: Gideon's ephod (8:27), tribal conflict (8:1–3; 12:1–6; 15:9–13), and inappropriate judgment in Samson's eyes (14:3, 7). Decline has been evident throughout the book. Othniel and Ehud are wholly positive figures, but ambiguity intrudes in the leadership of Barak, Gideon, and Jephthah, to say nothing of Samson. At first, women are positive and assertive figures: Achsah (1:11–15), Deborah (4:4–16), Jael (4:17–22; 5:24–7), and the woman of Thebez (9:53). However, then follows Jephthah's sacrifice of his daughter and Samson's problematic behavior with women. In the last chapters, the general breakdown in civic values is illustrated by violence against women (19:25–9; 21:11–12, 20–3).

Literary and thematic readings of Judges have flourished, and the women of Judges continue to exert fascination.[9] Judges has been used as a source for the social background, family structures, customs, and tribal/clan organization of the prestate period. However, much of what is described also could reasonably apply to the time of the monarchy as well, during which clan and tribal loyalties and rivalries continued, worship took place at multiple sanctuaries, and the danger of assertive neighboring peoples produced tales of renowned heroes (e.g., 2 Sam 23:8–12, 18–23). Weak ties of national unity (Judg 5:15–17), the authority of elders (cf. 8:14, 16; 11:5, 11), and an unwritten shared code of conduct (20:6) certainly continued after Judah and Israel become kingdoms. The stories in Judges thus portray a premonarchic period but do not necessarily reflect premonarchic circumstances accurately. In the last analysis, the so-called period of the judges was a construct of DH.

1 AND 2 SAMUEL

Samuel lacks tidy organization. Although for the most part its story is told in chronological sequence, even this breaks down with 2 Samuel 21–4. However, common themes are present throughout, such as kingship, God's word, and divine election.

The "Song of Hannah" near the beginning (1 Samuel 2) and two poetic pieces of David near the end (2 Sam 22:2–51 and 23:1–7) bracket Samuel and contribute thematic unity. Hannah celebrates what God can do, and David gives thanks for what God has done and promised. There are parallels between these poetic bookends: God is the "Rock of Israel" (1 Sam 2:2; 2 Sam 23:3) who brings low and raises up (1 Sam 2:7; 2 Sam 22:28), who thunders from heaven (1 Sam 2:10; 2 Sam 22:14), and who sustains the anointed king (1 Sam 2:10; 2 Sam 22:51). Hannah testifies that God is the key transforming factor in events, turning things upside down, and this is particularly clear in the stories that follow. The captured Ark defeats its enemies. Saul comes to power and is destroyed. The boy shepherd David rises to kingship, only to be nearly undone by family conflict.

Samuel presents the overlapping stories of three leaders: Samuel, Saul, and David. The pattern of overlap is Samuel alone (1 Samuel 1–8), Samuel and Saul (1 Samuel 9–15), Saul and David (1 Samuel 16–2 Samuel 1), and David alone (2 Samuel 2–24). The career of each leader begins with God's choice and call (1 Samuel 3, 9, and 16). The three major figures offer three contrasting portrayals of leadership. Samuel is a faithful and obedient hero. Saul is a tragic and despairing failure. David struggles with the ambiguities of faith and disobedience.

Samuel begins his career in a situation of religious corruption and Philistine domination. Unlike Samson, he is a proper Nazirite (1 Sam 1:11) whose victory over the Philistines completes what Samson had failed to achieve (7:13–14). The narratives about Samuel wrestle with the legitimacy of kingship. Problematic and faithless aspects of monarchy (8:1–22; 10:17–27; 12:12–25) alternate with more positive perspectives (9:1–10; 11:1–15). In the end, however, God proves willing to accept kingship as a flawed but tolerable institution (8:22; 10:1; 12:12–15, 20–5).

Saul's promising start is undone by (perhaps excusable) disobedience (1 Samuel 13, 15), leading into a long slide of divine abandonment, despair, and suicide. David's story divides into a positive beginning period described in 2 Samuel 2–8 (focused by 5:12) and a much more ambiguous, even negative portrayal in 2 Samuel 9–24 (leading up to and then developing Nathan's threat in 12:10–11). The transfer of the Ark to Jerusalem and a promise of an eternal dynasty mark the high point of the positive portrayal (6–7). The lowest point of the ambiguous second section is David's reaction to the death of Absalom (18:33), after which David's situation begins to improve (18–20). However, the chiastic summary section 2 Samuel 21–4 continues to stress ambiguity.

Given the book's complexity and its fascinating and deeply human characters, it is no surprise that Samuel has been the focus of many literary studies.[10]

I AND 2 KINGS

The book of Kings recounts the history of Israelite monarchy from the transition from David to Solomon up to an event during the exile of Jehoiachin. Individual kings are evaluated in relationship to the law of Deuteronomy (especially centralization and obliteration of the high places), the words of the prophets (e.g., 2 Kgs 17:13, 23; 24:2), and God's promise to David (1 Kgs 11:12–13, 36; 15:4–5; 2 Kgs 8:19; 19:34). Narratives about kings and prophets are set into a chronological framework constructed from opening and closing formulas for the reigns of the kings of Judah and Israel, treated in a synchronistic manner. These narratives may be short (1 Kgs 14:25–8) or long (2 Kings 18–19). The frameworks combine annalistic data derived from sources with theological judgments on each king. Judgments on the kings of Israel are uniformly negative and focus on generalized references to sins and Jeroboam as the founder of the kingdom. Judgments on the kings of Judah are mixed. Some are evil, the virtue of others qualified by a failure to remove the high places, and only Hezekiah and Josiah receive unqualified praise. Divergent patterns in these framework formulas have been used as evidence for different sources or a range of redactions, but such attempts have proved persuasive only when applied to the last four kings of Judah.

The structure of Kings treats the two kingdoms synchronically. First, the entire reign of a given king is recounted. When he dies, the narrative backtracks to cover the reigns of whatever king or kings of the other kingdom came to the throne during the first king's rule. Thus, 1 Kings 15:9–24 describes the long reign of Asa of Judah with opening and concluding formulas. Then the story goes back to pick up the reigns of five kings of Israel – kings who began their reigns during Asa's tenure (15:25–22:40). The last of these is Ahab. The narration then turns back to Jehoshaphat of Judah, whose reign began in Ahab's fourth year (22:41). Significantly, some stories fall outside the frames, notably the transfer of authority from Elijah to Elisha (2 Kings 2) and the illegitimate reign of Athaliah (2 Kings 11).

Other organizational structures include

- *Analogous or contrasting parallels:* God appears to Solomon (1 Kgs 3:4–15; 9:1–9), two contending mothers and the king (1 Kgs 3:16–28;

2 Kgs 6:26–31), the king and foreign visitors (1 Kgs 10:1–13; 2 Kgs 20:12–19), a son comes back to life (1 Kgs 17:17–24; 2 Kgs 4:18–37), and a wicked queen dies (2 Kgs 9:30–7; 11:13–16).

- *Pairing of kings and prophets:* Jeroboam and Ahijah (1 Kings 11–14), Ahab and Elijah (1 Kings 17–21), Jehoram (Israel) and Elisha (2 Kings 3–8), Jehu and Elisha (2 Kings 9–10), Hezekiah and Isaiah (2 Kings 18–20), and Josiah and Huldah (2 Kings 22–3).
- *Prophetic predictions and fulfillments:* kingdom divided (1 Kgs 11:29–39; 12:15), Bethel and Josiah (1 Kgs 13:1–3; 2 Kgs 23:15–18), the fall of Israel (1 Kgs 14:15–16; 2 Kgs 17:23), the fate of the Omri dynasty (1 Kgs 21:21–4; 2 Kgs 9:7–10; 10:17), and the fall of Judah (2 Kgs 21:10–15; 22:15–17; 24:2).

Two major evaluative turning points are 1 Kings 8 (Temple dedication) and 2 Kings 17 (fall of Israel). These texts review past events and point forward to future developments. Whereas Solomon's dedication prayer is open ended and positive about the future, 2 Kings 17 treats the fall of Israel as a harbinger of Judah's inevitable demise.

Josiah plays a central plot role, even though the story does not end with him. His elimination of the high places (2 Kgs 23:8–9) resolves the repeated criticism directed against most previous kings of Judah, while his desecration of the Bethel altar resolves the "sin of Jeroboam" transgression of the kings of Israel. His reforms explicitly cancel out the crimes of both Solomon (2 Kgs 23:13) and Manasseh (2 Kgs 23:5–7, 10–12).

Kings focuses on the Northern Kingdom to a remarkable extent. Prophetic threat and fulfillment relate predominantly to the kings and dynasties of Israel, and prophetic activity is concentrated in Israel, except for the figures of Isaiah and Huldah. In regard to Judah, narrative interest centers on cultic reforms (and not just high places) and the problematic consequences of foreign alliances, especially with respect to Assyria (Ahaz, Hezekiah, Manasseh, and Josiah).

Kings can be used (with care) as a source of useful historical data because one is often able to distinguish its sources from the surrounding redactional material. Some of these sources are folktales and prophet legends of questionable historical value and sometimes apparently set in the wrong period, but other sources have the flavor of genuine annalistic and chronological materials.

NOTES

1   Bernard M. Levinson, "The Reconceptualization of Kingship in Deuteronomy and the Deuteronomistic History's Transformation of Torah," *VT* 51 (2001): 511–34.

2 For the debate, see Thomas Römer and Albert de Pury, "Deuteronomistic Historiography (DH): History of Research and Debated Issues," in *Israel Constructs Its History: Deuteronomistic Historiography in Recent Research*, ed. by A. de Pury et al. (JSOTSup 306; Sheffield Academic, 2000), 24–141.

3 Thomas Römer, *The So-Called Deuteronomistic History: A Sociological, Historical and Literary Introduction* (New York: T & T Clark, 2005).

4 Marvin A. Sweeney, *1 and 2 Kings: A Commentary* (Louisville, KY: Westminster John Knox, 2007).

5 See most recently his collaboration with Mark A. O'Brien, *Unfolding the Deuteronomistic History: Origins, Upgrades, Present Text* (Minneapolis, MN: Fortress, 2000), 24–31.

6 See most recently A. Graeme Auld, *Samuel at the Threshold: Selected Works of Graeme Auld* (Aldershot, UK: Ashgate, 2004). For other issues, see Serge Frolov, "Succession Narrative: A Document or a Phantom?" *JBL* 121 (2002): 81–104.

7 Michael B. Dick, "The 'History of David's Rise to Power' and the Neo-Babylonian Succession Apologies," in *David and Zion: Biblical Studies in Honor of J. J. M. Roberts*, ed. by B. Batto and K. Roberts (Winona Lake, IN: Eisenbrauns, 2004), 3–19.

8 A. D. H. Mayes, "Historiography in the Old Testament," in *The Biblical World*, Vol. 1, ed. by John Barton (London: Routledge, 2002), 65–87.

9 For example, Elie Assis, "The Choice to Serve God and Assist His People: Rahab and Yael," *Bib* 85 (2004): 82–90.

10 For example, Serge Frolov, *The Turn of the Cycle: 1 Samuel 1–8 in Synchronic and Diachronic Perspectives* (BZAW 342; Berlin: de Gruyter, 2004); and Roy L. Heller, *Power, Politics, and Prophecy: The Character of Samuel and the Deuteronomistic Evaluation of Prophecy* (LHBOTS 440; New York: T & T Clark, 2006).

FURTHER READING

Geoghegan, Jeffrey C. *The Time, Place, and Purpose of the Deuteronomistic History: The Evidence of "Until This Day"* (BJS 347). Providence, RI: Brown Judaic Studies, 2006.

Guillaume, Philippe. *Waiting for Josiah: The Judges* (JSOTSup 385). London: T & T Clark, 2004.

Halpern, Baruch. *David's Secret Demons: Messiah, Murderer, Traitor, King.* Grand Rapids, MI: Eerdmans, 2001.

Hamilton, Victor P. *Handbook on the Historical Books: Joshua, Judges, Ruth, Samuel, Kings, Chronicles, Ezra-Nehemiah, Esther.* Grand Rapids, MI: Baker Academic, 2001.

McKenzie, Steven L. and M. Patrick Graham, eds. *The History of Israel's Traditions: The Heritage of Martin Noth* (JSOTSup 182). Sheffield Academic Press, 1994.

Mobley, Gregory. *Samson and the Liminal Hero in the Ancient Near East* (LHBOTS 453). New York: T & T Clark, 2006.

Nelson, Richard D. *The Historical Books.* Nashville, TN: Abingdon, 1998.

de Pury, Albert, Thomas Römer, and Jean-Daniel Macchi, eds. *Israel Constructs Its History: Deuteronomistic Historiography in Recent Research* (JSOTSup 306). Sheffield Academic Press, 2000.

Römer, Thomas, ed. *The Future of the Deuteronomistic History* (BETL 147). Leuven, Netherlands: Leuven University Press, 2000.

Satterthwaite, Philip, and Gordon McConville. *Exploring the Old Testament*, Vol. 2: *The Histories*. London: Society for Promoting Christian Knowledge, 2007.

11 The Latter Prophets and prophecy

MARVIN A. SWEENEY

OVERVIEW

The Latter Prophets of the Tanak (i.e., the Jewish form of the Hebrew Bible) are found within the second section of its tripartite structure (i.e., Torah-Prophets-Writings) and include the books of Isaiah, Jeremiah, Ezekiel, and the Twelve Prophets (Hosea, Joel, Amos, Obadiah, Jonah, Micah, Nahum, Habakkuk, Zephaniah, Haggai, Zechariah, and Malachi). The Old Testament (i.e., the Christian form of the Hebrew Bible) includes the Latter Prophets, called simply "Prophets," as its final section immediately prior to the New Testament, but this section also differs from the same section in the Tanak in that it includes the books of Isaiah, Jeremiah, Ezekiel, and Daniel and treats the twelve "Minor Prophets" as individual books.

The Latter Prophets of the Tanak and Old Testament each form an important component of their respective Bibles, one that plays a key role in expressing the respective theological outlooks of Jewish and Christian forms of the Bible. But each of the prophetic books also has a complex compositional history pointing to the significant roles that the individual prophets played within ancient Judean and Israelite society. The prophets are especially well known for their attempts to interpret the major historical, economic, and religious events of their day; to identify the divine will in relation to those events; and to call on the people of their times to follow the prophets' understanding of the divine will. Although prophets are frequently understood as figures who predict the future, their basic function is to persuade people to follow the divine will. Their efforts to envision the future were a means to indicate to people what possible consequences or outcomes their actions might hold, either for judgment or for blessing, and to convince them to adopt a course of action that was in keeping with the will of YHWH.

In an effort to provide a basis for understanding the prophetic books of the Hebrew Bible, this chapter examines (1) the phenomenon of prophecy in the ancient Near Eastern world, including speech and narrative forms, in order to demonstrate their importance for understanding prophecy in Israel and Judah, (2) each of the prophetic books of the Latter Prophets so as to discern their distinctive literary forms, compositional histories, and theological outlooks on the world of their time, and (3) the literary and theological significance of the Prophets in both the Jewish and Christian forms of the Bible.

PROPHECY IN THE ANCIENT NEAR EAST

Prophets were well known throughout the ancient Near Eastern world as figures who would serve as messengers or mouthpieces for the gods to communicate the divine will to their human audiences.[1] Most prophets were a professional class in the ancient world who generally served in temple complexes and frequently advised monarchs. Examples include the Mesopotamian *baru* priests and the Egyptian lector priests, who went through extensive training in ritual procedure, omens, sacrifice, the movements of stars and planets, reading and writing, and other necessary skills to perform their functions in the temples and royal courts of the ancient world.[2] Nonprofessionals also could function as prophets in certain instances, such as the young boy who displayed characteristics of trance possession to speak on behalf of the god Amon in the Egyptian narrative of the journey of Wen-Amon to Phoenicia.

The basic means by which prophets communicated the will of the gods was the prophetic oracle, in which the prophet would speak on behalf of the deity in question, sometimes characterizing the divine message in his or her own words or quoting the deity directly as if he or she embodied the deity. Mesopotamian *baru* priests were oracle divination priests who read smoke patterns from sacrificial altars, examined the livers of sacrificial animals, read the movements of heavenly bodies, and so on as preparation for the delivery of a divine oracle in a state of ecstasy or trance possession (see, e.g., Balaam ben Beor in Numbers 22–4). Ecstatic *muḫḫu* prophets from the Mesopotamian city of Mari drew blood from themselves and engaged in trance possession as part of their preparation for oracular speech (cf. the Baal prophets in 1 Kgs 18), and the *assinu* prophets of Mari were known for emulating feminine characteristics and dress as they prepared themselves to embody the goddess Ishtar of Arbela to speak on her behalf. The Egyptian lector priests engaged in analysis of the worlds of nature and human beings in preparation for the well-crafted poetic compositions that gave expression to the will of the gods that a new king should arise to restore order in the land.

Judean and Israelite prophets were also generally associated with temples, even if they were not priests, and they understood themselves (or they were understood by others) to function as messengers or mouthpieces for YHWH, the God of Judah and Israel. Each prophet understood the divine will in relation to a distinct theological tradition. Isaiah was heavily influenced by the royal Davidic/Zion tradition that viewed YHWH's eternal promises to the royal house of David and the city of Jerusalem as the foundation for Israel's and Judah's relationship with God. Jeremiah was a priest of the Elide line of Shiloh who held that adherence to divine Torah or instruction was the foundation of the relationship with God. Ezekiel was a Zadokite priest of the Jerusalem Temple who viewed the Temple as the center of creation and called on Israel and Judah to play their roles in maintaining both the ethical and ritual holiness of creation. Each of the twelve prophets likewise had his own distinctive theological worldview that provided the foundation of his respective understanding of Israel's and Judah's relationship with God.

Despite the variety of their theological worldviews, Judean and Israelite prophets employed standard forms of oracular language, often drawn from the prophetic speech forms of the larger ancient Near Eastern world, to express themselves.[3] Ecstatic behavior is not always evident in the prophetic books of the Bible, although figures portrayed in the Former Prophets, such as Saul (1 Sam 10:9–13; 19:18–24), sometimes engage in ecstatic behavior or trance possession. Elisha could call for musical accompaniment for his oracles (2 Kgs 3:9–20), and Chronicles views prophets as cultic functionaries who would sing the Temple liturgy (e.g., 1 Chr 25:5; 2 Chr 29:30; 35:15). Oracular speech forms appear frequently. A basic oracle form is the "prophetic pronouncement" (Hebrew, *maśśā'*), which appears especially in the oracles concerning the nations and elsewhere to articulate divine action, either current or projected, in the human world. One of the best known language forms is the so-called prophetic messenger formula, "thus says YHWH" (Hebrew, *kōh 'āmar yhwh*), which is also employed in Assyrian prophecy and appears to be derived from the language forms employed by messengers who speak on behalf of Assyrian kings. The oracular formula, "utterance/oracle of YHWH" (Hebrew, *nĕ'um yhwh*) can conclude or appear within oracular speech. The reassurance formula, "fear not!" (Hebrew, *'al tîrā'*), which is also known in Assyrian prophecy, appears in oracles of salvation, blessing, and restoration as a means to reassure the recipients of divine oracles in times of threat. The typical prophetic judgment speech, which lays out the grounds or reasons for punishment as well as the announcement of disaster or punishment itself, appears frequently among the Judean and Israelite prophets as a means to explain misfortune or to project it if the party in question fails to follow the prophet's understanding of the divine will.

Prophets are also well known for their visionary experiences, in which they may envision the divine presence in the Temple (e.g., Isaiah 6), in foreign lands (Ezekiel 1), or in the world of creation (Habakkuk 3) as part of the experience of the divine that leads them to speak. Often visionary experience is associated with temples and based on the observation of ritual acts, such as offerings presented at the altar of the Temple (Jeremiah 24) or even features of the Temple itself (Isaiah 6; Ezekiel 3), events in the natural world such as a locust plague (Amos 7:1–3; Joel 1–2), or mundane observations such as a man holding a plumb line while building a wall (Amos 7:7–9) or the pouring out of a cooking pot (Jer 1:13–15). Indeed, the question-and-answer schema employed in the vision reports of Amos, Jeremiah, and Zechariah suggests that visionary experience is based on the observation and interpretation of phenomena in the world as symbols of divine action and intent. Dream interpretation also may play a role in visionary experience, although this is disputed even among the prophets themselves (Jer 23:9–40).

Prophetic literature includes a number of narrative forms. Variations of the typical prophetic word formula, "the word of YHWH was (came) to me saying" (Hebrew, *wayhî děbar-yhwh 'ēlay lē'mōr*) frequently introduce narrative accounts of prophetic activity and play an important role in defining the literary structures of books such as Jeremiah and Ezekiel. Reports of symbolic actions portray a significant activity of prophets who engage in dramatic acts, such as walking about naked to symbolize subjugation to an enemy (Isaiah 20), carrying a yoke on the back for the same purpose (Jeremiah 27–8), or pointing to one's own marriage and children (Hosea 1–3), as a means to convey divine intent.

Finally, the prophetic book itself is a unique literary form in the Bible, one that presents the words and actions of a prophetic figure. The reading of prophetic books has emerged as a central concern in biblical scholarship as scholars increasingly recognize the significance of these books as coherent literary entities addressing central theological concerns.[4]

THE FOUR BOOKS OF THE LATTER PROPHETS

All four books of the Latter Prophets, that is, Isaiah, Jeremiah, Ezekiel, and the Twelve Prophets, appear together under the general rubric of prophets, but each book has a distinctive outlook based in part on the social identity of the prophet portrayed in the respective book.[5] Thus, Isaiah's royalist viewpoint relates to his role as royal advisor, Jeremiah's concern with the application of Torah stems from his role as a priest of the line of Eli or Ithamar, and Ezekiel's concern with reestablishment of the holy Temple relates to his identity as a priest of the line of Zadok that served as high priests of the Jerusalem Temple. Although the Book of the Twelve includes twelve originally discrete prophetic compositions, they are now arranged so that they function as a single composition with a pervasive concern for the city of Jerusalem. Indeed, the differences between the prophets are such that the books of Jeremiah, Ezekiel, and the Twelve Prophets frequently cite or allude to Isaiah and express their differences with Isaiah's views. Altogether the four books of the Latter Prophets each present their respective understandings concerning the significance of the fall of Jerusalem and the projected restoration of Jerusalem and the Temple for both Judah/Israel and the world at large.

Isaiah generally appears first in the order of the Latter Prophets,[6] and it functions as the most prominent dialogue partner for the other prophetic books.[7] Modern critical scholarship focuses on identification of the historical layers of the book, which results in reading Isaiah as a three-part composition. Isaiah 1–39 portrays the eighth-century prophet Isaiah ben Amoz, who argued that the Assyrian invasions of Israel and Judah constituted divine judgment owing to their failure to adhere to YHWH, but he also posited restoration under an ideal Davidic monarch in Jerusalem once the judgment was complete. Isaiah 40–55 presents the work of an anonymous prophet of the exile known as Deutero-Isaiah, who announced that the divine judgment of the Babylonian Exile was over and that the time for Israel to return to Jerusalem and restore the land of Israel was at hand. Isaiah 56–66 represents the work of anonymous prophets from the early Persian period, identified collectively as Trito-Isaiah, who discuss various aspects of the restoration of Jerusalem, Judah, and the Jerusalem Temple.[8] Although aspects of this historical paradigm may be disputed, it represents a largely sound model for reconstruction of Isaiah's compositional history and characterization of the individual prophetic figures whose works appear within the book. Nevertheless, an exclusively historical reading of the book impedes a full grasp of its literary and theological coherence.

A synchronic reading of Isaiah points to several fundamental concerns.[9] The book presents itself entirely as the vision of the eighth-century prophet Isaiah ben Amoz. Isaiah's vision therefore extends forward for some four centuries, from his own period during the time of the Assyrian invasions of Israel and Judah through the Babylonian Exile and the early Persian period, when Jews began to return to the land of Israel to reestablish their life in Jerusalem and Judah around a newly reconstructed Temple. Overall, it contends that both the destruction of Israel and Judah by the Assyrians and Babylonians and the restoration of Jerusalem under Persian rule are acts of YHWH designed to reveal YHWH's sovereignty over all creation and nations. Within this scenario, nations such as Assyria, Babylon, and Persia act as agents of the divine will. Of course, the famous "swords into plowshares" passage near the beginning of the book in Isaiah 2:2–4 signals that the nations will come to Jerusalem/ Zion, the site of YHWH's Temple, to learn divine Torah. Ultimately, the book of Isaiah envisions a future of world peace in which the Jerusalem Temple stands as the holy center of both Israel and the nations within a new creation.

Nevertheless, there are several remarkable dimensions to Isaiah's depiction of this ideal scenario, especially when the book is read from a synchronic standpoint. For one, the book is especially concerned with the issue of righteous Davidic kingship. Indeed, many have pointed to the ideological foundations of Isaiah's, Deutero-Isaiah's, and Trito-Isaiah's viewpoints in the royal Zion traditions of the house of David. A diachronic reading of the book points to each prophet's respective viewpoint: that is, Isaiah ben Amoz, the royal counselor, looks forward to an ideal, righteous Davidic king, perhaps Hezekiah; Deutero-Isaiah contends that the Persian monarch Cyrus is YHWH's anointed monarch as the Davidic covenant is applied collectively to all Israel; and Trito-Isaiah contends that YHWH is the true king, whose Temple in Jerusalem serves as royal throne and footstool in a new heaven and earth. At this level, the three major historical portions of the book are in debate with each other because each asserts its own respective view of ideal kingship for Israel. But when read synchronically, the three positions collapse into one, so that the book of Isaiah ultimately calls for Judah/Israel to submit to Persian rule (i.e., the rule of a non-Jewish king, as an expression of YHWH's ultimate sovereignty in the newly restored world of creation).[10] Certainly such a contention stands in contrast with the viewpoint of not only Isaiah ben Amoz but also the entire Davidic tradition (expressed in Samuel, Psalms, and elsewhere) that posited YHWH's eternal protection for both Jerusalem and the house of David.

Although the book of Isaiah's perspective finds agreement in the books of Ezra-Nehemiah, which portray reestablishment of a Temple-based Jewish community in Jerusalem under Persian rule as the fulfillment of the great prophet's vision, Isaiah's prophetic colleagues are hardly so accommodating. Jeremiah is a major case in point. The book of Jeremiah presents him as a prophet and Levitical priest like Moses.[11] He lives during the final years of the kingdom of Judah and sees the ultimate decline and destruction of Judah as the Babylonians destroy the city and the Temple and carry the people off to exile. Modern historical-critical scholarship has wrestled with the question of the interrelationship between the poetic oracles, prose sermons, and prose narratives of the book, generally concluding that the poetic oracles are Jeremian, the sermons are based on Jeremiah's oracles, and the narratives are the product of another author (perhaps Baruch or some other anonymous figures who are influenced by Deuteronomy or a Deuteronomistic school). The issue is complicated by the interrelationship between the Masoretic and Septuagint versions of the book and difficult questions concerning the redaction-critical reconstruction of the book and the prophet presented therein. In general, however, diachronic critical treatment contends that Jeremiah calls the Temple into question as a source for national security, sharply criticizes the house of David, and focuses especially on impending judgment against Jerusalem for a failure to observe divine instruction (while saying relatively little about the restoration of Jerusalem).

As interpreters begin to consider the synchronic literary dimensions of the book, additional issues come to light. One is the issue of intertextuality, particularly with regard to Jeremiah's relationship with the book of Isaiah.[12] Although interpreters have generally noted Jeremiah's relationship with the Deuteronomistic History as part of their efforts to demonstrate the Deuteronomistic editing of the book,[13] they have paid less attention to its links with Isaiah. Indeed, Jeremiah appears to cite or to allude to many passages from the book of Isaiah, most notably in the prophet's portrayal in Jeremiah 5–6 of YHWH's plans to bring a far-off nation to punish Judah, which draws heavily on Isaiah's similar statements in Isaiah 5 concerning YHWH's plans to bring a far-off nation to punish Israel. Although Jeremiah appears to agree with his senior colleague Isaiah about YHWH's intention to bring punishment, he disagrees on its ultimate timing and its target. Isaiah announced judgment against northern Israel and Jerusalem/Judah, but he never claimed that Jerusalem would be destroyed. Instead, Isaiah articulates YHWH's continuing commitment to Jerusalem as the holy center of creation.

The book of Jeremiah, however, presents the prophet quite differently. Jeremiah's well-known Temple sermon in chapter 7 presents a striking critique of the people's contention that the presence of the Jerusalem

Temple would guarantee the security of the city.[14] The narrative concerning his trial for sedition in Jeremiah 26 emphasizes the theme of Jerusalem's destruction when Micah's statement that Jerusalem will be destroyed (Mic 3:12) is cited in defense of Jeremiah. In true Levitical (and Deuteronomistic) fashion, Jeremiah maintains that security is achieved only insofar as the people abide by divine Torah; without adherence to YHWH's Torah, the city and the Temple will be lost, just as Shiloh was lost centuries before. Jeremiah's differences with Isaiah are also evident in his confrontation with the prophet Hananiah in Jeremiah 27–8. When Jerusalem falls under Babylonian rule, Hananiah contends that YHWH will act to deliver the city within two years. Jeremiah, by contrast, wears a yoke around his neck to symbolize his message that Jerusalem must submit to Babylon in keeping with the will of YHWH. During the ensuing confrontation, Hananiah breaks Jeremiah's yoke, but Jeremiah returns with an iron yoke to reiterate his message. With Hananiah's death, he is ultimately identified as a false prophet, and Jeremiah's message is confirmed by subsequent events. But readers must recognize that Hananiah's position is in fact that of Isaiah; that is, YHWH will act to defend the city.

Identification of Hananiah as a false prophet generally obscures an important point to be drawn from this confrontation: Jeremiah considers Isaiah's message of security for the city of Jerusalem to be false prophecy. In Jeremiah's view, Jerusalem would face war, destruction, and seventy years of exile. Although critical scholarship frequently denies passages concerned with restoration to the historical Jeremiah, a synchronic reading of the book indicates that restoration will come after the seventy years of exile. Jeremiah 30–1 employs the image of the weeping Rachel to portray Israel's return to Jerusalem, but it does so in the context of a new covenant in which Torah is inscribed on the hearts of the people. Whereas the book of Isaiah maintains the continuity of YHWH's covenant with David/Jerusalem/Israel as the basis for its portrayal of Jerusalem's restoration, the book of Jeremiah posits a change in covenant that will ultimately result in restoration of the city and its people. Interpreters might note that Jeremiah's vision of the future does – in contrast to the full form of the book of Isaiah – envision the restoration of a righteous Davidic monarch. Critical scholarship raises questions about the authenticity of the royal oracles in Jeremiah 23:1–8 and 33:12–26,[15] but a synchronic reading of the book necessarily concludes that Jeremiah envisions a restored Jerusalem ruled once again by a righteous member of the house of David. Whereas the book of Isaiah reinterpreted the Davidic covenant to justify submission to Persian rule, Jeremiah envisions a permanent Davidic covenant based in creation as part of the scenario for YHWH's new covenant with Israel/Judah.

Ezekiel is an erudite figure who cites both biblical and ancient Near Eastern mythological tradition as part of his effort to define the theological significance of the Babylonian exile and reconstruction of the Jerusalem Temple. Ezekiel is a Zadokite priest, and his education, practices, and use of Temple-based imagery (such as the use of imagery from the Holy of Holies of the Jerusalem Temple to describe the throne chariot of YHWH and the sacrificial destruction of Jerusalem in Ezekiel 1–11) point to this role.[16]

Again, a synchronic reading of the book enables readers to gain an understanding of its full theological significance. Modern critical scholarship has missed the mark in its efforts to separate priestly and prophetic elements in the book of Ezekiel. Indeed, the attempt to excise the prophet's vision of the restored Temple in Ezekiel 40–8 is fundamentally mistaken.[17] The vision clearly stands as the culmination of the book to express Ezekiel's understanding of divine purpose. YHWH first abandons the Temple so that it and the city might be purged of its impurity, and then returns to it so that it might stand once again as the holy center of creation. Ezekiel portrays the destruction of Jerusalem much like the offering of the scapegoat at the Temple on Yom Kippur (see Leviticus 16). The seven men dressed in white linen act as priests in carrying out the sacrificial ritual, by marking and recording those to be burnt, and by setting the fire much as one ignites the sacrifice on the altar (those left unmarked are killed in the destruction of the city; those marked are sent out to the wilderness of exile).[18] Ezekiel is after all a Zadokite priest, and he employs the imagery and conceptual categories for purification and holiness that are characteristic of the Zadokite priesthood.

He shares certain features with his prophetic colleagues. Like Isaiah, he envisions the future role of the Temple at the center of a transformed creation and nation Israel. He shares with Isaiah a theological foundation in the Zion tradition, although in contrast to Isaiah's interest in the house of David he focuses on YHWH's sanctification of Zion as the permanent site for the Temple. In this regard, he sees some diminishment of the role of the Davidic monarch, but he differs from Isaiah in that he does not dismiss the Davidic king entirely; instead, he clearly places the king under the authority of the Temple and its priesthood. He is able to employ Isaian motifs, such as the portrayal in Ezekiel 31 of Pharaoh as a high, lofty tree that must be brought down, much as Isaiah portrayed the Assyrian king in similar terms in Isaiah 10. Ezekiel likewise shares some concerns with Jeremiah. He employs the proverb, "the parents have eaten sour grapes and the children's teeth are set on edge," in Ezekiel 18 to illustrate his contention that people do not suffer for the sins of their parents – rather they suffer for their own wrongdoing – much as Jeremiah 31:27–30 uses the same proverb to make the same point. He might differ from his older contemporary (e.g., Ezekiel identifies Jaazniah ben Shaphan as one of those whose idolatrous worship profaned the holy Temple), but it was the Shaphan family that served as Jeremiah's primary supporters in his conflicts with the monarchs throughout his career.[19] Perhaps the Zadokite Ezekiel viewed Levitical supporters with suspicion as potential sources of corruption for the Temple and the people.

But Ezekiel's debate is not primarily with his prophetic colleagues; rather, it is with the tradition in which he has been trained to serve as a priest in the holy center of creation. Ezekiel cites and employs traditions that are well known in the Torah, but his understanding of those traditions differs to such an extent that in the Talmudic period Rabbi Hananiah ben Hezekiah burned three hundred barrels of oil working at night, attempting to reconcile the differences between Ezekiel and the Torah so that Ezekiel might be accepted as sacred scripture (b. Shabbat 13b; b. Ḥagigah 13a; b. Menaḥot 45a). For example, Ezekiel's discussion of individual moral responsibility in the above-cited Ezekiel 18 draws extensively on the so-called holiness code of Leviticus 17–26 to portray the actions of the righteous and the wicked in terms of the worship of idols, the slaughter and eating of meat, sexual activity, justice to the poor, and so on. But he differs markedly from the Torah by stating that an individual alone is responsible for his or her actions, whereas the Torah indicates that YHWH may punish later generations for the wrongdoing of their ancestors. His description of the restored Temple, its sacred precincts, and its altar differs markedly from the requirements of the Torah in many details – to the extent that the altar appears to represent a Babylonian stepped structure. He deliberately eats impure food to illustrate his life as an exile in a land that is not holy. His depiction of YHWH's throne chariot draws in part on the imagery of the Ark in the Holy of Holies in the Temple, but it also draws on motifs from the depiction of Mesopotamian gods such as Assur, who flies in his own throne chariot at the head of his armies.

Ezekiel employs traditions found in the Torah, but his differences suggest that he is in dialogue with them insofar as he changes them to meet the needs of a new situation. He is a Zadokite priest, raised for holy service in the Jerusalem Temple, but he finds himself with a life outside of that Temple, in a foreign land that can hardly be described as holy by

Temple standards. And yet he strives to act as a priest in very different conditions throughout his lifetime, to sanctify that land by demonstrating the reality of the divine presence even in Babylonia. In this respect, he demonstrates that YHWH is indeed sovereign over all creation. His portrayal of the restored Temple at the center of a restored Israel and a restored creation supports that contention.

Although Christian Bibles treat the Twelve Prophets as twelve discrete prophetic books, the Jewish Bible treats them as a single book that has twelve components. Indeed, modern critical scholarship has recently begun to consider both the compositional history and the literary form of the Book of the Twelve.[20] The issue is complicated by the existence of the Septuagint form of the book, which reflects its own distinctive hermeneutical perspective by presenting the Twelve Prophets in a different sequence from that of the Masoretic Text. Because the present concern is with the Tanak, the following will focus on the sequence of the Masoretic Hebrew Text (MT).

The MT sequence indicates a deliberate concern with Jerusalem and its relationship to YHWH and the nations of the world. The Book of the Twelve includes intertextual relationships with a wide variety of texts from the Bible (particularly the book of Isaiah), which facilitate consideration of the role of Jerusalem and its relationship with the nations in YHWH's plans for the future of the world.[21]

Thus, Hosea, a northern prophet from the latter eighth century, addresses the potential disruption in the relationship between Israel and YHWH but envisions resolution when Israel returns to YHWH and the house of David in Jerusalem.[22] Hosea uses his own marriage to Gomer bat Diblaim, whom he accuses of harlotry, and the birth of his own children to symbolize Israel's relationship as the bride of YHWH, who has abandoned her husband to seek other lovers. Although the abandonment of YHWH is a major religious theme, a close reading of the book indicates that Hosea objects to Israel's relationship with Assyria during the reign of Jeroboam ben Joash. This relationship called for Israel to trade with Egypt, its ancient enemy from the Exodus traditions. Hosea consequently calls for the overthrow of the Jehu dynasty so that Israel might realign with Aram, where its ancestors originated, and thereby restore its relationship with YHWH.

Joel, likely a fourth-century prophet, employs motifs from creation (e.g., locust plagues and images of grain) to focus attention on YHWH's defense of Jerusalem from the nations.[23] Ultimately, Joel looks to the Day of YHWH as the time when YHWH will defend Jerusalem from the nations that threaten it.

Amos is a mid-eighth-century prophet who points to the restoration of Jerusalem and Davidic rule following YHWH's punishment of Israel and the nations.[24] As a Judean farmer and sheep broker, Amos was compelled to bring his produce to the northern Israelite sanctuary at Beth El insofar as Judah was a vassal of Israel during the reigns of Jeroboam ben Joash of Israel and Uzziah ben Amaziah of Judah. Even though Judah suffered agricultural reverses, such as a locust plague and fire during the dry season that destroyed crops, Judean farmers were still compelled to bring their produce to northern Israel. Although the reason for such heavy taxation was Israel's need to pay tribute to its own ally, Assyria, Judeans such as Amos were left with little on which to survive. In Amos's view, YHWH would overthrow Jeroboam ben Joash and restore the rule of the house of David as in the days of Solomon.

Obadiah focuses on YHWH's judgment against Edom as a representative of the nations and on its submission to Israel at Zion on the Day of YHWH.[25] Although traditionalists sometimes identify Obadiah with Elijah's ninth-century associate (1 Kings 19), his references to Edom's role in the destruction of Jerusalem point to a setting at the outset of the Babylonian Exile.

Jonah tempers Obadiah's scenario of judgment by raising the question of YHWH's mercy to a repentant Nineveh.[26] Jonah ben Amittai is mentioned as a prophet from the time of Jeroboam ben Joash of Israel in 2 Kings 14:25, but the book appears to be a Second Temple literary work that reflects on the notions of divine mercy and judgment; namely, why should Jonah accept YHWH's forgiveness of Nineveh, the capital of Assyria, when Assyria will ultimately destroy his own homeland?

Micah, a late-eighth-century prophet from Judah's western border with Philistia, portrays the rise of a new Davidic monarch in Jerusalem who inaugurates a period of world peace after punishing the nations for their assaults on Israel.[27] But Micah is a war refugee who was forced to flee to Jerusalem when the Assyrians invaded Judah and devastated his homeland during Hezekiah's revolt against Assyria. He raises questions about how decisions made by the kings in Samaria and Jerusalem ultimately have consequences for the entire land. The full form of his book also anticipates a Davidic monarch who would defeat the nations that oppress Judah and Israel.

Nahum is a late-seventh-century Jerusalem prophet who celebrates the downfall of the oppressive Assyrian empire.[28] Although many modern interpreters decry Nahum's celebration of Nineveh's downfall, the Assyrian empire had destroyed northern Israel and sent large elements of its surviving population into foreign exile, never to return. The downfall of Nineveh in ancient times is essentially analogous to the downfall of Nazi Germany in modern times.

Habakkuk raises questions concerning divine justice as the Babylonians threaten Judah during the reign of Jehoiakim ben Josiah in 605 BCE.[29] Although many interpreters contend that Habakkuk condemns wicked Judeans, close analysis of his book indicates that he questions YHWH as to why the wicked Babylonians must oppress Judah. YHWH answers Habakkuk's questions by portraying Babylon's downfall at the hands of YHWH.

Zephaniah is a late-seventh-century Jerusalemite prophet who calls for a purge of Jerusalem and Judah on the Day of YHWH.[30] Although the placement of Zephaniah after Habakkuk and before Haggai signals a concern with the impending judgment of the Babylonian Exile, a close reading of the book indicates that Zephaniah spoke in support of King Josiah ben Amon's program of national restoration and religious reform. Zephaniah's portrayals of divine judgment against the wicked were designed to convince his audience to support Josiah's reforms.

Haggai was a late-sixth-century Jerusalemite prophet who calls on the returned people of Jerusalem to rebuild the Temple as the holy center of the nations during the early Persian period restoration of Jerusalem.[31] Like Isaiah, he was a royalist who envisioned the rise of a new Davidic monarch as a result of restoration of the Temple.

Zechariah was a late-sixth-century colleague of Haggai who portrays the process by which the nations will acknowledge YHWH at the Jerusalem Temple following a period of worldwide war.[32] Zechariah was also a Zadokite priest who envisioned the significance of rebuilding of the Temple in a series of eight visions that point to the significance of the restoration of Jerusalem. Although many contend that his final vision in Zechariah 6:1–15 was supposed to envision the restoration of a new Davidic king, the present text posits that Joshua ben Jehozadak, the high priest, will emerge as the new ruler who will wear the crown and sit in the throne with a priest by his side. Many contend that the royal figure was to be Zerubbabel ben Shealtiel, grandson of Jehoiachin, the last king of Judah, but Zerubbabel's unexplained disappearance from history left only the priest to rule Jerusalem in his place on behalf of the Persian Empire. Zechariah 9–14, often viewed as a later protoapocalyptic segment of the book, contains two prophetic pronouncements envisioning the return of a righteous Davidic king to Jerusalem and the ultimate defeat of the nations who will finally recognize YHWH at the Jerusalem Temple.

Finally, Malachi recaps the initial concerns of Hosea by calling for the observance of divine Torah, thereby rejecting calls for a disruption of the relationship between Israel and YHWH.[33] Interpreters question whether Malachi was actually a prophet because his name means simply "my messenger." His work is generally ascribed to the early Persian period following completion of the Temple, and it is viewed as a call for support of the Temple and its priesthood.

A prime example of the intertextual dialogue between the Book of the Twelve and the other prophetic books appears in the repeated references to the "swords into plowshares" passage appearing near the beginning of the book in Isaiah 2:2–4. Indeed, the passage plays important roles near the beginning, middle, and end of the MT sequence of the Twelve. Thus, Joel employs a reversal of its peaceful imagery in its portrayal of YHWH's call to battle against the nations that threaten Jerusalem on the Day of YHWH.[34] Micah employs a slightly different version of the Isaian passage in Micah 4:1–5 at the beginning of a sequence that calls for the rise of a new Davidic king who will confront and subdue the nations that have exiled Israel.[35] Zechariah employs the Isaian oracle in Zechariah 8:20–3 as a means of expressing the nations' proposal to seek YHWH at Zion, immediately prior to its depiction of world war in chapters 9 to 14, culminating in the submission of the nations to YHWH at the Jerusalem Temple.[36] Of course, there are many more allusions and citations both to Isaiah and to other biblical texts, but these examples suffice to demonstrate that the Book of the Twelve takes up concerns quite similar to those of Isaiah, that is, Jerusalem's role at the center of the world following a period of judgment. But it also differs markedly from Isaiah, which envisions Jerusalem's/Israel's submission to a foreign monarch as part of the divine plan for a restored creation. By contrast, the Book of the Twelve envisions a period of extensive conflict with the nations in which the nations will finally be subdued as they submit to YHWH. Although YHWH emerges as the ultimate sovereign of creation and Jerusalem serves as the site of YHWH's sanctuary, a new Davidic king and restored Judah/Israel play leading roles throughout the Book of the Twelve in realizing this goal.

THE LATTER PROPHETS WITHIN THE BIBLE

This survey of the Latter Prophets demonstrates that each addresses the problems of exile and restoration in its own distinctive way. Isaiah envisions a restored Jerusalem/Israel that will serve as a source for divine Torah and be ruled by a foreign monarch in the context of YHWH's recognition throughout the world. Jeremiah envisions the restoration of Israel to Jerusalem and the restoration of righteous Davidic rule based on divine Torah, following the punishment of the nation. Ezekiel envisions the purification of Jerusalem and the world at large as the process by which a new Temple will be built at the center of Israel and all creation. The Book of the Twelve anticipates a period of world conflict in which the nations will recognize YHWH at the Jerusalem Temple after their defeat by YHWH's Davidic monarch. Indeed, each takes up the problem of Israel's Exile as articulated in the Former Prophets by anticipating a restoration of Jerusalem/Israel at the center of a new creation. Each engages in debate, both with the tradition and with their prophetic colleagues, concerning the character of the future restoration.

The Latter Prophets therefore play a key role within the three-part structure of the Tanak, consisting of the Torah, which presents Israel arrayed around the Wilderness Tabernacle or Temple as the ideal culmination of creation; the Prophets (comprising both the Former Prophets and the Later Prophets), which reflect on the significance of the destruction and restoration of Jerusalem and the Temple; and the Writings, which focus once again on the Temple as the reconstituted holy center of Israel and creation.[37] Insofar as the Tabernacle/Temple serves as the ideal, holy center of creation in the Tanak,[38] its destruction by the Babylonians and the question of its restoration must stand as a central concern in the Prophets.[39] The first subsection of the Prophets (i.e., the Former Prophets or Joshua, Judges, Samuel, and Kings) presents a history of Israel's/Judah's existence in the land of Israel, from the time of the conquest under Joshua through the time of the Babylonian Exile, that reflects theologically on this history by demonstrating that the destruction of the Temple resulted from Israel's failure to abide by God's Torah.[40] The second subsection of the Prophets (i.e., the Latter Prophets or Isaiah, Jeremiah, Ezekiel, and the Twelve) likewise attempts to explain the destruction of the Temple as the result of Israel's/Judah's failure to abide by YHWH's expectations, but it also outlines divine plans to reestablish both the Temple and Israel/Judah at the center of creation once the period of punishment is over. In this regard, the Prophets play the central role in the Tanak insofar as they provide the link between the ideal portrayal in the Torah of creation, with Israel and the Temple at its center, and the reestablishment of that ideal in the Writings following its disruption.[41]

The Prophets also function within the Christian Bible as a key element in articulating the theological worldview of Christianity that understands the question of exile and restoration in a different manner.

The Prophets appear as the culminating segment of the four-part Old Testament that presents a historical progression from creation and takes up the problems posed by the destruction of Jerusalem and the Babylonian Exile but also looks forward to the future. Like the Tanak, the Christian Old Testament begins with the Pentateuch, which presents the early history of the world from creation through the granting of the mosaic covenant. The Historical Books (including Joshua, Judges, Ruth, 1–2 Samuel, 1–2 Kings, 1–2 Chronicles, Ezra, Nehemiah, and Esther) present the history of Israel from the time of entry into the land of Israel, through the Exile, and into the Persian period of restoration. The Wisdom and Poetic Books (including Job, Psalms, Proverbs, Ecclesiastes, and Song of Solomon) present the timeless concerns of reflection on the meaning and purpose of life and the human relationship with God. The Prophets (including Isaiah, Jeremiah, Lamentations, Ezekiel, Daniel, and the twelve Minor Prophets) interpret threats to Jerusalem and look forward to the future when God will be recognized throughout the world. Indeed, the placement of the Prophets at the conclusion of the Old Testament anticipates the New Testament in the Christian order of the Bible. For its own part, the New Testament displays a similar concern for progression through history to a future ideal. The Gospels present the foundational revelation of Jesus as the Christ figure in Christian theology within the context of the anticipated destruction of Jerusalem and the Second Temple by the Romans in 70 CE. The Acts of the Apostles present the early history of Christianity, focusing especially on the movement of early Christianity from Jerusalem to Rome. The Epistles of Paul and the other early Christian writers take up the timeless questions of Christian faith, understanding of covenant, and community organization. Finally, the apocalyptic book of Revelation points forward to the time when Christ will inaugurate the Kingdom of God at the end of time and thereby bring an end to the suffering of the world.

Whether read in relation to the Jewish Tanak or the Christian Old Testament, a fundamental concern for interpreting the basic patterns of exile and restoration in Israel's history, and the implications of those patterns for the world at large, is the hallmark of the Prophets, which have continued to inform and sustain both Christianity and Judaism throughout their respective histories.

NOTES

1   For discussion of prophecy in the ancient Near Eastern world, see esp. Marti Nissinen, with C. L. Seow and Robert K. Ritner, *Prophets and Prophecy*

in the Ancient Near East (SBLWAW 12; Leiden, Netherlands: Brill, 2003); Herbert B. Huffman, "Prophecy (ANE)," in *The Anchor Bible Dictionary*, Vol. 5, ed. by David N. Freedman (New York: Doubleday, 1992), 477–82.

2 For discussion of Mesopotamian *baru* or divination prophets, see esp. Frederick H. Cryer, *Divination in Ancient Israel and its Near Eastern Environment* (JSOTSup 142; Sheffield Academic Press, 1994).

3 For discussion of prophetic speech and literary forms, see Marvin A. Sweeney, *The Prophetic Literature: An Introduction* (IBT; Nashville, TN: Abingdon, 2005), 33–42.

4 For recent contributions to the discussion of prophetic books, see Ehud Ben Zvi, "The Prophetic Book: A Key Form of Prophetic Literature," *The Changing Face of Form Criticism for the Twenty-First Century*, ed. by M. A. Sweeney and E. Ben Zvi (Grand Rapids, MI: Eerdmans, 2003), 276–97;Terence Collins, *The Mantle of Elijah: The Redaction Criticism of the Prophetical Books* (BibSem 20; Sheffield Academic Press, 1993); Edgar W. Conrad, *Reading the Latter Prophets: Toward a New Canonical Criticism* (London: T & T Clark, 2004); David L. Petersen, *The Prophetic Literature: An Introduction* (Louisville, KY: Westminster John Knox, 2002); Sweeney, *Prophetic Literature*.

5 For introductions to each of the prophetic books that comprise the Latter Prophets, see in addition to Sweeney, *Prophetic Literature*, Joseph Blenkinsopp, *A History of Prophecy in Israel* (Louisville, KY: Westminster John Knox, 1996); Petersen, *Prophetic Literature*.

6 See the discussion of the order of the prophetic books in the Babylonian Talmud (b Baba Batra 14b), which identifies two different orders based on historical appearance (Isaiah, Jeremiah, Ezekiel, and the Twelve) and theological theme (Jeremiah, Ezekiel, Isaiah, and the Twelve).

7 See my studies "The Truth in True and False Prophecy," "Micah's Debate with Isaiah," and "Zechariah's Debate with Isaiah," all in *Form and Intertextuality in Prophetic and Apocalyptic Literature* (FAT 45; Tübingen, Germany: Mohr Siebeck, 2005), 78–93, 210–21, and 222–35. For discussion of the construction of the Book of the Twelve Prophets in relation to the book of Isaiah, see Erich Bosshard-Nepustil, *Rezeptionen von Jesaia 1–39 im Zwölfprophetenbuch* (OBO 154; Göttingen, Germany: Vandenhoeck und Ruprecht, 1997).

8 In addition to the studies on prophetic literature noted earlier, see the recent commentaries on Isaiah by Marvin A. Sweeney, *Isaiah 1–39, with an Introduction to Prophetic Literature* (FOTL 16; Grand Rapids, MI: Eerdmans, 1996); Brevard S. Childs, *Isaiah: A Commentary* (OTL; Louisville, KY: Westminster John Knox, 2001); Joseph Blenkinsopp, *Isaiah 1–39* (Anchor Bible 19; New York: Doubleday, 2000), and *Isaiah 40–55* (AB 19A; New York: Doubleday, 2002), and *Isaiah 56–66* (AB 19B; New York: Doubleday, 2003).

9 For attempts at synchronic readings of Isaiah, see Sweeney, *Isaiah 1–39*, 39–48, and *The Prophetic Literature*, 45–54; cf. Edgar W. Conrad, *Reading Isaiah* (OBT; Minneapolis, MN: Fortress, 1991); Thomas L. Leclerc, *Yahweh is Exalted in Justice: Solidarity and Conflict in Isaiah* (Minneapolis, MN: Fortress, 2001); Rolf Rendtorff, *The Canonical Hebrew*

Bible: A Theology of the Old Testament, trans. by D. E. Orton (Leiden, Netherlands: Deo, 2005), 167–201.

10 See my essays, "On Multiple Settings in the Book of Isaiah," in *Form and Intertextuality*, 28–35, and "Isaiah and Theodicy after the *Shoah*," in *Strange Fire: Reading the Bible after the Holocaust*, ed. by T. Linafelt (BibSem 71; Sheffield Academic Press, 2000), 208–19.

11 In addition to the introductions to prophetic literature cited earlier, see Louis Stuhlman, *Jeremiah* (AOTC; Nashville, TN: Abingdon, 2005); Jack Lundbom, *Jeremiah 1–20* (AB 21A; New York: Doubleday, 1999), *Jeremiah 21–36* (AB 21B; New York: Doubleday, 2004), and *Jeremiah 37–52* (AB 21C; New York: Doubleday, 2004).

12 See my essay, "The Truth in True and False Prophecy," for discussion of Jeremiah's reading of Isaiah; Ute Wendel, *Jesaja und Jeremia: Worte, Motive und Einsichten Jesajas in der Verkündigung Jeremias* (BibThSt 25; Neukirchen-Vluyn, Germany: Neukirchener, 1995).

13 E.g., Winfried Thiel, *Die deuteronomistische Redaktion von Jeremia 1–25* (WMANT 41; Neukirchen-Vluyn, Germany: Neukirchener, 1973), and *Die deuteronomistische Redaktion von Jeremia 26–45* (WMANT 52; Neukirchen-Vluyn, Germany: Neukirchener, 1981); Christl Maier, *Jeremia als Lehrer der Tora* (FRLANT 196; Göttingen, Germany: Vandenhoeck und Ruprecht, 2002); but see now Carolyn J. Sharp, *Prophecy and Ideology in Jeremiah: Struggles for Authority in the Deutero-Jeremianic Prose* (London: T & T Clark, 2003).

14 For the construction of Jeremiah's Temple speech as a levitical sermon, see the now classic study, E. W. Nicholson, *Preaching to the Exiles: A Study of the Prose Tradition of the Book of Jeremiah* (New York: Schocken, 1970), esp. 68–70.

15 For discussion of Jer 23:1–8; 33:14–36, see Lundbom, *Jeremiah 21–36*, 164–77, 534–46; cf. Yohanan Goldman, *Prophétie et royauté au retour de l'exil* (OBO 118; Freiburg, Germany: Universitätsverlag, 1992).

16 See my essays, "Ezekiel: Zadokite Priest and Visionary Prophet of the Exile," and "The Destruction of Jerusalem as Purification in Ezekiel 8–11," in *Form and Intertextuality*, 125–43, 144–55. For recent treatment of Ezekiel, see Daniel Block, *The Book of Ezekiel*, 2 vols. (NICOT; Grand Rapids, MI: Eerdmans, 1997–8); Katheryn Pfisterer Darr, "Ezekiel," in *The New Interpreter's Bible*, Vol. 6, ed. by L. E. Keck et al. (Nashville, TN: Abingdon, 2001), 1073–1607); Margaret S. Odell, *Ezekiel* (Smyth and Helwys Bible Commentary; Macon, GA: Smyth and Helwys, 2005).

17 Jon D. Levenson, *Theology of the Program of Restoration in Ezekiel 40–48* (HSM 10; Missoula, MT: Scholars Press, 1976).

18 Sweeney, "The Destruction of Jerusalem as Purification."

19 See Jay Wilcoxen, "The Political Background of Jeremiah's Temple Sermon," in *Scripture in History and Theology: Essays in Honor of J. Coert Rylaarsdam*, ed. by A. L. Merrill and T. W. Overholt (Pittsburgh: Pickwick, 1977), 151–66.

20 See now my commentary, *The Twelve Prophets* (Berit Olam; Collegeville, MN: Liturgical Press, 2000), esp. 1:xv–xlii; see also my "Sequence and Interpretation in the Book of the Twelve," in *Form and Intertextuality*, 175–209.

21 See Odil Hannes Steck, *The Prophetic Books and their Theological Witness* (St. Louis, MO: Chalice, 2000); Bosshard-Nepustil, *Rezeption von Jesaja 1–39 im Zwölfprophetenbuch.*

22 Francis Landy, *Hosea* (Readings; Sheffield Academic Press, 1995).

23 See also James L. Crenshaw, *Joel* (AB 24C; New York: Doubleday, 1995).

24 See Max E. Polley, *Amos and the Davidic Empire: A Socio-Historical Approach* (New York: Oxford University Press, 1989); Shalom Paul, *Amos: A Commentary* (Hermeneia; Minneapolis, MN: Fortress, 1991).

25 See also Ehud Ben Zvi, *A Historical-Critical Study of the Book of Obadiah* (BZAW 242; Berlin: Walter de Gruyter, 1996).

26 Uriel Simon, *Jonah* (JPS Bible Commentary; Philadelphia: Jewish Publication Society, 1999).

27 See also Mignon R. Jacobs, *The Conceptual Coherence of the Book of Micah* (JSOTSup 322; Sheffield Academic Press, 2001).

28 See also Klass Spronk, *Nahum* (HCOT; Kampen, Germany: Kok Pharos, 1997).

29 See also Robert D. Haak, *Habakkuk* (VTSup 44; Leiden, Netherlands: Brill, 1992).

30 See also Marvin A. Sweeney, *Zephaniah* (Hermeneia; Minneapolis, MN: Fortress, 2003).

31 See also David L. Petersen, *Haggai, Zechariah 1–8: A Commentary* (OTL; Philadelphia: Westminster, 1984).

32 See also ibid., and Petersen, *Zechariah 9–14, Malachi: A Commentary* (OTL; Louisville, KY: Westminster John Knox, 1995).

33 See also Petersen, *Zechariah 9–14, Malachi.*

34 Sweeney, "The Place and Function of Joel within the Book of the Twelve," in *Form and Intertextuality*, 189–209.

35 See my essay, "Micah's Debate with Isaiah."

36 See my essay, "Zechariah's Debate with Isaiah."

37 For discussion of the literary and theological structure of the Tanak and the Christian Old Testament, see Marvin A. Sweeney, "Tanak versus Old Testament: Concerning the Foundation for a Jewish Theology of the Bible," in *Problems in Biblical Theology: Essays in Honor of Rolf Knierim*, ed. by H. T. C. Sun et al. (Grand Rapids, MI: Eerdmans, 1997), 353–72.

38 For discussion of the role of the Temple in creation, see Jon D. Levenson, "The Temple and the World," *JR* 64(3) (1984): 275–98, and *Sinai and Zion: An Entry into the Jewish Bible* (Minneapolis, MN: Winston, 1985). See also the discussion of world order in Rolf P. Knierim, "Cosmos and History in Israel's Theology," in *The Task of Old Testament Theology: Substance, Method, and Cases* (Grand Rapids, MI: Eerdmans, 1995), 171–224, esp. 175–98, who points to the significance of sacred, cosmic space at the center of creation.

39 For discussion of the significance of the destruction of the Jerusalem Temple in 587 BCE and 70 CE and its relation to contemporary theological discussion of the *Shoah* or Holocaust, see Emil L. Fackenheim, *God's Presence in History: Jewish Affirmations and Philosophical Reflections* (New York: Harper Torchbacks, 1972); cf. Fackenheim, *The Jewish Bible after the Holocaust: A Rereading* (Bloomington: Indiana University Press, 1990), for general discussion of the question of a post-*Shoah* reading of the Bible.

40 For discussion of the Former Prophets or the Deuteronomistic history as
    they are known in modern scholarly parlance, see esp. Richard D. Nelson,
    The Historical Books (IBT; Nashville, TN: Abingdon, 1998), 67–148;
    Marvin A. Sweeney, *King Josiah of Judah: The Lost Messiah of Israel*
    (Oxford University Press, 2001), 33–177; Antony F. Campbell, S.J., *Joshua to
    Chronicles: An Introduction* (Louisville, KY: Westminster John Knox, 2004),
    15–105, 111–233.
41 Cf. Gerhard von Rad's treatment of the prophets in his acclaimed *Old
    Testament Theology*, 2 vols., trans. by D. M. G. Stalker (New York: Harper
    & Row, 1962–5). By devoting the entire second volume to the prophets, von
    Rad pointed to their central theological importance as the culmination of
    the Old Testament tradition, where they constitute the conclusion of the
    Old Testament and thus point to the New Testament in the Christian form
    of the Bible.

FURTHER READING

Joseph Blenkinsopp. *A History of Prophecy in Israel*. Louisville, KY: Westminster
    John Knox, 1996.
David L. Petersen. *The Prophetic Literature: An Introduction*. Louisville, KY:
    Westminster John Knox, 2002.
Martti Nissinen, with C. L. Seow and Robert K. Ritner. *Prophets and Prophecy in
    the Ancient Near East* (SBLWAW 12). Leiden, Netherlands: Brill, 2003.
Marvin A. Sweeney. *Form and Intertextuality in Prophetic and Apocalyptic
    Literature* (FAT 45). Tübingen, Germany: Mohr Siebeck, 2005.
    The Prophetic Literature (IBT). Nashville, TN: Abingdon, 2005.

12 The Psalms and Hebrew poetry

WILLIAM P. BROWN

Nowhere else in the Bible is there found such a varied and extensive collection of poetry than in the Psalter: 150 psalms in Hebrew, 151 in Greek. This corpus comprises a diverse array of literary forms including prayers, hymns, thanksgiving songs, and didactic poems, not to mention a royal wedding song and a judgment drama. Together, these psalms cover the span of Israel's national life (from monarchy to Second Temple), the breadth of Israel's religious practices (from centralized temple worship to local and family practices), and the gamut of human experience (from death and distress to life and jubilation). The Psalms, moreover, are noted for their introspective outlook as much as for their theological profundity. God and self are tightly interwoven in the book of Psalms.

Given the Psalter's diversity, it is no surprise that the Psalms have been studied from a variety of angles, from the fine poetic line to the Psalter's overall shape. This chapter explores some of these foci and notes how each highlights a significant aspect of the Psalter's common yet variegated character. We begin by examining the Psalms as poetry, proceed to exploring how they have been classified and organized, and conclude with broad questions of theological and anthropological interest.

PSALMS AS POETRY

The common denominator of all psalms is poetry. Whether ancient or modern, poetry is verbal art cast in condensed form. Like poetry in general, biblical poetry reflects a compact style of discourse, employs figurative language, and powerfully evokes emotion and thought. Although many poems exhibit rigidly set patterns of sonority and rhythm (e.g., rhyme and meter), poetry plays with language in creative ways. Innovative use of metaphor and imagery, for example, typically distinguishes poetry from prose. Structurally, poetry also sets itself apart from prose by its use of the poetic "line," the basic formal unit in poetry. A line is signaled by a pause or stop in the act of recitation, either completing a thought or running into the next line. The study of psalmist poetry thus can be divided into two domains: prosody and metaphor.

Prosody

The terse language of the Psalms, and of biblical poetry in general, tends to omit certain grammatical particles encountered in Hebrew prose, such as the definite article, relative pronouns, and the direct object marker. Conversely, certain features are present in poetry that prose material lacks, such as line structure, peculiar word order, repetition, chiasmus, unusual vocabulary, and word pairs. Note that meter is not included in the list. Hebrew poetry rarely adheres to consistent metrical systems. Attempts to adopt a system of iambic meter for Hebrew poetry have met with mixed results. In some cases, certain accentual rhythms have been identified, such as the *qînâ* or "lamentation," in which a divisible poetic line features an accentual beat of 3:2 (e.g., Amos 5:2; much of Lamentations; Ps 5:1–2). Some people read Psalm 117, the shortest in the Psalter, as reflecting a consistent accentual rhythm of 3:3.[1] But this is debatable, for such a count depends on how to assign the accents, particularly in construct chains. Others have counted syllables in order to discern a poem's prosodic regularity, again with mixed success. Although Psalm 113 reflects a syllabically consistent count,[2] most other psalms do not.

A more fruitful approach to prosodic analysis for Hebrew poetry is to examine the syntactic and semantic segmentation of lines. Hebrew poetry is characterized by the simple juxtaposition of poetic lines without subordinate clauses. Frequently absent are connective subordinate pronouns or causal markers, such as one finds in prose. Thus, parataxis (literally "placing side by side") is typical of Hebrew poetry, and the informed reader must ascertain by context how the lines fit together syntactically and semantically. The structured juxtaposition of lines, moreover, has to do with the central feature of Hebrew poetry, namely, *parallelismus membrorum*, as coined by Robert Lowth, professor of poetry at Oxford, in his 1753 lectures, *De sacra poesi Hebraeorum*. In his words, passages in Hebrew poetry "treat one subject in many different ways ... in different words or different things in a similar form of words."[3] In 1778, Lowth gave a more precise definition of this linguistic phenomenon in his introduction to Isaiah: "the *correspondence* of one Verse, or Line, with another, I call Parallelism."[4] Such correspondence is evident in the way the segments "repeat," "vary," and "amplify the same sentiment." Lowth placed these poetic correspondences or types of parallelism into three broad categories: synonymous, antithetic, and synthetic or constructive.

A few examples are in order. As Lowth noted, a poetic verse typically consists of paired lines, or cola, commonly called *bicola*, although less frequently *tricola*, and more elaborate patterns are also evidenced. In a typical poetic couplet, the second colon can repeat, intensify, modify, or complete the thought of the first colon. Furthermore, the relationship between the two cola may not always be obvious or even parallel. Yet such regular pairing of clauses conveys a sense of elegant symmetry. Take, for example, Psalm 30:11 (v. 12 in Hebrew):

> You have turned my mourning into dancing;
>> you have taken off my sackcloth and clothed me with joy.

The second line, or colon, amplifies the first: it expands the first both literally and figuratively. The first employs the language of religious behavior and emotion, whereas the second references articles of clothing. Nevertheless, a correspondence is clear, as evinced in the prosodic representation:

> A [a:b:c] / A' [a':b':a":c']

The second colon (A') features two complementary verbs (a' and a") to explicate the one verb (a) featured in the first colon (A), thereby illustrating in more graphic terms how God has transformed the speaker's emotional disposition. The negative verbal object "mourning" (b) in the first colon finds its parallel in the image of "sackcloth" (b'), and the positive image of "dancing" (c) is associated with the apparel of "joy" (c'). Given the parallel features, the verse as a whole builds up a semantic momentum from the first to the second colon.

While the preceding example illustrates Lowth's classification of "synonymous" parallelism, clearly more is going on within the corresponding segments than simply repetition. In the act of reading, a movement or dynamic interchange transpires between the two cola. Through the positive pairing of cola and their corresponding parts, the second line elaborates the first by providing more concrete imagery.

Examples of Lowth's "antithetical" form of parallelism can be readily seen in the following two examples:

> For you a lowly people deliver,
>> *but* haughty eyes you bring down.
>>> 18:27 [Heb v. 28]

Some in chariotry, others in horses,
> *but* we in the name of YHWH find our strength.[5]
>> 20:7 [Heb v. 8]

In each example, the telltale sign is clearly evident in English but not
so immediately clear in Hebrew. The connecting particle in Hebrew is
the same whether serving as a conjunctive ("and") or as an adversative
("but") in the second colon. Context is key. The correspondence in both
examples is clearly contrastive rather than synonymous: "humble people" and "haughty eyes" constitute an opposite pair, as well as the verbal
elements "deliver" and "bring down." Using for convenience the symbol of negation in logic (~), the relationship of correspondence can be
illustrated as A [a:b:c] ~ A' [b':c'], with "a" designating the independent
personal pronoun "you" in the first colon, which is absent in the second.
(The "you" in the second colon reflects a verbal inflection in Hebrew,
not an independent pronoun.)

The second example is syntactically more complex: A [a:b:a':b'] ~ A'
[a'':b'':c]. The elliptical first colon lacks a verb and comprises two clauses.
The second colon supplies the verbal phrase (c), which can be read back
into the first: "Some [find their strength] in chariotry; others [find their
strength] in horses." Thus, the second colon functions in part to fill the
syntactical gap of the first. As a whole, the first colon sets up the foil for
the second, which commends the true object of allegiance and source of
strength. In the first example, however, the foil is featured in the second
colon instead of the first. In both examples, the relationship between
the two cola is "antithetical," but as in the case of so-called synonymous parallelism, more is at work than a static correspondence between
opposites. Indeed, the two examples are contrastive in opposite ways.
Psalm 20:7 charts a movement from false trust to true allegiance, with
the latter exposing the former as illusory. The second colon, in short,
deconstructs the first. In Psalm 18:27, the "antithetical" relationship
between the two cola is different: both lines are held to be equally true –
the second is the converse and consequence of the first. Delivering the
lowly entails humiliation of the haughty.

As for synthetic parallelism, Lowth recognized examples of
Hebrew verse that do not fit into either of the two preceding categories.
Parallelism, whether synonymous or antithetical, does not apply in the
following examples:

Blessed be YHWH,
> who has not given us as prey to their teeth.
>> 124:6

From the rising of the sun to its setting,
   the name of YHWH is to be praised.

113:3

In the first example, the two cola are linked by a common subject, but that is as far as the syntactic similarity goes. The first colon invokes a blessing, for which the second, as a subordinate clause, provides the warrant. In the second example, the first colon prefaces the second, which provides its subject matter. This particular case of nonparallel lines exhibits poetic *enjambment* (literally "straddling"), whereby a sentence or thought does not end where the colon ends but continues naturally into the next colon.[6] Enjambment serves to propel the reader forward into the next line.

As a liability, Lowth's categories can foster a rigidly taxonomic approach that vitiates rather than elucidates the subtlety of Hebrew poetry. Nevertheless, his central point remains valid. Yes, the term "synonymous" is misleading. The same also can be said of "antithetical," and "synthetic" is much too general a classification to be helpful. Even the most synonymous-sounding poetic lines can deliver a semantic punch in the second colon. As James Kugel has formulated for so-called synonymous parallelism: "A is so, and *what's more*, B is so."[7] This *"more"* that belongs to the second colon, as Robert Alter observes, can indicate greater specification, unusual terminology, intensification, vividness, or figuration.[8] Kugel goes further to argue that there is no clear distinction between Hebrew poetry and prose: there are "poetic" passages lacking parallelism (see earlier), and there are "prosaic" passages that exhibit parallelism (e.g., Gen 22:12, 17).[9] There is, rather, a continuum of Hebrew style from prose to poetry. It is precisely here, however, that Kugel overstates the case. Although parallelism is itself not the defining mark of Hebrew poetry, it is, as Adele Berlin points out, the *"predominance* of parallelism, combined with terseness," that makes the difference.[10] To be sure, the difference between prose and poetry is a matter of degree; nevertheless, there remains a qualitative difference between "prosaic linearity and poetic contiguity."[11] With the exception of enjambed lines, correspondence between cola can exist on any number of linguistic levels, from phonology and morphology to syntax and semantics.[12]

Identifying various levels of correspondence between cola is one thing; charting the progression from one colon to the next is another, albeit interrelated, task. At root is a change of meaning. Robert Alter approvingly quotes Viktor Shklovsky regarding the purpose of parallelism: "to *transfer* the usual perception of an object into the sphere of a new perception – that is, to make a unique semantic modification."[13] By exploring the matrix of nuanced correspondences – from the patently obvious to the sublimely subtle – between poetic segments, parallelism generates progression of thought. Highlighting both the complexity of correspondence and the progression of semantic change, parallelism reveals "a dynamic microworld in which many different components function in relation to each other."[14] Every single colon in a given poem generates only provisional meaning. In isolation, cola supply only "half-meanings," reminding the reader of the need to keep reading through the poem, thoughtfully and imaginatively, to its conclusive end.[15]

Metaphor

In addition to the prosodic contours of Hebrew poetry, there are the visual dimensions that invite thoughtful attention. The evocative power of Hebrew poetry lies not only in its sonority and structure but also in its imaginative use of imagery and metaphor. A poetic analysis of any given psalm involves examining both the psalm's *verbal* texture and its *graphic* texture. As essential as parallelism, metaphor is a basic mark of Hebrew poetry. Indeed, both parallelism and metaphor have to do with the transference of meaning. In light of its Greek root, "metaphor" originally meant the "carrying over" of property (*meta* "trans" + *pherein* "to carry"). In the act of reading, metaphors facilitate the *transference* of meaning from something familiar to something new. Most definitions of metaphor include two elements that establish a correspondence or congruity. Janet Martin Soskice's definition is as good as any: "the metaphor is that figure of speech whereby we speak about one thing in terms [that] are seen to be suggestive of another."[16] How the "one thing" is related to "another" has been the pressing challenge for every literary theorist. Perhaps best known are the labels given by I. A. Richards: "tenor" and "vehicle," classifications that he himself admitted were "clumsy."[17]

Cognitive literary theorists George Lakoff and Mark Turner have introduced greater precision into the discussion of metaphor: "We use a metaphor to map certain aspects of the *source domain* onto the *target domain*, thereby producing a *new understanding* of that target domain."[18] The terms "target domain" and "source domain" not only acknowledge a certain parity of import between the metaphor and its referent; they also illustrate more precisely the *dynamic* that occurs when something is referenced metaphorically, namely, a superimposing or unilateral "mapping" of one domain (or "source") on another (i.e., "target").[19] Such transference of meaning results in a new understanding of the *target* domain.[20] To take a biblical example, the psalmist states that "YHWH God is a sun and shield" (84:12). The source metaphors, "sun" and "shield," map the character of divinity, the target. The image of the "sun" connotes effulgent blessing; military "shield" suggests sure protection. Together, both images inscribe God's nature as salutary.

To summarize: in the event of a metaphor, as in the phenomenon of poetic parallelism, there is a transference of meaning by which one mode of perception is superimposed on another, specifically a source domain onto its target domain. Such mapping generates a new understanding of the target, enabling "one to see similarities in what previously had been regarded as dissimilars."[21]

PSALMS AS SPECIES

The interpretation of psalms is by no means limited to individual poetic lines or even to isolated psalms. No psalm is an island unto itself. With few exceptions, a psalm shares features with other psalms. Not unlike a field biologist classifying various species of animals within the same genus, Hermann Gunkel (1862–1932) identified various types of psalms. Each type, Gunkel observed, is characterized by common form (*Gestalt*), content, and setting in life (*Sitz im Leben*), together constituting a particular psalm's genre (*Gattung*). Gunkel identified five major genres among the psalms: hymn, community lament, royal psalm, individual lament, and personal thanksgiving. He also identified various minor genres, including songs of pilgrimage, communal songs of thanksgiving, wisdom poetry, liturgy, and some mixed psalms. Put succinctly, genres establish family resemblances. For Gunkel, the original setting of the psalms was Israel's worship, which explains why the psalms "speak so generally."[22] Over time, however, these types became detached from their original settings in worship and came to be used in other ways. For Gunkel, most of the Psalms preserved in the Psalter are actually "spiritualized" imitations of old, now-lost cultic poetry.

Identifying the genre of a particular psalm, however, carries liabilities. It was thought that the form of a particular psalm directly reflected its setting in life, that is, its institutional context of usage (e.g., temple worship, educational setting, family setting, etc.). However, recent scholarship has shown no rigid correspondence between the form and setting of individual psalms. Psalms of similar structure may, and in fact do, reflect different settings of usage. Reception history has shown that a psalm can easily function in different settings, from public worship to individual devotion (see, e.g., Psalm 30, discussed later). Also, there is more generic fluidity among individual psalms than was typically acknowledged, with many being hybrids (to press the biological metaphor), or sharing elements of various genres.

Still, genre analysis is useful in at least two respects. On the one hand, a given genre conveys a set of expectations that prompts the reader to identify a psalm's constituent parts and to sense how a psalm typically moves from beginning to end. On the other hand, serving as a template, a genre can reveal how a particular psalm breaks the generic mold, thereby highlighting the psalm's uniqueness, or "the singularity of the poet's creation," to quote Gunkel.[23]

Scholars have been refining Gunkel's classifications ever since his groundbreaking work. Mention must be made of Claus Westermann, who dispensed with the formal-critical category of thanksgiving psalms. These psalms, Westermann argued, have so much in common with the psalms of praise or hymns that they are best considered as a type of praise psalm. As a result, Westermann distinguished two kinds of praise psalms or hymns: the psalm of "declarative praise," which focuses on what God *has done,* and the psalm of "descriptive praise," which focuses on what God *is* or *does.*[24] More refined is Frank Crüsemann's argument for retaining the classification "thanksgiving" for individual psalms because they have more in common with the individual prayers than with hymns.[25]

PSALMS AS PERFORMANCE

Gunkel's genre analysis not only carried forward the taxonomic impulse to categorize psalms but also launched great interest in the performative settings of psalms. From content alone, many psalms reflect the activity of worship: references are made to festal events (81:3), temple visits (5:7; 65:4; 122:1–2), processions (24:7–10; 42:4; 118:26–7), sacrifices (4:5; 51:19; 107:22; 116:17), and benedictions (115:14–15; 121:3–8; 134:3). Some psalms reflect antiphonal singing (118) and prescribe the use of various musical instruments in worship (149:3; 150:3–5). Many a superscription specifically designates some type of musical accompaniment or melody, such as "Deer of the Dawn" in Psalm 22, "The Dove on Far-off Terebinths" in Psalm 56, "Lily of the Covenant" in Psalm 60, and "Lilies" in Psalms 45, 69, and 80. Pending the discovery of a musical score from biblical times, we cannot reconstruct ancient Israel's sacred music. Nevertheless, it is clear that many psalms were crafted to be performed corporately and with music. Even the term usually translated as "meditate" or "meditation" carries a distinctly performative nuance (1:2; 19:14; 104:34). Private, silent reflection is not the aim of the Psalms.

The first to champion the performative dimensions of the Psalms was Norwegian scholar Sigmund Mowinckel (1884–1965). In his magisterial treatments, Mowinckel attempted to reconstruct a particular psalm's actual usage in worship, that is, the psalm's "cultic situation" with its attendant "ideological and liturgical complexity."[26] For Mowinckel, the cult designated "the socially established and regulated holy acts and words in which the encounter and communion of the Deity with the congregation is established, developed, and brought to its ultimate goal."[27] The simple act of prayer and invocation, consequently, originated outside the cult.[28] Thus, for Mowinckel, the cultic was preeminently public, and anything less than that was consigned to the worshiper's closet, as it were, including all forms of familial and "popular" piety unrelated to the temple. Mowinckel insisted that most of the Psalms were read in "the midst of the Great Assembly,"[29] as if cultic practice were exercised exclusively within this most centralized of sacred contexts. In so doing, Mowinckel attempted to reconstruct the rich choreography of movement, sound, and sight of First Temple worship.

By building on Gunkel's work, Mowinckel turned his teacher's developmental approach on its head: he saw cultic formulation as the culmination, not the beginning (and vanishing) point, of the Psalms' evolution in biblical Israel. In addition, Mowinckel was not convinced that the older instances of psalmist poetry were more pure. "Mixed types," rather, indicated greater antiquity; differentiation was the mark of later development. Mowinckel's "cult-functional" approach was informed by the anthropological work of his day, particularly that of V. Grønbech and A. van Gennep. From them, Mowinckel came to discern the dramatic, emotive dimensions of ancient ritual – what could be called the *pathos* of the cult – and thereby was able to recognize the personal within the public. Mowinckel successfully countered a prevailing prejudice that deemed liturgical compositions to be of a "certain inferiority."[30]

In addition to his clarion call for a cult-centered hermeneutic, Mowinckel is best known for his nearly singular concentration on the autumnal New Year's festival, the Israelite cousin of the Babylonian *akitu* festival. This central festival served as the occasion not just for the enthronement psalms, whose festal shout Mowinckel translated in a uniquely dramatic way ("Yahweh has become king!"), but also for much of the Psalter. He lodged this reconstructed enthronement festival, the festival of YHWH's epiphany, within the Feast of Tabernacles.

Regardless of whether he was correct in doing so,[31] Mowinckel demonstrated that the work of liturgy is more than the exercise of the worshiper's imagination; objective reality is itself shaped in the liturgical act. Therein lies the Psalms' performative power.

Historically and culturally, cultic performance in ancient Israel was by no means confined to the centralized festivals. In addition to the national Temple, the village and the family constituted bona fide ritual communities. Within these smaller settings, according to Erhard Gerstenberger, "small-group rituals" were conducted under the guidance of a "ritual expert."[32] The scope of Israel's cultic life thus cannot be limited to the Temple setting. "Cult" extends well beyond the "Great Assembly." Martin Buss aptly regards cult as a complex and varied set of expressions or "concrete operations" denoting a symbolic whole including everything from the "messy" major festivals at the sanctuary, to ritualized activity in the home, to an individual passing by a sacred spot.[33] In short, any definition of "cult," particularly for Psalms, must accommodate all forms of religious practice.

As the scope of Israel's cult has been significantly widened, so also has the idea of the Psalms' "life setting" (*Sitz im Leben*). While acknowledging his debt to Mowinckel, Walter Brueggemann has expanded the concept of "function" and "cult" in ways that make the Psalms accessible to modern readers. For Brueggemann, the cult is a world-creating drama, irrespective of its ancient ceremonial dynamics. By broadening the scope of what constitutes a "setting," Brueggemann classifies the Psalms in three broad categories: orientation, disorientation, and new orientation.[34] The first includes the psalms of descriptive praise (à la Westermann), the second includes the lament psalms, and the third comprises psalms of declarative praise (or "thanksgiving"). With these three categories, Brueggemann suggests a typology of psalmic movement, of the life of faith in which the transition to new orientation involves struggle, pain, and protest.

As research since Gunkel's taxonomic project indicates, the issue of genre remains quite fluid, ranging from reconstructing the choreography of ancient worship to discerning universal life settings of suffering and joy. Indeed, such fluidity is also indicated within the Psalter itself. Psalm 30, for example, presents itself as an individual thanksgiving psalm. The superscription, however, suggests that it was used to (re)dedicate the Temple. This startling example demonstrates that, in principle at least, no psalm can be tied to any particular setting. The notion of *Sitz im Leben* was never considered locked and final by the psalmists. Regarding a psalm's social setting and function, there are no copyright restrictions!

PSALMS AS CORPORA

Another avenue of interpretation is also comparative in nature. Unlike form-critical analysis, however, it does not seek out family resemblances among psalms of similar form or content. Rather, it takes seriously where and how psalms were placed within their received arrangement *ad seriatum*, despite their variety. Here a psalm's literary interaction with neighboring psalms is paramount, and one indication of such interaction is found in the psalmist superscriptions or titles.

One hundred and nineteen psalms in the Psalter bear various titles or superscriptions, from the terse to the elaborate. Through common formulations or attributions to common personages, many of the superscriptions suggest discrete subcollections. Other collections are indicated by common content or style:

1. Davidic collections	3–41; 51–72; 138–45
2. Korahite collection	42–9; 84–5; 87–8 (89?)
3. Asaphite collection	50; 73–83
4. Elohistic collection	42–83
5. Enthronement hymns collection	93; 95–100
6. Psalms of praise collection	103–7
7. Songs of ascents collection	120–34
8. Hallelujah collection	111–18; 135; 146–50

In addition to the Davidic collections, the other "personal" collections include that of the Korahites (literally "sons of Korah"), a guild of temple singers appointed by David,[35] and the collection attributed to Asaph, a temple singer also appointed by David.[36]

The so-called Elohistic collection includes a portion of the Korahite collection and all the Asaphite collection. These originally separate collections were partially combined in the Elohistic collection, whose defining feature is a distinct, albeit inconsistent, preference for the name "God" (*'ĕlōhîm*) over "LORD" (*yhwh*) in reference to the deity (cf. 14 and 53). Lacking superscriptions, the enthronement hymns collection is united by content and style: they celebrate YHWH's kingship over Israel and the nations, featuring among them the opening acclamation "YHWH reigns!" (93; 97; 99). The songs of ascents collection is distinguished by the unique superscription *šîr hamma'ălôt*, whose exact significance remains unclear.

Scholars have discerned some degree of thematic and stylistic continuity within these various collections. Several of the psalms attributed to the "sons of Korah," for example, acknowledge the ties that bind the speaker to Zion (e.g., 42:4; 43:3-4; 84:11), as one would expect from a Temple singer.[37] Their primary function may have been related to Temple service personnel.[38] Also prominent among these psalms is the theme of redemption from Sheol.[39] The twelve psalms of Asaph, likely of northern origin, lift up the theme of divine judgment and covenant (e.g., 50; 75; 76; 81; 83), Israel's history from Exodus to Exile (78-9), and religious instruction (73; 78).[40] The fifteen songs of ascents, perhaps also of northern origin, have evidently been redacted as psalms of pilgrimage to the Jerusalem Temple.[41]

Regarding the largest grouping of psalms, the Davidic superscription functions more as a hermeneutical entry point than as an ascription of authorship.[42] James L. Mays distinguishes three levels of Davidic interpretation in the Psalms: David as a model of piety, as one anointed by YHWH, and as "the source and patron of praise and prayer for the worship of the LORD."[43] The Davidic psalms illustrate, in part, how one should respond in situations of distress and adversity.[44]

Within larger collections, smaller, deliberately arranged collections have also been discerned. The grouping of Psalms 15-24 is a clear case in point. They are arranged in concentric or chiastic fashion[45]:

A	Psalm 15 (entrance liturgy)
B	Psalm 16 (song of trust)
C	Psalm 17 (prayer for help)
D	Psalm 18 (royal psalm)
E	Psalm 19 (Torah psalm)
D'	Psalms 20-21 (royal psalms)
C'	Psalm 22 (prayer for help)
B'	Psalm 23 (song of trust)
A'	Psalm 24 (entrance liturgy)

This subcollection is bracketed on the "outside" by two entrance liturgies; its center is the Torah psalm. The connections among these nine psalms run deep, as indicated by their symmetrical arrangement.

Frank-Lothar Hossfeld and Erich Zenger have identified thematic and redactional rationales for various clusters of psalms. They discern multiple redactional levels, from "messianic" redaction to one oriented toward the "piety of the poor" (*Armenfrömmigkeit* or *armentheologische Erweiterung*).[46] The resulting picture is a comprehensive account of the Psalter's complex growth.[47]

PSALMS AS CORPUS

Granted common features for the Psalter's various collections, what can be said about the Psalter as a whole? Can one speak of its final shape, and if so, can one account for its shaping? The issue over whether the Psalter is, to put it most pointedly, a random collection or a well-structured book is perhaps the most debatable issue in current Psalms research. However one arrives at an answer, one must begin by recognizing that the Psalter itself does reflect some degree of arrangement. It divides itself into five discrete units or "books," as indicated by the four doxologies that conclude each one: 41:13 (Heb 41:14); 72:18–20a; 89:52 (Heb 89:53); and 106:48.

Book I: Psalms 1–41
Book II: Psalms 42–72
Book III: Psalms 73–89
Book IV: Psalms 90–106
Book V: Psalms 107–50

The Psalter's structure, according to rabbinic tradition, finds correspondence with the Torah or Pentateuch (*Midrash Tehillim*, Psalm 1). Hence, one can speak canonically of a Davidic Torah as much as of a Mosaic Torah. Indeed, the paralleling of David and Moses can be found elsewhere in scriptural tradition: as Moses received the *tabnît* ("plan") from God for the Tabernacle on Sinai (Exod 25:9), so David received "from the hand of YHWH" the *tabnît* of the Temple, which he passes on to Solomon (1 Chr 28:11, 19).

Recent research has devoted great attention to the boundaries or "seams" between these "books" by noting the strategic positions of certain psalms. Most noted for this direction of research, Gerald Wilson has observed the placement of royal and "wisdom" psalms around these seams.[48] The Psalter's most decisive turning is found in the transition from Book III to Book IV in Psalm 89. For the first thirty-seven verses, this psalm gives praise for God's enduring *ḥesed*, or faithful benevolence (vv. 1–2; cf. 88:11). Such "steadfast love" is evidenced in God's covenant with David, which preserves "forever" the line of royal descendants (vv. 3–4, 28). God's incomparability (vv. 6–7; cf. 86:8), lordship over creation (vv. 9–12), and justice (v. 14) find their parallels in David's victory over his enemies, his rule over an extensive kingdom, and the enduring dynasty (vv. 19–37). But all this is undone in the second half of the psalm: the speaker complains of God's rejection of the covenant, evidenced in the king's defeat by his enemies (vv. 38–45), and concludes with bitter questions about God's reliability, the inescapability of death (vv. 47–48; cf. 88:4–6), and a desperate petition for God's *hesed* (vv. 46–51). Psalm 89, in short, performs the end of the Davidic kingdom from a covenantal standpoint.

Introducing Book IV, Psalm 90 is attributed to Moses and proclaims the Creator God as "our dwelling place" or refuge (v. 1). Lamenting the transience of human life, the psalm concludes with an appeal to God for *hesed* and prosperous work (vv. 13–14, 17). Following this psalm, God is proclaimed as king in the enthronement psalms, while utter silence settles over the earthly king. God's sovereignty, in effect, has trumped Davidic kingship.

Many interpreters have pushed Wilson's observations further by suggesting that the Psalter *as a whole* charts the history of Israel from the establishment of the monarchy (Books I–III), through its dissolution by exile (Book IV), to its restoration as a priestly kingdom (Book V).[49] Stephen Parrish speaks of the Psalter's historical-narrative movement that charts Israel's "emergence," "establishment," "collapse," and "reemergence."[50] A drawback to this metanarrative approach is that it selects only certain psalms that demonstrate narrative progression while neglecting other psalms that clearly do not. For example, the thirteen superscriptions that relate psalms to certain events in David's life stretch across nearly the entire Psalter, but without chronological ordering. Nevertheless, any attempt at accounting for the editorial shaping of the Psalter must discern the threads woven into and extending across the Psalms' great variety.

In addition to seeing the metanarrative thread of history tying the Psalter together, attempts have been made to trace the movement of certain themes and forms throughout the Psalter. James Mays, for example, notes the dispersal of Torah psalms (1; 19; 119), which provide an editorial frame of Torah instruction for much of the Psalter.[51] But that is not all: the liturgically oriented psalms bear equal, if not greater, thematic weight, suggesting a dual framework in which instruction and worship, study and performance, are tightly interwoven. In this light, the Psalter can be considered both a hymnbook *and* a textbook. Relatedly, a twofold theme is indicated at the Psalter's very introduction. Like the two pillars Jachin and Boaz flanking the entrance into the Temple (1 Kgs 7:21), Psalms 1 and 2 serve as a composite introduction to the Psalter by introducing two main themes that wend their respective ways throughout the book, namely, instruction (*tôrâ*) and kingship. Psalm 1 opens with a beatitude that sharply distinguishes the righteous from the wicked.

Likened to a well-nourished tree (see 52:8–9 and 92:13), the righteous individual flourishes by delightfully "meditating" on divine instruction day and night, whereas the wicked are tantamount to chaff driven away by the wind (1:3–4).

On a very different order, Psalm 2 plunges the reader into a scene of international conflict in which the foreign nations rally to attack Zion, YHWH's "holy hill" (2:1–6). The same verb for "meditate" in 1:2 is now used to describe the nations ranting and raving "in vain" (2:1). The king proclaims by divine decree that he is God's designated "son" and is established on Zion as one anointed to hold sway over the foreign nations (v. 9). The psalm ends with a dire warning: the kings are to "wise up" and serve YHWH with fear (vv. 10–11a); otherwise, they will "perish in the way" (v. 11), like the wicked in the previous psalm (1:4). As Psalm 1 began, Psalm 2 ends with a beatitude that commends taking refuge in God (v. 11b). Together, Psalms 1 and 2 conjoin various themes that pervade the Psalter: righteousness and royalty, way and refuge, instruction and dominion.

Regarding form, it is commonly noted that laments (or prayers for help) predominate in the first half of the Psalter, whereas praise psalms predominate in the second (particularly Books IV and V). Hence, in the last thirty psalms the "center of gravity" of the Psalter shifts in favor of praise, as well as from the individual to the community. The Psalter begins with a commendation to obedience (1) and ends in a lyrical summons to praise (146–50). In between unfolds a dramatic movement that scales the heights of praise by first descending into the depths of lament. The Psalter's climactic conclusion in the last six Psalms provides the precedent for Hebrew title of Psalms: "Praises" (*tĕhillîm*).

PSALMS AS "SOUL ANATOMY"

Because most of the Psalter is cast as human speech covering a wide-ranging variety of settings, the anthropological question, "What does it mean to be human?" is appropriate to pose. For the psalmist, the question is essentially theological: "What are human beings that you are mindful of them, mortals that you care for them?" (8:4). The answer lies in God's creating humankind "a little lower than" the divine realm, "crowned with glory and honor." The question of human identity in Psalm 8 is repeated in variant form in Psalm 144, but the answer is markedly different: human beings "are like a breath; their days are like a passing shadow" (v. 4). The psalmist testimony covers the extremes of the human experience: human beings are powerful and fragile, filled

with dignity and fraught with affliction. They are at once endowed with
nearly divine capacities and beset with physical and social debilitations.
Pain and death, the Psalms testify, constitute an integral part of life,
but so also wholeness and communion with God. Community is both
a blessing when peace reigns (e.g., 133) and a bane when alienation and
persecution are the norm (e.g., 22; 42; 55). The complaint prayers give
vivid testimony of abuse committed by the "wicked" with impunity.
Human beings exhibit the capacity to oppress others with a vengeance,
on the one hand, and to repent, show compassion, and work for reconciliation, on the other. As Athanasius noted, the Psalms are like a "mir-
ror"; together they portray "in all their great variety the movements
of the human soul."[52] As John Calvin stated even more succinctly: the
Psalter is "An Anatomy of all Parts of the Soul."[53]

The disparity between humanity's elevation and humanity's deprav-
ity suggests an eschatological orientation: human beings exist somewhere in between the now and the not-yet of their readiness to live into
God's image.[54] In the meantime, they long for communion with others
and with God. While the wisdom literature claims God as the ultimate
object of human learning, the Psalms render God as the ultimate object
of human yearning. The desire for divine presence, for deliverance and
communion, shapes the life of psalmist piety. For Bernd Janowski, the
Psalms feature two major existential movements: from life to death
and from death to life, not unlike Brueggemann's threefold movement.
Psalm 22 is perhaps paradigmatic of all three milestones on the journey
from life to death to new life. And what enables the passage from death
to new life is God's ḥesed.

PSALMS AS THEOLOGY

The varied attempts at articulating the Psalter's literary coherence have
added impetus to discerning a theological coherence in the Psalms. More
historically oriented approaches have sought to identify *the* theological origin and development of the Psalter, such as the divine warrior
tradition from the early Shilo Sanctuary[55] or the divine king's "saving
presence" at Zion.[56] More recent work has acknowledged the multiple
sources and developments associated with psalmist theology.[57] Although
Gerstenberger stresses the irreducible diversity of "theologies" in the
Psalter, his observations help to identify the theological perspectives
that shaped the Psalter.[58] There may be more to the Psalter's theology
than simply a catenation of various theological themes. The question
remains: Is there a generative theological core to the Psalter?

Several recent proposals have attempted to identify such a core. To be sure, identifying *the* "center" (*Mitte*) of the Psalms reveals as much about how the interpreter treats the Psalms in relation to his or her theological convictions as about how the Psalter is itself theologically structured. Several recent proposals have been offered. James Mays identifies divine kingship as the Psalter's "root metaphor."[59] Like Gerald Wilson, Mays finds the center of the Psalter lodged in Book IV, specifically in the enthronement psalms. Taking into account both the theological and anthropological dimensions of psalmist rhetoric, Jerome Creach identifies "refuge" as the Psalter's central metaphor.[60] God provides it; human beings seek it. This leitmotif occurs throughout Book I (2; 5; 17; 18; 31; 34; 36; 37) and the Korahite psalms, is redactionally prominent in Books III and IV, and is featured at the conclusion of the Psalter (144; 146).

Proportionally lacking in both proposals, however, are the instructional dimensions of the Psalms, as reflected in the Torah and didactic psalms. In these psalms and elsewhere the metaphor of "pathway" plays a prominent role. Both themes of "refuge" and "pathway" are interwoven in the first two psalms (1:1, 6; 2:12) and throughout the Psalter's multicolored tapestry. Thus, William Brown proposes a dual core or, better, framework to the Psalter, one that imbues the life of faith with both movement and destination, instruction and salvation, and discerns the God of the Psalms as both sovereign provider and divine pedagogue.[61]

There are, of course, other theological motifs to identify within the Psalter. Nearly every theological chord that resounds throughout the Old Testament can be heard in the Psalms, from covenant and history to creation and wisdom. In the Psalms, the God who commands is also the God who sustains. The God of royal pedigree and the God of the "poor and needy," the God of judgment and the God of healing, God's hidden face and God's beaming countenance – all are profiled in the Psalter. And so it is with good reason that Martin Luther called the Psalter "the little Bible."[62]

NOTES

1 See, e.g., Susan Gillingham, *The Poems and Psalms of the Hebrew Bible* (Oxford University Press, 1994), 57–9.
2 See J. P. Fokkelman, *Reading Biblical Poetry: An Introductory Guide* (Louisville, KY: Westminster John Knox, 2001), 18, 24.
3 Quoted in Adele Berlin, *The Dynamics of Biblical Parallelism* (Bloomington: Indiana University Press, 1985), 1.
4 Ibid. (emphasis added).
5 Read *nagbîr* for MT *nazkîr*.

6 For a full discussion with examples, see Wilfred G. E. Watson, *Classical Hebrew Poetry: A Guide to its Techniques* (JSOTSup 26) (Sheffield, UK: JSOT Press, 1986), 333.

7 James L. Kugel, *The Idea of Biblical Poetry: Parallelism and Its History* (New Haven, CT: Yale University Press, 1981), 8.

8 See Robert Alter, *The Book of Psalms: A Translation with Commentary* (New York: W. W. Norton, 2007), xxiii. For full discussion, see Alter, *The Art of Biblical Poetry* (New York: Basic Books, 1985), 3–26.

9 Kugel, *Idea of Biblical Poetry*, 3, 59.

10 Berlin, *Dynamics of Biblical Parallelism*, 5 (emphasis added).

11 Ibid., 15.

12 Ibid., 26. For a technical study of grammatical parallelism in Hebrew poetry, see Stephen A. Geller, *Parallelism in Early Biblical Poetry* (HSM 20). (Missoula, MT: Scholars Press, 1979).

13 Alter, *Art of Biblical Poetry*, 10 (emphasis added); Viktor Shklovsky, "Art as Technique," in *Russian Formalist Criticism*, ed. and trans. by Lee T. Lemon and Marion J. Reis. (Lincoln: University of Nebraska Press, 1965), 21.

14 Berlin, *Dynamics of Biblical Parallelism*, 2.

15 Mary Kinzie, *A Poet's Guide to Poetry* (University of Chicago Press, 1999), 49.

16 Janet Martin Soskice, *Metaphor and Religious Language* (Oxford, UK: Clarendon Press, 1985), 15.

17 I. A. Richards, *The Philosophy of Rhetoric* (The Mary Flexner Lectures on the Humanities 3) (New York: Oxford University Press, 1965 [1936]), 96–7.

18 George Lakoff and Mark Turner, *More than Cool Reason: A Field Guide to Poetic Metaphor* (University of Chicago Press, 1989), 38–9.

19 Lakoff and Turner's theory of metaphor effectively counters the traditional "interaction theory" of I. A. Richards and Max Black, who considered metaphorical movement to be "bidirectional," that is, from target to source *and* from source to target.

20 Soskice adopts a modified "interactive" theory of metaphor, specifically an "interanimation" theory (*Metaphor and Religious Language*, 43–51).

21 Soskice, *Metaphor and Religious Language*, 26.

22 Herman Gunkel with Joachim Begrich, *Introduction to Psalms: The Genres of the Religious Lyric of Israel*, trans. by James D. Nogalski (Macon, GA: Mercer University Press, 1998), 6.

23 Ibid., 8.

24 Claus Westermann, *Praise and Lament in the Psalms*, trans. by Keith R. Crim and Richard N. Soulen (Atlanta: John Knox Press, 1981), 34.

25 Frank Crüsemann, *Studien zur Formgeschichte von Hymnus und Danklied in Israel* (WMANT 32; (Neukirchen-Vluyn, Germany: Neukirchener, 1969).

26 Sigmund Mowinckel, *The Psalms in Israel's Worship*, 2 vols., trans. by D. R. Ap-Thomas (Grand Rapids, MI: Eerdmans, 2004 [1962]), 1.106.

27 Ibid., 1.15.

28 Ibid., 1.22.

29 Ibid., 1.8.

30 Ibid., 1.5, 12.

31 See J. J. M. Roberts's positive assessment in "Mowinckel's Enthronement Festival: A Review," in *The Book of Psalms: Composition and Reception*, ed.

by Peter W. Flint and Patrick D. Miller (VTSup 99; Leiden, Netherlands: Brill, 2005), 97–115.

32   Erhard S. Gerstenberger, *Psalms Part 1* (Forms of the Old Testament Literature 15) (Grand Rapids, MI: Eerdmans, 1988), 7–8, 14.

33   Martin J. Buss, "Meaning of 'Cult' and the Interpretation of the Old Testament," *JBR* 32 (1964): 320–2.

34   Walter Brueggemann, *The Message of the Psalms: A Theological Commentary* (Minneapolis, MN: Augsburg, 1984).

35   See, e.g., 1 Chr 9:19, 31; 26:1, 19; 2 Chr 20:19; cf. Num 16; 26:11.

36   See, e.g., 1 Chr 6:39; 15:17; 16:7; 26:1; 2 Chr 5:12.

37   Contra Michael D. Goulder, *The Psalms of the Sons of Korah* (JSPTSup 20) (Sheffield, UK: JSOT Press, 1982). See Martin J. Buss, "The Psalms of Asaph and Korah," *JBL* 82 (1963): 382–3, 387.

38   Buss, "Psalms of Asaph and Korah," 388.

39   David C. Mitchell, " 'God Will Redeem My Soul from Sheol': The Psalms of the Sons of Korah," *JSOT* 30(3) (2006): 365–84.

40   See Buss, "Psalms of Asaph and Korah," 384–5, 387; Michael D. Goulder, *The Psalms of Asaph and the Pentateuch: Studies in the Psalter III* (JSOTSup 233) (Sheffield, UK: Sheffield Academic Press, 1996); Harry P. Nasuti, *Tradition History and the Psalms of Asaph* (SBLDS 88) (Atlanta; Scholars Press, 1988).

41   Loren D. Crow, *The Songs of Ascents (Psalms 120–134): Their Place in Israelite History and Religion* (SBLDS 148; Atlanta: Scholars Press, 1996).

42   Indeed, the Hebrew ascription *lĕdāwîd* is grammatically ambiguous: "of/to/ for/concerning David."

43   James L. Mays, *The Lord Reigns: A Theological Handbook to the Psalms* (Lousville, KY: Westminster John Knox, 1994), 123–5.

44   Ibid., 143.

45   For full discussion, see Patrick D. Miller, "Kingship, Torah Obedience, and Prayer: The Theology of Psalms 15–24," in *Neue Wege der Psalmenforschung. Für Walter Beyerlin*, ed. by Klaus Seybold and Erich Zenger (HBS 1; (Freiburg, Germany: Herder, 1993), 127–42; Frank-Lothar Hossfeld and Erich Zenger, " 'Wer darf hinaufziehn zum Berg JHWHs?' Zur Redaktionsgeschichte und Theologie der Psalmengruppe 15–24," in *Biblische Theologie und gesell-schaftlicher Wandel*, ed. by Georg Braulik, Walter Gross, and Sean McEvenue (Freiburg, Germany: Herder, 1993), 166–82.

46   See Frank-Lothar Hossfeld and Erich Zenger, *Die Psalmen I: Psalm 1–50* (NEchtB; Würzburg, Germany: Echter Verlag, 1993), 1–14, and *Psalms 2: A Commentary on Psalms 51–100*, ed. by Klaus Baltzer, trans. Linda M. Maloney (Hermeneia: Minneapolis, MN: Fortress, 2005), 1–7.

47   See also J.-M. Auwers, *La composition littéraire du Psautier: un état de la question* (CRB 46) (Paris: J. Gabalda, 2000).

48   Gerald Henry Wilson, *The Editing of the Hebrew Psalter* (SBLDS 76) (Chico, CA: Scholars Press, 1985).

49   See Nancy L. deClaissé-Walford, *Introduction to the Psalms: A Song from Ancient Israel* (St. Louis: Chalice Press, 2004), 130–43.

50   V. Steven Parrish, *A Story of the Psalms: Conversation, Canon, and Congregation* (Collegeville, MN: Liturgical Press, 2003), 16 et passim.

51 James L. Mays, "The Place of the Torah-Psalms in the Psalter," *JBL* 106
    (1987): 3–12. See also J. Clinton McCann, "The Psalms as Instruction,"
    Interpretation 46 (1992): 117–28.
52 "The Letter of St. Athanasius to Marcellinus on the Interpretation of the
    Psalms," in Athanasius, *On the Incarnation: The Treatise De Incarnatione
    Verbi Dei*, 2nd ed. (Crestwood, NY: St. Vladimir's Seminary, 2003), 103, 105.
53 See John Calvin, "Introduction," in *Commentary on the Book of
    Psalms*, trans. by J. Anderson (Grand Rapids, MI: Eerdmans, 1949 [1845]),
    1.xxxvi–xxxvii.
54 James L. Mays, "The Self in the Psalms and the Image of God," in *Teaching
    and Preaching the Psalms*, ed. by Patrick D. Miller and Gene M. Tucker
    (Louisville, KY: Westminster John Knox, 2006), 55–6.
55 Hans-Joachim Kraus, *Theology of the Psalms*, trans. by Keith Crim
    (Minneapolis, MN: Augsburg, 1986).
56 Hermann Spieckermann, *Heilsgegenwart: eine Theologie der Psalmen*
    (Göttingen, Germany: Vandenhoeck und Ruprecht, 1989).
57 Erhard S. Gerstenberger, "Theologies in the Book of Psalms," in *The Book
    of Psalms: Composition and Reception*, ed. by Peter W. Flint and Patrick D.
    Miller (Leiden, Netherlands: Brill, 2005), 603–25.
58 See, e.g., Patrick D. Miller, "The Psalter as a Book of Theology," in *Psalms
    in Community: Jewish and Christian Textual, Liturgical, and Artistic
    Traditions*, ed. by H. W. Attridge and Margot E. Fassler (Atlanta: Society of
    Biblical Literature, 2003), 87–100.
59 James L. Mays, *The Lord Reigns: A Theological Handbook to the Psalms*
    (Louisville, KY: Westminster John Knox, 1994), 7.
60 Jerome F. D. Creach, *Yahweh as Refuge and the Editing of the Hebrew
    Psalter* (JSOTSup 217) (Sheffield, UK: Sheffield Academic Press, 1996).
61 William P. Brown, *Seeing the Psalms: A Theology of Metaphor* (Louisville,
    KY: Westminster John Knox, 2002), 15–53.
62 The designation is found in Luther's 1528 "Preface to the Psalter" (*Luther's
    Works*, vol. 35, ed. by E. Theodore Bachman [Philadelphia: Muhlenberg,
    1960], 254).

FURTHER READING

Attridge, H. W., and Margot E. Fassler, eds. *Psalms in Community: Jewish and
    Christian Textual, Liturgical, and Artistic Traditions*. Atlanta: Society of
    Biblical Literature, 2003.
Berlin, Adele. *The Dynamics of Biblical Parallelism*, 2nd ed. Grand Rapids,
    MI: Eerdmans, 2008.
Brown, William P. *Psalms*. Nashville, TN: Abingdon, 2010.
    Seeing the Psalms: A Theology of Metaphor. Louisville, KY: Westminster John
    Knox, 2002.
    The Oxford Handbook of the Psalms. Oxford: Oxford University Press, 2014.
Brueggemann, Walter. *The Message of the Psalms: A Theological Commentary*.
    Minneapolis, MN: Augsburg, 1984.
    The Psalms and the Life and Faith. Edited by Patrick D. Miller. Minneapolis,
    MN: Augsburg Fortress, 1995.

Creach, Jerome F. D. *Yahweh as Refuge and the Editing of the Hebrew Psalter* (JSOTSup 217). Sheffield, UK: Sheffield Academic Press, 1996.

The Destiny of the Righteous in the Psalms. St. Louis: Chalice Press, 2008.

deClaissé-Walford, Nancy L. *Introduction to the Psalms: A Song from Ancient Israel*. St. Louis: Chalice Press, 2004.

Holladay, William L. *The Psalms through Three Thousand Years: Prayerbook of a Cloud of Witnesses*. Minneapolis, MN: Fortress, 1993.

Kraus, Hans-Joachim. *Theology of the Psalms*. Translated by Keith Crim. Minneapolis, MN: Augsburg, 1986.

Mays, James L. *The Lord Reigns: A Theological Handbook to the Psalms*. Louisville, KY: Westminster John Knox, 1994.

Miller, Patrick D. *Interpreting the Psalms*. Philadelphia: Fortress, 1986.

Mowinckel, Sigmund. *The Psalms in Israel's Worship*. Translated by D. R. Ap-Thomas. Grand Rapids, MI: Eerdmans, 2004 [1962].

Westermann, Claus. *Praise and Lament in the Psalms*. Translated by Keith R. Crim and Richard N. Soulen. Atlanta: John Knox, 1981.

Wilson, Gerald Henry. *The Editing of the Hebrew Psalter* (SBLDS 76). Chico, CA: Scholars Press, 1985.

13 Wisdom

SAMUEL E. BALENTINE

The Hebrew term for "wisdom," *ḥokmâ*, occurs in various forms more than 300 times in the Old Testament, over half of which occur in Proverbs, Job, and Ecclesiastes. These three books, along with the deuterocanonical works of Sirach and Wisdom of Solomon, comprise the major corpus of what has been conventionally called the "wisdom literature" of ancient Israel. Both the term "wisdom" and the genre of material constituting "wisdom literature" point to salient characteristics that distinguish the preoccupations of Israel's sages. Along with prophets and priests (cf. Jer 18:18; Ezek 7:26), the sages devoted themselves to acquiring, understanding, and teaching fundamental truths about God, world, and humankind. Unlike their counterparts in this common endeavor, Israel's sages set their compass not to God's revealed commandments (Law or Torah) or to God's prescriptions for embodying them in ritual acts but instead to the pragmatic quest for knowledge through rational inquiry and human reason. Refusing to abandon reason for faith, they believed that God had created a world in which the wise, through disciplined study of observable phenomena, could discern and disseminate a way of living in consonance with the justice and righteousness on which God's "very good" creation (Gen 1:31) depended. Although the sages conceded the limitations of the human quest for the wisdom that God alone possesses (cf. Prov 19:21, 21:30; Job 28:12–13; Eccl 8:16–17), they believed that the quest was worth the effort.

As the sage who composed the "Wisdom of Jesus Son of Sirach" discerned, those who ponder the "great teachings ... given to us through the Law and Prophets should praise Israel for instruction and wisdom" (Sir, prologue). Those who would be wise, the sage continues, must learn to be "at home with the obscurities" of life in relation to God (Sir 39:3).

PROVERBS: "THE FEAR OF THE LORD IS THE BEGINNING OF WISDOM"

The final form of Proverbs, with all but one of the major text units clearly introduced by a title or superscription, provides an instructive entry into four major interpretive issues: (1) composition history, (2) literary forms, (3) social/historical context, and (4) thematic coherence.

1:1–9:18	"The proverbs of Solomon son of David, king of Israel" (1:1)
10:1–22:16	"The proverbs of Solomon" (10:1)
22:17–24:22	"The words of the wise" (22:17)
24:23–34	"These also are sayings of the wise" (24:23)
25:1–29:27	"These are other proverbs of Solomon that the officials of King Hezekiah of Judah copied" (25:1)
30:1–33	"The words of Agur son of Jakeh" (30:1)
31:1–9	"The words of King Lemuel. An oracle that his mother taught him" (31:1)
31:10–31	An untitled poem, structured as an acrostic (alphabetic) hymn praising the "capable woman"

Composition history

The different introductions mark this book as a compilation of various texts that have been stitched together over time. That parts are attributed to Solomon (1:1; 10:1) is more a recognition of his legendary embodiment of "the spirit of wisdom" exemplified by Moses and Joshua than a claim that he authored these texts (Deut 34:9; cf.1 Kgs 2:6; 3:3–28; 4:29–34; 10:1–25). The long legacy of Solomon's wisdom is evident both within this book, in its inclusion of the "copy work" attributed to Hezekiah's officials (25:1), who would have been active some two centuries after Solomon's death, and in other biblical (Eccl 1:1) and deuterocanonical books that extend the memory of Solomon's wisdom well into the first century CE (Sir 47:12–17; Wis 7–9). A part of this legacy connects Solomon's wisdom with that of other sages in the Eastern Mediterranean world (1 Kgs 5:1–18), which suggests that a collection titled the "Proverbs of Solomon" will likely draw on an international wisdom discourse. The book of Proverbs confirms this. The section introduced as the "words of the wise" (22:17–24:22) shows a creative dependence on the second-millennium Egyptian text "The Instruction of Amenemope." Both "the words of Agur son of Jakeh" (30:1) and "the words of King Lemuel" (31:1) are attributed to a foreigner from Massa (maśśā'; New Revised Standard Version [NRSV]: "oracle"), a region in Arabia.

To read Proverbs front to back, following the sequence of chapters preserved in its final form, is to know that this book has a complex compositional history spanning centuries. Absent any confirmable historical markers, scholars cautiously locate the Solomonic collections (10:1–22:16; 25:1–29:16) in the latter part of the First Temple period. This earliest form was then enlarged by the addition of other collections, with the framing pieces (1–9 and 31) likely added in the early Persian period. The LXX sequences parts of the collection differently (22:17–24:22 → 30:1–14 → 24:23–34 → 30:15–33 → 31:1–9 → 25:1–29:27 → 31:10–31), an indication that the final form of the book remained in flux during the Hellenistic period.

Rooted in the memory of Solomon's mythic wisdom, Proverbs looks back to Moses, the Israelite prototype of wisdom, and forward to the long trajectory of this wisdom centuries after Solomon died. It invites readers to enter a world of international discourse, where "learning about wisdom" (1:2) is an education in how to live in a world where geographical and cultural boundaries are permeable and religious commitments are responsive to changing historical circumstances.

Literary forms

The most distinctive literary form in wisdom literature is the "proverb" (māšāl). The word appears in the titles of the first two collections (1:1; 10:1), which illustrate the various forms proverbs take. The first collection consists of ten speeches (1:8–19; 2:1–22; 3:1–12; 3:21–35; 4:1–9; 4:10–19; 4:20–7; 5:1–23; 6:20–35; 7:1–27), couched as instructions, admonitions, warnings, and rebukes from a teacher, variously characterized, whose personal authority should persuade the hearer to heed the counsel offered. Proverbs 1:8–19 exemplifies parental advice to a child: "My child, if sinners entice you, do not consent ... do not walk in their way ... for their feet run to evil" (vv.10, 15, 16). If children accept this counsel, they will instead follow the "good path" of "righteousness and justice and equity" (2:9); they will "find wisdom" and "get understanding" (3:13); and their reward will be a long and "abundant life" (3:2), a "beautiful crown" (4:9) that symbolizes the nobility of a virtuous life. Alternatively, the child may be tempted to heed the siren call of seduction, personified as the "loose woman" whose "smooth words" (2:16) "drip honey" (5:3) but ensnare the one who partakes in "disgrace" that cannot be erased (6:33). Imbedded within these ten speeches are the words of another teacher, personified now as "woman wisdom," who counters the "loose woman," first by mocking those who refuse wisdom's invitation (1:20–33), and then by delighting in those who are wise enough to "keep my ways" (8:32), enter into her house, and feast on the food and wine at her bounteous table (9:5).

The 375 proverbial sayings in the second collection (10:1–22:16) exemplify a more succinct literary form, typically one-line maxims, divided into parallel halves, that advocate inviolable truths by means of three primary rhetorical strategies. The dominant form of the sayings in Proverbs 10–15 uses *antithetical parallelism* to draw a sharp contrast between two different ways of living, for example, being wise or foolish (10:1, 8), righteous or wicked (10:1, 2, 3, 6), lazy or diligent (10:4; 12:27; 13:4; 15:19), kind or cruel (11:12, 17), honest or deceitful (12:17, 19, 22; 14:25), "slow to anger" or "hot-tempered" (12:15; 14:29; 15:18), prudent or reckless with words (10:19; 12:18; 13:3; 14:3), greedy or gracious (11:24; 13:22; 14:31; 15:27). The sayings in Proverbs 16–22 are more often conveyed by a *synonymous parallelism* in which a truth is stated in the first half of the line, then essentially repeated with similar words in the second half; for example, "a false witness will not go unpunished and a liar will not escape" (19:5); "laziness brings on deep sleep; an idle person will suffer hunger" (19:15); and "differing weights are an abomination to the Lord; and false scales are not good" (20:23). A variation of this form, often labeled "progressive" or "synthetic parallelism," states a truth in the first half of the line and then extends or intensifies its meaning in the second half; for example, "gray hair is a crown of glory; it is gained in a righteous life" (16:17); "a fool takes no pleasure in understanding, but only in expressing personal opinion" (18:2); "whoever is kind to the poor lends to the Lord, and will be repaid in full" (19:17); and "wine is a mocker, strong drink a brawler, and whoever is led astray by it is not wise" (20:1). Integral to each of these types of one-line sayings is the assumption that an unambiguous truth is plain to see. It does not need to be argued, and compliance need not be commanded. Simple assertion, buttressed by the wisdom of collective experience, conveys its own imperative.

Scattered within and beyond the first two Solomonic collections are additional literary forms. "Better-than sayings" teach that one thing is preferable to another (e.g., 12:9; 15:16, 17; 16:8, 19; 19:1; 21:9; 25:7, 24; 27:5, 10c). Conditional sentences use an "if then" construction to accent the connection between deed and consequence (e.g., 23:13–14, 15; 24:10–12, 14; 25:16; 29:9, 12, 14). Rhetorical questions invite agreement with assumed answers (e.g., 24:12; 26:12; 29:20). Numerical sayings catalogue social and natural phenomena, thus widening the perspective for understanding (e.g., 6:16–19; 30:15–16, 18–19, 21–3, 24–8, 29–31). Metaphors and similes offer poetic analogies that engage and revitalize the imagination (e.g.,10:11, 20, 26; 11:22; 12:4, 18; 16:24; 17:8, 22; 18:4, 8; 22:14; 23:27–8; 25:11, 18; 26:11, 18–19; 28:3, 15).

A previous generation of scholarship made much of the difference between the longer speeches that dominate in Proverbs 1–9, which are framed by a distinctive theological linkage between the "beginning of wisdom" and the "fear of the Lord" (1:7; 9:10), and the various shorter-sentence forms that dominate in the other collections of the book, which were thought to be grounded primarily in empirical and practical observations. The sentence forms were correspondingly regarded as exemplars of older wisdom, which was rooted in antecedent Near Eastern traditions. The speeches, however, were thought to be a later theologized adaptation of international wisdom discourse. This distinction has largely collapsed for two reasons. First, it is now clear that ancient Near Eastern texts routinely connected wisdom with the gods who created the world and endowed it with principles of righteousness and justice (e.g., *maat*, "truth, justice, order" in Egyptian wisdom texts) that were instrumental for social order. The notion that "the fear of the Lord is the beginning of wisdom" (9:10) may be a distinctively Israelite conception, but it draws on a religious worldview with deep roots in contiguous cultures. Second, the distinction between the theological wisdom in the first part of Proverbs and the so-called secular wisdom of the other collections blurs on close inspection. The "fear of the Lord" is not only the beginning of wisdom in an abstract theological sense, as one might suppose from Proverbs 1–9, but also the source of "prolonged life" (10:27), "confidence" unencumbered by "the snares of death" (14:26–7), and material prosperity (15:16; 22:4). Moreover, "YHWH sayings" are not limited to Proverbs 1–9 but occur throughout the book (e.g., 16:1, 2, 9; 17:3; 20:24, 27; 21:31; 28:5, 25; 29:25, 26), a repeating reminder that wise and moral behavior – "righteousness, justice, and equity" (1:9; 2:9) – is necessarily informed, corrected, and sustained by devotion to the God who tuned the world to these requisite virtues.

Social/historical context

The discrete collections and the various literary forms are indicative of the different social and historical contexts in which proverbial material functioned in ancient Israel. Two primary contexts may be singled out.

The speeches in Proverbs 1–9 reflect a *family setting* in which a parent endeavors to shape a child's intellectual and moral development. This domestic setting for wisdom reflects the dynamics of Israel's prestate period, when parents were the locus of authority for a child's education and character formation. Persistent appeals such as, "My child, be attentive to my wisdom, incline your ear to my understanding" (5:1; cf. 1:6, 10, 15; 2:1; 3:1, 11, 21; 4:1, 11, 20; 5:7; 6:1, 3, 20), impart long-standing communal values. The template for these values is overviewed in 1:2–7, which serves as an introduction to both the first collection and the book as a whole. To become productive and responsible members of society, all persons – the "simple," the "young," even the "wise" – must acquire and develop the skill, prudence, and discernment (1:4–5) that enable them to make the right decisions in life. The objective is to embody the "righteousness, justice, and equity" (1:3) on which every family and, by extension, every community depends. The guidance offered in this familial context covers a wide range of areas, including, for example, being a good neighbor (3:27–31), marital fidelity (5:15–20), money lending (6:1–3), and diligent labor (6:6–11). The taproot of the learning and insight required to navigate each of these areas successfully is the wisdom that comes from devotion to God (1:7; 2:6; 9:10). Thus, the parent's instruction, like that of the parental character who personifies the very wisdom of God (1:20–33; 8:1–36; 9:1–17), makes a common appeal: "My child, do not despise the Lord's discipline or be weary of his reproof, for the Lord reproves the one he loves, as a father the son in whom he delights" (3:11–12).

The Solomonic collection (10:1–22:16), "the words" (22:17–24:22) and "sayings of the wise" (24:23–34), and the "other proverbs ... that the officials of Hezekiah copied" (25:1–29:27) reflect a *royal* or *court setting* for instruction in wisdom. Envisioned is the historical period of the monarchy, when the center of power and authority in Israel shifted from the family to the state, the official responsibility for education from the parent to a professional class of scribes and sages. The content of these various collections suggests that by the time of Hezekiah's reign, if not earlier, the national and international affairs of state required that those who served the king be educated in a wide range of matters, including table etiquette (23:1–8), the administration of impartial justice for the accused (e.g., 15:27; 17:15, 23; 18:5, 17; 24:23b; 28:21), economic policy, especially concerning obligations to the poor and disenfranchised (e.g., 13:23; 14:31; 15:25; 17:5; 19:17; 22:22–3), and the cult (e.g., 15:8, 29; 17:1; 21:3, 27; 28:9).

The king himself, despite his recognized ability to discern the wisdom God requires (25:2), is presumed to invite instruction and to be receptive to critique (28:3, 15–16; 29:4, 12, 14). According to the Lemuel collection (31:1–9), the king is also subject to the admonitions of his mother, who warns him that excessive consumption of alcohol will compromise his ability to speak clearly on behalf of the poor and needy who appeal for justice.

By and large, court wisdom promotes a politically and theologically conservative perspective on the world, reflecting the institutional status of the sages. Through antithetical proverbs, they envision a world where either-or choices are clear and their consequences unambiguous. One is *either* righteous *or* wicked, wise *or* foolish, and the rewards for choosing either path of life are predictably etched into the cosmic order by God, whom the king faithfully serves. There is little room and virtually no encouragement in court wisdom for questions or dissent. Edifying speech is prized (e.g., 10:11, 21; 15:4; 16:21, 23, 24), for "the lips of the righteous know what is acceptable" (10:32), but best of all, especially in the face of moral complexities, is silence (10:19; 11:12b; 12:23; 13:3; 17:28). Such silence is rooted in the abiding truth that the one who trusts God's inscrutable wisdom is safe (14:26; 16:3, 20; 18:10; 29:25), whatever the limits of human understanding (16:1, 9; 19:21; 21:30–1). There is sparing acknowledgment that the system of rewards and punishments sometimes seems upside-down (30:21–3), and that what is incomprehensible may drive a person more to lament than praise (30:1–4), but such thoughts are placed on the lips of foreigners, perhaps a subtle suggestion that while their wisdom has merit, it is not the norm. On this point, however, the sages who speak in Proverbs are not the only voices sitting at wisdom's table. Job (represented as another foreigner) will advance the lament and the protest that are barely audible in Proverbs; Qoheleth will press this lament to its outermost boundaries, where skepticism demands a hearing.

Thematic coherence

Because of its anthological character, scholars have typically conceded that Proverbs lacks any overarching thematic coherence. Superscriptions identify the beginning and ending of different sections; thematic emphases frame certain sections (e.g., "the fear of the Lord" in 1–9) and cluster together in others (e.g., kingship in 16:10–15). Repetitions, catchwords, and other rhetorical devices appear to create sophisticated literary subunits within the collection (e.g., 25–7). For all these individual structural and thematic markers, the book itself has long seemed to thwart the search for a rationale that explains its final arrangement.

Current scholarship is pressing beyond conventional assessments. Two exploratory trajectories will merit further investigation. First, a sustained argument has emerged in support of understanding Israel's creation theology as the center around which Proverb's various teachings about God, world, and humanity revolves.[1] A second probe acknowledges the centrality of creation theology but pushes its hermeneutical significance still further. The final form of Proverbs, with its various poetic maxims, may be construed as a "metanarrative" that tracks the pursuit of wisdom from its beginnings in a familial setting, to its extension to communal settings, to its ultimate contextualization as a virtue exemplified in the mother who "opens her hand to the poor and stretches her hand to the needy" (31:20).[2] Those who walk in this path, according to this reading, demonstrate the "fear of the Lord" that merits "praise" (31:30), which is the beginning of wisdom.

JOB: "BUT WHERE SHALL WISDOM BE FOUND?"

Proverbs begins and ends by affirming that the "fear of the Lord is the beginning of wisdom" (Prov 1:7; 9:10; 31:30). On first reading, the book of Job appears to endorse this affirmation. It begins with a prologue about a man named Job who steadfastly "feared God and turned away from evil" (1:1, 8; 2:3), despite horrendous and undeserved suffering, and ends with an epilogue recounting how God restored his fortunes and blessed him (42:7–17). This simple "all's well that ends well" story is, however, far more complex than it first appears. The text cited in the title for this section – "But where shall wisdom be found?" (28:12; cf. v.20) – is but a first clue that suffering like Job's had the capacity to turn the sages' affirmations into questions. The journey toward understanding the debate among the sages who produced this book begins by recognizing the tensions between the parts and the whole.

The *frame* of the book consists of a prose prologue (Job 1–2) and epilogue (42:7–17) that use a combination of speech and action to tell the story of a righteous man who suffers terrible misfortune, including the deaths of seven sons and three daughters "for no reason" (2:3), and in the end is rewarded for his unfailing fidelity. This story is likely the oldest part of the book, originating in legendary tales from the ancient Near East of exemplary righteous persons who served Israel's sages as models for the wise behavior they wished their students to embrace (cf. Ezek 14:14, 20). The figure of "the satan" is not identical to the later conception of Satan or the Devil but something like the prosecuting attorney of the heavenly council. It is not possible to date this version of the story with precision, but its depiction of Job's unquestioning affirmation of the sages' conventional retribution theology – God punishes the wicked and prospers the righteous – resonates with the optimism of the pre-exilic period, before the Babylonian conquest of Jerusalem.

The *center* of the book consists of an opening soliloquy by Job (Job 3), which sets in motion a series of dialogues between Job and his friends (Job 4–27), a second soliloquy by Job (29–31), and a final round of dialogues between Job and God (38:1–42:6). These chapters are written in poetry, not prose, and are dominated by the speech of the characters, not their actions. There is widespread consensus that a later sage, most likely writing from the Babylonian Exile (586–538 BCE), when the collapse of Jerusalem seeded hard questions about the justice of God, spliced these speeches into the existing Joban narrative to protest its affirmations, now thinned by the painful realities of brokenness and loss. The template for this wisdom dialogue about the pious sufferer would have been readily available in existing literature from Babylon (compare the text "I Will Praise the Lord of Wisdom," also known as the "Babylonian Job" and "The Babylonian Theodicy").

The speeches draw primarily on the genres of lament and disputation. Now juxtaposed with the prologue/epilogue, they convey quite different profiles of Job, the friends, and God. Instead of blessing without question the God who gives both the "good" and "bad" (1:21; 2:10), Job curses his life and, by implication, the creator of all life (3:1–10), and repeatedly raises the question that demands an answer from every character in the ensuing dialogues, including God: "Why?" (3:11–26).

On first seeing the enormity of Job's suffering, the friends are silent and sympathetic (2:11–13). Once Job curses and questions God, they become increasingly strident. In three cycles of dialogues (4–14, 15–21, 22–7), they move from counterquestions designed to comfort Job by assuring him that his righteousness will result in his ultimate vindication (4:2–6; 8:2–7; 11:2–6), to questions that warn and rebuke him for "doing away with the fear of God" (15:4; cf. 18:4; 20:4–11), to questions that deny his innocence (22:1–11) and press him toward the only option left for those condemned as guilty: "Agree with God, and be at peace" (22:21).

One by one, Job refuses the wisdom of his friends. He insists that he is innocent (6:28–30, 9:21; 10:7; 16:7) and that the friends have "whitewashed" the truth (13:4) and spoken "falsely" for the God they defend (13:7). He wonders if there is any place in heaven or on earth where the cries of the innocent can be justly addressed (16:18–22). He returns again and again to the idea that his only recourse is to summon God as a defendant to a courtroom trial where he could ask, "What are you doing?" (9:12), where an impartial "umpire" will ensure that neither party has unfair advantage (9:33), and where a "witness" in heaven will corroborate the truth of his testimony (16:19). Even if "there is no justice" in a court where the judge has already declared him guilty (19:6–7), Job clings to a faintly conceived hope that there is a "redeemer" – whether heavenly or human he does not know – who will come to his rescue (19:25–7). To that end, Job concludes his last extended speech by swearing his innocence and demanding that God respond to his subpoena to appear before the bar of justice: "Here is my signature! Let the Almighty answer me!" (31:35).

The center of the book also profiles God differently. In the prologue and epilogue, God speaks *about* Job's exemplary fidelity but never *directly* addresses Job. After accepting the satan's wager by saying, "Very well, he [Job] is in your power; only spare his life" (2:6), God retreats in silence, never once uttering a word throughout the course of the dialogues between Job and his friends. When God speaks next, the words come "out of the whirlwind" (38:1). The structure of God's first and only "dialogue" with Job (38:1–42:6) is clear – God has two speeches (38:1–39:40; 40:1–34 [Heb 41:26]); Job offers two responses (40:3–5; 42:1–6) – but the discourse is fraught with complexity. God speaks for 123 verses, Job for only 9. God comes *asking* his own questions, not *answering* the questions Job has persistently raised throughout the dialogues. In the first speech, the questions focus on God's "counsel" or "plan" for the world (38:2: ʿēṣâ), with specific attention to cosmic boundaries (38:4–18), meteorological phenomena (38:19–38), and five pairs of animals (38:39–39:30). Job responds by saying, "I am small," and then placing his hand over his mouth (40:3–5), a gesture that symbolizes his retreat into silence, though whether of shame, futility, or disapproval remains open to interpretation. In the second speech, the questions focus on God's governance of the world (40:8: mišpāṭ), with special attention to a sixth and final pair of animals, Behemoth (40:9–15) and Leviathan (41:1–34 [Heb 40:25–41:26]). Job responds by stating what he now knows and sees about God and himself (42:1–6). The NRSV's translation of 42:6 is but one of many that suggest Job's final words should be interpreted as a confession of sin: "therefore I despise myself and repent in dust and ashes." This reading is deeply ingrained in interpretive history, but grammatical ambiguities deny it the certainty it claims.[3]

Two subsequent additions to the frame and center betray the internal debate the book generated among the sages. First, the poem on wisdom in Job 28 is cast as an anonymous soliloquy. Unlike the previous speeches, it addresses no one directly, and it receives no response from the other characters in the book. It is generically similar to other sapiential poems that discuss wisdom's place in the world and the ability of humans to discover it (cf. Proverbs 8; Sirach 1, 24; Baruch 3–4), but it differs from them by emphasizing wisdom's elusiveness rather than its availability. A twice-repeated question – "where shall wisdom be found?" (vv. 12, 20) – sets the table for the sage's answer: "mortals do not know" (v. 13); "he [God] knows" (v. 23). The last verse echoes the prologue's conventional commendation of Job's piety: "the fear of the Lord, that is wisdom, and to depart from evil is understanding" (v. 28; cf. 1:1, 8; 2:3). In the view of this later sage, perhaps writing from the Persian period when more traditional forms of wisdom thinking regained their dominance, the truly wise will accept without question what an inscrutable God "gives" and "takes away" (1:21), both the "good" and the "bad" (2:10). They will not follow the example of the Job of the dialogues, who complains and challenges God.

Whatever the sage's intention, the location of Job 28 does not resolve the existing tensions within the frame and center of the book; it adds to them. On the other side of this soliloquy, Job resumes his discourse, once again defending his integrity, protesting his mistreatment, and demanding that God respond to his quest for wisdom, however arrogant and inadequate it may be (29–31).

The speeches of Elihu (32–7), a fourth friend, elsewhere unmentioned, constitute a still later addition to the book, perhaps from a sage of the late Persian or early Hellenistic period. The substance of the speeches resonates with the intellectual climate of late wisdom texts such as Ecclesiastes and Sirach and protoapocalyptic texts such as Daniel 1–6, which are set against a political backdrop of foreign domination that calls into question long-held convictions about God's power, justice, and compassion. Both Elihu's narrator (32:1–5) and Elihu as a character in his own right (32:6–22, 33–7) suggest that what this story needs is a sage who can definitively "answer" Job's questions (32:1, 3, 5, 6, 12, 17, 20). According to the narrator, it is Elihu's anger at the friends' failure that compels him to speak (32:3, 5). When the constructed Elihu speaks for himself, however, he claims that he is motivated not by anger but by divine inspiration (32:8, 18; 33:4). *The* answer, Elihu argues, is that God has inscribed both divine silence (35:5–13) and human suffering into a revelatory process calibrated to invoke Job's confession (33:14–20) and awe (36:26–37:13) before the Almighty.

Speaking for 159 verses, Elihu commands center stage for longer than any other character in the book, including God, except Job. His speeches, however, receive no response in the final form of the book. Couched as invitation to dialogue (33:5, 32), they effectively substitute monologue for dialogue and debate. Read against God's assessment of Job's friends in the epilogue – "you have not spoken of me what is right" (42:7, 8) – Elihu's "answer" invites further questions. Is his anger righteous and therefore worthy of imitation? Or is it self-interested inspiration, folly masquerading as wisdom?

How should interpreters tally the sum of the various parts of the book? The sages who composed the prologue/epilogue commend Job's unflinching piety in the face of inexplicable suffering. Those who constructed the dialogues between Job and his three friends subjected this commendation to intense scrutiny; they honor hard questions about divine justice but falter when trying to resolve them. The sages who added the poem on wisdom and the speeches of Elihu try to break the stalemate but succeed only in widening the rift between what God alone knows (28:23) and the answers of those who claim to speak on God's behalf (36:3). They add wisdom to wisdom in an effort to teach a compelling new truth, and in the end it is the truth of the old lesson that judges them a failure. It is Job's prayers that rescue them from foolishness, not their wisdom (42:8–9).

Both chronologically and thematically, the book of Job represents an important crossroad in wisdom thinking. On the one hand, it looks back to Proverbs and to the conventional affirmation that "the fear of the Lord *is* the beginning of knowledge." On the other, it anticipates Qoheleth's skepticism: "what advantage have the wise over fools?" (6:9). Faced with the Joban problem, the sages who constructed this book from a sum of vexed and vexing parts themselves exemplify, perhaps inadvertently, a central proverbial truth: the "one who moves too hurriedly misses the way" (Prov 19:2).

ECCLESIASTES: "ALL IS VANITY AND A CHASING AFTER WIND"

The search for answers to conventional introductory questions about the book of Ecclesiastes – authorship, date, setting, and form – confronts interpreters with a number of difficult problems at the outset. The initial verse ascribes authorship to "Qoheleth [NRSV: 'Teacher'], the son of David, king in Jerusalem." David did not have a son named Qoheleth, however, so we must reckon from the beginning with a literary fiction that invites hearing these words *as if* they convey a royal perspective. The fiction is reinforced and complicated by the seven occurrences of the word "Qoheleth" throughout the book, as a personal name (1:1, 2, 12), with the definite article, thus as a reference to one's title or function

(7:27; 12:8), and as a sage who studied and taught wisdom (12:9, 10). The noun, a feminine participle from the verb *qāhal*, "to convoke, assemble," appears to refer to one who collects wisdom sayings and, by extension, to a "speaker" (Revised English Bible [REB]), "teacher" (NRSV, New International Version [NIV]), or "preacher" (Luther: *Prediger*; cf. the LXX title for the book, "Ekklesiastes," "one who leads a congregation [*ekklēsia*]"). Jerusalem may be the geographical locus of the author, but Qoheleth's Hebrew, which includes Aramaic and occasional Persian loanwords, suggests a date not in the Solomonic period (tenth century BCE) but instead in the Persian or, more likely, Ptolemaic period (c. 250 BCE).

A date in the mid-third century correspondingly suggests that the author is well acquainted with ideas circulating in a cultural milieu shaped to a large extent by Egyptian and Greek influence. Both the form and the content of the book bear this out in a variety of ways. One finds traditional genres well represented in other biblical wisdom books: for example, proverbs, in isolation (1:14) and in a series (7:1–13; 10:1–20), didactic poems (1:3–11; 3:1–15), parables (11:7–12:8), rhetorical questions (2:3, 19, 25; 3:9, 21, 22; 4:11; 5:6, 11, 16; 6:8, 11; 7:13, 16, 17; 8:1, 4, 7; 10:14), and "better than" sayings (4:3, 6, 9, 13; 5:5; 6:3, 9; 7:1, 2, 3, 5, 8; 9:4, 16, 18). There are also autobiographical sayings that resemble royal testaments and tomb inscriptions from Egypt, wisdom instructions that recall Mesopotamian texts such as "The Gilgamesh Epic" and "A Dialogue About Human Misery" (also known as "The Babylonian Ecclesiastes"), and reflections on the tragic dimensions of life that connect with Greek philosophical skepticism from Homer and Hesiod to Sophocles, Euripides, and the post-Socratic schools of the Cynics and Stoics.[4]

Although there is no consensus on many of these important conventional introductory issues, interpretive traction can be achieved by attending to what James Crenshaw has called Qoheleth's "fiction in the service of a rhetorical plan."[5] Most agree that the rhetorical plan includes an editorial frame consisting of a prologue and epilogue(s) (1:1; 12:9–14), a beginning and concluding thematic statement – "vanity of vanities" (1:2–3, 12:8) – and two poems (1:4–11; 11:7–12:8). Inside this frame, the book divides generally into two halves. The first half, 1:12–6:12, picks up on the thematic statement in 1:2–3 and develops it with a refrain that repeats seven times, "all is vanity and a chasing after wind" (1:14; 2:11, 17, 26; 4:4, 16; 6:9). The second half, 7:1–11:6, extends Qoheleth's search for what is "good" in life (2:3; 6:12; cf.1:2) with another set of repeating refrains, "cannot find out" / "who can find out?" (7:14, 23;

8:1, 7, 16) and "do not know" / "no knowledge" (9:1, 5, 10; 10:14, 15; 11:2, 5, 6). A number of other refrains occur throughout the book, none more structurally or theologically decisive than the statement that there is "nothing better for mortals than to eat, drink, and find enjoyment in their toil," which repeats seven times (2:24–6; 3:12–13, 22; 5:18–20 [Heb17–19]; 8:14–15; 9:7–10; 11:7–12:1).

This general outline illustrates a major rhetorical strategy of the book, the repetition of key words and phrases that signal central themes in Qoheleth's teaching. The thematic statement in 1:2, "*All* is vanity," sets the table. The word "all" (*kōl*) occurs ninety-one times in Ecclesiastes, roughly 41 percent of its total 222 verses, a disproportionate frequency for a book this size (cf. Job, forty-two chapters and seventy-three occurrences; Proverbs, thirty-one chapters and seventy-seven occurrences). Qoheleth's objective, these statistics suggest, is to explore the totality of life, everything that happens "under the sun," a phrase that repeats twenty-nine times (e.g., 1:3; 2:3; 3:1; 4:1; 5:12; 6:1; 8:9; 10:5). It is a pursuit of knowledge and understanding about human existence that exceeds anything else in Israel's wisdom tradition. Even God, whose domain is "in heaven" (5:2 [Heb.5:1]) and whose ways defy all human understanding (11:5), is subject to Qoheleth's intellectual inquiries. Among the various subjects to which Qoheleth returns again and again, the following deserve special attention:

> "Vanity" (*hebel*). This noun, which provides a thematic refrain for the book (1:2; 12:8), occurs thirty-eight times, roughly 60 percent of the total occurrences of the word in the Hebrew Bible. A wide semantic range must be considered when interpreting individual occurrences, but a baseline for all is the literal meaning "vapor/breath," which Qoheleth uses as a metaphor for something that is ephemeral, present one moment but gone the next – in short, something both too impermanent and too unreliable to give meaning to life. Even if one has the unlimited resources of a king, as Qoheleth claims for himself in 2:1–11, and is able to build houses, plant vineyards, and acquire wealth that exceeds all others, his legacy will not last; among the living, "there is no enduring remembrance of the wise or fools ... in the days to come all will have been long forgotten" (2:16). Toil and labor produce riches, but the gain is erased when one dies, for the wealth will be left to someone else, who may be more foolish than wise (2:17–18; cf.3:9; 5:10–17; 6:1–9). Companionship adds pleasure and security to life, but it does not prevent anyone from needing help, for there is always trouble lurking somewhere (4:7–12).

"A threefold cord is not *quickly* broken" (4:12b), but when adversity comes, it is the qualifying adverb that hints of the weak link in the chain. Life is better than death, so "seize the day," but because "all is vanity," there will be times to "hate life" rather than enjoy it (2:17), times when "the dead … are more fortunate than the living" (4:2–3), times when "chance" stops humans in their tracks, like fish caught in a net or birds in a trap (9:11–12).

"Fate, chance" (*miqrê*). Seven of the ten occurrences of this noun in the Old Testament are in Ecclesiastes (2:14, 15; 3:19 [three times]; 9:2, 3; cf. verbal forms in 2:14, 15; 9:11). The basic meaning is "fate" or "chance," which conveys the idea that things happen to people over which they have no control. It is impossible to know in advance what will occur; hence it matters little what one does. It is better to be wise than foolish, even if wisdom is always beyond one's grasp (7:23–4), but if ultimately what happens to one happens also to the other, then why expend the effort (2:15)? It is better to be righteous than wicked, but the same fate comes to both (9:2–3). If one's behavior has no bearing on the way God treats people, then is not compromise rather than adhering to principle the wiser course to pursue? Qoheleth counsels a middle course: "Do not be too righteous, and do not act too wise; why should you destroy yourself?" (7:16). Chance, not choice, determines what happens in life, Qoheleth says, and this is "an evil in all that happens under the sun" (9:3).Until death, the ultimate fate, lays its claim on all persons, "madness is in their hearts while they live" (9:3b; cf.2:2).

"Joy" (*śimḥâ*). Qoheleth uses the term in the seven *carpe diem* (Latin, "seize the day") refrains, which many regard as the leitmotif of the book (2:24–6; 3:12–13, 22; 5:18–20; 8:14–15; 9:7–10; 11:7–12:1; for additional occurrences, see 2:1, 2, 10; 4:16; 10:19), to identify the potential for joy in four things: labor, eating and drinking, love, and youth. He examines the joy that people may create for themselves out of their own resources by building, planting, and acquiring possessions but concludes that their only dividend is to leave people asking the question, "What use is it?" (2:2). He commends instead the simple pleasures of life, eating and drinking, essential aspects of conviviality and pleasure that have nothing to do with earned gain or profit (e.g., 2:24; 3:13, 22; 5:18; 8:15). Sufficient bread, wine, clothes, and oil make life worth living. Having someone to love increases joy by adding companionship for "all the fleeting days of life that have been granted to you under the sun – all your fleeting days. For that alone is what you can get out of life and out of the means you acquire" (9:9; New Jewish Publication Society Bible [NJPS]). Old age, harbinger of death, stalks life relentlessly, grinding away at every joy God grants, so the time to maximize pleasure is when one is young and the consequences for following "the inclinations of your heart and the desire of your eyes" are too distant to matter (11:9).

Qoheleth's commendation of joy invites different assessments. On the one hand, he advocates joy as a gift, not an achievement, a perspective that frees one to enjoy the moment, to work, love, and live fully and without reservation in the present, irrespective of what may come next. On the other hand, he concedes that the gift of joy may be no more than an anesthetic that masks the pain of life but does not remove it. One interpretation tilts toward the "mysteriously incidental quality" of God's providence, which can be trusted, if not always understood.[6] The other tilts toward the concession that God teases humans with ephemeral joy only to afflict them with permanent pain.[7]

"[The] God" ([hā]'ĕlōhîm). Qoheleth always uses the generic word 'ĕlōhîm for God (forty times), over half the occurrences with the definite article, "the God." This designation betrays a distance between Qoheleth and the God he experiences as hidden behind an impenetrable veil of secrecy. He acknowledges that God "gives" (nātan; 1:13; 2:26; 3:10, 11; 5:18–19; 6:2; 8:15; 9:9; 12:7) wisdom, knowledge, work, wealth, possessions, joy, love, and life itself; that God "makes" ('āśâ; 3:11, 14; 7:14, 29; 8:17; 11:5) everything in the world the way it is, with the caveat that no one can understand what God is doing or why. Both the giver and the gifts are capricious, which undermines the rationale for ethical behavior or piety. Qoheleth never prays, sacrifices, or makes vows to the God, though he commends caution to those who do (5:1–6). He neither praises nor protests the oppression and violence he sees in the world God has made; instead, he says that no one should be surprised at such things (5:8). To ponder the works of God is to confront a question – "Who can make straight what he has made crooked?" (7:13) – and to resign oneself to its implicit truth: "In the day of prosperity be joyful, and in the day of adversity consider, God has made the one as well as the other" (7:14). In what may be an allusion to Job, who refuses the similar counsel of his friends, Qoheleth warns against arguing with those who are stronger (6:10). He never uses the conventional wisdom phrase "the fear of God," but he urges "fear" when standing before the deity, counsel that blurs reverence and awe with terror (3:14; 5:7 [Heb. 5:6]; 7:18; 8:12; cf.12:13).

The hidden God is nonetheless palpably present to Qoheleth. Denied full comprehension of the divine, he understands that God has placed a sense of the whole in the human heart (3:11). The "memory of transcendence,"[8] an elusive but abiding image of what is eternal, enables humans to be satisfied with the "portion" (*ḥēleq*; 2:10, 21; 3:22; 5:17, 18; 9:6, 9) of the whole God has given them. To live meaningfully in the world God has made is to be completely immersed in what "God has given to everyone to be busy with" (3:10). The past is beyond retrieval; the future is unknown. Only the present is available, and its gifts, limited as they may be, are only accessible to the living.

The first "commentary" on Ecclesiastes appears in the epilogue (12:9–14). Whether from one or multiple authors, these last words explain how a book that claims "all is vanity" has the capacity to speak "truth plainly" (12:10). Like "goads" and "nails" (12:11), wisdom stings, jolting with an unexpected and often unwelcomed clarity that puts everything in a different perspective. The new perspective may increase the vexation that comes with learning life's painful lessons (1:18), so one must weigh the gain of wisdom's truth against the cost of laughing with foolish indifference at its imperatives (7:5–6a). "This also is vanity," Qoheleth says, so one must wait for the "end" before assessing the "beginning" (7:8). And when we come to "the end of the matter," the epilogist says, humans will be judged by the way they have tuned their lives to a grammar that begins with the words "all is vanity" and ends with the words "fear," "the God," "judgment," the "whole duty of everyone," and "good or evil" (12:13–14).

NOTES

1   E.g., Leo G. Perdue, *Wisdom and Creation: The Theology of Wisdom Literature* (Nashville, TN: Abingdon, 1994), 77–122; *Wisdom Literature: A Theological History* (Louisville, KY: Westminster John Knox, 2007), 37–76; and *The Sword and the Stylus: An Introduction to Wisdom in the Age of Empires* (Grand Rapids, MI: Eerdmans, 2008), 85–116.

2   William P. Brown, *Character in Crisis: A Fresh Approach to the Wisdom Literature of the Old Testament* (Grand Rapids, MI: Eerdmans, 1996), 22–49.

3   See, e.g., Carol Newsom, *The Book of Job* (NIB, Vol. IV; Nashville, TN: Abingdon Press, 1996), 629, who cites five different translations as legitimate possibilities.

4   For an overview of extrabiblical texts and their relevance for contextualizing Qoheleth, see Perdue, *Wisdom Literature*, 161–216; and *The Sword and the Stylus*, 198–255.

5   James L. Crenshaw, "*Nuntii Personarum et Rerum*: Qoheleth in Historical Context," *Biblica* 88 (2007): 297.

6   Brown, *Character in Crisis*, 136–40.
7   Crenshaw, "Nuntii Personarum et Rerum," 294–5.
8   Ibid., 298.

FURTHER READING

Brown, William P. *Wisdom's Wonder: Character, Creation, and Crisis in the Bible's Literature.* Grand Rapids, MI; Cambridge, UK: William B. Eerdmans, 2014.

Clifford, Richard J. *Wisdom Literature in Mesopotamia and Israel* (Symposium Series 36). Atlanta: Society of Biblical Literature, 2007.

Crenshaw, James L. *Old Testament Wisdom: An Introduction*, rev. and enlarged ed. Louisville, KY: Westminster John Knox, 1998.

Dell, Katherine. *"Get Wisdom, Get Insight": An Introduction to Israel's Wisdom Literature.* Macon, GA: Smyth and Helwys, 2000.

Gammie, John G., and Leo G. Perdue, eds. *The Sage in Israel and the Ancient Near East.* Winona Lake, IN: Eisenbrauns, 1990.

Murphy, Roland E. *The Tree of Life: An Exploration of Biblical Wisdom Literature*, 3rd ed. Grand Rapids, MI: Eerdmans, 2002.

Penchansky, David. *Understanding Wisdom Literature: Conflict and Dissonance in the Hebrew Text.* Grand Rapids, MI; Cambridge, UK: William B. Eerdmans, 2012.

Perdue, Leo G. *Wisdom Literature: A Theological History.* Louisville, KY: Westminster John Knox, 2007.

    The Sword and the Stylus: An Introduction to Wisdom in the Age of Empires. Grand Rapids, MI: Eerdmans, 2008.

Rad, Gerhard von. *Wisdom in Israel.* Nashville, TN: Abingdon, 1972.

Sneed, Mark R. *The Social World of the Sages: An Introduction to Israelite Wisdom Literature.* Minneapolis: Fortress, 2015.

    ed. *Was There a Wisdom Tradition? New Prospects in Israelite Wisdom Studies.* Atlanta: SBL Press, 2015.

Weeks, Stuart. *An Introduction to the Study of Wisdom Literature.* New York; London: T and T Clark, 2010.

14   Late historical books and rewritten history

EHUD BEN ZVI

"NATIONAL" HISTORIES

Among the historical books in the Hebrew Bible, two are later than the rest: Chronicles and Ezra-Nehemiah.[1] Like the "Deuteronomistic History" (= Joshua, Judges, Samuel, and Kings; hereafter DH) and the "Primary History" (Genesis–2 Kings; hereafter PH), both Chronicles and Ezra-Nehemiah belong to the genre of "national histories."[2] In ancient Israel, national histories were the norm at least from the Persian period on.[3] This stands in contrast to the situation in the rest of the ancient Near East prior to the Hellenistic era, in which such historical narratives are not attested.[4]

Books or collections of books that are "national histories" contain prominent, well-individualized characters (e.g., Ezra and Nehemiah in Ezra-Nehemiah; David, Solomon, and Hezekiah in Chronicles; Joshua in the book of Joshua). From the general perspective of the book of Chronicles or Ezra-Nehemiah as a whole, though, it is indisputable that the central protagonist of the overall historical narrative is Israel, not Ezra, Nehemiah, or David. Similarly, Joshua may or may not be the main protagonist in the book of Joshua,[5] but within the context of the entire DH or PH, the story is certainly about Israel, not Joshua.

The two main characters in all ancient Israelite historiography, including Ezra-Nehemiah (in its present form) and Chronicles, are Israel and YHWH. Most significantly, the story is never really about political Judah or Yehud, any polity past or present, or any particular leader but about a religious ethnocultural and transtemporal group and its deity. The religious ethnocultural group is a theologically conceived Israel, with whom the authors and readers of these historical narratives identified and which, in return, gave them an ideological/theological identity. This Israel was asked to remember, and remember it did – hence, national memories. Memories, reports, and expectations related to its past, present, and future interactions with YHWH played a pivotal role in its discourse.

From an actual (and remembered) spatial perspective, this was an Israel at whose center Jerusalem and Judah had stood since David's time but that nevertheless conceived itself as "exilic" Israel. This was an Israel whose memory and self-identity were deeply influenced by a central metanarrative about a sequence of grievous sinning and punishment associated with exile that leads to a present, but not by any means full, restoration.

National histories in ancient Israel (and other places in the Hellenistic period; cf. Berossus and Manetho) represented a response of cultural peripheries to interactions with imperial centers (e.g., the Achaemenid or later Hellenistic empires).[6] They were an important ideological resistance tool that contributed to the maintenance, development, and enhancement of local traditions. These traditions were upheld (and reshaped) by local elites, and conversely, the elites were strengthened by them. National histories contributed to the self-identity and sense of self-worth of local elites and those who identified with their narratives.

Transcultural historical studies lead to an expectation that in this type of interaction between imperial and peripheral centers, ideas, symbols, and images pertaining to imperial discourses are being reconfigured to support the claims of groups in the periphery. In Chronicles and Ezra-Nehemiah, the prestige and power of the empire are explicitly co-opted and placed at the service of the ideology and institutions of Jerusalem, supported by the implied authors of these books and by those who identified with the positions of these authors. Thus, for instance, Cyrus was construed as a king for whom YHWH is *the* God of heaven, who openly acknowledged that YHWH has given him all the kingdoms of the earth and charged him to build him a house at Jerusalem (2 Chr 36:23).[7] This characterization of Cyrus supports the ideological discourse of the implied author of the book (and its actual readers) in general terms but also provides an explicit explanation of historical causality that elucidates the reason for the emergence of the central empire: the deity of the readers of the book, YHWH, stirred up Cyrus's spirit in fulfillment of prophecies given to Israel in the past and (implicitly) for its sake.[8] Similarly, in Ezra-Nehemiah, the power and prestige of the empire were co-opted into the service of the ideology of and the central institutions supported by the implied author (see, e.g., Ezra 6:3–5; 7:12–26). It is important to stress that up to a point, however, the process was a two-way street. Local ruling groups and their intellectual retainers had a vested interest in ideologically co-opting the prestige of the empire to legitimize their institutions (and themselves), but the imperial center could only benefit if its central personages and institutions were presented and accepted as supporting pillars for local elites and their own ideologies and institutions.[9]

National histories deal, of course, with matters (or myths) of origins and with explanations about how the present came to be. They are meant to strengthen the national identities of those who write and read them. As they do so, they "naturally" tend to shape, reinforce, and communicate boundaries meant to separate (true) insiders from outsiders. The main goal of this discourse about boundaries is not to set limits between clear insiders and outsiders (e.g., between Israelite worshipers of YHWH and Babylonian worshipers of Bel), but to separate (or integrate) groups whose boundaries are contested, permeable, and up for contested reconfigurations.

Both Chronicles and Ezra-Nehemiah are excellent examples of this tendency. Both books deal with boundaries between Israel – as understood by their implied authors and the readers who identify with them – and those who likely understood themselves as Israel, too, but were placed either in a peripheral position or outside Israel.

Chronicles, time and again, advanced an image of a transtemporal and seemingly all-inclusive Israel. But it also conveyed an *emphatic* sense of center and periphery, and assigned all of non-Judahite/Yehudite Israel to the latter. This peripheral Israel, whether in the present or the remembered past (e.g., the northern kingdom of Israel), was fully removed from the main historical narrative of Israel. Because peripheral Israel was still Israel, it was construed in Chronicles as being required to follow YHWH's teaching in its "true" form, namely, as this teaching was understood by the Jerusalem-centered implied author of Chronicles and the Jerusalemite literati who identified with him. Thus, those of peripheral Israel (e.g., Samarians) were imagined within this discourse as compelled ideologically to "Jerusalemitize" themselves, that is, to relinquish their own traditions, accept a Jerusalem-centered perspective, and behave accordingly. This said, since they are, after all, peripheral to the large national narrative, if they do not act as desired, nothing of significance will happen to central Israel (i.e., Judah/Yehud) or to its core institutions/spaces (i.e., Temple or city) – as Chronicles' recounting of the history of the monarchic period clearly shows.

Ezra-Nehemiah seems far more hostile toward Samarians than Chronicles, but it also keeps the door open for those who accept the perspective of the Jerusalemite center, as envisioned by the implied author of the book and the literati who identify with him.[10]

The main difference between Ezra-Nehemiah and Chronicles on the matter of boundaries involves the question of whether people identified as outside the "lineage of Israel" may be integrated into the community (should they adopt the theological premises and cultural-religious behavior of the Israelites as understood by the center in Jerusalem). Chronicles – in line with, among others, the Pentateuchal narratives, the DH, and Ruth – emphatically answers the question in a positive way. For instance, not only foreign women appear as wives and mothers of Israelites in all these texts, but in Chronicles, the same holds true for a foreign father who married an Israelite woman.[11] YHWH is implicitly construed as blessing these "mixed marriages."

In sharp contrast, Ezra-Nehemiah advances a notion of "holy seed" (Ezra 9:2) that denies such a possibility (and such a construction of YHWH). From the perspective of the implied author of Ezra-Nehemiah, the entire question is framed around concepts of purity and defilement that find no parallel in Chronicles. Not only does the latter not share these particular concepts, it also tends not to appeal to concepts of purity and defilement as a means of constructing the identity of the community and the boundaries around it.[12]

This difference between the two national histories is not a marginal matter. The exclusion of foreigners from the community is not a minor theme in Ezra-Nehemiah. To the contrary, it is central to the message of the implied author. It is saliently expressed by (1) the prominence given in the book to the expulsion of foreign wives and their "mixed progeny" and (2) the effort to present the directly related innovations in purity laws that it advances as the authoritative meaning of the accepted tradition.

To be sure, this exclusionary position of Ezra-Nehemiah and its purity underpinnings are unique to this book in the Hebrew Bible.[13] Moreover, although it likely influenced some groups in the late Second Temple period, it was categorically rejected by early Judaism, which invented the procedure of *giyyur* ("conversion"), which contradicts the very essence of Ezra-Nehemiah's position.[14] From a political perspective, however, the exclusionary position of Ezra-Nehemiah was not unique in the region because it resembles Pericles's citizenship law, according to which Athenians are those born to two Athenian parents.

In other words, Chronicles and Ezra-Nehemiah are both late biblical national histories. As national histories, both serve to create boundaries through the narration (and inculcation) of past events. But none of this requires that their boundaries be the same or that they would support them with similar types of discourse. Although the Temple is central to Chronicles – as well as to Ezra-Nehemiah – matters of purity rarely come to the forefront in the book. Moreover, Chronicles and Ezra-Nehemiah do not share the same understanding of purity. This distinction is important because it suggests that although their vocabulary may be similar, these two histories did not share the same concepts. References to "Temple" or "community" did not evoke the same range of meanings among the readers of these two late national histories.

Moving to other aspects of national histories, they are not required to provide a comprehensive historical narrative, from mythical origins to present times or to some event construed as a turning point for the community. Ezra-Nehemiah simply provides separate snapshots, as it were, of what the book portrays as periods of crucial importance for Judah and Jerusalem during the Persian era.

A segmented history conveys important messages beyond its direct focus on what it explicitly narrates. For instance, it asks the readers to create meaningful historical trajectories linking the explicit references. To illustrate, Ezra-Nehemiah conveys the message that the project of establishing a stable and proper Temple and community was not accomplished by Zerubbabel. It required Ezra and Nehemiah, but above all, it required a proper Torah and a leadership bent on leading the community in the observance of this Torah,[15] which is what Ezra and Nehemiah exemplify. This book communicated to its readers that a stable and proper Temple required continuous vigilance because people, even leaders of the community, tend to and do go astray. Therefore, the community needs not only the Torah that Ezra brings and teaches but also leaders such as Ezra and Nehemiah. Significantly, these two leaders are characterized as coming from outside the Jerusalemite community and as supported by (as well as being supporters of) the Achaemenid center. They are neither Davidides nor members of any locally rooted Yehudite/ Jerusalemite elite. They are, by definition, outsiders who know far better than the supposed insiders what the community should be. And they do not hesitate to act in order to achieve their goal. In the case of Ezra, matters go beyond that, and as much as the text offers a parallel between his entrance to the land and the Exodus from Egypt, he and his group become an embodiment of Israel, to the exclusion of the others already living in the land, who within this symbolic universe become akin to Canaanites, even if they are also Israel and worship in the Jerusalemite Temple.

Chronicles has a much larger historical perspective. It begins with Adam, explains the place of Israel among the nations and its composition in terms of genealogical lineages, but it quickly moves to David. Because it is clearly informed by the PH, the omission of central historical, formative narratives that were well known among the literati of late Persian Yehud or the early Hellenistic period is salient. The omitted historical narratives include the patriarchal stories, those about the Exodus and the stay in the wilderness, the conquest of land in Joshua, and the stories of judges and pre-Davidic leaders. Moreover, Chronicles omits any reference to the actual rebuilding of the Temple and the community in Yehud. In fact, the entire history of Yehud is just outside the national narrative that the book advances.

Of course, these omissions did not erase knowledge that already firmly existed within the community, nor could this have been the goal.[16] Instead, as in any segmentary national history, the point is to evoke among the readers new links and trajectories among well-known memories of the past within the community. The reconfiguration of trodden paths connecting particular memories about individuals, places, and events carries strong ideological implications. For example, in Chronicles, a clear teleology governs these paths. They lead quickly and directly to *David and the Temple* and then slowly, through a meandering monarchic history, to *Cyrus and the Temple*. YHWH's Torah and David's commands concerning the Temple stand large over and make sense of the entire path, along with the related question of their observance (or lack thereof) in the past and, by implication, the present and future. Within this strong teleology, there is no room for narrative detours about the leadership of Moses, Joshua, or any other non-Davidic leader.

Both Chronicles and Ezra-Nehemiah related a national history, advanced myths of beginning for the community, carried a strong teleological message, and were free to skip over historical events and periods from their main narrative to achieve rhetorical and ideological goals. But they did so in different ways.

Because the narrative of Chronicles ends where that of Ezra-Nehemiah begins, and given that the matter is particularly emphasized by the partial textual overlap between 2 Chronicles 36:22–3 and Ezra 1:1–2, it is clear that despite all the differences between these two books – and they are many, as indicated earlier – a clear intertextual connection binds them together.[17] It suffices at this point to state that this connection (along with the shared use of late Biblical Hebrew) may have suggested to at least some ancient readers that the two works could be read as part of one large national history collection (cf. the PH, which is also a collection of separate books, which by themselves belong simultaneously to other collections, such as Pentateuch, Joshua-Judges, Samuel-Kings, or DH).[18]

REWRITTEN HISTORY AND SOCIAL MEMORY

Chronicles is a second national history. The literati among whom and for whom the book was written already had the DH and the PH. Chronicles uses, among others, Samuel and Kings (DH) – though not necessarily always in the exact form in which they appear in the MT. It emulates them while at the same time presenting itself as different from them, even at the basic level of its linguistic profile: The book of Chronicles is written in late biblical Hebrew (hereafter LBH); Samuel and Kings in standard biblical Hebrew (hereafter SBH). This shift in language already conveyed to readers a sense that Chronicles was late and secondary to DH (as well as to PH). In addition, because Chronicles extensively quotes these preexisting texts, it could not but evoke them and, accordingly, present itself as a rewritten national history.

Why would the literati of the late Persian or early Hellenistic period accept within their repertoire a second, rewritten history? Which social needs would such a history serve? To be sure, few historians would dispute that every history is written from a present perspective, with every past constituting a "present past," and this being so, any "history" (along with any construction of the past) is by necessity continuously resignified and, for all practical purposes, rewritten in any living community.[19] But none of this fully explains why Chronicles was accepted or required in ancient Yehud. What is noteworthy about Chronicles is that the rewriting of memory is textually inscribed in a new book rather than in interpretive comments on existing written material. The question is even more intriguing because Chronicles was written within a community that was very poor in resources, low in population, and possessed only a few bearers of high literacy.[20] Why would two separate, written, and extensive national histories be accepted, read, and reread within a very small community of readers?

A potential starting point to address this question is the common observation that the goal of rewritten history is often to legitimize the present by projecting it into the far past.[21] In terms of Chronicles, this likely translates into an effort to legitimize the ordinances governing the Temple during the time in which Chronicles was written by associating them with David, and by doing so to legitimize the existing Temple by portraying it as Davidic. The corollary of this process is the legitimization of Jerusalem as the only legitimate religious center of Israel.

This approach is heuristically helpful, even if it is not clear whether Chronicles actually portrays the way in which the Temple of the late Persian or early Hellenistic Jerusalem actually worked, or some utopian version (see the role of the Levites), or perhaps more likely a combination of both. Whatever the case may be, Chronicles projects an image of Chronicles' Temple into the mythic past and anchors it to David.[22]

As helpful as this position is, it represents an overly narrow approach to Chronicles and above all to its function in society as a second historical narrative. To begin with, Chronicles as a whole is not only or even mainly about particular Temple regulations or the role of the Levites in certain cultic circumstances. As for the legitimacy of the Jerusalemite Temple itself (and the city as its extension), it is very doubtful that such legitimacy required the writing of an extensive second national history. The existing DH was probably enough. DH and the prophetic literature emphasized, time and again, the role of the Jerusalemite Temple and of the city. Moreover, the DH and prophetic literature provided an interpretative key to understand the Pentateuch in a Jerusalem-centered way. In fact, it is hard to imagine that the question of the centrality of Jerusalem and its Temple was an issue of contention among *Jerusalemite* literati of the late Persian or early Hellenistic period for whom Chronicles was written. Of course, Chronicles reinforced the inner discourse of these literati against the positions of Samarians and other Yhwistic groups that rejected the exclusivist claims of Jerusalemite literati, but can one find in such a role a sufficient reason for writing and continuously rereading a second national history?

Another potential avenue for approaching the question mentioned earlier is to compare Chronicles and its sources. What are the main differences between them? In terms of its scope (and, one may say, *conceptually*), Chronicles does not resemble any of the books it uses as sources but certainly references books, in particular the PH. As such, Chronicles serves as proof positive that books were read and reread, at least for particular purposes, not only as separate works but also within a frame informed by various collections of books.

Moreover, Chronicles starts, as in Genesis and 2 Kings, with a mythical beginning (in one case the creation of the universe, in the other of humankind), but it, unlike the PH, concludes with an important, though brief, reference to Cyrus and a command to rebuild the Temple. This is a significant difference, which is made significant by other features of the book.

As mentioned earlier, Chronicles is to some extent a segmented history because it does not recount all the history of Israel. Instead, and following an introduction, it focuses on the period from David's reign to Cyrus's declaration. As with all segmented histories, it shapes and conveys important messages by choices of exclusion and inclusion, foregrounding and backgrounding. Chronicles moves from the monarch who established – even if he did not actually build – the Temple to the monarch who commanded the rebuilding of the Davidic Temple (even if he did not actually rebuild it either). One may say that Chronicles moves from one pregnant beginning to another: from David to Cyrus and back to David. It conveyed to its readers a sense of restoration of the old beginning, except that the Israelites who participate in the (ongoing) second beginning were made acutely aware of the story of the first beginning and of what followed it (by reading Chronicles and through social or cultural memory). Likewise, they are aware that David was no Cyrus, nor Cyrus any David.

This said, it is difficult to assume that the only reason for developing and maintaining a complete second national history within the community would come *explicitly* to the forefront only in the last three verses of a book as extensive as Chronicles.[23] Moreover, if this were the *only* reason for developing and maintaining Chronicles as a second national history, what role does 1 Chronicles 1–9 play in this scheme?

The previous attempts to answer the central question posed at the beginning of this section shed light on important ideological messages of Chronicles, but they fail to advance a compelling, comprehensive answer to the original query. They provide important but only partial responses.

The path for a more comprehensive answer lies most likely in a more general approach to the role and message of Chronicles within the ancient community instead of those based on crucial (but still particular) ideological issues. A good starting point for such an approach is the observation that both Chronicles and the DH[24] are *not* cultural memories but rather texts used to evoke, shape, and reshape cultural memories among those who read them through the very process of reading and rereading the texts. Chronicles and the DH served as coexisting communal tools for imagining and reimagining the past. Chronicles neither tried nor could have tried to replace or even significantly displace the DH or the PH within the community. The latter were far more authoritative or classical than Chronicles. But a readership informed by Chronicles read Samuel and Kings, for instance, differently than it would have without Chronicles. Of course, the process worked both ways, and readers of Chronicles were also informed by the DH and the PH, but this was a given from the outset. The presence of a second historical narrative was necessary not only to reshape some memories of the past; to add to the range of images and characterizations of places, events, and personages to be remembered and imaginatively visited by the readers; to create new links among remembrances; or to advance new causal explanations, even if it did all of this. Chronicles was necessary to allow the community that shared, read, and reread its past to create a dense tapestry of interacting, intertwining, and partially overlapping memories. By doing so, by informing and being informed by the images of the other historical narratives, the addition of Chronicles to the mix allowed for an enhanced, multiple, and continuous renegotiation of social memory. The latter, in turn, facilitated social reproduction and created space for the necessary interpretative freedom to reimagine the past.

Chronicles is a source for evoking, shaping, and reshaping memories that unavoidably interacted with other memories, but it is also a *book*, that is, a written text. As a text that derives from and uses others, it appropriates, reuses, and resignifies texts taken from the major historical narratives and other texts (e.g., Psalms) within the literary repertoire of the community within which it emerged. As Chronicles appropriated and resignified these texts, not only did it reconfigure some "facts" about the past, it also emplotted them in a new narrative. The result is a new set of implicit or explicit causal relations between events and portrayed actions, characters, and situations. Thus, Chronicles contributed not only to an increasingly rich universe of intertwined historical memories but also to an ideological mind-set in which representations of historical causality informed and balanced each other. This matter is far from trivial given (1) the importance of causal relations for historical writing and (2) the social and socializing roles that such writing fulfills. To illustrate, the adoption of a second historical narrative with its own causal claims relativizes any categorical claims of knowledge about historical causality that may seem to emerge from any authoritative historical narrative. Thus, the authoritative (co-)presence of Chronicles raised within the community – and particularly its literati – the issue of limitations on achievable, secure knowledge. Furthermore, because claims of historical causality within the discourse of ancient Israel involved YHWH directly or indirectly, these considerations have a direct bearing on the community's construction of its images of YHWH.

Do all these considerations fully explain why a second national history was written by Jerusalemite literati during the late Persian or early Hellenistic period? Perhaps not, but at least they shed light on what the presence of a second national history did for and to the community that accepted it. Perhaps our historical reconstructions can go as far as reconstructing the reasons for the reception rather than those for the creation of this second history.

To the best of our knowledge, Ezra-Nehemiah does not parallel existing historical narratives in the community.[25] However, it also incorporated, replotted, and resignified many source texts. This is true at the level of particular units within the book,[26] as well as at the level of the book as a whole.[27] Here the historical process led the community to cease transmitting the original sources as separate documents (once they became subsumed in the developing or newly developed book).[28] Two caveats are in order, however. First, Ezra 1–6 evokes a memory that interacts with the one evoked by Haggai and Zechariah 1–8 in terms of the process of and the circumstances associated with Temple rebuilding. Second, Ezra-Nehemiah was previously combined in such a way that maintained a sense of being two related but also separate books, as the opening of Nehemiah clearly indicates. At times, this bifurcation substantially contributes to the emergence of multiple memories informing each other (cf. Ezra 9 and Nehemiah 7).

STUDY OF CHRONICLES: FACING THE TWENTY-FIRST CENTURY

Once upon a time, though not too far away from the present, the book of Chronicles was very boring. It was deemed to be simplistic, secondary in importance for all practical purposes, and dull at best from a literary perspective. All this has changed in recent decades.[29] To understand the shift, one has to look into the reasons for which Chronicles was once characterized in such a negative way and found so interesting today.

The negative evaluation of Chronicles in the past was at least in part the result of the control exerted on its interpretation and evaluation by (1) comparisons with the DH and (2) its link with Ezra-Nehemiah. To begin with, Chronicles was already considered inferior to the DH on the grounds that it repeats much of it. But Chronicles was considered not only inferior, but *far* inferior to the DH on account of the sections in which it did not repeat the DH. These sections were more often than not considered of tainted quality because (1) they were less historically reliable than those in the DH for reconstruction of the history of the monarchy and (2) they were assessed as theologically flat.

The first consideration implies an approach according to which good historical narratives in ancient times should reflect "historicity" (construed, of course, in modern terms), and therefore, the more "historical" they are, the better they are. This approach was common in the late nineteenth century when some foundational works for the critical study of the Old Testament were written, and it has held sway for most of the twentieth century. It is a telling fact that during this period, there was little debate about whether the authors of the DH were historians but much discussion on whether the Chronicler (meaning the historical author of Chronicles) could be described as a historian or not. After all, if the latter is the case, then he committed one of the gravest sins a historian can commit: intentionally and forcibly twisting history and (to make matters even worse) doing so to advance a flattening theological viewpoint. Of course, if he was simply a pious theologian, but not a historian, he would have been absolved of the sin of falsifying history. But his value would not have increased by much. In the common pecking order held at the time, a historian such as the one responsible for the DH was assigned a far higher status than a (petty) theologian with no sense of the importance of what actually happened.

This is not the place to discuss the ideological assumptions underpinning the system of evaluations mentioned earlier. For present purposes, it is better to focus on the fact that the devaluation of Chronicles reflected a sense that (1) the history of the monarchic period (for which the narrative in Samuel-Kings was considered a better source) was of far greater importance than the Persian period (for which Chronicles was considered a better, though indirect source) and (2) direct portrayals of past periods in historical narratives are better and more reliable sources than implied messages shaping the ways in which the historical narrative is emplotted.

The theological flatness of Chronicles involved a negative evaluation of central aspects of what was then generally accepted to be the theology of the Chronicler. Significantly, this theology was constructed *not* on the basis of the book of Chronicles as whole but in the main on an academically reconstructed text that included only (or mainly) the sections in Chronicles without parallel in other biblical books, particularly the DH.[30]

Most commonly, and despite minor caveats, the Chronicler was imagined as advocating a simplistic doctrine of immediate and personal retribution. In addition, he emphasized Temple and ritual over charisma and divine revelation, and preferred (late) priestly concerns over monarchic period Deuteronomic ideals. These last two preferences were considered theologically deficient by many scholars at the time.

Chronicles was inferior as a historical source and as a theological document, as well as from a literary perspective. It was not only that the genealogies in 1 Chronicles 1–9 were considered dull and boring, but unlike the DH, Chronicles used LBH, not SBH, and it was SBH that was then lionized as the language of the great prophets, poets, historians, and theologians of Israel. LBH employed a far less worthy language than SBH. In fact, LBH was construed as a sign and symbol of cultural decline. Moreover, at the time, it was claimed that Chronicles also flattened the heroic characters of Israel's past (e.g., David and Solomon), and thus created one-dimensional, almost cartoonish pious personages.

The control that Ezra-Nehemiah exerted over the interpretation and evaluation of Chronicles worked in a different way. It was not only (or even mainly) that Ezra-Nehemiah and Chronicles were considered one work, but rather that the (perceived) voice of Ezra-Nehemiah silenced what would have been the voice of Chronicles if it had been read by itself. (Interestingly enough, interpreters did not allow the voice of Chronicles to silence that of Ezra-Nehemiah.) Thus, Chronicles became anti-Samaritan and an anti-foreigner book in general – following the common interpretation of Ezra-Nehemiah as a closed-minded, antiforeigner document. This reconstruction of the message of Chronicles played well with the (then) common reconstruction of the Persian period as one of ethnoreligious ("Jewish") isolationism, which, in turn, was negatively evaluated from a theological perspective.

All the considerations and attitudes mentioned earlier have been challenged in recent decades. Surely, there is no doubt that Chronicles repeats much of the material in the DH, but the emphasis has shifted today to explanations about the social roles that a situation of "double history" played in ancient Israel and to the ways in which the DH and Chronicles informed each other. Moreover, studies in the resignification of older texts in Chronicles (through emplotment techniques) by necessity raise the question of whether Chronicles actually "repeats" the DH at any particular place.

As for historicity, although it remains widely accepted that Chronicles is a problematic source for historical-critical reconstruction of the monarchic period, the same applies to use of the DH for the premonarchic and monarchic periods. Certainly theology or ideology played central roles in the shaping of both the DH and Chronicles. In an ironic way, Chronicles, although influenced by P, now seems more Deuteronomistic than the DH. In any event, the conceptual gap that once separated the DH from Chronicles has narrowed considerably.

In a related development, the Persian period has become more and more a central focus of interest in ancient Israelite history, and along with this shift, there is greater concern for Chronicles as a product of that period. Evaluations of historical narratives in terms of a simplistic understanding of "historicity" continue to exist, but they are becoming more and more a matter of the past, not only because of the "literary turn" in historiographical studies or postmodernist sensitivities in historical methodology, but also because they do not reflect the way in which ancient societies worked and the evaluations and roles of historical narratives among them. Their main function in society was not to retell history as it actually happened (whatever that might be), but to shape the social memories deeply involved in socialization processes, constant identity shaping and reshaping, and above all, social cohesion.

Literary studies on Chronicles have pointed out how carefully construed implicit or explicit rhetorical arguments contributed much to the persuasive power of the narratives in Chronicles. These studies have shown that numerous sophisticated literary devices were at work. Even the genealogies, rather than being a repetitive and numbing device, have been reevaluated as direct and sturdy statements of hope, social identity, and above all, of a successful process of social reproduction that has overcome all calamity.

In other words, renewed study has shown how Chronicles communicates a sophisticated system of multivocal claims informing and balancing each other, rather than simplistic and flat approaches to matters such as divine retribution, temple, and so on.

Disentangling Chronicles from Ezra-Nehemiah and reading it as a book in its own right allowed for a hearing of Chronicles in its own voice. The resulting Chronicles was certainly not anti-Samaritan/Samarian. Moreover, it became clear that on some critical issues, such as mixed marriages, it runs contrary to Ezra-Nehemiah. This reassessment of the message of Chronicles, in turn, led unavoidably to reassessments of common reconstructions of the world of ideas in the Persian period, but that is still a work in progress.

The more the focus is on Chronicles by itself, the more its view on some important ideological issues becomes a central resource for historical reconstructions of the world of ideas within the late Persian/early Hellenistic Jerusalemite literati. But Chronicles' message, because of its system of balanced approaches (i.e., both/and rather than either/or) becomes more and more difficult to categorize in simplistic terms. For instance, is Chronicles a royalist book that conveys a sense of hope that the house of David will come back to power one day through the normal process of history? Is it a messianic/eschatological book? Or does it convey a sense that there is no need in the present and in the foreseeable future for a Davidic royal restoration? Or is it a theocratic rather than royal book? Ancient (and modern) readers could find support for any of these positions in Chronicles because such support was conveyed in various units of the book. Rereading the book raises the issue of balance and interrelation among all these tendencies.

Such matters bear direct influence on reconstruction of the social location within which Chronicles emerged. Is it a utopian book? Does it represent the position of the ruling elite or only of some segment among the literati? What if it is a marginally utopian book? That is, what if it raises utopian matters (and an implicit but critical attitude toward the present), but only on the margins and for the most part reflecting the dominant discourse of the time?[31] Given all these considerations and questions, it comes as no surprise that there is much effervescence today in the study of Chronicles.

STUDY OF EZRA-NEHEMIAH: FACING THE TWENTY-FIRST CENTURY

Studies on Ezra-Nehemiah have also experienced renewal. Although often with caveats, Ezra-Nehemiah was regularly used as the main source for a reconstruction of the history of Yehud in the Persian period. In fact, most histories of the period have been, in one way or another, a kind of (rationalized) renarration of Ezra-Nehemiah. However, questions about the historicity of Ezra-Nehemiah have become more and more prominent in recent years. Debates based on linguistic and literary criteria have been part of this process,[32] but the most important contribution is probably that of archaeology.[33] Matters are not settled, and perhaps never will be, but critical renarrations of Ezra-Nehemiah are becoming increasingly problematic as present-day historical narratives about Yehud. If Ezra-Nehemiah ceases to play the defining role in historical reconstructions of the Persian period, then a substantial reconfiguration of the latter is to be expected, and in fact, is already in the works and contributes much to the present excitement in Persian period studies.

To be sure, Ezra-Nehemiah remains a problematic book for many contemporary readers.[34] At the same time, there is a much better historical understanding of its ideology in general, and its view on cultic purity and the construction of the community that follows it in particular. Some contemporary scholars have focused their attention on the goals of Nehemiah's policies (as portrayed in the book) and concluded that they were necessary in their time to establish "a fully independent province of Judah, and a new Jewish identity, and self-confidence."[35]

Of course, these policies, at least from the perspective of the implied author of Ezra-Nehemiah, were not based on political but religious and, in particular, purity considerations. As expected in discourses of traditional societies, and despite the unique character of many of the latter, Ezra-Nehemiah claims not to innovate on these matters but to represent traditional laws. To do so, the book (or its implied author) has to engage in Pentateuchal exegesis. Thus Ezra-Nehemiah has become an important source for research on ancient exegetical modes of reading because it provides a window into the actual understanding of the contents of the traditional text/Torah in antiquity, as it was adopted by a particular group, as well as into the process of reading and understanding the Torah that led to such exegesis.[36]

Ezra-Nehemiah presents itself as the text of a group within the community. Of course, from the perspective of the author, this one is the "correct" group, but nevertheless a group that constantly stands in opposition to others. Ezra-Nehemiah likely reflects the thoughts of a segment of the literati (of the population in general?) and evokes fragmentary memories (i.e., memories that are unlikely to belong to the entire community). It has been suggested that some of the positions in Ezra-Nehemiah are more likely to reflect the viewpoint and experience of minority communities living in exile (e.g., a Babylonian community or some segment of it). These exilic/minority communities (or "traditionalist" segments of communities) confronted challenges that majority communities did not. For instance, perceived or actual threats to self-identity were seen differently in Yehud than in these exilic minority communities or traditionalist segments of communities. Cross-cultural studies show that the latter tend to stress boundaries between "self" and "other," to emphasize the related concept of "purity of lineage" and endogamous marriage, and to favor interpretations of the received traditions that harden and heighten religio/cultural/social boundaries rather than those that might conceivably lower them.[37] The explicit and emphatic diasporic background of both Ezra and Nehemiah, as portrayed in the book, not only reflects elements of cultural memory but also offers a key interpretative consideration for understanding the positions of the group embodied by the implied author of the book and its main two heroes. This said, the community within which and for which Ezra-Nehemiah was composed resided most likely in Judah, not Babylon. In other words, this approach leads by logical necessity to a historical reconstruction of a social group that continued to hold and develop minority diasporic viewpoints in social and political circumstances that were substantially different from the ones in which those viewpoints originated. Was this a kind of sectarian group that conceived of itself as a minority group,[38] but whose writings eventually became part of the majority tradition? And if so, when and how did all these social and religious processes influence the composition and contents of Ezra-Nehemiah?

Unlike the case of Chronicles, for which studies about its redactional layers and compositional forerunners do not take central stage, research in Ezra-Nehemiah continues to focus to a large extent on redactional layers, sources, literary forerunners, and compositional strategies. The reason is simple: it is difficult to think that Ezra-Nehemiah was originally composed in a form that closely resembles the present-day book. Even the bipartite structure of the book and the title in Nehemiah 1:1 speak against this possibility. Traditions from the Hellenistic period refer to Ezra or Nehemiah but not to both of them at the same time, raising even more questions about the original unity of the book. A further question is whether the memory of one was always intertwined with the memory of the other, as the final edition of the book seems to suggest. In addition, there are substantial differences even within the "book of Ezra" and the "book of Nehemiah" that by themselves have led to numerous efforts at developing redactional models that reconstruct the processes involved in the development of the text. To be sure, such studies bear implications for the dating of each of the literary units and subunits in Ezra-Nehemiah and, eventually, for Ezra-Nehemiah as a whole, which in its present form is far more likely to be the product of the Hellenistic period than the Persian period. All these potential dates involve different social locations and historical circumstances, which, in turn, play a role in any reconstruction of the possible meaning or meanings of each of these proposed texts and their history. The difficulties involved in this process are clear and hint at the limits of secure historical knowledge about the book, and they explain the increased interest in the book.

The question of the meaning(s) of the intertextual link between Ezra-Nehemiah and Chronicles can now be addressed, though not resolved. Even if it were possible to identify the group that created this literary bridge, their social location and the purpose they had when they created it, and to establish which precise text/book was intertextually linked to Chronicles – none of which is in fact possible with any degree of certitude – we would remain with multiple answers to this question. The crux of the matter is that the meanings of the link depended on the perspective of the ancient observers, even if they agreed that the link asked them to read the two books as part of a single historical collection, as was likely the case. What does it "do" to readers to view these books as part of one collection? Does it mean that they should read Chronicles in the light of Ezra-Nehemiah and thereby relativize some of Chronicles' main ideological positions? Or vice versa?[39] Social locations, ideological positions,

and the particular settings or purposes of particular readings may have all
played an important part in choosing one mode of reading the collection
over the other. Groups that favored a more integrative approach have continually read one book in the light of the other and then vice-versa.

NOTES

1 Ezra-Nehemiah in its present form is one book.
2 The question of whether or in which sense one may use the term "nation"
   in relation to ethnocultural groups in antiquity is open. My goal here is to
   portray even if in rough strokes the "Israel" that these texts referred to and
   helped to construe. On the issue of "ancient nations," see, e.g., A. D. Smith,
   *The Nation in History: Historiographical Debates about Ethnicity and
   Nationalism* (Hanover, NH: University Press of New England, 2000); and
   cf. S. Grosby, "Borders, Territory and Nationality in the Ancient Near East
   and Armenia," *JESHO* 40 (1997): 1–29; and his *Biblical Idea of Nationality.
   Ancient and Modern* (Winona Lake, IN: Eisenbrauns, 2002).
3 The same holds true in late Second Temple Jewish historical writing; see
   Josephus and Pseudo-Philo. The ancient Israelite historical collections
   referred to as the DH and the PH emerged in the Persian period. Chronicles is
   likely dated to the late Persian period but might be from the early Hellenistic
   period. The potential forerunners of main sections within Ezra-Nehemiah
   (e.g., Ezra 1–6; the "Nehemiah Memoir/Memorial") are usually dated from
   late Persian to Hellenistic period. Ezra-Nehemiah in its present form may
   well be much later than Chronicles.
4 This does not mean that there was no communal self-awareness or that such
   self-awareness carried no memories in the rest of the ancient Near East.
   See A. Kuhrt, "Israelite and Near Eastern Historiography," in *Congress
   Volume: Oslo 1998*, ed. by A. Lemaire and M. Sæbø (VTS 80; Leiden,
   Netherlands: Brill, 2000), 257–79. But extensive national historical narratives comparable to the DH or PH are not attested.
5 This depends on the way the book was read.
6 Cf. A. Momigliano, "Eastern Elements in Post-exilic, Jewish, and Greek
   Historiography," in his *Essays in Ancient and Modern Historiography*
   (Middletown, CT: Wesleyan University Press, 1977), 25–35. Compare and
   contrast Kuhrt, "Israelite and Near Eastern Historiography," *Congress
   Volume: Oslo*, esp. 268–76. For examples of historiographic works by and about
   "peripheries" in Hellenistic times, see the works of Berossus and Manetho.
7 Cf. Isa 44:28; 45:1–25.
8 It is important that, from the perspective of these readers, their deity did not
   overlap with any other deity or deities. Thus, from their point of view, these
   claims were imagined as exclusionary.
9 Cf. Cyrus's cylinder.
10 See Neh 9:2, which, when read within the context of Nehemiah 9, allows
   for descendants of the northern tribes to join the community – if their ideology is identical to that of the Yehudites portrayed in the book, and if they
   behave accordingly.

11 See 1 Chr 2:34 and contrast with Lev 24:10, which implies that the son of a foreign father is not to be considered an Israelite.

12 On these concepts in Ezra-Nehemiah, see S. M. Olyan, "Purity Ideology in Ezra-Nehemiah as a Tool to Reconstitute the Community," *JSJ* 35 (2004): 1–16.

13 It is even subtly and partially undermined within Ezra-Nehemiah itself. See my "Re-negotiating a Putative Utopia and the Stories of the Rejection of the Foreign Wives in Ezra-Nehemiah" in *Worlds that Could Not Be. Utopia in Chronicles, Ezra and Nehemiah*, ed. by S. J. Schweitzer and F. Uhlenbruch (LHBOTS 620; London: Bloomsbury T&T Clark, 2016), 105–28, esp. 115–24.

14 It is worth stressing that Ezra-Nehemiah is interested in the composition of the community, which it interprets in terms of cultic purity. It has no problems with nations other than Israel per se. For instance, the Persian authorities who certainly have no interest in joining the cultic community around the Jerusalemite Temple are clearly praised in the book as a whole. The same holds true for people from other nations (see Ezra 1:6). In addition, Ezra-Nehemiah condemns groups that it construes as "outsiders" (those who live in the near-abroad of Yehud and wish either to join in or to preempt the building of the Jerusalemite Temple – a central institution in the book). From the perspective of the implied author of Ezra-Nehemiah and those who identify with him, these outsiders represent a threat to establishment of the proper Temple. Those who would like to join in would render the Temple (and its community) impure. Those who would preempt its building, of course, would deny the community of its Temple and, within the ideology of the book, also the explicit orders of Achaemenid kings. Thus, they are construed as standing against god and king.

15 To be achieved by persuasion but also as the result of a forceful use of power within the community.

16 Chronicles implies that its intended (and primary) readers would be aware of these stories. How could they not be?

17 Cf. G. N. Knoppers, *1 Chronicles 1–9* (AB 12; New York: Doubleday, 2004), 72–89, 135–7.

18 During the Persian and early Hellenistic periods (and perhaps later), individual books could be associated with more than one collection. The interest or purpose of a particular reading within the community would activate or deactivate these links and the collections they created. One may imagine a kind of library in which scrolls are placed on one shelf for particular reading purposes and on another for other reading purposes.

19 See my "Reconstructing the Intellectual Discourse of Ancient Yehud," *SR* 39(1) (2010): 7–23. To be sure, the same holds true for contemporary professional historians studying and constructing any past community.

20 This stands in sharp contrast to the far wealthier and more populous Judah of the late Second Temple period, in which parabiblical texts that involved the rewriting of biblical texts were composed.

21 Transcultural studies in cultural or social memory support this observation.

22 The difference is that in one case it would be legitimizing the present Temple as is, without any call for change in some of its regulations. The other case would be tantamount to a call for a change in some of these regulations. In the first case, Chronicles would reflect the position of the ruling group in the

Temple; in the other, it would be a document reflecting the aims and view-point of a (less enfranchised) segment among the literati.

23 Chronicles is the largest book in the HB.

24 Or the PH for that matter.

25 Unless, of course, one brings into the picture Esdras, but this book is probably later than Ezra-Nehemiah. The matter is, however, somewhat debatable.

26 H. G. M. Williamson proposes that the author of Ezra 1–6 had at his disposal Ezra 7–Nehemiah 13 "in substantially its present form" and "a number of primary sources of such nature as could well have been preserved in an official archive, and he also knew several other relevant works which are not found in the Old Testament. ... There is nothing in Ezra i–vi which cannot be explained on this minimal assumption" ("The Composition of Ezra i–vi," *JTS* 34.1 (1983): 1–30 (29–30).

27 Ezra-Nehemiah in its present form is most likely the final outcome of a very lengthy and complex process of composition and redaction.

28 For a cross-cultural example of the tendency toward the disappearance of (older) texts that became "embedded" in newer texts, see D. Mendels, *Memory in Jewish, Pagan and Christian Societies of the Graeco-Roman World: Fragmented Memory–Comprehensive Memory–Collective Memory* (LSTS 45; London: T & T Clark, 2004), esp. 1–29.

29 Several works in the seventies opened the door for this development. Among them, one may mention H. G. M. Williamson, *Israel in the Books of Chronicles* (Cambridge University Press, 1977); S. Japhet, *The Ideology of the Book of Chronicles and Its Place in Biblical Thought* (BEATAJ 9; Frankfurt, Germany: P. Lang, 2009 [2nd rev. ed., 1997; 1st English ed., 1989; orig. Hebrew ed., 1977]); R. Mosis, *Untersuchungen zur Theologie des chronistischen Geschichtswerkes* (FTS 92; Freiburg, Germany: Herder, 1973); and T. Willi, *Die Chronik als Auslegung* (FRLANT 106; Göttingen, Germany: Vandenhoeck und Ruprecht, 1972). Two, now classic English-language commentaries on Chronicles by two of the main trailblazers of the 1970s contributed much to the dissemination of a renewed, and far more positive, evaluation of Chronicles. See H. G. M. Williamson, *1 and 2 Chronicles* (NCBC; Grand Rapids: Eerdmans, 1982; and S. Japhet, *I and II Chronicles* (OTL; Louisville, KY; Westminster John Knox, 1993).

30 Needless to say, such a "book" of nonparallel texts never existed in ancient Israel. No ancient literati ever read such a "book."

31 See S. J. Schweitzer, *Reading Utopia in Chronicles* (LHBOTS 442; London: T & T Clark, 2007). His position has been criticized, but the question of whether there are utopian elements in Chronicles, and if so, which they are, remains open. In fact, even the lengthy genealogy of the Davidic lineage may be understood as an implied voice asking readers to involve themselves in utopian thinking. Yet other readings of this list are possible as well. Reading and rereading Chronicles has led time and again to the identification of an authorial voice that expresses itself through carefully balanced multivocality.

32 See, e.g., D. Schwiderski, *Handbuch des nordwestsemitischen Briefformulars: ein Beitrag zur Echtheitsfrage der aramäischen Briefe des Esrabuches* (BZAW 295; Berlin: de Gruyter, 2000); but cf. R. C. Steiner, "Why Bishlam (Ezra 4:7) Cannot Rest 'In Peace': On the Aramaic and

Hebrew Sound Changes That Conspired to Blot Out the Remembrance of Bel-Shalam the Archivist," *JBL* 126 (2007): 392–401.

33 Issues go far beyond general agreement that the image of a single large immigration to Yehud is historically impossible. For the kind of matters raised by recent archaeological studies of the Persian Yehud, see H. Geva, "Estimating Jerusalem's Population in Antiquity: A Minimalist View," *EI* 28 [Teddy Kollek Volume] (2007): 50–65 (Hebrew); Y. Finkelstein, "Jerusalem in the Persian (and Early Hellenistic) Period and the Wall of Nehemiah," *JSOT* 32 (2008): 501–20, and "Archaeology and the List of Returnees in the Books of Ezra and Nehemiah," *PEQ* 140 (2008): 1–10; O. Lipschits, "The Size and Status of Jerusalem in the Persian and Early Hellenistic Periods," in *Judah between East and West: The Transition from Persian to Greek Rule (ca. 400–200 BCE)*, ed. by O. Lipschits and L. L. Grabbe (LSTS 75; London: T & T Clark, 2011), and *The Fall and Rise of Jerusalem* (Winona Lake, IN: Eisenbrauns, 2005), esp. 258–71; C. E. Carter, *The Emergence of Yehud in the Persian Period: A Social and Demographic Study* (JSOTS 294; Sheffield Academic Press, 1999); A. Kloner, "Jerusalem's Environs in the Persian Period," in *New Studies on Jerusalem*, ed. by A. Faust and E. Baruch (Ramat Gan, Israel: Ingeborg Rennert Center for Jerusalem Studies, 2001), 91–5 (Hebrew).

34 One can easily imagine why it would not be a preferred scripture reading for children of today's "mixed marriages."

35 See, R. Albertz, "Purity Strategies and Political Interest in the Policy of Nehemiah," in *Confronting the Past: Archaeological and Historical Essays on Ancient Israel in Honor of William G. Dever*, ed. by S. Gittin, J. E. Wright, and J. P. Dessel (Winona Lake, IN: Eisenbrauns, 2006), 199–206.

36 See, among others, M. Fishbane, *Biblical Interpretation in Ancient Israel* (Oxford, UK: Clarendon Press, 1988); S. M. Olyan, "Purity Ideology in Ezra-Nehemiah," and bibliography. Cf. J. R. Shaver, *Torah and the Chronicler's History Work* (BJS 196; Atlanta: Scholars Press, 1989).

37 This reference is the "tip of the iceberg" in terms of new approaches to Ezra-Nehemiah that are strongly informed by sociological or anthropological models.

38 See earlier on the constant portrayal of the two heroes as outsiders and its symbolic implications.

39 Much of the history of research in Chronicles has been influenced by one of these readings, namely, by that of Chronicles in the light of Ezra-Nehemiah. Whether this was the case in ancient times is debatable.

FURTHER READING

Albertz, R. "Purity Strategies and Political Interests in the Policy of Nehemiah," pp. 199–206 in *Confronting the Past: Archaeological and Historical Essays on Ancient Israel in Honor of William G. Dever*. Edited by Seymour Gitin, J. Edward Wright, and J. P. Dessel. Winona Lake, IN: Eisenbrauns, 2006.

Becking, B. *Ezra, Nehemiah, and the Construction of Early Jewish Identity* (FAT 80). Tübingen, Germany: Mohr Siebeck, 2011.

Beentjes, P. C. *Tradition and Transformation in the Book of Chronicles* (Studia Semitica Neerlandica 52). Leiden, Netherlands: Brill, 2008.

Ben Zvi, E. *History, Literature and Theology in the Book of Chronicles.* London: Equinox, 2006.

"Chronicles and Its Reshaping of Memories of Monarchic Period Prophets: Some Observations," pp. 167–88 in *Prophets, Prophecy, and Ancient Israelite Historiography.* Edited by M. J. Boda and L. M. Wray Beal. Winona Lake, IN: Eisenbrauns, 2013.

Ben Zvi, E. and D. V. Edelman, eds. *What Was Authoritative for Chronicles?* Winona Lake, IN: Eisenbrauns, 2011.

Blenkinsopp, J. *Ezra-Nehemiah: A Commentary* (OTL). London: SCM Press, 1989.

Boda, M. J. and P. L. Redditt, eds. *Unity and Disunity in Ezra-Nehemiah: Redaction, Rhetoric and Reader.* (Hebrew Bible Monographs 17). Sheffield Phoenix Press, 2008.

Eskenazi, T. C. *In an Age of Prose: A Literary Approach to Ezra-Nehemiah* (SBLMS 36). Atlanta: Scholars Press, 1988.

Frevel, C., ed. *Mixed Marriages: Intermarriage and Group Identity in the Second Temple Period* (LHBOTS 547). New York: T & T Clark, 2011.

Japhet, S. *I and II Chronicles* (OTL). Louisville, KY: Westminster John Knox, 1993.

The Ideology of the Book of Chronicles and Its Place in Biblical Thought. (BEATAJ 9). Frankfurt, Germany: P. Lang, 2009.

Kalimi, I., ed. *New Perspectives on Ezra-Nehemiah: History and Historiography, Text, Literature, and Interpretation.* Winona Lake, IN: Eisenbrauns, 2012.

The Reshaping of Ancient Israelite History in Chronicles. Winona Lake, IN: Eisenbrauns, 2005.

Klein, R. W. *1 Chronicles* (Hermeneia). Minneapolis, MN: Augsburg Fortress, 2006.

2 Chronicles (Hermeneia). Minneapolis, MN: Augsburg Fortress, 2012.

Knoppers, G. N. *1 Chronicles 1–9* (AB 12). New York: Doubleday, 2004.

1 Chronicles 10–29 (AB 12A). New York: Doubleday, 2004.

"Ethnicity, Genealogy, Geography, and Change: The Judean Communities of Babylon and Jerusalem in the Story of Ezra," pp. 147–71 in *Community Identity in Judean Historiography: Biblical and Comparative Perspectives.* Edited by G. N. Knoppers and K. A. Ristau. Winona Lake, IN: Eisenbrauns, 2009.

"The Relationship of the Deuteronomistic History to Chronicles: Was the Chronicler a Deuteronomist?," pp. 307–41 in *Congress Volume Helsinki 2010* (VTS 148). Edited by M. Nissinen. Leiden, Netherlands: Brill, 2012.

Person, R. F. *The Deuteronomic History and the Book of Chronicles: Scribal Works in an Oral World* (SBLAIL 5). Atlanta: SBL, 2010.

Schweitzer, S. J. *Reading Utopia in Chronicles.* New York: T & T Clark, 2007.

Williamson, H. G. M. *Studies in Persian Period History and Historiography* (FAT 38). Tübingen, Germany: Mohr Siebeck, 2004.

"The Aramaic Documents in Ezra Revisited." *Journal of Theological Studies* 59(1) (2008): 41–62.

1 and 2 Chronicles. Grand Rapids, MI: Eerdmans, 1982.

Wright, J. L. *Rebuilding Identity: The Nehemiah-Memoir and Its Earliest Readers* (BZAW 348). Berlin: Walter de Gruyter, 2004.

15 The biblical short story

LAWRENCE M. WILLS

The imaginative narratives of the Hebrew Bible, perched at the edge of history writing, are often gathered and studied together as "short stories," "novellas," "historical novels," and so forth. Were these narratives in fact seen as similar in the ancient world, or is it the modern fascination with fiction and the short story that motivates this grouping? It seems likely that although these stories can be grouped in different ways, with different sets of implications about their generic function in ancient Judaism, they did have a literary relationship that would have been experienced as such, consciously or unconsciously, by the ancient audience. Here I treat the Joseph story of Genesis 37–50, Ruth, Jonah, the prose frame of Job, Esther, Daniel 1–6, Susanna, Bel and the Dragon, Judith, Tobit, and the international *Story of Ahikar* as well. Since there are no comments in the ancient world on these texts as a genre, we are left to draw our own conclusions as to how they functioned in their original setting. They provide the kind of enjoyment and "out of history" experience that we associate with fiction, including wild exaggerations, contradictions, impossible famous personages, and logical absurdities. Yet they were all brought into at least one of the canons of the Bible, and so we are left to ask whether the ancients had a more flexible notion of what is appropriate for biblical texts or the biblical texts had come to be considered historical. Although the former is not impossible – Esther, for instance, is enjoyed in Jewish tradition as a carnivalesque reading for Purim – some are quoted authoritatively at Qumran and in the New Testament, and Josephus, writing at the end of the first century CE, included most of these narratives in his history of Israel. (He does, however, correct some of the "mistakes" that were originally part of their fictional world.) It will be my contention, then, that with the possible exception of the Joseph story, the earliest audiences did not see these stories as historical fact, and it was only later that they took on a different kind of authority, that of a written legend for Jewish heroes and heroines. It was because the stories were "biographical" or even "hagiographical" that they also could come to be "historical"; that is, hagiographa was the switch point between fiction and history.

A striking feature of these short stories, like the Wisdom tradition with which they are sometimes associated, is that they are international in scope and origin. They all play on the theme of innocents abroad. In many cases, there are parallel texts from other cultures – *Tale of the Two Brothers* for Joseph, *Ahikar* for the Jewish court narratives, or narratives now found in Herodotus or the Persian epic. The experience of the Jew in a larger world seems to motivate them. But the affinity of fiction and internationalism is not just a Jewish or Israelite phenomenon. From a very early period there were various ancient Near Eastern texts that were probably read as fictional, from royal autobiographies written in Akkadian to the Egyptian traditions of the national hero, *Sinuhe* in the nineteenth century BCE and *Wenamun* in the eleventh century BCE. In the Hellenistic period, the latter gave rise to a series of fictionalized accounts: *Sesonchosis, Setne Khamwas, Petubastis,* and *Nektanebos.*[1] In addition, Greek novelistic literature has an international setting or orientation, as if it is on the boundaries that the ironic muse comes alive.[2]

Preliminary to all discussions of ancient fiction are two questions. First, what is the relation of these stories to oral tradition? While some scholars have insisted that the narratives here in view must have arisen in an oral tradition and are shaped by those compositional forces, others have countered that throughout the Near East there was a practice of composing, editing, and altering stories at the written level as well.[3] However, it is a false either/or to posit these two possibilities as strict alternatives. It is clear that the composition, transmission, and alteration of tradition occurred on both levels, which were likely mutually influencing. This is most clearly seen in the multiple versions of the Esther and Daniel texts. Whether from oral or written origins, some of the later texts also reflect a progressive novelization; that is, they are expanded and acquire novelistic elements, such as physical description, psychological interest, dialogue, and the fascination with everyday elements. By 100 BCE, there also emerged a fairly standard size for the novellas Greek Esther, Greek Daniel, Tobit, and Judith.[4] They have been expanded from shorter versions to achieve this length, some by adding duplicate scenes, subplots, dialogue, or poetic sections (Joseph, Esther, Jonah, Tobit, and Judith), and others mainly through the device of collecting cycles of originally oral legends together in one new novella (Daniel). The second question is this: in their written form (regardless of origin), what is their class or social function – that is, who read them and under what performance conditions? This last question is prompted by the observation that the literacy rate was so low and writing materials so expensive that a specialized situation must be imagined, usually among the wealthy, for the fostering of gentle fictions. Morton Smith attempted to provide a social and class context for these texts by characterizing them as "belletristic," that is, *belles lettres* that emanated from "a lay circle enjoying wealth, leisure, and considerable culture."[5] There has been no way to confirm or disprove his thesis, but it is quite plausible.

In addition to their literary qualities, the theology and social function of the narratives have attracted much of the scholarly attention. Some have found in the lines of these narratives teachings that accord with biblical wisdom: steadfastness in the Lord, rewards for the pious and punishment for the wicked, and so on.[6] Yet it is sometimes argued that this connection is overstated. Is it simply a loose association between a popular narrative pattern and a fond theological belief in the ways of God? At the very least, the narratives are didactic and depict the happy ending of those who abide in God. (Jonah may accomplish this in reverse by describing the plight of one who refuses to take God's plan seriously.) The relations with Gentiles in the Diaspora in some of the narratives also suggested to one scholar that some of these narratives should be classified as "diaspora novella" (*Diasporanovelle*), and another argues that they advocate a "lifestyle for diaspora." Still others have leaned more on modern literary categories and suggested "novella" and "short story".[7] The label is not as important as deciding the role of genre in an ancient setting: which texts would seem to the ancient audience to be similar? What does this genre typically communicate?

We may proceed by listing texts that fall into the broad rubric of "short story," noting some of the salient characteristics that have drawn them into our grouping. The texts may be divided into an early period and a late period. The Joseph story, Ruth, Jonah, and the prose sections of Job, along with the non-Jewish *Story of Ahikar*, were all likely composed before 400 BCE. The later texts include Daniel and Esther with their Deuterocanonical additions, Judith, and Tobit.

EARLY TEXTS

Joseph story

The Joseph story has long been considered "novelistic" because of some of the ways in which it differs from the individual patriarchal sagas. The length of the Joseph story – and the long time period covered – allows for the sweep of movement and change. Although there are doublets and discrepancies that suggest that it was composed of two strands, they are somewhat different from the strands generally attributed to J and E. In the shorter J and E episodes concerning Abraham, Isaac, and Jacob, God or messengers are constantly present, but in the Joseph story, God's role is mainly seen in the providential way that things work out. Joseph, and later Daniel, must use a special means of understanding God's hidden meanings – dream interpretation – and in each case, a central point is emphasized: the dream interpreters of the other nations are inept beside the truly wise man, whose wisdom comes from God. Another difference between the Joseph story and the previous patriarchal narratives is the more direct moral model that Joseph provides.[8] The previous patriarchs were not depicted as moral paragons, no matter how much later tradition might have viewed them in this way, but as men who married women from the right families; endogamy (marrying within a particular group) is destiny in these early chapters. Joseph, however, struggles more directly with domestic morality, which, as we shall see, spurs for the audience an interest in character development. And yet, for all that, the Joseph story will play its usual role as the outlier for *any* theory of literary development of the early traditions.

Ruth

Ruth is an idyll or a pastoral poem-in-prose that focuses on the love between two women.[9] As in the Joseph story, there is little reference to direct divine intervention, but it is knowingly suggested throughout. Aside from its ending, which may have been added later, it is one of the few ancient stories that achieves that social realism that Erich Auerbach called the "divine in the concrete" – that is, true experience, suffering, and tragic potential in someone who was not aristocratic.[10] All these aspects justify Goethe's remark that it is "the loveliest little epic and idyllic whole which has come down to us."[11] Ruth is composed in a classical Hebrew style and uses a number of literary, even grammatical techniques that indicate it was to be understood as fictional: (1) it begins in the "middle" of the narrative, introduced with *wayhî*, (2) it is set in an artificial time, "when judges ruled," (3) most of the names have meanings, (4) there is an artificial digression to explain "now the custom was," (5) there is an important role for coincidence, and (6) there is extra dialogue or detail to carry the story's meaning (2:19–20, 3:7–9), more here than in any other biblical narrative.[12]

It is only at the idyll's end that we are told how Ruth's story relates to Israelite history. Not only is this not relevant within the story proper, neither is there any interest raised in the fact that Ruth is a Moabite, a violation of the marriage rules of Deuteronomy 23:3. The Moabites here are simply another people. This suggests that the original story may not have been about an ancestor of David but simply a poor widow. Was the concluding genealogy added, or was the reverse the case: namely, a genealogical problem – David was descended from a forbidden union – gave rise to a narrative to fill out the special nature of this particular Moabite over whom God kept watch? Further, is there here an implicit counterargument to those, like Ezra and Nehemiah, who wanted to exclude foreign wives? It is difficult to be certain about these possibilities, but if the story is reacting to Ezra's reforms, it is not a clear or committed response.[13] The classical beauty of the book of Ruth also makes it difficult to date. The Hebrew is typical of standard biblical Hebrew, but that could be recreated in a romanticized story set in a distant past "when judges ruled."

Jonah

Although the book of Jonah probably takes as its personage the prophet Jonah named in 2 Kings 14:25, this narrative is a satire of the prophet, a story of an antiprophet. When Jonah is called by God to prophesy against Nineveh, capital of Assyria, he flees the other way as far and as fast as he can. When he does finally prophesy destruction for Nineveh, and the people surprisingly repent and are forgiven, Jonah is outraged. A number of literary techniques allow this short narrative to weave a rich tapestry. As in the story of Joseph, real and metaphorical descent is depicted throughout: Jonah goes to the bottom of the boat, he is swallowed by a fish, and he says in prayer that he has been brought down to Sheol. Signs of the fictional nature of the story abound, especially in its irony and extravagance of untruths. Jonah is vomited by the great fish at the edge of Nineveh – but Nineveh was 400 miles from the sea. Nineveh is said to be three days' walk across – but no city was that large in circumference. Jonah's religiosity is ultimately less sympathetic than that of the gentile sailors in the boat – or the Ninevites! And it is not only the people who fast and wear sackcloth; it is also the animals. Other prophets have pages of courageous, eloquent oracles that meet with no success, while the weak and directionless Jonah invokes one short oracle and thereby elicits the greatest repentance in the entire Bible. God cares here for a city that does not know God (4:11), but the readers know that, first, it was famous for capturing and destroying the northern half of Israel, and second, Nineveh itself was ultimately destroyed long before the text was written. The ludicrousness of this short story renders it a satirical parable.[14] We are to learn something from the story, but like every good parable, it does not hand us an easy lesson expressed in explicit terms. Surely the pompous prophet is satirized, but is the audience's self-righteousness as well? A strict retributive justice is mocked, but also a complacent belief in Israelite superiority? As is typical of a parable, there is no resolution at the end; we never hear Jonah's reaction. The point is not his redemption, but the reader's response to his shallow sense of justice. This simple story thus allows for differing, complex readings.

Jonah and Ruth are finely sculpted, evocative, and haunting, all in five pages. Most of the plot developments, especially in the beginning, are told in the fewest number of words possible; the *fact* that they happened is all the reader needs to know. (It is for this reason that I do not use the term "novelistic" for these texts.) Like Ruth, Jonah is sometimes said to be opposing the restrictive new policies of Ezra and Nehemiah or, if not these reforms in particular, the stricter boundaries with Gentiles in general. But the debate is not directly engaged in the text; Jonah may be more indirect. The text dashes expectations and transgresses normal views of the prophet, in this case a particular personage probably known as a *good* prophet. At a very early point, Christians revered Jonah as a prophet (Luke 11:29–30) and interpreted his deliverance from the belly of a fish as a symbol of resurrection (Matt 12:40). Jonah also became a common image in early Christian art, symbolizing not resurrection but prayer and deliverance. These various interpretations lent it hagiographical authority over the satirical fictitious reading.

Job

The prose frame of Job is a court narrative transposed to the court of heaven. It differs so dramatically from the long poetic dialogue of Job and his interlocutors that it likely reflects a separate text history. The poetic sections of Job, like Joseph, Ruth, and Jonah, allow for the interpenetration of good and evil. Job thunders against God because there is no clear separation of rewards for good and evil behavior, and Job has been cheated of his reward. In the prose frame, however, Job never wavers from his faith in God and, though tested, is ultimately rewarded. Our praise for the prose story may be somewhat muted when it is compared with the magnificent poetic sections, but it reflects some of the same fictional techniques as Ruth, simply lacking the moral complexity of the other early short stories.

Story of Ahikar

The *Story of Ahikar* is included because it was discovered in a Jewish military colony in Elephantine, Egypt, and seems generically compatible with Jewish stories. Ahikar was a well-known figure – whether real or fictitious we cannot say – from the Assyrian court, and his story of imprisonment on trumped-up charges and vindication was told in many different nations and languages.[15] He could even be transformed into an Israelite in Tobit 1:21–22 and an Ammonite convert to Judaism in Judith 5:5, 14:10. The existence of *Ahikar* among Jewish books and the adoption of the character in the novellas also reinforce the general sense that the fictitious narratives were telling a "wisdom" story, even when satirical.

LATE TEXTS

The later texts – Daniel and Esther with their Deuterocanonical additions, Judith, and Tobit – are characterized, among other things, by more consistent motifs, especially their court setting and important women characters. To be sure, the Joseph story and *Ahikar* are set in the court, and Ruth features strong women, but in the late texts, these two motifs are almost universal. A striking and fascinating aspect of most of the early short stories is the interpenetration of good and evil; a doctrinaire division of the world into good and evil people, or even people of God and others, is simply absent. This is not the case with most of the later texts, where the interpenetration of good and evil is unthinkable.

Daniel

Daniel can be divided neatly between the legends concerning Daniel and his three companions in the first half, described in the third person (Daniel 1–6), and his apocalyptic visions in the second half, told in the first person (Daniel 7–12). Here we will only be concerned with the former. After chapter 1, which introduces the protagonists and their situation in the court of Nebuchadnezzar, the legends can be divided again into court contests (Daniel 2, 4, and 5) and court conflicts (Daniel 3 and 6). In the contests, the faithful Jewish hero proves that he is more accomplished at some important task of courtly wisdom, whether interpreting the king's dreams (Daniel 2 and 4) or mysterious writings on the palace wall (Daniel 5). In the court conflicts, the protagonist inspires jealousy in the non-Jewish courtiers, is persecuted, and ultimately vindicated while they are punished.

Interesting for our discussion is the way in which the Daniel tradition provides a laboratory for the study of the growth of originally oral legends into a makeshift novella merely through the process of collection. Daniel is a novel by agglutination, a development found elsewhere in the Hellenistic East.[16] Daniel 4–6 probably circulated as a separate short collection before it was expanded first into Daniel 1–6, then Daniel 1–12, and finally Deuterocanonical Daniel with Susanna, the Prayer of Azariah and the Song of the Three Jews, and Bel and the Dragon. The artifice of such a process is seen, first, in the fact that at times the characters are unaware of what happened in the previous stories, but second, in the corrections of this inconcinnity that begin to appear. Small notations have evidently been added at points to sew the cycle of stories together; Daniel 5:11, for example, recalls the events of Daniel 4. As in contemporary novelistic traditions in the indigenous nations of the Greek world (e.g., *Satne Khamwas* and *Petubastis* in Egypt), so here as well the popular, assertive narratives of a colonized people find a new function in a longer written form.

Yet, despite the prevailing scholarly view that the Daniel legends were at least in some cases fictional – "Darius the Mede," for instance, in Daniel 5:31 must have been seen as an impossible personage – we must note that Daniel was placed with the prophets in the earliest Christian Bibles, and at Qumran, Daniel was already treated as a prophet, as he was also in Matthew 24:15. Josephus calls Daniel one of the greatest prophets (*Antiquities* 10.266), and Daniel 1–6 is spliced in seamlessly as part of his history of Nebuchadnezzar (10.139, 186–218). Like the appropriation of Jonah, a strong emotional resonance in Daniel – his proud prophetic stance and near martyrdom in the court of the foreign king – likely defictionalized the text for a new authoritative function. Hagiographa trumps fiction.

Esther

The entertaining mock history of Esther has had a fitful role in Jewish and Christian tradition. Barely canonized and not often quoted in early centuries, Esther has nevertheless remained popular for Jews because of its role in Purim festivities. It has often been seen as marginal or even negative by Christians. It makes use of the structure of the court conflict but places it in the service of a farcical send-up of Persian court protocols. The trappings of the court are emphasized and exaggerated to comic effect, and the king over it all, Ahasuerus, is more interested in revelry than in governance. The foreign setting comes to dominate so thoroughly that Judah, Jerusalem, the Temple, and even God are never mentioned.

The enjoyable story is carried along by a number of devices. The pace is brisk as a result of abrupt changes in status and quick reversals of fortune: Vashti falls, Esther rises, Haman rises and then falls, and Mordecai falls and then rises.[17] The characters are often paired or contrasted: Vashti/Esther, Mordecai/Esther, Mordecai/Haman, and Haman/Zeresh. There is a succession of banquets with the generous imbibing of wine. Much of the plot is also carried by constant reference to letters and decrees; they emphasize the power of the king, the extent of the empire, and the mix of nations. The inflated and repetitive style of the narrative has been viewed by many as inferior, but it is *"faux Persian"* and actually quite appropriate to the ethos of the story.

And yet, though God and strictly "religious" symbols are lacking, there is a new emphasis on the meaning of "Jew" and "Judaism," a rallying cry for a "Jewish identity" that is realized in the face of the threats to it – a very "modern" notion that nevertheless goes back to Nehemiah 4. It is stated that Mordecai is a Jew and wears his identity proudly (sometimes as a moniker, "the Jew Mordecai" 6:10), while Esther hides her Jewish identity and will have to *learn*, in the process of the narrative, to identify as Jewish. Character development, we are often told, is something that did not exist in ancient literature and was only discovered with the invention of the modern novel,[18] but it appears at times in these texts. It should be noted that character development here (Esther 4) is depicted *specifically* in regard to Jewish identity. An aspect of the narrative that has been very uncomfortable for modern readers is the account of what appears to be forced conversions: many "acted as Jews for fear of the Jews." The number of references to Jewish identity – but never to God! – is astounding. God, once again, is moved out of the foreground, but there are also suggestions of God's role. The vague reference of help to come from another quarter (4:14) is often noted, but even the fast of the Jews at 4:16, not explicitly an appeal to God, could only have been understood in that way. The purpose for biblical fasts was to demonstrate a self-affliction *in order to be visible to God*.[19] Even more suggestively, Haman's wife Zeresh "prophesies" to her husband, "If Mordecai is Jewish, you will fall before him."[20]

The book of Esther is often dated to the Persian period, but its emphasis on Jewish identity and enforced "Judaizing" is more understandable after the Maccabean Revolt, about the middle or end of the second century BCE. The lack of Greek loan words is no argument for an earlier date; Daniel 7–12 lack Greek words as well, and Greek words, though common in rabbinic literature, are rare in the Hebrew Dead Sea Scrolls. They were noticeable enough to be filtered out when desired.

Tobit
Tobit begins with a brief court conflict but, after this initial scene setting, takes up and reinterprets a folktale similar to the well-known

"Grateful Dead Man," in which a traveler discovers the corpse of a man killed by robbers, buries the body, and is accompanied on his journey by a mysterious stranger – the ghost of the dead man – who dispenses magical boons. The accompanying ghost of the tale is in this case an angel of God, Raphael, and this keeps God and Tobit's piety at the center of this story, but the exaggerations, humor, magical cures, and happy ending breathe the air of fiction. Is there an interpenetration of good and evil in the satirizing of Tobit's self-righteousness? Perhaps, but scholars disagree, and either way the book of Tobit remains a typical late novella.

Judith

Judith also brims with fictional elements – impossible personages ("Nebuchadnezzar, king of the *Assyrians*"), incorrect or unknown place names, wildly exaggerated military features, and preposterous actions of the enemy general Holofernes. God is brought more explicitly into this text, at the same time that the heroine transgresses every rule of traditional piety for women. The story is something of an outrageous experiment: because Judith, the ideal of virtue, is defending her people, she can come out of seclusion and enter into a zone of parody where she can lie, be sexually provocative, and "unman" an enemy general by decapitating him – all without ruffling a feather. Still, by the end, her liminal experience of transgression is over, and she is returned to a position of aristocratic decorum. She, too, becomes heroized by the end of the first century CE (1 Clement 55.4–5).

LITERARY STRUCTURE OF THE LATER TEXTS

There are different ways in which one might group these texts, and each analysis reflects assumptions about what the essential similarities are, how the texts functioned, and how they were "performed" in an ancient setting. Yet it was in turning to these later narratives that scholars began to think more in terms of a repeatable pattern and a popular genre. Certain occasional motifs from the earlier texts – a court setting, for example, or the role of female protagonists – are now encountered in every text. In the Hellenistic period, there was a novelistic development not only in Jewish literature but also in other ancient Near Eastern and Greek literature that favored a female protagonist as the focus of moral decision making.[21] The later texts in most cases likely reflect both an origin in oral storytelling and a new social function as written, novelistic texts in the brave new world of Hellenistic empires.

Genres are often identified by a simple cataloging of commonly occurring motifs, such as a court setting or women characters, but in addition, a number of studies have tried to see the commonality of the texts in terms of repeating structures in the stories, that is, to identify a model of the *relation* of elements placed in a particular order. This approach uses a method introduced into folklore studies by Vladimir Propp.[22] In a Proppian analysis, the elements themselves – such as a particular lack that is experienced or how the lack is liquidated – are quite variable, but the narrative tension *between* a lack and its liquidation is common across many examples. Despite general agreement on the value of a Proppian approach, however, various groupings have been proposed that emphasize different story structures. Susan Niditch and Robert Doran selected a subset of the texts in question, Genesis 41 from the Joseph story, Daniel 2, and *Ahikar* 5–7, in an effort to arrive at a more specific structure for these narratives. The sections that they analyzed all fall into the category of court contests[23]:

1. A person of lower status is called before a person of higher status to answer difficult questions or to solve a problem requiring insight.
2. A person of high status poses a problem that no one seems capable of solving.
3. The person of lower status does solve the problem.
4. The person of lower status is rewarded for answering correctly.

Hans-Peter Müller turns to a different grouping of texts (the prose frame of Job, Daniel 1–6, Tobit, Esther, and *Ahikar*) and analyzes them as examples of didactic or wisdom narrative (*weisheitliche Lehrerzählung*).[24] He notes that these stories are diverting, yet each bears a strong moral message, partly communicated through the common structure:

1. Introduction
    a. Protagonist's virtue
    b. Symbolic deed of virtue
    c. Antagonists and intermediaries
2. Body
    a. Conflict arising from virtue
    b. Testing and proving of virtue
3. Conclusion
    a. Punishment of antagonists
    b. Rewarding of protagonist
    c. Miraculous demonstrations

Note that he emphasizes the *conflict* stories in Daniel and the *conflict* section of *Ahikar*, whereas Niditch and Doran draw together a *contest* from Daniel and the *contest* section from *Ahikar*.

And yet a somewhat fuller structural pattern can be discerned if we focus on the conflict narratives as a group: *Ahikar*, Esther, Daniel 3 and 6, Susanna (set in a local court), and Bel and the Dragon. Even the Joseph story is similar if we imagine Joseph and his brothers as parallel to court- iers. The structure of the conflicts then can be rendered as

1. The protagonist is among equals in the court of the king, reflecting a false sense of stability.
2. Either the protagonist *or* the antagonist ascends within the court, giving rise to or merely revealing instability.
3. An edict or demand is invoked to the detriment of the protagonist.
4. The protagonist performs a courageous act of conscience in defiance.
5. Other courtiers conspire or accuse the protagonist.
6. The execution of the protagonist is set.
7. The execution of the protagonist is attempted.
8. The protagonist escapes death and is vindicated.
9. The antagonist is punished by his or her own device.
10. The protagonist is promoted or exalted in court, resulting in true stability.[25]

An interesting confirmation of a Proppian approach can be observed here: an apparent difference in motifs at the beginning – the ascent of the protagonist *or* one of the courtiers – is now seen as structurally the same in that in both cases the false stability of the court is disturbed. And yet it is ironic that although a sense of "true stability" is found at the end of the individual court conflicts, when they are collected and "novelized" in the book of Daniel, the "true stability" at the end of one conflict disappears by the beginning of the next (Susanna; Daniel 3, 6; Bel and the Dragon).[26]

CONCLUSIONS

Although it is not possible to isolate a precise genre of the short story or novella, one can speak of a general rubric that evolves over time. The stories have a number of important traits in common, even if we are forced at times to set the Joseph story aside as an interesting outlier. They are relatively short prose narrative texts that existed outside of epic and history. They have the appeal of imaginative stories cross-culturally and were likely viewed as fictional. Even where they downplay the intervention of God on an explicit level, there is a clear, happy, and divinely sanctioned resolution that is, alas, not apparent in real life – and that is precisely the point of the story: divine providence is not apparent in real life but is true nevertheless. Like modern romantic comedies, these stories function as a reassurance to those who live in some uncertainty, and like romantic comedies, they either reconstitute the proper orders of society or satirize them.

In a number of these stories, the protagonist undergoes some character development, a literary theme that was supposedly unknown in the ancient world. Joseph grows up and changes from impolitic to politic. When he gets a second chance to interact with his brothers, his treatment of them is altered and broadened by his own experiences. Ahikar (at least in late versions of the text) experiences rudimentary character development from trusting and passive to wily and active. But more significant, Esther changes within one chapter (Esther 4) from petulant and ineffectual to authoritative, ready now to risk her own life in order to save her people. As Mordecai suggests, perhaps she is the very person who can now find it within herself to save her people. Many of the early stories also depict the interpenetration of good and evil (or at least the lack of a separation of good and evil), but in the later texts, good and evil are generally kept strictly separated. To be sure, the book of Judith opens the floodgates temporarily, and the book of Tobit may satirize our self-righteous protagonist, but the general pattern is one of separation. This may correlate with several other developments: some motifs, such as the court setting and the role of women, become more common; the plot structures become more formulaic; and the texts are collected and expanded by a process of novelization. Biblical scholars in the past have chiefly looked to the Bible for theology, history, and great literature. The late texts, however, stand outside the theological masterpieces of the Hebrew Bible, maddeningly confuse all attempts at historical reconstruction, and are often considered inferior in terms of literary quality. Yet, in our age of social and cultural approaches to historical reconstruction, they may now engage a new audience.

NOTES

1   Tremper Longman III, "Israelite Genres in Their Ancient Near Eastern Context," in *The Changing Face of Form Criticism for the Twenty-First Century*, ed. by Marvin Sweeney and Ehud Ben Zvi (Grand Rapids, MI: Eerdmans, 2003), 190; Lawrence M. Wills, "The Jewish Novellas," and John Tait, "Egyptian Fiction in Demotic and Greek," both in *Greek Fiction: The*

Greek Novel in Context, ed. by J. R. Morgan and Richard Stoneman (London: Routledge, 1994), 203–22 and 223–38; Mu-chou Poo, *Enemies of Civilization: Attitudes Toward Foreigners in Ancient Mesopotamia, Egypt, and China* (Albany: State University of New York Press, 2005). Robert Alter, *The Art of Biblical Narrative* (New York: Basic Books, 1981), 23–46, speaks of biblical narrative in general as "fiction," but he intentionally uses a very loose definition of fiction as a plastic narration. The genre boundary between fiction and history is also porous because we note how in the Greek period the conquered nations produced exuberant histories that we cannot divide easily into fiction or nonfiction; cf. especially the *Ninus Romance*, the *Nektanebos* tradition, and among Jews, *Artapanus*.

2   The colonial boundary, as argued by Homi Bhabha, *The Location of Culture* (London: Routledge, 1994), esp. 38, is the zone of creativity, and it becomes as well the principal zone in which identity is contested.

3   The two opposing positions can be represented by Susan Niditch, *Oral World and Written Word: Ancient Israelite Literature* (Louisville, KY: Westminster John Knox, 1996), 113, and Karel van der Toorn, *Scribal Culture and the Making of the Hebrew Bible* (Cambridge, MA: Harvard University Press, 2007), 140.

4   They are still smaller than the standard biblical scroll. On observing that the novelistic texts discovered at Qumran were transmitted on smaller scrolls, J. T. Milik dubbed them the "paperbacks of antiquity" ("Les modèles araméens du livre d'Esther dans la grotte 4 de Qumrân," *RQ* 59 [1992]: 363–5).

5   Smith, *Palestinian Parties and Politics that Shaped the Old Testament* (New York: Columbia University Press, 1971), 157–63. He includes in this analysis Job, Ecclesiastes, Ruth, Jonah, Judith, Tobit, Esther, Song of Songs, and the rewriting of Proverbs.

6   Hans-Peter Müller, "Die weisheitliche Lehrerzählung im Alten Testament und seiner Umwelt," *Die Welt des Orients* 9 (1977): 77–98; Gerhard von Rad, "The Joseph Narrative and Ancient Wisdom," in *The Problem of the Hexateuch and Other Essays* (New York: McGraw-Hill, 1966), 292–300; Shemaryahu Talmon, "Wisdom in the Book of Esther," *VT* 13 (1963): 419–55; and Lawrence M. Wills, *The Jew in the Court of the Foreign King: Ancient Jewish Court Legends* (Minneapolis, MN: Fortress, 1990), esp. 23–38.

7   Arndt Meinhold, "Die Gattung der Josephsgeschichte und des Estherbuches: Diasporanovelle, I, II," *ZAW* 87 (1975): 306–24; *ZAW* 88 (1976): 79–93; W. Lee Humphreys, "A Life-Style for Diaspora: A Study of the Tales of Esther and Daniel," *JBL* 92 (1973): 211–23, and "Novella," in *Saga, Legend, Tale, Novella, Fable: Narrative Forms in Old Testament Literature*, ed. by George W. Coats (Sheffield, UK: JSOT Press, 1985), 82–96; Edward F. Campbell, "The Hebrew Short Story: A Study of Ruth," in *A Light Unto My Path*, ed. by H. N. Bream, R. D. Heim, and C. A. Moore (Philadelphia: Temple University Press, 1974), 83–101.

8   Reinhard G. Kratz, *The Composition of the Narrative Books of the Old Testament* (London: T & T Clark, 2005), 274–9; Walter Dietrich, *Die Josephserzählung als Novelle und Geschichtsschreibung: zugleich ein Beitrag zur Pentateuchfrage* (Neukirchen-Vluyn, Germany: Neukirchener, 1989), 53–66.

9   Ilana Pardes, *Counter-Traditions in the Bible: A Feminist Approach* (Cambridge, MA: Harvard University Press, 1992), 98–117.

10 Erich Auerbach, *Mimesis: The Representation of Reality in Western Literature* (Princeton, NJ: Princeton University Press, 1953). Auerbach would not have accepted this judgment, but his criteria are clearly met in Ruth.

11 See Jack M. Sasson, *Ruth: A New Translation with a Philological Commentary and a Formalist-Folklorist Interpretation* (Baltimore, MD: Johns Hopkins University Press, 1979), 196.

12 Edward F. Campbell, Jr., *Ruth: A New Translation and Commentary* (Garden City, NY: Doubleday, 1975), 3–18.

13 Saul Olyan, *Rites and Rank: Hierarchy in Biblical Representations of Cult* (Princeton, NJ: Princeton University Press, 2000), 90–2, argues that Ruth responds to Ezra; John J. Collins, *Introduction to the Hebrew Bible* (Minneapolis, MN: Fortress, 2004), 533, 535, expresses doubts.

14 See the excellent but inconclusive discussion by Phyllis Trible, "The Book of Jonah," in *The New Interpreter's Bible*, Vol. 7, ed. by Leander E. Keck (Nashville, TN: Abingdon Press, 1994–2001), 467–71.

15 Wills, *Jew in the Court*, 44–9.

16 Tait, "Egyptian Fiction;" David Konstan, "The *Alexander Romance:* The Cunning of the Open Text," *Lexis* 16 (1998): 123–38.

17 Sidnie White Crawford, "The Book of Esther," in *New Interpreter's Bible*, Vol. 3, 857; Jon D. Levenson, *Esther* (Louisville, KY: Westminster John Knox, 1997), 8.

18 Michael E. Vines, *The Problem of Markan Genre: The Gospel of Mark and the Jewish Novel* (Atlanta: Society of Biblical Literature, 2002), 86–8, probably correctly concerning Greek and Roman literature. Michael V. Fox, *Character and Ideology in the Book of Esther* (Columbia: University of South Carolina Press, 1991), emphasizes the character development found in Esther.

19 David Lambert, "Fasting as a Penitential Rite: A Biblical Phenomenon?," *HTR* 96(4) (2003): 477–512. Matthew 6:16 is an exception and an innovation in Jewish and Christian tradition.

20 Crawford, "Book of Esther," Vol. 3, 867.

21 Lawrence M. Wills, *The Jewish Novel in the Ancient World* (Ithaca, NY: Cornell University Press, 1995). The feminism of the female characters must be seen in the context of the narrative worlds created and their relation to the social world. Strong female characters appear in both the Hebrew Bible and classical Greek literature, but this may not indicate that women played a more visible role in society. Susan Niditch, "Short Stories: The Book of Esther and the Theme of Woman as a Civilizing Force," in *Old Testament Interpretation, Past, Present and Future: Essays in Honor of Gene M. Tucker*, ed. by James Luther Mays, David L. Petersen, and Kent Harold Richards (Nashville, TN: Abingdon Press, 1995), 195–209, points out the folklore parallels to this; that is, the role of women as a civilizing or salutary force in tales cross-culturally.

22 Vladimir Propp, *Morphology of the Folktale*, 2nd ed. (Austin: University of Texas Press, 1981); Wills, *Jewish Novel*, 21–3. To be sure, some of the early

texts were brought into these studies, but it was the discernment of a traditional pattern in the later texts that spurred the structural analysis of the narratives. In regard to Ruth, however, see Sasson, *Ruth*.

23 Susan Niditch and Robert Doran, "The Success Story of the Wise Courtier," *JBL* 96 (1977): 179–93. Two of their texts are early, but Niditch and Doran were responding to Humphreys's categories for late texts.

24 Müller, "Die weisheitliche Lehrerzählung."

25 See the discussion in Lawrence M. Wills, "Response to 'The Genre and Function of the Markan Passion Narrative,'" in *George W. E. Nickelsburg in Perspective: An Ongoing Dialogue of Learning*, ed. by Jacob Neusner and Alan J. Avery-Peck (Leiden, Netherlands: Brill, 2003), 504–12. Nickelsburg's article, pp. 473–503, gathers most of these texts and adds Wisdom of Solomon 2–5, 3 Maccabees, 2 Maccabees 7, and Mark; the group as a whole enacts the narrative of the persecuted righteous person.

26 This reflects the variety and repeatability of legend – unlike epic, nothing is really established in legend except the *character* of the hero and God's graces working through him.

FURTHER READING

Campbell, Edward F. "The Hebrew Short Story: A Study of Ruth," pp. 83–101 in *A Light Unto My Path*. Edited by H. N. Bream, R. D. Heim, and C. A. Moore. Philadelphia: Temple University Press, 1974.

Craven, Toni. *Artistry and Faith in the Book of Judith*. Chico, CA: Scholars Press, 1983.

Fox, Michael V. *Character and Ideology in the Book of Esther*. Columbia: University of South Carolina Press, 1991.

Humphreys, W. Lee. "A Life-Style for Diaspora: A Study of the Tales of Esther and Daniel." *JBL* 92 (1973): 211–23.

"Novella," pp. 82–96 in *Saga, Legend, Tale, Novella, Fable: Narrative Forms in Old Testament Literature*. Edited by George W. Coats. Sheffield, UK: JSOT Press, 1985.

Müller, Hans-Peter. "Die weisheitliche Lehrerzählung im Alten Testament und in seiner Umwelt." *Die Welt des Orients* 9 (1977): 77–98.

Niditch, Susan. *Oral World and Written Word: Ancient Israelite Literature*. Louisville, KY: Westminster John Knox, 1996.

"Short Stories: The Book of Esther and the Theme of Woman as a Civilizing Force," pp. 195–209 in *Old Testament Interpretation, Past, Present and Future: Essays in Honor of Gene M. Tucker*. Edited by James Luther Mays, David L. Petersen, and Kent Harold Richards. Nashville, TN: Abingdon Press, 1995.

Niditch, Susan and Robert Doran. "The Success Story of the Wise Courtier." *JBL* 96 (1977): 179–93.

Sasson, Jack M. *Ruth: A New Translation with a Philological Commentary and a Formalist-Folklorist Interpretation*. Baltimore, MD: Johns Hopkins University Press, 1979.

Trible, Phyllis. "The Book of Jonah," pp. 461–529 in *The New Interpreter's Bible*, 12 vols. Edited by Leander E. Keck. Nashville, TN: Abingdon Press, 1994–2001.

Wills, Lawrence M. "The Book of Judith," pp. 1073–1183 in *The New Interpreter's Bible*, Vol. 3. Edited by Leander E. Keck. Nashville, TN: Abingdon Press, 1994–2001.

The Jew in the Court of the Foreign King: Ancient Jewish Court Legends. Minneapolis, MN: Fortress, 1990.

The Jewish Novel in the Ancient World. Ithaca, NY: Cornell University Press, 1995.

"The Jewish Novellas," pp. 203–22 in *Greek Fiction: The Greek Novel in Context*. Edited by J. R. Morgan and Richard Stoneman. London: Routledge, 1994.

16 Apocalyptic writings

STEPHEN L. COOK

The eschatological hope of apocalypticism centers on God's renewal of the cosmos, nature, and humanity, thus establishing perfect shalom and joy. The renewal is physical and material, not symbolic and ethereal. It ushers in a marvelous world beyond anything that humans have ever known (see, e.g., Zech 14:6–7; Isa 25:8; 26:19). Heretofore, few indeed have glimpsed God's resurrected world (see 2 Kgs 2:11–12), and even prophets have struggled to accept a vision of Sheol's defeat (2 Kgs 2:16–18).

Within the Hebrew Bible, Daniel (especially chapters 2, 7–12) is the primary "apocalypse," a type of writing attested more fully in the wider Jewish and Christian world of Hellenistic and Greco-Roman times.[1] The book of Daniel includes a visionary, with angels' help, grappling with the "Beyond." The seer (Daniel) explores a superior reality, parallel to human experience, which is on a collision course with history. The writings of the book have little to do with the tried and true. Rather, Daniel's apocalyptic imagination exposes transpersonal evil, uncovers primal conflicts of existence, and evokes humanity's awe before God.

The visions of Daniel 7–12 disclose a heavenly world and an imminent culmination to history. They contain pulsing images on a mythic scale; they predict the ultimate triumph of good over evil. A steady increase of worldwide evil is inevitable, according to the visions, but there will follow an end-time triumph of God over its forces. God is about to intervene in history, destroying the dehumanizing spirit embedded within the world's empires. When that happens, God will overthrow wholesale all imperial systems of control, establish an everlasting dominion on earth, and reward the faithful.

Beyond Daniel, the First Testament also contains an assortment of texts enlivened by an apocalyptic imagination but lacking the standardized features of the Hellenistic apocalypses. These texts exhibit apocalyptic thinking and may be designated as early apocalyptic or "protoapocalyptic" literature. They presuppose a cognitive grid for interpreting the world where the contested reign of God verges on manifesting itself in open power, ushering in a transformation of embodied existence. Radical additions to several prophetic books fall under the rubric "protoapocalyptic" (e.g., Ezekiel 38–9; Isaiah 24–7), as do the entire books of Haggai, Zechariah, Joel, and Malachi.

Scholars of the Hebrew Bible have some catching up to do in relation to their New Testament counterparts in granting legitimacy to the idea of apocalyptic thinking outside the traditional Hellenistic-era apocalypses. New Testament scholars realize that John the baptizer, who never wrote an apocalypse or, indeed, any surviving literature, certainly adopted the cosmological and eschatological perspective of the apocalypse genre (see Matt 3:7, 10, 12). Jesus of Nazareth did not write an apocalypse either, but approximately half the biblical guild currently affirms the historicity of Jesus's apocalyptic preaching of the reign of God (see Mark 1:15; Matt 4:17; 11:11).

DEFINITIONS AND SCOPE

Perhaps the best entrée into defining apocalyptic thinking is to draw some contrasts between it and mythological thought. If by mythological thinking we mean a culture's accounting for the present world, a symbolic expression of nature's cycles and paradoxes in which stability must win out, then mythology is antithetic to the apocalyptic imagination. As Jindo writes, "Myth expresses the longing for the eternal, the durative, the perpetual, i.e., the unchanged."[2] In contrast, apocalypticism in no way "accounts" for the world and assures its stability. Rather, it prepares for its radical change through an invasion by otherness. After this invasion, the preternatural Beyond incarnates itself incontestably in human existence.

Near Eastern mythological polytheism envisioned the world as the battlefield or playground of immanent supernatural forces. By the time of the apocalyptic literature, biblical thought had charted a very different understanding of existence. The "mythological" feel of apocalyptic texts is not a prescientific grappling with hustling, immanent superpowers, but the literature's means of opening windows into God's transcendent truths (understood as mustering themselves).

The Greek verb *apokalyptein* means "unveil, reveal, or disclose." Exactly what is revealed? Apocalyptic insight reveals how the world and its immediate future look from within an experience of transcendence, from a perspective immersed in absolute reality. The influential twentieth-century Jesuit theologian Karl Rahner cogently articulated such a perspective. Rahner described workaday human knowledge as but a tiny floating island adrift in a vast unknown sea that bears all life and consciousness on the island.[3] The lamp of normal human observation and common sense illuminates the island in a relatively acceptable manner. Most people live primarily or exclusively by this light. Apocalyptic visionaries, by contrast, dive into the sea of mystery and observe how things look from the depths. They observe the depths churning, transcendence whipping up a storm. Life on the island is fragile and cannot long perdure.

The sovereign finality of absolute reality will imminently prove incontestable, apocalyptic visionaries observe. Just "one moment yet" (New American Bible [NAB]), the Hebrew idiom of Haggai 2:6 specifies, and God will shake the sky and the earth, the sea and the dry ground. "I am about to shake the heavens and the earth," God reiterates in Haggai 2:21. Isaiah 56:1 sounds the same note: salvation is "soon." Joel 2:1 echoes the theme: "The day of the Lord is about to come. Indeed, it is near!" (New English Translation [NET]).

Apocalypticism is neither mythic nor polytheistic, but it relies heavily on the images and oppositions of mythology. Again, Karl Rahner's thought provides our key for understanding. Rahner explains that the truths of transcendent reality have a backdoor entrée into perception via the shared archetypes of the preconscious human mind and their symbolic expression in human dreams, nightmares, and mythologies. In his philosophy, the archetypes of the collective unconscious are a prethematic, "natural" witness to the transcendent plane. Apocalyptic literature naturally avails itself of them as windows or openings out into the Absolute, as representations of basic ontological truths.

APOCALYPTICISM OUTSIDE THE APOCALYPSES?

The popular mind takes a conceptual approach to what counts as an "apocalyptic" Scripture. The public generally tags as "apocalyptic" those biblical texts that speak of massive terrestrial cataclysms. (Sometimes people realize that such texts also entail celestial victories ushering in God's reign.) The dominant scholarly approach, by contrast, is often hesitant to speak of Israelite apocalypticism outside those works that fit the literary genre "apocalypse." Over several decades, Klaus Koch, John J. Collins, and others mapped out the parameters of the apocalypse genre with real success. An apocalypse proper narrates a supernatural intermediary's revelations to a human recipient about the imminent eruption of

God's salvation in history, establishing God's reign on earth. This salvation emanates from a transcendent realm, which is both spatially separate from earthly reality, paralleling it, and temporally removed from the present in that history must wait for salvation to manifest itself decisively. The consensus definition succeeds in encompassing the standard corpus of Hellenistic and Greco-Roman apocalypses.

It is certainly legitimate to pursue a literary-critical investigation of the generic apocalypse. This is the logical entry point into apocalypticism for scholars specializing in the religions of late antiquity, when apocalypses emerged as a key element of the milieu in which the early Jewish sects, including Christianity, took shape. For those interested in the variety of apocalyptic literature within the Hebrew Bible, however, maintaining a sustained focus on the literary genre of the apocalypse proper has limitations.

The generic apocalypse only made its appearance in late antiquity. We finally see it emerge in parts of *Enoch* and the book of Daniel at the tail end of the Hebrew Bible's history of composition. If one takes the full-blown genre as one's point of departure and touchstone, one must expend real effort working backward to elucidate the genre's earlier biblical antecedents. The historical and social scientific data for mounting such an effort is largely lacking, and there is wide disagreement about which scholarly constructs should inform the attempt. One may well end up neglecting earlier apocalyptic Scriptures, even though these texts bear a recognizable apocalyptic imagination. And it is strange to see mainstream scholars of apocalypticism sideline Ezekiel's description of Gog of Magog (Ezekiel 38–9) and Joel's description of a swarming horde of foes (Joel 2:1–11), when modern lay readers instinctively sense their apocalyptic energy and when the Apocalypse of John latches onto precisely these descriptions in its portrayals of earth's last days (Rev 9:1–12; 19:17–21; 20:7–9).

Even if texts such as Ezekiel 38–9 and Joel 2:1–11 are recognized as protoapocalyptic literature, approaching them with an orientation on literary genre may predispose the scholar to negative value judgments. Scholars often come away from the apocalypses of late antiquity impressed with their air of obscurantism, paranoia, and fantasy, and may automatically transfer such impressions to any canonical literature that they understand as parallel.

Apocalyptic writings bear a family resemblance to each other with regard to literary character but also resemble one another on a conceptual basis. Characteristic formal features go hand in hand with overlapping material features, including overlapping and crisscrossing concepts of cosmology, otherworldly salvation, and the consummation of history. The ideas of apocalypticism are hardly secondary in understanding the phenomenon. Apocalyptic revelations transmit specific content from the beyond, unveiling the churning sea of mystery about to engulf our island world.

A social scientific approach to apocalyptic literature compares the biblical apocalyptic visionaries with what anthropologists term "millennial" (or "millenarian") groups and movements. Cross-cultural comparison reveals that such groups use a great variety of literary and oral forms to express the apocalyptic imagination of their membership. The millennial message is recognizable across eras and cultures, but the media used to covey the worldview are surprisingly variable. The apocalypse is by no means the primary formal vehicle. To prioritize the generic apocalypse as the core vehicle of the apocalyptic message is to limit one's database artificially.

This is not to say that millennial groups across cultures have avoided apocalypse as a genre. They do indeed produce apocalypses, the point of departure and touchstone of genre-oriented scholars of apocalypticism. Confirming our assumptions about the modus operandi of biblical visionaries, they pen these works as expressions of a literal belief in a fast-approaching, miraculous judgment and salvation of this world. They bear witness to their beliefs through many media beyond apocalypses, however, attesting to the plethora of vehicles available for airing an apocalyptic worldview.

Lester Grabbe provides two clear examples.[4] He cites an apocalypse by Rabbi Nathan of Gaza, associated with the millennial movement surrounding the seventeenth-century CE Jewish messiah, Sabbatai Ṣevi. Jump-starting the Sabbatian movement, Rabbi Nathan penned a pseudepigraph describing revelations of a celestial mentor to an aged rabbinic sage named Abraham from four centuries earlier. These revelations identified Sabbatai Ṣevi as the true messiah who would subdue the chaos dragon and usher in an eternal kingdom on earth. Beyond writing this apocalypse, Nathan expressed his apocalyptic message through many alternative vehicles, including conversations, preaching, letters, and commentaries. He even uttered ecstatic prophecy from a trance state, during which he stripped and fainted.

Grabbe also cites the apocalypses of the Seneca Native American figure known as Handsome Lake. The code of Handsome Lake's millennial movement, the *Gaiwiio* ("Good Message"), records certain commissioning visions of the prophet that fit the apocalypse genre proper. In these visions, which occurred between June 1799 and February 1800

CE, Handsome Lake tours heaven and hell with three beautiful messengers acting as guides and interpreters. The guides summon him to preach repentance to his people, based on a coming fiery end of the earth. Beyond its sections on Handsome Lake's visionary journeys, the apocalyptic content of the Good Message takes other forms than the generic apocalypse. It contains moral teaching on social life, ceremonial regulations, and a great deal of the biography behind the prophet's visions.

THE QUESTION OF PERSIAN INFLUENCE

From the beginning of the twentieth century, researches have recognized the possibility of Persia's influence on Western scriptural traditions (e.g., Lawrence Mills, George Carter, and Hubertus von Gall). The History of Religions School adopted the position that such influence was thoroughgoing, and this view is far from dormant in contemporary scholarship. Robert Carroll even argues that a "Persian shaping of Jewish thought was one of the most fundamentally creative forces in determining the roots of Second Temple Judaism."[5]

Apocalyptic beliefs, such as a dualism of good and evil, a coming resurrection of the dead, and an eschatological judgment of every human individual, appear to have characterized Zoroastrian religion already during Israel's restoration era. Plutarch, in the first century CE, attests to an apocalyptic Zoroastrian cosmology and eschatology, and he attributes his understanding of the religion to the fourth-century BCE historian Theopompus. Other Greek writers corroborate the legitimacy of using Theopompus as a source of knowledge about early Zoroastrianism. Persian apocalypticism was thus early enough to have influenced the development of apocalypticism in the Judeo-Christian tradition, and contact with Zoroastrian belief would have been inevitable in the Second Temple period, when Jews and Persians interacted at many levels.

Acknowledging that Zoroastrianism likely stimulated Israel's apocalyptic thinking, however, does not mean that Scripture has lifted or borrowed chunks of alien theology without discrimination. To the contrary, the biblical visionaries tended to stick to their own alternative eschatological schemes, betraying no interest in Iranian patterns of faith. It is erroneous, for example, to consider Daniel 12:1–3 and its vision of resurrection as discontinuous with preceding biblical tradition and a likely by-product of Israel's contact with Zoroastrianism.

In Daniel 12, the dead "awake" to the resurrection from their "sleep in the dust of the earth." No such sort of resurrection is found in

Zoroastrianism, which shuns the burial of corpses as potentially defiling of the earth. The Persians did not imagine the rising of buried corpses but a re-creation of bodies from the bare elements of nature. Three centuries before the writing of Daniel 12, Herodotus attests the Zoroastrian practice of exposing dead corpses to be picked clean by vultures and dogs (*Hist.* 1.140).

Instead of looking to Zoroastrianism for the roots of Daniel 12, its antecedents are more naturally discovered in texts such as Isaiah 26:19; 53:10–11; and 66:22–24, as further discussion shall reveal. Indeed, Israel was apparently comfortable with resurrection already by the time of the Babylonian Exile, long before the notion's supposed surprise appearance in Daniel 12, long before Theopompus's era, and even long before Palestine first began to settle into Achaemenian rule. I am referring to the vision of resurrection in Ezekiel 37, which stems from a time and place (Babylonia around 580 BCE) unlikely to have felt much Zoroastrian influence.

Ezekiel 37 uses resurrection as a metaphor, but the implications of this use are momentous. The prophet is assuming that his readers will relate to his metaphor and find it persuasive. He would certainly not have chosen resurrection as the literary vehicle of his message if the idea had been a foreign and unintelligible concept in the minds of his exilic audience. Ezekiel's use of resurrection language is symbolic, to be sure, but it demonstrates how rising from death was far from an anomalous idea in Hebrew tradition.

Social scientific insights cast further doubt on the idea that some external influence, such as an influx of Persian religion, must account for the rise of Israelite apocalypticism. Across cultures, apocalyptic beliefs, including beliefs in resurrection, regularly arise autochthonously out of native religious building blocks, especially archetypal symbols of creation. No foreign influences were at play in 1890 CE, for example, when the Ghost Dance arose among Native Americans with its vision that a messiah was now on earth and a resurrection of ancestors was imminent. The Ghost Dance initially developed indigenously; Zoroastrianism had nothing to do with it!

The likeliest cases where Persian religion may have had a genuinely creative influence within Israel occur within the apocalypses of the Hellenistic era. Long after the rise of Israelite apocalypticism during Achaemenid times, Hellenistic texts from after 170 BCE begin to exhibit some telltale Persian motifs, such as Satan as God's archenemy, an elaborate demonology, and a predetermined, detailed periodization of history. We know that Persian thought was of real interest to many

Greek intellectuals, who may have mediated some of its content to circles within early Judaism.

THE RELATIONSHIP OF EARLY BIBLICAL APOCALYPTICISM TO PROPHECY

Cross-cultural study of millennialism shows that many different types of groups develop an apocalyptic imagination. Within Israel, prophetic circles seem to have been the first to have hosted such a thought complex. Scripture's earliest apocalyptic writings – texts such as Isaiah 56–66 and Ezekiel 38–9 – are nestled within prophetic collections.

Despite this open fact, scholarly literature continues to caution against assuming any straightforward growth of apocalypticism out of prophecy. Such cautions have their point but are easily overdrawn. Prophecy and apocalypticism are far from blatantly discontinuous, as many contend. Although it attends to the complications of ordinary life and history in a way different from apocalypticism, biblical prophecy cannot be reduced to bare politics and activism. The Hebrew God of prophecy no more fits a humanly construed idea of plain history and real politics than the God of apocalypticism. Rather, Israelite prophecy tended to rip apart all boxes for confining God, boldly directing history toward an extraordinary telos.

The eschatological vision of prophecy often resembles apocalypticism in its embrace of sweeping divine promises of shalom for Israel and for earth. The difference is that apocalypticism recapitulates God's hopes for the world and projects them to the bounds of existence. As Moltmann writes, "In apocalyptic the whole cosmos becomes interpreted in the light of truth learned from God's revelation in Israel's history."[6]

Any suspicions that Hebrew prophecy mostly confines itself to the historical-political realm are immediately dispelled by a glance at Isaiah. Isaiah's trenchant call is to abandon diplomacy and place all trust in "the gently flowing waters of Shiloah" (Isa 8:6). Jerusalem and its rivers manifest God's cosmic mountain, Isaiah insists, a supraterrestrial realm walled off from quotidian reality. A transcendent blessing is attached to Isaiah's Jerusalem, which defies chaos, decay, and death, and radically challenges human historical experience with symbols of an alternative divine reality. The blessing even includes inklings of human immortality (cf. Ps 52:8; 92:12–15).

The prophetic notion of all God's people receiving a new heart and a new spirit (Ezek 36:26) hardly fits the parameters of plain history. By the same token, one strains to imagine the nations no longer training for war

(Mic 4:3) as something historically realistic. And who can routinize the idea of God's backing of the Servant figure of Isaiah's book even beyond death (Isa 53:11, see New International Version [NIV], Dead Sea Scrolls [DSS]; cf. Ps 22:15, 24)? One could multiply examples of such suprahistorical expectations within prophecy.

The history of the tradition in Isaiah 11:1–10 provides one clear example of a trajectory from prophecy into early apocalypticism. This messianic text speaks of ideal perfections of government finally realized in a superhuman vicar (3–4; cf. Isa 9:6), including a spirit-imbued righteousness, reverence, and strength. Under the reign of this supermonarch, an alien shalom will appear, including among wildlife. Even if the language is figurative, the text still confronts us with our experience transformed.

Later texts within Isaiah expand on Isaiah 11 and its otherworldly hope. Isaiah 42:1–9 alludes to the passage through half a dozen verbal and thematic correspondences and interprets it to possess global ramifications (the "land" of Israel in 11:4 becomes the entire "earth" in 42:5). Eventually, the tradition proves foundational in the apocalyptic vision of Isaiah 65. After announcing God's imminent apocalyptic creation of new heavens and a new earth (17), Isaiah 65 stipulates that God's coming reign will see the vision of Isaiah 11 fully and literally realized (25). Isaiah 65:25 directly references and affirms Isaiah 11:6–9, summarizing the passage in an alternative postexilic Hebrew idiom.

THE ORIGINS OF THE APOCALYPTIC IMAGINATION IN ISRAEL

Apocalypticism emerged in Israel when the transcendent potentials of Israel's traditional theological ideals and symbols finally came into their own. Intimations of otherworldly salvation embedded in biblical tradition now asserted their tension with mundane reality in the starkest possible fashion and with shocking immediacy. Contradictions aplenty surfaced as a series of unbearable antitheses. Finally, lines got drawn in the sand.

The archetypal imagery of the "Divine Warrior" was grist for the mill in the postexilic ripening of apocalyptic understandings. Such symbolism bore the germs of a fundamental refusal to tolerate this world's ugliness, sterility, and strife. As in the original creation, the Divine Warrior now achieves a decisive cosmic victory that will defeat chaos and pave the way for beauty, harmony, and human community.

Israelite prophecy envisioned the Divine Warrior raging against chaos, driving chariots of salvation to victory, causing mountains to quake and the sky to pour down water (see Hab 3:8–10). The Divine Warrior reappears in apocalyptic texts with new import and urgency. Now the Warrior eschews human instrumentality and intervenes on earth in an open and literal fashion, all possible human mediators of salvation being deemed absent or unqualified (Isa 59:16). The Warrior declares, "I have trodden the winepress alone"; "no one was with me" (Isa 63:3, cf. v. 5). His direct intervention has a universal scope that extends justice to the ends of the earth (Isa 59:18), to all "peoples" (Isa 63:6). His duel is with a suprahistorical reality: "Edom" understood as evil embodied (Isa 63:1; cf. Isa 34; Mal 1:2–5), similar to Ezekiel's "Gog" (Ezekiel 38–9).

Mythic and archetypal motifs and themes, such as the myth of a duel between God and chaos, form crucial building blocks of the apocalyptic imagination. In apocalyptic thinking, mythic reality is precisely that transcendent reality that invades history as the end times emerge. Apocalypticism thus "leans on" mythology while disavowing Near Eastern mythological polytheism, which envisioned the world as a showground for supernatural forces to interact and clash.

In the ontological dualism of apocalypticism, God reigns over the cosmos well above the fray of the fearful "multiverse" of Near Eastern religions. To return to my paradigm based on Karl Rahner's philosophy, God's supernatural reality in apocalypticism's understanding is fully transcendent over everything tangible or immanent. God's reality is the great churning sea that lies off the shores of what Rahner calls our "tiny island of experience."

The first appearances of Israelite apocalypticism date to the exilic and postexilic eras. The exilic period, when Israel's entire world was inverted, brought an intense, focal concentration of Israel's eschatological hopes. It reawakened Israel's primal fears and poetic dreams, and it provoked a new orientation toward Israel's archetypes of creation and divine blessing. At this time, the traditional expectations and spiritual goals of Israel's Torah, the classical prophets, and the sapiential literature blossomed under the new, imaginative "sheltering canopy" of apocalypticism.

This same era saw the emergence of a new medium of revelation that relied on an intertextual and mantic study of Scripture. A considerable collection of authoritative, sacred writings was in place by Second Temple times, to which Israel's new apocalyptic visionaries made ready reference. Far from signifying religious decline (as Wellhausen once assumed), their learned, scribal mode of operation was spiritually fruitful. This mode of channeling revelation forged a compelling apocalyptic imagination from echoes and allusions to earlier Scriptures. It both validated Israel's heritage and made its radical realization and fulfillment a source of orientation and adrenaline for the faithful.

Recent scholarship, including work on the Isaian apocalypse by J. Todd Hibbard, helps us to appreciate how a new apocalyptic mosaic may simultaneously sustain and transform the tiles that coalesce in its creation.[7] Hibbard shows how Isaiah 24 reached into sacred tradition to reference earlier texts such as Hosea 4:9, Amos 5:2, and Isaiah 17:6. Such texts took on an altered, global scope in their new Isaian context. God's character and purposes are received as constants but now extend in a radically totalizing fashion.

Social scientific study of millennial groups reveals that their apocalyptic imaginations may coalesce in many varieties of social arenas. Apocalypticism emerges in eras of calm and eras of disruption, in stable societies and amid the encounters and clashes of cultures, and in peripheral or colonized peoples and in dominating or colonizing powers. Scholars must abandon the commonplace view that apocalypticism is a religion of marginal, deprived, and oppressed peoples. Just consider the apocalyptic zeal of certain Franciscan parties among the Spanish colonizers of the New World. Gerónimo De Mendieta, a sixteenth-century Franciscan missionary, drove the indigenous population of New Spain to accept colonization as a preparation for God's dawning millennial reign.

The sixth-century BCE apocalyptic texts of Haggai and Zechariah 1–8 arose in a milieu of international calm and Persian benefaction. These Scriptures cannot be considered a means of coping with disruptions or restrictions. Rather, according to the texts, "Lo, the whole earth remains at peace" (Zech 1:11). The Persian monarch Darius I had quelled all revolts, restored security, and established the Davidic heir Zerubbabel in power in Yehud. "In the second year of King Darius" (Hag 1:1), preparations for God's reign could begin. Learned study of Jeremiah 25:11–12 and 29:10 left no doubt that God's prescribed seventy years of exile were concluding, that God was now coming into Jerusalem's midst (Hag 1:13; 2:4–7; Zech 8:3).

THE VARIED GROUP PROVENANCES OF SCRIPTURE'S APOCALYPTIC LITERATURE

The prophetic school of Ezekiel may have been the first Israelite circle to generate a protoapocalyptic text: Ezekiel 38–9, the oracles against Gog of Magog. The prophet and his followers who edited and preserved his prophecies were members of a specific lineage of priests in Israel known as the Zadokites (see Ezek 44:15–31). At the time of Ezekiel's exile, the Zadokites dominated the authority structures and rites at the Jerusalem Temple. Going into exile, the prophet carried a specific *priestly* theology, one preserved elsewhere in the Hebrew Bible as a source of the Pentateuch known as the "Holiness School" (HS).[8]

Who else but members of the Zadokite priestly elite would have penned an eschatological vision of purifying Israel through months of burying bones (Ezek 39:11–16)? In keeping with their provenance, the entire thrust of these apocalyptic oracles is predicated on Zadokite thinking, on emphases of the HS (cf. Lev 17:15–16; 18:25–8; 22:4). The existence of Zadokite apocalypticism belies the commonplace view, following in the wake of the scholarship of Otto Plöger, Paul Hanson, and others, that Israel's priestly elite advocated a realized eschatology, that they suppressed millennialism.

Sixth- and fifth-century protoapocalyptic texts in Zechariah and Joel draw on the Gog oracles. Zechariah 2:4 (MT 2:8) interprets Ezekiel 38:11 very literally, using it to explain why an ideal Jerusalem will have to lack walls. Joel 2:20's term "northerner" pins an apocalyptic motif from Ezekiel 38:6, 15; 39:2 on a locust and sirocco crisis. Joel depends on Ezekiel, and not the other way around, because Joel's disasters came out of the eastern desert. The term "northerner" is applied to them solely because Joel viewed his crises as portents of Gog's attack. Joel 2:20 also includes exegesis of Ezekiel 39:11, clarifying its reference to a locale "east of the sea." Joel 3:17 (MT 4:17) contains a crabbed misreading of Ezekiel 39:11's mythic language, which speaks colorfully of Gog's dead horde clogging up Sheol's entrance. It narrows Ezekiel's wide purview down to Jerusalem's environs, where Joel lived and worked (1:13–14; 2:1, 15, 32; 3:1, 16–17).

The early apocalyptic book of Malachi (c. 465 BCE) comes from a different priestly line, namely, the Levitical priesthood. This line bore the theology that lies behind the E strand of the Pentateuch and Deuteronomy. Malachi was outraged at the failure of rival priestly factions within postexilic Jerusalem to respect Deuteronomy's ideals. Styling himself a humble Levite in Deuteronomy's mode (e.g., Deut 12:12, 18; 14:27; 16:11), he assumed a defensive posture vis-à-vis upper-echelon priests (the very posture seen in Deut 18:6–7). He spoke up as an outsider against claimants to a strictly circumscribed priesthood.

Malachi 3:1 stresses the sudden, momentous arrival of the Lord God in a fiery epiphany, which provokes the pentateuchal E strand's desired human response of reverent "fear" of God on earth (see Mal 3:5; cf. Gen 20:11 [E]; 22:12 [E]; 28:17 [E]; Deut 4:10; 5:29; 8:6). The Lord's apocalyptic epiphany is preceded by the coming of the angel of the Exodus. This is the supernatural being whom the E strand describes as leading the Israelites out from slavery in Egypt (note the parallel language of Exod 23:20; 33:2). Malachi also announces the arrival of a third figure, "the messenger of the covenant" (Mal 3:1). He plays the role of the Mosaic prophet described in Deuteronomy 18:15–19 and Numbers 12:6–8 (E).

Early apocalyptic writings within the book of Isaiah link to yet another priesthood: the circle of Aaronide priests standing behind the "Priestly Torah" (PT). The authors of PT are surely Aaronides, whose theology of reverence differs markedly from the hierarchical "holiness" thinking of the Zadokites. In the apocalyptic writings of Third Isaiah, old class distinctions topple at the coming of God's apocalyptic reign. Foreigners even become priests (Isa 56:6; 66:21), a development barely conceivable within the tradition of HS and Ezekiel (see Ezek 44:7, 9; Num 18:1–10, 22), but fully in line with PT's propensity to level distinctions (e.g., Gen 17:27). A universal congregation bows to the Lord at the eschaton (Isa 66:23), an eventuality in keeping with PT's vision of Jacob spawning an assembly of nations (Gen 35:11).

The book of Daniel represents a nonpriestly species of apocalypticism, a millennialism borne by mantic sages.[9] Both major sections of the book hint of such authorship by the "wise." Daniel 1:4 celebrates the heroes of Daniel's court tales as "young men ... versed in every branch of wisdom, endowed with knowledge and insight." Daniel 11:33, 35 and 12:3, 10 likewise celebrate "the wise." These verses within the book's second half specially esteem these figures, who give instruction and understanding to their people during earth's last days.

The term "mantic" refers to the skill of these sages in deciphering obscure revelations, such as omens or dreams. The Daniel authors likely operated as royal advisers in the foreign courts of their exile, in the tradition of this type of professional wisdom. Because the Daniel authors treasured scriptural traditions, the mantic specialty took a particularly interesting turn among them. The puzzles most intriguing to the group were the enigmas of the Scriptures, especially Scriptures that remained unfulfilled. Group members wrestled with how the unfulfilled ideals and symbols of the Bible would eventually find definitive realization. This is why Daniel echoes Isaiah so much.

Initially, life at court was competitive and full of pitfalls for the Daniel authors but did not involve targeted persecution. The monarchs of the court tales expose Daniel and his companions to danger due primarily to royal incompetence and inanity. For his part, in fact, King Darius tears his hair out all night to come up with a plan for delivering

344 *Stephen L. Cook*

Daniel from the famed lions' den. Eventually, the Daniel group returned to Judea, their ancestral homeland, where they recorded apocalyptic visions (chapters 7–12). At this period, after 198 BCE, their expanding apocalyptic imagination increasingly exposed them to the ire of officials. Nevertheless, they did not hide; they did not use the name Daniel as a cloaking device ("pseudonymity"). They used it, rather, to claim their noble calling as wise scribes and to assert the divine origin of their revelations. They were fearless. They used the apocalyptic imagination to challenge all imperial efforts to control, mesmerize, and dehumanize.

AFTERLIFE AND THE RESURRECTION OF THE DEAD

The question of how the biblical writers understood the fate of human beings after death is sometimes at the heart of debates over the nature of apocalyptic literature. John Collins, for example, has argued forcefully that an expectation of a personal judgment of each individual after death is the pivotal difference between prophetic eschatology and apocalyptic eschatology.[10] Resurrection and individual judgment, he opines, arose in the late, full-blown apocalypses as something radically new for Israel. Similar notions are commonplace among scholars, yet this position is vulnerable on a number of fronts.[11] Most significantly, much inner-biblical evidence attests to the organic growth of the expectation of resurrection out of native Israelite ideals and hopes.

The biblical writers consistently embrace shalom over chaos and Sheol, spirit-directed life over disobedience and destruction, corporate worship over stillness and thanklessness, and purity and holiness over uncleanness and corpses. From early on, Israel upheld the joy and fulfillment of embodied human community as a core ideal, and individual Israelite kin groups worked to preserve ties with their living-dead. What is more, Israel was long familiar with the idea that the dead might awaken (cf. 1 Kgs 17:17–24; 2 Kgs 4:8–37; 13:21; Hos 6:2; Ezek 37; Isa 53:9–10), and texts such as Hosea 13:14a understand God to be capable of destroying death's sting. In the Second Temple period, such ideals, longings, and convictions joined up and surfaced in Israel's conscious faith. Deep currents within Israelite tradition flowed together and poured forth in an explicit expectation of eschatological resurrection.

Second Temple–era eschatology develops a firm doctrine that God will eventually destroy death and release its prisoners. It will not forever cast its shroud over the joy of human, embodied togetherness. Isaiah 25:8 declares that death, well known for a voracious appetite (cf., e.g., Isa 5:14; Hab 2:5), is about to get its payback. It is going to be swallowed up for all time. From the same era, editing added to Psalm 22 describes a coming universal embrace of the Lord, which will include not only all nations of earth but also all peoples in the netherworld (27–9). The thought of Psalm 22:29 is captured well by the NAB version: "All who sleep in the earth will bow low before God / All who have gone down into the dust will kneel in homage."

In like manner, Isaiah 26:19 attests to the doctrine of the resurrection of the dead already at home in restoration-era protoapocalyptic literature.[12] Isaiah 26:7–21 is a communal lament and petition for God's intervention against the wicked on behalf of the righteous. The people confess their powerlessness in and of themselves to infuse Israel's family tree with life (18). An oracle of salvation (19), however, startles Israel to hope. In shocking encouragement, it cries "But friends, your dead ones will live! Israel, still alive and in prayer" (11–18). Israel receives assurance that its faithful dead (a plurality in the Hebrew, not a "collective" or "political" singular) will miraculously return to earth. The dead and buried will hear the command as a corpse: "Wake up! Sing!"

The final colon of Isaiah 26:21 supports this line of interpretation. It reveals, at least partially, which dead Israelite family members verse 19 has in mind. The netherworld, the verse declares, will soon cease covering over *the murdered*. These "slain," the murdered ones of verse 21, would appear to be those killed by God's adversaries (11), that is, by the "other lords" of verse 13. The casualties of the Babylonian destruction of Jerusalem and of the Exile might well be center stage in the authors' minds.

The reference to *rĕpā'îm* (New Revised Standard Version [NRSV]: "those long dead") at the end of Isaiah 26:19 is significant. The text speaks of the rising of dead *rĕpā'îm* in part to convey nuances of Israel's ancient founders leading a stream of rebirths up from the netherworld. Israelite ancestors and rulers, such as Abraham, Jacob, and Josiah, will lead the deceased children of "Daughter Zion" out from the burial chambers. Such a belief fits the era of the Isaiah apocalypse. In Third Isaiah, the restoration community explicitly laments its alienation from the living-dead souls of the ancestors. The people are in the sorriest of straits because "Abraham does not know us and Israel does not acknowledge us" (Isa 63:16).

Isaiah 26 draws a sharp contrast between the fate of Israel's *rĕpā'îm* and the fate of enemy *rĕpā'îm*. For the enemies of Israel to invoke their own *rĕpā'îm* is futile, verse 14 declares. God has made sure these "shades do not rise." In verses 11–14 God finishes off the tyrants, kills them a second time, by eliminating the invocation of their names. The erasure of remembrance, the "death after death" of the enemy rĕpā'îm, paves the way for the miracle of verse 15. Extermination of the royal dead allows Israel to multiply and the borders of the land to extend. As when Israel destroyed the rĕpā'îm at the conquest (Deut 3:11; Josh 17:15), the land's present owners/occupiers are disenfranchised as their dead are wiped away. To wipe out all memory of the dead (Isa 26:14–15) is to eliminate their power to aid and abet living descendants. It is to release all enemy hold on Israel's land.

In this context of wrestling over the fate of real spirits and their possible influence on earth, Israel's corpses, buried in the dust (Isa 26:19), cannot be mere symbols. Verse 19's dead Israelites are no more figurative of something else than are their counterparts, the putatively divinized shades of the enemy (14). The text holds the two sets of souls in antithetical tension. In each case, actual living-dead souls are at issue.

NOTES

1 Outside the Hebrew Bible, some generally recognized apocalypses include Revelation, *1 Enoch* 1–36, *2 Enoch*, *2 Baruch*, *3 Baruch*, *Jubilees* 23, *4 Ezra*, the *Apocalypse of Abraham*, the *Testament of Levi* 2–5, the *Testament of Abraham* 10–15, and the *Apocalypse of Zephaniah*.

2 Job Y. Jindo, "On Myth and History in Prophetic and Apocalyptic Eschatology," *VT* 55 (2005): 412–25 (412).

3 Karl Rahner, *Foundations of Christian Faith: An Introduction to the Idea of Christianity*, trans. by W. V. Dych (New York: Crossroad, 1978), 22.

4 Lester L. Grabbe, "The Social Setting of Early Jewish Apocalypticism," *JSP* 4 (1989): 27–47, esp. 30, 37–8.

5 Robert Carroll, "Israel, History of (Post-Monarchic Period)," in *The Anchor Bible Dictionary*, Vol. 3, ed. by David N. Freedman (New York: Doubleday, 1992), 574.

6 Jürgen Moltmann, *Theology of Hope*, trans. by J. W. Leitch (New York: Harper & Row, 1967), 137, quoted in John N. Oswalt, "Recent Studies in Old Testament Apocalyptic," in *The Face of Old Testament Studies: A Survey of Contemporary Approaches*, ed. by D. W. Baker and B. T. Arnold (Grand Rapids, MI: Baker, 1999), 375.

7 J. Todd Hibbard, *Intertextuality in Isaiah 24–27: The Reuse and Evocation of Earlier Texts and Traditions* (FAT II/16; Tübingen: Mohr Siebeck, 2006). Also see Mark J. Boda and Michael H. Floyd, with a major contribution by Rex Mason, *Bringing Out the Treasure: Inner Biblical Allusion in Zechariah 9–14* (JSOTSup 370; Sheffield Academic Press, 2003).

8 For an introduction to the HS strand and the PT strand (discussed later), see Jacob Milgrom, *Leviticus 1–16: A New Translation with Introduction and Commentary* (AB 3; New York: Doubleday, 1991), 1–2, 13–42, 48; Israel Knohl, *The Sanctuary of Silence: The Priestly Torah and the Holiness School*

(Minneapolis, MN: Fortress, 1995), and *The Divine Symphony: The Bible's Many Voices* (Philadelphia: Jewish Publication Society, 2003).

9 Robert R. Wilson, "From Prophecy to Apocalyptic: Reflections on the Shape of Israelite Religion," in *Anthropological Perspectives on Old Testament Prophecy*, ed. by R. C. Culley and T. W. Overholt (*Semeia* 21; Chico, CA: SBL, 1981), 81–3, 88; Paul L. Redditt, *Daniel* (NCBC; Sheffield Academic Press, 1999), 14–18; Jin Hee Han, *Daniel's Spiel: Apocalyptic Literacy in the Book of Daniel* (Lanham, MD: University Press of America, 2008), 75–6.

10 John J. Collins, "Prophecy, Apocalypse and Eschatology: Reflections on the Proposals of Lester Grabbe," in *Knowing the End from the Beginning: The Prophetic, the Apocalyptic and their Relationships*, ed. by L. L. Grabbe and R. D. Haak (JSPSup 46; London: T & T Clark, 2003), 47, 49–50; cf. Collins, "Apocalyptic Eschatology as the Transcendence of Death," *CBQ* 36 (1974): 21–43. For an overview of ancient Israel's thorough familiarity with existence beyond death, see Stephen L. Cook, "Funerary Practices and Afterlife Expectations in Ancient Israel," *Religion Compass* 1(6) (November 2007): 660–83, available at: http://www.blackwell-synergy.com/doi/abs/10.1111/j.1749-8171.2007.00045.x.

11 It is particularly misleading that many scholars continue to construe Israel's resurrection faith as a mechanism for coping with the martyrdoms of the Maccabean era. The fact that the righteousness of the faithful issued directly in their deaths in that age surely raised questions about divine justice, but we cannot trace the idea of resurrection to such dissonance. Texts from pre-Maccabean times, especially *1 Enoch* 27:1–4, already predict resurrection.

12 See the astute analysis and bibliography in Jon D. Levenson, *Resurrection and the Restoration of Israel: The Ultimate Victory of the God of Life* (New Haven, CT: Yale University Press, 2006), 197–200.

FURTHER READING

Blenkinsopp, Joseph. *Opening the Sealed Book: Interpretations of the Book of Isaiah in Late Antiquity.* Grand Rapids, MI: Eerdmans, 2006.

Carey, Greg. *Ultimate Things: An Introduction to Jewish and Christian Apocalyptic Literature.* St. Louis, MO: Chalice, 2005.

Collins, John J. *The Apocalyptic Imagination: An Introduction to Jewish Apocalyptic Literature,* 2d ed. Grand Rapids, MI: Eerdmans, 1998.

Cook, Stephen L. *The Apocalyptic Literature* (IBT). Nashville, TN: Abingdon, 2003.

"Eschatology of the OT," pp. 299–308 in *The New Interpreter's Dictionary of the Bible,* Vol. 2. Edited by K. Sakenfeld et al. Nashville, TN: Abingdon, 2007.

"Mythological Discourse in Ezekiel and Daniel, and the Rise of Apocalypticism in Israel," pp. 85–106 in *Knowing the End from the Beginning: The Prophetic, the Apocalyptic and their Relationships* (JPSup 46). Edited by L. Grabbe and R. Haak. London: T & T Clark, 2003.

Prophecy and Apocalypticism: The Postexilic Social Setting. Minneapolis, MN: Fortress, 1995.

Grabbe, Lester L., and Robert D. Haak, eds. *Knowing the End from the Beginning: The Prophetic, the Apocalyptic and their Relationships* (JPSup 46). London: T & T Clark, 2003.

Hill, Craig C. *In God's Time: The Bible and the Future.* Grand Rapids, MI: Eerdmans, 2002.

Levenson, Jon D. *Resurrection and the Restoration of Israel: The Ultimate Victory of the God of Life.* New Haven, CT: Yale University Press, 2006.

Sweeney, Marvin A. *Form and Intertextuality in Prophetic and Apocalyptic Literature* (FAT 45). Tübingen, Germany: Mohr Siebeck, 2005.

Tigchelaar, Eibert J. C. *Prophets of Old and the Day of the End: Zechariah, the Book of Watchers, and Apocalyptic* (OtSt 35). New York: Brill, 1996.

17 Deuterocanonical/apocryphal books

SHARON PACE

The terminology "Deuterocanonical/apocryphal" refers to Jewish literature of the Second Temple period found outside of the twenty-four books of the biblical canon of the Hebrew Scriptures. It is not clear what the connotations of the word "apocrypha" (from the Greek ἀπόκρυφα, "hidden things") may have been in its earliest usages. Perhaps it was used pejoratively – the books were considered hidden owing to their deficient or problematic nature. Alternatively, the connotations may have been mystical; the books were hidden because one needed special knowledge or revelation to understand them.[1] Because the canon of Scripture is distinct for Jews, Orthodox Christians, Roman Catholics, and Protestants, the contents of each community's Apocrypha are unique, as is its usage of the term. For Jews, none of the apocryphal books are considered canonical. Catholics refer to this collection as "Deuterocanonical books" (second canon) and the Orthodox Church as "Anagignoskomena" (that which is read). In Catholic and Orthodox Christian Bibles, these books are interspersed among the Old Testament books or are found as additional chapters of canonical books.[2] Because the Apocrypha are not canonical for Protestants, they are either omitted in their printed Bibles or are placed in a separate section.

LISTING OF THE APOCRYPHA IN THE NEW REVISED STANDARD VERSION (NRSV)

In 1991, the NRSV included the following books and additions to canonical books in its Apocrypha, printed in between the Old and New Testaments:

1. Books included in the Roman Catholic, Greek, and Slavonic Bibles, namely, Tobit, Judith, Additions to Esther (the entire Greek Esther is included), Wisdom (or the Wisdom of Solomon), Sirach (or Ben Sira or Ecclesiasticus), Baruch, the Letter of Jeremiah, the Additions

to Daniel (namely, the Prayer of Azariah and the Song of the Three Young Men [or Song of the Three Jews]; Susanna; and Bel and the Dragon), 1 Maccabees, and 2 Maccabees

2. Books included in the Greek and Slavonic Bibles, namely, 1 Esdras, the Prayer of Manasseh, Psalm 151, and 3 Maccabees

3. One book included in the Slavonic Bible and in an appendix to the Vulgate, namely, 2 Esdras

4. One book included in an appendix to the Greek Bible, namely, 4 Maccabees

Considered as a whole, the apocryphal books date to the period of the third century BCE–first century CE and have their roots in the land of Israel, Antioch (Syria), Alexandria (Egypt), and perhaps Persia. Some were originally written in Aramaic or Hebrew; others were composed in Greek.

To say that the term "Apocrypha" refers to books outside "the biblical canon" should not be taken to imply that the canon was fixed at the time the books were composed. In the late Second Temple period, evidence for a precise content of the "canon" – understood as an authoritative, closed list of Scripture, whose books were vetted and accepted by the believing community – is wanting. Although an earlier generation of scholars argued that the Apocrypha came from an Alexandrian canon (used by the Diaspora Jewish community in Egypt), as opposed to a Palestinian canon of the Hebrew Scriptures, no verification of any definitive, authoritative *canon* exists for this period.[3] However, there are data that point to the beginnings of a *canonical process*. Eugene Ulrich describes this textual situation as follows:

> The canonical process is the journey of the many disparate works of literature within the ongoing community of Israel (including both rabbinic Judaism and Christianity, each claiming to be the true Israel) from the early stages when they began to be considered as somehow authoritative for the broader community, through the collection and endorsement process, to the final judgment concerning their inspired character as the unified and defined collection of scripture – i.e., until the judgment of recognition that constituted the canon.[4]

Thus, although there is no authoritative canonical list, there is the idea of scriptural *books* being authoritative in the first half of the Second Temple period. In the later Second Temple period and in the decades following the destruction of the Temple, we also find evidence of a nascent tripartite classification of the Hebrew Scriptures and of the number of books that were counted within it. Not until the Babylonian Talmud is there a substantiation of twenty-four books in the Hebrew canon listed by name. Earlier references to twenty-two books (by Josephus) and twenty-four books (4 Ezra) do, however, suggest a correlation to the Talmudic listing but leave open the question of the exact books accepted by earlier Jewish communities. The following texts appear to have been included or excluded inconsistently: Esther, Ben Sira, the Song of Songs, Psalm 151, *Jubilees*, *1 Enoch*, and the *Temple Scroll*.

Except for 2 Esdras, the books of the Apocrypha are found in three Greek codices that witness to the Septuagint. Strictly speaking, the Septuagint refers to the Greek translation of the Pentateuch, but it has taken on the meaning of the entirety of the Greek translations of the Hebrew Scriptures. Each of these Septuagint codices, namely, Alexandrinus, Sinaiticus, and Vaticanus, has a distinct collection of apocryphal books, but with considerable overlap. Although Greek-speaking Jews were responsible for the translation of the Septuagint, these codices that witness to it come from Christian hands. There are no Jewish canonical records or codices from the Second Temple period, books were instead written on individual scrolls, and there was no one authoritative group to make any definitive list.[5] Nonetheless, Greek-speaking Jews revered their Scriptures in Greek and believed the translation of the Torah/Pentateuch to be accurate, as the *Letter of Aristeas* demonstrates. Although the account is legendary, the explanation that seventy-two elders translated the Torah of Moses into Greek in the time of Ptolemy Philadelphus (285–167 BCE) shows the esteem with which the Septuagint was considered.[6] Some scholars conclude that the many citations and allusions to apocryphal books in early Christian writings reflect an Egyptian Jewish usage of religious literature.[7]

The Qumran scrolls provide important evidence for the developing notion of canon because fragments of most of the books later known as part of the Jewish canon were found there. In addition, several books later known as apocryphal and pseudepigraphal by the various Christian canons are attested at Qumran, namely, Psalm 151, Sirach, Tobit, the Letter of Jeremiah (Baruch 6), *1 Enoch*, *Jubilees*, and parts of the *Testament of the Twelve Patriarchs*. At Qumran, as well as in other Jewish and Christian sources, some of these texts are appealed to or quoted as authoritative – just as are other biblical books. Ben Sira is quoted in early Jewish literature with the standard introductory phrase, "As it is written in the book of Ben Sira."[8] James VanderKam argues that *1 Enoch* may have been authoritative at Qumran because its subject matter regarding the sinful angels who fathered giants with women is interpreted in other Qumran texts, because its calendar serves as a paradigm for Qumran calendars, and because it possibly was the subject of the *Apocalypse of Weeks*. Fragments from fourteen manuscripts of *Jubilees* were found at Qumran. It is quoted in the *Damascus Document* and possibly alluded to in one additional Qumran text (4Q228 ["Text with a Citation of *Jubilees*"]).[9]

In certain cases, the unique interpretations offered by sectarian documents show a conviction that particular mysteries of Scripture were being revealed for the first time. Nonetheless, a belief that the community's exegeses ultimately were based on Moses' revelation made unique interpretations worthy – Scripture itself was seen as the starting point. From scriptural texts come the phrases, allusions, and key ideas that permeate much of the Qumran nonbiblical texts; in addition, scriptural texts are often cited with introductory formulas that presuppose their authority.[10]

In addition to this developing notion of canon, Jews in the late Second Temple period were classifying their holy writings in a tripartite manner as "Torah," "Prophets," and a third category variously called "the rest of the books," "Psalms," or "the writings of David." In addition, there are two references to the number of books counted as sacred writings by Jews. The following evidence is commonly cited:

> *Ben Sira (Sirach, Ecclesiasticus).* Originally written in Hebrew (first quarter of the second century BCE), this book was translated by the author's grandson into Greek, as he explains in the prologue, which he added to the text. In this prologue, he speaks of his grandfather's study of "the Law, Prophets, and other books" of their ancestors. He also refers to the differences in the original Hebrew and Greek translations of these same divisions.

> *The Halakhic Letter* (4QMMT, *Miqṣat ma'aśê ha-Torah*). This work, regarding various legal disputes, refers to "the book of Moses [and] the book[s of the pr]ophets and David ... [the annals of] each generation" (4QMMT C 9–11). Although the complete reading is reconstructed, the first two categories of Scripture are clear (the book of Moses and the prophets). The phrase "(the books of) David" apparently refers to the Psalms, although some suggest that it may indicate a broader collection of what is later known as the Writings.[11] It is not known whether "[the annals of] each generation" is to be understood together with the phrase "(the books of) David" or as a distinct (fourth) grouping.[12]

2 Maccabees. 2 Maccabees 15:9 (dated to 124 BCE) refers to the Law and Prophets in its report of Judas Maccabeus' speech to his troops: "Encouraging them from the law and the prophets, and reminding them also of the struggles they had won, he made them the more eager" (see also 2 Macc 2:13).

Philo's De Vita Contemplativa 25. In discussing the practices of the Therapeutae, Philo (20 BCE–50 CE) remarks that they study nothing but "laws and oracles prophesied by the prophets and hymns and the others." To be sure, the last phrase "the others" lacks specificity; it is debated whether it could possibly refer to the Writings.[13]

The New Testament. Luke 24:44 refers to the Law, Prophets, and Psalms. The references in Matthew 5:17; 7:12; 22:40 refer to the Law and Prophets. Not much should be made by the absence of a third category; perhaps it simply was not relevant to the evangelist's argumentation.

Josephus's Contra Apionem 1.37–43. Although Josephus does not list the titles of the books of the Jewish Scriptures, he does refer to "twenty-two books" formed by the time of "Artaxerxes who succeeded Xerxes as king of Persia." Joseph Blenkinsopp argues that Josephus's statements about the twenty-two books in the Jewish corpus presuppose a closed list that included, arguably, the books of Moses, Joshua, Judges (with Ruth), Samuel, and Kings (later known as the Former Prophets), the four lengthy prophetic books (Isaiah, Jeremiah, Ezekiel, and the Twelve), Job, Daniel, Ezra-Nehemiah, and Chronicles.[14]

2 Esdras (4 Ezra). Some manuscripts of 2 Esdras 14:45 have the reading: "make public the twenty-four books that you wrote first." It is possible that Josephus's twenty-two books are the equivalent to this reference to twenty-four books, if Josephus counted Lamentations with Jeremiah and Ruth with Judges.

Mishnah and Talmud. Many biblical scholars of the late nineteenth to twentieth centuries held that the discussion of Scripture in *m. Yad.* 3:5 was tantamount to a "council" held at Jamnia (Yabneh, Yavneh), in which the canon of the Jewish Scriptures was closed. However, the consensus of biblical scholars today is that this *mishnah* is much narrower in scope; rather than formalizing the books of the canon, it discusses the issue of inspiration. The text begins with the statement, "all Scripture renders the hands unclean" – in other words, Scripture imparts a ritual holiness that necessitates ceremonial washing. Although it is true that the discussion in this text is limited to whether Ecclesiastes and the Song of Songs are revelatory or authoritative, it is also true that this 200 CE text assumes a concept of Holy Scripture. Thus, although we do not know exactly which books constituted Scripture, and although there is no canonical list offered here, the rabbis do consider whether these two particular works are constituent of God's written corpus of revelation, presupposing that this to be an appropriate question to consider. Similarly, a later text, *b. Meg.* 7a (fourth century CE), discusses the status of Esther.

It is not until the Babylonian Talmud (550 CE) that we find a listing of the contents of the three divisions of Scripture. In *b. B. Bat.* 14b–15b, the prophets are identified as Joshua, Judges, Samuel, Kings, Jeremiah, Ezekiel, Isaiah, and the Twelve. The Writings are comprised of Ruth, Psalms, Job, Proverbs, Ecclesiastes, Song of Songs, Lamentations, Daniel, Esther, Ezra, and Chronicles. Only with this text can we be certain which books comprised the Jewish listing of twenty-four and in which of the three divisions of the Hebrew Bible they were placed.

The Church Fathers. The use of the books of the Apocrypha by various church fathers shows a lack of uniformity. We note the following examples. Origen included the Letter of Jeremiah and Baruch in his understanding of what constituted the book of Jeremiah-Lamentations, but he does not identify his judgment concerning the canonical status of other biblical books. In his letter to Africanus, Origen argues that it is the church's authority that justifies the use of Tobit for edification, even though it is not so used by Jews (*Ep. Afr.* 13), suggesting that Tobit was not found in the nascent canon of the Jewish community with which he was familiar. Athanasius, Cyril of Jerusalem, and Epiphanius considered Baruch and the Letter of Jeremiah as part of Jeremiah-Lamentations. Some sources include Wisdom and Sirach among the books of the New Testament. Epiphanius lists Wisdom and Sirach; Canon Muratori has Wisdom; and the Table of Contents for Codex Alexandrinus lists the Psalms of Solomon as its last entry, following the New Testament.[15] Two distinct lists come from Pseudo-Chrysostom; one contains Sirach, and the other has Tobit, Judith, Wisdom, and Sirach.[16]

Jerome. Jerome, translator of the Hebrew Scriptures into the Latin Vulgate, spoke of two categories of holy books – those that were canonical and those that were "ecclesiastical," that is, those useful for edification as opposed to doctrine. Jerome held these ecclesiastical books worthwhile and maintained that he had Hebrew copies of Sirach, Tobit, 1 Maccabees, *Jubilees*, and an Aramaic copy of Judith.[17] Jerome understood the Hebrew Bible as being comprised of the Law, Prophets, and Hagiographa, with five, eight, and eleven books, respectively (*Praef. Vulg. Dan.*).

Augustine. In *Doctr. Chr.* 2.8.12–13, Augustine included a broader listing of books familiar as the Septuagint of his time, namely, Tobit, Judith, 1 and 2 Maccabees, Wisdom, Sirach/Ecclesiasticus, and Baruch (as part of Jeremiah).[18]

Council of Carthage. When listing the books of the Bible, the Council of Carthage (397 CE) included Tobit, Judith, 1 and 2 Maccabees, and "the five books of Solomon," which would have included the Wisdom of Solomon and Ecclesiasticus, along with the other three books ascribed to Solomon, namely, Proverbs, Song of Songs, and Ecclesiastes.[19]

Luther. With Luther's insistence that Scripture alone must be the source of faith and doctrine – and not church teachings or traditions – disagreements about the role of the Apocrypha came to the forefront. In debates with Luther, contemporaries used Tobit 4:7–11 to support the Catholic position that almsgiving is useful for salvation and 2 Maccabees 12:43–5 to defend the practice of saying prayers for the souls in purgatory – beliefs that Luther opposed. In this polemical context, Luther argued that the books of the Apocrypha were not properly considered Scripture. Thus, in his German translation of the Bible, Luther placed the Apocrypha between the Old Testament and New Testament, remarking: "these are not held to be equal to the sacred Scriptures yet are useful and good for reading."[20]

Other developments. It is only with the Council of Trent (1546) that the Roman Catholic Church proclaimed a definitive list of the canon of Scripture, which included the longer versions of Esther and Daniel as well as the following books of the Apocrypha: the Wisdom of Solomon, Ecclesiasticus, Tobit, 1 and 2 Maccabees, Judith, Baruch, and the Letter of Jeremiah. It did not include 3 and 4 Maccabees, the Prayer of Manasseh, and 1 and 2 Esdras. Nevertheless, the Prayer of Manasseh and 1 and 2 Esdras are included in an appendix to the Vulgate. This was the first *ecumenical* council to make such a pronouncement. For Eastern Orthodox churches, the Trullan Council (692 CE) accepted a range of opinion on whether individual books should be considered canonical or useful.[21] Protestant churches exhibit a diversity of usage. While none accepts the apocryphal books as part of the canon per se, they differ on whether these books should be included in printed editions of the Bible or lectionary. The Authorized King James Version (1611) included them in an appendix. Early Calvinists did not accept the Apocrypha as part of the canon, as reflected in the Westminster Confession of 1646.²² Today, the common lectionary of the United Methodists and Presbyterians does not contain the Apocrypha. The Lutheran lectionary includes the Song of Three Young Men as a canticle.²³ The Anglican tradition considers the Apocrypha useful – if not for matters of doctrine – and includes readings from the Apocrypha in liturgy.

We now turn to a description of the contents of the eclectic list of the Apocrypha as found in the NRSV²⁴:

Tobit. Identified as a historical novel or romance, Tobit is a second-century BCE work that portrays the importance of remaining loyal to God's law while encountering the hardships and tragedies of exile by using Assyria's conquest of Israel (eighth century BCE) as its literary setting. Sinaiticus and Vaticanus attest to a longer form, considered original, and Alexandrinus to a shorter version. In addition, four versions in Aramaic and one in Hebrew were found at Qumran. The book weaves together the hardships of two families who will eventually be united: the household of Tobit and Anna, and that of Raguel and Edna. Tobias (the son of Tobit and Anna), Gabriel (the angel sent to assist Tobit), and Sarah (the daughter of Raguel and Edna) bring healing to the two families, resolving illness, hardship, impending death, and tragedy.

Tobit and Anna live in Nineveh, having been exiled from Israel with the Assyrian invasion. Tobit, who is particularly loyal to the commandments, suffers from poverty and blindness. His faithfulness is underscored by his willingness to bury the dead, even when this commandment is outlawed by the Assyrians. In addition, Tobit teaches his son, Tobias, the importance of endogamous marriage and of providing for the poor. Tobit sends Tobias on a journey to retrieve funds whose access was blocked because of the vicissitudes of Assyrian rule. Concerned for his safety, the father hires one Azariah as a guide for his son; unbeknownst to them, Azariah is really the angel Raphael. Along the journey, Tobias is attacked by a giant fish, yet Raphael teaches him to save its organs as a cure for Tobit's blindness as well as for the peril that soon awaits Tobias.

The danger comes from the trials of another family exiled to Assyria, Raguel, Edna, and their daughter Sarah. Sarah, widowed seven times because of the vengeful demon Asmodeus, seeks another husband. Armed with the instructions of Raphael, Tobias wards off the demon and becomes Sarah's husband without suffering harm. The story ends with the safe return of the couple to Tobias's family, the cure of Tobit, and Tobit's instructions to his son, which remind him of the rewards and blessings that come from obeying God's commandments. In addition, hope is expressed for the future of all of Israel: repentance, return from exile, and restoration of the Temple that will serve as a beacon to all nations.

Judith. The book of Judith describes the defeat of Holofernes, general of Nebuchadnezzar's army, by the courage and intrigue of a single Jewish woman, Judith. Because of the various historical inaccuracies of the book (most notably, identification of Nebuchadnezzar as the king of Assyria, residing in Nineveh), the work is identified as a historical novel. The book's portrayal of Nebuchadnezzar, who is proclaimed as the lord of all the earth and worthy of devotion, finds common ground with the portrayal of Darius in the book of Daniel (Dan 6). It is possible that Judith's Nebuchadnezzar is really a cipher for Antiochus IV Epiphanes.

Judith, whose name means "Jew" (f.) and her city, Bethulia, whose name means "virgin," represent the people and land of Israel. Nebuchadnezzar plots to destroy Bethulia by the invasion of Holofernes, in retaliation for Israel's refusal to become his vassal and fight in his empire's campaigns. Bethulia's leadership is ineffective; the people assume that the impending siege is due to their sin. Confident that Israel is no longer idolatrous, Judith sees the siege as a test from God – one that requires the faithful response of prayer, fasting, and action. Paralleling Jael (Judg 4:18–22; 5:24–7), who, by deception, brought victory to Israel by killing Sisera singlehandedly, Judith also saves her people by beheading Holofernes, who is smitten by her beauty. Throughout her ordeal with the enemy of Israel, Judith remains loyal to the commandments, even bringing her own properly prepared food. By posting the head of Holofernes for the entire army to see, Judith spreads panic throughout Nebuchadnezzar's legions; the Assyrians flee, harming neither Jerusalem nor the Temple. Like Miriam of old, Judith leads her people in praise of God (Exod 15:20–1). Throughout the book, confidence is shown in the God of Israel who accepts repentance, who will return the exiles to the land, and who stunningly defeats Israel's enemies in the most surprising of ways – through a supposedly innocuous widow.

The additions to Esther. The additions to Esther enhance the plot line of the canonical book, answering questions that the text proper raises. The book of Esther tells the account of how King Ahasuerus's vizier, Haman, plotted to kill the entirety of the Jewish population in the Persian Empire, ostensibly because one Jewish man, Mordecai, refused to bow to him. Was there another reason why Haman hated Mordecai? The additions show another tradition in which the king immediately praised and promoted Mordecai for discovering the plot against his life. Although this intrigue also is presented in the canonical text proper, the additions enhance the king's recognition of Mordecai's courageous loyalty and underscore Haman's treasonous acts. The canonical text shows that King Ahasuerus, unwittingly, has chosen a Jewish woman, Esther, as his new queen. Did Esther remain loyal to the commandments? What did Esther think of King Artaxerxes (Ahasuerus), her Gentile husband? The additions show that she kept the food laws, offered prayers, and observed Shabbat; in addition, she states in prayer, "[I] abhor the bed of the uncircumcised and of any alien" (Esth [Gk.] 14:15). In the canonical text, through a series of amazing coincidences and fortuitous events, Haman undermines his own plot, and Esther is able to intercede for her people. The book of Esther never mentions God directly, yet the coincidences are reminiscent of the story of Joseph in Egypt, wherein everything works out according to God's plan for good. Did some readers doubt that God had been directly involved? The additions emphasize that all proceeded by divine providence; indeed, the contest between Haman and Mordecai and the intervention of Esther are portended in a dream. In the canonical story – although she hesitates at first, fearing for her life – Esther intercedes on behalf of her people at the prodding of Mordecai. What was it like for Esther to approach the king? The additions portray her as overcome with fear, yet courageous nonetheless.

There are six specific additions to the text of Esther. Two of these, scholars are confident, were originally written in Greek; the other four originally may have been composed in Hebrew. In the face of Haman's heinous decree, which was prompted by the unique nature of the faith and practices of the Jewish people, the author declares that the community lives by noble and righteous laws as the children of God. Esther herself sees that although the people have sinned, it is also true that the Gentiles have perversely gone beyond God's plan by plotting to turn Jerusalem into a city of idols; in addition, they themselves disobey God's decrees.

The Wisdom of Solomon. Why do the innocent suffer and the wicked prosper? Does God reward the righteous and punish the wicked? What values should be held most dear – spiritual or material? These eternal questions that trouble the person of faith are probed throughout the Wisdom of Solomon (the book of Wisdom). This work explores what is only briefly mentioned or hinted at throughout the Hebrew Scriptures, namely, that the righteous are rewarded with immortality. A key ingredient of living a righteous life is the discovery of God's gift to the world: wisdom. Wisdom, the underlying plan for all of reality, is analogous to the spirit of God, and present with God at the very creation of the world. Emanating from God and personified as female, Wisdom can be sought through prayer. Already present with God at creation, wisdom accompanied the Israelites throughout their history, from the call of Abraham, to the Exodus, to the entrance into the Promised Land. It is the source of all righteousness and linked to the cardinal virtues known from Greek philosophy: prudence, justice, courage, and temperance. Wisdom is the ultimate source of faith and enables one to act with justice and kindness toward one's fellow. The righteous, who follow wisdom's guidance, serve as a constant challenge to the ungodly. Their pursuit of justice and righteousness – spiritual, eternal values – critiques the materialism and self-centeredness of the wicked, who eschew wisdom's call. In their idolatry, they oppress the widow and the orphan, trusting in their own power and the works of their own hands. The righteous, by contrast, may suffer on this earth, but their trials are tests from God and provide discipline, allowing them to be rewarded for their merits in eternity.

The Book of Wisdom was written in Greek and evidences a melding of Greek philosophy and Jewish teachings. Its emphasis on the Israelites' experience in Egypt and the folly of Egyptian idolatry makes it possible that it was written in the Jewish Egyptian Diaspora.

Sirach/Ecclesiasticus. "To fear the Lord is the beginning of wisdom" (Sir 1:14). This statement encapsulates the essence of the book written by Jesus ben Sirach in the early second century BCE in Jerusalem. This writer, familiar with the wisdom traditions of his neighbors, combines secular wisdom with the wisdom of Torah, the latter always taking precedence. Fidelity to the Torah may bring hardship or ridicule, but it is the only true value worth pursuing, even if it leaves one impoverished. Ultimately, the rewards of Torah fidelity will be great. The Torah brings one into right relationship with God and allows for people to live with justice and righteousness in all their affairs – business, government, family relationships, and friendships.

Concretely, a wise relationship with God is characterized by one's acknowledgment of the Creator of the universe, who chose the patriarchs and Israel to fulfill a unique mission. Sirach sees God as merciful, deserving of trust. God is the distributor of blessings, calling one to be prudent and cautious in economic and social relationships. Wisdom teaches one to exercise one's free will for good and prompts repentance. It cautions one to be careful with one's speech, to limit destructive emotions and passions, and to use one's time and talents for good. Such positive acts include almsgiving, the pursuit of social justice, and prudent business practices. This work teaches respect for persons, even if the book's statements about women reflect prejudicial gender stereotyping.

Wisdom, whose very origins come from the Creator, is described as the equivalent of the Torah, as a beautiful woman, and as dwelling in the Temple. Although following wisdom may bring suffering in the short term, it brings knowledge, delight, and blessing in the end. Those who abandon it will find death and destruction, but it gives life to those who never forsake its quest.

Baruch. Likely written in the second century BCE, the literary setting of this book is the Babylonian Exile of the sixth century BCE. A pseudonymous work, it purports to have been written by Baruch, Jeremiah's scribe, who accompanied his compatriots to Babylon. The book consists of an introduction, which links the exilic and Jerusalem communities, a prayer of repentance, an account of Wisdom, and a poem about the role of Zion. As depicted in the introduction, Baruch reads his work to the exiled King Jeconiah and to the community, prompting their sorrowful repentance in prayer and fasting, and their practical response of collecting alms for the Jerusalem community. Baruch returns to the Jerusalem community, bringing replacement Temple vessels and instructions for the use of donations on behalf of sacrifices in the Temple. Like Jeremiah, Baruch asks the community to pray for Nebuchadnezzar and his "son" Belshazzar (cf. Dan 5), as well as for the exilic community, and to read his work at designated times. The prayer of the exiles underscores both the justice and mercy of God. In this prayer is found the Deuteronomistic pattern of sin, punishment, repentance, and hope for future salvation. In the poem about Wisdom, features common with Sirach are seen, namely, a female personification and an equation with Torah. Finally, the poem about Zion offers solace to the Jewish people for their suffering, encouragement for the exilic community to return, and an expression of hope for salvation. At the time of salvation, all nations who have disobeyed God will themselves be punished, and the righteous of Israel will return to the land in joyful deliverance.

The Letter of Jeremiah. This sermon argues that the God of Israel is the only divinity; rival claims of other deities are false – they are only human-made idols. The wise person of faith will hold fast to God alone. Because this work lists many specifics of the nations' futile rituals with their idols, we are able to see how Israel saw (and polemicized about) specific practices. Idols are dressed in beautiful clothing but unable to stop thieves from stealing them. They hold scepters and swords yet are powerless to set up and depose kings, as does the God of Israel. Such idols are humiliated – tarnished, smoke damaged, and desecrated by impure women and animals. Defenseless, they must be hidden in times of war. In order to avoid reproach and shame, the person of faith will avoid idols, believing instead in the one God of righteousness and justice who controls the destinies of kings, sends the rain in its appointed time, and delivers the righteous.

Additions to Daniel. The Greek versions of Daniel include three additions not found in the Masoretic Text (MT), namely, the Prayer of Azariah and the Song of the Three Young Men, Susanna, and Bel and the Dragon.[25] Identification of the original language (or languages) of the Prayer of Azariah and the Song of the Three Young Men is debated; it is possible that they reflect a Semitic original. The Prayer of Azariah and the Song of the Three Young Men (considered to be one addition) include Azariah's words of praise to God while he walks about in the fire (Pr Azar 1–22 [24–45]), a prose insert describing the angel's actions in stopping the flames (Sg Three 23–7 [46–50]), and the poetic praise of God by the three for their deliverance (Sg Three 28–68 [51–90]). Azariah's words evidence a theology of God's justice in which Israel suffers exile because of its sins, yet they also express the hope that God will continue to show mercy, echoing similar hymns of praise (Ps 103, 136, 148). The Song of the Three Young Men concludes with the specific recognition that God delivered the three near martyrs from death. In this composition we find another example of Nebuchadnezzar being presented as the embodiment of political evil: "You have handed us over to our enemies, lawless and hateful rebels, and to an unjust king, the most wicked in all the world" (Pr Azar 9 [32]). It is possible that this reference is a cipher for Antiochus IV, the cruel Seleucid king who persecuted the Jewish people and whose reign forms the context of Daniel's visions (Daniel 7–12).

The account of Bel and the Dragon, dated to the second or first century BCE, preserves another tradition about Daniel being threatened by lions. As in the canonical book of Daniel, a test is proposed that would compromise Daniel's loyalty to God; he is commanded by the (unnamed) king to worship the great serpent that the Babylonians revered as a god. Daniel counters that he "will kill the serpent without sword or club" (Bel 26), thus proving that it is not divine. Just as the narrative of Daniel 6 portrays a larger population (all the satraps and viziers) conspiring against Daniel, so here, too, on hearing of Daniel's success, the surrounding populace rises against him, demanding that the king cast Daniel into the lions' pit. Similar to the account in Daniel 6, the weak king of Bel and the Dragon readily capitulates to their demands. As in Daniel 6, the king calls out to Daniel – whom the lions have spared – acknowledges Daniel's God, and throws the accusers into the pit for the same death proposed for the innocent Daniel.

The narrative of Susanna, composed in approximately the third century BCE, reflects the concerns of a Hellenistic Jewish community. It is unknown whether this account comes from a Semitic original. The story of Susanna shows that even in unpredictable times of living without any independent power, Jews not only critiqued their foreign rulers, they also continued their long-standing biblical tradition of introspection. Far from restricting their critique of injustice to their foreign overlords, the Hellenistic Jewish community probed their own tradition and treatment of one another. Susanna tells the moving account of a married Jewish woman of considerable means who becomes the object of two judges' voyeurism. The story assumes that Jews have autonomous rights to judge one of their own in some matters – here the issues are adultery and bearing false witness. The judges give Susanna an ultimatum: she must have sex with them or they will accuse her of committing adultery with an unspecified lover. Susanna chooses to submit to their false accusation, claiming that she is trapped. These judges think they have a foolproof plan to ensure a capital sentence for Susanna because they can provide the required testimony of two witnesses. Although she has a wealthy husband, respected parents, hundreds of servants, and four children, no one questions the false testimony of these men or takes steps to ensure that their words are honest. The turning point in the story comes when Susanna prays. God indeed hears the cry of the innocent, and the young Daniel is stirred to come to her defense. Even before Daniel begins questioning the men, he knows that they are guilty (perhaps God has revealed this to him), and he gathers proof that the judges are providing false testimony by questioning them separately, catching them in their lies. The community, happily, believes Daniel, and Susanna is saved.

The account of Susanna illustrates the importance of key legal procedures that must be pursued if there is to be justice and an ideal community is to be created: witnesses must be properly cross-examined; perjurers must be punished according to the intended punishment for their victim, as the law of Moses specifies; and the community must guard against corruption among its leadership. This account targets both the lecherous judges and the uncritical community, which is far too quick to judge. With its clever plot, delightful word play, and the drama of a detective story, it entertains yet also challenges its audience. If all are on guard against injustice, the rewards are not only the protection of the innocent but also the formation of a community built according to God's plan, yielding a preview of the ideal age in the present.

1 Maccabees. This interpretive history presents an account of the Maccabees, or Hasmoneans, namely, Mattathias, his five sons, and their descendants. These rebel fighters provided the moral leadership and military prowess to fight against the abuses of Hellenism in the second and first centuries BCE. The roots of the revolt began with the acquiescence and, in some circles, the enthusiastic embrace of Hellenistic practices by Jews who had been encouraged by the usurper high priests Jason and Menelaus, who succeeded the ousted, legitimate priest Onias III. These priests had challenged Jewish law and disregarded Jewish prohibitions in order to buttress Hellenistic institutions. When Antiochus IV, prompted by his defeat in Egypt and his rage against the attempt of Jason's supporters to oust Menelaus, began his persecutions of Jews, the pious Mattathias and his sons began an armed revolt – not only against the king but also against other Jews, who had abandoned their faith in favor of Greek religion and philosophy. The Maccabees, under the leadership of Mattathias's son Judah, employed guerilla tactics to fight the armies of Antiochus IV and successfully pressured his successor, Antiochus V, to remove the idolatrous cults from the Jerusalem Temple. The book praises Judah for his loyalty to the commandments and to the

Jewish way of life, crediting "Heaven" for Judah's victories. Under the direction of Jonathan, Judah's brother, the Maccabees later ousted the Seleucids from power in Judea (166–160 BCE) and set up an independent dynastic state that endured until 37 BCE, finally succumbing to the power of Rome.

2 *Maccabees.* This work presents a theological interpretation of Maccabean history wherein all history, all meaning, and all eternity are unequivocally under God's control. Particular villains who oppressed the Jewish people are singled out for study, and Jews themselves are placed under scrutiny.

Various events are emphasized in order to show how God protects Israel with divine guidance. During the reign of Seleucus IV, a dispute arose between Simon (an overseer of the Temple) and his compatriot – the high priest Onias III – that escalated into a community-wide disaster. Simon, angry with Onias, told Seleucus that the Temple treasury was stocked with immeasurable wealth. Seleucus sent his minister, Heliodorus, to raid the Temple funds. But a trio of divine warriors assaulted Heliodorus, thereby protecting the Temple.

Nonetheless, Onias' position eventually was taken over by his brother, Jason, who presented Antiochus IV with a substantial bribe. Jason's goal, the author laments, was to make the people more accommodating to Hellenistic practices. A significant number of Jews received privileges for adopting the ways of the state. The author expresses particular disdain for the gymnasium and the games because the search for approbation ultimately gave their Greek (Seleucid) rulers an easier path to set up their idols and outlaw Jewish practice. The author even reports that Jason sent money to offer sacrifices to the god Hercules (2 Macc 4:19). After three years as high priest, Jason was ousted by Menelaus, who obtained his position by bribery (and who consequently raided Temple funds), setting the stage for riots by outraged fellow Jews. The disarray reached a climax when Jason, on hearing a false rumor of Antiochus' death, returned to Jerusalem to oust Menelaus and recapture his position as high priest, resulting in terrible civil unrest. The author laments the deaths of Jews by a fellow Jew; in addition, Jason not only was unsuccessful and met an ignominious death but also set the stage for Antiochus's revenge. Believing that the entirety of the Jerusalem populace was rebelling against him on his return from Egypt, he crushed the Jews with merciless assault. Horrors included massacres, violence, and capture for slavery. Any practice or acknowledgment of

Jewish faith was deemed a capital offense. Moreover, Antiochus IV polluted the Temple, dedicating it to a foreign god. This holiest of places became the location of forbidden offerings and festivals to pagan gods, a practice that began in December of 167 BCE and lasted until December of 164 BCE.

2 Maccabees relates particular stories of martyrs, including the pious Eleazar and a mother with seven sons. These accounts are particularly interesting theologically because they speak of divine judgment, resurrection for the righteous, and atoning suffering. Judah offers sacrifice on behalf of his compatriots who have died in battle, thereby "making atonement for the dead, so that they might be delivered from their sin" (2 Macc 12:45). The practice of offering prayers for the dead, supported by this verse, was quite contentious in the history of Judaism and Christianity.

The author credits God as the just judge who punished the idolater Antiochus IV with an excruciating death in which he recognized his hubris. God is the one who ensured that the king's successor, Antiochus V, allowed Jews to live "free from disturbance ... [and] according to the customs of their ancestors," with their Temple restored (2 Macc 11:22–25). When a later Seleucid king, Demetrius I, and his appointed governor, Nicanor, threaten the Temple and the Jewish way of life, God once again brings the Maccabees to victory.

1 Esdras. 1 Esdras presents an account of Israel's experience from the days of King Josiah (seventh century BCE) to the time of Ezra's leadership among the returning exiles in Jerusalem (sixth century BCE). Probably written in the second century BCE, it survives in Greek but may be a translation of a combined Hebrew/Aramaic original. In the main, this work repeats the content of 2 Chronicles 35–6, the book of Ezra, and Neh 7:6–8:12, with minor variations, along with the addition of a court tale in chapters 3 and 4. Compared to the biblical parallels, the role of Zerubbabel, leader of the first group of exiles who returned to Jerusalem, is enhanced. The main concern of the book is the importance of keeping Israel's unique identity when it is under threat of assimilation from both the power of Persia and the subterfuge of the local population in the former land of Judah – now a Persian province. In order to rebuild the once-exiled community, the necessity and continuity of Temple worship, the integrity of the priesthood, and the reading of and commitment to the commandments are emphasized. God is understood as the just judge who exiled the people because of their own sins and the sins of their leaders. God is also the merciful one, directing all of human history according to a divine plan. In addition, great care is taken to link people's fidelity to their family lineage. Descendants of persons who never left the land are considered suspect as true members of the faith; indeed, they are portrayed as attempting to thwart the building of the Second Temple, and willing to incite the king's ire against the returnees by presenting them as traitors. The leadership of the beleaguered returnees views the presence of foreigners among the community as so threatening to the faith that they command the men to dissolve marriages with foreign women.

A unique court tale is found within the broader historiography. Based on what was surely an independent wisdom account, three of the king's bodyguards propose a contest in which each would identify to their sovereign that which is the strongest thing known to humankind. The king, identified as Darius, will then decide who was correct and reward the winner with great riches. The first bodyguard identifies wine, because it puts both wise and foolish, weak and strong, rich and poor on the same plane. The second identifies the king, for he is the one all obey, even to the point of going to war. The third, who is identified as Zerubbabel, claims two things: women and truth. Women are the strongest because men are dependent on them for life itself (birth), and because all of men's actions are motivated by desire for women, their pleasure, and approval. Yet, added to this identification, making an originally non-Jewish tale didactic for a Jewish audience, is truth. Zerubbabel convincingly argues to his superiors that truth is ultimately the strongest because it comes from God. He refuses any reward; instead, he pleads with the king to be true to his word and allow the exiles to return. Darius complies not only with his permission but also by contributing resources to support the returnees on their journey and in the reconstruction of their Temple.

The Prayer of Manasseh. Most likely composed in Greek, this work is found in some Septuagint manuscripts. Canonical for Orthodox Christians, it is also found in an appendix to the Vulgate. The king who recites the prayer, Manasseh, is known in the Hebrew Scriptures as the worst of Israel's sovereigns; his idolatry was one of the main causes of the Exile. According to 2 Chronicles 33:12–13, while exiled, he appealed to God, but no details are provided. In this prayer, Manasseh is the model of a sincere penitent. He approaches God with the memorable phrase, "I bend the knees of my heart" (Pr Man 11). Addressing God as Creator and sovereign of the universe and admitting the severity of his sins, he appeals to God's mercy. By presenting even the most evil of kings as a prayerful petitioner, the author shows that God is open to the repentance of all.

Psalm 151. Originally composed in Hebrew, as found in the Dead Sea Scrolls, the Greek text is found in Codex Sinaiticus as part of a canonical listing of "the 151 psalms of David"; in Alexandrinus and Vaticanus, it follows the canonical listing of 150 psalms. Credited to King David, this psalm recounts his victory against Goliath, a victory that was, in effect, for all Israel. God's saving activity was accomplished through the surprising choice of its first king: he was the youngest and weakest in his family, a shepherd, and a musician.

3 Maccabees. This theological history presents two accounts of King Ptolemy IV Philopator's torments of Jews – on one occasion in Jerusalem and another in Egypt. In Jerusalem, he insisted on entering the Holy of Holies, defying Jewish law. Paralleling the account of Heliodorus, who was vanquished by the divine trio of warriors on trying to enter the Temple (2 Macc 3:25–26), Philopator (221–204 BCE) was stricken by an act of God, rendering him incapable of even speaking. Yet, in Egypt, he proves himself not only able to defy God but also to threaten the entirety of Egyptian Jewry. Reminiscent of Haman's proposed annihilation of the Persian Jewish community dramatized in the book of Esther, Philopator demands that all Egyptian Jews submit to the worship of Dionysius or face death. The sorrow of the people who face slavery and torture is poignant and chilling.

Gathering all the faithful in the hippodrome of Alexandria, the king threatens them in an outrageous manner. He provides elephants with wine and frankincense to intoxicate them; the animals were then to crush the people. However, angels appear to frustrate the elephants and save the community. Throughout the account, Philopator is one moment menacing, the next benign. Thus, this text stresses the capricious dangers of Diaspora living. Not only kings but also the wider population of Gentiles can threaten at a moment's notice. In addition, the threat of idolatry is ever present. The community faces destruction not only from without but also from within, because some Jews are lured to worship the emperor's gods in hopes of advancing their lot. These vicissitudes are particularly consternating because, although unique Jewish practices label them as threatening to the state, they are, in fact, loyal and dependable subjects. Yet God listens to prayers, intervening to save the people even during the worst of threats. In a great reversal, Philopator acknowledges the power of the Most High God.

There are no other accounts of a threat to Jews in Egypt during the time of Philopator. Josephus, however, records that a similar event occurred during the reign of Ptolemy VIII Physcon (146–117 BCE), in which a number of Jews were killed by intoxicated elephants (*C. Ap.* 2.53–5). It also has been suggested that the reigns of Augustus (c. 24 BCE) or Caligula (37–41 CE) inspired the account.

2 *Esdras.* A composite work, 2 Esdras consists of a Jewish apocalypse, composed in the first century CE (chapters 3–14), and two Christian additions. The first addition (chapters 1 and 2), written in the second century CE, and the second addition (chapters 15 and 16), either contemporaneous with the first or up to a century later, portray the Church as the true successor to an Israel that spurned God and contain oracles of doom against those who persecute Christians. Chapters 3–13 of 2 Esdras are also known as 4 Ezra, chapters 1 and 2 as 5 Ezra, and chapters 15 and 16 as 6 Ezra. The apocalypse was originally written in Hebrew; the additions were composed in Greek. The most complete manuscript survives only in Latin; in addition, there are Armenian, Ethiopian, and Georgian translations. 2 Esdras is canonical in the Slavonic canon (where it is known as 3 Esdras) and found in an appendix in the Latin Bible (where it is known as 4 Esdras).

The apocalypse ponders the justice of God in the face of terrible suffering. While the literary setting is the Exile in Babylon, the text was written in the time period of Roman rule, reflecting the soul searching that occurred as Jews faced terrible losses of life, freedom, and the institutions of their faith, including the Temple – the very dwelling place of God. At the same time, they were surrounded by the glory and success of Rome (Babylon). The answer of the angel Uriel to Ezra's poignant questions is epitomized in this quotation: "Go, weigh for me the weight of fire, or measure for me a blast of wind, or call back for me the day that is past" (2 Esd 4:5). Just as God's voice in the whirlwind teaches Job, the angel instructs Ezra that the human mind is insufficient to understand the ways of God. God's providential care of the universe is just nonetheless. Although it cannot yet be seen, in the fullness of time, wrongs will be righted. This coming age, the author believes, will arrive soon, as is shown to the seer in a series of visions that include imagery of a mother weeping for her only son (symbolic of Zion weeping for Jerusalem), an eagle (Rome), and the triumph of the messiah. The seer's persistent questioning and sadness concerning the lot of humanity – most of whom are destined to perish without an eternal reward – evidence the continual trials of faith that plagued the author's community.

4 Maccabees. As Jews encountered both the attractions of Greek culture and threats to their way of life by rulers who could exercise
tyranny on a whim, questions about the integration of religion
and secular philosophy were endemic. 4 Maccabees, composed in
Greek in the first century BCE, proposes a solution. The wisdom of
Judaism and the wisdom of Greek philosophy are not incompatible.
Among the Greek virtues of prudence, justice, courage, and temperance, one of them – prudence – can be understood as devout reason.
Torah informs reason and permits the other virtues to come to complete fruition. Taking the examples of the Maccabean martyrs who
endured the persecutions of Antiochus IV, the author underscores
how their unshakeable belief in the truths of the Torah allowed
them to remain devoted to God, even in the midst of unspeakable
horrors. They died a noble death because their foundation in the
Torah (i.e., their faith) gave them an unencumbered rational judgment to cling to what is ultimately valuable. For Jews, only a life
lived in accordance with the teachings of their faith made sense.
Such a Torah-filled life would be rewarded by a just God who would
give the righteous everlasting life. The martyrs – Eleazar, the mother,
and her seven sons – evidence how devout reason enables the faithful to argue against the so-called wisdom of tyrants and to endure
any suffering, even a tortuous death.

NOTES

1   Bruce M. Metzger, "Introduction to the Apocryphal/Deuterocanonical
    Books," in *The New Oxford Annotated Bible with the Apocryphal/
    Deuterocanonical Books*, ed. by Bruce M. Metzger and Roland E. Murphy
    (New York: Oxford University Press, 1991), iii AP.
2   R. W. Cowley delineates two main ways of listing the Old Testament books
    of the Ethiopian canon: a narrower list of forty-six and a broader canon of
    fifty-four. Note that *Jubilees, 1 Enoch*, and Josippon's *History of the Jews*
    are found in the Ethiopian canon. See "The Biblical Canon of the Ethiopian
    Church Today," *Ostkirchliche Studien* 23 (1974): 318–23.
3   See the discussion in Albert C. Sundberg, "The Bible Canon and the
    Christian Doctrine of Inspiration," *Interpretation* 29(4) (1975): 352–6.
4   Eugene Ulrich, "The Notion and Definition of Canon," in *The Canon
    Debate*, ed. by Lee Martin McDonald and James E. Sanders (Peabody,
    MA: Hendrickson, 2002), 30.
5   James E. Bowley, "Rethinking the Concept of 'Bible': Some Theses and
    Proposals," *Henoch* 25 (2003): 5–6.
6   R. Zuurmond, "The Structure of the Canon," in *The Rediscovery of the
    Hebrew Bible*, ed. by J. W. Dyk et al. (*ACEBTSup* 1; Maastricht, Netherlands:
    Shaker, 1999), 143.

7   Albert Sundberg, "The Septuagint: The Bible of Hellenistic Judaism," in *Canon Debate*, 82–3.

8   *b. Ḥag.* 13a; *b. Yebam.* 63b; *b. Erub.* 54a. Furthermore, some of the quotations of Ben Sira are specified as coming from the Writings.

9   James C. VanderKam, "Authoritative Literature in the Dead Sea Scrolls," *DSD* 5(3) (1998): 382–402 (398–9). See, also, VanderKam, "Questions of Canon Viewed through the Dead Sea Scrolls," in *Canon Debate*, 105–7.

10 VanderKam, "Authoritative Literature in the Dead Sea Scrolls," 382–96.

11 See the discussion in Sundberg, "The Septuagint: The Bible of Hellenistic Judaism," 87.

12 VanderKam, "Authoritative Literature in the Dead Sea Scrolls," 387.

13 Julio Trebolle Barrera, "Origins of a Tripartite Old Testament Canon," in *Canon Debate*, 131–2.

14 Joseph Blenkinsopp, "The Formation of the Hebrew Bible Canon: Isaiah as a Test Case," in *Canon Debate*, 54.

15 Sundberg, "The Bible Canon and the Christian Doctrine of Inspiration," 357, n. 28.

16 Daniel Harrington, "The Old Testament Apocrypha in the Early Church and Today," in *Canon Debate*, 199.

17 Sundberg, "The Septuagint: The Bible of Hellenistic Judaism," 88.

18 Harrington, "The Old Testament Apocrypha in the Early Church and Today," 204.

19 See Everett Ferguson, "Factors Leading to the Selection and Closure of the New Testament Canon," in *Canon Debate*, 319–20; and Sundberg, "The Bible Canon and the Christian Doctrine of Inspiration," 357.

20 Sundberg, "The Bible Canon and the Christian Doctrine of Inspiration," 354.

21 See David A. deSilva, *Introducing the Apocrypha: Message, Context, and Significance* (Grand Rapids, MI: Baker Academic, 2002), 39.

22 Marvin E. Tate, "The Old Testament Apocrypha and the Old Testament Canon," *RevExp* 65 (1968): 339–56, 353.

23 deSilva, *Introducing the Apocrypha*, 40.

24 See the following studies: Daniel Harrington, *Invitation to the Apocrypha* (Grand Rapids, MI: Eerdmans, 1999); and deSilva, *Introducing the Apocrypha*.

25 There are two Greek versions of the additions to Daniel, namely, the Old Greek (Septuagint) and Theodotion. The Old Greek is known to us from the Hexapla of Origen – a multicolumn translation in which Origen preserved this earliest Greek text. The Hexapla was compiled in the third century CE, but its origins go back to the late second or early first century BCE. In addition, Codex Chisianus (ms. 88, ninth–eleventh centuries CE) and Papyrus 967 (the Chester Beatty papyrus, second century CE) attest to the Old Greek. Theodotion, which dates from the second century CE, was composed to bring the Greek into greater compliance with the developing Hebrew/Aramaic text.

FURTHER READING

Charles, R. H., ed. *The Apocrypha and Pseudepigrapha of the Old Testament*, Vol. 2: *Pseudepigrapha*. Oxford, UK: Clarendon Press, 1913; reprint, Berkeley, CA: Apocryphile Press, 2004.

Charlesworth, James H., ed. *The Old Testament Pseudepigrpha*, 2 vols. Garden City, NY: Doubleday, 1983–1985.

Collins, John J. *Between Athens and Jerusalem: Jewish Identity in the Hellenistic Diaspora*, 2nd ed. Grand Rapids, MI: Eerdmans, 2000.

deSilva, David A. *Introducing the Apocrypha: Message, Context, and Significance.* Grand Rapids, MI: Baker Academic, 2002.

Harrington, Daniel J. *Invitation to the Apocrypha.* Grand Rapids, MI: Eerdmans, 1999.

Metzger, Bruce M. *An Introduction to the Apocrypha.* New York: Oxford University Press, 1977 [1957].

McDonald, Lee Martin, and Sanders, James A. Sanders, eds. *The Canon Debate.* Peabody, MA: Hendrickson, 2002.

Nickelsburg, George W. E. *Jewish Literature between the Bible and the Mishnah: A Historical and Literary Introduction*, 2nd ed. Minneapolis, MN: Fortress Press, 2005.

Nickelsburg, George W. E. and Stone, Michael E. *Early Judaism: Text and Documents on Faith and Piety*, rev'd. ed. Minneapolis, MN: Fortress Press, 2009.

Rost, Leonhard. *Judaism Outside the Hebrew Canon: An Introduction to the Documents.* Nashville, TN: Abingdon Press, 1976.

Sparks, H. F. D., ed. *The Apocryphal Old Testament.* Oxford, UK: Clarendon Press, 1985.

Stone, Michael E. *Ancient Judaism: New Visions and Views.* Grand Rapids, MI: Eerdmans, 2011.

Part V

Reception and use

18 The Hebrew Bible in Judaism

FREDERICK E. GREENSPAHN

The Hebrew Bible (Old Testament) lies at the very heart of Judaism. This is why Mohammad spoke of Jews (and Christians) as "people of the book" (Arabic *ahl al-kitab*). It is a fitting title. Almost every aspect of Jewish life relates to the Bible. For example, Jewish liturgy is filled with Scripture. Prayer services include numerous excerpts from the Bible, most notably, though not exclusively, from the book of Psalms. Among these are many biblical passages that are not really prayers at all. One of the best known is the *Sh'ma* (Deut 6:4), which proclaims the uniqueness of God. It is also included, along with other excerpts from the Bible, in the *tefillin* ("phylacteries") that are worn during daily prayer and the *mezuzot* that Jewish families hang on the doorposts of their homes. Over the course of a year, every word of the Pentateuch (the first five books of the Bible) is read out loud in Hebrew during Sabbath services, along with thematically related selections from the prophetic books called *haftarot* and all five of the festival scrolls (Song of Songs, Ruth, Lamentations, Ecclesiastes/Qohelet, and Esther). In traditional synagogues, an individual (called a *gabbay*) stands alongside the reader to ensure that each word is pronounced correctly.

Biblical language pervades Jewish life outside the synagogue as well. The names of many places in Israel come from the Bible. For example, the words "Tel Aviv" come from a vision in Ezekiel 3:15, where they refer to a place in Babylonia. Book titles, too, are frequently drawn from the Bible. The sixteenth-century code of Jewish law that has become normative for Jewish practice is called the *Shulchan Aruch*, which means "set table," because it lays out all the laws governing Jewish life in an orderly way. However, the phrase itself comes from Ezekiel 23:41. Likewise, the Yiddish "women's Bible" came to be known as *Tseene Ureene*, two feminine verbs that appear in Song of Songs 3:11.

Jews also derive their identity from the Bible, which they understand as the story of their origins. During the Passover *seder*, a ritual meal that commemorates the Israelites' flight from Egypt thousands of years ago, the head of the household explains that the holiday is observed "on account of what the Lord did for *me* when *I* came out of Egypt" (emphasis added). In fact, Jews believe themselves to be biologically descended from Abraham; converts are, therefore, called sons or daughters of Abraham and Sarah in order to include them in that lineage, if only symbolically.

In addition, much of Jewish religious literature is devoted to identifying the biblical source of later practices such as lighting candles on the Sabbath, a ritual never mentioned in the Bible, and the holiday of Hanukkah, which commemorates events that took place after the Bible was complete. In its early years, the Zionist movement, which was largely secular in its orientation, rejected the British offer of land in Africa because of the powerful hold that the Bible's promise of Israel has held over the Jewish people from earliest times. That same hold is evident in both the movement's name (Zion is a biblical term for Jerusalem) and the decision to call the country that it eventually created "Israel," with Hebrew, the language of the Bible, as its national tongue.

Despite the Bible's centrality in Jewish life, the fact of the matter is that many Jewish practices are not derived from it. Modern Israel is not the monarchy of biblical times, nor do Jews observe Passover by slaughtering a lamb and then eating it as the book of Exodus commands. The theology of Jewish prayers, though couched in biblical phrases, is often not biblical at all. In fact, the very idea of reciting fixed prayers in a synagogue on a regular schedule is quite different from the sacrifices that the Bible requires one to bring to priests at the Jerusalem Temple.

The list of Jewish practices that differ from what the Bible calls for could easily be expanded because Judaism as we know it today and as it has been observed for the last 2,000 years is not the religion of the Bible. Instead, it was shaped by rabbis, a role that did not come into existence until several centuries after biblical times. The rabbis were the spiritual heirs of the Pharisees, a religious party that emerged during the period of the Second Temple. The ancient historian Josephus reports that they followed "certain regulations handed down by former generations and not recorded in the Laws of Moses."[1] These regulations evolved into what is now called the "Oral Law." To be sure, they are not entirely unrelated to the Bible, which, after all, does call for Sabbath observance (even if not by lighting candles), and it certainly mentions Passover, though it was the rabbis who determined how a *seder* (or Passover observance) should be run.

The rabbis routinely justified their practices by connecting them to specific biblical passages, regardless of whether or not they actually originated there. For example, they traced the idea of praying three times each day to the biblical patriarchs, based on biblical references to Abraham's actions in the morning (Gen 19:27), Isaac's in the afternoon (Gen 24:63), and Jacob's in the evening (Gen 28:11). Even practices that they knew were not based on the Bible were linked to biblical texts. Where the connection was weak, the biblical text was called an *asmakhta* ("support"). As the Mishnah observes, some of its regulations "are like mountains which hang by a hair," whereas others "have nothing [biblical] on which to lean" (*m. Ḥag.* 1:8).

The relationship between Judaism and the Bible is therefore more complicated than we usually acknowledge. While there is no doubt that Jewish practice and belief developed out of the Bible, they frequently differ from biblical requirements and expectations in several significant ways, even though rabbinic tradition sought to root almost every component in the Bible, including those that did not exist in biblical times. Thus, the rabbis told stories about how Abraham discovered monotheism, an innovation that Genesis never suggests. In so doing, they turned Abraham into the founder of the Jewish religion and not just the ancestor of the Israelite people in the way that he is in the Bible. Similarly, they called Moses "our rabbi," as if to emphasize their belief that he was the originator of their own religious ideas.

To justify these positions, the rabbis explained that alongside the written Torah (the Pentateuch), the Jewish people had received another, equally valid strand of tradition from God at Mount Sinai. They called this the "Oral Torah" because they believed that it had not been written down initially but was transmitted orally for over a thousand years; only then was it collected and transcribed in the Talmud, which includes both the Mishna, a code of Jewish practice from the second century CE, and the Gemara, a collection of early rabbinic discussions on the Mishna.

This terminology introduces several complications in understanding the Bible's role in Judaism. Jewish rhetoric uses the term "Torah" for both the Written and the Oral Laws, making it difficult to be sure what that word means in any particular context. Sometimes it refers to the first five books of the Bible (the five books of Moses); elsewhere, it designates the whole Bible or even all of Jewish tradition (i.e., the written and oral Torah combined); and sometimes, it refers to a cosmic entity that preceded these both physically and conceptually.

Moreover, the relationship between the Oral Torah and the more familiar written one (Genesis–Deuteronomy) has been conceived in different ways. Sometimes the Oral Torah is thought of as existing in parallel to the Written Torah. According to this view, its contents were revealed to Israel at the same time as those of the Written Torah and are therefore every bit as authoritative. The only thing that distinguishes these two bodies of revelation is the way they have been transmitted – one in writing and the other orally. The rabbis reflected this belief when they described practices for which they could find no biblical basis as "Moses' law from Sinai" (*halacha le-Moshe mi-Sinai*), meaning laws that came from Sinai even though they are not part of the written Torah. At other times, however, they presented the Oral Torah as an expansion of the written one, in other words, as spelling out the details that are implicit in its general principles. This is the line of reasoning that led them to search for "prooftexts," that is, passages in the Written Torah to which these later practices could be tied. A well-known example is their linking the mandate of keeping meat and dairy products separate to the biblical commandment that a kid not be seethed in its mother's milk (Exod 23:19, 34:26; Deut 14:21).

However the relationship between these two bodies of law was described, the rabbis attributed higher authority to the Written Torah. They were, therefore, less stringent with practices they considered rabbinic (*d'rabbanan*) than with those based on the Bible (*d'oraita*). But their practice did not always conform to this theory; the Oral Law frequently overshadowed the Written Law. The Jerusalem Talmud states that "Mishna takes precedence over the Bible" (*j. Hor.* 3:7, 48c). It even asserts that "the Oral Torah is more precious than the Written" (*j. Pe'ah* 2:6, 17a), while the Babylonian Talmud acknowledges that sometimes "the *halakha* goes beyond and uproots Scripture" (*b. Soṭa* 16a).

Over time, Talmud study came to displace attention to the Bible. Jewish authorities justified this move by explaining the Talmud's designation *bavli* (Babylonian) as a reflection of the fact that it combines (*bll*) Scripture, Mishna, and Talmud (*b. Sanh.* 24a). There was, therefore, no need to study the Bible separately. As the brother of Judah Loew, a prominent sixteenth-century rabbinic authority who was known as the Maharal of Prague, observed, "Our holy ancestors, especially the Ashkenazi pietists, saw fit to direct their sons to Talmud alone."[2] The consequences of that attitude are evident in a widespread joke about Eastern European yeshiva students, whose knowledge of the Bible was limited to its citations in the Talmud.[3] But this was no joking matter;

traditional Jews, particularly in Ashkenazi communities, were often unfamiliar with the Bible as an important document in itself.

As a result of these attitudes, rabbinic Judaism has repeatedly been charged with having ignored and even deviated from the Bible. The ancient Sadducees used that argument against the Pharisees. It was revived in the eighth century by the Karaite movement, whose name literally means "biblicists"; they accused the rabbis, who were the intellectual heirs of the Pharisees, of having manufactured their additional teachings. The charge was then picked up by various Christian polemicists, who used it against Judaism, and, in the eighteenth and nineteenth centuries, by enlightened German Jews, who wanted to purge Judaism of its "legalistic trivia" in favor of the ethical monotheism that they attributed to the prophets. When early Zionists rebelled against what they perceived as the passivity of Eastern European Jewry, they sought to bring Jews back to their understanding of the biblical ideal. Ironically, all these movements eventually developed traditions of their own alongside those of the Bible; many times they returned to the rabbinic (Talmudic) teachings they had initially rejected.

Because of the Torah's centrality in Jewish tradition, it has received a great deal of theological attention. The Mishna warns that those who deny the Torah's divine origin (*torah min hashamayim*) will have no place in the world to come; sharing that fate are "Epicureans," those who do not accept the biblical basis for the doctrine of resurrection and even, according to some, people who read noncanonical works, utter charms over wounds, or pronounce God's name (*m. Sanh.* 10:1).

Denying the Torah's divine origin is different from denying that it was revealed at Sinai, although the two frequently have been equated. In fact, some authorities taught that God had revealed the Torah incrementally throughout the forty years that Israel wandered in the desert (*b. Giṭṭin* 60a). According to this view, it was not finished until shortly before the Israelites were ready to enter the Promised Land.[4] There are also divergent opinions as to whether God had dictated it word for word or only inspired those who did the actual writing. What was not questioned was the rabbis' belief that all Holy Writings, not just the Torah, were the product of the "Holy Spirit."[5] This meant that the entire Bible had been produced by prophets, who were the only ones believed capable of receiving divine inspiration. And so the rabbis expended considerable energy in efforts to identify the authors of individual biblical books; many of the names we now use for those books are the result of that project (e.g., Joshua, Samuel, and Jeremiah).

However, Jews have long recognized that these beliefs about the Bible's sanctity and authority raise many problems. The Bible's contents are not entirely consistent, and some sections rest on theologically troubling positions. Later books of the Bible show traces of efforts to address these issues. For example, the book of Chronicles requires that the Passover lamb be "boiled in fire" (2 Chr 35:13), thereby merging the conflicting mandates of Exodus 12:9 and Deuteronomy 16:7. Ezekiel insists that "a child shall not share the burden of a parent's guilt" (18:20), apparently repudiating the Ten Commandments' explicit statement that God "visits the guilt of the parents upon the children, upon the third and upon the fourth generations" (Exod 20:5).

The rabbis also developed techniques for dealing with contradictory biblical passages. One of Rabbi Ishmael's thirteen principles of interpretation is devoted to how contradictions between biblical verses should be resolved (Sifra 3a). Jewish tradition also preserves several lists of problematic passages in the Bible, including one compiled by a heretic named Ḥivi, who lived in Khorasan (Persia/Afghanistan) during the ninth century.[6]

To demonstrate the Bible's theological cohesion, the rabbis sometimes provide three separate verses to illustrate a particular point, taking one from each of the Bible's three sections. However, they accorded a higher status to the first five books ("the Torah") than the rest, citing them more often than the others and arguing that the later sections of the Bible (the Prophets and the Writings) merely reiterate points first stated there.

According to classical rabbinic theology, God had created the Torah before He undertook the other activities described in Genesis 1, in other words, before He made anything else. The rabbis saw this as comparable to the way architects prepare blueprints before embarking on a building project. This meant that the Torah was available to assist in the process of creation. What happened at Sinai was not, therefore, really the creation of a new document but the transmission of one that already existed from heaven to earth. In fact, the rabbis delighted in relating how many nations turned down God's Torah before the Israelites, who had just escaped from Egyptian slavery, accepted it. Moreover, they did so with the words, "We will do and [then] we will understand" (Exod 24:7). Another tradition attributes this response to God's having held Mount Sinai over their heads.

This conception of the Torah as primordial developed shortly after the biblical period. It implies that the physical scroll Jews use during worship is an earthly counterpart to a heavenly object. This explains the great reverence with which Jews treat it. In synagogues it is kept in a special cabinet, called an 'aron, the same term that the Bible uses for the chest in which the Ten Commandments were carried through the desert. Worshipers rise when the 'aron is opened during worship and touch the scroll as it is paraded by before being read. A special pointer is used so that the reader does not touch it directly, and a widely cited tradition mandates a forty-day fast for anyone who drops it or even, sometimes, for those who witness such an event.[7]

Jewish tradition understands the Psalmist's statement that "God's Torah is perfect" (Ps 19:8) to mean that it contains all knowledge and that everything in it is exactly the way it is supposed to be. Even the decorative marks on individual letters have meaning, not to mention unusual spellings, passages that seem repetitive, and ostensibly trivial statements, such as the Bible's extensive genealogical data. And so the sages insisted, "Turn it and turn it because everything is in it" (*m. 'Avot* 5:22). And turn it they did, subjecting the Bible to minute examination in an effort to uncover teachings on everything from ethics and ritual to science and philosophy. An entire school of thought, commonly associated with the second-century sage Akiva, developed techniques to identify and explain the significance of every detail. There are also several lists itemizing elaborate interpretive techniques that can be applied to the Bible. These range from the seven that are attributed to Hillel, the legendary first-century rabbi, to Rabbi Ishmael's thirteen and the thirty-two (or thirty-six) said to have come from the Galilean Rabbi Eliezer. An alternative approach associated with Akiva's contemporary Rabbi Ishmael takes a more accommodationist stance, attributing the Torah's inconsistencies and theologically problematic statements to its use of human modes of expression.

In the process of exploring these issues, Jewish thinkers produced a vast body of commentary. Gershom Scholem, the great scholar of Jewish mysticism, remarked that commentary is "the characteristic expression of Jewish thinking about truth."[8] There is much truth to this assertion, for commentary holds a high status in Jewish life. Since medieval times, Jews have conventionally read the Bible in editions called *Mikra'ot Gedolot* (literally "Big Bibles"), in which a variety of commentaries, primarily from the Middle Ages, are printed alongside the actual text. This format survives to the present day in the Bibles that the major Jewish denominations provide worshipers in their synagogues. Numerous other works, ranging from Maimonides' philosophical masterpiece, the *Guide of the Perplexed*, to the *Zohar*, which is the classic text of Jewish mysticism, are in large part constructed as commentaries on the Bible.

The process of interpreting the Bible had begun before the biblical period was over. The book of Daniel explains how Jeremiah's prophecy that Israel would suffer for seventy years under Babylonian oppression (Jer 29:10) really means seventy "weeks" (i.e., units of seven) of years (Dan 9:2, 24), in other words, four hundred and ninety (70 × 7) years. Other writings from the same period treat other biblical passages similarly.

Toward the end of the biblical period, Jews began writing works that retell accounts in the Bible. Both Chronicles and Deuteronomy are early versions of that genre, which includes the later books of Jubilees, the *Biblical Antiquities* mistakenly attributed to the philosopher Philo (hence "Pseudo-Philo"), Josephus's *Antiquities*, and several of the Dead Sea Scrolls. Those scrolls also include the oldest writings to be constructed as actual commentaries, quoting and then explaining biblical passages in sequence, one after the other. The Qumran community in which these works originated believed that the interpretations had themselves been revealed by God, albeit to their leader rather than to the original prophet. As their commentary to the biblical book of Habakkuk explains, "God told Habakkuk to write down what was going to happen to the final generation, but He did not let him know when time would come to an end." Instead, the commentary continues, it was "the Teacher of Righteousness to whom God made all the mysteries of the words of His servants the prophets known" (1 QpHab 7:1–5). In other words, the author of this commentary believed that the biblical prophets had not been given the full meaning of the messages they received; instead, they thought that God waited centuries before revealing the meaning of these earlier prophecies to the leader of their community. In effect, this turns the interpretation of these passages into a second revelation. Later generations would accord a similar status to Rashi's interpretation of the Bible.[9]

Jewish tradition allows for the possibility that the Torah can have several meanings; even individual passages may be interpreted in multiple ways. The Talmud grounds this position in the prophet Jeremiah's statement, "Behold My word is like a fire – declares the LORD – and like a hammer that shatters rock" (23:20). The rabbis took this to mean that "just as a hammer shatters rock into numerous splinters, so may a single biblical verse yield a multiplicity of meanings" (*b. Sanh.* 34a, cf. *b. Shabb.* 88b). And so they claimed that any given passage could have as many as seven or seventy or even 600,000 meanings.

According to the classical Jewish tradition, there are four ways of interpreting the Bible. These are represented by the acronym "PaRDeS," which stands for *peshat, remez, derash,* and *sod.*

The most extensive approach is the homiletical one (*derash*). These are interpretations that elaborate on the biblical text for didactic or aesthetic purposes. Some simply fill out the biblical account, giving the names of characters who are anonymous in the Bible or describing events that took place during periods that the Bible ignores. Others impart ethical, ritual, or theological lessons. The stories of how Abraham discovered monotheism are one example of this. Not only do such stories credit the founder of the Israelites with this fundamental theological idea, but they also provide information about Abraham's childhood, a period about which the Bible itself has nothing to say. Other interpretations apply elaborate techniques, treating biblical words as acronyms (*notarikon*) or codes in which each letter represents a numerical value (*gematria*).

The most extensive allegorical interpretations (*remez*) come from the first-century philosopher Philo. He viewed biblical figures as representing different personality types. For example, the patriarchs signify ways of achieving virtue, with Abraham symbolizing learning; Isaac, nature; and Jacob, training. The Song of Songs, with its explicit erotic imagery, was particularly susceptible to this treatment, which takes it to be a symbolic representation of the history of Israel's relationship with God. A related approach has come to be called "typology." It treats various accounts as foreshadowing or symbolizing events that came later. As the medieval exegete Nahmanides put it, "What happened to the ancestors is a sign of what their descendants would experience." The patriarchal stories were understood as indicative of events that would affect the Israelites centuries afterwards.

The Kabbalistic tradition presents the most prominent mystical interpretations (*sod*). There the Bible is understood as a (cryptic) description of events within the divine realm. As the Zohar explains, "Each particular narrative, seemingly a mere story or fact ... teaches us not only its own limited lesson, but supernal ideas and recondite doctrines" (Zohar 3 *Beha'alotekha* 149b). Adherents of this approach understand the patriarchs as representing different facets of God. Thus, when the Bible says that Abraham and Isaac walked together to the place God had told him (Gen 22:8–9), it is really referring to the unification of the two divine aspects that these characters represent.

The fourth and final approach, *peshat*, originally meant the authoritative understanding of the Bible. However, since the Middle Ages, it has been understood as the straightforward interpretation, what we today consider the Bible's original meaning. The medieval French commentator Rashi and his disciples were the first to give priority to this kind of interpretation, but it was carried out most extensively in medieval

Spain, under the impetus of the Karaite movement and the influence of Islamic study of the Qur'an. It has achieved particular importance in modern times, after becoming prominent within Protestantism, which was itself heavily influenced by medieval Jewish scholarship.

Christian interpretation has long been a powerful motivator for Jewish biblical studies, although Jewish heretics such as those mentioned earlier also played a role. The resulting disputes had serious political ramifications, especially in the Middle Ages. The Provencal interpreter David Kimchi was particularly committed to refuting Christian views. Modern Jewish biblical scholarship also has carried a defensive edge. In a famous speech, Solomon Schechter described contemporary biblical scholarship as "the higher anti-Semitism," while his contemporary Benno Jacob complained that "our Bible is no longer our Bible."

Modern biblical scholarship arose in the wake of Protestantism and the scientific method. The former emphasized studying Scripture on its own (*sola scriptura*), and the latter elevated reason over revelation, leading to the Bible's being treated like any other book. Several general conclusions emerged from those premises: (1) that the traditional Hebrew text of the Bible is not always accurate, (2) that some biblical books (especially Isaiah and the Pentateuch) are composite, (3) that the authors of the Bible had religiopolitical agendas, which their writings sought to promote, and (4) that the Bible must be viewed within the context of the ancient Near East. This last position gained particular strength in light of the archeological discoveries that began to multiply toward the end of the nineteenth century.

Although the New Testament was subjected to similar techniques, the conclusions of these studies were often presented in ways that seemed inimical to Judaism, even when the real targets were internal to Christianity. For example, many scholars taught that the Bible's most profound teachings had originated much later than the Bible itself claims or had been borrowed from other cultures. This meant that the Bible's most important ideas had originated among non-Israelites or developed in relatively late periods of Israelite history, before degenerating after the Exile until they could be restored by Christianity. Biblical scholars also dismissed traditional Jewish interpretations as inaccurate and irrelevant; only modern insights and discoveries were thought capable of illuminating the Bible.

In such an environment, it is no wonder that Jewish scholars felt attacked. Some reacted by retreating into the Talmud or the ghetto; however, others felt the importance of finding a response. Among the nineteenth-century pioneers who addressed these issues were Samuel

David Luzzatto and David Zvi Hoffmann, who lived in Italy and Germany, respectively. In the twentieth century, Israeli scholars Yehezkel Kaufmann and Umberto Cassuto, who had been born in the Ukraine and Italy, respectively, produced several substantial works echoing European biblical studies but in a Jewish mode. Kaufmann's contentions that the ancient Israelites had invented monotheism and that the Bible's charge of Israelite infidelity to God was due to its misunderstanding of paganism have an almost nationalistic tone, whereas Cassuto drew on the ancient Near Eastern materials then becoming prominent. Another scholar who sought to relate the Bible to its surrounding cultures was the American Cyrus Gordon; he tried to find connections between the biblical world and other ancient Mediterranean civilizations.

Over the past generation, much has changed. Today's Jewish scholars are more comfortable with the larger field of biblical studies than were their predecessors. Following in the footsteps of such luminaries as Moses Mendelssohn, Franz Rosenzweig, and Martin Buber, they pay increasing attention to the Bible's literary features and the history of Jewish biblical interpretation. Meanwhile, non-Jewish scholars have begun to draw on the Jewish interpretive tradition while becoming more conscious of the ideological assumptions that lie behind their own work.

Although Judaism is usually said to have grown out of the Bible, it might be more useful to emphasize the reverse: that the Bible is itself a product of Judaism. To be sure, there was no Judaism as we know it today in biblical times, but neither was there a Bible. Figures such as Abraham, Moses, David, and the prophets did not have a Bible, though later traditions argued otherwise. The book of Jubilees, which was written during the intertestamental period, goes so far as to claim that Abraham had been given commandments based on heavenly tablets, whereas the later rabbinic tradition asserted that various biblical figures had actually studied Scripture. But neither of these views accords with either the biblical account or historical facts.

Not only did the Bible not exist as such during the biblical period, but neither were any of the various books that came to be part of it written for that purpose. Instead, they were composed for various reasons over a span of 1,000 years. Only toward the end of that period did the process of selection (canonization) begin. Most scholars believe that it took place in stages, with the Pentateuch coming to be authoritative some time after the Judeans returned from the Babylonian exile in 538 BCE, then the Prophets by the year 200 BCE, and the Writings several centuries after that. Moreover, different versions of biblical books existed side by side until at least the second Christian century, when one of these ("the Masoretic Text" or MT) came to be accepted as authoritative. Even then, several hundred years would pass before vowels and punctuation were added to the original consonantal text in an effort to ensure that the Bible was always read properly. It took even more time until all twenty-four (or thirty-nine, depending on how you count) books of the Hebrew Bible were bound together in a single volume as they are today, although, as we have seen, Jewish tradition had long regarded them as a cohesive theological unit. In recent centuries, this collection has come to be called *Tanakh*, an acronym for its three sections: Torah, Prophets (*Nevi'im*), and Writings (*Ketuvim*).

Thus, Judaism existed before the Bible as we know it today, though not before the individual books it contains. The process of selecting books for inclusion in what became the Bible was carried out by Jews, even if we do not know all the details of how that occurred. In other words, it was the Jewish community that elevated these books to the status of Scripture and then joined them together. Jews, therefore, not only created the Bible – but even the idea of a Bible. To be sure, other cultures had holy books; but no earlier religion or culture had a Bible. The sacred books that Jesus considered his Scripture, and that were eventually incorporated into the Christian canon, were therefore a Jewish collection. This is also the Bible that has been cherished, preserved, and given life by the Jewish community in the myriad ways described here, including the Bible's elevation as the source for all rabbinic teaching, as given by God on Mount Sinai.

As much as Judaism has evolved beyond the Bible over the past 2,000 years, it invariably returns to it. In Schechter's words, the Bible is Jews' "sole *raison d'être*."[10] Scholars such as Kaufmann and Cassuto have tried to understand it and the world from which it comes. Thinkers such as Joseph Soloveitchik and Martin Buber have grounded their teachings in it. Halakhists such as Moshe Feinstein and Solomon Freehof have cited it. Preachers such as David Wolpe and Irwin Kula have used it to illustrate their message. Whatever the complications, the Bible, which after all describes fully half of Jewish history, lies very much at the heart of Judaism in all its various manifestations.

NOTES

1   *Antiquities* 13:10.6 (§297); cf. 13:16.2 (§408) and Mark 7:3.
2   Quoted by Adolf Neubauer in *HaMagid* 37 (September 29, 1869), 293b.
3   Jakob J. Petuchowski, "The Bible of the Synagogue, the Continuing Revelation," *Commentary* 27 (February 1959): 149.

4 Cf. Abraham Joshua Heschel, *Heavenly Torah as Refracted through the Generations* (New York: Continuum, 2006), 626–31.
5 See *t. Yad.* 2:14.
6 Judah Rosenthal, "Ḥiwi al-Balkhi, A Comparative Study," *JQR* 38 (1947–8): 317–42.
7 Daniel Z. Feldman, "The Development of Minhag as a Reflection of Halakhic Attitude: Fasting for a Fallen Sefer Torah," *Tradition* 33(2) (1999): 19–30.
8 Gershom Scholem, *The Messianic Idea in Judaism and Other Essays on Jewish Spirituality* (New York: Schocken Books, 1971), 290.
9 Cf. Moshe Idel, *Kabbalah: New Perspectives* (New Haven, CT: Yale University Press, 1988), 238–9.
10 Solomon Schechter, *Seminary Addresses and Other Papers* (New York: Burning Bush Press, 1959), 37.

FURTHER READING

Attias, Jean Christophe. *The Jews and the Bible.* Stanford: Stanford University Press, 2014.
Berlin, Adele and Marc Zvi Brettler, eds., *The Jewish Study Bible,* 2nd ed. *New York: Oxford University Press,* 2nd ed. *2014.*
Ginzberg, Louis. *The Legends of the Jews,* 2nd ed. Philadelphia: Jewish Publication Society of America, 2003.
Halbertal, Moshe. *People of the Book: Canon, Meaning, and Authority.* Cambridge, MA: Harvard University Press, 1997.
Harris, Jay M. *How Do We Know This? Midrash and the Fragmentation of Modern Judaism.* Albany: State University of New York Press, 1995.
Heschel, Abraham Joshua. *Heavenly Torah as Refracted through the Generations.* New York: Continuum, 2007.
Holtz, Barry. *Back to the Sources: Reading the Classic Jewish Texts.* New York: Summit Books, 1984.
Jacobs, Louis. *Jewish Biblical Exegesis.* New York: Behrman House, 1973.
Satlow, Michael L. *How the Bible Became Holy.* New Haven: Yale University Press, 2014.
Silver, Daniel Jeremy. *The Story of Scripture: From Oral Tradition to the Written Word.* New York: Basic Books, 1990.
Sperling, S. David. *Students of the Covenant: A History of Jewish Biblical Scholarship in North America.* Atlanta: Scholars Press, 1992.

19 The Old Testament in Christianity

R. W. L. MOBERLY

Some issues in life are not capable of final resolution. Questions such as 'What is the good life?' and 'How can we get good government?' and 'Whom can I trust?' are not amenable to definitive answers in the same way as many mathematical and scientific questions. Rather, such fundamental questions of living recur afresh in every age. Part of the thesis of this chapter is that the role of the Old Testament in Christianity is, in essence, such an irresolvable issue. Christians ancient and modern have not found unanimity or finality in understanding and using the Old Testament – and this may be a sign not of failure but rather of the intrinsic variety of the challenges that the Old Testament poses for Christian faith. A collection of religious literature that is pre-Christian in origin, written over centuries and initially compiled by Jews (as Israel's Scriptures), and only subsequently appropriated by Christians (as the Old Testament), inherently poses intriguing, albeit enriching, questions to Christians.

Lack of definitive resolution therefore should in no way call into question the importance of wrestling with understanding the Old Testament within Christian faith. A. H. J. Gunneweg, for example, wrote

> It would be no exaggeration to understand the hermeneutical problem of the Old Testament as *the* problem of Christian theology, and not just one problem among others.... If the interpretation of holy scripture is an essential task for theology, and if the Bible is the basis of Christian life, the foundation of the church and the medium of revelation, then it is of fundamental importance for the theologian to ask whether and why the collection of Israelite and Jewish writings to which the Christian church has given the name Old Testament are part – indeed the most substantial part – of the canon of scripture and what their relevance is. This question affects the extent and also qualitatively the substance of what may be regarded as Christian.[1]

Thus, engagement in debates about the understanding and appropriation of the Old Testament – debates which in practice probably take place more in contexts of worship and everyday life than in formal academic contexts – is itself part of what constitutes Christian faith.

DIVERGENT ATTITUDES

Some of the recurrent issues can readily be set out. On the one hand, the Old Testament contains much that is constitutive of Christian faith: there is one God, creator of the world, who is personal, good, sovereign, and the appropriate recipient of human trust and allegiance; human life has intrinsic dignity and value ('in the image of God'); human knowledge of, and relationship with, God is always initiated by God ('grace', 'revelation'); God's purposes within the world focus on, though are not restricted to, the loving call of a people whose call entails faithful service ('election'); prayer is an essential means of communication between humans and God; human life entails, in important respects, imitating God through displaying qualities of moral integrity, justice and mercy – one should love God and one's neighbour. Without such content, there would be no Christian faith.

Of course, some of the content of the Old Testament has no continuing constitutive role within Christianity, as already becomes clear in the New Testament with regard to circumcision and the dietary laws (both of which symbolise Israel's distinctiveness vis-à-vis the Gentiles), even though the covenant symbolised by circumcision is said to be given 'in perpetuity' (Gen 17:7, 13), that is, with no termination or revocation envisaged. But these points simply recognise, in essence, how the death and resurrection of Jesus mean that Christians approach the Old Testament differently from Jews.

On the other hand, the Old Testament contains material that appears problematic. Most notoriously, God's instructions to Israel for the occupation of Canaan appear to sponsor murderous 'ethnic cleansing' (Deutereonomy 7, Joshua 1–12), and to be at some remove from God's self-giving in Jesus; Elijah calls down fire from heaven to incinerate a hundred soldiers and their captains so as to teach proper respect for a prophet (2 Kings 1; contrast Luke 9:52–5); the psalmists utter imprecations on enemies (e.g., Psalm 58; contrast Matt 5:44). Assumptions are made whose enduring value is doubtful, not least about the relative worth and roles of male and female (e.g. Lev 27:1–8). There are questions as to how far, if at all, the Old Testament can be appropriated in the light of modern science and history. And so on.

Such issues have received extensive discussion down the ages. Sometimes closer study can show how some positive features may be more problematic, and some negative features less problematic, than they appeared initially.[2] It is also usually most helpful to try to grasp an overall frame of reference within which Christians approach the Old Testament (as in a chapter such as this) so that the discussion of particular issues progresses in dialectical interchange with an understanding of the whole. Nonetheless, even though real progress in understanding the Old Testament is possible, debate about the nature and extent of its appropriation within Christianity remains ongoing.

Some measure of the diversity can be gauged by considering the following statements by eminent twentieth-century Protestant theologians (one of the historical distinguishing marks of Protestant Christianity being its emphasis upon the importance of the Bible). Adolf von Harnack, who operated within a Lutheran frame of reference that has sometimes tended to ambivalence towards the Old Testament,[3] wrote a major book on Marcion, who c. AD 150 had proposed a form of Christian faith entirely without the Old Testament, on the basis that the deity it portrays is other than, and inferior to, the God of Christian faith of whom Paul speaks. In it, Harnack proffers this much-quoted dictum:

> To reject the Old Testament in the second century was a mistake which the Church rightly repudiated; to retain it in the sixteenth century was a fate which the Reformation could not yet avoid; but to continue to keep it in Protestantism as a canonical document after the nineteenth century is the consequence of religious and ecclesiastical paralysis.[4]

To be sure, Harnack's own proposal was not the abandonment of the Old Testament within Christianity (as Marcion had sought) but rather its downgrading, that the Old Testament should lose its canonical status and be placed among books that are 'good and useful to read', which was how Luther classified the Apocrypha. Nonetheless, it is clear that Harnack sought a renewed form of Christian self-definition with minimal input from the Old Testament.

By contrast, Brevard Childs, who stood in the Reformed tradition of Calvin and Barth, which has probably been the strand within Protestantism that has consistently placed the highest value on the enduring significance of the Old Testament for Christian faith, says this when discussing how to speak of God:

> I do not come to the Old Testament to learn about someone else's God, but about the God we confess, who has made himself known to

Israel, to Abraham, Isaac and to Jacob. I do not approach some ancient concept, some mythological construct akin to Zeus or Moloch, but our God, our Father. The Old Testament bears witness that God revealed himself to Abraham, and we confess that he has broken into our lives. I do not come to the Old Testament to be informed about some strange religious phenomenon, but in faith I strive for knowledge as I seek to understand ourselves in the light of God's self-disclosure. In the context of the church's scripture I seek to be pointed to our God who has made himself known, is making himself known, and will make himself known.[5]

The God whose self-revelation to Abraham is attested in the Old Testament is the God who is known in Christian faith today. There is both continuity and familiarity for Christians who read the Old Testament in faith, for its story is their story, its God is their God. Christian faith is in principle formed by substantive input from the Old Testament.

Although Childs undoubtedly expresses a classical Christian understanding in a way that Harnack does not, numerous Christians still express doubts about the Old Testament comparable to those of Harnack – which can give ongoing debates about the Old Testament a sharp edge.

THE OLD TESTAMENT IN RELATION TO JESUS AND THE NEW TESTAMENT

Christian faith in God focuses on Jesus and has come to understand Jesus as the key not only to understanding and encountering God but also to understanding and being able to realise what human life is really about – as summed up in the shorthand affirmation (itself summarising the Council of Chalcedon in AD 451) that Jesus is truly divine and truly human. Yet Jesus himself was rooted within and formed by Jewish faith in God that receives its fundamental formulation in Israel's Scriptures. This means that the faith that Christians have in Jesus is not identical with the faith that Jesus himself had; Jesus himself was not a Christian but a Jew.[6] Yet Christians have generally felt it important that there should be continuity between the faith of Jesus himself and faith in Jesus. Arguably, it is in the complex dynamics of holding these together that many core issues of Christian faith relating to the Old Testament also can be seen.

Consider the differences between the synoptic gospels which portray Jesus' earthly ministry and message, and the Pauline letters which depict Christian proclamation about Jesus. For example, in Matthew's account of Jesus' encounter with the rich young man (Matt 19:16–22),[7] Jesus answers the young man's question about eternal life with 'If you wish to enter into life, keep the commandments' (19:17). When the young man asks the clarifying question 'Which ones?', Jesus responds by citing scriptural commandments, primarily some of the Ten Commandments (Exod 20:13–16, Deut 5:17–20), but also the injunction to 'love your neighbour as yourself' (Lev 19:18). The young man says that he has observed these and asks the further question 'What do I still lack?' This appears to depict him as someone who has done all the right things and yet for whom the realities of God have for some reason not come alive. So Jesus offers a way ahead through issuing a challenge that should, as it were, break the log jam – the young man should give up all his wealth and follow Jesus as a disciple. In this, Jesus speaks as one for whom God's commandments as set out in Israel's Scripture ('law', *torah*) contain the way of life – what matters is to live out, and find life in, what God has already said. Jesus' challenge to sell up and follow involves no particular belief about himself, beyond recognition of him as someone in touch with God, and the emphasis is upon an action whose radical demand will bring alive the realities of God as set out in Israel's law.

However, Paul in Galatians 3 puts a markedly different challenge to his readers: 'Did you receive the Spirit by doing the works of the law or by believing what you heard?' A strong antithesis between believing a message about the crucified Jesus and doing particular deeds in obedience to Israel's law runs throughout Paul's argument. Strikingly, Paul roots this antithesis within Israel's Scriptures themselves, positing an antithesis between Abraham and the law. Paul appeals to Abraham as one who believes and has this faith reckoned as righteousness (Gen 15:6). His righteousness thereby constitutes a model for others, too, who by believing receive the promise of blessing which was also given to Abraham (3:6–9, 15–18). The law, by contrast, was a temporary expedient whose purpose was fulfilled with the coming of Christ in whom God's promise to Abraham is now received by faith (3:19–26). Far from commending obedience to the Ten Commandments, Paul's dialectical argument about the nature of Christian faith revolves around God's promise to Abraham, believing, receiving the Spirit, and being baptised into Christ (whose crucifixion is fundamental, 3:1; 6:12, 14).

On any reckoning, the tenor of Paul's argument is markedly different from that of Jesus' words in Matthew's portrayal.[8] The question then becomes how one should understand the relationship between the two, not least because both are part of the New Testament, which is authoritative for Christian faith. I have heard more than one preacher argue that the words of Jesus to the rich young man could not really mean what they appear to mean – presumably because that would conflict too much with what is taken to be a Pauline understanding of salvation – and so must be understood ironically, perhaps as a way of helping the young man to see that obedience to the law can only end in failure (in the sense of still lacking something), for which Jesus then provides the remedy. In effect, Luther's antithesis between law and gospel provides a way of prioritising Pauline theology and re-conceptualising the synoptic portrayal of Jesus within a Pauline frame of reference.

At a more sophisticated level, Rudolf Bultmann put his finger on this issue in his own distinctive way at the outset of his *Theology of the New Testament*:

> The message of Jesus is a presupposition for the theology of the New Testament rather than a part of that theology itself.... Christian faith did not exist until there was a Christian kerygma; i.e., a kerygma proclaiming Jesus Christ – specifically Jesus Christ the Crucified and Risen One – to be God's eschatological act of salvation. He was first so proclaimed in the kerygma of the earliest Church, not in the message of the historical Jesus.[9]

In other words, Paul gives authentic Christian theology, while Jesus' words are historical background to that theology. Of course, all this is not as such a difference between the Old and New Testaments, for the difference is located within the New Testament. But conceptually Bultmann removes that which precedes the Christian message of Christ crucified and risen from being integral to, and constitutive of, the content of Christian faith. What applies to the teaching of Jesus in his ministry assuredly applies even more so to the Old Testament,[10] as Bultmann consistently argued in two well-known essays.[11]

Bultmann reads the Old Testament with a distinctive, indeed idiosyncratic, hermeneutic, inspired by a particular reading of Pauline theology. First, because 'Jesus is God's demonstration of grace in a manner which is fundamentally different from the demonstrations of divine grace attested in the Old Testament',[12] the prophetic hope of the Old Testament 'is fulfilled in its inner contradiction, its miscarriage'; though 'the miscarriage of history actually amounts to a promise', for the failure of the human way gives an opening to God's way in Christ.[13] Secondly, the manner in which the Old Testament functions for Christians is not different from what can be found elsewhere:

> The exodus from Egypt, the giving of the Law at Sinai, the building of Solomon's Temple, the work of the prophets, all redound to our benefit in so far as these are historical episodes which form part of our Occidental history. In the same sense, however, it can be said

that the Spartans fell at Thermopylae for us and that Socrates drank
the hemlock for us.[14]

The Old Testament's lack of special theological significance is essentially because 'everywhere the possibility is present for man to become
aware of his nothingness and to come to humility or despair.'[15]

Bultmann, like Harnack, offers a revisionist proposal in the name of
'faith that is specifically Christian';[16] only, in so doing, he has played off
differing voices in the canon of both Old and New Testaments against
each other in a way that leaves a rather thin Christianity. As Francis
Watson puts it,

> The polyphonic witness of both Testaments to God's definitive
> self-disclosure in Jesus Christ has been *replaced* by the monotony
> of the kerygma, the single word that can only be repeated, over and
> over again.[17]

In sum, it should be clear that an understanding of the role of the Old
Testament within Christianity necessarily involves wide-ranging and
complex theological judgements, which are not separable from judgements about how best to comprehend the differing theological emphases
in relation to Jesus found within the New Testament.

DIFFERING USES OF THE OLD TESTAMENT IN MATTHEW'S GOSPEL

A simpler example of some of the issues concerning the Old Testament
within Christianity can be found in a consideration of the use of the
Old Testament specifically within Matthew's Gospel. There are two
recurrent emphases in Christian debate about the Old Testament. One
is that there is profound moral and theological content within the Old
Testament such that Christian neglect leads to spiritual impoverish-
ment.[18] Another is that much Christian appeal to the Old Testament is
fanciful, taking passages out of context and using them arbitrarily. Within
Matthew's Gospel, one can see grounds for both of these contentions.

On the one hand, there is Jesus' use of the Old Testament as portrayed by Matthew,[19] a use that is consistently searching. When, for
example, the nature of Jesus' ministry as Son of God is being tested,
Jesus responds to temptations to use God's power to make things easier
for himself by appeal to precepts in Deuteronomy: relieving his hunger
is less important than the obedience to God that is constitutive of true
human living; promises of divine protection should not be used in such

a way as to diminish the trust they are meant to engender; realisation of God's promises should not be sought in seemingly speedy ways that compromise loyalty to God (Matt 4:1–11). Jesus twice highlights a fundamental prophetic sentiment, 'I desire mercy, not sacrifice' (Hos 6:6; cf. 1 Sam 15:22), and challenges his interlocutors, who, of course, are familiar with the notion, to go away and learn what it really means (Matt 9:13, 12:7). Jesus critiques a preoccupation with detailed niceties of religious observance through a challenge to attend to 'the weightier matters of the law: justice and mercy and faithfulness' (without neglecting detailed observances [Matt 23:23]). Most famously, Jesus specifies that the two most important commandments are to love God and one's neighbour, and that these are a key to the Old Testament as a whole (Matt 22:34–40).

On the other hand, there is Matthew's own use of the Old Testament in his framing some of the episodes in his narrative. With small variations of wording, there are nine occurrences of the formula 'This was to fulfil [or "then was fulfilled"] what was spoken by the prophet, saying...'.[20] The most famous of these is the first, 1:22–3, where the angel's message to Joseph that Mary has conceived a child by the Holy Spirit is said by Matthew to be in fulfilment of Isaiah 7:14 (in the Septuagint), 'Behold the virgin shall conceive...'. Commentators ancient and modern have regularly pointed out that the sense of Isaiah 7:14 in its own context (in Hebrew) neither implies virginal conception nor envisages a long-range prediction only to be realised many centuries later. In other words, the Isaiah text is given a re-contextualisation by Matthew that leaves unclear the sense in which this 'fulfils' what the Old Testament says. Modern interpreters vary widely in their evaluation of Matthew's fulfilment formulae. To some, these formulae represent arbitrary and forced proof-texting, the kind of thing which gives Christian use of the Old Testament a bad name; to others, they represent a subtle and imaginative drawing out of larger patterns within the Old Testament. Either way, this is a use of the Old Testament strikingly different from the use made by Jesus. The puzzle is that Matthew wrote both.

A CHRISTIAN APPROACH TO THE SHEMA

Another instructive example is afforded by characteristic Christian approaches to that passage which Judaism has considered foundational, the Shema (Deut 6:4–9):

> Hear, O Israel: YHWH our God, YHWH is the one and only.[21] So you shall love YHWH your God with all your heart, and with all your

being, and with all your might. These words that I am commanding
you today are to be in your heart; repeat them to your children, and
speak of them when you are at home and when you are away, when
you lie down and when you get up. Bind them as a sign on your
hand, and let them be as emblems on your forehead, and write them
on the doorposts of your house and on your gates.

Judaism has historically focussed upon this as a key text for Jewish identity and practice,[22] which seems in line with the intrinsic significance
of the text. Deuteronomy contains theological perspectives which are
formative for much of the Old Testament; the verses cited are the key-
note of Moses' address to Israel in the light of his appointment to speak
for YHWH (Deut 5:22–33), and the content of this passage, both the proclamation of YHWH as the sole recipient of Israel's undivided allegiance
and the importance attached to the pondering, teaching, and displaying
of this proclamation, highlight the text's intrinsic significance. Down
the ages, Jews have framed their activities and their sense of time by
reciting these words at the end and beginning of each day (in line with
verse 7b), and for many, these words have been their dying utterance,
often in contexts of martyrdom, from Aqiba under the Romans (b. Ber
61b) to countless Jews under the Nazis. Moreover, although Jews have
disagreed over the precise understanding of the injunctions to 'bind' and
'write' and have varied in their practices, it has nonetheless been characteristic that these words have led to specific practices symbolic of Jewish
identity and allegiance.

So, for example, the Mishnah, the first authoritative post-biblical
codification of Jewish thought and practice, begins with tractate
Berakoth, whose opening line is 'From what time in the evening may the
Shema' be recited?'[23] There is no question whether the Shema should
be recited; Jewish practice in conformity with the biblical injunction
is presupposed, and so the question concerns when. If the biblical text
indicates recital in evening and morning, the first question to discuss
is the parameters of evening and morning: how late or early can one
be in relation to each and still count as fulfilling the requirement?
The tractate then moves on to consider possible distractions, difficulties and hard cases,[24] all with a view to clarifying and enabling faithful observance of this core religious obligation. In continuity with this
perspective, a modern scholarly Jewish commentary on Deuteronomy,
such as that of Jeffrey Tigay,[25] devotes considerable space not only to
interpretation of the biblical injunctions but also to discussing issues
of practical observance (even if primarily in a historical rather than a
contemporary mode).

A Christian approach is, unsurprisingly, rooted in the gospel portrayal of Jesus. According to Matthew and Mark (Matt 22:34–40; Mark 12:28–34)[26] Jesus, when asked which commandment in the law took pre-eminence, responds with the injunction to love God wholly and unreservedly (Deut 6:5), to which he conjoins the command to 'love your neighbour as yourself' (Lev 19:18). Although in speaking thus Jesus stands firmly within Jewish tradition,[27] Christian tradition has often fixed on this double love commandment as a convenient shorthand summary of the Christian life. Augustine, for example, in his *On Christian Teaching*, took the command to love God and neighbour as the key to, and purpose of, biblical interpretation as a whole. Moreover, the double-love commandment has received frequent use within Christian liturgies. Although this does indeed direct Christian attention to the Shema, it does so peculiarly. Not only is there some tendency (as already in Matt 22:37) to refer to loving God without the preceding affirmation about Israel's God as the one and only, which can diminish the sense of loving God as a realisation of Israel's true identity; the injunctions about remembering, teaching, displaying, and writing the all-important preceding words also become separated and get lost.

By way of contrast with the Mishnah's opening concern with practical observance, it is instructive to consider a recent anthology of early Christian commentators on Deuteronomy 6:4–9, who are generally somewhat later in date than the Mishnah but remain comparable as representatives of antiquity.[28] The editor provides extensive discussion of verses 4 and 5 by numerous commentators who focus both on the oneness of God and on love. Yet, on verses 6–9, no early Christian commentator is quoted, and although the section is headed '6:4–9 The Great Commandment', only the text of verses 4 and 5 is cited by the editor at the head of the section; verses 6–9 have disappeared. Even if the anthology is not exhaustive, it is surely representative; as such, its disinterest in verses 6–9 is telling of Christian assumptions.

Among modern Christian commentators on the Old Testament, Gerhard von Rad is widely recognised as outstanding, not least in his concerns to relate the Old Testament to Christian faith. In his commentary on Deuteronomy, von Rad devotes 581 words to 6:4–9.[29] Of these, 451 words are devoted to verses 4 and 5, whilst only 130 words are devoted to verses 6–9. He notes the problem of the referent of 'these words' in verse 6a; he remarks on the 'intensity of the spirituality' in verses 6–9; and he concludes

It is not clear what significance is attached to the tokens which were to serve as reminders and so forth. Probably we still have to do here with a figurative mode of expression, which was then later understood literally and led to the use of the so-called phylacteries.

Von Rad seems not greatly interested in the text. Neither analogous ancient Near Eastern practices nor extensive Jewish debates and varying practices merit any mention. Many other Christian commentaries on the text display proportions comparable to those of von Rad in their allocation of space. Whilst the more scholarly linger a little on whether verses 8 and 9 are metaphorical or literal, with some inclination towards recognising that the original sense may well have been literal,[30] some of the more popularly oriented treatments have hardened von Rad's 'probably ... figurative' into a bald assertion of fact,[31] in the kind of way which may imply that predominant historic Jewish practice, which has sought actually to do what the text says, shows a misunderstanding based on a regrettable legalistic attachment to the letter of the text rather than its spirit.[32]

Surely this disinterest in verses 6–9 is a corollary of Christians feeling under no obligation to do what the text says – despite verses 6–9 being one of the more extended and emphatic sets of related injunctions in the Old Testament. When Christians do feel under obligation to do what the biblical text says, then the engagement with the text becomes endlessly more extensive – if one considers, for example, Christian commentary down the ages on the Lord's Prayer or the eucharistic words of Jesus. This Christian 'sitting light' to verses 6–9 is rooted partly in the disappearance of these verses in Christian usage of verses 4 and 5, and more substantively in the fact that Christian identity centres on the person of Jesus. The words that Christians most regularly recite are the words that Jesus taught his disciples, the Lord's Prayer; and the symbol of identity and allegiance that Christians display on their person and their buildings is the cross. A centre of gravity other than that envisaged in Deuteronomy leads to a set of practises other than those envisaged in Deuteronomy.

Yet it is worth asking why Christian practice should replace, rather than supplement, the Deuteronomic prescription. If one asks ordinary Christians why they do not do what the biblical text specifies as well as saying the Lord's Prayer and displaying a cross,[33] the prime answer tends to be some form of 'Well, we just don't'; that is, the practice is not a recognised part of Christian tradition. Another answer is 'That's what Jews do' – because doing what Deuteronomy prescribes is a recognised distinctive of Jewish identity, Christians feel that they should not do something that implies Jewishness. Either way, although Christians still (in principle) seek to practice, teach and display love for the one and only God, they do not obey the Deuteronomic prescription because of the growth of a distinctively Christian identity and practice from earliest times.

All this revealingly illustrates something of the intrinsically differentiated Christian stance towards the Old Testament. The content is appropriated unevenly and comes to function differently in its Christian context – a fact to which, of course, attention is often drawn in relation to issues more contentious than the Shema, not least, at present, Christian use of the Old Testament for formulating appropriate disciplines for sexual (including homosexual) practises. Although one can formulate a kind of general Christian rationale along the lines of 'adopt and apply the principles more than the practices', this stance does not really do justice to the complexities involved when the Old Testament is read and appropriated in contexts where the focus upon Jesus entails a re-contextualisation and re-configuration of those scriptures in ways which they themselves do not envisage.

CLASSIC CHRISTIAN HERMENEUTICAL STRATEGIES

The recognition that Christian faith leads to a re-contextualisation of Israel's Scriptures has been foundational to classic Christian approaches down the ages. A paradigmatic example is Luke's account of the risen Jesus' pointing the puzzled disciples on the Emmaus Road to 'Moses and all the prophets' (Luke 24:25–7). In context, where the disciples know clearly the facts of Jesus' ministry and of angelic reports of an empty tomb, and yet are miserable (24:17–24), the risen Jesus is offering that which will enable them at last to understand him. And since he has returned from the dead and might be expected to be able to make startling new revelations on that basis, it is the more striking that he appeals to existing Scripture as that which is necessary to understanding; that is, Jesus cannot be understood without the Old Testament. But since the disciples were already thoroughly familiar with the Old Testament yet had not hitherto managed to understand Jesus on this basis, it is clear that some fresh way of reading related to Jesus' passion is required (24:26); that is, the Old Testament cannot be understood without Jesus. This dialectic between Jesus and Israel's Scriptures, each necessary for the understanding of the other, implies that Christian reading of the Old Testament has as its corollary a Jesus-centred frame of reference.

To be sure, modern historical-critical scholarship has emphasised the benefits, practical and existential, as well as academic, of understanding the texts within the Old Testament as ancient texts with meanings related to their world of origin. Nonetheless, this does not deny that when the texts are read and appropriated within Christian contexts, there may still be necessary re-contextualisations. Rather, it clarifies that there is a dual task for contemporary Christian faith, both to do justice to the texts in their originating pre-Christian frame of reference and within their acquired Christian frame of reference.[34] It must be recognised, however, that for much of Christian history this distinction was not clearly made; the latter task obscured the former.

One classic Reformation strategy, with older roots, was to introduce accessible conceptual distinctions in order to clarify how and why the Old Testament still functions within a Christian context. As the Thirty Nine Articles in the Anglican *Book of Common Prayer* put it, in Article VII about the Old Testament,

> Although the Law given from God by Moses, as touching Ceremonies and Rites, do not bind Christian men, nor the Civil precepts thereof ought of necessity to be received in any commonwealth; yet not-withstanding, no Christian man whatsoever is freed from the obedience of the Commandments which are called Moral.

The logic is plain: the ceremonial/ritual has been fulfilled in the sacrificial death of Christ, the civil applied to the context of ancient Israel, whilst the moral is enduringly valid. It has often been observed that such distinctions do not do justice to, and can indeed impede understanding of, the Old Testament laws in their originating frames of reference, whose conceptualities are quite other. Nonetheless, the distinctions were not devised in the service of ancient historical understanding but rather to serve as a comprehensible rule of thumb for Christian appropriation.

Moreover, although a clear distinction between originating frames of reference and Christian frames of reference is in principle helpful, in practice there are many grey areas, especially relating to the fact that already within the Old Testament there is extensive re-contextualisation of material. This can encourage metaphorical and analogical modes of reading which anticipate certain characteristic Christian modes of reading. If the titles which relate many of the Psalms to David and to particular episodes in his life are, as appears likely, secondary additions which attest an imaginative shift within the understanding and use of the Psalms already within the Old Testament period, then the classical Christian relating of the Psalms to David and the Messiah is already adumbrated by such re-contextualisation.[35]

Another interesting example is afforded by the paradigm problem of 'ethnic cleansing' in Joshua 1–12. A characteristic Christian mode of reading is exemplified by Origen (c. 185–c. 254), from whom we have the oldest extant corpus of Christian homilies on the Old Testament. Origen recognised that the text of Joshua was about warfare and that, as such, it could incite its readers to violence (which he states pejoratively as a matter of fact):

> When that Israel which is according to the flesh read these same Scriptures before the coming of our Lord Jesus Christ, they under-stood nothing in them except wars and the shedding of blood, from which their spirits, too, were incited to excessive savageries and were always fed by wars and strife.[36]

However, Origen is clear that the coming of Jesus changes things; Jesus 'teaches us peace from this very reading of wars',[37] which happens when the biblical text is read metaphorically in terms of moral and spiritual warfare:

> We shall not fight in the same manner as the ancients fought. Nor are the battles in our land to be conducted against humans 'but against sovereigns, against authorities, against the rulers of darkness of this world' [Eph 6:12]. Certainly you understand now where you must undertake struggles of this kind.[38]

And again:

> And therefore, according to the teaching of our Lord Jesus Christ, when we indeed read these things, we also equip ourselves and are roused for battle, but against those enemies that 'proceed from our heart': obviously, 'evil thought, thefts, false testimony, slanders' [Matt. 15:19], and other similar adversaries of the soul. Following what this Scripture sets forth, we try, if it can be done, not to leave behind any 'who may be saved or who may breathe' [Josh 10:40].[39]

Modern biblical scholarship has sometimes been dismissive of such a reading of the text as a forced evasion of its plain sense. Yet Origen's clear concern is with how the texts should be read in a Christian frame of reference: that is, re-contextualised in the light of Jesus.

Moreover, modern biblical scholarship itself has made the reading of the Joshua narratives less straightforward. On the one hand, there is a picture of incomplete Israelite occupation of Canaan in the book of Judges, which has long been recognised to stand in some tension with the narrative of Joshua 1–12. Also, archaeological evidence has generally been recognised not to support the historicity of the conquest account. On the other hand, scholars are inclined to date the composition of the narrative to centuries after the scenario it envisages. What if, therefore, one were to posit that the Joshua narrative might never have been intended to tell the history of the conquest (as that might be understood today) but rather was meant to serve a different purpose?

Within the storyline, the interest is not in the details of battles or body counts[40] but rather in certain episodes set within the conflict. The most detailed narrative is Joshua 2, which features a Canaanite prostitute – an entirely unpromising figure in Old Testament terms. Yet Rahab offers a full acknowledgement of YHWH (2:9–13) – and deals with the Israelite spies in a way that exemplifies 'steadfast love' (*ḥesed*, v. 12), a prime quality of YHWH himself (Exod 34:6–7), so that both she and her family are spared and become part of Israel (6:22–5). The only narrative that depicts explicit sin features Achan, who has an impeccable pedigree within the tribe of Judah, yet brings death upon himself and his family (7:1–26). The one who should be killed acts faithfully and lives; the one who should live acts faithlessly and dies. Just as the 1997 film *Titanic* uses the known story of the sinking of the *Titanic* to portray a love story set against the backdrop of the ship's voyage, it may be that Joshua 1–12 is a narrative about the paradoxical boundaries of Israel's identity as the people of YHWH in relation to living by *torah*, set against a backdrop of demarcating conflict.[41]

At the very least, the reading of Joshua appears to be intrinsically open to more possibilities than may initially be suggested by concerns about 'ethnic cleansing'. Indeed, it would be a pleasing irony if modern scholarship began to find common ground with Origen in terms of reading the text metaphorically.

CONCLUSION

'The more things change, the more they remain the same.' This epigram could well sum up the role of the Old Testament in Christianity. Although the modern debates have complexities undreamed of in antiquity, and although there are no straight lines from Marcion to Harnack and Bultmann or from Irenaeus to von Rad and Childs, there are nonetheless real continuities, continuities which sometimes become clearer the deeper one goes into the debates. Moreover, I have suggested that the continuing debates are a sign of life, evidence of engagement with the challenges of what really constitutes authentic Christian living and thinking.

In conclusion, it would be appropriate to note the capacity of the Old Testament to surprise and enrich its Christian readers in unanticipated ways. Three features from recent years may be noted. First is the re-discovery of the value of the lament psalms as potent resources for honest expression of some of the difficulties of trusting God in a world that is often painful and puzzling. Second is the re-discovery of the principle of debt remission, the Jubilee (Leviticus 25), which recently played a significant role in a major international campaign to ease the debt problems of poor countries today. Third is the re-discovery of the value of Jewish tradition and interpretation, which has helped many Christians escape from negative stereotypes about what Jews mean by faithful adherence to *torah*, as part of learning to recognise important common ground between Christians and Jews. If there are comparable re-discoveries yet to come in the years ahead, the role of the Old Testament within Christianity should continue to be richly fruitful.

NOTES

1   A. H. J. Gunneweg, *Understanding the Old Testament*, trans. by John Bowden (OTL; London: SCM Press, 1978), 2. Gunneweg is writing in the context of introducing his book on the subject, so one might suspect a degree of rhetorical over-statement. Nonetheless, his basic point, that understanding the role of the Old Testament is integral to the content and self-understanding of Christian faith, is unarguable.

2   E.g., both the command to love YHWH unreservedly (Deuteronomy 6) and the command to put to the ban the seven nations of the land (Deuteronomy 7) are less straightforward in meaning than they may initially appear (see my 'Toward an Interpretation of the Shema' in *Theological Exegesis: Essays in Honor of Brevard S. Childs*, ed. by Christopher Seitz and Kathryn Greene-McCreight [Grand Rapids, MI: Eerdmans: 1999], 124–44).

3   It is not possible to do justice to the subtlety and complexity of Luther (still less his appropriation in nineteenth- and twentieth-century liberal Lutheranism) in a few words. Nonetheless, to put matters baldly, Luther developed a foundational theological dialectic between law and gospel; and, although he found both law and gospel in the Old Testament, he found there more of the former than the latter, and this generated ambivalence towards the Old Testament.

4   Adolf von Harnack, *Marcion: das Evangelium vom fremden Gott. Eine Monographie zur Geschichte der Grundlegung der katholischen Kirche* (Darmstadt, Germany: Wissenschaftliche Buchgesellschaft, 1921), 248f, as cited in Heikki Räisänen, 'Attacking the Book, Not the People: Marcion

and the Jewish Roots of Christianity' in his *Marcion, Muhammad and the Mahatma* (London: SCM Press, 1999), 64–80 (77).

5 Brevard S. Childs, *Old Testament Theology in a Canonical Context* (London: SCM Press, 1985), 28.

6 This point has often been made in modern biblical scholarship, though only in recent years has it led to a new respect for Jewish faith and tradition both ancient and modern. Julius Wellhausen famously wrote, 'Jesus was not a Christian, but a Jew' ('*Jesus war kein Christ, sondern Jude*', in his *Einleitung in die drei ersten Evangelien* [Berlin: Reimer, 1905], 113), and yet was notoriously negative towards Judaism.

7 In my paraphrase here I cannot do justice to all the distinctive Matthean emphases within the telling of the story.

8 Of course, Paul elsewhere says other, more positive things about the law (Rom 7:12) and can speak of fulfilling the commandments (Rom 13:8–10). So the tenor of Paul himself varies from context to context. My use of Galatians 3 is heuristic, to highlight the challenge of diversity within the New Testament with reference to pre- and post-Easter contexts.

9 Rudolf Bultmann, *Theology of the New Testament*, vol. I, trans. by Kendrick Grobel (London: SCM Press, 1952), 3.

10 Bultmann observes: 'Thus Luther has already rightly perceived that Jesus, in so far as he is engaged in teaching, is not different from the Old Testament prophets; rather, like them, he proclaimed the Law and consequently belongs within the Old Testament' ('The Significance of the Old Testament for Christian Faith', in *The Old Testament and Christian Faith*, ed. by Bernhard W. Anderson [London: SCM Press, 1964], 8–35, 12).

11 'Prophecy and Fulfilment', in *Essays on Old Testament Interpretation*, ed. by Claus Westermann (London: SCM Press, 1963), 50–75; 'Significance', 8–35.

12 'Significance', 29.

13 'Prophecy', 72.

14 'Significance', 31.

15 Ibid., 17.

16 Ibid., 12.

17 Francis Watson, *Text and Truth: Redefining Biblical Theology* (Edinburgh, UK: T & T Clark, 1997), 168.

18 Ronald Heine offers the image of a 'message of Jesus' that is 'largely severed from its roots in the Old Testament Scriptures' as being a 'cut-flower faith' (*Reading the Old Testament with the Ancient Church* [Grand Rapids, MI: Baker Academic, 2007], 11).

19 My use of "Matthew" is conventional, without prejudice towards questions of ancient authorial identity.

20 Matt. 1:22–3, 2:15, 2:17–18, 2:23, 4:14–16, 8:17, 12:17–21, 21:4–5, 27:9–10. A tenth example is 2:5–6, though this is set on the lips of characters within the narrative.

21 I have discussed the construal of *'eḥad*, and other interpretive issues, in my 'Toward an Interpretation of the Shema', 124–44.

22 I am oversimplifying the practice of morning and evening prayers, where Deut 6:4–9 is recited in conjunction with Deut 11:13–21 and Num 15:37–41.

23 Herbert Danby, ed., *The Mishnah* (Oxford, UK: Clarendon Press, 1933), 2.

24 E.g., 2:5, 'A bridegroom is exempt from reciting the *Shema* on the first night, or until the close of the [next] Sabbath if he has not consummated the marriage. Once when Rabban Gamaliel married he recited the *Shema* on the first night. His disciples said to him, "Master, didst thou not teach us that a bridegroom is exempt from reciting the *Shema* on the first night?" He said to them, "I will not hearken to you to cast off from myself the yoke of the kingdom of heaven even for a moment."'

25 Jeffrey Tigay, *Deuteronomy* (JPS Torah Commentary; Philadelphia: Jewish Publication Society, 5756/1996), 76–9, 438–44.

26 There are complexities within the tradition, for only in Mark's account does Jesus cite Deut 6:4, whilst in Luke's account (Luke 10:25–28) it is the questioning lawyer, rather than Jesus, who links the two love commandments.

27 The Lukan portrayal of the lawyer linking the commandments, together with the scribe within the Markan account instantly acknowledging the rightness of Jesus' double love commandment (rather than expressing astonishment), implies that the linkage of the love commandments was not a novelty on Jesus' part but rather an articulation of a live issue of understanding and interpreting Scripture among his contemporaries.

28 Joseph T. Lienhard, ed., *Ancient Christian Commentary on Scripture: Old Testament III: Exodus, Leviticus, Numbers, Deuteronomy* (Downers Grove, IL: IVP Press, 2001), 282–5.

29 Gerhard von Rad, *Deuteronomy: A Commentary*, trans. by Dorothea Barton (OTL; London: SCM Press, 1966), 63–4. For convenience, my word count is based on the English translation.

30 E.g., A. D. H. Mayes, *Deuteronomy* (NCB; London: Marshall, Morgan and Scott, 1979), 177.

31 'What was given originally as a metaphor became for later Jews a literal injunction' (J. A. Thompson, *Deuteronomy* [Tyndale Old Testament Commentaries; London: IVP Press, 1974], 123); 'originally this order was understood metaphorically, but later it was interpreted literally and led to the wearing of phylacteries' (Anthony Phillips, *Deuteronomy* [CBC; Cambridge University Press, 1973], 57–8.

32 In recent years, however, there is more distancing from this pejorative attitude with a corresponding finding of more significance in the text. So, for example, Christopher Wright says, 'Christian readers of 6:8–9 may be tempted to dismiss the Jewish use of *tefillin* ... and *mezuzot* ... as unnecessary literalism.... However, the question is whether we are any more serious or successful in flavoring the whole of life with conscious attention to the law of God (v. 7, which is not at all "symbolic") as a personal, familial, and social strategy for living out our commitment to loving God totally' (*Deuteronomy* [NIBCOT; Peabody, MA: Hendrickson, 1996], 100).

33 I have asked this question on a number of occasions but confess that my 'research' is anecdotal rather than systematic.

34 There is a triple task if one includes understanding and respecting Jewish interpretation and appropriation.

35 The classic modern essay is Brevard S. Childs, 'Psalm Titles and Midrashic Exegesis', *JSS* 16 (1971): 137–50.

36 Origen, *Homilies on Joshua*, Homily 14:1, ed. by Cynthia White; trans. by Barbara Bruce (FC 105; Washington, DC: Catholic University of America Press, 2002), 130.
37 Ibid.
38 Homily 12:1 in *Homilies*, 121.
39 Homily 14:1 in *Homilies*, 130.
40 In the account of Jericho (Joshua 6), the interest is overwhelmingly in Israel's ritual actions and the exceptional treatment allowed for Rahab and her family. The actual overthrow of Jericho is told briefly; the accounts of victories in Joshua 10–12 become increasingly brief and stylised.
41 See further Douglas S. Earl, *Reading Joshua as Christian Scripture* (Journal of Theological Interpretation Supplements 2; Winona Lake, IN: Eisenbrauns, 2010); also, in more popular format, Earl, *The Joshua Delusion? Rethinking Genocide in the Bible* (Eugene, OR: Cascade, 2010).

FURTHER READING

Anderson, Bernhard W., ed. *The Old Testament and Christian Faith*. London: SCM Press, 1964.
Bright, John. *The Authority of the Old Testament*. Nashville, TN: Abingdon, 1967.
Childs, Brevard S. *Old Testament Theology in a Canonical Context*. London: SCM Press, 1985.
Gunneweg, A. H. J. *Understanding the Old Testament* (OTL). Translated by John Bowden. London: SCM Press, 1978.
Levenson, Jon D. *The Hebrew Bible, the Old Testament, and Historical Criticism*. Louisville, KY: Westminster John Knox, 1993.
Mowinckel, Sigmund. *The Old Testament as Word of God*. Translated by Reidar B. Bjornard. Nashville, TN: Abingdon, 1959.
Pontifical Biblical Commission. *The Jewish People and Their Sacred Scriptures in the Christian Bible*. Boston: Pauline Books and Media, 2002.
Seitz, Christopher R. *Word Without End: The Old Testament as Abiding Theological Witness*. Grand Rapids, MI: Eerdmans, 1998.
Thompson, John L. *Reading the Bible with the Dead: What You Can Learn from the History of Exegesis That You Can't Learn from Exegesis Alone*. Grand Rapids, MI: Eerdmans, 2007.
Westermann, Claus, ed. *Essays on Old Testament Interpretation*. Edited and translated by James Luther Mays. London: SCM Press, 1963.
Young, Frances M. *Biblical Exegesis and the Formation of Christian Culture*. Cambridge University Press: 1997.

20 The Hebrew Bible in Islam

WALID A. SALEH

The earliest Islamic creed preserved in the Qur'an states that Muslims 'believe in God, His angels, His scriptures, and His messengers' and that Muslims should make 'no distinction among any of His messengers' (Q. 2:285). The formulation of this creed has much to do with the introduction of monotheism to Arabia. Although neither scripture nor prophecy was given credence as a paradigm of human interaction with the gods by the pre-Islamic Arabs, they were to become essential elements of the new faith. Thus, much energy and time are devoted in the Qur'an to defending the existence of divinely revealed scriptures and the office of prophecy. This terse creed is used also in polemical retorts with the Jews and Christians who were telling Muslims to 'become Jews or Christians, and you will be rightly guided'. The Muslims are asked to say, 'No, ours is the religion of Abraham, the upright, who did not worship any god besides God. So say: "We believe in God and in what was sent down to us and what was sent down to Abraham, Ishmael, Isaac, Jacob and the Tribes, and what was given to Moses, Jesus, and all the prophets by their Lord. We make no distinction between any of them, and we devote ourselves to Him"' (Q. 2:135–136). The creed asks Muslims to uphold the truth of the Scripture of Judaism but sees in that commitment no barrier to accepting the Qur'an as Scripture of the same status.

As a matter of faith, then, Muslims are supposed to believe that God sent revelation to humanity. The most important examples given in the Qur'an of such revealed Scriptures are the Torah of Moses (*tawrāt*), the Gospels of Jesus (*injīl*, here the Qur'an gives to Jesus what he never claimed to have), and the Psalms of David (*zābūr*). Many of the arguments in the Qur'an use the existence of these models as evidence for the divine origins of the new Scripture being revealed to the Arabs. Indeed, the nature of the Qur'an as Scripture is understood in the self-presentation of the Qur'an to be the same as that of the Torah and the Gospels.

Attempting to characterise the position of the Qur'an towards the Hebrew Bible is anything but simple. First, it is not clear how much of the Hebrew Bible the Qur'an has in mind when it refers to 'the book of Moses', the Torah. Although the Qur'an is mainly concerned with Moses and the Patriarchs, it does know of David and Solomon; moreover, the knowledge in the Qur'an of Jewish Scripture is mediated through a mid-rashic prism. A precise answer to this question, that is, how much of the Torah the Qur'an knows, is thus impossible.[1] To argue, however, that the Qur'an knows of the Bible only what it presents is also indefens-ible. One could conceive of Muhammad knowing much of the Hebrew Bible yet choosing not to make much of it part of his presentation. There is actually an ambivalence in the Qur'an towards certain periods of Israelite religious history, notably the period of the judges.[2] Whatever was the case, the presentation of biblical material in the Qur'an is done with utter conviction about the veracity of the version being told. There is no hesitation or self-doubt. God is telling Muhammad *the* story (cf. Q. 20:99, 40:78).

Second, there are contradictory, though not irreconcilable, positions expressed in the Qur'an vis-à-vis the authority and authenticity of the Scriptures of Judaism and Christianity. There are many instances where these Scriptures are called upon to vindicate Muhammad; they are called 'light and guidance', and their truth is such that they make manifest the truth of the Qur'an. Muhammad pleads with his people to query the 'People of the Book', a phrase invented by the Qur'an. The People of the Book are in a position to vouchsafe for the truth of the prophecy of Muhammad. Yet there are verses where the authenticity of these very Scriptures is called into doubt. The Jews are accused of tampering with their Scripture, corrupting it and violating God's will. How do we under-stand these statements, and more importantly, how were they under-stood by successive generations of Muslims?

THE SCRIPTURES OF GOD

Rudi Paret has spoken of the tendency of the Qur'an to standardise (*typi-sieren*) monotheistic history.[3] Human history is seen as a series of simi-lar prophetic eras: God sends a prophet to a nation to guide it to Him, only to repeat this process again; usually these prophets have Scriptures and miracles to vindicate them. Muhammad is one such prophet in this history. The Meccans, meanwhile, did not regard prophecy as a legitimate phenomenon. The thrust of the arguments in the Qur'an is thus not whether Muhammad is a true or a false prophet, alternatives that presuppose in the first place an acceptance of the notion of proph-ecy, but whether prophecy itself, which entailed in this case scriptural authority, is a valid phenomenon. The same attitude held for divinely revealed Scriptures – the Meccans denied the existence of such a thing as revealed books. In defending its claims, the Qur'an raises repeatedly the histories of Judaism (particularly the story of Moses and the Patriarchs) and Christianity (the life of Jesus and his Gospel). What Muhammad is doing has been done before. Moreover, the Qur'an presents Jews and Christians as possessors of knowledge (*dhikr*, *'ilm*) and books (*kitāb*). They had already experienced the prophetic phase that the Arabs were now experiencing, and each already possessed a book. Confused Arabs should ask them about the claims of Muhammad.

Chapter 16 of the Qur'an, *sūrat al-naḥl*, is a good example of the use of Jewish and Christian antecedents to argue for the veracity of Scripture and prophecy. Verse Q. 16:24 records the mockery of the Meccans regarding Scripture: 'When they are asked, "What has your Lord sent down?" they say, "Ancient Fables." ' This is an oft-repeated sarcasm levelled by the Meccans against Muhammad's new scripture. It is not divine; it is nothing but fables. Prophecy is defended in Q. 16:36 by reference to the prophetic paradigm of human history: 'We sent a messenger to every community, saying, "Worship God and shun false gods." ' Both prophecy and Scripture are again defended in verse Q. 16:43–5, when the Qur'an asks the Meccans to query people of knowledge (*dhikr*): 'All the messengers We sent before you were simply men to whom We had given the Revelation: you people can ask those who have knowledge if you do not know. We sent them with clear signs and scriptures.' There is no doubt that Jews and Christians are denoted by the epithet 'people who have knowledge'. The word *dhikr* ('knowledge', 'scripture') is used extensively in the Qur'an, and it clearly is connected to Scripture and revelation (cf. Q. 21:7 also).

Indeed, many of the arguments presented in another chapter (13) are cemented by the testament of those who 'have been given the Book'. They, meaning those who possess Scripture, are overjoyed with what Muhammad has been receiving from God (Q. 13:36). Those who have the knowledge of the Book are called upon to act as witnesses to the truth of Muhammad's prophethood (Q. 13:43): 'They say, "You have not been sent." Say, "God – and those who have knowledge of the Scripture – are sufficient witness between us." ' These instances of calling upon Christians and Jews to step forward to support Muhammad's claims are remarkable in so far as they are not mixed with reservations or qualifications. The tone of the Qur'an towards Jews and Christians would soon harden considerably as Muhammad realised that being a monotheist did not win him any support.

We should not be surprised, however, to see such a positive attitude towards the Scriptures of Judaism and Christianity at the outset of Muhammad's career. The whole message of the Qur'an, as the Qur'an tirelessly repeats, is nothing but a recapitulation of the same essence of the Jewish and Christian faith in Arabic for the Arabs. The Qur'an is to be the Scripture of the Arabs, just as the Torah and the Gospels were the Scripture of the Jews and the Christians, respectively. Drawing an analogy between the history of the Jews and the Christians, on one hand, and the history of Muhammad with his fellow Arabs, on the other, was essential for the claims of the Qur'an. In many ways, Jewish history is pivotal for Muhammad's claims, just as Jewish Scripture is said to be the vindication of the Qur'an. The Qur'an at no point hides or belittles the connection to its Jewish paradigm. Ultimately, the Qur'an saw itself as the continuation of the history of Judaism and Christianity.

The Meccans were not swayed by this affinity. Faced with the parallels Muhammad was drawing between himself and Moses, the Meccans mockingly insisted on a replication of the Mosaic model, a book descending physically from heaven unto Muhammad – this was one among many demands placed on Muhammad to prove his prophetic identity. Neither Muhammad nor the Qur'an could answer to such a challenge because both refused performing miracles as a precondition for faith. The Qur'an, however, insists on calling its verses *āyah* ('signs' or 'miracles'), thus turning the table on the Meccans. Now Scripture itself is taken to be a sign of God. Revelation, a verbal inspiration that prophets proclaimed to their people, is *the* sign from God. In the case of Muhammad, it would be the sufficient sign; he would refuse to perform any of the miracles demanded of him, although the Qur'an does admit that Moses and Jesus performed such deeds – a contradiction that places the Qur'an in an unenviable position. Muhammad's Qur'an is to suffice. Scripture is thus made central in the world of the Qur'an, the sole connection between God and humanity.[4] Moreover, Scripture is both the message (a promise of salvation) and the medium (its very word is miraculous).

There is thus a rather developed notion in the Qur'an of what Scripture is, what it should look like, and what its supposed function is in monotheistic history – what has been called the 'self-referentiality' of the Qur'an.[5] The Qur'an speaks of itself as a Scripture and demands to be treated as one. This understanding of Scripture is projected back onto the Torah and the Gospels, and it determines how the Qur'an understands what the Torah is and what the Gospels are. In this sense, the past is made into the image of what Muhammad was experiencing. There is a lot of such backward projection in the Qur'an. The life of Moses is seen as a replication of Muhammad's life and the previous Scriptures as earlier Qur'ans. Earlier Scriptures were verbal inspirations to the prophets on hand (i.e., Moses and Jesus), proclaimed to their peoples, and enshrined as books. These books therefore must be scrupulously preserved. To later Muslims, any deviation from this model meant that the Jewish and Christian Scriptures were no longer divine.

Scriptures are also placed at the centre of any religious community. Thus, the Qur'an calls the Torah a 'guidance and light', a book of rules to be followed that guarantees salvation (Q. 4:44), just as it would call the Qur'an. Indeed, the Qur'an reserves much of its poetic language for extolling the potency of Scripture, its effect on believers, its over-whelming cosmic power and its sheer salvific fiat (cf. the famous verse Q. 59:21 'If We had sent down this Qur'an upon a mountain, you would have seen it humbled and split apart in its awe of God; and those similitudes – We strike them for men, so that they may reflect'). Obeying the word of the Scriptures becomes a central issue in the Qur'an; the role of the prophet (nabī) is equated, if not relegated, to that of a 'messenger' (rasūl), a herald of God's will expressed in verbal utterances that convey the divine commands. Finally, Scriptures vindicate each other; thus, the Gospels were sent down to vindicate the Torah (Q. 3:50, 5:46), just as the Qur'an is sent down to vindicate the Gospels and the Torah (Q. 27:76).

THE JUDGEMENT OF THE QUR'AN

The Qur'an, however, regards itself as more than just a vindication of the Torah; it is also a judge and an arbitrator of its authenticity. The Qur'an outlines this position (Q. 5:48) in the following manner:

> We sent to you [Muhammad] the Scripture with the truth, confirm-ing the Scriptures that came before it, and with final authority over them: so judge between them according to what God has sent down. Do not follow their whims, which deviate from the truth that has come to you. We have assigned a law and a path to each of you. If God has so willed, He would have made you one community, but He wanted to test you through that which He has given you, so race to do good: you will return to God and He will make clear to you mat-ters you differed about.

This quotation sums up what could be called the 'constructive ambiv-alence' of the Qur'an towards the Scripture of Judaism and Christianity. The Qur'an acknowledges the status of the Torah, its divine origin, and its central character: it is a book of guidance and divine command. It is also the law of its nation, the foundation of its life. Coming so late after Christianity and Judaism, Islam could hardly deny the Torah its standing. The Qur'an is, nevertheless, ambivalent about how much authority it wants to accord to the Bible. There are clear statements in the Qur'an that the Torah was a good enough book for the Jews; they should follow it, and God will be pleased with them (Q.5:66–9). As such, there is no abrogation of 'the book of Moses', just a restriction of its efficacy to the Jews. The Qur'an is asking the Jews to believe in Muhammad to the degree that it is confirming their faith, not replacing it. The Qur'an sees the Torah as a book for a nation, which means that other nations have the right to their own books.

One could describe the judgements of the Qur'an on the status of the Torah as situational. The Qur'an can issue a damning judgement if the issue is the denial of Muhammad's prophecy or the truthfulness of the Qur'an. To the degree that the Jews are claiming their Torah is not in agreement with the Qur'an, then either they are hiding the true Scripture or the Scripture they claim to quote is falsified. Repeatedly, the Qur'an claims that Muhammad was foretold in the Scriptures, and the Jews' denial of such a foretelling is a clear sign of the corruption they have brought to God's word.

THE CHARGE OF FALSIFICATION

A major dent in the authority of the Bible is thus the Qur'an's accusation that the Jews have tampered with it. The Qur'an raises this charge repeatedly, using different terms in different contexts. Most prominent among the contentious issues is the foretelling of the coming of Muhammad in the old Scriptures. The Qur'an insists that the coming of Muhammad was foretold in the Torah and the Gospels. Having the pagan Meccans as his enemies was one thing, for Muhammad could always point to Judaism and Christianity as his spiritual brothers; having the Jews mount arguments against his preaching was far more grave. Muhammad could ill afford not to answer. The points of reference are now different. Muhammad was insisting that his message was nothing short of a repetition of the old monotheistic creed, whether Jewish or Christian. He made it a point to urge his Arab opponents to ask the Jews and the Christians about him. Yet the Jews of Medina, Muhammad's new abode after Mecca, were not eager to accept Muhammad as a prophet, let alone the idea that he could bring another Torah. Moreover, there were marked differences between the retelling of biblical stories in the Qur'an and their counterparts in the Bible. The Jews were eager to point these out. It is in light of this new opposition from the Jews of Medina that the Qur'an insists on the fact that Muhammad is proclaimed in the Torah and that the Jews are hiding this fact. The tone of the Qur'an now hardens, and the Jews are accused of many a crime.

Take, for example, this description of what the enemies of Muhammad were doing with Scripture (Q. 2: 77–9): 'Do they not know that God is well aware of what they conceal and what they reveal? Some of them are uneducated, and know the Scripture only through wishful thinking. They rely on guesswork. So woe to those who write the Scripture with their own hands and then claim, "This is from God", in order to make some small gain. Woe to them for what their hands have written! Woe to them for all that they have earned.' Or his Jewish opponents are said to twist God's word, deliberately changing its meaning (Q. 4:46, 5:13). In verse Q. 6:91, the Qur'an takes aim at both the Meccans and the Jews: 'They have no grasp of God's true measure when they say, "God has sent nothing down to a mere mortal." Say, "Who was it who sent down the Scripture, which Moses brought as a light and a guide to people, which you made into separate sheets, showing some but hiding many?"' The Jews are accused of mispronouncing, hiding, and fabricating new Scripture. This accusation of falsification, known in Arabic as *taḥrīf*, in truth became the prism through which later Muslims understood the status of the Bible. In many ways, the Qur'an poses an almost impossible dilemma here: the Torah is divine; the Torah is corrupted. The status of the Hebrew Bible is ever suspended, and the tension between its divinity and its corruption is never resolved. In this sense, the Qur'an sets the stage for the sustained ambivalence towards the Bible that characterises all subsequent Islamic literatures. Indeed, a Muslim could never be sure what to think of the Bible in so far as any judgement was always fraught with uncertainties.[6]

Yet, even the concept of falsification was not clear to Muslims themselves. There were at least four positions taken by medieval scholars regarding the scope of the falsification of the Torah. The first position held that all the Torah is falsified, and nothing of its original divine form was left. The second maintained that most of the Torah was corrupted. The third opinion, entertained by a majority of scholars, insisted that only a small part of the Torah was corrupted, whilst the fourth camp believed that the Torah was divine, and only the interpretations given to it are corrupted. According to the latter view, the wording of the Torah was still the originally revealed word of God; the Jews simply did not give the correct interpretation.[7] Given these four differing views, an

'Islamic' position towards the Bible can be very difficult to predict; a scholar may espouse any of these positions and defend it. The issue, however, was always the implications that the upholding of each such position would entail.

This ambivalence also was translated into the legal realm, where Muslims were asked to withhold judgement on any particular biblical pericope. They should not reject it for fear it was divine, and they should not accept it for fear it might be corrupted.[8] An example of the complex set of anxieties that confronted Muslim jurists when dealing with the holiness of the Torah can be illustrated from an historical incident in the tenth century that produced a *fatwa* ('religious ruling').[9] Camilla Adnag has studied this *fatwa* and translated it. Here is the problem: a Muslim slave who was owed money by a Jewish merchant asked for the return of his money. The Jewish merchant swore by the Torah that he was unable to pay him at that time. To this oath, the Muslim slave said: 'May God curse the Torah.' This altercation was witnessed by one individual only. Another witness stepped forward saying that he met the slave after the altercation, and the slave said to him that he 'cursed the Torah of the Jews'. The judge presiding over a complaint brought by the Jewish community against the Muslim slave was of the opinion that the slave should be put to death for his blasphemy, but since the punishment was so grave and the situation unclear – did the slave curse *the* Torah or the Torah of the Jews – he decided to consult a jurist (or *mufti*, a customary habit in the Shariah system). The slave meanwhile was languishing in jail awaiting resolution of the matter. The *mufti* rejected the slave's defence of feeble-mindedness or ignorance, on the grounds that he had the capacity to remember his money and ask for it. The issue of what to do with him for cursing the Torah, however, remained uncertain. There was only one witness who saw the altercation and reported that the slave cursed the Torah; the other witness had a different version of the story. Capital punishment required unambiguous, clear testimony from at least two reliable witnesses. After mulling over the matter further, the *mufti* gave this most ambivalent decision:

> I have thus shown you that I am obliged to be ambiguous in the answer I give. If someone is liable to the maximum punishment, i.e. execution, but there is an obstacle which renders the death sentence problematic, this person should not be released from prison, but neither should his prison term be extended if he has spent an appropriate length of time in jail. Moreover, he may be relieved of carrying more chains than he can bear. Perhaps God will show us a

reply concerning this issue that the heart can be at peace with, and that is supported by evidence from God's proof (the Qur'an) and the proof of His Messenger. This is what I hold, and in God is success.[10]

THE POST-QURANIC LITERATURE AND THE BIBLE

The main result of the Qur'an's ambivalence is that the Hebrew Bible never became an official part of the Scripture of the new faith. Relying as much as it did on the Bible, the new religion was nonetheless able to break away from it. However, this shift did not prevent the Bible from being admitted into Islamic religious tradition in a different guise. It is important to point out that even while the Hebrew Bible did not ultimately reach the status of Scripture, biblical lore was nevertheless enshrined as part of the Islamic traditions. The charge of falsification did not prevent Muslims from acquiring the biblical lore that was needed to flesh out the Quranic references to biblical stories. Indeed, a massive cultural and religious acquisition was undertaken by the early generations of Muslims, resulting in a wholesale transference of Jewish lore to Islam. Much of this activity was carried out by converts from Judaism.[11] In this sense, Muslims acquired the complete story, with material from the Hebrew Bible as the basis of that complete story, from Adam to Muhammad. The lore acquired by Muslims was extensive, and it appeared in many forms, as prophetic traditions (*ḥadīth*) ascribed to Muhammad; as specifically Jewish lore, called in Arabic *isrā'īliyyāt* ('Israelite material'); as biographies of the Patriarchs (the Patriarchs in Islam were considered prophets, and the Arabic name for this genre is 'Tales of the Prophets'); and as part of universal histories written by Muslim historians.[12] In this sense, the Bible was made part of the Islamic tradition, even though its absorption into the tradition is not always readily apparent.

There are two areas where this biblical lore played a major role. The first is in Qur'an commentary literature, and the second is in the genre of Tales of the Prophets. The Qur'an has a substantial amount of material retelling biblical stories – from Adam, Noah, Abraham, the Patriarchs, Moses, David, and Solomon, to the destruction of the Temple. These retellings are referential; that is, they presume a certain familiarity with these stories in advance. Thus, the commentary tradition felt the need to fill in the details omitted in the Qur'an. Again, Jewish converts to Islam played a major role in supplying the material with which commentators sought to fill this void. This material, as might be expected, has had a checkered history of reception, oscillating on the one hand between complete acceptance and attempts on the other at purging it from the tradition. Yet, because of its intimate connection to a central genre in Islam, it has proved impossible to uproot *isrā'īliyyāt* from the tradition.[13]

The other area where biblical material left its impact is in the genre of Tales of the Prophets. This is a genre of literature that presents human history as salvation history, centred on stories of men whom Islam came to consider prophetic figures. These works usually began with the creation of the world, the story of Adam, Noah, and most of the patriarchal history of the Hebrew Bible, and included also the life of Jesus, all presented as a preamble to the life of Muhammad.[14]

An example of the interaction of the Qur'an, the Hebrew Bible and Islamic literature

Q. 11:69–73 offers an example of how the Qur'an retells biblical stories and how the shadow of the Hebrew Bible informs Muslims' understanding of their Scripture. This is a retelling of the story of the Angels announcing to Abraham the birth of his son Isaac:

> To Abraham, Our messengers brought good news. They said, 'Peace.' He answered, 'Peace', and without delay he brought in a roasted calf. When he saw that their hands did not reach towards the meal, he found this strange and became afraid of them. But they said, 'Do not be afraid. We have been sent against the people of Lot.' His wife was standing nearby and laughed. We gave her good news of Isaac, and after him, of Jacob. She said, 'Alas for me! How am I to bear a child when I am an old woman, and my husband here is an old man? That would be a strange thing!' They said, 'Are you astonished at what God ordains? The grace of God and His blessing be upon you, people of this house! For He is worthy of all praise and glory.'[15]

The biblical and midrashic background of this retelling is unmistakable. Yet, when Muslim exegetes came to interpret this paragraph, they were not bound by the biblical archetype, or at least they found it easy to relegate it to a subordinate position. The wording in Arabic of the text has Sarah laughing *before* she is told that she is going to have a son. This order in the text allowed Muslim commentators the possibility of speculating about other reasons for her laughter (in addition to the fact that she was too old to become pregnant). It is not that they did not know the biblical archetype; rather, the archetype was simply not paramount. Sarah could have laughed for many reasons, and all of these were given, as is typical of the art of medieval interpretation where one meaning was not enough.[16]

If one reads the hundreds of Qur'an commentaries written across the centuries, one might come to the conclusion that the story as told in the Bible is not operative here. Yet this is not the case. The Hebrew Bible, with its ambivalent position in Islam, can make a sudden appearance and be re-integrated into the tradition; it takes only one exegete to decide to go back to the biblical source to change the picture. Such a figure did exist. In the fifteenth century, a Muslim exegete, al-Biqāʿī, decided to use the Bible to interpret the Qur'an – re-positioning the Hebrew Bible as central to understanding of the biblical material in the Qur'an.[17] When interpreting the preceding pericope, he had no doubt about why Sarah was laughing, as he explicitly cites the Hebrew Bible and another Quranic passage (Q. 51:29).[18] All other interpretations are refused. The Hebrew Bible thus has a continuous presence in the Islamic religious imagination.

This example highlights another important aspect of the position of the Hebrew Bible in Islam. Despite the forgoing comments on Jewish lore, the Hebrew Bible was never appropriated as such; to Muslims, it remained a Scripture in Hebrew (or its official rabbinic or Karaite Arabic translation), and thus in the custody of the Jews. While Muslims were able to have access to it (because Jewish populations in the central Muslim lands were remarkably literate), Muslims were always cognizant that this was the Scripture of another faith. Its use in Islam had to be negotiated away from Judaism. Muslims knew that they could issue a judgement against the Bible itself, but they were not foolish enough to think that this judgement would carry weight with the faithful. The Bible in this sense, as a text belonging to the Jews, was never appropriated; it had its custodians, the Jews themselves. Muslims could attack it, but to do so in a credible manner, they had to contend with its Jewish custodians.

POLEMICAL ANTI-BIBLE LITERATURE

One of the most sustained engagements Muslims have had with the Hebrew Bible was in polemical treatises written against the Jews. Here all the scholarship of medieval Islam was brought to bear on the Hebrew Bible, and a systematic dismantling of the text was carried out. The legacy of this interaction with the Hebrew Bible has been studied extensively.[19] Hava Lazarus-Yafeh believes that since Muslims did not uphold the sanctity of the Hebrew Bible, they brought 'an almost scholarly critical study' to the Old Testament, as well as to the New Testament. She has also suggested that 'Muslim Bible criticism drew heavily on pre-Islamic pagan, Christian, Gnostic, and other sources, and later may have been transmitted – through both Jewish and Christian mediators – to early modern Bible criticism.'[20] This assessment highlights the sophistication that medieval Muslim polemicists brought to their study of the Bible.

Lazarus-Yafeh identifies four arguments that Muslims used against the Bible: falsification (*taḥrīf*), abrogation (*naskh*), lack of reliable transmission of the text (*tawātur*), and novel biblical exegesis.[21] The first two were already used in the Qur'an. The third, the nature of the transmission of the Torah, was developed later after a theory of 'universal transmission' was developed by Muslim theologians. The fourth category, advancing novel interpretations of the Hebrew Bible, was mainly used to prove that the Torah already predicted the coming of Muhammad.

The Iberian Ibn Ḥazm (d. 1064) was the first to offer a systematic presentation of the corruptions in the Hebrew Bible to prove the charge of falsification that the Qur'an raised.[22] His main arguments have been grouped by Lazarus-Yafeh into three categories: chronological and geographical inaccuracies, theological impossibilities and preposterous behaviour. For each of these categories Ibn Ḥazm supplies a long list of examples. The story of Joseph, he insists, shows such chronological inconsistencies that it cannot be true on its own or composed by God. He also points out the anthropomorphic passages in the Torah to highlight its theological faults. Other theological issues that he raises are the sins of the prophets: cheating Jacob, incestuous Lot, and lying Abraham. These were all blasphemous accusations against holy men that cannot have been true. Finally, the instances of fornication that filled the biblical account of Israelite history were too unsettling for Ibn Ḥazm. The list he brandishes is long, and he is full of indignation that such lies can have been levelled against a genealogy God chose to bless.[23]

The belief that there was a lack of a reliable transmission history for the Bible came to play a major role in anti-Jewish polemics. Unlike the Muslims, Ibn Ḥazm insisted, Jews could not offer clear evidence showing that the Bible was transmitted faithfully, and that tampering and collusion to corrupt the text had been avoided. Ibn Ḥazm transferred this criterion from native Muslim scholarship, where it was used to assess the veracity of the Muslims' own religious tradition. Muslims had devised a theoretical model for transmitting historical information and texts, explaining how texts are preserved and how they are corrupted. Highest in the methods of transmission of a text was 'universal transmission', or what is known in Arabic as *tawātur*. This is transmission of a text from one generation to the other such that a text could not become corrupted, because its transmission has been witnessed and (done) by all. This stringent condition has only been met by the Qur'ān and very few other prophetic traditions. The Torah was not transmitted in this fashion, Ibn Ḥazm insisted. Wars, exile, and destruction of the Temple all point to the impossibility of an unbroken chain of transmission of the Torah.[24] Muslim polemicists highlighted the role played by Ezra in reconstituting the Hebrew Bible. Ibn Ḥazm, Lazarus-Yafeh writes, 'was the first to make Ezra into a wicked scoundrel who intentionally corrupted the Scriptures', thus raising 'the general Islamic argument against the Bible to an essentially higher level of systematic textual criticism'.[25]

THE BIBLE REHABILITATED

It would be safe to state that the Bible, apart from a small window of time early on in the history of Islam, had a tangential relationship to the Islamic religious tradition. Yet, as has been shown, this statement also needs to be qualified because biblical influences in fact continued to be abundant. Moreover, Muslims cultivated an intimate polemical knowledge of the Bible. The fact that the Bible was not part of the Scripture of Islam, or part of the curriculum of its theological training, did not mean that intellectuals and religious scholars could not access it. The presence of an active Jewish community in the central Muslim lands (Arabia, Persia and Turkey) meant that copies of the Hebrew Bible (in their official Arabic translations) were accessible. Periodical Jewish conversion to Islam meant that specialised knowledge could be codified in polemical treatises – since many converts wrote polemical treatises against their previous faith. Yet the ambivalence inherent in the Islamic position vis-à-vis the Bible meant that the ordinarily negative tones of this polemic could be overturned, permitting a more positive appreciation of the Bible that was always latent in the Islamic religious imagination.

In 1457, a Muslim exegete residing in Cairo, al-Biqāʿī, embarked on the composition of a massive new Qur'an commentary. By then the genre was almost 800 years old, and a revolutionary work was unexpected. For reasons that remain mysterious, however, al-Biqāʿī decided to re-admit the Hebrew Bible as the proof-text for interpreting biblical material in the Qur'an. He thus turned his back on the Islamicised biblical lore that was by then the only available source to explicate the biblical material in the Qur'an and instead made a daring return to the biblical sources. Moreover, al-Biqāʿī, whom I have called a Muslim Hebraist, was using a rabbinically trained Jewish friend to help him navigate the Hebrew Bible.

He managed to use three Arabic Bible versions: the rabbinic translation by Saadia Gaon, a Karaite translation (by Yafet ben Eli?), and an Arabic Christian version of the Septuagint.[26] When in doubt, he compared the Arabic version to the Hebrew original with the help of his informant. He moreover kept his extensive citations in the original Judeo-Arabic register, thus refusing the temptation to Islamise the phraseology of the Hebrew Bible (it was customary to 'Quranise' the language of the Bible). Nothing of this sort had been seen before. It is not that biblical material was not admitted into Islam, for, as stated earlier, the biblical material in the religious Islamic tradition is extensive. But it was always admitted through mediation: re-phrased, re-told and never attributed to the Hebrew Bible as the Jewish Hebrew Bible.

So unusual was al-Biqāʿī's practice that soon a controversy erupted as to whether it was Islamic and legal to quote the Bible in order to interpret the Qur'an. This was a major theological controversy, and al-Biqāʿī felt compelled to write an apologia in defence of his practice.[27] This apologia preserves the most extensive known debate in Islam about the status of the Bible. Polemicist that he was, al-Biqāʿī also solicited the opinions of the major intellectuals, judges, and scholars of the city – who were his friends. We thus have an extensive amount of material on the issue of the Scriptures of other religions and their status in Islam. Al-Biqāʿī stood his ground and fearlessly defended the sanctity of the Hebrew Bible but also, more importantly, a Muslim's right to use it in a religious context.

The major argument that al-Biqāʿī employed to rehabilitate the Hebrew Bible was not that it was uncorrupted, for he did believe that a very small part was falsified. Rather, being in a position to judge the Hebrew Bible, al-Biqāʿī argued that a Muslim scholar should be able to use it. Using the Qur'an as a criterion to ferret out the falsified from the genuine in the Hebrew Bible, a Muslim should go ahead and use any part of the Bible, as long as his readers are warned in the case of corrupt material. Indeed, al-Biqāʿī goes a step further. Even when unable to assess the pericope in question, a Muslim should go ahead and use it for edification and exhortation. In other words, the Hebrew Bible should receive the benefit of the doubt, al-Biqāʿī insists. Since it is the word of God, then it is worthy of use in religious context.

This rather accommodating view of the Hebrew Bible is not unusual; it must be remembered that there was always one camp of Muslim intellectuals who upheld the sanctity of the Hebrew Bible. Yet, even when so valued, the Hebrew Bible remained outside the parameters of Islamic education; holding a high opinion of the Hebrew Bible usually did not translate into any meaningful interaction with the text. Here is where al-Biqāʿī was radically innovative. He insisted on using the Hebrew Bible in the most sacred of Islamic literatures, Qurʾanic commentaries.[28] He quoted copiously from the Torah as well as from the Prophets and the Writings in the Hebrew Bible. He knew what to look for and what to quote. He exhibited a knowledge of the intricacies of the Hebrew Bible which remains unique among the medieval scholars of Islam. Finally, this affinity for the Hebrew Bible came at a cultural moment when Muslim lands were not occupied or under threat from Europe – before humanism and before the Hebrew Bible became a classical work of literature in secular modernity. This was an Islamic development which was the result of religious factors intrinsic to the long history of Islamic religious tradition.

THE MODERN PERIOD

The modern history of the Hebrew Bible in Muslim countries has yet to be studied systematically, and what follows simply highlights what I consider to be significant elements of a yet-to-be told story. The increased influence of Europe upon Muslim societies during the past two centuries, whether through trade, colonisation, missionary activity, or educational outreach, meant that Muslims were exposed to more aggressive methods of encountering the Hebrew Bible (now usually as the 'Old Testament', regarded as part of the Christian Bible). Anti-Qurʾan polemical literature proliferated, and many Muslims felt besieged, although 'higher criticism' was a boon for Muslim polemicists, and Muslims showed remarkable awareness of the modern literature on the Bible, especially the Muslims of India.

In contrast to this negative re-encounter with the Hebrew Bible, the nascent nationalisms of the Muslim world were invested in making the religious minorities of their countries feel part of their respective nations. This entailed a celebration of unity, with the concomitant acceptance of the Scripture of Judaism and Christianity as part of the national heritage. The Bible was on its way to becoming a classic in the Muslim world. Soon intellectuals would not be caught without having read the Bible, even though Muslims were not in the habit of reading it.

One still finds the old positions surviving, if not dominating, in most of the population (e.g., the Bible has been falsified). But new factors have made for radical developments. Not least is the wide availability of the Bible. In the Muslim world, all the mass-produced Bibles are Christian Bibles, which means that Muslims are reading the Hebrew

Bible as part of Christian Scripture. Any educated individual now has access to the Bible. Far more significant is the fact that, especially in the Arab World, the new nineteenth-century American Protestant translation of the Bible into Arabic was of immense cultural significance far beyond the numerical percentage of Christians in the native population. To quote a famous nineteenth-century statement, 'the Arabic language was Christianized.' Since the new Protestant translation owes much to Saadia Gaon's Arabic translation – much more than is admitted – the Judeo-Arabic of the Hebrew Bible translation was far more influential than Christian-inflected Arabic. Modern Standard Arabic owes much to the Protestant translation, which revolutionised modern Arabic. The Bible was thus enshrined as part of the modern Arabic sensibility and became an essential component of the Arabic renaissance. Indeed, since many of the modern Arab poets were Christians, and since their Arabic was highly shaped by the new translation, modern Arabic is infused with biblical language. The presence of Arabs in the new state of Israel also meant that one now had native speakers of Hebrew who are Arabs. Mahmoud Darwish, one of the most famous modern Arab writers, spoke and read Hebrew as a native tongue and publicly admitted the influence of the Hebrew Bible on his poetry.

In the religious sphere, the Muslims started to publish the medieval polemical literature on the Hebrew Bible. Meanwhile, they also developed new polemical strategies against the Bible, most significantly the deployment of the findings of higher criticism, to cast doubt on the integrity of the Hebrew Bible.[29] But there were also more serious attempts to come to terms with the Bible as Scripture. Indeed, in the nineteenth century we witness the first attempt by a Muslim to give a full commentary on the Bible. Sayyid Ahmad Khan (1817–98) was a Muslim Indian intellectual who witnessed an increasingly bitter polemical war between Muslims and Christian missionaries in India. Part of his response to this charged atmosphere was an attempt to come to terms with the origins of the Christian faith through a thorough investigation of the Bible. The first section of his project was a commentary on the Hebrew Bible.[30] He confirmed the integrity of the text of the Hebrew Bible, insisting on its prophetic origins and rejecting the common understanding of the notion of taḥrīf ('falsification'). He also attempted to answer the question of 'how should Muslims understand their belief in prophetic revelation so that full justice be done to the superiority of the Qur'ānic revelation and the truths of pre-Islamic revelations at the same time?'[31] The answers of Sayyid Ahmad Khan betray an honest attempt to keep a coherent Islamic outlook while according the Scriptures of Judaism and Christianity their religious validity. In this regard, he is continuing an old Islamic question: How is the Qur'an divine in light of the precedence of the Hebrew Bible?

NOTES

1   All translations of the Qur'an are from M. A. S. Abdel Haleem, *The Qur'an: A New Translation* (Oxford University Press, 2004). The classical study on the parallels between the Bible and the Qur'an is Heinrich Speyer, *Die biblischen Erzählungen im Qoran* (Hildesheim, Germany: G. Olms, 1988, reprint of 1931 ed.).
2   See Walid A. Saleh, 'What if You Refuse, When Ordered to Fight? King Saul (Ṭālūt) in the Qur'ān and Post-Quranic Literature', in *Saul in Story and Tradition*, ed. by Carl S. Ehrlich (Tübingen, Germany: Mohr Siebeck, 2006), 261–83.
3   Rudi Paret, *Mohammed und der Koran* (Stuttgart, Germany: W. Kohlhammer, 1991), 99.
4   On the Qur'an as the end of a long process of development of the notion of Scripture in the Near East, see Wilfred Cantwell Smith, 'Scripture as Form and Concept: Their Emergence for the Western World', in *Rethinking Scripture*, ed. by Miriam Levering (Albany: State University of New York Press, 1989), 29–57.
5   See the articles in *Self-Referentiality in the Qur'ān*, ed. by Stefan Wild (Wiesbaden, Germany: Harrassowitz, 2006).
6   This ambivalence is also reflected in the prophetic *hadith* literature; see M. J. Kister, 'Ḥaddithū 'an banī isrā'īla wa-lā ḥaraja: A Study of an Early Tradition', *Israel Oriental Studies* 2 (1972): 215–39.
7   On these positions, see Walid A. Saleh, 'A Fifteenth-Century Muslim Hebraist: Al-Biqā'ī and His Defense of Using the Bible to Interpret the Qur'ān', *Speculum* 83 (2008): 629–54, 649.
8   On this formulation, the suspension of judgement on the Bible, see ibid., 646.
9   See Camilla Adang, 'A Fourth/Tenth Century Tunisian Muftī on the Sanctity of the Torah of Moses', in *The Intertwined Worlds of Islam: Essays in Memory of Hava Lazarus-Yafeh* (Jerusalem: Ben Zvi Institute, 2002): vii–xxxiv.
10 Ibid., xvi.
11 See Steven M. Wasserstrom, *Between Muslim and Jew: The Problem of Symbiosis under Early Islam* (Princeton, NJ: Princeton University Press, 1995).
12 An example of this literature with an extensive bibliography is Roberto Tottoli, *The Stories of the Prophets by Ibn Muṭarrif al-Ṭarafī: Edited with an Introduction and Notes* (Berlin: Klaus Schwarz, 2003). See also Jacob Lassner, *Demonizing the Queen of Sheba: Boundaries of Gender and Culture in Postbiblical Judaism and Medieval Islam* (University of Chicago Press, 1993).
13 For bibliography, see John C. Reeves, ed., *Bible and Qur'ān: Essays in Scriptural Intertextuality* (Atlanta, GA: Society of Biblical Literature, 2003).

14   For an example in English of this literature, see *Lives of the Prophets as Recounted by al-Tha'labī*, trans. and annotated by William M. Brinner (Leiden, Netherlands: Brill, 2002).

15   See Speyer, *Erzählungen*, 147–51. See also the works of Tottoli, *Stories of the Prophets*.

16   See S. P. Stetkevych, 'Sarah and the Hyena: Laughter, Menstruation, and the Genesis of a Double-Entendre', *History of Religion* 35 (1996): 13, 41.

17   On this exegete, see Walid A. Saleh, 'A Fifteenth-Century Muslim Hebraist', *Speculum* 83(3) (2008): 629–54.

18   See al-Biqāʿī, *Naẓm al-durar* (India, 1976), v. 9:331.

19   See Hava Lazarus-Yafeh, *Intertwined Worlds: Medieval Islam and Bible Criticism* (Princeton, NJ: Princeton University Press, 1992), and, more recently, Camilla Adang, *Muslim Writers on Judaism and the Hebrew Bible: From Ibn Rabban to Ibn Hazm* (Leiden, Netherlands: Brill, 1996).

20   Lazarus-Yafeh, *Intertwined Worlds*, xi.

21   Ibid., 19.

22   The literature on Ibn Ḥazm is immense; there is the classic work by M. Asin Palacios, *Abenházam de Córdoba y su historia critica de las ideas religiosas*, 5 vols. (Madrid: Real Academia de la Historia, 1927–32). See also Adang, *Muslim Writers*, 59–69, where more literature is cited.

23   Lazarus-Yafeh, *Intertwined Worlds*, 34.

24   Ibid., 41–7.

25   Ibid., 68.

26   See Walid A. Saleh, ' "Sublime in its Style, Exquisite in its Tenderness": The Hebrew Bible Quotations in al-Biqāʿī's Qur'ān Commentary', in *Adaptations and Innovations*, ed. by Y. Tzvi Langermann and Josef Stern (Paris: Peeters, 2007), 333–4.

27   See now the treatise and the history of the controversy, Walid A. Saleh, *In Defence of the Bible: A Critical Edition and an Introduction to al-Biqāʿī's Bible Treatise* (Leiden, Netherlands: Brill, 2008).

28   For the Hebrew Bible quotations in his Qur'an commentary, see Saleh, ' "Sublime in its Style." '

29   For an example of such a method, see Mohammad Abu-Hamdiyyah, *The Qur'ān: An Introduction* (London: Routledge, 2000).

30   On the life and works of Khan, see Christian W. Troll, *Sayyid Ahmad Khan: A Reinterpretation of Muslim Theology* (New Delhi: Vikas Publishing, 1978).

31   Ibid., 85.

FURTHER READING

Bell, Richard. *The Origin of Islam in Its Christian Environment: The Gunning Lectures, Edinburgh University, 1925.* London: Macmillan, 1926.

Birkeland, Harris. *The Lord Guideth: Studies on Primitive Islam.* Oslo, Norway: H. Aschehoug, 1956.

Bravmann, M. M. *The Spiritual Background of Early Islam: Studies in Ancient Arab Concepts.* Leiden, Netherlands: Brill, 1972.

Cook, Michael. *The Koran: A Very Short Introduction.* Oxford University Press, 2000.

Déroche, François. *La transmission écrite du Coran dans les débuts d l'islam: le codex Parisino-petropolitanus.* Leiden, Netherlands: Brill, 2009.

Donner, Fred M. *Narratives of Islamic Origins: The Beginnings of Islamic Historical Writing.* Princeton, NJ: Darwin Press, 1998.

Jeffery, Arthur. *The Foreign Vocabulary of the Qur'ān.* Leiden, Netherlands: Brill, 2007.

Neuwirth, Angelika. *Der Koran als Text der Spätantike: ein europäischer Zugang.* Berlin: Verlag der Weltreligionen, 2010.

Nöldeke, Theodor, Friedrich Schwally, Gotthelf Bergsträsser and Otto Pretzl. *The History of the Qur'ān. Edited and translated by Wolfgang H. Behn.* Leiden, Netherlands: Brill, 2013.

Speyer, Heinrich. *Die biblischen Erzählungen im Qoran.* Hildesheim, Germany: G. Olms, 1961.

DAVID LYLE JEFFREY

The distinctive imposition of the second commandment notwithstanding, the Hebrew Bible has a great deal to say about art. Moreover, it
promotes poetry and has been a source of inspiration for all the arts in
Western culture to a degree surpassed only by the New Testament.

TENSION IN TEXT AND COMMENTARY

While Jewish artists from patriarchal times observed careful scruples
where the human image (closely associated with the divinity, Gen
1:26–7) was concerned, the actual term used by the text of Exodus (20:4)
makes it clear that "graven image" (from the Hebrew *pāsal*, "to carve
from wood or stone") refers specifically to three-dimensional rather than
two-dimensional images. Typically, these three-dimensional images
were used as idols.[1] That there is no ban on other forms of representa-
tional imagery is clear from the same book of Exodus, in which the Lord
reveals to Moses that he has called Bezalel of the tribe of Judah, filling
him "with divine spirit, ability, intelligence, and knowledge of every
kind of craft, to devise artistic designs, to work in gold, silver, bronze,
and in cutting stones for setting, woodcarving and every kind of craft"
(31:1–5). The artistic provisions for the beauty of the Tabernacle are
intensified when Solomon deputizes Hiram of the tribe of Naphtali to
be the master artisan for the far more elaborate artwork of the Temple (1
Kgs 7:13–51). There, not only carved candlesticks and cherubim but also
bas relief and sculpted gold pomegranates, lilies, lions, oxen, wheels, and
palm trees were all arranged in splendor. The association of Solomon's
wisdom with the beauty of artistic endeavor, moreover, was embedded
in the very term for the artist: the artist is "filled with divine spirit" and
wisdom. Indeed, the characteristic trait of the artist is to be *ḥăkam-lēb*
("wise-hearted"; Exod 31:2–6, 35:30–6; 1 Kgs 7:14, etc.). Ezekiel speaks
comparably of "the beauty of wisdom" (28:7). After the Babylonian
captivity, God commands Cyrus to rebuild the Temple using beautiful

materials (Ezra 1:2), and two hundred singers go back to the ruins of Jerusalem to provide choral accompaniment for Temple worship (Ezra 2:65). It is impossible to read the text of the Hebrew Bible for long without appreciating the deep affection for artistic expression in its pages.

Biblical poetry was itself a fountain of inspiration for artistic and worshipful enterprise long after the Psalmists and their successors, including the poet of the Song of Solomon and Isaiah, ceased to compose. In their works, beauty is a divine property (cf. Zech 9:17); moreover, the Lord is said to desire beauty (Ps 45:11). The Psalm writers speak of a "beauty of holiness" (Ps 29:2; 96:9), a divine beauty to which the poet himself aspires (Ps 90:17). Beauty in both the visual and literary spheres shares a common aesthetic in the Hebrew Bible, one that suggests a love for the careful workmanship of the jeweler, and a corresponding lapidary precision and intricacy in the craft of the writer: "A word fitly spoken is like apples of gold in pictures of silver" (Prov 25:11).

This is not to deny that there is a strain of iconoclasm and even antiaestheticism in apocryphal Jewish texts and Talmudic commentary. One luminous example is the apocryphal Wisdom of Solomon, most probably an Alexandrian Greek text written sometime between the second century BCE and the reign of Caligula (c. 40 CE). Chapters 13–15 of this work are devoted to counteracting Hellenic secularizing influences. And though there is tacit acceptance that human artistry expresses genuine wisdom (14:2), the text argues that art initiates a slippery slope leading to talismanic, then political and moral idolatry. Here idolatry is found alike in the funerary art commissioned by grieving parents and political sculpture, in which the artist has every incentive to "enhance" the attractiveness of his patron. Visual hyperbole leads, in turn, to a kind of worship in which "people, in bondage to misfortune or to royal authority, bestow on objects of wood or stone the name that ought not to be shared" (14:21). The desire to eschew idolatry represents in itself, of course, an indubitable plank of biblical wisdom ("for the worship of idols not to be named is the beginning, cause, and end of every evil"), but is here so totalizing in its reach that it seems to contradict both the letter and spirit of the canonical texts. The writer boasts a Karaite purity: "for neither has the evil intent of human art misled us, nor the fruitless toil of painters, a figure stained with various colors whose appearance arouses yeaning in fools so that they desire the lifeless form of a dead image" (15:4–5). Similar strains of Puritanism can be found in Talmudic texts such as a *baraita* in Middot, which says that at the time of Enosh, images and immorality were introduced by the descendants of Cain (32 Middot; cf. Yalkut 1:47; cf. Gen 4:21–2; Judg 8:22–35).

Yet the critical distinction preserved in the canonical text of Exodus pertains to reference, not to artistic form. The same gold that Bezalel will use to adorn the Tabernacle was first used, in Moses' absence, to fashion the golden calf – idolatry *simpliciter* (Exodus 32). Even the astringent Wisdom of Solomon comprehends the instrumental rather than idolatrous use of the brazen serpent set up by Moses in the wilderness (Num 11:31–5; 21:6–9), saying "the one who turned toward it was saved, not by the thing that was beheld, but by you, the Savior of all" (16:7). This basic teleological distinction would seem to have underwritten the later, otherwise perhaps surprising, flourishing of two-dimensional figuration painted on synagogue walls and in Haggadic manuscripts.

ART FOR THE SYNAGOGUE

Apart from some uncertainly dated Roman tombs – where, in the manner of Jewish coins, grave sites may be adorned with symbols (almond branch, menorah, *lulav, ethrog*)[2] – there is no surviving evidence of Jewish pictorial art from the first two centuries CE reflecting biblical narrative. The third century produces artifacts of a remarkably developed narrative character, however, that must have had some precedents, now lost. The most complete extant example is from the synagogue at Dura Europos, an ancient city between Syrian Aleppo and Baghdad. Excavated along with a nearby Christian church, also with painted walls (of inferior quality), the Dura Europos synagogue (c. 240 CE) features biblical sequences *al fresco* of Abraham sacrificing Isaac (Genesis 22), Moses and the Israelites crossing the Red Sea (Exod 14:20–31), the Ark of the Covenant and the shattered god Dagon (1 Samuel 5), and Elijah confronting the prophets of Baal (1 Kgs 18:30–40) – in versions influenced directly by the elaborated midrash.[3] After the fourth century, elaborate mosaic synagogue floor tile art begins to be widespread. The mosaics featured biblical narrative only occasionally, as at Sepphoris in the early fifth century, and typically incorporated a modified Hellenistic zodiac as the centerpiece. Such syncretistic elements, including a figure of the sun god Helios riding his chariot at the hub of the zodiac (perhaps a double for the figure in Ps 19:4–6), were also incorporated into liturgical poetry.[4] Though such visual representations were two-dimensional, it is clear that at many points in the history of Judaism such artwork in a synagogue would have seemed a breach of the commandment against idolatry.

At least as interesting for a consideration of the influence of the Hebrew Bible is the rich legacy of medieval illuminated manuscripts of the Haggadah for Passover. The best surviving manuscripts of this type are illuminated in the manner of the *Vienna Genesis*, a seventh-century Christian manuscript, though they date from the fourteenth and fifteenth centuries. The Haggadah manuscripts employ a wider range of colors in their vivid depictions of the *akedah* (Genesis 22, the binding of Isaac), the flight of Jacob and his family into Egypt (dressed in medieval garb, and driving with horses and wagons of the period), the making of bricks, a celebration of the first Passover, Samson defeating the lion, David hacking off Goliath's head, Judith doing the same with Holofernes, and Esther interceding before the king, followed by the hanging of Haman.[5] Here, too, one finds evidence of the sort of iconographic fusion of pagan and biblical motifs that characterize medieval Christian art. For example, the beautifully illustrated Israel Museum manuscript 180/51 (fol. Lv) opens with a large depiction of King David, seated and playing his harp in a garden or grove of fruit trees, surrounded by deer, rabbits, and birds who are attentive to his song: the identification of the Psalmist with Orpheus, also to become prominent in medieval Christian iconography, is evident (Figure 21.1).[6] It seems probable that Christian illuminated Bibles, such as the magnificent *Bible Moralisée* with its 5,000 small medallion illustrations (c. 1240) of Old Testament types and New Testament antitypes, paired and explicated, had some influence on the Haggadic artists of the next two centuries.[7]

ART AND TYPOLOGY IN THE MEDIEVAL CHRISTIAN CHURCH

Christian iconography from the catacombs through the Middle Ages develops along lines parallel to its Jewish counterpart, as the Dura Europos finds and the extensive paintings of the catacombs from a century later would suggest. But in Christian contexts, the use of narrative from the Hebrew Bible depends on typological, Christological readings, as the *Bible Moralisée* most extensively illustrates. At first, these depictions function symbolically, as in Jewish funerary art: a "good shepherd" from the third century fuses a Roman bucolic image and a Christian biblical motif; a second-century tomb mosaic featuring Christ as the Sun God in his chariot resembles the mosaic floors of Levantine synagogues. When human figures first occur, they are nonbiblical as well as biblical. But the sacrifice of Isaac, Jonah being swallowed by the whale,

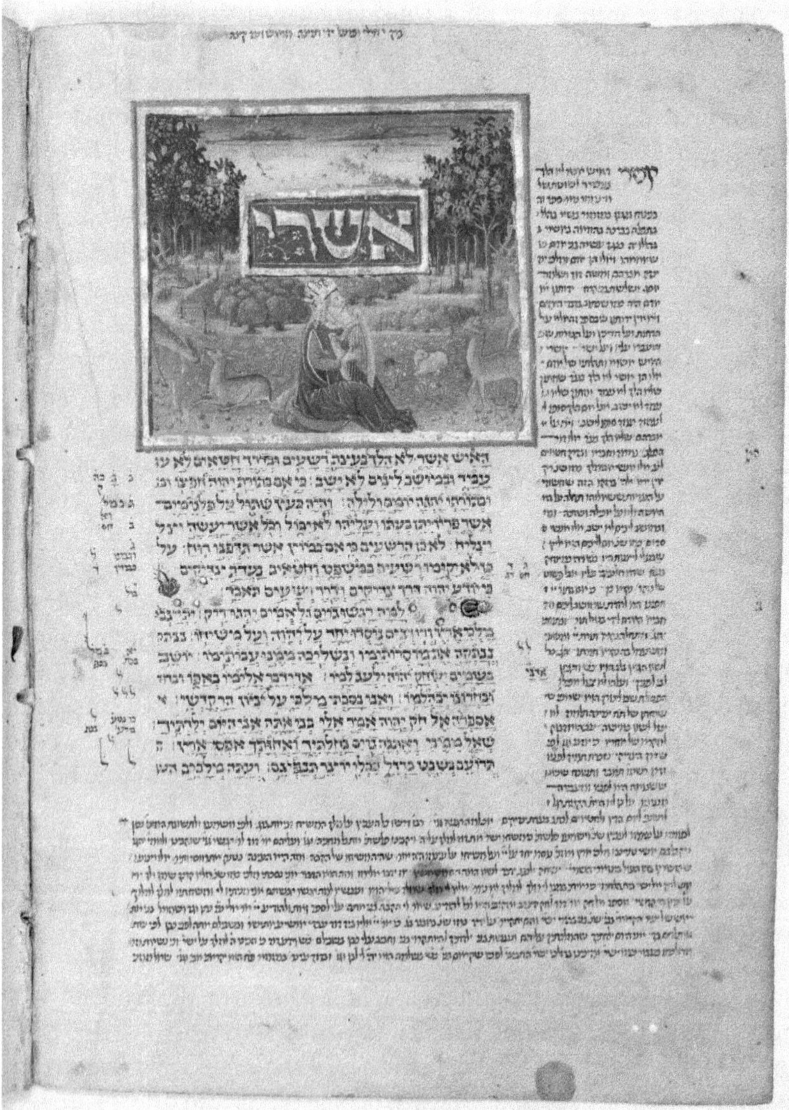

Figure 21.1. *Ashray* (Psalm 1), Israel Museum, Jerusalem. MS 180/51 fol. Lv. By permission of the Israel Museum, Jerusalem.

and Moses receiving the tablets of the Law, occur frequently in associations that indicate how the first is to be seen as a type of Christ, the second a figure for the Resurrection, and the third a reminder of Christ as fulfillment of the Law.[8] Later, other narratives from the Hebrew Scriptures, as distinctively developed in Christian exegesis, begin to appear as well – Byzantine mosaics with Abraham and his three visitors (suggestive of the Trinity), sarcophagi with Noah receiving the dove, or the three youths in Nebuchadnezzar's fiery furnace, with each narrative being read as confirmation of God's protection of his elect. The churches of Ravenna and S. Maria Maggiore in Rome offer fine examples of the typological development in mosaic art. Later medieval churches make lavish use of scenes from the Hebrew Bible in similar fashion, especially in the sculpture of portals and capitals but also, of course, in stained glass and interior painting. The extent of this art is so massive that even a selection of major representative studies can do no more than hint at the richness of the typological use of the Old Testament in later medieval art and architecture.[9]

THE HEBREW BIBLE AND MEDIEVAL POETRY

A rich body of Jewish medieval poetry, heavily influenced by Arabic verse, developed in medieval Europe, especially Spain.[10] Poets Shmuel HaNagid (993–1056), Solomon Ibn Gabirol (1021–58), Moshe Ibn Ezra (1055–c. 1135), and Yehuda Ha Levi (1075–1141), attentive as they are to Moorish models, also demonstrate the pervasive influence of both Bible and Talmud. This appears in continuous allusion functioning as paroemia, and in the structuring of whole books of poetry as a species of contemporary commentary on the biblical source. In Shmuel HaNagid, for example, poems are organized into three volumes entitled *Ben Tehellim* ("After the Psalms"), *Ben Mishle* ("After Proverbs"), and *Ben Koholet* ("After Ecclesiastes").[11] HaNagid's sense of his kinship to Moses and his claim to poetic prowess "superior to the Levites" make clear his intent to contribute to a specifically biblical tradition of wisdom literature. This determination is reflected also in the recommendation of Ibn Ezra: "Gather for yourselves from the verses of the Bible however much you like and find pleasing.... As for me, in every speech I gave, in every letter I wrote and in every poem I composed, I followed this course when I found it in Holy Scriptures."[12]

In medieval Christian poetry, it is less in the lyric than in longer narrative poetry and drama that the influence of the Hebrew Bible is most prominently felt. In Anglo-Saxon poetry, the earliest examples (the so-called Caedmonian poems) are loose paraphrases drawn from the Latin Old Testament: Caedmon's "Creation Hymn," "Genesis A," "Genesis B," "Exodus," and "Daniel." Old Testament narrative, with its themes of exile and pilgrimage, the struggle between good and evil forces, and exemplars of heroism, such as appear in the Old English poem "Judith," was initially more attractive than New Testament material to the Anglo-Saxon poets.[13]

Later narrative poetry likewise featured Old Testament stories: the elegant and learned poet of the Middle English "Pearl" also wrote "Patience," a retelling of the story of Jonah, and "Cleanness," a treatise against sin and profanation that features Sodom and Gomorrah, and the fall of Babylon after Nebuchadnezzar. Medieval drama, from the Anglo-Norman *Jeu d'Adam* through all the cycle plays (e.g., *N-Town*, *York*, *Chester*, *Lincoln*, and *Wakefield*), makes heavy use of those Old Testament narratives featured in the lections of the liturgical year as episodes in the *humana historia salvationis*.[14] English writers, especially in the north, made much more use of Old Testament narrative than did the Christian poets of France or Italy, among whom – as in Dante, Chaucer, Jean de Meun, and Chrétien de Troyes – basic literary inspiration beyond the New Testament tended to come from classical Roman poets such as Virgil, Ovid, and Statius.

Another notable feature of the use of Old Testament narratives by English poets is adaptation via implied or actual allegory as a species of partisan political argument. In the fourteenth-century Middle English "Pistel of Swete Susan," for example, the apocryphal narrative appendix to Daniel (chapter 13 in the Vulgate), the story of a woman sexually threatened and then libeled, is retold with vivid clarity in such a way as to highlight the Wycliffite argument that the Law of God, being just, requires interpreters and "justisis of ech lawe" who are righteous and "clene of liif," if biblical law is to be honored in its application.[15] This is an argument against the prevalent disposition of both civil and religious power, and it presages other adaptations of Old Testament narrative in political criticism three centuries later, as in John Dryden's "Absolom and Achitophel" (1681).

RENAISSANCE AND REFORMATION

After the Reformation, literary use of the Old Testament in Europe tended to be heavily marked by Calvinist typology and polemical anti-Catholic invective. Calvinist theology focused on the covenant (Hebrew *běrît*) in such a way as to characterize the Calvinist elect as the New Israel, and it prompted interest in Old Testament narratives not featured prominently in the traditional Roman lectionary. In England, Tudor plays, many now lost, were written about Ruth, Esther, Darius, Hezekiah, Jephthah, Joshua, Samson, Absalom, and Susanna, as well as Abraham, Jacob, and Esau. Elizabethan plays like *Susanna* (1569) by Thomas Garter, Thomas

Watson's *Absalon*, and George Peele's *King David and Fair Bethsabe* (1594), as well as John Milton's *Samson Agonistes*, manage to combine a strong sense of the intrinsic drama of much biblical narrative with a high estimation of their protagonist's heroic and sometimes tragic proportions; almost all of these works have a political register.[16] Milton's retelling of the story of the Fall in *Paradise Lost* (1667) and his use of Job in *Paradise Regained* (1671) are more obviously imbued with deep theological instruction and apologetic. As Harold Fisch has shown, in the seventeenth century in general, Puritan writers showed a depth of literacy in the Hebrew Bible unmatched by other contemporaries. Moreover, like Milton, they were glad to borrow from Jewish commentary in their reading of these texts.[17]

THE HEBREW BIBLE AND LATER POETRY

After Robert Lowth, Professor of Poetry at Oxford, published his *De sacra poesi Hebraeorum* (1753), a consciousness of the particular character of biblical poetry (and the remarkable capturing of much of it in the King James translation of 1611) became influential well beyond the circles of biblical scholarship. The dominant characteristics of Hebrew poetry identified by Lowth were rhythm and parallelism, and while critical attention has refined our understanding of these features since then, Lowth's basic thesis has been maintained.[18] Ironically, while prominent English poets such as William Blake, Samuel Taylor Coleridge, and Matthew Arnold were excited by Lowth's findings, the actual effect of his stylistic discovery on their own poetry was limited. In Blake's case, the influence of the Hebrew Bible shows primarily in his reading (and rewriting) of the prophets, especially Isaiah and Ezekiel.[19] Christopher Smart's imitations of the Psalms and *Jubilate Agno* much more directly attempt to capture the cadence and parallelism of the biblical prototypes. In these and other poets, the oratorical idiom of the King James translation is evident.

French skeptic Richard Simon's *Critical History of the Bible* (translated into English in 1682) and John Locke's philosophical writings, followed by the work of the Hegelians in Germany and their admirers (such as Matthew Arnold in England), tended over the next century to force Old Testament narrative from center stage. Thus, despite playful allusions in novels such as Henry Fielding's *Joseph Andrews* (1742), and the counterpoint of romantic rebellion expressed in Lord Byron's *Cain* (1821), interest in the Hebrew Scriptures waned in England even as it waxed in the Colonies.

Here, too, the Calvinistic appropriation of biblical narrative plays a decisive role, especially perhaps in America. The reason, as Sacvan Bercovitch and others have shown, is the Pilgrims' extension of Calvinist typology to America itself as not only the "New Israel" but also as an eschatological embodiment of the millennial kingdom.[20] Biblical analogies and allusions to the Exile, Babylonian captivity, Israel's wilderness journey, and Promised Land are warp and woof in the writings of William Bradford, John Winthrop, Roger Williams, Michael Wigglesworth, Cotton Mather, Samuel Sewall, Samuel Willard, and Jonathan Edwards. Thomas Hooker's *The Covenant of Grace Opened* (1651), Edward Johnson's *Wonder-working Providence of Sion's Savior in New England* (1654), and Yale President Timothy Dwight's epic poem, *The Conquest of Canaan* (1775), all read as though America was the Promised Land pledged by God to Abraham in Genesis.

By the twentieth century, American nationalistic historiography and jeremiad begins to give way to use of the Hebrew Scriptures as a means of framing novels and plays with themes pertaining to social justice and cultural criticism. In George Cabot Lodge's *Cain* (1904), F. E. Pierce's *The World that God Destroyed* (1911), William Ford Manley's *The Mess of Pottage* (1928), Richard Burton's *Rahab* (1906), Scholem Asch's *Jephthah's Daughter* (1915), Marc Connelly's *Green Pastures* (1929), Eugene O'Neill's *Belshazzar* (1958), and Archibald MacLeish's adaptation of Job in *J.B.* (1958) and his poem collection *Songs for Eve* (1954), there is a wide diversity of appropriations and, on the whole, much more creative, nuanced, and less catechetical use of the source texts in question. In Canada, the poet A. M. Klein was by the mid-twentieth century writing poetry and fiction that, in their sophisticated midrashic appropriation of texts of the Hebrew Bible, recollect the Jewish poets of the Golden Age more than perhaps any intervening exemplars. Klein's poem "Five Characters," for example, is a penetrating analysis of the book of Esther, and his "Koheleth" reads Ecclesiastes in the company of centuries of rabbinic commentary. His "The Psalter of Avram Haktani" (1948) and "A Voice Was Heard in Ramah" of the same year exhibit a fertile scholar's command of Talmudic sources as well as a knowledge of the rich lineaments of traditional Hebrew poetry. His novel, *The Second Scroll* (1951), is a double narrative, with five books named for the books of the Torah and a brilliant narrative *chumash* for each. Much like Adele Wiseman's *The Sacrifice* (1956), Klein's *Second Scroll* combines core biblical narratives with postholocaust experience; each in its own way challenges the thesis of fellow-Canadian Emile Fackenheim in his *The Jewish Bible after the Holocaust* that Jews can never go back to reading the Hebrew Bible in a deeply inscribed religious way as revelation.[21]

In British and American poetry, drama, and fiction in the second half of the twentieth century, there are no real equivalents to Klein or Wiseman, except perhaps for Howard Nemerov, in whose *Collected Poems* (1977) angular commentary of a high order may be observed in some of the later poems especially, namely "Moses," "Ahasuerus," "Lion and Honeycomb," "Endor," "Cain," and "Nebuchadnezzar, Solus."[22] The novels and short stories of many American Jewish writers, among them Chaim Potok, Isaac Bashevis Singer, Philip Roth, Bernard Malamud, and Saul Bellow, make allusion to the Hebrew Scriptures, even as do Gentiles such as Rudy Wiebe in *Blue Mountains of China* (1970), Margaret Atwood in *The Handmaid's Tale* (1985), and Toni Morrison in *Beloved* (1987) and *Song of Solomon* (1977), but in nothing like the deeply learned and textured way one finds in the earlier traditions. If there is an exception in the novel, it would be Thomas Mann's masterful four-volume series *Joseph and His Brothers* (1933–44, trans. 1949), rich in its integration of both Jewish and Christian exegetical commentary and reliably informed by ancient literature and anthropology. More often than not in the modern novel, however, a biblical title is largely a pre-text for other matter. Here one may consider as thin an evocation as that by Josef Ponten in *Der Babylonische Turm* (1918) or the more textured reflection in Raymond Abellio's *La Fosse de Babel* (1948) and *Les Yeux d'Ezechiel Sont Ouverts* (1949).

THE HEBREW BIBLE IN PAINTING SINCE
THE RENAISSANCE

If it is impossible to do more than to sketch out general lines of historical development for literature influenced by the Hebrew Bible, it is for similar reasons – mostly sheer amplitude – difficult to do much more for painting than isolate a limited number of highlights and popular themes, and then, by way of conclusion, metonymically to illustrate the deep interconnection between biblical text and exegetical tradition in the work of distinguished visual artists.

Artistic subject matter in this period is increasingly a function of patronage. From the Reformation and Counter-Reformation forward, Western painting was overwhelmingly dominated by Christians. Postmedieval Jewish constraint in respect of the Second Commandment made this more or less inevitable. In the sixteenth and early seventeenth centuries, patronage of art was still predominantly ecclesiastical, except in Protestant countries such as Holland and England, where there was growing lay patronage from the ranks of the prosperous burgher middle class and landed gentry, respectively. Domestic patronage, largely Protestant, brought with it new topics. Royal patronage and political focus also increased. By the eighteenth century, the market was increasingly for secular rather than religious subject matter. The influence of the Hebrew Bible on painting tended with rare exceptions to wane.

But in the Renaissance it was still at its zenith. In Italy, where Catholic typological appropriation continued to characterize the depiction of Old Testament narrative, an almost ideal tutorial is available in the Sistine Chapel. On the upper south and north walls, facing each other across the chapel, are depicted the life and mission of Moses and the life and mission of Christ, respectively. Painted by Perugino, Botticelli, Roselli, and Ghirlandaio, these massive mirroring programs in fresco illustrate the parallels of type and antitype (humble births, attempts on the infant life, the theme of Passover and liberation, Mount Sinai and the Sermon on the Mount, the brazen serpent and the Cross, Moses being "taken up" and the Resurrection and Ascension of Christ, etc.) – the most basic framework of Christian reinterpretation of the Jewish "grand narrative."[23] The entrance wall depicts Jacob and Joseph as the patriarchal progenitors, while Michelangelo's magnificent ceiling affords originary representations of the Creation of the world, Adam and Eve, the Fall and Expulsion from Eden, and Noah and the Flood. Additionally, there are echoing narratives of Israel's deliverance from subsequent perils. Yet all these patriarchal episodes, as A. M. Klein's overawed yet scandalized narrator in his novel, *Second Scroll*, discovers, are subsumed into a traditional Catholic refiguration, in which Jewish biblical narrative is merely propaedeutic to the Christian metanarrative of creation, redemption, and finally, the terror of last judgment on Michelangelo's east wall.

Michelangelo's work can be taken, albeit imperfectly, as a reification of the older Christian typology that had come to characterize Counter-Reformation artistic use of the Hebrew Scriptures. When he sculpted his statue of Moses for the tomb of Pope Julius II (1513), he reiterated the ossified iconography by which, since the later Middle Ages (see the *Biblia Pauperum*), Moses was depicted as having goatlike horns. Though by this time understood to reflect a medieval mistranslation of Exodus 34:30 (Latin *quod cornuta esset facies sua*, with the Hebrew read as "horned" rather than "beaming"), it had become such a conventional means of identifying Moses (and indeed a source of bizarre exposition in some quarters) that it was retained despite an overall context of unprecedented artistic realism.

Moses is the central figure of the Hebrew Bible on the traditional Catholic view, and the events of his life receive, accordingly, frequent representation, incident by incident. There are numerous paintings of the finding of Moses in the bullrushes, among which the versions by Vermeer (1570), Poussin (c. 1638), Rembrandt (1635), Hogarth, and Tiepolo (1730) are notable; later the subject becomes increasingly secularized, sentimentalized, and even eroticized, as in versions by Sir Lawrence Alma-Tadema (1904) and Edwin Longsden Long (1886). The latter type of painting makes use of the biblical narrative as a pretext for lush and sometimes prurient focus on Pharoah's daughter and her female attendants. Such developments had been anticipated in the late Middle Ages in the depiction, for example, of Lot and his daughters (Benozzo Gozzoli, Campo Santo fresco, 1470; see also Rubens, 1625), and certainly in paintings of Susannah and Bathsheba by Rubens, Caravaggio, and others, the Pre-Raphaelites had precursors. This taste is in striking contrast to the nude depictions of Adam and Eve by Dürer, Cranach, and Bosch, for example, or the powerful *Expulsion from Eden* fresco by Massaccio (1426).

Nicholas Poussin was the most notable of late Counter-Reformation painters drawn to the life of Moses. Between 1626 and 1645 he painted a series of scenes: the burning bush encounter, the changing of Aaron's rod into a serpent, crossing the Red Sea, gathering manna, and the golden calf. Perhaps only Rembrandt in this period paints Moses more powerfully; in *Moses with the Tablets of the Law* (1659), Rembrandt's choice of dramatic *chiaroscuro* marks the Dutch master's Protestant focus on the individual character.

Catholic painters of the seventeenth century exhibit a keen interest in the narratives concerning the Ark of the Covenant and its role at the heart of Jewish sacred observance. Poussin's *The Plague of Ashdod* and *The Fall of Dagon* are powerful explorations of conflict between the sacred and the profane. Sebastian Bourdin's *The Return of the Ark from Captivity* and Luca Giordana's *David Dancing before the Ark* (both late seventeenth century) are charged with Counter-Reformation interest in the connection between authentic liturgy and divine presence.

In another feature of traditional Catholic salvation history, the triumph of David over Goliath becomes a master sign of God's deliverance of his people. Michelangelo's Sistine Chapel painting (1512), not so powerful as his famous sculpture, still makes of David a heroic Greek god;

Bernini and Donatello's more slender and boyish sculptures are at once more plausibly biblical or at least more attuned to the theological exegesis usually given, namely, that God's presence in a mere shepherd boy brings the very mightiest of men to a bad end.[24] But heroes of the Hebrew Bible whose strength is sometimes a compromised virtue also fascinate Catholic painters: Pisano, Guido Reni, and Rubens all did representations of Samson, and the complexity of these works should occasion more study than it has. Meanwhile, another complex biblical narrative of redemption important in early Christian iconography, namely, the Jonah story, fades away. Between Michelangelo's Sistine depiction, in which Jonah languishes as the great fish begins to nibble on his thigh, and modern comical treatments in literature, such as James Bridie's satirical comedy, *Jonah and the Whale* (1932), and Wolf Mankowitz's *It Should Happen to a Dog* (1956, bilingual pun intended), there is little of compelling interest.

Other figures from the Hebrew Bible become artistically important because of typological association: for example, of Esther with the Virgin Mary (tacit in Fillipino Lippi's [c. 1470] series of Esther paintings, more explicit in Michelangelo's inclusion of Esther pleading for her people in the Sistine Chapel [c. 1510], foreshadowing Mary's intercession for the Church). Poussin, famous for his series of paintings emblemizing the Seven Sacraments, includes the story of Ruth and Boaz for the *Summer* panel of his *Four Seasons* (1660–4), probably because of the homiletical association of marriage with redemptive grace.

But the story of Ruth and Boaz is in fact treated far more frequently in this period by Protestant – especially Dutch – painters than by painters commissioned by Catholics. Moreover, figures from the Hebrew Bible largely neglected for the first millennia and half of Christian art become increasingly of interest because of Calvinist exegesis of the narratives in question. The story of Judah and Tamar, for instance, was painted to the point of cliché in Holland. More prominent examples include those of Ferdinand Bol (1644), Gerbrand van den Eeckhout (1645), Barent Fabritius, Aert de Gelder, and Pieter Lastman. In France, by contrast, it is only in the Orientalist fashion of the post-Napoleonic period that this subject appears prominently, notably in a painting by Horace Vernet (1840).

Protestant artists were fond of the prophets, and Rembrandt's *Jeremiah Lamenting the Destruction of Jerusalem* (1630) is an example of the growing introspection in Protestant exegesis as it begins to reveal itself in art; this aged, dejected Jeremiah is strikingly different from Michelangelo's muscular, looming figure in the Sistine Chapel. Elijah had emerged into prominence in Franciscan iconography in the thirteenth century, reflecting the Joachimite-flavored history of that order; Netherlandish painter Dieric Bouts makes intriguing typological use of *Elijah in the Desert*, depicting *Five Mystic Meals* in his *Altarpiece of the Holy Sacrament* (1464–8), while the Protestant emphasis on "speaking truth to power" emerges later in works such as Thomas Matthews Rooke's *Elijah Confronting Ahab* (1878). Other aspects of Protestant versus Catholic polemic appear in Pieter Breughel the Elder's two versions of the *Tower of Babel* (1563, 1568), in which the *ziggurat* has been cast as a clearly recognizable version of the Roman Colosseum. In a different vein, Job, under the pen of William Blake (twenty-one watercolors, 1818–20), could be subpoenaed as a witness against both the Almighty and the Crown. In Rembrandt's Holland, it seems that some distinctively Jewish stories held potential as allegory of political resistance, namely, the resistance of the Dutch Calvinists to their Catholic Spanish enemies.[25]

But there is more to it than political allegory. In Holland, where there was a well-respected Sephardic Jewish community, especially in Amsterdam, a philosemitic group grew up among the Dutch Protestants and included in their number such artists as Govert Flinck, Jan Lievens, and, most eminently, Rembrandt himself. These men were familiars of leading Jewish families, holding them and their distinctive approaches to the Hebrew Bible in affectionate regard. It is a sense of filiation, rather than supercession, that marks the paintings of Rembrandt especially, allowing him to become the greatest of all painters of Jewish biblical narrative before Chagall. His paintings include, unsurprisingly, many biblical subjects – *Balaam and his Ass* (1626), *David's Parting from Jonathan* (1642), *The Angel Appears to Hagar* (1655), *Esau Sells his Birthright* (1649), *Jacob Wrestling with the Angel* (1660), and *Jacob Blesses the Sons of Joseph* (1656) – all of which feature prominently in Calvinist covenant theology. His two paintings of Joseph being tempted by Potiphar's wife (1634, 1655) might equally, perhaps, have found a place in a Catholic context. But there are other deeply empathetic paintings that in their evocative realizations bear little relationship to the formalities of either Calvinist or Catholic schema. They do, however, reflect narratives central to Jewish commentary: for example, *The Departure of the Shunamite Woman* (1640), *David Sends Uriah Away* (1666), *The Reconciliation of Jacob and Esau* (1655), *The Blinding of Samson* (1636), and more than twenty drawings, five paintings, and three etchings based on the book of Tobit. Rembrandt's *The Sacrifice of Isaac* (1635) is a more powerful rendering of the terror of the *akedah* and near immolation of Abraham's son than anything since Caravaggio (1597), to which it is indebted, and nowhere is the horror so effectively realized from a Jewish point of view. Finally, Rembrandt's second rendition of *Bathsheba* (1654) seems likely indebted to Rembrandt's personal and surprisingly intimate interest in Judaism and Jewish ways of reading biblical narrative.

ART, EXEGESIS, MIDRASH

Traditional Christian characterizations of David's adultery with Bathsheba, for reasons of typology as well as of heroic celebration, find ingenious ways of minimizing, if not exculpating, David from the scandal of his offense. Sometimes the technique is allegory, as when the *Glossa Ordinaria*, following Pope Gregory I, makes Bathsheba a type of the Law, needing to be liberated from the "carnal letter of legalism." Peter Riga, in his *Aurora*, goes so far as to describe Bathsheba as the "denuded law," divested of legalistic trappings, hence that *candida scripturum* (Latin), which is loved by Christ. Alternatively, the narrative may be interpreted tropologically, as by Augustine (*On the Psalms* 51:2–4), as a general warning against lustful temptation.

In Protestant exegesis, the primacy of focus on David tended to mean that one minimized the obvious. Martin Luther's *The Estate of Marriage* regards the king's adultery at the literal level as not worth much attention. Calvin, while he clearly condemns David's act, is not interested in Bathsheba but rather in demonstrating how the divine purpose in salvation history does not depend on human virtue; he takes the opportunity to associate that misconception explicitly with Jews (*Harmony of the Gospels* 1.59).

Depictions of Bathsheba bathing appear frequently in Protestant Bible illustration and books of catechism. There, as in Lucas Cranach's painting (1526), David and his court typically look down from a balcony on a fully clothed Bathsheba washing merely her feet; the pictorial modesty is made possible by learned Protestant appreciation of the Hebrew euphemism "feet" for genitalia (*regel*; cf. Ezekiel 16:25) and an understanding that postmenstrual purification was a likely occasion for Bathsheba's ablutions.

After the sixteenth century, both modesty and moral instruction give way to frank interest in the erotic potential of the story, even by such stalwarts of the Counter-Reformation as Peter Paul Rubens. His *Bathsheba at the Fountain* (1635) presents frontally a young, sexually aroused Bathsheba eagerly receiving from a royal page the note summoning her to the king's bed. The little spaniel, barking at her feet, is a jovial echo of a symbol frequently indicative of a worthy woman's fidelity in medieval iconography; here the dog is evidently ineffectual, and the viewer of the painting is invited to enjoy a frankly erotic scene without the slightest risk of typology or further moral instruction. Rembrandt painted his first *Bathsheba at her Toilette* (1643) in a not dissimilar way, though with a less overt eroticism. His second attempt came at a point when he was living in the Jewish quarter of Amsterdam and enjoying the friendship of several distinguished Jewish intellectuals, including the physician and poet Ephraim Bonus, of whom he did two portraits, and Rabbi Manasseh ben Israel, who lived directly across the street and whose advice resulted, among others things, in the accurate Aramaic inscription in his painting of *Belshazzar's Feast*. Rembrandt was raised as a Calvinist, but his fascination with Jewish culture, religious observance, and gracious Amsterdam communal life, has been shown to have provided him with much of his Jewish subject matter (though only 1 percent of Amsterdam's population at the time, Jews constitute 20 percent of his painterly subjects).[26]

It is noteworthy that while in Jewish exegesis, as in much Christian iconography, David is to some degree exculpated, Bathsheba (in sharp distinction to both Catholic and Reformation commentary) is herself the focus of sympathy and even admiration. She is regarded as one of the "twenty-two virtuous women" and in some accounts as the wise woman of Proverbs 31, the "mother of Lemuel" or of Solomon (Sanh. 70b; Mishle 30, 107–8; 31, 112, etc.).[27] She is a paragon of opulent beauty (*bat-šebaʿ*, "daughter of fullness," or "well endowed"), and while later commentary mutes this emphasis somewhat (Sanh. 107a etymologizes her name as "a fine quality of figs"), approbation of her beauty is still evident. In striking contrast to the conventional Calvinist or more secularizing versions of his contemporaries, Rembrandt's *chiaroscuro* turns the light on what Bathsheba herself might have felt, in all the tragic complexity of her dilemma. In what Simon Schama (1999) calls "the most beautiful nude of his career," Rembrandt's 1654 *Bathsheba* has downcast eyes; the crumpled, oft-read summons betrays her sadness and sense of entrapment. Here Rembrandt lends her a dignity that, far from exculpating David, nonetheless ennobles her as the mother-to-be of Solomon. This is a nude, but it is not erotic. It offers a much less simplistic way of looking at the mysteries of divine providence, we might think, than the reading of Calvin, and is less reflective of exegesis in that vein than of a midrash on the aggadic narrative (Figure 21.2). Rembrandt, though not himself Jewish, in this respect helps us to appreciate the midrashic use of the Hebrew Bible by Marc Chagall, the most celebrated of modern

Figure 21.2. *Bathsheba at Her Bath*, by Rembrant Harmensz van Rijn (1654). Louvre, Paris. Photo credit from Réunion des Musées Nationaux, by permission of Art Resource, New York.

Jewish painters, himself something of a crossover between Jewish and Christian religious imagination.

Marc Chagall (1887–1985) is the most important recent painter of subjects drawn from the Hebrew Bible. Though he grew up in a Hassidic mysticism of the sort associated with the Baal Shem Tov, and he remained imbued with its sense that all of Creation was filled to the point of overflowing with the love of God, he was not conventionally religious but something of a universalist. Yet, in his own words, "Ever since my earliest childhood I have been captivated by the Bible. I have always thought, and still think, that it is the greatest source of poetry of all time ... [and] have sought this reflection in life and in art."[28] His biblical subjects, as may be seen in his massive program for the Musée National Message Biblique in Nice, are among those most frequently treated by Christian painters after the Renaissance. The twelve large pictures in the main gallery include *The Creation of Man* (1962), *Paradise*

(1962), *Adam and Eve Driven Out* (1954–67), *Noah Releasing the Dove* (1931), *Noah and the Rainbow* (1931), *Abraham and the Three Angels* (1954–67), *The Sacrifice of Isaac* (1931), *Jacob's Dream* (1954–67), and *Jacob Wrestling with the Angel* (1931), as well as *Moses before the Burning Bush, Moses Striking the Rock,* and *Moses Receiving the Tables of the Law.* Additionally, Chagall's five oil paintings on themes from the Song of Songs (1960) are in this collection, as well as a mosaic clearly imitative of the early floor mosaics from fifth-sixth century synagogues, except that, strikingly, at the hub of the zodiac wheel where we expect to find Helios or the figure from Psalm 19, there appears rather the prophet Elijah. In this fashion, Chagall reveals his deep knowledge of the biblical art tradition, yet at the same time turns a *pesel* (Hebrew "image") of the ancient past into a *pēšer,* an artist expression, the messianic exegesis central to Hassidic tradition.

Other biblical pieces in the same collection include a striking *Cain and Abel* (1911), in which a powerful and uncircumcised Cain beats down a sexless Abel, *Noah Receiving the Order to Build the Ark* (1931), and the stained-glass depiction of *The Creation of the World.* Elsewhere in private collections one may find, in addition to Chagall's powerful *Exodus* (1952–66), representations of King David as the Psalmist, playing his harp in a nuptial setting that evokes Psalm 45 (1962–3), paired with a beautiful *Bathsheba* that emphasizes only the tenderness of David's devotion to her (1962–3).[29]

It is well known that images of the Crucifixion of Jesus hover in many of Chagall's works, representing the Suffering Servant of Isaiah (Isaiah 53) as a recurrent sign of Jewish experience, but inevitably – and deliberately – evoking the New Testament emblem par excellence of the overarching meaning of biblical grand narrative. This has been the occasion of discomfort to many of his admirers and is mirrored in at least one modern novel, Chaim Potok's *My Name Is Asher Lev* (1972), the story of a boy who grows up to become a painter in a Hassidic community (Potok was also a painter). It is more probably the case that Chagall has in many of his works effectively reversed the polarity of Christian typology in such a way as to say (as in his *Yellow Crucifixion* of 1943) that the meaning of the *bĕrît* (Hebrew "covenant"), and even of the Torah and the prophets, is illuminated by the crucifixion as atonement.[30] But Chagall's *Elijah,* centering the zodiac, marks in its way the ultimate universality of biblical influence in Western painting and literature, and compels a recognition, even as in Rembrandt, that the power of biblical narrative to shape art cannot finally be divorced from its power to shape lives.

NOTES

1   The Hasmoneans (168–134 BCE) built decorated tombs, including martial imagery (ships, armor, and weapons), but clearly eschewed representation of the human form. See L. Y. Rachmani, "Ancient Jerusalem's Funerary Customs and Tombs: Part Three," *Biblical Archaeologist* 45(1)(1982): 43–53. See also the excellent chapters by Steven Fine, "Jewish Art and Biblical Exegesis in the Greco-Roman World," in *Picturing the Bible: The Earliest Christian Art*, ed. by Jeffrey Spier (New Haven, CT: Yale University Press, 2007), 25–49.

2   Cf. b. Sanh. 21b; Azariah de' Rossi, *The Light of the Eyes* (New Haven, CT: Yale University Press, 2001), 665–8.

3   See Carl H. Kraeling, *The Excavations at Dura Europos, Final Report VIII, Part 1, The Synagogue* (New Haven, CT: Yale University Press, 1956), 137–41; Fine, "Jewish Art and Biblical Exegesis," 41–2.

4   Fine, "Jewish Art and Biblical Exegesis," 46–9.

5   One of the most beautiful is the *Ashkenazi Haggadah*, a Hebrew manuscript from the fifteenth century illuminated by Joel ben Simeon (Jerusalem, Israel Museum MSS Rothschild 24). Israel Museum MS 180/51; Wroclaw University Library MS. M1106; British Library Add. MS 11639; Hamburg, Staats, und Universitäts Bibliothek, Cod. Hebrew 37, and a Haggadah kept in the National Museum of Sarajevo are others. Illustrations from these and other manuscripts are reproduced in Dominique Speiss, *An Illustrated Bible* (Laussane, Switzerland: Edita, 1993). See Malachi Beit-Arié, "Joel ben Simeon's Manuscripts: A Codicologer's View," *Journal of Jewish Art* 3(4) (1976–7): 25–39; and Sheila Edmunds, "The Place of the London *Haggadah* in the Work of Joel ben Simeon," *Journal of Jewish Art* 7 (1980): 25–37.

6   See Paul Corbey Finney, "Orpheus-David: A Connection in Iconography between Greco-Roman Judaism and Early Christianity, *Journal of Jewish Art* 5 (1978): 6–15.

7   See A. de Laborde, *La Bible Moralisée Illustrée Conservée a Oxford, Paris et Londres*, 5 vols. (Paris: Société francaise de reproductions de manuscrits à peintures, 1911–27), 1011–1917.

8   Robin M. Jensen, "Early Christian Images and Exegesis," in *Picturing the Bible*, 65–85; and Mary Charles-Murray, "The Emergence of Christian Art," in ibid., 51–2.

9   See "Chapter further reading" for some useful sources. An excellent study of a single art object is Catherine Brown Tkacz, *The Key to the Brescia Casket: Typology and the Early Christian Imagination* (South Bend, IN: University of Notre Dame Press, 2002).

10 Ross Brann, *The Compunctious Poet: Cultural Ambiguity and Hebrew Poetry in Muslim Spain* (Baltimore, MD: Johns Hopkins University Press, 1991).

11 See the *Selected Poems of Shmuel HaNagid*, trans. by Peter Cole (Princeton, NJ: Princeton University Press, 1996).

12 Adele Berlin, *Biblical Poetry through Medieval Jewish Eyes* (Bloomington: Indiana University Press, 1991), 24.

13 David Fowler, *The Bible in Early English Literature* (Seattle: University of Washington Press, 1976), and *The Bible in Middle English Literature* (Seattle: University of Washington Press, 1984).

14 V. A. Kolve, *The Play Called Corpus Christi* (Stanford, CA: Stanford University Press, 1966); Murray Roston, *Biblical Drama in England: From the Middle Ages to the Present Day* (Evanston, IL: Northwestern University Press, 1968): Rosemary Woolf, *The English Mystery Plays* (Berkeley: University of California Press, 1972).

15 Ellen Spolsky, ed., *The Judgment of Susanna: Authority and Witness* (Atlanta, GA: Scholars Press, 1996), 57–72. In early Christian art (see C. B. Tkacz), Susanna could be a type of Christ.

16 Ruth Blackburn, *Biblical Drama under the Tudors* (The Hague: Mouton, 1971).

17 Harold Fisch, *Jerusalem and Albion: The Hebraic Factor in Seventeenth Century Literature* (New York: Schocken, 1964).

18 See Robert Alter, *The Art of Biblical Poetry* (New York: Basic Books, 1985); also Adele Berlin, *Biblical Poetry through Medieval Jewish Eyes*, 11–15 and especially Adele Berlin, *The Dynamics of Biblical Parallelism* (Bloomington: Indiana University Press, 1992 [1985]).

19 See Leopold Damrosch, *Symbol and Truth in Blake's Myth* (Princeton, NJ: Princeton University Press, 1980).

20 Sacvan Bercovitch, *Typology and Early American Literature* (Amherst: University of Massachusetts Press, 1972); Giles Gunn, ed., *The Bible and American Arts and Letters* (Philadelphia: Fortress, 1983).

21 *The Collected Poems of A. M. Klein*, ed. by Miriam Waddinton (Toronto: McGraw-Hill Ryerson, 1974), and *The Second Scroll* (Toronto: Macmillan, 1951); Adele Wiseman, *The Sacrifice* (Toronto: Macmillan, 1956); Emile Fackenheim, *The Jewish Bible after the Holocaust* (Bloomington: Indiana University Press, 1990).

22 *The Collected Poems of Howard Nemerov* (University of Chicago Press, 1977).

23 See Jean Daniélou, *From Shadow to Reality: Studies in the Typology of the Fathers*, trans. by D.W. Hibbard (London: Burns & Oates, 1960).

24 Except, of course, for the spurious hat – which serves to remind us that even a beautifully executed nude can be made to look ridiculous by the addition of a superfluous item of clothing.

25 See Michael Zell, *Reframing Rembrandt: Jews and the Christian Image in Seventeenth Century Amsterdam* (Berkeley: University of California Press, 2002); Helen Webberly, *The Book of Esther in Seventeenth-Century Dutch Art* (AAANZ National Conference Proceedings, Art Gallery of New South Wales, 2002); D. Wavre, *Rembrandt: The Old Testament* (Nashville, TN: Thomas Nelson, 1996); Steven Nadler, *Rembrandt's Jews* (University of Chicago Press, 2003).

26 Zell, *Reframing Rembrandt*, and Nadler, *Rembrandt's Jews*; also Franz Landsberger, *Rembrandt, The Jews and the Bible*, trans. by Felix N. Geson (Philadelphia: Jewish Publication Society, 1946).

27 The association of Bathsheba with the wise woman of Proverbs 31, familiar from rabbinic commentary, begins to appear in Protestant writing only in the

early seventeenth century, e.g., in Robert Cleaver's *Bathsheba's Instructions to her Son Lemuel* (1614).

28   Quoted in François le Targat, *Marc Chagall* (New York: Rizzoli, 1985), 16.
29   Ibid., 18.
30   David Lyle Jeffrey, "Meditation and Atonement in the Art of Marc Chagall," *Religion and the Arts* 16(3) (2012): 211–30.

FURTHER READING

Alter, Robert. *The Art of Biblical Poetry*. New York: Basic Books, 1985.

Berlin, Adele. *Biblical Poetry through Medieval Jewish Eyes*. Bloomington: Indiana University Press, 1991.

 The Dynamics of Biblical Parallelism. Bloomington: Indiana University Press, 1992 (1985).

Brann, Ross. *The Compunctious Poet: Cultural Ambiguity and Hebrew Poetry in Muslim Spain*. Baltimore, MD: Johns Hopkins University Press, 1991.

Fine, Stephen, "Jewish Art and Biblical Exegesis in the Greco-Roman World," pp. 25–49 in *Picturing the Bible: The Earliest Christian Art*. Edited by Jeffrey Spier. New Haven, CT: Yale University Press, 2007.

Fisch, Harold. *Jerusalem and Albion: The Hebraic Factor in Seventeenth-Century Literature*. New York: Schoken, 1964.

Gutman, Joseph. *No Graven Images: Studies in Art and the Hebrew Bible*. New York: Schocken, 1971.

 "The Illustrated Midrash in the Dura Europos Synagogue Paintings: A New Dimension for the Study of Judaism." *Proceedings of the American Academy for Jewish Research* 50 (1983): 91–104.

Landsberger, Franz. *Rembrandt, the Jews and the Bible*. Translated by Felix N. Geson. Philadelphia: Jewish Publication Society, 1946.

Nadler, Steven. *Rembrandt's Jews*. University of Chicago Press, 2003.

Spier, Jeffrey. *Picturing the Bible: The Earliest Christian Art*. New Haven, CT: Yale University Press, 2007.

Zell, Michael. *Reframing Rembrandt: Jews and the Christian Image in Seventeenth-Century Amsterdam*. Berkeley: University of California Press, 2002.

22 The Old Testament in public: the Ten Commandments, evolution, and Sabbath closing laws

NANCY J. DUFF

INTRODUCTION: IDENTIFYING THE ISSUE

When I was a child riding in the car with my father through East Texas farm country, we would occasionally spot a cow grazing on the side of the road. Seeing an animal that had obviously broken through a fence and strayed from the farm where it belonged always prompted my father to declare that legally we were required to return the cow to its owner. Of course, we never stopped to capture a stray animal, locate its owner, and return it home, for we could not possibly have accomplished such a feat. My father was aware this was an obsolete law that made sense when local farmers knew each other and traveled in wagons equipped to put a cow or horse on a lead, but had now become impossible to honor. Decades later, when I was co-teaching a course on the ethics of the Ten Commandments, my colleague, Patrick Miller, delivered a lecture titled, "The Economics of the Straying Ox," on Deuteronomy 22:1–4, which reads in part, "You shall not watch your neighbor's ox or sheep straying away and ignore them; you shall take them back to their owner."[1] It seemed to me there was a good chance that the law my father referred to all those decades ago was based on this Old Testament passage.

That there are laws in the United States that have drawn on biblical commandments is certain. The extent to which biblical commandments contributed to the foundation of the system of law in the United States, however, is in dispute. Some people, including certain Supreme Court justices, believe that the Bible's influence on the formation of the US legal system was extensive. William Rehnquist, for instance, argued in favor of government-sponsored displays of the Ten Commandments based on the "substantial contribution" they had made to secular legal codes.[2] Others, however, argue that while there are individual cases of biblically based civil law, the claim that our legal system was profoundly influenced by the Bible and, more specifically, the Ten Commandments is simply wrong. Steven Green, for instance, provides a convincing account of how English common law and rationalism rather than the Bible formed the basis for American law, arguing that the Bible's overarching influence on the US Constitution is a commonly held misconception.[3]

This chapter looks at three instances where the Old Testament has entered into cultural and legal debates in the United States: (1) posting the Ten Commandments in the public realm, (2) teaching evolution in the public schools, and (3) Sabbath closing laws. Claims regarding the Bible's actual as well as appropriate influence on US civil law play a role in all three cases, which raise constitutional issues with respect to the freedom of religion. These cases also represent serious differences regarding how to interpret the Old Testament texts themselves. Arguments over biblical interpretation, however, are often overlooked by the media, which focus more attention on the clash between church and state than on disputes over the integrity of the Bible. Only occasionally does one hear debates about the interpretation of the biblical texts themselves.

The contention here is that Christians especially should be concerned not only about the issue of constitutionality but also about the meaning of the biblical texts, and that this concern necessarily defies actions that allow secular authority and contexts to give meaning to essentially religious texts. Christians who challenge the wall of separation between church and state are actually handing over the meaning of biblical texts and certain aspects of the Christian faith to secular sources and contexts. No matter how sincere their faith (and I do not doubt that their faith is sincere), as they seek to Christianize American society, they are unwittingly secularizing the Christian gospel.[4]

Because the three issues examined here have spawned heated debates regarding the Bible and the US Constitution, one must consider the American people's knowledge of both. While some Americans argue that evolution and creationism should be taught in the public schools,[5] a Pew survey showed that only 63 percent of Americans know Genesis is the first book of the Bible.[6] While this is a marked improvement from an earlier poll revealing that less than half could make this identification, one might expect to see a greater awareness of this fundamental biblical fact.[7] The Pew survey also shows that over a quarter of Americans do not know "Keep the Sabbath holy" is among the Ten Commandments and the Gold Rule ("Do unto others as you would have them do unto you") is not.[8] Equally important is the American people's knowledge of the Constitution. A vast majority cannot correctly name all five rights guaranteed by the First Amendment.[9] While battles over issues involving the clash between church and state are fueled by passionate convictions, those convictions are not always well informed.

Correcting ignorance of the Bible may require, as Stephen Prothero suggests, a nationwide introduction to religious studies in the public schools,[10] but the content of the First Amendment of the Constitution is brief and straightforward: "Congress shall make no law [1] respecting an establishment of religion, or prohibiting the free exercise thereof; or [2] abridging the freedom of speech, [3] or of the press; [4] or the right of the people peaceably to assemble, and [5] to petition the government for a redress of grievances." Expertise in constitutional law may be required to determine whether a specific law upholds or violates the freedom of religion, speech, press, and assembly or the right to express grievances, but surely a larger percentage of US citizens should know what the five basic components of the First Amendment are.[11]

It is the guarantee of the freedom of religion that most pertains to the issues addressed here. Significantly, two clauses make up the freedom of religion. The "Establishment Clause" prohibits the enactment of any law that seeks to establish a particular religion and is the clause most often invoked in the debates under discussion. The "Free Exercise Clause" rules unconstitutional any law that interferes with a citizen's right to exercise religion freely, and it occasionally enters into the debates as well. The issues explored in this chapter will identify some key aspects of the ongoing constitutional debate. Attention also will be given to the equally important issue of the interpretation of the biblical texts themselves, and whether Christians should want the secular arena to influence that interpretation. Two additional prefatory comments are necessary before exploring these specific issues.

First, this chapter is presented almost exclusively from a Christian perspective because Christians most often initiate arguments in favor of laws that support biblical teachings. Furthermore, Christian interpretations of these laws, and the assumption that US civil laws arise from the Christian Bible and Christian tradition, have often bolstered these arguments. Jewish perspectives therefore will be mentioned only in passing. A project that engages Jewish interpretation of these texts from the Hebrew Bible, as well as the perspective of Jewish ethicists involving these public debates, is worthy of further attention.

Second, while the perspective given here argues for a separation of church and state on both constitutional and biblical grounds, this chapter is *not* proposing that Christians separate their faith from their civil responsibilities. How to allow one's faith to guide responsibilities in the public realm, however, is a complicated question that this chapter does not seek to answer in full. The argument given here makes one significant claim regarding this issue: when Christians seek to express their faithfulness to God in the public arena, they should not ignore the US Constitution or encourage the state to interpret or lend meaning to essentially religious texts.

POSTING THE TEN COMMANDMENTS IN THE PUBLIC REALM

The debate over whether the Ten Commandments should be displayed in public arenas provides a clear example of how constitutionality *and* biblical interpretation are significant when the Old Testament fuels cultural debate. Although the debate over the public display of the Decalogue usually focuses on the issue of constitutionality, Christians should consider *of equal importance* the question of whether such a display is actually true to the meaning of the Ten Commandments themselves.

Interpreting the Constitution

Supporters of the constitutionality of the public display of the Ten Commandments have tended to employ one of three arguments. First, some people claim that the writers of the Constitution never intended to prohibit the government from supporting specifically Christian expressions in the public realm. Others, however, insist that while the Decalogue originates within the Judaeo-Christian tradition, it also carries an inherent secular meaning that allows public displays to comply with the Establishment Clause of the US Constitution. The third argument claims that artistic value sometimes prevents government-sponsored displays of the Ten Commandments from being unconstitutional. It will be argued here that while the first two claims are highly problematic, the third claim does not necessarily violate the First Amendment.

One example of the first argument, which claims that the Constitution supports government-sponsored expression of religious ideas, is provided by the "Ten Commandments judge" and former Chief Justice of the Alabama State Supreme Court, Judge Roy Moore. Justice Moore, who placed a granite monument of the Ten Commandments in the rotunda of the Alabama state judicial building, claimed that this action was not only allowed by the US Constitution but was consistent with his duty as a judge. According to Justice Moore, it was his responsibility *as a judge* to promote the belief that the sovereignty of God is "the source from which all morality springs," a belief, he said, that was recognized by the Founders of the nation.[12] That Chief Justice Moore believes that God and not government ultimately "gave us our rights" should not generate concern. Both the freedom of religion and the freedom of speech guaranteed in the First Amendment allow him to express this belief. To use his office as a state supreme court justice, however, to encourage "a return to the knowledge of God in our land" by displaying the Ten Commandments in a government building, should occasion grave concern. Whatever one believes about the influence the Bible had on the Founding Fathers, the First Amendment to the Constitution says that no law will be used to establish religion. Appeal to the original intention of the writers of the Constitution is troublesome, because it suggests that no development regarding interpretation of the Constitution has merit. Not only does this argument assume that the Framers of the Constitution were never in error, logically it could encourage neglect of the amendments to the Constitution, as if their nonoriginal status makes them less significant for US law. Whether the Framers of the Constitution intended to promote Christian perspectives or not, government-sponsored displays of a religious text for a specifically religious purpose violate the Establishment Clause of the First Amendment.

Other supporters of the public display of the Ten Commandments do not argue for the government's right to promote religious claims but argue instead that the Ten Commandments have a secular meaning separate from their religious origin. This argument, however, is at best only partially true. While one could possibly give a secular interpretation of the last six commandments for honoring parents and prohibiting stealing, lying, killing, and coveting, a secular interpretation *cannot* be given to the first four: to have no other gods than the one, true God, not to take God's name in vain, not to make graven images of God, and to honor the Sabbath. These commandments are without question *religious* in nature; no secular interpretation can uncover their meaning.

The third argument, that some displays of the Ten Commandments are justified by their artistic value, carries more weight than the first two, but not without complications. A good case in point is found in depictions of Moses as lawgiver located inside and outside the Supreme Court building of the United States. Supporters of the public display of the Ten Commandments sometimes point to these images of Moses, arguing that if they are allowed in the US Supreme Court building, then the Ten Commandments can be displayed in other public locations. Although some people claim that the historical influence of the Ten Commandments on US law makes such displays legal (invoking the debate over the influence of the Ten Commandments on US law), a stronger argument points to their artistic value, because the images are part of the architecture of the building, which was erected in 1935. This argument, which has merit, nevertheless could potentially be expanded to claim that every display of the Ten Commandments has artistic value.

Such a move, however, overlooks the fact that Moses does not stand alone in these depictions in the Supreme Court building. While Moses is displayed in a portrait medallion at the front of the building as a lawgiver, so is the lawgiver Hammurabi, as well as eight other figures, including Cicero, Aristotle, and Gaius, who represent advocates, philosophers, and jurists. Moses again appears as a lawgiver on a frieze inside the building, but so do Solon (an Athenian lawgiver), and the Roman and Greek gods Minerva and Zeus. Moses is also depicted in the south-wall frieze along with another Old Testament figure, Solomon, but also with Hammurabi, Confucius, Octavian, and others. The fact that no one religion's representative is alone displayed in the Supreme Court building is consistent with present US society, which includes adherents to Christianity, Judaism, Islam, Native American religions, and a host of others – as well as those who adhere to no religious beliefs at all. If a symbol displayed on public grounds represents only one or two religious views (e.g., Christianity and Judaism when Moses and the Ten Commandments are depicted), then claims for artistic value would be hard pressed to demonstrate that the artist did not intend to promote religious views through artistic means. Such an argument also would not stand up well against legal challenges claiming that artistic expressions of other religious views should be given equal time and space.

Giving equal space to other religious views presents its own set of problems, as demonstrated by a recent case in Utah. At issue was whether the display of the Ten Commandments in a public park in Pleasant Grove City, Utah, represented a private donation when the Fraternal Order of Eagles placed it there in 1971. If so, would not freedom of speech dictate that private donations representing other views have to be accepted as well? With this question in mind, the Summum religion sued the city for the right to display the "Seven Aphorisms of Summum," which it claims were on the first stone tablet that Moses destroyed on Mount Sinai. Similarly, in Casper, Wyoming, Fred Phelps wanted to place a monument concerning Matthew Shepard, the young gay man who was murdered in Laramie in October 1998, next to a display of the Ten Commandments. The new monument would read, "MATTHEW SHEPARD Entered Hell October 12, 1998, in Defiance of God's Warning 'Thou shalt not lie with mankind as with womankind: it is abomination.' Lev. 18:22."

The decision made by the Supreme Court in *Pleasant Grove City v. Summum* applied to the case in Casper as well. The Court unanimously upheld the right of local government to reject a donated monument, arguing that this is not an issue of individual free speech, but government speech, because the government, not the donor, owns the monument. Freedom of speech is not violated by the rejection of a donation because people can still protest in a public park by giving public speeches, organizing rallies, or distributing leaflets, activities that are temporary compared to the more permanent statement offered by a monument or plaque. The Court also argued that government has the right to display monuments that represent the values of the government and of the community, as long as those displays do not violate the rights of citizens.[13]

Interpreting the Bible

Turning from the Constitution to the Bible, it seems that those whose faith leads them to honor the Ten Commandments should readily agree that the Ten Commandments cannot be rightly understood apart from their biblical context, which is exactly what happens when they are put on display in the public realm. The monument in Alabama, for instance, diverges from the Bible by beginning with the words, "I am the Lord thy God," and then moving directly into the First Commandment, "Thou shalt have no other gods before me." Significantly, the words that identify who God is – the One "who brought you out of the land of Egypt, out of the house of slavery" – are omitted, just as they tend to be omitted from all such monuments that stand on government property. The Jewish community includes this claim as part of the First Commandment itself, while most Christians recite it as a prologue to the First Commandment. In both cases, it is only after the pronouncement of who God is and what God has done that we read and hear the commandment, "Have no other gods before me" and each commandment that follows.

These identifying words are a reminder that the Ten Commandments are located within a specific biblical context, that is, the story of God calling Moses to lead the people of God out of slavery and into the Promised Land. The Commandments do not arise from rational considerations of what will best sustain civil society, as important as such considerations are, nor do they arise from a general concept of God as a so-called higher power. The Commandments are rightly understood only *within the story* of who God is and what God has done. Do believers really want to give up the biblical affirmation that these Commandments are given by *this* God? Do Christians want to promote the idea that one can keep the commandments as a list of rules separated from the biblical story of the Exodus rather than obeying the living God who gave the commandments?

In a pluralistic society that protects the free expression of religion and prohibits the establishment of any one religion by the state, there may indeed be room for the public display of various religious symbols under certain limited circumstances. An argument, then, for artistic value can be used to support the images of Moses on the Supreme Court building. This secular value, however, is the only one that Christians should be willing to concede to the Ten Commandments, which are in content and meaning appropriately understood from the perspective of faith in the one God who gave them. To allow, much less expect, the state to support the church through public displays of the Ten Commandments (and a bastardized version at that, without the prologue) should be unthinkable to Christians before they even consider whether or not such a display is constitutional.

READ YOUR BIBLE: EVOLUTION VERSUS CREATIONISM

In 1925, in Dayton, Tennessee, John Scopes was found guilty of defying the Butler Act, which prohibited teaching evolution in Tennessee public schools.[14] The six-day trial pit William Jennings Bryan (the lead prosecuting attorney) and Clarence Darrow (the lead attorney for the defense) against each other. By the end of the trial, it appeared that Darrow (and the American Civil Liberties Union that hired him) had lost the battle. Scopes was found guilty of violating the Butler Act, and Darrow failed to bring the question of constitutionality to bear on the case. Nevertheless, the trial actually represented a setback for the anti-evolutionary forces of the time. William Jennings Bryan's enthusiastic support from spectators at the beginning of the trial dwindled dramatically before it was over. Nevertheless, arguments involving the claims of science against literal interpretations of the creation story in Genesis retain remarkable familiarity today as the controversy continues.[15]

At the beginning of the trial, Clarence Darrow succinctly summarized that aspect of the debate that placed science and religion against each other in his objection to a banner that hung in the court where the jury could clearly read it.

> Your honor, before you send for the jury, I think it my duty to make this motion. Off to the left of where the jury sits a little bit and about ten feet in front of them is a large sign about ten feet long reading, "Read Your Bible," and a hand pointing to it. The word "Bible" is in

large letters, perhaps a foot and a half long.... I just want to make this suggestion.... We might agree to get up a sign of equal size on the other side and in the same position reading, "Hunter's Biology," or "Read your evolution."[16]

With this image of dueling banners, the trial clearly represented the clash between science and religion that crystallized at the time. Advances in science and the rise of philosophical rationalism in the years prior to 1925 helped to spawn the beginnings of fundamentalism in the United States, along with sparking people's fear that science and rationalism posed threats to Christian doctrine and the moral fabric of the nation. The lead attorneys on both sides fell clearly into the divide between science and religion, at times representing the worst arguments of their respective positions. Bryan made Christianity appear narrow and anti-intellectual. Darrow was overly optimistic about the tenets of science and sounded, as Allan Dershowitz has said, like an "antireligious cynic."[17]

Simply to characterize this debate as one between the claims of science and religion or science and the Bible, however, is too simplistic. The debate stands between science and *a certain type* of biblical interpretation. The debate not only pits scientists against Christians, but Christians against Christians. For instance, Dudley Field Malone, another attorney for the defense, argued that tenets of evolutionary theory and the truths revealed in Scripture do not conflict.

> The defense maintains that there is no more justification for imposing the conflicting views of the Bible on courses of biology than there would be for imposing the views of biologists on courses of comparative religion. We maintain that science and religion embrace two separate and distinct fields of thought and learning. We remember that Jesus said: "Render unto Caesar the things that are Caesar's and unto God the things that are God's."[18]

Although Malone's stark separation of religious and civil concerns would rightly be questioned by many Christians, he demonstrates that there are faithful Christians who see no conflict between the biblical story of creation and the scientific theory of evolution. Strictly speaking, the Old Testament account of Genesis in itself has *not* resulted in religious opposition to evolution. Rather, a particular *interpretation* of the creation story has. For those who hold to that interpretation, the issue can be described as a fight between science and religion; for others, however, biblical interpretations that lead to conflict with science actually *contradict* the creation story's most powerful truths. For them there is no contradiction between the claims of science regarding evolution and the tenets of faith.

Legal arguments against teaching evolution in public schools have taken at least three forms since the *Scopes* trial in 1925.[19] First, just as with public displays of the Ten Commandments, Christian opponents of evolution have argued that the Constitution defends Christian beliefs and supports the right to teach religious ideas in public schools. The Butler Act itself represents such a view. When constitutional challenges to teaching religion in public schools began to succeed, the argument shifted to the claim that belief in the Genesis story of creation has scientific validity. "Creationism" or "creation science" was presented as another scientific view, as equally valid as evolution. The argument shifted a third time when creationism was replaced by arguments for "intelligent design," which was again touted as a scientific theory comparable to evolution. While these latter two arguments are similar in that claims about God as creator are presented as science, creationism and intelligent design are not the same thing.

In the *Scopes* trial, one sees a clear representation of the first argument, for it is assumed that the United States is a Christian nation and that Darwin's theory of evolution, which many people believed challenged the creation account in Genesis, could not be allowed to corrupt the minds of students. Other aspects of the trial represented the belief that US law upholds the Christian faith. Another attorney for the prosecution, Ben McKenzie, defended the banner to which Darrow objected by asking, "Why should we remove the sign cautioning the people to read the Word of God just to satisfy the others in the case?" Furthermore, the judge invited local pastors to open the trial with prayer every day, and he appealed to the power of Christ to forgive when he withdrew his threat to fine the prosecution for contempt. That same judge refused to allow scientific experts to be called as witnesses, but he allowed William Jennings Bryan to take the stand and be questioned by Clarence Darrow regarding his tendency to interpret the Bible literally. It was, indeed, a different era. None of those practices is likely to occur in a court of law now.

When court decisions began to challenge the constitutionality of laws that prohibited the teaching of evolution, the debate shifted, and arguments were put forward that creationism and intelligent design are scientific theories. In both cases, the reverse charge is made that evolution is "only a theory." This argument, however, misrepresents the meaning of the word "theory." In everyday, nonscientific use, "theory" indeed indicates that something is conjectural and still uncertain, or at least not yet thoroughly tested. In science, however, the word "theory" indicates a general proposition that has been so thoroughly examined and established that it is now used as a principle of explanation. If one challenges the validity of a scientific explanation on the grounds that it is "just a theory," one would have to challenge Einstein's theory of relativity, the theory of gravitation, and the claim that germs cause illnesses, otherwise known as the "germ theory."

This scientific understanding of theory, just as the nature of science itself, makes it impossible to uphold the claim that either creationism or intelligent design is a scientific theory. Creationism draws on the creation stories of Genesis 1–3 and is often tied to a literal reading of the Bible, although some proponents, such as William Jennings Bryan, have modified the notion of a literal reading by conceding that a "day" mentioned in the Bible may not indicate a twenty-four-hour period but thousands of years instead. Others, who do give a literal rendering to the twenty-four-hour claim, say that there is scientific evidence for a "young earth" that backs their understanding of the claims of Genesis. Attempts are also made to find plausible scientific evidence to support biblical references to a worldwide flood, which, in turn, is used to explain fossil records. Further arguments are put forward as scientific evidence that human beings came into the world *ex nihilo* (Latin "out of nothing") or "fixed in kind."

Intelligent design, which also lays claim to being a science, does not depend on the Bible. It is, in fact, a classic form of apologetics, offering logical proof for the existence of God. William Paley, a nineteenth-century Anglican priest and teacher in Cambridge, England, was not the first to put forward such an argument, but his use of the image of a divine watchmaker is often invoked in the contemporary debate. According to this reasoning, if someone came upon a watch without knowledge of what it was or who made it, the discoverer would have to conclude that such a complex mechanism was the result of a designer; luck or happenstance could never have resulted in such an intricate design. Similarly, the argument continues, there are things in nature so intricate in design that reason dictates an intelligent designer must have produced it. While the argument does not claim that the intelligent designer is the God of the Bible, most antievolutionists use it to lend support to the creation story in Genesis. But whether they make this move or not, arguments for intelligent design seek to insert concepts of God into science.

When arguments for God are given so-called scientific status and evolution is described as "only a theory," the stage is set for arguing that public schools should "teach the controversy" in their science classes.

Former US President George W. Bush supported this position. The problem (besides the misrepresentation of what is meant by "theory") is that supernatural explanations do not belong in science. Although a leading spokesman for intelligent design, William Dembski, denies that the supernatural constitutes part of the argument for intelligent design, his subsequent insistence that "God may have left tangible evidence of His involvement in creation" and that "intelligence is needed to explain life's origin and development" seems to indicate otherwise.[20] Once the word "God" enters the conversation, one is no longer in the realm of science – unless one has already turned the definition of science on its head, for scientists look for natural, not divine, explanations of things.[21] The scientist, *who also may be a person of faith*, cannot invoke God as a cause because God does not constitute a scientific explanation of things. To say otherwise constitutes bad science and, as will be argued later, bad theology as well.

Biblical interpretation

The truth revealed in the Bible neither contradicts science nor needs science to uphold it. The very first line of the Bible demonstrates that this is so. "In the beginning," the Bible tells us, "God created the heavens and the earth." The profound theological meaning of this claim resides in the Hebrew word for "created" (*bārā'*), which is used only with God as subject. While human beings create many things, God creates in a way unique to God. Nothing human beings do can enable them to lay claim to being the Creator. That designation belongs only to God. The Bible tells us nothing *from a scientific perspective* about how the world was formed. Rather, it identifies *who* formed the world. Dietrich Bonhoeffer understood that the Bible does not yield scientific data:

> Whether the creation occurred in rhythms of millions of years or in single days, this does no damage to biblical thinking. We have no reason to assert the latter or to doubt the former; the question as such does not concern us. That the biblical author, to the extent that the author's word is a human word, was bound by the author's own time, knowledge, and limits is as little disputed as the fact that through his word God, and God alone, tells us about God's creation.[22]

Bonhoeffer warned Christians not to use God to explain otherwise inexplicable things, for this results in a notion of God as a stopgap to incomplete human knowledge. If science can later explain what only the concept of God could once provide, then God is pushed ever further to the periphery of life. God does not belong on the periphery of human knowledge, Bonhoeffer said, but at the center of life.[23]

The scientist Kenneth Miller, perhaps unwittingly, maintains Bonhoeffer's rejection of the god of the gaps when he objects to the notion that religious meaning and purpose in life can only found in "areas of scientific ignorance" or in the "dark recesses of what science cannot explain."[24] Miller refuses to make scientific claims for religion in its capacity for explaining things that science has not yet explained. "We should find our being, our value, and our meaning as human beings," he says, "not in the darkness but in the bright areas of knowledge that science illuminates."[25] Bonhoeffer could not have said it better. For the faithful, belief in God should stand at the center of life rather than being reduced to explaining things that cannot be explained any other way.

SABBATH CLOSING LAWS

In 1869, the Reverend Benjamin M. Palmer of the First Presbyterian Church in New Orleans proclaimed in a Thanksgiving Day sermon that the same demon who opposed Sabbath closing laws also supported the French revolution, abolition, and human rights. Few supporters of Sunday closing laws have actually taken their stance in order to curtail civil rights, as Palmer did. Sabbath laws, sometimes called "blue laws," have existed since Colonial days and endure in some form in every US state today, except Alaska.[26]

In 1610, laws in the Colony of Virginia prohibited people from working on the Sabbath and required them to attend two worship services every Sunday. The penalty for violating the law was one week's provisions for the first offense and another week's provision, plus being whipped, for the second. A third offense resulted in death.[27] Despite this severe penalty, the law resulted in such widespread disregard that by 1623 penalties in Virginia were reduced to payments in tobacco, one pound for the first offense, and fifty pounds for missing "a month of Sundays."[28] Sunday laws still exist, varying from limiting hours for the sale of alcohol on Sundays, to prohibiting the sale of cars, to the curtailment of fishing on government property. Breaking Sabbath laws is commonly treated today as a misdemeanor. The most stringent law still enforced is found in Paramus, New Jersey, where all "worldly employment" is prohibited, which means that four major shopping malls are closed on Sundays throughout the year, even at Christmas. However, the reason for the survival of this law may have more to do with traffic control on the always congested Route 17 than with worshiping God.

Interpreting the Constitution

As with the preceding two issues, Sabbath laws have been based on the belief that US law should support Christian practices. A more common argument, however, assumes a secular interpretation of the commandment as protecting something that everyone needs, namely, rest from work. Human beings, animals, and the earth itself need the cycle of day and night, wakefulness and sleep, work and rest. Whether one believes that such rest is commanded by God, or mimics divine activity at Creation, or should be accompanied by worship, the need for rest is simply a fact of life. In fact, labor unions have sometimes argued in favor of Sunday closing laws for this reason.

While this argument has merit, it overlooks the fact that Sunday closing laws dictate that such rest must occur on *Sunday*, the day of rest identified by most, though not all, Christians. Seventh Day Adventists and Jews identify Saturday as the Sabbath, and Muslims observe the Sabbath on Friday. Laws that protect the sanctity of Sunday by curtailing activities on that day can place an economic burden on those who wish to observe Sabbath on Friday or Saturday, but cannot afford to take off work on Sunday as well. Despite this argument, four cases that came before the Supreme Court, and were jointly decided in 1961, failed to bring a decision against the constitutionality of Sunday closing laws.[29]

Of course, there are also citizens who do not choose to observe any day of the week based on a religious understanding of Sabbath, but who still want time off from work. Concern for the rights of these workers was in part represented in a Supreme Court decision of 1985, *Thornton v. Caldor*. The Supreme Court concurred that a Connecticut statute giving employees an absolute right not to work on their chosen Sabbath violated the Establishment Clause of the First Amendment.[30] Although the law may at first appear to be a reasonable compromise because it does not designate a particular day for the Sabbath, it requires the state to determine whether someone is legitimately asking to observe a Sabbath for religious reasons and, in turn, denies nonreligious workers the same privilege. It was its specifically religious motivation that led to the decision that the law violated the Establishment Clause. The law still sought to uphold a religious practice even if honoring that practice was made flexible enough to accommodate different religions instead of supporting the tradition of only one.

From the perspective of the Constitution, it seems that communities need to address the complex matter of providing workers with time for rest, and even providing communities with respite from the sometimes frenetic challenge of 24/7 commerce. To be in compliance with the First Amendment of the Constitution, however, these laws must address citizens' need for rest without supporting any particular religion or curtailing the observance of religious practices.

Biblical interpretation

The biblical command to observe the Sabbath (Exod 20:8–11; Deut 5:12–15) has three clearly identifiable meanings. The commandment describes the need for humans and even animals to enjoy rest from labor. It also addresses the obligation and privilege of setting aside time to worship God. Finally, it speaks to issues of social justice, in that the demands of work cannot justify abuse of humans or animals who contribute to labor. There is, of course, no secular interpretation for setting aside time to worship God, unless once again Christians want to allow the secular arena to define the God who is worshiped as a generic "higher power" to whom each worshiper gives homage and perhaps even definition in his or her own way.

The point here is not to belittle those who find meaning in the concept of a higher power – rather to insist that the Sabbath commandment was not (according to the Bible) delivered by a nameless entity or force, but by the God who brought God's people out of the house of slavery. Christians should be motivated by this divine command to advocate for labor laws limiting the number of hours in a given week that people are required to work. At the same time, serving this God and following this God's commandments does not require them, as the Reverend Palmer believed, to deny the civil rights of others. If churches can only motivate their members to honor the Sabbath by depending on the state to enforce it, then Christians might as well acknowledge that they are first and foremost US citizens, abiding by laws imposed on them, rather than Christians who freely and joyfully seek to serve God by making holy the Sabbath day.

Modern society is more complicated than that envisioned (and sometimes enjoyed) by groups of Christians wishing to order their lives in such a way that the entire community can enjoy rest from labor and together praise God. There were, nevertheless, always citizens who wished to be free from obligatory worship, as well as those who wanted to be free to worship and rest on a day other than Sunday. What better way is there for Christians to honor the God who delivers from slavery than by supporting secular laws protecting the rights and freedoms of all their neighbors?

CONCLUSION

When considering the constitutional issues presented here, Christians need to acknowledge what some of their Christian forebears could not, that the United States is *not* equivalent to ancient Israel. Current US citizens do not as a group constitute the people of faith addressed by the Bible. For Christians, the community of faith that stands parallel to ancient Israel is the Church, not the nation, just as for Jews that community is represented by the Synagogue or Temple. Although Christians are continually challenged to seek ways to be faithful as people of God, even as they remain citizens of the United States, surely they do not want to allow their identity as Christians to be subsumed under their identity as US citizens. People of faith do not need, nor should they expect, the state to support their beliefs and practices, though they certainly should expect the state to give them the freedom to worship God. Nor should they desire the state to wield coercive power, forcing their beliefs on others, although they certainly should expect the state to protect their freedom to give witness to what they believe. The Establishment Clause and the Free Exercise Clause of the Constitution guarantee them these freedoms, while the Bible encourages them to be true to who they are – believers in the One who brought them out of the house of slavery and commanded their obedience in love and freedom.

NOTES

1   The full title of his lecture was "The Economics of the Straying Ox: Property and Possessions." The parallel passage is Exodus 23:4: "When you come upon your enemy's ox or donkey going astray, you shall bring it back." Now see Patrick D. Miller, *The Ten Commandments* (Interpretation; Louisville, KY: Westminster John Knox, 2009), 323–4.

2   For reference to Rehnquist's argument, see my essay, "Should the Ten Commandments Be Posted in the Public Realm? Why the Bible and the Constitution Say, 'No,'" in *The Ten Commandments: The Reciprocity of Faithfulness*, ed. by William P. Brown (Louisville, KY: Westminster John Knox, 2004), 165. Also see Rehnquist, C. J., dissenting, Supreme Court of the United States, *City of Elkhart v. William A. Books et al.*; available at: http://www.law.cornell.edu/supct/html/00-1407.ZD.html.

3   Steven K. Green, "The Fount of Everything Just and Right? The Ten Commandments as a Source of American Law," *Journal of Law and Religion* 14(2) (1999–2000): 525–58.

4   Dietrich Bonhoeffer understood that when Christians set out to Christianize the world, they secularize the Gospel instead. Dietrich Bonhoeffer, *Discipleship* (Dietrich Bonhoeffer Works 4; Minneapolis, MN: Fortress, 2001), 54.

5   A 2005 poll conducted by the Pew Forum on Religion and Public Life and the Pew Research Center for the People and the Press showed that two-thirds of the American people believe both creationism and evolution should be taught in public schools. See Laurie Goodstein, "Teaching of Creationism Is Endorsed in New Survey," *New York Times*, August 31, 2005; available at: http://www.nytimes.com/2005/08/31/national/31religion.html. In 2014, *Slate* magazine published a map indicating which public schools in the United States teach creationism; available at: http://www.slate.com/articles/health_and_science/science/2014/01/creationism_in_public_schools_mapped_where_tax_money_supports_alternatives.html.

6   "US Religious Knowledge Survey Executive Summary," Pew Research Religion Public Life Project, September 28, 2010; available at: http://www.pewforum.org/2010/09/28/u-s-religious-knowledge-survey/.

7   Susan Jacoby, "Blind Faith," *Washington Post*, March 4, 2007, a review of Stephen R. Prothero, *Religious Literacy: What Every American Needs to Know and Doesn't* (San Francisco: HarperSanFrancisco, 2007); available at: http://www.washingtonpost.com/wpdyn/content/article/2007/03/01/AR2007030102073.htm.

8   "US Religious Knowledge Survey Executive Summary," Pew Research Religion Public Life Project, September 28, 2010.

9   According to a July 2013 survey conducted by the First Amendment Center at Vanderbilt University, 59 percent of those surveyed identified freedom of speech as one of the rights guaranteed by the First Amendment; freedom of religion was identified by 24 percent; 14 percent named freedom of the press; 11 percent named freedom to assembly, and only 4 percent could identify the freedom to petition.

10 Prothero, *Religious Literacy*.

11 Prior to writing this chapter, I could not myself name all five freedoms guaranteed by the First Amendment.

12 The monument also exhibits excerpts from American documents and quotations from English and American statesmen, but the Ten Commandments are most prominently displayed. For Judge Moore's arguments, see the Petition for a Writ of Certiorari to the United States Court of Appeals for the Eleventh Circuit, Roy S. Moore, *Petitioner*, v. Stephen R. Glassroth, *Respondent*; available at: www.morallaw.org/PDF/Cert._Petition_Moore_v._AJIC_7.29.04.pdf.

13 See *Pleasant Grove City et al. v. Summum*, October Term 2008; available at: http://www.supremecourt.gov/opinions/08pdf/07-665.pdf. See also Nancy J. Duff, "Should the Ten Commandments Be Displayed in Public?" participant handout for an adult study; available at: http://www.TheThoughtfulChristian.com.

14 The Butler Act was passed by the State of Tennessee in 1925 and read, in part: *"Be it enacted by the General Assembly of the State of Tennessee, That it shall be unlawful for any teacher in any of the Universities, Normals*

and all other public schools of the State which are supported in whole or in part by the public school funds of the State, to teach any theory that denies the story of the Divine Creation of man as taught in the Bible, and to teach instead that man has descended from a lower order of animals." Violating the act was a misdemeanor that carried a fine of $100 to $500.

15 Many people's awareness of the trial is based on the 1955 play, *Inherit the Wind*, by Jerome Lawrence and Robert Edwin Lee, and the 1960 movie staring Spencer Tracy. The play, however, is fiction, written in part to counter McCarthyism. For facts, one must study the trial itself. For a website devoted exclusively to the *Scopes* trial, see Douglas O. Lindner, "Famous Trials in American History: *Tennessee vs. John Scopes*, 'The Monkey Trial,' 1925" (2008); available at: http://www.law.umkc.edu/faculty/projects/ftrials/scopes/scopes.htm.

16 Lines omitted from the quotation have to do with the judge disputing that the letters were as large as Darrow claimed and a response from one of the prosecuting attorneys, Ben B. McKenzie. See "Scopes Trial: Excerpts from the Court Transcripts, Day 7"; available at: http://faculty.smu.edu/jclam/science_religion/trial_transcripts.html.

17 Even the ACLU feared that Darrow had alienated potential supporters. See Douglas O. Lindner, "Clarence Darrow (1857–1938)" (2004; available at): http://www.law.umkc.edu/faculty/projects/ftrials/scopes/darrowcl.htm.

18 Douglas O. Lindner, "Excerpts from Scopes Trial"; available at: http://www.law.umkc.edu/faculty/projects/ftrials/scopes/day4.htm.

19 Charles A. Israel, "How the Anti-Evolution Debate Has Evolved," George Mason University's History News Network, December 21, 2005; available at: http://hnn.us/articles/19613.html.

20 William A. Dembski, "First-Person: The Difference 'Expelled' Will Make," *Baptist Press: News with a Christian Perspective*, April 18, 2008; available at: http://www.bpnews.net/BPFirstPerson.asp?ID=27872.

21 Dembski does, in fact, want to change the scientific definition of what is "natural," leaving room for the concept of an intelligent designer.

22 Dietrich Bonhoeffer, *Creation and Fall: A Theological Exposition of Genesis 1–3* (Dietrich Bonhoeffer Works 3; Minneapolis, MN: Fortress, 1997), 49.

23 Dietrich Bonhoeffer, *Letters and Papers from Prison*, enlarged ed. (New York: Macmillan, 1971), 310, 341, 359–60.

24 Kenneth Miller, "In Defense of Evolution," from *NOVA*, "Judgment Day: Intelligent Design on Trial," © 1996–2007 WGBH Educational Foundation; available at: http://www.pbs.org/wgbh/nova/id/defense-ev.html.

25 Ibid.

26 Two explanations have been offered for the designation of Sunday closing laws as "blue laws." Some say that the code of law in the colony of New Haven in 1665 was written on blue paper. Others say that for Puritans blue represented faithfulness, based perhaps on the staying power of blue dye. See David N. Laband and Deborah Hendry Heinbuch, *Blue Laws: The History, Economics, and Politics of Sunday-Closing Laws* (Lexington, MA: Lexington Books, 1987), 8.

27 Ibid., 30.

28 Ibid.
29 The four cases were *McGowan v. Maryland*, 366 U.S. 420 (1961); *Gallagher v. Crown Kosher Super Market of Mass., Inc.*, 366 U.S. 617 (1961); *Braunfeld v. Brown*, 366 U.S. 599 (1961); and *Two Guys from Harrison vs. McGinley*, 366 U.S. 582 (1961).
30 See *Estate of Thornton v. Caldor, Inc.* (No. 83-1158) from Supreme Court Collection, Cornell University Law School; available at: http://www.law .cornell.edu/supct/html/historics/USSC_CR_0472_0703_ZO.html.

FURTHER READING

Barth, Karl. "The Holy Day," §53 "Freedom before God," pp. 47–72 in *Church Dogmatics, Vol. III, Chap.4: The Doctrine of Creation.* Edinburgh: T & T Clark, 1961.

Duff, Nancy J. "Should the Ten Commandments Be Posted in the Public Realm? Why the Bible and the Constitution Say, 'No,'" pp. 159–70 in *The Ten Commandments: The Reciprocity of Faithfulness.* Edited by William P. Brown. Louisville, KY: Westminster John Knox, 2004.

Green, Steven K. "The Fount of Everything Just and Right? The Ten Commandments as a Source of American Law." *Journal of Law and Religion* 14(2) (1999–2000): 525–58.

Heschel, Abraham. "A Palace in Time," pp. 214–22 in *The Ten Commandments: The Reciprocity of Faithfulness.* Edited by William P. Brown. Louisville, KY: Westminster John Knox, 2004.

Larson, Edward J. *Summer for the Gods: The Scopes Trial and America's Continuing Debate over Science and Religion.* Cambridge, MA: Harvard University Press, 1998.

Lawrence, Jerome, and Robert Edwin Lee. *Inherit the Wind.* New York: Ballantine Books, 2007.

Lindner, Douglas O. "Famous Trials in American History: Tennessee vs. John Scopes, 'The Monkey Trial,' 1925." 2008; available at: http://www.law .umkc.edu/faculty/projects/ftrials/scopes/scopes.htm.

McCrossen, Alexis. *Holy Day, Holiday: The American Sunday.* Ithaca, NY: Cornell University Press, 2000.

Miller, Patrick D. *The Ten Commandments* (Interpretation). Louisville, KY: Westminster John Knox, 2009.

23 The Theology of the Hebrew Bible/ Old Testament

JOHN GOLDINGAY

Biblical theology, with Old Testament theology as an eventual subset, was a relative latecomer on the scene of biblical study. It emerged as a discipline distinguishable from systematic or dogmatic theology in the seventeenth century, with the role of providing the biblical evidence for the assertions of systematic or dogmatic theology. In the eighteenth century it began to assert itself as a discipline that should define its own categories rather than simply act as handmaid to systematics, and in 1787, Johann Philipp Gabler delivered a lecture that is commonly seen as a key articulation of this conviction, 'An Oration on the Proper Distinction Between Biblical and Dogmatic Theology and the Specific Objectives of Each'.[1] A number of nineteenth-century Old Testament theologies worked with Gabler's prescription, though they also continued to be influenced (consciously or unconsciously) by the categories of systematics, by the philosophical views of the day, and by New Testament priorities that led to an emphasis on marginal topics, such as resurrection, and a neglect of topics prominent in the Old Testament but not in Christian faith. It became customary for Old Testament theologians to draw attention to the way their predecessors were affected by the presuppositions of their time but not to recognize the same dynamics in their own work. In the twenty-first century, post-colonial or feminist or other postmodern perspectives are equivalents to the evolutionism, rationalism or romanticism of the nineteenth century. These provide frameworks that theologians bring to their study, which both illumine it and skew it.

WALTHER EICHRODT

Another such framework is the assumption that Old Testament theology needs to be approached historically, and it became common for theologies to comprise two parts, one tracing Israel's history and the other covering the theological implications of the literature in topical fashion.

Indeed, the energy in nineteenth-century Old Testament study came to lie in tracing the history of Israel and its religion against their Middle Eastern background. This preoccupation rather left hanging the question of the Old Testament's ongoing religious and theological significance. It was after the 1914–18 war in Europe, and parallel to the work of Karl Barth in Christian dogmatics, that some Old Testament scholars began once more to think in theological terms. This development came to a climax in the 1930s with the *Theology of the Old Testament* by Walther Eichrodt, a colleague of Barth in Switzerland.[2] It was the first great modern attempt to synthesise the thinking of the Old Testament, and the first Old Testament theology that remains enlightening in what it says about the Old Testament, rather than being of interest purely as part of the history of the discipline.

Ironically, this judgement holds despite the fact that Eichrodt fails to achieve either of his two stated aims. There is regularly a disparity between the statements about aims and method with which Old Testament theologians begin their works and the insights and implications about method that emerge from those works themselves, and Eichrodt illustrates this phenomenon well.

Eichrodt aims to identify the constant fundamental nature of Old Testament religion, the system of faith that underlies the entire Old Testament, and to demonstrate how this faith links distinctively with that of the New Testament. In this connection, he emphasises Yhwh's covenant, which Eichrodt takes as key to understanding the relationship between Yhwh and Israel, though not to understanding Yhwh's relationship with the world (which he treats in his second volume). Although aiming to make a cross-section of Old Testament faith, in his chapters on different topics he commonly takes an historical approach, seeking to show how understandings of (for instance) the covenant, priesthood or sacrifice changed over the centuries (and a notable weakness here was his perpetuation of the traditional Christian assumption that Old Testament faith degenerated as time passed).

Further, it soon becomes clear that his image of one faith 'underlying' the whole Old Testament does not work. There is no indication within (for instance) Exodus, Ecclesiastes, and Nahum that they have the same underlying convictions. A better way to picture the idea that there is one Old Testament faith is to think in terms of a theology issuing from the Old Testament as a whole rather than one underlying the whole. A 'big picture' emerges from the Old Testament, to which Genesis, Esther, the Song of Songs, and Isaiah all make their distinctive contributions.

Eichrodt's distinctive emphasis on covenant as the center of Old Testament theology highlights two key elements in this big picture. The Old Testament is about Yhwh and Israel, the two parties involved in that covenant relationship.

YHWH

A fundamental Old Testament challenge is, 'Acknowledge that Yhwh is God' (Ps 100:2). While the Old Testament can use the generic Hebrew word 'ĕlōhîm to refer to supernatural beings other than Yhwh, it is clear that Yhwh is God *par excellence*. 'Yhwh is the great king over all gods' (Ps 95:3). Yhwh is not just one god among gods but *the* 'God of gods' (Deut 10:17). Yhwh's relationship to other deities is traditionally formulated in terms of the development of monotheism (or belief in only one God), but this way of framing the question imposes a perspective from the later history of Christian thought. The Old Testament question was not 'how many gods are there' (one or three or a thousand), but 'who is God' (Baal or Marduk or Yhwh). And the Old Testament's attitude towards the 'gods' that other nations worshiped was not to deny their existence, but to demote them to Yhwh's servants. Only Yhwh is truly God.

In Leviticus 19:2, Yhwh offers in person an illuminating self-definition nuancing the declaration that only Yhwh is God: 'I Yhwh your God am holy'. First, Yhwh is not merely 'God' but 'your God'. This emphasis underscores that relationship involved in the covenant. Yhwh's being 'your God' implies a mutual commitment between Yhwh and Israel. Yhwh is committed to Israel, and thus acts on its behalf when it is in need; 'I am Yhwh your God who brought you out of the land of Egypt, out of the household of serfs' (Exod 20:2). And Israel is (supposed to be) committed to Yhwh: 'You shall have no other gods over against me' (Exod 20:3). Israel was Egypt's servant; now it is Yhwh's. Yhwh *is* king and lord, sovereign in the heavens and on earth. Yhwh *is to be* Israel's king and lord, its sovereign, but also its protector. ('Yhwh' comprises the consonants of this name; the Hebrew alphabet has no vowels. Jewish practice gave up pronouncing the name, and no one is sure any longer how to pronounce it, though 'Yahweh' is the usual assumption. Following Jewish custom, most English translations of the Old Testament replace the name by the common noun 'the Lord'. This convention gives the impression that Old Testament reference to God focuses much more on the image of God as Lord than is actually the case.)

In Leviticus 19:2, however, 'I Yhwh your God' is but the subject of a sentence that continues 'am holy'. Arguably, this is the most elemental statement that can be made about Yhwh. Indeed, it is close to being a tautology. In Christian usage, 'holiness' came to be a moral category, like purity or righteousness. But in Old Testament usage, 'holiness' is a metaphysical category, a term for a kind of being. To say that someone or something is holy is to say that the person or object is set apart as belonging to the supernatural realm. So to say 'Yhwh is holy' has very similar significance to saying 'Yhwh is supernatural'. It would not in itself indicate that Yhwh is upright or faithful (e.g., a Canaanite or Babylonian god could be described as holy without being upright or faithful).

Yet the word 'holy' did come to have those connotations of uprightness and faithfulness because *in Yhwh's case*, being God or being holy *does* involve moral qualities. Comments by two prophets illustrate the point. Isaiah 5:16 declares, 'Yhwh of Armies has been majestic in exercising authority, and the holy God has shown himself holy in doing the right thing'. The frightening implication in context is that Judah has been ignoring Yhwh's expectations for its community life and is in the midst of paying for it. Bringing the nation down will be an expression of Yhwh's holiness because it is an act of integrity and uprightness.

In contrast, Isaiah's contemporary, Hosea, has Yhwh declaring an intention of similarly putting down the northern kingdom, but then facing the impossibility of doing this 'because I am God and not a man, in your midst as the holy one' (Hos 11:9). Here Yhwh's holiness is expressed in refraining from punishment, not in punishing, and in mercy, not in judgement. The point is taken further subsequently in Isaiah, when Yhwh as the holy one *of Israel* comes to be described as Israel's restorer or redeemer (e.g., Isa 41:14). The basis for Israel's restoration is not that Israel deserves it; no change has come over the people. Its basis is simply that Yhwh is Israel's holy one, the God committed to Israel, and will restore the people because of that commitment. Once more, Yhwh's holiness expresses itself in faithfulness and mercy.

In another self-description, Yhwh personally sums up the two sides to this holiness without actually using the word 'holy' (Exod 34:6–7): 'Yhwh, God compassionate and gracious, long-tempered and big in commitment and steadfastness, keeping commitment to thousands, carrying waywardness, rebellion, and shortcoming, not at all acquitting, attending to the waywardness of parents on children and on grandchildren to thirds and to fourths'. The self-description does not explain the relationship of the two sides of Yhwh's character, and while Israel can often see a logic to Yhwh's faithfulness and wrath, frequently Yhwh is merciful when one might have expected trouble, and sometimes Yhwh sends trouble when Israel cannot see the reason.

The origin of the distinctive name 'Yhwh' is obscure. In recounting the revelation of this name to Moses, Exodus 3 makes a link with the verb 'to be', though the significance of this link is also obscure, and the Old Testament hardly again refers to it. For Israel, 'Yhwh' is simply a name. Exodus 3 and the subsequent revelation in Exodus 6 focus on a different point, that the God who reveals this name is not a new God. Yhwh appears as the God of Israel's ancestors, the God of Abraham, Isaac, and Jacob. Yhwh appears as the one they also knew as El Shadday – and as El Elyon and by means of other such compound names in Genesis.

The explanation in Exodus 3 does perhaps point to Yhwh's capacity to 'be there' for Israel in whatever ways different contexts require. This would link with another characteristic feature of Yhwh. While the Old Testament makes clear that Israel often made images of Yhwh, it never approves of this. Yhwh cannot be imaged. Yhwh is a being who speaks and acts. An image cannot convey that; it can only mislead. The rationale for banning images is thus not that Yhwh is spiritual rather than bodily, though if we interpret Yhwh's being 'spirit' in the Old Testament's own terms, that would underline this point, as Yhwh's spirit stands for Yhwh's dynamic power.

ISRAEL

And what is Israel? Having lifted the Israelites out of serfdom in Egypt and brought them to Sinai, Yhwh declares that if they now live by the covenant expectation that Yhwh lays down, 'you will be my personal possession from among all the peoples, because all the earth is mine, but you – you will be for me a kingdom of priests and a holy nation' (Exod 19:5–6).

So Israel is one of the 'peoples' of the world; 'the people Israel' is a common expression. Israel is an ethnic group, and other words describing Israel also suggest that it is like a family writ large. It is a 'household', a collection of 'clans', comprising 'ancestors' (fathers and mothers and grandfathers and grandmothers) and 'descendants' (children and grandchildren). As the King James Version has it, these people are 'the children of Israel'. Israel does not comprise a collection of people who decided to join it, so that the faith decisions of individuals are decisive to what it is. You do not *have* to be born into this people; you can be adopted into it and then become as real a family member as someone who was born into it. But the people exist independently of such individual choices, a sign of the fact that Israel exists by God's choice and not by human initiative, that its existence as a corporate body is prior to its being made up of discrete individuals, and also that its members are expected to relate to one another like the members of a family.

In Exodus 19:5–6, Yhwh adds a series of other descriptions of Israel. As well as being a people, Israel is a 'nation', a political entity relating to other political entities. It functions not merely in the familial realm but also in the realm of history. In being freed from Egypt, it is not freed from involvement in the world of the nations of which Yhwh is Lord. What kind of nation it is will vary; it begins as one in which leadership is diffused, then it becomes a monarchic state, and then it is the subaltern of an imperial power. But it never ceases to be an entity involved in history and international relations.

Standing in some tension with this is the fact that Israel is a 'kingdom'. There is some appropriateness in its being a nation in which power is diffused because its king is Yhwh. Yhwh reigns over it. The covenant puts Yhwh in the position of an imperial power that lays down its expectations of subordinate powers; the people of Israel are expected to be utterly loyal to the Great King and not to submit themselves to any other power. There is then some tension with Israel's being either a monarchic state with human kings or the subaltern of an imperial power. Yet Yhwh allows both these political arrangements as consequences of Israel's resistance to having Yhwh alone as king.

Further, Israel is a kingdom of priests. Other peoples had priests who could draw near to their gods in a way that ordinary people could not, and could mediate the gods' instructions to their people. Israel was designed to be a people who could all draw near to God, and could all hear God speak. There is thus again some tension with the idea that Israel, too, will soon have a priesthood, by God's decree and by the people's desire (Exod 20:16).

And Israel is a 'holy' nation. There is some ambiguity about these statements concerning what Israel is destined to be. It *is* a kingdom where Yhwh reigns; it is *to be* a kingdom where Yhwh reigns. It *is* a holy nation, and it is *to be* a holy nation. As is the case where the word 'holy' applies to Yhwh, the term describes Israel's metaphysical position or nature, not its moral nature. Yhwh has already made the point in calling Israel Yhwh's 'personal possession'. As well as controlling state resources, a king had his own private, personal wealth (extra significance thus attaches to his giving from his possessions; see 1 Chr 29:1–4). All the nations likewise belong to Yhwh, but Israel is Yhwh's special personal possession; no one can trespass on that. To speak of Israel as 'holy' makes the same point. Its association with Yhwh means that it shares in Yhwh's distinctiveness, over the rest of the world. It is no ordinary people. But, as is the case with Yhwh, its holiness comes to have moral implications. Israel is to be like Yhwh in also being characterized by uprightness and faithfulness.

THE WORLD

In a variety of ways, the Old Testament makes clear that putting Israel in a special position does not mean Yhwh has written off the rest of the world. Israel exists within the context of Yhwh's intention so to bless Abraham that all earth's families will make that blessing the paradigm for the blessing they seek (Gen 12:1–3). While this affirmation highlights what Yhwh will do for Abraham, it appears in the setting of a narrative that presupposes Yhwh's concern for all the nations. Thus, it also indicates what Yhwh will do for them. Indeed, all the Old Testament's talk of what Yhwh will do for Israel links to Yhwh's intentions for the world. That psalm urging acknowledgement of Yhwh as God actually addresses all the earth, and like many psalms, it makes the assumption that what Yhwh has done for Israel is good news for the world. Among the prophets, all three parts of the book of Isaiah speak of Yhwh's involvement with the whole world. Assyria and Egypt will come to share Israel's position as 'my people' and 'my handiwork' (19:24). 'Turn to me and be delivered, all earth's extremities', Yhwh urges the nations passing from Babylon's suzerainty to Persia's (45:22); again, the context emphasises how the world's acknowledgement of Yhwh is good news for Israel, but in doing so indicates Yhwh's concern for the world. And Isaiah almost ends with these survivors becoming Yhwh's emissaries, with some of them turned into priests in the Temple (66:18–21).

Yhwh is also involved with and concerned for the non-human world. The Old Testament's opening makes this clear in relating the week's work that God undertook in creating the world. Humanity has no place until Friday afternoon, created then to subdue the animate world on God's behalf, but not free to eat from it. It re-expresses the point in the subsequent story of the orchard (usually reckoned to be an older story, on which Genesis 1 is then a kind of midrash). There humanity is formed first to 'serve' this orchard. The picture of a world with its own significance before God, independent of that of humanity, is taken further in the Psalms (e.g., Psalm 104). These also call the animate and inanimate world into worship of Yhwh (e.g., Pss 148–50). When Yhwh finally appears to Job, it is to observe how much bigger the world is than Job has allowed. It has its own importance independent of Job; if Job has a fault, it is reckoning that the world revolves around him. Yhwh does also note that elements within the world are resistant to Yhwh's lordship. Yhwh's words correspond to the perspective of the Psalms and the commission to subdue the earth. Yhwh's project in creating the world is not completed, but Yhwh will bring it to completion.

GERHARD VON RAD

After Eichrodt, Old Testament theology in the mid-part of the twentieth century came to a climax with the work of Gerhard von Rad, another Old Testament professor in Germany, who produced his *Old Testament Theology* in the 1950s.[3] Eichrodt had acknowledged the diverse way the Old Testament handled individual themes, but put the emphasis on there being one faith implicit in the Old Testament as a whole. Von Rad reversed this. He acknowledges the possibility of drawing a picture of Israel's understanding of God, of God's relationship of the world, and so on, and his *Theology* includes sections on subjects such as 'Israel's Ideas about Time and History' and 'The Law', but he reckons it more appropriate to focus on the way Israel actually spoke of Yhwh. And the distinctive way it did that was by telling the story of Yhwh's activity in its history. This takes one form in the gargantuan narratives that dominate the Old Testament; it takes another form in the distinctive way the prophets talk about Yhwh's activity in history not as a past event but a future one.

Von Rad deals with those parts of the Old Testament that do not relate very clearly to Yhwh's activity in history, notably the wisdom books, at the end of his first volume under the rubric 'Israel before Jahweh (Israel's Answer)'. But subsequently he wrote a whole book entitled, *Wisdom in Israel*,[4] which, in effect, constitutes a third volume of his *Theology*. It stands in tension with the emphasis on history that dominates his *Theology*, yet heralds the way wisdom and forms of creation thinking would come back to life in the last decades of the twentieth century. Both on the large canvas, then, and in his study of individual parts of the Old Testament, von Rad emphasised the diversity of Israel's faith.

His focus on Yhwh's activity in history draws attention to a key feature of Old Testament faith, though it does so for contextual reasons. For modernity as a whole, history was of supreme importance. His work has its own place in European history. Although he wrote his *Theology* in the 1950s, he did the creative critical work on which it was based in the 1930s (when Eichrodt was also writing his *Theology*), during the context of Barth's rejection of natural theology; indeed, Barth sometimes refers to von Rad. It is no coincidence that von Rad subordinates creation to the history of Yhwh's acts on Israel's behalf. His emphasis on history also parallels the emphasis on 'God's acts in history' in the 'biblical theology movement' in the United States.[5] But whereas US scholarship worked against the background of a conservative estimate of the Old Testament's historical value, von Rad worked against the background of the more critical estimate of his teacher, Albrecht Alt.[6] He thus recognises the problem of the gap between the story the Old Testament tells and the events that underlie this story. But his work involves more a recognition of this problem than a resolution of it.

Von Rad also tried to think through questions about the relationship of the Old Testament to Christian faith. His opening assertion in this discussion is that the Old Testament is a book of ever-increasing anticipation. It looks not merely for the restoration of the past but for a whole new future. Thus, the way the Old Testament is in due course 'absorbed in the New' is the logical end of a process begun by the Old. And the very fact that this absorption was possible also shows that it was appropriate; the Old Testament contained 'pointers to Christ'. There was a true parallel between what God was doing in Israel and what God was then doing in Christ 'in a more intensified form'. The first prefigures or typifies the second; the second fulfils the first.

BREVARD CHILDS AND WALTER BRUEGGEMANN

In the English-speaking world at least, the last part of the twentieth century belongs to Brevard Childs and Walter Brueggemann, professors of Old Testament in the United States. The US biblical theology movement came under increasing pressure in the 1960s, and in 1970, Childs pronounced it to be in crisis.[7] The proliferation of diverse methods of interpretation in the period that followed (e.g., liberationist, feminist, deconstructionist, post-colonial) made this no exaggeration. His proposal was that Old Testament and New Testament theological scholarship needed to pay renewed attention to the fact that these writings are the canonical Scriptures of the church. In various subsequent publications, Childs works with different implications of this fact. The most fundamental is that the Scriptures are concerned to make statements about God. Biblical commentaries, even the most theological, are inclined to confine themselves to statements about what Israel believed about God. Childs urges that they should make present-tense truth affirmations about God. It is in this connection that we should consider his emphasis on recovering the church's exegetical tradition, the way Chrysostom, Augustine, Calvin or Luther interpreted Scripture. Likewise, for Childs, 'doing theology in a canonical context' means working with the framework of the 'rule of the faith', and with the categories and questions of Christian theology, so he begins his *Old Testament Theology in a Canonical Context*[8] with a series of chapters on the notion of revelation, a subject that has been important in theology, though not (in this sense) within the Old Testament.

Childs urges that the proper object of theological study is the biblical text itself as we have it in its canonical form, not a hypothetical earlier version (J or P or Second Isaiah). One reason for this stance is the perceptible fact that the biblical text has been shaped to function as canon. It did not come into being through a merely literary process but through a religious one, a process designed to convey the significance of the text for the believing community. He urges that the link between Old and New Testaments within one canon makes the New Testament's use of particular texts (e.g., Psalm 8) an appropriate topic for biblical theological reflection. And it makes it appropriate to bring together the varying biblical material on a given subject (Old Testament and New Testament).

Childs and Brueggemann see themselves and are often seen by others as very different.[9] While Brueggemann also emphasises the Old Testament's theological significance for the church, he refuses to assimilate the Old Testament to church faith. Further, he stands within the dominant late-twentieth-century strand of mainstream scholarship rather than seeking to redirect it. Really, he stands within two dominant streams: study of the literary and rhetorical nature of the Old Testament documents, and of the way they create alternative worlds, and study that uses the tools of sociology to analyze how writing and propagating (or canonizing) texts are a means of exercising power. One of his key insights about Old Testament theology is his identification of the tension between theology that affirms order and theology that questions it. This then corresponds to a reality within society. There are forces that emphasise God's undergirding of order in the world, God's ensuring that obedience to God and blessing in experience are linked; these are forces that hold power in society and have a vested interest in the idea that things are all right as they are. And then there are forces that emphasise God's subverting of order and leading the oppressed to freedom, that protest the fact that obedience does not lead to blessing; these are forces that hold no power in society and have a vested interest in the idea that things are not all right as they are and need to change. The conviction that the Old Testament holds together beliefs that are in intense mutual dialogue underlies his *Theology of the Old Testament*, tellingly subtitled *Testimony, Dispute, Advocacy*.[10]

The fact that Brueggemann approaches the Old Testament as a whole in light of this conviction about society affects his approach to all its texts, as the approaches of Eichrodt, von Rad, and Childs affect their approach to all its texts; one can predict how their interpretation will come out. Nevertheless, Brueggemann has one key characteristic that matches the stance of Childs, his insistence on paying sustained attention to the text of the Old Testament itself. This links with another conviction they share, that the Enlightenment or modernity led theology astray, though whereas Childs then wants to go behind modernity, Brueggemann wants to go forward beyond it. In commentaries, he, too, deals with the actual texts of Genesis, Samuel, Psalms, and Jeremiah, and does not seek to identify earlier versions or identify the historical events that underlie the texts. And he insists on facing the demands of all the texts he studies, including ones that are not very congenial to Western Christians, such as the account of Joshua's destruction of Hazor, the frightening prayers in Psalms 109 and 137, or the stress on Yhwh's holiness in Ezekiel.

OLD TESTAMENT THEOLOGY AS A CHRISTIAN ENTERPRISE

To Christians, it may seem strange that Old Testament theologies have all been written by Christians (indeed, almost exclusively by Protestants). Yet the very expression 'Old Testament theology' suggests a major reason for this. This phrase presupposes a particular way of looking at the Hebrew-Aramaic scriptures. They are the first part of a twofold canon. Further, the expression 'old testament/covenant' comes from a New Testament passage that unfavorably contrasts this 'old testament/covenant' with the 'new testament/covenant'. It says of Israel at Sinai, 'their minds were blinded: for until this day remaineth the same veil untaken away in the reading of the old testament; which veil is done away in Christ' (2 Cor 3:14 King James Version [KJV]; cf. 2 Cor 3:6; Heb 3:15). So the expression 'Old Testament' suggests something inferior that has now passed away.

Great Old Testament theologians such as Eichrodt and von Rad are interested in the Old Testament because they believe it has intrinsic theological value. Yet they are also committed to the view that there is an essential link between the Old Testament and the New. Eichrodt sees Old Testament theology's aim as to construct 'a complete picture of the OT realm of belief', but also to show how the Old Testament drives forward towards Christ, 'in whom the noblest powers of the OT find their fulfilment. Negative evidence in support of this statement is afforded by the torso-like appearance of Judaism in separation from Christianity'. So Old Testament theology is concerned 'to see that this comprehensive picture [of the Old Testament realm of belief] does justice to the essential relationship with the NT'.[11] Eichrodt both undergirds and undermines his point by critiquing the Old Testament itself where he sees it manifesting features that characterise Judaism and not Christianity, such as its stress on a life of detailed obedience to God. In other words, a strain in his work looks anti-Jewish, and involves representing Judaism in a way that does not correspond to its own self-understanding.

Von Rad, in turn, dedicates his last hundred pages to 'the Old Testament and the New' and asks, does not reading the Old Testament as 'an object that can be adequately interpreted without reference to the New Testament, turn out to be fictitious from a Christian point of view?'[12] Old Testament theology only counts as theology when it makes explicit links between the Old Testament and the New, and is able to make people believe that the two testaments belong together.[13]

Childs, too, strongly affirms that 'the discipline of Old Testament theology is essentially a Christian discipline' presupposing a relationship between the life and history of Israel, and that of Jesus Christ.[14] In contrast, however, Brueggemann sees the Hebrew-Aramaic Scriptures as 'intransigently Jewish' in their 'openness to ambiguity and contradiction',[15] though Childs declares that 'the irony emerging from his description of God is one that no serious, religious Jew can tolerate.'[16] Where once Christian scholars minimised the Jewishness of the Old Testament, now they almost seem to be competing to say 'I'm more Jewish than you'.

JEWISH BIBLICAL THEOLOGY

The Christian assumptions of Old Testament theology make it unsurprising that Jewish scholars have not felt drawn to the discipline. It has seemed doubtful whether Jews and Christians can discuss biblical theology, because for Christians 'biblical theology is concerned with christological issues in a way that excludes the Jew.'[17] Other factors have also likely contributed. Whereas Christians have often assumed that they have a two-part canon while Judaism just reads the Hebrew-Aramaic

Scriptures, actually, Jews are not much more involved with these Scriptures than Christians are. As Christians pay more lip service than real attention to the Old Testament, so Jews focus more on the Mishnah and Talmud than on the Scriptures. And they read the latter through that lens of the Mishnah and Talmud, even as Christians read them through the lens of the New Testament. That links with Judaism's focus on faithfulness in living the right kind of life rather than in believing the right sort of things (orthopraxy rather than orthodoxy), or on faith as trust in God rather than faith as a collection of doctrines.[18] The category of biblical theology, with Old Testament theology as a subset, is related to Protestant stress on 'Scripture alone'. Its development was an aspect of the development of biblical criticism, whose own concern was to distance biblical study from commitment to the church's traditional ways of interpreting Scripture. But, like Roman Catholicism, Judaism takes a much more positive view of the community's accumulated tradition concerning the interpretation of Scripture, and assumes that Scripture and this tradition form a continuous stream of insight, so that it is neither appropriate nor necessary to consider the two separately. 'There can be no Jewish biblical theology; there can only be Jewish theology.'[19]

Yet it can also be said that 'the native theology of traditional Judaism is a biblical theology'.[20] Judaism has long engaged in theological study of its Scriptures, as the work of twentieth-century figures such as Martin Buber, Yehezkel Kaufmann and Jacob Milgrom indicates, even if they, of course, did not call it 'Old Testament theology'.[21] The chapter headings of Louis Jacobs's *A Jewish Theology*[22] would hardly raise eyebrows as the chapter headings for an Old Testament theology.

The end of the twentieth century in fact saw developing Jewish interest in what it is appropriate for Jews to call 'biblical theology'.[23] Arguably this involved not so much an increase in Jews thinking theologically about the Scriptures, but their doing it in dialogue with Christian scholars, as both an aspect and result of the way general scholarly study of the Scriptures had become more inter-confessional. For better or for worse, Jews thus became drawn into scholarly debate about method in doing biblical theology instead of simply doing it. This likely reflected factors such as the increased involvement of Jews in biblical scholarship, the development of Jewish-Christian dialogue, and Jewish resistance simply to let Christian views stand without being questioned. At the beginning of the twentieth century, Solomon Schechter urged Jews to fight the 'intellectual persecution' that was attempting to destroy the Jewish community's Bible by means of anti-Semitic higher-critical theories and 'to think out our theology for ourselves'.[24] To date, one of the editors of this volume has published a theologically oriented introduction to the Bible,[25] with more such efforts likely to appear, and a number of Jewish scholars have produced interesting and far-reaching individual studies that come close to offering a wide-angle perspective.[26]

THE DIFFERENCE THAT FAITH MAKES

Can biblical theology then be done only by (Jewish or Christian) faith so that it is not an objective exercise? There are several aspects to this question. Whether Yhwh brought about Judah's deliverance from Sennacherib is a matter of faith, but whether and how Isaiah thought it did so is surely not. Whether Yhwh is God is a matter of faith; what is Yhwh's personality profile in the Scriptures is surely not. Interpreters may disagree about the nature of that personality profile, but such disagreement is not very different from other interpretative differences among readers. And Jewish reflection on the theological significance of the apparently non-historical nature of much of the Scriptures is similar to Christian reflection.[27]

However, particular faith positions do make one see certain things, and differences between conclusions may indicate that their advocates started from a particular faith position. It is a fundamental insight of hermeneutics that what we see is decisively shaped by who we are and what we already think. It is always easier to perceive this in other people and generations than in ourselves. We have noted that the history of Old Testament theology up to the present day illustrates the point. This is not a reason for despair. The assumptions, frameworks, and questions that make us misconstrue some things do enable us to see other things. The dynamics of this process are a reason to be open to looking at issues from varying angles.

Whereas for Christians these Scriptures are 'the Old Testament', for Jews, they are 'the Torah, the Prophets, and the Writings' or (to use an acronym for the Hebrew phrase) 'the Tanak'. For Christians, they move from the past (the narrative from Genesis to Esther), through the present (Job to Song of Songs), to the future (Isaiah to Malachi, neatly closing with promises of a forerunner that the New Testament can apply to John the Baptist). For Jews, they move from Israel's establishment as a Torah-shaped community (the Torah), through its failure and promised renewal (the Former and Latter Prophets), to its ongoing life with God (the Writings). The Protestant Old Testament follows the order of the Greek Bible but the contents of the Tanak (omitting the works not accepted in the Jewish community). It may be that in origin both arrangements go back to Jewish communities, but it looks significant which arrangement each community chose.[28]

Looking at these Scriptures in light of Jewish rather than Christian faith, one sees new emphases. The Torah (not 'law') becomes a gift; the Jewish community has never perceived it as a burden (as von Rad had noted). The wilderness sanctuary and the Temple gain new significance. Sacrifice gains a new profile; it is not merely a (temporary) solution to the problem of sin but a wide-ranging means of giving outward expression to our worship. Interesting questions arise concerning the relationship of Sinai and Zion. It becomes clear that the land is a very prominent theme (Brueggemann had seen this).[29] The individual human being and individual salvation become less important; the community and the Israelite people become more important. A doctrine of universal human sinfulness becomes rather insignificant; a challenge to human obedience becomes rather more significant. In prayer, an acknowledgement of sinfulness also becomes less significant than a freedom to challenge God. However, the importance of eternal life and the Messiah parallel for some strands of Judaism the importance they have had for much Christian study, even though they are not very prominent in the Scriptures themselves.

Jewish biblical theology and Christian Old Testament theology each see the Hebrew-Aramaic scriptures from different angles and perceive different aspects to them, aspects that the other study misses. The Hebrew-Aramaic Scriptures are a rich and varied collection of narratives, insights, and biddings regarding God, Israel, the world, and life. Both the Mishnah, the Talmud and other Jewish traditions, on the one hand, and the New Testament and Christian traditions of theology and spirituality, on the other, allow themselves to be shaped by aspects of that collection, ignore other aspects, and subvert yet other aspects, as does any attempt to write an Old Testament theology (excluding, one inevitably imagines, one's own).

NOTES

1   English translation in Ben C. Ollenburger, ed., *Old Testament Theology: Flowering and Future*, rev'd. ed. (Winona Lake, IN: Eisenbrauns, 2004), 497–506.

2   In English, Walther Eichrodt, *Theology of the Old Testament*, 2 vols. (London: SCM/Philadelphia: Westminster, 1961–7).

3   In English, Gerhard von Rad, *Old Testament Theology*, 2 vols., trans. by D. M. G. Stalker (Edinburgh: Oliver and Boyd/New York: Harper, 1962–5).

4 In English, Gerhard von Rad, *Wisdom in Israel* (London: SCM/Nashville: A bingdon, 1972).

5 See especially George Ernest Wright, *The God Who Acts* (London: SCM/ Chicago: Regnery, 1952).

6 Albrecht Alt, *Essays on Old Testament History and Religion* (Oxford, UK: Blackwell, 1966).

7 Brevard S. Childs, *Biblical Theology in Crisis* (Philadelphia: Westminster, 1970).

8 Brevard S. Childs, *Old Testament Theology in a Canonical Context* (London: SCM, 1985; Philadelphia: Fortress, 1986).

9 Brueggemann's *The Book that Breathes New Life* (Minneapolis, MN: Fortress, 2005), 165–79, includes his review of Childs and Childs's review of him.

10 Walter Brueggemann, *Theology of the Old Testament: Testimony, Dispute, Advocacy* (Minneapolis, MN: Fortress, 1997).

11 Eichrodt, *Theology of the Old Testament*, 1: 25–7 (the first and last phrases are italicised).

12 Ibid., 2:321.

13 Ibid., 2:428–9.

14 Childs, *Old Testament Theology in a Canonical Context*, 7.

15 Walter Brueggemann, 'Biblical Theology Appropriately Postmodern', in *Jews, Christians, and the Theology of the Hebrew Scriptures*, ed. by Allis Ogden Bellis and Joel S. Kaminsky (Atlanta: SBL, 2000), 97–108 (104).

16 See his review of Brueggemann's *Theology of the Old Testament* in Brueggemann, *Book That Breathes New Life*, 174.

17 Jon D. Levenson, 'Why Jews Are Not Interested in Biblical Theology', in *Judaic Perspectives on Ancient Israel*, ed. by Jacob Neusner et al. (Philadelphia: Fortress, 1987), 281–307 (295). The sentence is interestingly omitted from the reprint of this article in Levenson, *The Hebrew Bible, the Old Testament, and Historical Criticism* (Louisville, KY: Westminster John Knox, 1993), 33–61.

18 Cf. Martin Buber, *Two Types of Faith*, reprint (New York: Harper, 1961); Leo Adler, *The Biblical View of Man* (Jerusalem: Urim, 2007), 9–10.

19 Benjamin D. Sommer, 'Unity and Plurality in Jewish Canons', in *One Scripture or Many?*, ed. by Christine Helmer and Christof Landmesser (New York: Oxford University Press, 2004), 108–50 (149). See further his paper, 'Dialogical Biblical Theology: A Jewish Approach to Reading Scripture Theologically', in *Biblical Theology*, ed. by Leo Perdue (Nashville, TN: Abingdon, 2008).

20 Michael A. Fishbane, *Judaism* (San Francisco: Harper, 1987), 58.

21 See Sommer's survey in 'Dialogical Biblical Theology'.

22 Louis Jacobs, *A Jewish Theology* (New York: Behrman, 1973).

23 Tikva Frymer-Kensky, 'The Emergence of Jewish Bible Theologies', in *Jews, Christian, and the Theology of the Hebrew Scriptures*, ed. by Alice Ogden Bellis and Joel S. Kaminsky (SBLSS 8; Atlanta: Society of Biblical Literature, 2000), 109–21.

24 S. Schechter, 'Higher Criticism – Higher Anti-Semitism', in *Seminary Addresses and Other Papers* (Cincinnati, OH: Ark, 1915), 35–9 (see 38);

cf. Levenson, 'Why Jews Are Not Interested in Biblical Theology', in *The Hebrew Bible, the Old Testament, and Historical Criticism*, 43.

25 Marvin A. Sweeney, *Tanak: A Theological and Critical Introduction to the Jewish Bible* (Minneapolis, MN: Fortress, 2012).

26 See Isaac Kalimi, ed., *Jewish Bible Theology: Perspective and Case Studies* (Winona Lake, IN: Eisenbrauns, 2012), as well as the work of Jon Levenson in *Sinai and Zion* (Minneapolis, MN: Winston, 1985), and *Creation and the Persistence of Evil* (San Francisco: Harper, 1988); also *The Death and Resurrection of the Beloved Son* (New Haven, CT: Yale University Press, 1993); *Resurrection and the Restoration of Israel* (New Haven, CT: Yale University Press, 2006). James Barr comments that Levenson's discussion of 'Why Jews Are Not Interested in Biblical Theology' is undermined by the fact that 'no one looks more like a successful Jewish biblical theologian than he himself does' (*The Concept of Biblical Theology* [Minneapolis, MN: Fortress, 1999], 294).

27 See Marc Zvi Brettler, 'Biblical History and Jewish Biblical Theology', *Journal of Religion* 77 (1997): 563–83.

28 See Marvin A. Sweeney, 'Tanak versus Old Testament', in *Problems in Biblical Theology*, ed. by Henry T. C. Sun et al. (Grand Rapids, MI: Eerdmans, 1997), 353–72.

29 See Walter Brueggemann, *The Land: Place as Gift, Promise, and Challenge in Biblical Faith* (Philadelphia: Fortress, 1977).

FURTHER READING

Bellis, Allis Ogden, and Joel S. Kaminsky, eds. *Jews, Christians, and the Theology of the Hebrew Scriptures* (SBLSS 8). Atlanta: SBL, 2000.

Brueggemann, Walter. *Theology of the Old Testament*. Minneapolis, MN: Fortress, 1997.

Childs, Brevard S. *Biblical Theology in Crisis*. Philadelphia: Westminster, 1970.

Eichrodt, Walther. *Theology of the Old Testament*, 2 vols. London: SCM, 1961 and 1967.

Goldingay, John. *Old Testament Theology*, 3 vols. Downers Grove, IL: IVP 2003, 2006, 2009;Carlisle, UK: Paternoster 2006, 2006, 2009.

Ollenburger, Ben C., ed. *Old Testament Theology: Flowering and Future*, rev'd ed. Winona Lake, IN: Eisenbrauns, 2004.

Perdue, Leo, ed. *Biblical Theology*. Nashville, TN: Abingdon, 2008.

Rad, Gerhard von. *Old Testament Theology*, 2 vols., trans. by D. G. M. Stalker. Edinburgh: Oliver and Boyd, 1962 and 1965.

Index

abduction marriage, biblical
    scholarship on, 173–75
Abellio, Raymond, 435
Abraham
    as founder of Judaism, 377,
    382–84
    intersection of Qur'an, Hebrew
    Bible and Islamic literature
    on, 416–17
    narrative of, 118–19, 153–56,
    167, 194–95
Abraham Ibn Ezra, 191–92
ʾabrogation *(naskh)* of Bible, Islamic
    charges of, 417–19
Absalom (son of David), 152–53,
    155–56, 161, 227–29
Absalon (Watson), 432–33
Absolom and Achitophel
    (Dryden), 431–32
Achaemenes, 74
Achaemenid Dynasty, 74–76
Achenbach, Reinhard, 207
acquired/ascribed honor, in biblical
    narrative, 154–55
acquired shame, 155–56
acronyms *(notarikon),* biblical words
    as, 382–84
Adad-nirari III (King), 69–70
Adam, A. K. M., 140
Add. 1846, University Library
    Cambridge (Samaritan
    Pentateuch), 12–13
Adnag, Camilla, 412–15
Africanus, 354
afterlife, in apocalyptic
    writing, 344–46

Ahab of Israel, 69–70
    Deuteronomistic History
    and, 218–19
    disguise of, 150–51
    in 1 Kings, 222–23, 229–30
    in non-biblical texts, 120–23
Ahaz of Judah, 69–70
Ahikar. See Story of Ahikar
    court narratives and, 314–16
Ahriman (deity), 76
Ahura-Mazda (deity), 76
Akhenaten (Amenhotep IV)
    (Pharaoh), 65–66
Akhetaten city-state, 65–66
Akiva (sage), 380–81
Akkadian texts
    Babylonian Empire in, 73–74
    deciphering of, 57–59, 87–90
    exiled Jews in, 74–76
    history of, 59–60
    narrative fiction in, 314–16
    in Old Babylonian period, 60–61
Alalakh texts, 62–63
Albertz, Rainer, 94, 96
al-Biqāʾī (Muslim exegete), 419–21
Albright, William Foxwell,
    129–30, 132–33
Aleppo Codex, 9–10
    canon included in, 47n13
Alexander the Great (Alexander of
    Macedon), 76–78
Alexandria (Egypt), founding of, 76–78
Alexandrian canon, 350–51
Alexandrinus Codex. *See* Codex
    Alexandrinus
al frescos, in synagogues, 428–29

Printed in the USA
CPSIA information can be obtained
at www.ICGtesting.com
LVHW012221300823
756711LV00003B/8